The Mind's Construction

The Mind's Construction

The Ontology of Mind and Mental Action

Matthew Soteriou

OXFORD
UNIVERSITY PRESS

OXFORD
UNIVERSITY PRESS

Great Clarendon Street, Oxford, OX2 6DP,
United Kingdom

Oxford University Press is a department of the University of Oxford.
It furthers the University's objective of excellence in research, scholarship,
and education by publishing worldwide. Oxford is a registered trade mark of
Oxford University Press in the UK and in certain other countries

First Edition published in 2013

Impression: 1

published in the United States of America by Oxford University Press
198 Madison Avenue, New York, NY 10016, United States of America

British Library Cataloguing in Publication Data
Data available

ISBN 978–0–19–967845–7

Printed and bound in Great Britain by
CPI Group (UK) Ltd, Croydon, CR0 4YY

For my parents

Contents

Part II. Conscious Thinking

Acknowledgements

Some of the material in this book draws on, and develops, work of mine that has been previously published. The relevant papers are the following: 'Mental Action and the Epistemology of Mind', *Nous* (2005), volume 39, issue 1, pages 83–105; 'The Subjective View of Experience and its Objective Commitments', *Proceedings of the Aristotelian Society* (2005), volume 105, issue 2, pages 193–206; 'Content and the Stream of Consciousness', *Philosophical Perspectives* (2007), volume 21, issue 1, pages 543–68; 'The Epistemological Role of Episodic Recollection', *Philosophy and Phenomenological Research* (2008), volume 77, issue 1, pages 472–92; 'Mental Agency, Conscious Thinking and Phenomenal Character', in *Mental Actions* (2009), edited by L. O'Brien and M. Soteriou. Oxford University Press; 'Cartesian Reflections on the Autonomy of the Mental', in *New Waves in Philosophy of Action* (2010), edited by J. Aguilar, A. Buckareff, and K. Frankish. Palgrave Macmillan; 'The Perception of Absence, Space and Time', in *Perception, Causation and Objectivity, Issues in Philosophy and Psychology* (2011), edited by J. Roessler, N. Eilan, and H. Lerman. Oxford University Press; 'Perceiving Events', *Philosophical Explorations* (2010), volume 13, issue 3, pages 223–41; 'Occurrent Perceptual Knowledge', *Philosophical Issues* (2011), volume 21, issue 1, pages 485–504.

I am very grateful to colleagues at the Philosophy Department at Warwick University for many helpful discussions of this work, and in particular I should like to thank Bill Brewer, Stephen Butterfill, Quassim Cassam, Naomi Eilan, Christoph Hoerl, Guy Longworth, Matthew Nudds, and Johannes Roessler. To Hemdat Lerman I owe special thanks for taking the time to write up extremely useful comments on an earlier draft of this book. My heartfelt thanks to Tom Crowther for his encouragement, support, advice, the detailed and invaluable written comments, and the many conversations we've had about these issues, from which I've learnt so much. For helpful discussions, encouragement, and advice I should also like to thank Tim Crane, Paul Faulkner, Mark Kalderon, Lucy O'Brien, Ian Phillips, Hannah Pickard, Maja Spener, and Scott Sturgeon. I have benefited enormously from insightful and helpful written comments that were prepared by Alan Millar, and an anonymous referee for Oxford University Press. I am very grateful to them, and also to Peter Momtchiloff at Oxford University Press for his help and guidance in overseeing the publication of this book.

One inevitably accumulates many intellectual debts when one tries to engage seriously with the work of others, but there are a couple in particular that I should like to single out and acknowledge here. Michael Martin was my supervisor when I was a postgraduate at UCL. He was an inspirational teacher, his work continues to be a source of inspiration, and I am very grateful to him for the support he has shown me over the years. As will soon become obvious to those who read on, this work also owes a great debt to the work of Brian O'Shaughnessy. It was enthralled readings and re-readings of

Brian O'Shaughnessy's extraordinary books, *The Will: A Dual Aspect Theory* and *Consciousness and the World*, that prompted me to try to develop many of the lines of thought that are to be found in this book.

Finally, I should like to express my deepest gratitude to those I owe the most, for what matters most: Sandra, Enjoli, Luke, and my parents, Kay and Andrew Soteriou, to whom this book is dedicated.

Introduction

Not all aspects of mind fill time in the same way. For example, some elements of our mental lives *obtain* over intervals of time, others *unfold* over time, some *continue to occur* throughout intervals of time, and so on. These distinctions of temporal character are often highlighted in work on the ontology of mind, where it is suggested that they play a crucial role in determining which ontological category a given aspect of mind belongs to—e.g. in determining whether that aspect of mind is a mental state, a mental event, or a mental process. In this book I try to show how these ontological distinctions can be put to work in ways that can help to illuminate a number of other debates in the philosophy of mind. In particular, I discuss various ways in which the application of these distinctions can help inform philosophical accounts of both sensory and cognitive aspects of our conscious mental lives.

The book is divided into two parts. Part I focuses on aspects of sensory consciousness—conscious perceptual experience, bodily sensation, and acts of perceptual imagination and perceptual recollection. Part II of the book is concerned with varieties of conscious cognitive activity that self-conscious subjects can engage in—such as conscious calculation, conscious deliberation, suppositional reasoning, and self-critical reflection. A key aim in Part I is to establish that work in the ontology of mind that focuses on distinctions of temporal character has much to contribute to philosophical accounts of the phenomenology of various elements of sensory consciousness. In Part II, I try to show how these ontological considerations can also inform our understanding of conscious thinking, as well as the form of self-conscious consciousness that we have as subjects capable of engaging in such activity, by helping to account for and explain the respect in which agency is exercised in conscious thinking. This in turn, I argue, brings into clearer view the place and role of mental action in an account of the metaphysics of mind. In what follows I'll map out the contours of some of the main issues I engage with over the course of the book.

Part I: sensory consciousness

Philosophical accounts of sensory consciousness often invoke claims that are supposed to be grounded in the perspective that each of us has on his or her own conscious mental life. For example, philosophers often invoke the claim that there is something that it is like for one to have any given conscious sensory experience, and that what it is like for one to have such an experience is somehow manifest to one as the subject of that experience. This often gets expressed in terms of the claim that conscious sensory experiences have phenomenal properties that determine what it is like for one to be the subject of them. In such discussions the focus of enquiry tends to be directed more or less exclusively on the nature of these phenomenal, what-it-is-like properties, and it is rarely made explicit how we are to think of the temporal profile of the experiences to which such properties are attributed. For example, it's not often made explicit whether the bearers of these phenomenal properties are mental events, or mental states, or mental processes. Moreover, there isn't much discussion of the relevance that these ontological considerations might have in accounting for our knowledge of what it is like to have conscious experiences. Implicit is the assumption that such matters have little to contribute to a philosophical account of sensory consciousness. One of my principal aims in Part I of the book is to show otherwise.

I begin my exploration of the ways in which these ontological concerns are relevant to an account of sensory consciousness by picking up on some remarks that Geach once made when he argued against William James' suggestion that our conscious mental lives include a 'stream of conscious thought' (James 1890: 233). Geach (1969) argued that although conscious *sensory* aspects of mind may be stream-like, mental acts of thinking thoughts and making judgements are not. The question of what it is for an aspect of mind to be 'stream-like' is related to a question about its temporal character—the question of how that aspect of mind fills time. Geach's suggestion is, in effect, that conscious sensory aspects of mind and conscious thoughts do not fill time in the same way. According to Geach, this becomes clear once we attain the correct understanding of the way in which mental acts of thinking thoughts are individuated by their propositional contents.

Many now hold that conscious perceptual experiences are individuated by representational contents that have veridicality conditions. A number of those who take this stance note that there are important distinctions to be drawn between the propositional content of thought and the representational content of experience. But does Geach's argument have the resources to show that such accounts nonetheless end up making conscious perceptual experience too thought-like—by failing to accommodate the distinctive way in which our conscious experiences fill time? I broach this issue in Chapter 2, where I connect it with debates about the relation between the representational content and phenomenal character of conscious experience. In doing so, I introduce a general proposal about the ontology of conscious sensory experience that I develop and put to work in a number of ways in the subsequent chapters of Part I. This proposal invokes both conscious sensory states and conscious sensory occurrence, and it suggests how we should think of the relation between them. Here I also begin to introduce the ontological category of conscious 'occurrent state', which plays a key role in many of the arguments I present throughout the book.

Over the course of Part I, I indicate various ways in which these ontological concerns, which depend on distinctions of temporal character, can contribute to our understanding of phenomenal consciousness. In Chapter 2, I suggest how they can be used to help diagnose the intuition that there is an 'explanatory gap' associated with attempts to understand the relation between the phenomenal and the physical (and functional) features of conscious sensory experience. In Chapter 3, I explain how they can inform an account of the phenomenology of bodily sensations, such as pains—aspects of mind that are often thought to be paradigmatic of those mental occurrences and states that only a phenomenally conscious subject can be the subject of. In Chapters 4, 5, and 6, I focus on aspects of the temporal phenomenology of conscious sensory experience. Here I discuss debates about our experience of events, debates about the so-called 'specious present', the 'continuity' of consciousness, and debates about whether there is a respect in which we can be said to experience the 'passage' of time. Over the course of this discussion I argue that the right account of the ontology of conscious experience can help resolve certain puzzles that arise in these debates and that in doing so it can help illuminate a distinctive form of conscious contact with time that phenomenally conscious subjects have. My suggestion is that the right account of the ontology of conscious experience has a key role to play in accommodating the distinctive temporal texture of the phenomenology of our conscious sensory encounter with the world, and that this is an important, but often overlooked, ingredient in an account of phenomenal consciousness.

In Chapter 7, I discuss the similarities and differences between the phenomenology of conscious perceptual experience and the phenomenology of acts of perceptual imagination and recollection. I propose an account of the ontology of perceptual imagination and perceptual recollection that can accommodate and explain these similarities and differences, and I also explain how this proposal can capture the intuition that these are mental acts that only a phenomenally conscious subject can engage in. In the final chapter of Part I, I apply these ontological considerations in providing an account of a variety of knowledge that only a phenomenally conscious subject can possess—knowledge of what it is like to have conscious sensory experience.

The aim in Part I is to build up to an account of the ontology of sensory consciousness that fits the phenomenology, as well as the knowledge that we have of that phenomenology, and in the course of building up to an account of that ontology I also engage with the question of whether we should accept that a psychological relation of perceptual acquaintance has an indispensable role to play in an account of the phenomenal character of conscious sensory experience. I argue that we should (Chapter 4). According to the sort of relational view of experience that I defend, important explanatory roles are assigned to structural features of the relation of perceptual acquaintance (Chapter 5). I suggest we should appeal to these structural features in accounting for certain aspects of the phenomenology of our experience of space, time, and absence. I try to show that these structural features of the relation of perceptual acquaintance are relevant to some of the phenomenal differences between some of the different modalities of sense perception (e.g. vision and bodily awareness); and I also argue that they are relevant to debates about the extent to which our conscious sensory experiences may be said to be 'transparent' when we attempt to introspect them.

A major challenge faced by the sort of relational view I defend is that of providing a satisfactory account of hallucination. The key to meeting this challenge lies in unpacking the various ways in which disagreements about the phenomenal character of experience can intersect with disagreements about self-knowledge—e.g. disagreements about what we can know about the phenomenal character of an experience when we have it and what puts us in a position to acquire such knowledge. I suggest that in order to settle these disputes we not only need the right account of the ontology of our conscious sensory experiences, we also need the right account of the ontology of our knowledge of their phenomenology. So in my defence of a relational view of conscious sensory experience, ontological considerations are brought into play once again.

Part II: conscious thinking

In many of the standard current philosophical accounts of mentality, emphasis is placed on the notion of psychological subject as bodily agent. Such accounts do not deny the reality of a subject's inner mental life, but they hold that a subject's inner mental life will necessarily be anchored in publicly observable bodily behaviour that expresses, and that is an effect of, that subject's mentality. For example, a number of functionalist and interpretationist accounts of the mental incorporate this idea in different ways. Those advocating these approaches rarely address explicitly the question of the place and role of mental action in an account of the metaphysics of mind. Functionalist approaches to mind that take the individuation of a mental state to be determined by its causal relations to sensory stimulations, other mental states, and behaviour, are usually confined to treating the relevant behaviour in question as bodily behaviour. This doesn't mean that such accounts are incompatible with the idea that we can perform mental as well as bodily actions, but the implicit assumption often seems to be that agential mental behaviour is to be explained and characterized in terms of the prior notions of sensory stimulation, bodily behaviour, mental states, and the events that are transitions between such states that contribute to the causal explanation of bodily behaviour. Similarly, under interpretationist approaches to the mental, the focus is invariably on mental state attributions that rationalize and causally explain *bodily* behaviour.

The implicit assumption is that although bodily behaviour is to be taken as basic, mental behaviour is not. So for instance, under such views mental events with phenomenal properties are not usually regarded as constituting mental behaviour that is the output of the functional roles that mental states characteristically play; nor are they regarded as occurrences constituting mental behaviour that needs to be rationalized and explained by mental state attributions. Moreover, a number of philosophers have pointed out that under such views it's not clear that we need to appeal to the phenomenal properties of mental events and states when it comes to explaining the publicly observable bodily manifestations of our mentality and agency. In consequence, it is sometimes suggested that a subject who is not phenomenally conscious may be capable of doing whatever the phenomenally conscious subject is capable of doing—the implicit assumption being that phenomenal consciousness is not only inessential to bodily action, it is also inessential to mental action. The thought here is that were we to strip our mentality of phenomenal properties, we would still have mentality and agency, and we would still be psychological subjects, and agents, no less autonomous than we are now. The underlying methodological assumption, then, is that accounts of mentality and agency can proceed without a solution to the so-called 'hard problem' of *phenomenal* consciousness, which requires its own special and separate treatment. Given the way in which so much of the current theorizing about consciousness is dominated by a concern with the nature of phenomenal consciousness, this helps to reinforce an assumption that considerations regarding mental action can at best be of marginal significance to a philosophical account of consciousness. It also helps reinforce an assumption that considerations regarding phenomenal consciousness do not have a central role to play in an account of the kind of autonomous agency that we are capable of exercising as self-conscious subjects. In the account of conscious thinking that I develop in Part II, I try to show why some of these assumptions should be challenged. The key to seeing why they should be challenged, I argue, lies in uncovering the ways in which mental agency is exercised in conscious thinking, and in uncovering the ways in which an account of this mental agency depends on the right account of the ontology of conscious thinking.

In my investigation into the place and role of mental agency in conscious thinking I start by considering suppositional reasoning and self-critical reflection. In the *Meditations*, Descartes suggests that when one is engaged in these activities, which are the essential elements of his method of doubt, 'the mind uses its own freedom'.[1] In a similar vein, O'Shaughnessy suggests that the capacity to engage in these activities provides the self-conscious, thinking subject with a form of 'mental freedom' that allows her to 'transcend the condition of animal immersion' (2000: 110). In Chapter 11, I try to articulate what is right in this suggestion, and in identifying where we should locate the role of mental agency in these forms of conscious reasoning I provide a critique of Galen Strawson's (2003) suggestion that the role of mental action in thinking and reasoning can at best be 'merely catalytic' and 'indirect' (2003: 231). I also question certain general assumptions that are sometimes made in philosophical accounts of action—in particular, the assumption that the factors that determine whether a subject's behaviour is agential are simply to be located in the initiating causes of that behaviour—initiating causes which are themselves non-agential.

In Chapter 12, I argue that mental action also has an important role to play in an account of a distinctive variety of agency—namely the sort of autonomous agency that we, as self-conscious agents, are able to exercise in having the capacity to engage in practical deliberation and make decisions. I also try to outline ways in which mental action should be central to an explanation of the distinctive practical and epistemic perspective that we have on our own futures and future actions as self-conscious, autonomous agents.

---

[1] Descartes makes this claim in the Synopsis of the *Meditations*.

In Chapter 13, I turn to the epistemology of mental action, and consider its relevance to our understanding of the epistemology of mind in general. I argue that the right account of the epistemology of mental action has a crucial role to play in an account of our knowledge of what we are doing when we are consciously thinking. I connect the proposal I make with some claims that O'Shaughnessy (2000) has made about the role of the 'mental will' in an account of the state of wakeful consciousness in the self-conscious subject—in particular, some claims he makes about the differences between dreaming and wakeful states of consciousness. In the final chapter of the book, I go on to consider how this proposal bears on an account of one's knowledge of one's standing attitudes, and in particular, one's knowledge of what one believes. Here I also address some further epistemological questions about the connections between the activity of conscious thinking and the standing attitude of belief. I explore some of the ways in which an account of the ethics of belief may be affected once various ontological and agential considerations regarding the activity of conscious thinking are properly accommodated.

As I have said, central to the various proposals I make about the role of mental agency in conscious thinking is the account of the ontology of conscious thinking that I offer. This is introduced in Chapter 10. Here I reconsider Geach's argument for the claim that there is no stream of conscious thought. I defend an account that acknowledges that there is a respect in which there can be said to be a stream of conscious thought, but which nonetheless preserves the idea that there are important ontological distinctions to be drawn between the conscious cognitive and conscious sensory aspects of our mental lives, and which also accommodates a point that Geach and others have been concerned to emphasize: that we should reject the suggestion that 'to think certain thoughts is to have certain images, feelings, unspoken words etc. passing through one's mind' (1969: 34).

Over the course of Part II, I try to make a case for the following proposal: with the right account of the ontology of conscious thinking in place, we can attain a clearer view of the way in which agency is exercised in conscious thinking, and an account of this mental agency can serve as an important connecting thread linking issues in the epistemology of mind, an account self-conscious consciousness, and an account of the kind of autonomous agency that only self-conscious subjects can exercise. This in turn, I suggest, brings into clearer view the place and role of mental action in the construction of our conscious mental lives.

PART I

Sensory Consciousness

1

The Manifest Image of Sensory Consciousness

As a self-conscious subject one is often in a position to know at least something about the sensory experience one is having at any given time, and it seems reasonable to assume that this variety of first-personal self-knowledge can potentially serve as a source of evidence when it comes to theorizing about sensory perception. There are, however, a number of reasons for thinking that any such source of evidence may be rather limited in scope. For instance, there are various processes underlying one's capacity to sense the world whose occurrence and nature one is not in a position to discern simply on the basis of introspective reflection. So it is not obvious that this first-personal source of evidence should serve as the starting point of philosophical theorizing about sense perception, and it is not obvious that this source of evidence should somehow serve to fix what it is that an account of sense perception should seek to explain. Nonetheless, there has been a persistent and prevalent tendency among philosophers to assume that the distinctively first-personal knowledge we have, or can have, of our sensory experiences when we have them has a special and significant role to play when it comes to offering a philosophical account of *conscious* sensory experience, and that an appeal to introspection and phenomenology is legitimate when theorizing about the nature of such experience in a way it perhaps isn't when theorizing about thought. In consequence, one often finds that philosophical claims about the nature of conscious sensory experience are intertwined with claims about the sort of knowledge that we, as self-conscious subjects, have, or can have, of those experiences when we have them.

The underlying assumption here seems to be something like the following: one's conscious sensory experiences have a *sensuous* character, this sensuous character that they have is somehow manifest to one as a self-conscious subject when one has them, the nature of that distinctive sensuous character is a legitimate object of enquiry, and introspective reflection on one's conscious sensory experience has a significant role to play in an investigation of that character. Those endorsing this assumption need not be committed to the idea that introspective reflection alone determines what it is that an account of sense perception should seek to explain, and they may concede that there is a great deal that introspective reflection cannot reveal about the nature of conscious sensory experience.[1] But the thought here seems to be that introspective reflection does at least have a legitimate role to play when it comes to articulating what we might call the 'manifest image' of conscious experience, in contrast to its 'scientific image', and that the sensuous character of conscious experience is a crucial aspect of that manifest image.

The labels 'manifest image' and 'scientific image' allude to Wilfrid Sellars' paper 'Philosophy and the Scientific Image of Man'.[2] In that paper, Sellars contrasts the 'manifest image of man-in-the-world' and the 'scientific image of man-in-the-world', and he discusses problems involved in attempting to see how these different conceptions 'fit together in one stereoscopic view' (2007: 373). Over the course of the paper, Sellars elaborates in quite specific ways how he wants us to understand his use of these labels. My use of the labels 'manifest image' and 'scientific image' here is somewhat looser, but in adopting the labels I do have in mind certain remarks that Sellars makes. Sellars says that in employing the term 'image' he doesn't mean to be denying to either or both 'images' the status of 'reality', although he does introduce the labels in a way that leaves open the possibility that a number of different stances may be taken on the relation between them, including the possibility that the manifest image of man-in-the-world turns out to be the 'tracery of an explicable error' (2007: 377), and that the contrast between the manifest image and the scientific image is the contrast between 'man as he falsely believes himself to be' and 'man as he discovers himself to be in the scientific enterprise' (2007: 376). Sellars also notes that his use of the term 'image' is a metaphor for 'conception', but by calling these different conceptions 'images' he is 'transforming them from ways of experiencing the world into objects of philosophical reflection and evaluation' (2007: 373).

This last remark is particularly relevant to what I have in mind when referring to the 'manifest image' of conscious sensory experience. One of the points I want to emphasize is that the step to articulating the 'manifest image' of conscious sensory experience is not philosophically innocent. I suggested that many philosophers seem to assume that the sensuous character of conscious sensory experience is a crucial aspect of its manifest image. But the claim that 'sensory' experiences have a 'sensuous' character borders on the trivial, and saying something more substantive about what that sensuous character consists in is far from straightforward. Among those who share the intuition that the sensuous character of conscious sensory experiences is somehow manifest to one—i.e. somehow subjectively accessible to one as a self-conscious subject when one has them— there is disagreement over the question of how best to articulate what it is that is manifest to one. The attempt at articulation appears to require not only the employment of one's 'attentional tweezers', as O'Shaughnessy puts it, but also the employment of

---

[1] For discussion of the history of appeals to introspection in psychology and the criticisms that have been levelled at such appeals, see Hatfield 1990, chapters 4–5, Kusch 1999, and Hatfield 2005.

[2] This paper was first published in 1962. Page references in what follows are to the reprint in Sellars 2007.

'conceptual tweezers aided and abetted by argumentation' (2000: 452). In consequence, differences in the background theoretical frameworks that different philosophers adopt can affect how these philosophers articulate what is manifest to one in having a conscious sensory experience. And this, in turn, can affect the way in which questions are posed about the relation between the manifest image and the scientific image of conscious sensory experience.

These disagreements about how to articulate the manifest image of conscious experience can be quite basic and fundamental. There are disagreements over the general shape of the manifest image of conscious sensory experience, and not just disagreements over the fine details. For example, there are disagreements over whether or not we need to appeal to a distinctive kind of psychological relation that obtains when we have conscious sensory experience; whether or not we should just appeal to the occurrence/obtaining of a mental event/state that has certain distinctive properties. And such disagreements about how to articulate the manifest image of conscious experience often intersect with disagreements about self-knowledge—disagreements about what one is, and is not, in a position to know about the conscious sensory experience one is having at any given time, as well as disagreements about what puts one in a position to know what one does know.

In much of Part I of this book I shall be focusing on claims made about the 'manifest image' of conscious sensory experience, and how these claims intersect with views about the kind of knowledge we can have of our conscious sensory experiences as self-conscious subjects of them. One of my aims in Part I is to suggest various ways in which issues in the ontology of mind can contribute to our philosophical understanding of sensory consciousness, and a recurring theme of the book is that these issues in the ontology of mind are also relevant to our understanding of the sort of knowledge we have of our own experiences and thoughts as self-conscious subjects. I shall introduce some of these ontological issues in the next chapter, where I shall be discussing the idea that there are various distinctions to be marked between different aspects of mind that are determined by the different ways in which those aspects of mind fill time. I shall be arguing for the significance of these ontological distinctions when it comes to attempting to articulate appropriately the manifest image of conscious sensory experience. Appropriate articulation of that manifest image, I shall be suggesting, will depend on finding an ontology that fits both the phenomenology and the knowledge that we have of it—and one that can hopefully make sense of the existence of disagreement about that phenomenology. The attempt to discern the appropriate ontology can't simply depend on something like the inner glance of introspection alone. It will depend on the use of appropriate 'conceptual tweezers aided and abetted by argumentation'.

In this chapter I shall be sketching out some of the prominent and conflicting claims that philosophers have made about what is manifest to one in having a conscious sensory experience, and I shall be commenting on how differences in these articulations can affect the direction taken by philosophical enquiry and influence the kinds of questions about sensory experience that it is considered important to address. This will set

the stage for subsequent discussion of various ways in which the application of ontological distinctions of temporal character can engage with and contribute to these more
familiar debates.

1.1   Introspection, 'diaphanous' experience, and the relation of perceptual acquaintance

It can seem like a relatively small and innocent step to move from the claim that (a) conscious sensory experience has a sensuous character that is somehow subjectively accessible to the subject who has that conscious sensory experience, to the claim that (b) a
conscious sensory experience is a mental state/event that has some sensuous quality that
the subject of that sensory experience can introspectively attend to. However, the latter
claim has courted controversy. One difficulty that has been raised for it is the following.
When one has a conscious sensory experience, that experience does seem to put one in
a position to attend directly to certain qualities—certain *sensory* qualities, as we might
call them; for example, in the case of vision, colours and shapes, and in the case of audition, timbre and pitch. However, these sensory qualities do not strike one as being qualities of one's experience. For example, it doesn't seem right to say that the experience
itself seems to be shaped and coloured. So the sensory qualities that one's experience
appears to put one in a position to attend to directly do not seem to be the sensuous
qualities of experience mentioned in claim (b).

In his early and influential paper 'The Refutation of Idealism',[3] Moore warns against
the danger of equivocating between what I am calling the 'sensory qualities' that an
experience can put one in a position to attend to and the 'sensuous qualities' of the
experience itself. According to a view that Moore sets out to challenge,

The 'sensation of blue'... differs from a blue bead or a blue beard in exactly the same way as the
latter two differ from one another: the blue bead differs from the blue beard, in that while the
former contains glass, the latter contains hair; and the 'sensation of blue' differs from both, in that,
instead of glass or hair, it contains consciousness. The relation of the blue to the consciousness is
conceived to be exactly the same as that of the blue to the glass or hair: it is in all three cases the
quality of a *thing*. (1903: 38)

One might think Moore's warning unnecessary, for there is little temptation to suppose
that our mental episodes or states are actually blue in colour. However, one could see
Moore as challenging a related view as well—a view which may be more tempting. One
might think that when one has a sensory experience of blue there is at least *some* quality
one is in a position to attend to directly, and that quality may not be the quality of some
object in the world, distinct from the experience itself, with which one is acquainted.
For it could be that one is hallucinating and aware of no such object. Or perhaps there is
reason to think that objects in the world are not really blue. In which case, one might

---

[3] Moore 1903. The page references in what follows are to the reprint in Moore 1993.

think, the quality that one's sensory experience puts one in a position to attend to directly must be a quality of the experience itself. Even if that quality is not that of being the colour blue, it is, nonetheless, a sensuous quality of the experience that we might label a 'blue★' sensational quality or quale, or the sensuous quality of sensing in a 'blue★-ish' way. Part of Moore's warning here, I think, is that even if one's experiences have such 'blue★' sensational properties, even if there is a sensuous quality of sensing in a 'blue★-ish' way, the quality that one's sensory experience seems to put one in a position to attend to directly doesn't strike one as being any such property. The quality that one's experience seems to put one in a position to attend to directly is the colour blue—a property that it is unlikely that one's experience actually possesses.

Moore famously notes what appears to be an obstacle to our attempts to attend directly to what I am calling the sensuous qualities of a conscious sensory experience.

The moment we try to fix our attention upon consciousness and to see *what*, distinctly, it is, it seems to vanish: it seems as if we had before us a mere emptiness. When we try to introspect the sensation of blue, all we can see is the blue: the other element is as if it were diaphanous. (1903: 41)

There is a negative point being made in this part of Moore's discussion. The expectation that one will be able simply to attend directly to, and read off and describe, the sensuous qualities of one's conscious sensory experience is likely to be thwarted when one undertakes that endeavour. However, the points that Moore is concerned to make in his discussion of the way in which consciousness appears to be 'diaphanous' are not entirely negative. When he says that the conscious element of the sensation of blue seems to one to be diaphanous, Moore adds, 'Yet it *can* be distinguished if we look attentively enough, and if we know that there is something to look for' (1903: 42). When he is articulating his own positive proposal, Moore writes,

When we know that the sensation of blue exists, the fact we know is that there exists an awareness of blue. And this awareness is not merely...itself something distinct and unique, utterly different from blue: it also has a perfectly distinct and unique relation to blue. (1903: 40).

The sensation of blue includes in its analysis, beside blue, *both* a unique element 'awareness' *and* a unique relation of this element to blue. (1903: 41)

One significant aspect of Moore's discussion is the way in which it brings to the fore the idea that sensory experience somehow involves some kind of psychological *relation* of awareness, and not simply some psychological event, process, state, or property. In this context, to say that the relation of awareness is a psychological one isn't simply to say that one of the relata of the relation is a psychological subject—a bearer of psychological properties—for there are also non-psychological relations that psychological subjects can stand in to things. The suggestion appears to be that when one has a sensory experience there obtains a distinctive psychological relation that one stands in to some sensory quality, where that sensory quality is not a quality of the psychological relation. The awareness of blue is not itself blue.

Once one has in play the idea that conscious sensory experience may involve the obtaining of a distinctive kind of psychological relation, then we can see how the simple argumentative step mentioned earlier may not be so innocent and uncontroversial—i.e. the move from the claim that (a) conscious sensory experience has a sensuous character that is somehow subjectively accessible to the subject who has that sensory experience, to the claim that (b) a conscious sensory experience is a mental state/event that has some sensuous quality/property that the subject of that sensory experience can introspectively attend to. For the sensuous character of sensory experience mentioned in (a) may be explained, at least in part, by a distinctive psychological relation that obtains when one has a sensory experience, and not simply some sensuous quality of some mental event or state.

However, this proposal, as it stands, just raises more questions than it answers. Suppose one were to accept the idea that the sensuous character of conscious sensory experience is to be explained, at least in part, by a distinctive psychological relation that obtains when one has a conscious sensory experience. How should one go about trying to articulate what is distinctive of that psychological relation? Should one be seeking to describe certain features of the relation, and is one able to attend directly to features of the relation when one has a conscious sensory experience? Should one be seeking to characterize distinctive psychological properties of oneself, as a psychological subject, that one has when one stands in that psychological relation? Should one be seeking to characterize distinctive properties of a psychological event that occurs when one stands in that distinctive psychological relation? These ideas are not all equivalent, and it is not clear that introspective reflection alone can deliver answers to these questions.

I suggested earlier that the differences between the various ways in which philosophers articulate the manifest image of conscious sensory experience can affect the direction taken by philosophical enquiry and influence the kinds of questions it is considered important to address. At one stage, in part under Moore's influence, it became the orthodoxy to suppose that conscious sensory experience involves a fundamental psychological relation, and that an analysis of sensory experience would need to make mention of that psychological relation. One of the tasks undertaken by many of those who took this idea seriously was the attempt to say more about the nature of that psychological relation. For example, Russell held that experience is constituted by a relation of 'acquaintance' or 'awareness' (Russell 1992: 35), but he also held that there is reason to suppose that 'there are several species of the general relation of acquaintance'—for example, different varieties of the relation obtain, according to Russell, in the cases of memory and imagination (1992: 38). At one stage in his thinking, Russell uses the label 'sensation' to pick out a particular species of that general relation. Sensation, he says, implies acquaintance, but is not identical with acquaintance (1992: 63). He entertains the hypothesis that 'sensation' is 'acquaintance with particulars given as simultaneous with the subject' (1992: 58), but then warns that 'It is not a definition of sensation that it is acquaintance with an object which is in fact simultaneous with the subject: the simultaneity must be not merely a fact, but must be deducible from the nature of the experience involved in the sensation' (1992: 63). He then goes on to suggest that 'sensation must be a special relation of subject and object different from any relation which does not show that the object is at the present time', and that 'it is natural to take "sensation" as an ultimate, and define the present time in terms of it' (1992: 64).

At this stage, I don't intend to try to assess Russell's specific proposals. The aim is just to give some indication of the way in which a given theoretical framework can emerge and thereby affect the direction taken by philosophical discussions of sensory experience. In a theoretical framework within which an appeal to a distinctive psychological relation of acquaintance is thought to be fundamental and crucial, one question that naturally arises is whether more can be said about what is distinctive of that relation. Part of what is going on in Russell's discussion of 'sensation', I take it, is the attempt to do just this—to say something more about distinctive features of a psychological relation that obtains when one has a perceptual, sensory experience.

Broad was another philosopher working under the same general theoretical framework, and he too attempts to say something about what is characteristic of a psychological relation that obtains in a 'perceptual situation', as he calls it, in contrast to a 'thought-situation'. He mentions the idea that the psychological relation involved in the perceptual situation has an 'intuitive' character, as opposed to a 'discursive' character, which somehow puts one 'in more immediate touch with its object' than in a thought-situation; and like Russell, he emphasizes the idea that 'it is the essence of the perceptual situation that it claims to reveal its object as it is at the time when the situation is going on' (Broad 1925: 145). He also suggests that 'sensation' plays an indispensable role in the perceptual situation. These sensations, he says, are not possible to define, but they contribute to the 'sensuous' character of the perceptual situation.

To give one more example, Price (1932) also appeals to a psychological relation of acquaintance in his account of perceptual consciousness. For Price, acquaintance involves the 'intuitive apprehension' of particular existents, and not simply the apprehension of facts, or states of affairs. He claims that this relation of acquaintance is never more than an element in our total state of mind, but it is, nonetheless, an element of perceptual consciousness, and an essential one. He labels the entities we are acquainted with 'sense-data', and claims, 'It is impossible from the nature of the case to prove that there are sense-data . . . The utmost we can do is to remove misunderstandings which prevent people from searching for them and acknowledging them when found. After that, we can only appeal to every man's own consciousness' (1932: 6). He also suggests that there is a characteristic common and peculiar to sense-data, which he calls 'sensuousness', and adds 'This is obvious on inspection, but it cannot be described' (1932: 6). We see Price here appealing to introspective reflection in support of the claim that sensory experience involves the obtaining of a distinctive psychological relation of acquaintance that is an essential element of perceptual consciousness. We see him trying to say something about its distinctive character, and one of the suggestions he makes is that 'sensuousness' is a characteristic of the *objects* of that relation—i.e. a characteristic of the entities with which we are acquainted.

As the latter point suggests, once one has in play the notion that there is a distinctive and fundamental sort of psychological relation that obtains when one has sensory experience, questions inevitably arise about the nature of the entities to which one is so related. Are they material objects and their properties? Are they surfaces, or parts of surfaces, of material objects? What are the entities to which one is psychologically related when one hallucinates, or experiences a perceptual illusion? If they are not material objects, or parts of material objects, then exactly what sort of entity has now been introduced into our ontology? What properties do they have? Are we aware of the same sorts of entities in all cases of sensory experience? If so, how are we to understand the relation between our awareness of such entities and our perceptual consciousness of material objects?

Different sense-datum theorists offer different answers to these questions, and I don't propose to examine those different answers here. Again, the aim at this stage is just to indicate the way in which a given theoretical framework can influence the direction taken by philosophical discussions of sensory experience and hence the sorts of questions that it is considered important to address when theorizing about sensory experience. One point is worth noting though—a point to which I shall return—and that concerns the role of introspective reflection in such accounts. One finds sense-datum theorists appealing to introspective reflection in support of the idea that a distinctive psychological relation obtains when one has sensory experience;[4] introspection is also appealed to in support of claims that are made about what is distinctive of that relation—e.g. the claim that it is a relation to particulars, and the way in which Russell and Broad attach importance to the idea that this psychological relation appears to reveal its objects as *temporally present*. Introspection is also appealed to in support of certain claims that are made about some of the features possessed by the entities to which we are psychologically related—e.g. the claim that in the case of vision, the entities to which we are related have colour properties. However, once theoretical considerations and questions are introduced, and a more rarefied specification of the entities to which we are so related is attempted, one finds critics complaining that introspection ends up undermining these theories. For it is suggested that the sorts of entities we appear to be related to, and which we are in a position to attend to when we introspect, are material objects and their features, and not the sorts of entities that sense-datum theorists are led, by theoretical and argumentative considerations, to posit as objects of acquaintance.[5]

---

[4] See also the role played by the 'phenomenal principle' in Robinson's (1994) arguments for a sense-datum theory.

[5] Certain sense-datum theorists were aware of this. For example, Price (1932) held that the intuitive apprehension of sense-data was an *element* of perceptual consciousness, and not the only element, and the fact that we appear to be perceptually aware of material objects is to be explained by other features of perceptual consciousness. (See also the concessions Price makes about this in the preface of the 1954 reprint of *Perception*.)

1.2 Representational content and the properties of conscious experience

We have since seen the emergence of a rather different framework within which questions about sensory consciousness tend to get addressed. Within that framework, sense-datum theories are no longer as popular as they once were. The idea that the sensuous character of conscious sensory experience is to be explained, in part, by appeal to a distinctive psychological relation that obtains when one has conscious sensory experience no longer dominates theorizing about the nature of sensory experience. It is generally agreed that perceptual illusions and hallucinations are conscious sensory experiences, but most philosophers now dismiss the idea that we need to provide some account of entities possessing sensory qualities, such as colour and shape, to which we are psychologically related when we hallucinate or experience a perceptual illusion, and so arguments from illusion and hallucination are no longer treated as seriously as a basic philosophical challenge that an account of perception must address. In the philosophy of perception there has been a tendency for the focus of enquiry to shift away from questions about the objects of sensory experience, and the nature of the distinctive psychological relation we bear to them, to questions about the properties of sensory experience.

Martin (2000) makes some interesting suggestions about this shift in the focus of debates about perception in the context of offering a diagnosis of the way in which the argument from illusion lost its pre-eminence as a serious philosophical challenge that an account of perception must meet. The question he addresses is this. What made the argument from illusion so persuasive to so many philosophers given that the argument is now thought, by the majority of philosophers, to be so easy to dismiss?[6] Martin's concern here isn't simply that of tracing and commenting on the history of the subject. The proposal he offers has a philosophical point. His suggestion is that an appeal to introspective reflection played a significant role in persuading philosophers of the conclusion of the argument from illusion and in leading them to adopt a sense-datum theory. Martin suggests that given that many now think that introspective reflection undermines sense-datum theories, this 'reflects something at the heart of the problem of perception, something which is rarely made fully articulate in discussion of it...that the more fundamental problem here is one concerning our knowledge of our own minds' (2000:198).

Martin's proposal, very roughly, is that there is introspective evidence that can be appealed to in support of sense-datum theories, and there is also introspective evidence that can be appealed to in arguing against them, and the background intellectual climate of the time affects and influences the kind of introspective evidence that is appealed to and emphasized in theorizing about perception. So as the background intellectual climate changes, the kind of introspective evidence that is cited changes, and the argument from illusion loses its appeal.

---

[6] See also Snowdon 1992.

More specifically, Martin's suggestion is this. Introspective reflection provides one with a source of evidence for some kind of sense-datum theory, in so far as it offers support for a relational conception of the sensory. However, introspective reflection offers a source of evidence against sense-datum theories, in so far as it offers support for the idea that we are directly aware of mind-independent material objects, and not the sorts of entities that sense-datum theorists posit in their accounts. At the time when the sense-datum approach was more popular, philosophers were preoccupied with the problematic status of common-sense realism—the problem of accommodating the apparent presence to mind of sensory qualities that are not part of the scientific view of the world. Moreover, there was not at that time the same resistance as there now is to the consequences of positing objects of awareness in the case of hallucination. For a commitment to physicalism, and in particular the completeness of physics, was not as widespread as it now is. These aspects of the background intellectual climate of the time influence the emphasis placed on the introspective evidence that supports a relational conception of the sensory. However, the ascendancy of a commitment to physicalism brings with it a greater resistance to the positing of non-physical objects of awareness; and so the introspective evidence that undermines sense-datum theories is now appealed to and emphasized.[7]

Not all of these ideas are uncontroversial, and some of the more controversial ideas will be discussed in more detail in later chapters. But a point that I think many will agree with is that the dominance of the question of whether some kind of physicalist view is correct has had a profound effect in shaping the way in which we approach the philosophy of mind in general (for physicalists and non-physicalists alike), and the sorts of philosophical questions we raise about sensory consciousness in particular. But another hugely important factor, I think, has been the development in our understanding of thought. The significant development I have in mind is the notion that thoughts are to be individuated in terms of propositional contents, and in particular a number of claims concerning what such a view amounts to that find their first crystallized formulation in the work of Frege.

The Fregean view of thought is associated with a series of claims about the contents of our thoughts and propositional attitudes—the contents in terms of which we individuate such aspects of mind—that still dominate much of our thinking in this area. These include the following: the idea that such contents, as the objects of our propositional attitudes, can be judged and agreed upon by different thinkers, so there is inherent in the notion the idea of the objectivity or shareability of such contents; the claim that the notion of content that we need to employ when theorizing about thought is one according to which such contents have truth conditions; the idea that these contents are composite, structured entities, and that one understands their structural nature

---

[7] It should be said that among the early sense-datum theorists there was a live debate as to whether or not sense-data should be regarded as non-physical. See, for example, Russell 1914, and the discussion of this issue in Nasim 2008.

and their components in terms of the contribution of such components to the truth conditions of the contents they compose, and their contribution to preserving truth in deductive inference.

Many of these ideas were prefigured in the work of earlier philosophers, but Frege provided us with a logic that made it possible to make headway with them in a way that was previously unavailable. Although the impact of the Fregean account of thought on philosophical accounts of sensory experience was not immediate, and although many disagreed, and still do disagree, with various aspects of the Fregean account, a cluster of ideas associated with the Fregean view eventually became the centre of gravity of philosophical discussions of intentionality in general—the mind's directedness on the world. Given that perceptual experience is, in these broad terms, intentional—directed on the world—this eventually leads to the suggestion that we should understand the intentionality of sensory experience in terms of a notion of intentional/representational content that is similar in certain important respects to the Fregean notion of thought. There are a number of claims associated with this notion of the intentional/representational content of sensory experience that mirror, in certain respects, some of the claims made about Fregean thought—e.g. the idea of the objectivity of such intentional contents; the idea that such contents have veridicality conditions; the idea that these contents are structured composite entities; the idea that the structure of these contents marks structural aspects of the capacities embodied in the perceptual states/events that they individuate, which are revealed, in part, in the kinds of transitions between mental states/ events with intentional content in which they partake.[8]

One significant consequence of this development in our understanding of thought is the way it impacts on our understanding of the relation between sensory experience and thought—the question of whether and how sensory experiences cause, ground, and rationalize our perceptual judgements and beliefs and the concepts that constitute the contents of those judgements and beliefs. The notion that sensory experiences have intentional contents with veridicality conditions appears to throw new and illuminating light on these issues. It also appears to offer a useful way of thinking about the way in which sensory experience can causally explain and rationalize perceptually guided action.

Another advantage of this picture is the way in which it provides a helpful framework within which scientific theorizing about sense perception can be fruitfully pursued. For example, one of the tasks of an empirical investigation of the senses becomes that of determining and explaining the processes by which perceptual systems form perceptual states/events with specific veridicality conditions from specific types of stimulation of a subject's sensory receptors. The invocation of mental states/events with intentional contents that have veridicality conditions offers a useful way of thinking of what is to be

---

[8] Those who endorse the idea that experiences have intentional contents with veridicality conditions include Evans (1982), Searle (1983), Harman (1990), Peacocke (1992), Burge (1991 and 2010), Tye (1992 and 1995), Pautz (2010), and Siegel (2011).

explained—the obtaining/occurrence of perceptual states/events with intentional contents that have certain veridicality conditions—and it also offers a way of thinking of
distinctively psychological processes that are involved in their formation—e.g. unconscious cognitive processes involved in the formation of perceptual states/events with
veridicality conditions that respond to the stimulus values that the subject's sensory
receptors transduce.[9]

With this general understanding of the intentionality of sensory experience in play,
illusion and hallucination can now be seen as akin to false belief in certain important
respects. When a subject hallucinates or experiences a perceptual illusion there
obtains/occurs a perceptual state/event with an intentional content whose veridicality conditions are not satisfied. There is no need to posit the existence of non-physical
entities—sense-data—to which the subject is psychologically related. The 'problem'
of hallucination and illusion is no longer seen as a distinctive and pressing problem
that an account of sense perception must address, in so far as it is seen as just an
instance of a more general question about the intentionality of mental states/events
with intentional contents that are false/non-veridical, and so the argument from illusion loses its pre-eminence as a distinctive challenge that a philosophical account of
sensory experience must address.

I noted that appeals to introspection seem to have played a significant role in motivating sense-datum theories. So within this new framework have appeals to introspection
disappeared? Even in the scientific study of sense perception introspection is still used as
a source of evidence. For example, in perceptual and cognitive psychology the perceived
qualities of objects and the effects of experimental manipulation on experience are
sometimes investigated by techniques that rely on subjects' introspectively mediated
responses to what they experience, and this can be used as a source of evidence in investigating the underlying psychological processes involved in sense perception.[10] But what
is more, one also finds that a number of philosophers who address questions about sensory experience within the new framework appear to endorse something like the
assumption about the role of introspective reflection that I invoked earlier: i.e. the
assumption that conscious sensory experiences have a distinctive sensuous character
that is manifest to one as a self-conscious subject when one has them, the nature of that
distinctive sensuous character is a legitimate object of enquiry, and introspective reflection on one's conscious sensory experience plays a significant role in an investigation
of that sensuous character.

One might think that developments in our understanding of thought (and hence
belief and judgement) may allow us to accommodate adequately the intuition behind
the assumption regarding the distinctive role of introspection in theorizing about

---

[9] The suggestion that the relevant sub-personal processes are to be understood in terms of transitions
between mental states with veridicality conditions is not uncontroversial. For discussion, see Hatfield 1991
and 2009, chapter 1.

[10] For discussion of this issue, see Hatfield 2005.

conscious sensory experience by enabling us to provide an account that focuses on explaining the *judgements* and *beliefs* about sensory experience that our introspective reports express. And in providing such an account we need not assume that the assumption about the distinctive role of introspection is true. In other words, in providing an account of the judgements and beliefs about sensory experience that our introspective reports express we need not assume that conscious sensory experiences actually have a distinctive sensuous character whose nature is to be discerned and articulated via introspection.

However, I think that part of the intuition behind the assumption is that the appeal to introspection is, in a sense, self-justifying. That is to say, the intuition about the legitimacy of the role of introspection in discerning and articulating a distinctive sensuous character of conscious sensory experience is itself grounded in introspection. In consequence, any attempt to accommodate the intuition behind the assumption about the legitimacy of the role of introspection in discerning a distinctive sensuous character of conscious sensory experience that does not commit to the truth of that assumption can appear simply to depend on presupposing the falsity of that intuition. As a result, the feeling is that the intuition behind the assumption will have been neither accommodated nor adequately diagnosed, and so the intuition persists, and so even within the new framework vestigial questions about the nature of the distinctive sensuous character of conscious sensory experience remain.

But the new framework within which debates about sensory experience are addressed affects the way in which questions are posed about the distinctive sensuous character of conscious sensory experience. Debates about the sensuous character of conscious sensory experience are now no longer usually framed in terms of the question of what is distinctive of a particular kind of psychological relation that obtains when one has conscious sensory experience, but rather in terms of the question of what properties conscious sensory events/states have, and disagreements about the sensuous character of conscious sensory experience are usually thought of as disagreements about the properties of these mental events/states.

Within this framework, the positions taken by different philosophers can diverge in a variety of ways. For example, there are disagreements about the kind of intentional content that sensory experience has (e.g. whether the content is conceptual or nonconceptual, and disagreements over exactly what that distinction amounts to); there are disagreements over whether certain non-psychological, e.g. causal, relations between the environment and the experience must obtain if that experience is to have a given intentional content; there are disagreements about the functional role of these sensory events/states; and there are also disagreements over whether these mental events/states have non-representational/sensational properties (or qualia) in addition to having an intentional content with veridicality conditions. The latter issue often gets posed in terms of a question about the relation between the phenomenal (or 'what-it-is-like') properties of sensory experience and the representational properties of experience.

Some suggest that introspective reflection supports the contention that one fails to accommodate adequately the distinctive sensuous character of conscious sensory experience if one simply appeals to the idea that our conscious experiences are mental states/events that have intentional contents with veridicality conditions. They propose that one needs, in addition, to appeal to non-representational properties/qualia that our experiences possess. In response to this, something akin to Moore's appeal to the respect in which conscious experience is 'diaphanous' is sometimes invoked in these debates. Some suggest that an appeal to the 'transparency' of experience can help undermine the contention that we need to appeal to non-representational properties of experience (or qualia) in order to accommodate adequately the distinctive sensuous character of conscious sensory experience. The thought here, very roughly, is that when one attempts to attend introspectively to the posited non-representational properties of experience one will fail. The attempt to attend introspectively to one's experience only reveals the objects, properties, and relations that are *represented* by one's experience. In this context, debates about the extent to which experience may or may not be transparent are not usually thought to turn on the question of whether we need to appeal to a psychological relation of perceptual acquaintance in an account of the sensuous character of conscious experience, but rather on the question of whether our conscious sensory experiences have non-representational as well as representational properties.

As the question of whether we should accept physicalism has come to the fore in the philosophy of mind, one key concern has been whether, and how, accounts of the sensuous character of conscious sensory experience fit into a physicalist view of the world. While there are significant differences of opinion on this issue, something like a consensus has emerged concerning how such questions should be posed. In particular, it is often assumed that this issue centres on the question of whether the phenomenal/what-it-is-like properties of conscious sensory states/events supervene on the physical. And central to that debate, for many, is the question of whether we need to appeal to non-representational properties of conscious experience, in addition to the representational properties of experience, in order to provide an account that adequately accommodates the phenomenal character of conscious sensory experience.

As progress is made in scientific empirical investigations of the mind, questions can be posed about the relation between the manifest image of mind and the scientific image of mind at more fine-grained levels of specification. For example, questions can be posed about the relation between the 'manifest image' of conscious sensory experience that is subjectively accessible to introspective reflection and the postulates of theories of sense perception proposed by empirical psychologists and brain scientists, where such postulates might include sub-personal informational processes and mechanisms, neural events and states, and neuro-chemical properties. And here there often appears to be some kind of consensus on the general shape the manifest image should take—conscious sensory experiences are to be thought of as personal-level mental states/events that have representational properties and, for some, non-representational properties as well.

Once we pose questions in terms of the relation between the 'manifest image' of mind and the 'scientific image' of mind, a number of issues emerge concerning how these perspectives on the mind can and should have an impact on one another. For example, should we try to articulate the manifest image independently of scientific enquiry and should the postulates of the manifest image be treated as data to be explained by a scientific theory? Should we rather think of the 'manifest image' as a crude, naïve first approximation of something that the more sophisticated, scientific image of mind can elaborate on, refine, correct, and perhaps ultimately replace? To what extent is the mind's image of its own construction merely a construction of the mind? These sorts of issues turn, in part, on questions of self-knowledge—questions concerned with what we can and cannot know about our own minds independently of scientific enquiry.[11] This, in turn, suggests that questions about self-knowledge are right at the heart of questions about the manifest image of mind and its relation to the scientific image. And as an instance of that, questions about self-knowledge appear to be right at the heart of questions about the manifest image of conscious sensory experience. So disagreements about the manifest image of conscious sensory experience and its relation to the scientific image may depend on disagreements about what we can and cannot know about our conscious sensory experiences when we have them. This takes us back to Martin's proposal—that puzzles about self-knowledge lie at the heart of philosophical disagreements about conscious sensory experience.

1.3 The re-emergence of relational views

I said that there appears to have emerged something of a consensus concerning the general shape that the 'manifest image' of conscious sensory experience should take. Debates about the sensuous character of conscious sensory experience are generally no longer framed in terms of the question of what is distinctive of a particular kind of psychological relation that obtains when one has conscious sensory experience, but rather in terms of the question of what properties conscious sensory events/states have, and disagreements about the sensuous character of conscious sensory experience are usually thought of as disagreements about the properties of mental events/states. However, the recent re-emergence of relational views of sensory experience can be seen as a challenge to this consensus.[12]

These relationalists endorse the idea that we need to appeal to the obtaining of a distinctive kind of psychological relation when characterizing the manifest image of conscious sensory experience—i.e. when characterizing the sort of distinctive sensuous character of conscious sensory experience that is manifest to one when one has a conscious sensory experience. In this, they appear to agree with sense-datum theorists.

---

[11] As well as questions about what we can and cannot know about the minds of others independently of scientific enquiry.

[12] See e.g. Martin 2002, Campbell 2002, Brewer 2011.

However, they reject sense-datum theories of perception, for they claim that the relevant psychological relation is one that subjects bear to material objects and their features, and not to the sorts of entities posited by sense-datum theorists. This psychological relation to material objects and their features cannot plausibly be held to obtain when a subject hallucinates. So according to these relationalists, when a subject hallucinates, although it may seem to that subject as though she is having a conscious sensory experience that involves the obtaining of a distinctive psychological relation to material objects and their features, she isn't. And so the sort of conscious sensuous character that seems to the subject of the hallucination to be introspectively accessible to her, is not in fact introspectively accessible to her.

What this relationalist proposal amounts to is, I think, a radical challenge to what has become the more orthodox view of the general shape of the manifest image of conscious sensory experience. It reintroduces the idea that the sensuous character of conscious sensory experience is to be articulated (at least in part) by appeal to a distinctive psychological *relation* that obtains when one has conscious sensory experience, and not simply by appeal to the occurrence/obtaining of a mental event/state that has certain distinctive properties. I will be discussing the proposal in more detail in later chapters. But what I want to emphasize and signal at this point is the way in which this rather different claim about the general shape of the manifest image of conscious sensory experience intersects with a view about self-knowledge—a view about what a subject is in a position to know about her conscious sensory experience when she has it, and what puts her in a position to know it. It involves the idea that an account of what one can know about the sensuous character of the conscious sensory experience one has when one successfully perceives the world, and one's account of what puts one in a position to know it, cannot be straightforwardly and symmetrically applied to the case of hallucination. This can be thought of as an instance of the general idea mentioned earlier—that disagreements about the manifest image of conscious sensory experience and its relation to the scientific image may depend on, and intersect with, disagreements about what we can and cannot know about our conscious sensory experiences when we have them.

I have suggested that despite the significant changes in the frameworks in terms of which questions about sensory experience tend to get addressed, a basic intuition about the special and significant role that introspection should play in providing a philosophical account of the *sensuous* character of *conscious* sensory experience has persisted; but differences in the background theoretical frameworks that different philosophers adopt can affect how these philosophers articulate the manifest image of conscious sensory experience, which in turn can affect the way in which they pose questions about the sensuous character of conscious experience, as well as the way in which they pose questions about the relation between the manifest image and the scientific image of conscious sensory experience. Although debates about the extent to which conscious experience may or may not be 'transparent' are now often framed in terms of questions about whether conscious experiences have non-representational properties (qualia) as well as representational properties, within a framework that involves appealing to the obtaining of a psychological relation of perceptual acquaintance questions about the transparency of experience can be framed in somewhat different terms. For example, for those who adopt a relationalist approach to conscious sensory experience, a question that connects with the issue of the extent to which conscious experience may or may not be transparent is the following: how much of the conscious character of conscious sensory experience is to be explained by appealing to the nature of the objects of perceptual acquaintance, and how much by the manner in which one is perceptually acquainted with them?

This, in turn, connects with the following general issue: if one is a relationalist, how should one go about trying to articulate what is distinctive of the sort of psychological relation that obtains when one has conscious sensory experience? Should one be seeking to describe certain general features of the relation? Should one hold that there are different things to be said about different features of the relations that obtain in different modalities of sense perception? For example, the sense-datum theorist Price (1932) denied that there are different kinds of sensing. He held that the difference between the senses seems to be wholly on the side of the data that are sensed. Is this something that all relationalists should accept? I noted ways in which the sense-datum theorists Russell and Broad attached importance to the idea that the psychological relation of perceptual acquaintance appears to reveal its objects as temporally present. Is this something that the new relationalist theories should appeal to? And if so, is this to be somehow explained by the nature of the psychological relation of perceptual acquaintance, rather than the objects of that psychological relation? And how does this aspect of the temporal phenomenology of perceptual experience bear on the question of the extent to which conscious sensory experience is 'transparent' when one attempts to attend introspectively to it?

1.4 Articulating the manifest image of sensory consciousness

In what follows I shall be suggesting various ways in which issues in the ontology of mind—and in particular, ontological distinctions that can be marked by the different ways in which different aspects of our mental lives fill time—can engage with and contribute to these debates about the manifest image of sensory consciousness that I have sketched. So far, I've talked very generally about an intuition that introspection has a significant role to play in investigating the 'sensuous character' of 'conscious sensory experience'. Philosophers discussing conscious sensory experience often focus on the character of conscious *visual* experience, and refer less frequently to other sensory modalities. But if one shares this intuition, then one is likely to think that something like this intuition also applies when it comes to an investigation of the conscious character of sensations, such as tickles, itches, and pains. It is also intuitive to think that perceptual imagination and perceptual memory have something in common with the sensuous character of conscious sensory experience. So can the account one gives of what I have been calling 'the general shape' of the manifest image of conscious visual experience be straightforwardly applied to these other aspects of mind? If not, why not? These issues will also be addressed in Part I, and again, in addressing them I shall be emphasizing the importance of various ontological distinctions between different aspects of mind that are determined by the different ways in which those aspects of mind fill time.

I shall start by examining in more detail the way in which the appeal to the notion of an intentional content with veridicality conditions has affected debates about sensory experience, and in particular debates about the sensuous character of conscious sensory experience. My suggestion is going to be that a fruitful route to exploring these issues is to look at how the notion of propositional content affected views about the nature of thought at a time when it was not yet the orthodoxy to appeal to an intentional content with veridicality conditions in providing an account of sensory experience. In particular, the idea is to go back to a time when the significant development in our understanding of the nature of thought that Frege initiated was appealed to as a way of highlighting an important *difference* between thought and sensory experience. Such an appeal is to be found in Geach's work on the mental acts of thinking thoughts and making judgements.

Geach argued, *contra* William James, that there is no *stream* of conscious thought. Although sensory processes may be stream-like, mental acts of thinking thoughts and making judgements are not, and according to Geach this becomes clear once we acknowledge that such mental acts are individuated by their propositional contents. Geach's argument offers what I think is an interesting angle on the question of the differences between, and the relations between, the cognitive and the sensory. The question of what it is for an aspect of mind to be 'stream-like' raises issues in the ontology of mind—namely the question of how the temporal features of an aspect of mind, the way in which it fills time, are relevant to its ontological category. The suggestion is that a consideration of such ontological issues can be a fruitful way of thinking about the differences between thought and sensory experience. I shall be suggesting in what follows that these matters are also relevant to current debates about sensory experience that are now framed in terms of the relation between representational content and phenomenal character. In particular, in the next chapter I shall introduce ways in which these ontological concerns can contribute to a familiar debate that centres on the following question: to what extent, if any, do purely representationalist accounts of conscious sensory experience fail to accommodate the distinctive sensuous character of conscious sensory experience?

2

Occurrence, State, Content, and Character

In the previous chapter I contrasted, at a very general level, two opposing views of the general shape of the manifest image of conscious sensory experience: a view according to which we need to appeal to a distinctive psychological relation that obtains when we have conscious sensory experience, and a view according to which we should just be appealing to distinctive properties of mental states/events. In this chapter I shall be introducing the idea that there are further important distinctions to keep in mind when articulating the general shape of the manifest image of conscious experience.

One issue that is discussed in the ontology of mind is the following: what is it that distinguishes the general ontological categories of mental state, mental event, and mental process? Those addressing this issue often appeal to the idea that these ontological distinctions are to be marked by the different ways in which these different aspects of mind fill time. For example, it is suggested that mental states *obtain* over, and throughout, intervals of time, and at times; whereas mental events and processes *occur/happen/unfold* over time and/or at times. The idea here is that even when a mental state and a mental event (or process) have the same temporal extension—even when they occupy the same interval of time—they don't have the same temporal character. They will fill that interval of time in quite different ways. For example, in her book on the ontology of mind Helen Steward writes:

> In merely giving the temporal dimensions of an existent thing–in specifying the beginning and end-points of its existence–one does not thereby determine its temporal character. For vastly more important than these temporal reference points, in determining the ontological category of any item, is the way in which that item fills the relevant period of time– whether it persists through time, or occurs during the time, or obtains throughout the time etc. (1997: 73).

I shall be arguing that these issues in the ontology of mind can contribute to our philosophical understanding of sensory consciousness. In this chapter I shall introduce a general proposal about the ontology of conscious sensory experience that I will be developing and putting to work in various ways in subsequent chapters. My starting point will be to explore how these issues in the ontology of mind may bear on debates that are framed in terms of the question of the relation between the representational content of a conscious sensory experience and its phenomenal character.

2.1 The temporal profiles of thought and experience

Debates about the conscious character of conscious sensory experience now often start with the idea that there is 'something it is like' for the subject to have such experiences. It is then suggested that a conscious sensory experience has 'what-it-is-like' properties, often called 'phenomenal' properties, that determine what it is like for the subject to have the experience. The claim is that a conscious sensory experience has a phenomenal character that is determined by the experience's phenomenal/what-it-is-like properties.

For those who hold that experiences are mental states/events that have intentional contents with veridicality conditions, one question that arises in this context is whether the phenomenal character of a conscious sensory experience can be exhaustively explained in terms of the idea that it is a mental event/state that has an intentional content with veridicality conditions. This sometimes gets expressed in terms of a question about the relation between an experience's representational properties and its phenomenal properties. In such discussions it is rarely made explicit how we are to think of the temporal profile of the conscious sensory experiences to which such properties are attributed. Implicit is the assumption that such matters do not bear directly on the question of the relation between the representational content of a conscious sensory experience and its phenomenal character.

This debate about the relation between an experience's representational properties and its phenomenal/what-it-is-like properties is a relatively recent one. But there is a much older debate to which it appears to be related, and within that older debate it has been suggested that these ontological concerns are relevant and important. The older debate I have in mind is the long-standing question of the differences between thought and experience, thinking and sensing, or more generally, the cognitive and the sensory. Philosophical debates about the differences between the cognitive and the sensory have arisen in a number of different contexts. These debates often get framed in quite different ways, reflecting the different theoretical frameworks that are assumed during the different periods in which they are conducted; but within such debates one finds both theories of thought and theories of experience being criticized for failing to respect and reflect the differences between the cognitive and the sensory. One such debate, which is not discussed much now, arose when Geach objected to William James' notion of the 'stream of conscious thought'. James wrote,

Consciousness...does not appear to itself chopped up in bits. Such words as 'chain' or 'train' do not describe it fitly as it presents itself in the first instant. It is nothing jointed: it flows. A 'river' or a 'stream' are the metaphors by which it is most naturally described. *In talking hereafter, let us call it the stream of thought, of consciousness, or of subjective life.* (James 1890: 233)

Geach presented an argument designed to 'call . . . attention to the discontinuous character of thought', and 'the complete inappropriateness of James' expression "the stream
of thought"' (1969: 34). Geach suggested that those who think that there is a *stream* of
conscious *thought* are making the mistake of assuming that 'to think certain thoughts is
to have certain mental images, feelings, unspoken words etc., passing through one's
mind' (1969: 34). He suggested that although *sensory* aspects of mind may be 'stream-
like', acts of thinking thoughts are not; and this becomes clear, according to Geach,
once we attain a correct understanding of the way in which acts of thinking are to
be individuated in terms of their propositional contents.

Geach's argument offers an interesting angle on these older debates about the differences between, and relations between, the cognitive and the sensory. The question of
whether an aspect of mind is 'stream-like' connects with the ontological question of the
manner in which that aspect of mind fills time. What we find in Geach's argument is, in
effect, the suggestion that acts of thinking do not fill time in the way that sensory aspects
of mind fill time, and his suggestion is that this becomes clear once we have a correct
understanding of the way in which thoughts, in contrast to sensory aspects of mind, are
to be individuated in terms of their propositional contents. How might these concerns
be relevant to the more recent debate framed in terms of the question of the relation
between an experience's representational properties and its phenomenal character?

In the previous chapter I said that there are a number of claims associated with the
notion of an intentional/representational content of sensory experience that mirror, in
certain respects, some of the claims made about Fregean thought. One concern to which
such accounts give rise is whether they end up making sensory experience too thought-
like, and in particular, whether they fail to accommodate the distinctive sensuous character of conscious sensory experience. The debate framed in terms of the question of
the relation between an experience's representational properties and its phenomenal
character can be seen as engaging with these concerns. Geach's argument against the
notion of a conscious *stream* of thought is in effect targeting accounts of thought that he
thinks fail to mark adequately the distinction between thought and the sensory. But
they may also be relevant to debates about the relation between an experience's representational content and its phenomenal character in suggesting the following possibility.
A purely representationalist account of conscious sensory experience may end up making conscious sensory experience too thought-like, by failing to accommodate and
respect the way in which conscious sensory experience, in contrast to thought, is
'stream-like'. So what would be lacking in a creature for which a representationalist
account of sensory experience was true would be a *stream* of sensory consciousness.
The idea that such a creature's mental life would lack a stream of sensory consciousness
may, in turn, impact on intuitions as to whether the creature would be phenomenally
conscious.

I said that issues in the ontology of mind—questions concerned with how aspects of
mind fill time—are relevant to the question of whether an aspect of mind is 'stream-
like', and so relevant to the question of whether a subject's mental life includes a stream

of consciousness. So such considerations introduce a new angle on the question of the relation between the representational properties of a conscious sensory experience and its phenomenal character that may get missed if we simply focus on the question of what properties conscious sensory experiences have *independently* of the question of the temporal profile of the bearers of those properties. In what follows I shall be investigating whether this line of thought really can throw any light on the debate about the relation between the representational content of a conscious sensory experience and its phenomenal character. I start by examining Geach's argument against James' notion of a stream of conscious thought.

2.2 Geach on the discontinuous character of thought

In an essay called 'What Do We Think With?', Geach writes,

Thinking consists in having a series of thoughts which can be counted off discretely–the first, the second, the third,...–; which, if complex, must occur with all their elements present simultaneously; which do not pass into one another by gradual transition. (1969: 35)

He goes on to claim that 'thoughts occur not in a Jamesian stream, but...as a series in which certain thought-contents successively occur, with no succession within any one thought and no gradual transition from one thought to another' (1969: 35–6).

In unpacking Geach's argument for 'the complete inappropriateness of James' expression "the stream of thought"', we'll need to address the following questions. (i) What does Geach mean by the claim that (a) there is no succession within any one thought? (ii) What does Geach mean by the claim that (b) there is no gradual transition from one thought to another? (iii) Why does Geach think that (a) and (b) show that there is no 'stream of conscious thought'? What assumptions is he making about what it would be for the thinking of thoughts to be 'stream-like'? I start with (i).

Geach's argument for the claim that 'there is no succession within any one thought' depends upon his understanding of the idea that acts of thinking are to be individuated in terms of their propositional contents, and in particular his understanding of the idea that the propositional content in terms of which we individuate any given act of thinking is a 'non-successive unity'. It is helpful here to look at what Geach says in *Mental Acts* when he is warning against the danger of carrying too far an analogy between thought and speech. In this passage he points to 'an important difference between speech and thought as regards temporal duration':

Spoken words last so long in physical time, and one word comes out after another; the time they take is, as Aquinas would say, the sort of time that is the measure of local motion–one could sensibly say that the utterance of the words was simultaneous with the movement of a body, e.g. the hand of a clock, from one place to another. The same would go for the duration of mental images of words, or any other mental images; one could sensibly say "I rehearsed the words in my head as I watched the beetle crawl from one side of the table to the other".

With a thought it is quite different. Even if we accepted the view...that a judgement is a complex of Ideas, we could hardly suppose that in a thought the Ideas occur successively, as the words do in a sentence; it seems reasonable to say that unless the whole complex content is grasped all together–unless the Ideas...are all simultaneously present–the thought or judgement just does not exist at all. (1957: 104)

In a similar vein, in 'What Do We Think With?' Geach writes,

even if a thought has a complex content, this does not mean that the elements of this complex can occur separately and successively...Unless the whole content of the thought is simultaneously present to the thinker no such thought occurs at all. (1969: 34)

The important point to highlight here is the idea that the propositional content in terms of which we individuate an act of thinking may be complex—that is to say, it may have structure, parts, and elements; however, according to Geach, there can be no question of these parts 'occurring in *any* temporal order' (1957: 105). In that sense the propositional content should be thought of as a 'non-successive unity'.

In the case of a mental state like belief, or a mental act of judging, that is specified in terms of a propositional content with truth conditions, it is common to think of the propositional content in question as having a complexity—it has structure, and parts, or elements. The components of the propositional content and the way in which that propositional content is structured are relevant to the logical and rational relations that obtain between the different propositional contents in terms of which we type-individuate different beliefs and judgements. So in specifying a property of a mental state/episode in terms of its propositional content we are specifying a property of that mental state/episode in terms of something that has structure, parts, and elements. We can therefore think of the attribution of such a property as involving the attribution of a range of different properties. For example, if S believes that 'John is tall', then S has a belief about John. Being a belief about John may be common to other beliefs S has, as well as beliefs that other subjects have, so we can think of this as a property of the belief that it shares with other beliefs with different propositional contents. But when S has a belief about John, this is because he has a belief about John that can be specified in terms of a whole content with truth conditions. S can't simply have a belief that 'John'.

Likewise, although the propositional content of an act of judging that 'John is tall' may have a part that is about John, one can't simply judge 'John'. In that sense, the parts of the propositional content do not occur separately.[1] And since they do not in this way occur separately, they do not occur successively, in so far as one cannot first judge 'John', and then judge 'is tall'. In contrast, when one asserts something in speech, the spoken words one utters can occur separately and successively. One can simply say 'John', and when one asserts that John is tall, then one can first say 'John', and then say 'is tall'.

---

[1] It is considerations of this kind that lead Mouton (1969) to claim, in his discussion of Geach's argument, that there is 'no such thing as a partial thought', and that 'It is impossible in principle for one to get halfway through a thought and stop' (64).

The spoken words uttered are temporally ordered, but the parts of the propositional content in terms of which we individuate an act of judging are not temporally ordered. In a similar vein, one can say that although the words on a written page are spatially ordered, the parts of the propositional content they may express are not to be thought of as standing in spatial relations to one another.

Since spoken words can occur 'separately and successively', they can, in principle, be uttered in any temporal order. According to Geach, that makes it possible for one to talk nonsense in a way in which one cannot think nonsense.

If you write down a nonsensical *that* clause after 'Smith has the thought...', the whole sentence will be nonsense and thus cannot be a true report of what Smith thought; but there is no such difficulty about quoting the nonsense that Smith talks. (1969: 35)

What Geach's argument seems to get us so far, is the idea that we should reject a certain mistaken picture of those acts of thinking that are individuated in terms of propositional contents. According to that mistaken picture, a mental act of, say, judging that p is thought of as filling an interval of time that can be broken down into sub-intervals of time in each of which there occurs a temporal part of that mental act that is to be speci-fied in terms of a part of the propositional content that p that is judged. When Geach claims that 'there is no succession within any one act of thinking a thought' he means us to reject this mistaken picture of what is involved in an act of thinking a thought. When a subject judges that p, there is no sequence of successive thinkings of different parts of the content that p. Hence, Geach writes,

The thought that the pack of cards is on the table occurs all at once or not at all ... (What kind of ideas the contrary view leads to may be seen from William James' fantasy: that the thought lasts for the whole time of the sentence 'the pack of cards is on the table', and goes through successive phases, in which bits of the thought corresponding to the successive words are prom-inent–including bits corresponding to 'the' and 'of'). (Anscombe and Geach 1961: 96)

Now to our second question: (ii) What does Geach mean by the claim that 'there is no gradual transition from one thought to another'? I think that Geach takes this to follow from the idea that there can be no question of the *temporal* order of the parts of the propositional content in terms of which we individuate an act of thinking. For example, suppose that a subject successively thinks two thoughts that are individuated in terms of their propositional contents. The first act of thinking is a judging that p and the second act of thinking is a judging that q. Suppose that the propositional content that p and the propositional content that q have a part in common—suppose that both judgements are about John. If one held that the parts of the propositional content judged occur sepa-rately and successively, one might think it possible for the judgement that p and the judgement that q to share a *temporal* part—the part that is about John. And so in that sense there could be a gradual transition from one act of judging to the next. On this view, one thought could unfold into the next, and so in that sense these conscious thoughts would not be 'discrete' and 'discontinuous'. However, given that the parts of the propositional content judged are not temporally ordered, it would be a mistake to think that when the propositional contents of two judgements have a part in common it is thereby possible for them to have a temporal part in common. So, in that sense, there can be no gradual transition from one thought to another. Again, what is underlying this claim is the rejection of a certain picture of what is involved in thinking a thought that is individuated in terms of its propositional content—a picture according to which when a subject judges that p there is a sequence of successive thinkings of different parts of the content that p.

So when Geach contrasts sensory aspects of mind with what he takes to be the correct understanding of what is involved in an act of thinking that is individuated in terms of a propositional content, what he seems to have in mind is the following. It is intuitive to think that when sensory aspects of mind fill an interval of time (where these sensory aspects of mind include conscious sensory experiences, sensations, and acts of sensory imagining), that interval of time can be thought of as an interval that can be broken down into sub-intervals in each of which there occurs some successive phase of that sensory episode. For example, a visual experience as of a beetle crawling across a table might be thought of as filling an interval of time that can be broken down into sub-intervals in each of which there occurs an experience as of the beetle occupying a different position on the table. Successive phases of experience are not 'discrete' and 'discontinuous', but rather unfold into one another. Similar remarks apply to episodes of imagining the beetle crawl across the table. And when one imagines saying 'John is tall' in inner speech, it is intuitive to think that there is a temporal phase of the overall episode that involves saying 'is' in inner speech, where that phase of the episode can be thought of as being a temporal part that is common to the earlier phase of saying 'John is' in inner speech and the later phase of saying 'is tall' in inner speech.

As I said earlier, Geach appeals to the claim that (a) there is no succession within any one thought and the claim that (b) there is no gradual transition from one thought to another in arguing for 'the complete inappropriateness of James' expression "the stream of thought"'. But why should claims (a) and (b) make trouble for the notion of a stream of conscious thought?

I have suggested that what Geach's defence of (a) and (b) delivers so far is just the rejection of a certain mistaken picture of what is involved in an act of thinking a thought that is individuated in terms of its propositional content—a picture according to which when a subject thinks (e.g. judges) that p, there is a sequence of successive thinkings of different parts of the content that p. But one could reject the mistaken picture and consistently hold that the activity of thinking (e.g. calculating whether p) involves a series of transitions between successive mental *states*. On this sort of view, each mental state may have temporal duration—perhaps each mental state occupies a very short interval of time—but as a mental state, this aspect of mind does not unfold over the interval of time it occupies. Rather, it obtains throughout that interval of time. On this view, there need be no commitment to the mistaken view of thinking thoughts that Geach's argument targets. If the propositional content of one of these mental states is 'John is tall', then it is not as though the first phase of that mental state is to be individuated in terms of a part of that propositional content—'John'—and the second phase in terms of another part of the propositional content—'is'—and so on. Rather, at each instant that falls within the interval of time that that mental state occupies, there obtains a mental state that is to be individuated in terms of the whole propositional content—'John is tall'.

This view of what is involved in thinking thoughts accommodates Geach's points (a) and (b). But it is also consistent with the suggestion that conscious cognitive activity, such as calculating whether *p*, involves a *process* that occurs over an interval of time and which is constituted by series of successive mental states each of which (and each temporal part of which) is to be individuated by a whole propositional content with truth conditions. So now in what respect is this view of conscious thinking inconsistent with the notion of a *stream* of conscious thought? This takes us to our third question: (iii) Why does Geach think that (a) and (b) show that there is no 'stream of conscious thought'? What assumptions is he making about what it would be for the thinking of thoughts to be 'stream-like'? In particular, what assumptions are being made about the way in which 'stream-like' aspects of mind fill time? In attempting to answer these questions it will help to turn to O'Shaughnessy's remarks on the stream of consciousness in his *Consciousness and the World*.

2.3 The ontology of the stream of consciousness

O'Shaughnessy writes, 'The "stream of consciousness" is such as to necessitate the occurrence of processes and events at all times' (2000: 43); 'It is not the mere existence of flux... that is distinctive...: it is the *necessity* of flux' (2000: 44). In the realm of the stream of consciousness, 'whatever endures necessarily does so processively' (2000: 44). O'Shaughnessy uses the term 'experience' to pick out those aspects of mind that make up the stream of consciousness, and according to him, 'experiences are essentially in a condition of flux. What this means is that all experiences of necessity happen or occur or are going on: in a word are either events, or processes or both' (2000: 49).

'Experiences' are, then, to be contrasted with mental states. Mental states obtain for periods of time, but they do not go on, nor are they undergone, for periods of time. Implicit in the metaphor of the stream of consciousness is the idea that aspects of mind that make up the stream must unfold over time in a way that mental states, like belief, do not. 'Experience' is 'occurrent to the core' (2000: 49), whereas mental states are not happenings. The continuities that make up the stream of consciousness are processive in character; they unfold over time, or occur throughout intervals of time, whereas the continuity of a mental state is, by contrast, non-processive.

Even when experience does not change in type or content it still changes in another respect: it is constantly renewed, a new sector of itself is then and there taking place. This is because experiences are events or processes, and each momentary new element of any given experience is a further happening or occurrence (by contrast with (say) the steady continuation through time of one's knowing that 9 and 5 make 14). (2000: 42)

O'Shaughnessy goes on to claim,

continuation of the knowledge that 9 and 5 make 14 does not as such necessitate the occurrence of *anything*...[it] is not for an extended event of knowing to have occurred. Rather, a state of knowing endured for that time. (2000: 43)

One might object to the suggestion that the 'continuation of the knowledge that 9 and 5 make 14 does not as such necessitate the occurrence of *anything*', for even though a subject may retain that knowledge through dreamless sleep, one might doubt whether a subject could retain that knowledge in the absence of *any* brain activity, or without the occurrence of any life-sustaining biological events and processes. However, even if the continuation of a subject's knowledge that 9 and 5 make 14 does, after all, necessitate the occurrence of some events/processes, we should still agree with O'Shaughnessy that the continuation of that knowledge does not amount to the occurrence of an extended event of knowing. One's knowledge that 9 and 5 make 14 is a mental state. So what this suggests is the following: one cannot determine the ontological category of an aspect of mind by simply looking to the ontological categories of the biological and physical things on which it may supervene. This is an important point that I will have cause to return to later.

O'Shaughnessy makes a further, and important, qualification regarding the ontological profile of 'experiences'—those aspects of mind that make up the stream of consciousness. According to O'Shaughnessy, experiences are processive in character, they unfold over time, or occur throughout intervals of time, and what is more, they are not processes that are analysable in terms of states and events that are simply changes to, or in, those states. Consider a mental state that obtains over an interval of time t1 to tn. We might think of the temporal boundaries of the obtaining of the state as marked by the occurrence of events—namely the event of the mental state's acquisition and the event of its extinction. A mental process of some kind could be constituted by a series of such events—e.g. the acquisition of mental state M1 at t1 and the event of its extinction at t5, the event of the acquisition of mental state M2 at t5, and the event of its extinction at t10, and so on. We might think of this as a mental process constituted by a series of transitions between mental states. Note also that these mental states may be rather short-lived, as the question of whether an aspect of mind should be regarded as a mental state or a mental event/process isn't determined by the amount of time it fills, but rather by the way in which it fills the relevant interval of time. According to O'Shaughnessy, this sort of mental process would not amount to an 'experience'—i.e. an aspect of mind that makes up the stream of consciousness—as it is analysable in terms of mental states and events that are simply changes in those states.

As O'Shaughnessy notes, 'processes can occur in the non-experiencing sector of the mind'. For, as he puts it, 'states are not immutable' (2000: 46). Furthermore, certain events that are changes *to* states can have temporal duration, and these changes may take gradual and continual form. Take, for example, a case of forgetting that happens gradually and continuously, or a case in which one's degree of belief in a proposition changes gradually and continually, as one becomes more and more convinced of something. According to O'Shaughnessy, we can specify a 'non-experiential' psychological process by simply specifying a psychological state, positing an event consisting in a change in that state, and positing continuity as the mode in which the change is realized. Such processes, although they unfold over time, are not elements in the stream of consciousness. They are not 'experiences', for 'experiences' are not analysable as a series of continual and gradual changes in, or to, states. According to O'Shaughnessy, 'No experiences are states. None can be and of necessity' (2000: 47). He asks, 'If no psychological states are experiences, how can there be a state whose continuous change constitutes experiential process?' (2000: 47). And so he concludes that 'experiences' cannot be constituted out of psychological states.

O'Shaughnessy's discussion of continuities in the stream of consciousness provides us with an interesting proposal about what would be absent in a creature whose mental life did not include a stream of consciousness. According to this proposal, the mental life of such a creature would lack mental continuities that are processive in character but which are not analysable in terms of mental states and events and processes that are simply changes to/in those mental states. With this proposal in mind we can return to Geach's objection to the notion of a *stream* of conscious thought.

Perhaps Geach is assuming something like O'Shaughnessy's proposal—the proposal that those aspects of mind that constitute a stream of consciousness are not mental states and events/processes that are analysable in terms of changes to/in mental states. In which case, perhaps Geach thinks something like the following: those who think that there is a conscious stream of thought are assuming that the activity of thinking is not analysable in terms of mental states and events/processes that are changes to/in mental states, and their assumption rests on a mistaken picture of the act of thinking a thought. According to this mistaken picture, there is succession within each act of thinking which allows that there can be a gradual transition from one act of thinking to another. The mistaken picture might lead one to think that an act of thinking (e.g. an act of judging that *p*) unfolds over time. It involves the successive unfolding of thinking different parts of the content judged, which in turn would allow for the possibility of a continual unfolding of one act of thinking to the next act of thinking, with each successive act of thinking sharing a temporal part with the next act of thinking.[2]

---

[2] Note that someone could hold that there are other reasons for thinking that conscious thinking is not analysable in terms of mental states and events/processes that are changes to/in mental states. For example, suppose one holds that (a) conscious thinking requires the occurrence of sensory imagining, and (b) sensory imagining is not analysable in terms of mental states and events/processes that are changes to/in mental states. Someone who holds this view need not be committed to the mistaken view of the act of thinking a thought that Geach rejects. So this view is not ruled out by that part of Geach's argument that I have discussed so far. Geach has other reasons for rejecting this view. I put them aside for now, as they will be discussed in detail in Part II.

Let us briefly summarize some of the main points covered so far, before turning to the question of how these points may bear on the debate about the relation between the representational content of sensory experience and its phenomenal character. Geach suggests that acts of thinking do not fill time in the way that sensory aspects of mind fill time. His suggestion is based on a certain understanding of the idea that acts of thinking are individuated in terms of their propositional contents. This leads Geach to suggest that although there may be a stream of sensory consciousness, it is a mistake to think that there is a stream of conscious thought. Behind Geach's argument lies an assumption about the temporal profile of those aspects of mind that make up a stream of consciousness. I looked to O'Shaughnessy's discussion of continuities in the stream of consciousness to help identify what that assumption might be. That discussion led to a proposal about what would be lacking in a creature whose mental life did not include a stream of consciousness—the proposal that that creature's mental life would lack mental continuities that are processive in character but which are not analysable in terms of mental states and events/processes that are simply changes to/in those mental states.

What Geach's argument brings into play is the idea that the differences between the cognitive and the sensory aren't simply to be explained in terms of differences in the properties possessed by each. For the suggestion is that there is an important difference between the cognitive and the sensory that turns on the further issue of how these aspects of mind fill time. At this stage, these ideas are all just suggestive, and we're not yet in a position to draw any definite conclusions from them. However, as far as their relevance to the debate about the relation between representational content and phenomenal character is concerned, some pertinent questions that these suggestive ideas invite are the following.

(A) Given the similarities between the idea that sensory experience is to be individuated in terms of a representational content with veridicality conditions and the idea that acts of thinking are to be individuated in terms of a propositional content with truth conditions, is there reason to think that purely representationalist accounts of sensory experience are committed to the idea that a subject's perceptual psychological life is analysable in terms of mental states and events/processes that are simply changes to/in those mental states?

(B) If purely representationalist accounts of sensory experience are committed to the idea that a subject's perceptual psychological life is analysable in terms of mental states and events/processes that are simply changes to/in those mental states, do such accounts fail to capture the different ways in which thought and experience fill time and thereby fail to capture the idea that there is a *stream* of sensory consciousness?

(C) If purely representationalist accounts fail to capture the idea that there is a stream of sensory consciousness, do they thereby fail to accommodate the fact that such sensory aspects of mind are phenomenally conscious?

As far as the last question is concerned, we should note the following. One might have the intuition that if a creature's mental life does not include a *stream* of consciousness, then that creature is not *phenomenally* conscious. However, according to O'Shaughnessy's proposal, a creature's mental life would be lacking a stream of consciousness if that creature's mental life did not include mental continuities that are processive in character but which are not analysable in terms of mental states and events/processes that are changes in/to mental states. So those inclined to give an affirmative answer to question (C) will need to respond to the challenge expressed in the following question.

(D) Shouldn't we grant that there are such things as phenomenally conscious mental *states*; and if we do, shouldn't we grant that there can be such a thing as a phenomenally conscious creature whose mental life *is* analysable in terms of mental states and events/processes that are changes to/in those mental states?

This is a question I shall return to at the end of the chapter. First though, I want to start by considering question (A): is there reason to think that purely representationalist accounts of sensory experience are committed to the idea that a subject's perceptual psychological life is analysable in terms of mental states and events/processes that are simply changes to/in those mental states? In the next section I shall consider some potential difficulties faced by representationalist accounts of conscious sensory experience that attempt to resist the claim that a subject's perceptual psychological life can be analysed in this way.

2.4 Representational content and the ontology of experience

Let us suppose that the representationalist claims that a subject's conscious experience is a mental *occurrence*—a mental event or process that occurs/happens/unfolds over and/or at times. On this view, in talking of the representational content of a sensory experience one is specifying what kind of mental occurrence it is. The occurrence in question may have temporal extension—it may be an occurrence that unfolds over an interval of time—in which case in specifying the representational content of the experience one is specifying the kind of occurrence that unfolds over that interval of time.

The first thing to note about this sort of representationalist view is that although the posited experiential occurrence may be something that unfolds over time, and so something that has different temporal parts and successive phases, we should not accept that this is equally true of the content with veridicality conditions in terms of which we individuate that mental occurrence. There are reasons for thinking that the intentional content with veridicality conditions in terms of which the unfolding occurrence is individuated is what Geach called a 'non-successive unity'. Recall Geach's argument that although the propositional content of a judgement can be thought of as being complex, and having parts, it would be a mistake to think that the parts of the propositional content that *p* occur 'separately and successively' when one judges that *p*. Similar remarks apply to the components of an intentional content with veridicality conditions in terms of which a conscious perceptual occurrence is type-individuated. The parts of the intentional content of conscious experience do not occur separately. If over an interval of time t1–t5 S underwent an experience with the content 'That F is G', it would be a mistake to think that from t1 to t2 S underwent a conscious experience with the content that 'That F', and over the interval of time t3–t5 S underwent a conscious experience with the content that 'is G'. If the experience occurs over an interval of time t1–t5, then at t2 a temporal part of the event of experiencing that p may have occurred, but it would be wrong to say that from t1 to t2 S underwent a conscious experience that can be specified in terms of part of the content that p. Contents with veridicality conditions may be used to specify the kind of conscious experience undergone by a subject over an interval of time, but such intervals are not to be thought of as intervals that can be broken down into sub-intervals in each of which there occurs a conscious experience that is to be specified in terms of some part of the content experienced, where such parts lack veridicality conditions.

The second thing to note about this representationalist view is the following. If we appeal to an intentional content with veridicality conditions in individuating an experiential occurrence undergone by a subject, we thereby specify properties of the experiential occurrence undergone by that subject; but if we assume that the experiential occurrence that we are individuating in terms of an intentional content with veridicality conditions is a conscious, personal-level mental occurrence, there is a question to be addressed about the connection between the properties of the experiential occurrence undergone by the subject (properties that are specified in terms of an intentional content with veridicality conditions) and properties of the *subject* undergoing the occurrence.

The significance of this point can be illustrated by considering a proposal that Tye makes in his (2003) discussion of the diachronic unity of consciousness. Suppose that over the course of a day a subject continually undergoes perceptual experience, from the moment she wakes to the moment she falls asleep. What determines an answer to the question of how many perceptual events occurred during the course of that day? Tye suggests that 'The simplest hypothesis compatible with what is revealed by introspection is that, for each period of consciousness, there is only a single experience—an experience that represents everything experienced within the period of consciousness as a whole (the period, that is, between one state of unconsciousness and the next)' (2003: 97). On one reading of this hypothesis, we are to attribute to the single perceptual experience undergone by the subject over the course of a day, a single content that p—which represents the conjunction of everything that the subject experiences as being the case during that day.[3] However, the attribution of such a content to the subject's experience begins to look unwarranted when we consider the question of the

---

[3] For criticism of Tye's view, see Bayne 2005 and 2010. Tye's view will be further discussed in Chapter 6, where I shall be considering an alternative reading of this 'one experience' view.

relation between (a) the intentional content of the perceptual experience undergone by the subject and (b) what perceptually seems to the subject to be the case in undergoing an experience with that intentional content.

It is generally accepted that when a subject undergoes a conscious, personal-level experiential occurrence with a content that p, it perceptually seems *to the subject* that p. In the case we are considering, p is supposed to be a content that represents the conjunction of everything that a subject experiences as being the case during the course of a day. But it would be wrong to claim that in the case of this subject it perceptually seemed to the subject that p *for the whole day*. Moreover, there is no reason to think that there is a time, during the course of the day, at which it perceptually seems to the subject that p.

When we report the fact that it perceptually seems to a subject that p we are attributing to that subject a psychological property that we specify in terms of the content that p. So there is a direct connection between the properties of the conscious, personal-level mental *occurrence* that we specify in terms of an intentional content with veridicality conditions, and psychological properties of the *subject* undergoing that occurrence; and it's not clear that we are warranted in attributing to a conscious, personal-level experiential occurrence properties specified in terms of an intentional content that p unless we are also warranted in attributing to the subject undergoing that occurrence a psychological property that is specified in terms of an intentional content that p.

The problem with the suggestion that we should attribute to a subject's day-long perceptual experience a single content that p (where p represents the conjunction of everything that the subject experiences as being the case during the course of the day) is that there is no reason to attribute to the subject a psychological property that is to be specified in terms of that intentional content. Over the course of the day, a subject's psychological properties will change a great deal. Some of her beliefs, desires, and intentions may be retained over the course of the day, but she will typically undergo a series of changes to her *perceptual* psychological properties. For example, many of the subject's perceptual psychological properties that obtain in the morning will no longer obtain in the afternoon. So the representationalist should say that we have no reason to attribute to the experience that the subject undergoes over the course of the day a single content that p, for we have no reason think that for the whole day the subject had a perceptual psychological property that is to be specified in terms of the content that p. The attribution of such a property is not needed to explain anything that the subject thinks, believes, or does, and it is not needed to explain the phenomenology of the experience she undergoes. The representationalist should instead claim that an account of the conscious perceptual experience a subject undergoes over the course of a day should reflect the respect in which the subject's perceptual psychological properties change over the course of the day, and that we should appeal to different intentional contents, with different veridicality conditions, when it comes to specifying the different perceptual psychological properties of the subject that obtain when she undergoes her day's perceptual experience.

The perceptual psychological property of a subject that obtains when she undergoes a conscious experiential occurrence can be regarded as a mental state of that subject. So what this suggests is that there is reason to think that representationalists who hold that their appeal to the representational content of experience is being used to type-individuate a conscious, personal-level mental occurrence should also hold that the representational content appealed to type-individuates a mental state of the subject that obtains when she undergoes that kind of occurrence. So this representationalist should accept that their appeal to representational content is being used to specify not only properties of the conscious, personal-level experiential occurrence that the subject undergoes, but also properties of a mental state of the subject that obtains when she undergoes it.

But how stable is this latter position? If the representationalist needs to hold that the representational content of experience type-individuates a mental state of the subject, why should she think that it *also* type-individuates a mental occurrence that the subject undergoes when she is in that mental state? Isn't the appeal to the mental occurrence now redundant? In which case, is there any good reason for the representationalist to deny that conscious sensory experience is analysable in terms of mental states and events/processes that are simply changes to/in those mental states?

We can note that the considerations that Geach's argument introduces show that the following would *not* be a good reason for thinking that a subject's conscious sensory experience is a mental occurrence: being committed to a view on which a subject's conscious sensory experience involves the successive unfolding of different temporal parts of a conscious mental occurrence each of which is to be thought of as a conscious experience that is to be specified in terms of some part of a representational content, where such parts lack veridicality conditions. Another bad reason for thinking that a subject's sensory experience must be a mental occurrence, as opposed to a mental state, would be that of appealing to the idea that each distinct experience is short-lived, for as has been pointed out already, the question of whether an aspect of mind is a mental state or a mental event/process isn't determined by the amount of time that it fills, but rather by the way in which it fills the relevant interval of time.

No doubt events do occur when we have conscious sensory experience, for no doubt events are among the effects caused in us by the environment when we perceive. But from the fact that events occur when we have conscious sensory experience it does not automatically follow that a conscious sensory experience is itself an event. For example, the fact that neural and/or sub-personal informational events/processes occur when a subject has a sensory experience does not in itself give one reason to think that a subject's conscious experience is itself a mental occurrence rather than a mental state; for as was mentioned earlier, it is a mistake to think that one can determine the ontological category of an aspect of mind by simply looking to the ontological categories of the things on which it supervenes. These points together put pressure on the representationalist to accept the following claim. Under a representationalist account of experience, a subject's perceptual psychological life is analysable in terms of mental states and events/processes that are simply changes to/in those mental states, and any other events/processes that occur when a subject has a sensory experience are simply to be thought of as events upon which the subject's perceptual states supervene.

There may yet be ways for the representationalist to resist this claim. But the general conclusion I want to suggest we should draw at this stage is the following. The representationalist should accept that the representational content of conscious sensory experience type-individuates a perceptual state of the subject that obtains when she has a sensory experience. And representationalists who want to claim that a subject's perceptual psychological life is not analysable in terms of mental states and events/processes that are simply changes to/in mental states should explain why any further occurrences that they posit are not simply to be thought of as events/processes upon which the subject's perceptual states supervene.

With this general conclusion in mind I now want to consider how these issues may bear on the question of the relation between the representational content of sensory experience and its phenomenal character.

2.5 Representational content and phenomenal character

Questions posed about the phenomenal character of conscious sensory experience are sometimes framed in terms of what it is like for one to *undergo* them, or what it is like for one when they *occur*.[4] But they are also sometimes framed in terms of what it is like for one to *be* in a certain perceptual state, or what it is like for one to stand in a certain kind of perceptual relation—e.g. what it is like for one to see the colour red?[5] When asked a question about phenomenal character posed in the first kind of way, it is natural to interpret it as a question asking about the sort of mental state that obtains when a certain kind of event/process occurs. That is, it looks as though one provides an answer to the question when one specifies a state, or perhaps a perceptual relation, that obtains when the event/process occurs. For example, one can answer the question by saying something of the form, 'it seems to me that *p*', or 'I seem to be aware of an F'. When one reflects upon one's perceptual experience, considered as an event, or process, and one is asked what it is like for one to be undergoing such an experience, one ends up specifying, picking out, mental states or perceptual relations that obtain. You are asked to attend to a perceptual event and to say something about its features, but you end up saying something about yourself—something true of S, where S is not an event, but a subject of experience. But this shouldn't be so puzzling, for the relevant features of the event you are asked to characterize are features of the event that modify you in various ways. You are characterizing what it is like *for you* when such an event occurs. So you are thereby

[4] For example, this formulation can be found in Byrne 2001 and 2004.
[5] For example, this formulation can be found in Siewert 2002 and Chalmers 2004.

specifying features of the event in terms of what is true of you when such an event occurs.[6] So the assumption behind this kind of answer to the first kind of question seems to be that one can say something about the phenomenal features of an event by saying something about oneself. We make sense of this when we realize that these features of the event are ones that we specify in terms of some state of oneself that obtains in virtue of the occurrence of such an event.

But then once one has answered the first kind of question in this way, the second sort of way of asking a question about phenomenal character can be posed: what is it like for one to be in that state? What is it like for one to stand in that perceptual relation? And such questions strike us as legitimate, for surely there *is* something it is like for one to be in such a state, to stand in such a relation? For example, there is something it is like for you to see the colour red. The assumption in play here, then, seems to be the following. One can characterize what it is like for one when a perceptual event occurs by describing what state one is in, or what perceptual relation one stands in, but in doing so, one has left something out, for someone can then ask what it is like for one to be in such a state, or to stand in such a relation—as if more needs to be said. So what lies behind the thought that more needs to be said?

Intuitively, we want to mark a distinction between the phenomenally conscious mental states and the mental states that are not phenomenally conscious. Conscious sensory states are among the phenomenally conscious ones. But what makes such states phenomenally conscious? One might think that the obvious, albeit trivial, answer is that the phenomenally conscious mental states have phenomenal properties, whereas the mental states that are not phenomenally conscious do not have such properties. But then once one has conceded this much, one might ask about the nature of such properties. What are they? Assuming that your mental state has phenomenal, what-it-is-like properties, tell us what they are, describe them. Hence the question, 'what is it like for you to be in that mental state?' This can then lead to debates about the nature of the phenomenal properties of these mental states.

The sorts of mental states that standardly get cited in answering questions about what it is like for one to undergo a conscious perceptual occurrence are mental states that are intentionally directed on the world. When we then turn to the question of what it is like to be in those intentional mental states, and we take this question to be asking about the nature of the phenomenal properties of these mental states, debates arise as to whether the mental states in question have non-intentional properties, as well as intentional properties, which contribute to their phenomenal character—i.e. which contribute to determining what it is like to be in those mental states. The debate as to whether or not

---

[6] Compare the discussion of committed and uncommitted allorepresentation in Travis 2004. We may say, for example, when asked to characterize the features of a perceptual event x: (i) in virtue of x it seems to me that *p*; or (ii) x is such that it seems to me that *p*; or (iii) x is such that it represents it to be the case that *p*. But in the latter case, we are implicitly saying one of the other two things: x is such that it represents it to be the case that *p, because* x is such that it seems *to me* that *p*, or in virtue of x it seems *to me* that *p*.

conscious experiences have non-representational phenomenal properties, as well as representational properties, can be thought of as an instance of this.[7]

Some argue that the phenomenal properties of a perceptual state cannot be identified with representational properties of that state on the grounds that a state could have the relevant representational properties and yet not be a phenomenally conscious one.[8] For those adopting this stance, questions can then be posed about the kind of relation that obtains between the representational and non-representational properties of the state (or, more broadly, the intentional and non-intentional properties of the state). For one might want to accommodate an intuition that these kinds of properties are distinct, but preserve the intuition that there is an intimate connection between them. For example, some argue that the representational properties of the state obtain *in virtue* of the phenomenal properties of the state, as a way of accommodating an intuition that the phenomenal properties of the state could not obtain without the representational/intentional properties. The representational properties supervene on the phenomenal properties. Fix the phenomenal properties of the state and one has thereby fixed its representational properties.[9]

However, others argue that once one specifies the representational/intentional properties of the relevant perceptual state, there is nothing left over for introspection to discover—there are no further properties, over and above the representational properties, that are salient, that one can attend to, and whose intrinsic nature one can specify. And one might think that, if any properties are discoverable through introspection, surely the phenomenal properties are. If we think that the representational properties of a perceptual state obtain *in virtue of* the non-representational phenomenal properties of the state—that is, if we think that the representational properties supervene on the non-representational phenomenal properties of the state—this in itself does not entail that we cannot identify the non-representational phenomenal properties without reference to the representational properties. For when we think that one set of properties supervenes on another set of properties, we don't usually think that it follows from this that we cannot specify the latter without reference to the former. If the phenomenally conscious perceptual state has non-representational phenomenal properties upon which the representational properties of that state supervene, then it might be argued that we should be able to discern introspectively those non-representational phenomenal properties and specify their nature independently of the representational properties that supervene upon them.

I don't propose to engage with these arguments now. At this stage I merely want to highlight some assumptions behind this way of framing debates about the phenomenal character of conscious sensory experience. One assumption is that our focus of concern

---

[7] See e.g. Harman 1990, Tye 1992 and 1995, Dretske 1995, Lycan 1996, Carruthers 2000.

[8] See e.g. Block 1978, 1990, 2003, Chalmers 1996.

[9] See McGinn 1988, Siewert 1998, Horgan and Tienson 2002, Chalmers 2004. See also the discussion of this issue in Byrne 2001 and also in Crane 2003.

should ultimately be directed towards questions about the nature of phenomenal properties of a mental state—whether they are representational properties of a mental state, whether they are non-representational properties of a mental state, whether they are a combination of both, and how one might think of the relation between the representational and non-representational phenomenal properties of such mental states. When the focus is in this way directed on a question about the nature of *properties* of a mental *state*, the question of whether we might also need to posit conscious *occurrence* in our account of the phenomenal character of experience is not thought to be especially significant. The assumption is that there are such things as phenomenally conscious mental states, it is the phenomenal properties of such states that make them phenomenally conscious, and so there can be no good reason for thinking that we would fail to accommodate the fact that a subject's perceptual experiences are phenomenally conscious if we commit to an account on which that subject's perceptual psychological life is analysable in terms of mental states and events/processes that are simply changes to/in those states. In consequence, the assumption is that there is no good reason to think that if an account of conscious sensory experience fails to capture the idea that such aspects of mind have an ontological temporal profile that makes them suited to feature in a *stream* of sensory consciousness, then that account thereby fails to accommodate the way in which such aspects of mind are phenomenally conscious.

In the next section I shall start to introduce an alternative approach—one which brings into play the suggestion that these issues in the ontology of mind should be central to philosophical concerns with the phenomenal character of conscious experience.

2.6 An ontological proposal: occurrence, state, and explanatory circularity

I shall start by sketching in outline a proposal about the ontology of conscious sensory experience. According to this proposal, we need to accommodate the idea that there is a *stream* of sensory consciousness, and in order to accommodate the idea that there is a stream of sensory consciousness we need to appeal to the occurrence of conscious events/processes that are not analysable as changes to/in mental states. It is accepted, on this view, that we will need to appeal to the obtaining of conscious sensory states, as well as conscious sensory occurrence, but a particular stance is taken on how we are to think of the relation between the conscious sensory states and occurrences that are posited.

In section 2.4 I considered whether representationalist accounts of sensory experience end up being committed to the idea that a subject's perceptual psychological life is analysable in terms of mental states and events/processes that are simply changes in or to those states. The general conclusion I reached was the following: the representationalist should accept that the representational content of sensory experience type-individuates a perceptual state of the subject that obtains when she has a sensory experience; and representationalists who want to claim that a subject's perceptual psychological life is not analysable in terms of mental states and events/processes that are simply changes to/ in mental states should explain why any further occurrences that they posit are not simply to be thought of as events/processes upon which the subject's perceptual states supervene. The view of the ontology of conscious experience I now want to sketch posits both perceptual states and perceptual occurrence, but it denies that the relation between them is simply that of supervenience. That is to say, it denies that the experiential occurrences that it posits are simply to be thought of as events/processes upon which perceptual states supervene.

In the previous section I suggested that when it comes to specifying what it is like to undergo a phenomenally conscious perceptual occurrence, one generally does so by citing some perceptual mental state (or perceptual relation) that obtains when a perceptual event/process of that kind occurs. You specify what it is like *for you* when an event of that kind occurs. You specify features of the event that modify you in various ways. So you thereby specify phenomenal features of the event in terms of what is true of you when such an event occurs. The proponent of the view I now want to introduce agrees with the proposal that when it comes to characterizing what it is like for one to undergo a phenomenally conscious perceptual occurrence one does so by specifying the kind of mental state that obtains when one undergoes that kind of occurrence. As I also said in the previous section, it is natural to think that there is something it is like for one to be in that sort of mental state (or to stand in that sort of perceptual relation), and it is also tempting to think that what it is like for one to be in such a mental state is something that is determined by certain properties of that mental state—its phenomenal properties. With that assumption in play it becomes unclear why it should be necessary to posit phenomenally conscious occurrence at all in one's account of the phenomenal character of a subject's perceptual life. For all the relevant work appears to be taken on by certain properties of mental states. The appeal to phenomenally conscious occurrence appears ultimately to be redundant. According to the alternative ontological proposal I'm now introducing, the claim that the appeal to phenomenally conscious occurrence is *not* redundant is connected with the suggestion that the relation between the perceptual states and perceptual events/processes that it posits isn't simply that of supervenience, as I shall now explain.

Consider the conscious sensory states one appeals to when characterizing the phenomenal features of a perceptual occurrence—i.e. the perceptual states one appeals to when specifying what it is like to undergo that kind of perceptual occurrence, such as the perceptual state one appeals to when saying something of the form 'it seems to me that p'. These conscious sensory states can, in principle, be individuated at different levels of abstraction. At one level of abstraction, one types the kind of state that obtains without making any reference to the kind of mental event in virtue of whose occurrence that state obtains. In typing such a state in this way, one allows that such a state could in principle obtain without the occurrence of a mental event of that kind. Now we imagine a creature whose mental life consists in the obtaining of such states—perceptual states that obtain without the occurrence of these perceptual events. In the case of this creature, there are no mental phenomenally conscious continuities that are processive in character and that are not reducible to changes to mental states. So the mental life of such a creature does not include aspects of mind that fit the ontological profile of an element of the stream of consciousness. The *stream* of consciousness is simply absent.

Now suppose instead we do not individuate perceptual states at this level of abstraction, but rather we individuate the kind of perceptual state that obtains in terms of the kind of mental event in virtue of whose occurrence that state obtains. Individuating perceptual states at this level of abstraction commits one to the idea that such states are of the same kind only if they obtain in virtue of the occurrence of phenomenally conscious perceptual events of the same kind. On this proposal, phenomenally conscious sensory states obtain in virtue of the occurrence of phenomenally conscious mental events/processes, and if we do not individuate such states by making reference to the kind of event/process in virtue of whose occurrence that phenomenally conscious mental state obtains, then we do not individuate those states at the right level of abstraction. That is, we do not individuate a phenomenally conscious state *as such*. So we need to individuate the kind of phenomenally conscious state that obtains in terms of the kind of mental event/process in virtue of whose occurrence the state obtains. Otherwise we are simply individuating a state whose obtaining is *entailed* by the obtaining of a phenomenally conscious mental state, but which can obtain without that phenomenally conscious mental state, and so which can obtain without the occurrence of a phenomenally conscious mental event/process—without a stream of phenomenal consciousness. On this proposal there is then a *necessary* connection between the occurrence of a phenomenally conscious perceptual event/process and the obtaining of a phenomenally conscious perceptual state. A given kind of phenomenally conscious perceptual state obtains if and only if a given kind of phenomenally conscious perceptual event/process occurs.

On this view, the relation between the perceptual state and perceptual occurrence in question isn't simply that of supervenience. Phenomenally conscious states do not merely supervene on the occurrence of certain events/processes that occur when one has conscious sensory experience. The relation between perceptual state and occurrence is more intimate than that. For the natures of these phenomenally conscious states are to be specified, at least in part, in terms of the kinds of phenomenally conscious events/processes that occur when those phenomenally conscious states obtain. On this view, although there are such things as phenomenally conscious perceptual states (and indeed, although we need to posit phenomenally conscious perceptual states in an account of the ontology of conscious sensory experience), a subject's psychological perceptual life is not analysable in terms of mental states and events/processes that are simply changes to/in those perceptual states. This is due to the intimate way in which phenomenally conscious mental states and phenomenally conscious mental events/processes are related. The latter cannot occur without the obtaining of the former, and the former cannot obtain without the occurrence of the latter. On this view of the ontology of conscious experience, phenomenally conscious states are to be specified in terms of the kind of event/process in virtue of whose occurrence they obtain. When characterizing phenomenally conscious states as such, reference to unfolding phenomenally conscious occurrence is, then, ineliminable. So in that sense, although we should grant that there are phenomenally conscious mental states, it doesn't follow that there can be a phenomenally conscious creature whose mental life is simply analysable in terms of mental states and events/processes that are changes to/in mental states.

This view of the ontology of conscious sensory experience has further significant consequences. According to it, the nature of the phenomenally conscious state that obtains when one has a conscious experience is to be specified, at least in part, in terms of the kind of phenomenally conscious event/process that occurs when that perceptual state obtains. But now what are the features of such events that we should appeal to in so individuating perceptual states? Let us assume they are the phenomenal properties of the events in question. But then what are these phenomenal properties of the events? As we have already noted, they are features of the event we characterize in terms of the kind of state that obtains in virtue of their occurrence. So on this view we are to understand the ontology of conscious sensory experience in the following way. Conscious sensory experience involves both the occurrence of a certain kind of conscious event/process and the obtaining of a certain kind of conscious state. The event/process and state in question have a certain kind of *interdependent* status. For the nature of the event/process in question is to be specified in terms of the kind of state that obtains when it occurs, and the nature of the state in question is to be specified in terms of the kind of event/process that occurs when it obtains. The interdependent status of event/process and state introduces a certain kind of explanatory circularity. We cannot explain the nature of the mental event/process that occurs independently of the kind of state that obtains when it occurs, and we cannot explain the nature of the state that obtains independently of the kind of event/process that occurs when the state obtains.

The kind of explanatory circularity that is a consequence of this view of the ontology of conscious sensory experience is significant, as it can potentially be used to diagnose certain intuitions that are often appealed to in debates about the conscious character of perceptual experience. Suppose one is attempting to characterize what it is like for one to have a given conscious sensory experience and one does so by citing functional and/or representational features of a perceptual state that obtains when one has that experience. Some have the intuition that such attempts to capture the phenomenal character of the experience are ultimately incomplete. They omit some crucial ingredient. For the intuition is that a subject could in principle be in a perceptual state with those functional and/or representational properties and yet that subject's perceptual state could nonetheless fail to be a phenomenally conscious one (or alternatively, the suggestion is that that subject's perceptual state could nonetheless have a different phenomenal character.)

This intuition is accommodated by the ontological proposal that I've just outlined. For according to it, in simply specifying the functional and/or representational properties of a perceptual state that obtains when one has a conscious sensory experience, one does omit a crucial ingredient. For one thereby types the perceptual state that obtains when one has a conscious experience in a way that allows that such a state can in principle obtain without the occurrence of a phenomenally conscious event/process. In typing at this level of abstraction the kind of perceptual state that obtains when one undergoes a phenomenally conscious perceptual event/process, one fails to individuate a phenomenally conscious state *as such*. One individuates, rather, a kind of perceptual state whose obtaining is merely entailed by the obtaining of a phenomenally conscious perceptual state.

According to the ontological proposal I've outlined, in order to specify the nature of the phenomenally conscious event/process that occurs when one has a conscious sensory experience one needs to do so in terms of the kind of perceptual state that obtains when that kind of phenomenally conscious event/process occurs. The relevant perceptual state is one that is intentionally directed on the world. So this proposal also accommodates the intuition, which many have, that one cannot specify any of the phenomenal properties of conscious sensory experience independently of (i.e. without making reference to) the experience's intentional properties.

The fact that this ontological proposal gives rise to a form of explanatory circularity may also be relevant to the intuition that there is an 'explanatory gap' associated with attempts to understand the relation between the phenomenal and physical/functional features of these aspects of mind.[10] As I have said, the proposal accommodates the intuition that in merely specifying the functional and/or representational features of a perceptual state that obtains when one has conscious sensory experience, one omits something crucial. However, on this proposal there is a problem of explanatory circularity when it comes to specifying what it is that has been left out; and this is a consequence of the *interdependent* status of the occurrence and the state in question. We cannot explain the nature of the phenomenally conscious event/process that occurs independently of specifying the kind of phenomenally conscious state that obtains when that phenomenally conscious event/process occurs, and we cannot explain the nature of the phenomenally conscious state that obtains independently of specifying the kind of phenomenally conscious event/process that occurs when the state obtains. The phenomenally conscious event and state are to be specified in terms of one another.[11]

Note that accepting that there are phenomenally conscious events and states that have this sort of interdependent status does not in itself commit one to denying that the occurrence and obtaining of these interdependent events and states supervenes on the physical. For all that has been said, acceptance of the ontological proposal I've outlined may be consistent with accepting the idea that there is a set of physical conditions the

---

[10] For discussions of the 'explanatory gap', see Levine 1983, McGinn 1989, Van Gulick 1993, Shear 1997, Block and Stalnaker 1999, and Chalmers and Jackson 2001.

[11] Note that this need not entail that one cannot know what it is like to have such a conscious experience. I turn to the question of what this knowledge consists in towards the end of Part I.

obtaining of which is sufficient for both the occurrence of an event and the obtaining of a state that have this interdependent status. However, the proposal does suggest that simply knowing that those physical conditions obtain (and knowing the functional roles of the psychological states that obtain in virtue of those physical conditions) won't in itself inform one about the nature of the interdependent event and state that supervene on those physical conditions. In order to acquire knowledge of the nature of the event and state one needs to break into the explanatory circle. And knowledge of the physical and/or functional properties of the event and state does not in itself suffice for this. In consequence, the ontological proposal gives rise to a kind of 'explanatory gap'.

2.7 The interdependence thesis

At the end of the previous chapter I suggested that appropriate articulation of the manifest image of conscious sensory experience will depend on finding an ontology that fits the phenomenology and the knowledge we have of that phenomenology. In this chapter I have introduced a general proposal regarding that ontology. The proposal is that (i) conscious sensory experience involves the occurrence of mental events/processes; (ii) when such a mental event/process occurs, the subject undergoing it has psychological properties that she wouldn't otherwise possess—she is in a psychological state that wouldn't otherwise obtain; (iii) the nature of the mental event/process is to be specified in terms of the sort of psychological state of the subject that obtains when the mental event/process occurs; and (iv) at a certain level of abstraction, the nature of this psychological state is to be specified in terms of the kind of event/process in virtue of whose occurrence it obtains. The event/process and state in question have a certain kind of *interdependent* status. The nature of the one is to be specified, at least in part, in terms of the nature of the other. In consequence, this view of the ontology of conscious sensory experience gives rise to a certain kind of explanatory circularity. I have suggested how the existence of this form of explanatory circularity can be used to diagnose certain intuitions that often get cited in debates about the phenomenal character of perceptual experience. Moreover, the proposal I've outlined can accommodate the idea that there is a stream of sensory consciousness; and it can accommodate the idea that a subject whose mental life does not include a stream of consciousness will not be phenomenally conscious, while also accommodating the claims that (a) there are phenomenally conscious states and (b) the mental life of a phenomenally conscious subject cannot be analysed simply in terms of mental states and events/processes that are changes to/in those mental states.

Do we have reason to accept this general picture of the ontology of conscious sensory experience? It is not obvious that an appeal to introspection alone can straightforwardly settle the matter. Relevant to this point is a warning that G.E. Moore (1925) once issued about the quick and easy importation of metaphysical assumptions when characterizing conscious sensory experience—assumptions that may not be warranted by the simple deliverances of introspection alone. He wrote:

Although I know for certain both that I have had many experiences, and that I have had experiences of many different kinds, I feel very doubtful whether to say the first is the same thing as to say that there have been many events, each of which was an experience and an experience of mine . . . The proposition that I have had experiences does not necessarily entail the proposition that there have been many events which were experiences; and I cannot satisfy myself that I am acquainted with any events of the supposed kind. (1925: 123)[12]

In what follows I shall be suggesting that the question of whether we should accept the ontological proposal that I have sketched should largely depend on what explanatory work it can do. In subsequent chapters I shall be suggesting that this view of the ontology of conscious sensory experience can be put to work in a variety of ways. I shall be suggesting that it can help to illuminate a distinctive form of conscious contact with time that phenomenally conscious subjects have; I shall be suggesting that it can help to illuminate the respect in which there are certain things that only phenomenally conscious subject can do—e.g. engage in acts of perceptual imagining; I shall be suggesting that it can help provide an account of a variety of knowledge that only phenomenally conscious subjects can have—e.g. knowing what it is like to have a conscious sensory experience; and in the next chapter I shall be arguing that this general view of the ontology can inform our account of the phenomenology of bodily sensations—aspects of mind that are generally thought to be paradigmatic of those mental occurrences/states that only a phenomenally conscious subject can be the subject of.

This discussion of bodily sensation will give rise to issues that begin to re-engage with a question that I introduced and left hanging in Chapter 1—the question of whether we need to appeal to the obtaining of a distinctive kind of psychological relation when characterizing the manifest image of conscious sensory experience, i.e. when characterizing the sort of distinctive sensuous character of conscious sensory experience that is manifest to one when one has a conscious sensory experience.

---

[12] Page references are to the version reprinted in Moore 1993.

3

The Phenomenology and Ontology of Bodily Sensation

In the previous chapter I introduced a general proposal about the ontology of conscious sensory experience—the 'interdependence thesis'. According to this proposal, conscious sensory experience involves the occurrence of mental events/processes and when such mental events/processes occur the subject undergoing them has psychological properties that she wouldn't otherwise have—she is in psychological states that wouldn't otherwise obtain; the nature of the mental event/process is to be specified in terms of the sort of psychological state of the subject that obtains when the mental event/process occurs; and at a certain level of abstraction, the nature of this psychological state is to be specified in terms of the kind of event/process in virtue of whose occurrence it obtains. The event/process and state in question have a certain kind of interdependent status. I suggested how this proposal about the ontology of conscious sensory experience can give rise to a certain form of explanatory circularity.

If the proposal purports to be an account of the ontology that fits the phenomenology, then an objection to it that we will need to consider in due course is this. When one has a conscious sensory experience and attempts to attend introspectively to the posited mental occurrence, it is far from clear that one succeeds. One's conscious sensory experience appears to put one in a position to attend to various entities—objects, events, their features, and relations that those entities stand in to one another. However, those entities strike one as being distinct from one's experience of them. So it is not clear that one can introspectively attend directly to the posited experiential occurrence itself. This point is reflected in the passage I quoted from Moore (1925).

The proposition that I have had experiences does not necessarily entail the proposition that there have been many events which were experiences; and I cannot satisfy myself that I am acquainted with any events of the supposed kind. (1925: 123)

The point that Moore is raising in the quoted passage can be connected with his (1903) suggestion about the respect in which conscious sensory experience appears to be 'diaphanous'. The sensory qualities that one's conscious sensory experience appears to put one in a position to attend to directly do not strike one as being sensuous qualities of the experience itself.

> The moment we try to fix our attention upon consciousness and to see *what*, distinctly, it is, it seems to vanish: it seems as if we had before us a mere emptiness. When we try to introspect the sensation of blue, all we can see is the blue: the other element is as if it were diaphanous. (1903: 41)

Do these remarks present a problem for the general proposal about the ontology of conscious sensory experience that I outlined in the previous chapter? That is a question I shall be returning to in later chapters. In this chapter I want to discuss aspects of mind for which Moore's remarks do *not* seem to apply straightforwardly, namely bodily sensations such as pains, tickles, and itches, and I'll be focusing in particular on the bodily sensation of pain.

I will first outline various respects in which the phenomenology of these sensations is distinctive and puzzling, and how this presents difficulties when it comes to the task of articulating the 'manifest image' of bodily sensation. I will then be suggesting how the general proposal about the ontology of conscious sensory experience outlined in the previous chapter can be put to work in accommodating and explaining these distinctive aspects of the phenomenology and resolving the puzzles to which that distinctive phenomenology gives rise. Here I shall be invoking the interdependence thesis—the thesis that there are phenomenal occurrences and phenomenally conscious mental states that have a certain kind of interdependent status. But I shall be suggesting that what is distinctive of bodily sensation (in contrast, say, to visual experience) is that among the phenomenal events that have this interdependent status, we need to invoke *bodily* events with phenomenal properties that occur at different parts of one's body—namely the parts of one's body where one feels the relevant sensations to be located.

3.1 The phenomenology of pain

Let us start with an attempt to articulate and make explicit various aspects of the phenomenology of the experience of a bodily sensation of pain.[1] Consider a case in which you feel a stabbing pain in your knee. In this sort of case it *is* intuitive to think that you are acquainted with, you are directly aware of, an occurrence that is a sensation—i.e. the stabbing pain that you feel to be *in your knee*. The stabbing sensation strikes one as being an occurrence one is directly aware of, and which one can attend to directly. In the case of a visual experience of something blue, the attempt to attend directly to the occurrence of a conscious event that has phenomenal qualities seems to be thwarted. As

---

[1] In attempting to articulate various aspects of the phenomenology of the experience of bodily sensation I shall sometimes make claims about what 'seems to one' to be the case in having the relevant experience. But in doing so I am not assuming that these claims characterize the intentional contents of mental states that inevitably obtain when one experiences a bodily sensation. At this stage I am leaving open what account might best accommodate the claims I make about the phenomenology of the experience.

Moore put it, 'all we see is the blue', and the blue thing one appears to be in a position to attend to doesn't strike one as being a conscious event, and its blueness does not strike one as being a property of that conscious event. But when one feels a stabbing pain, it is far more intuitive to think that it is possible to attend directly to the occurrence of an event that has phenomenal qualities. For example, the phenomenal features of a stabbing pain in your knee that distinguish it from a tickling sensation in your knee seem to be directly available for you to attend to.

A number of philosophers have pointed out that there are good reasons to hold that the experience of located bodily sensations (e.g. the experience of a pain in one's knee, or an itch on one's nose) should be thought of as being a form of bodily awareness. When you have such an experience, the experience involves (or seems to involve) an awareness of your body, or some part of it. An aspect of the phenomenology of these bodily sensations that is sometimes remarked upon is the fact that it does not seem to one as though one feels these sensations to be in space but not in a body.[2] Furthermore, it does not seem to one as though one feels these sensations to be in different bodies. Rather, it seems to one as though one feels the sensations to be in different parts of one body. In feeling more than one sensation as located in different places one thereby senses (or at least seems to sense) different parts of one's body.

Importantly, it seems that the location of the sensation is felt to be where some part of one's body is. In feeling the sensation as located one thereby senses (or at least seems to sense) some part of one's body—the part of the body where the sensation is located. Moreover, when you feel a located bodily sensation it seems to you that you are aware of a region of space within which such sensations are located only in so far as you are aware of some thing (your body) occupying that region of space. Your awareness of the spatial location of a bodily sensation isn't, and does not seem to you to be, simply a matter of your awareness of something occupying a spatial location that just happens to be coincident with the spatial location of some part of your body that you also happen to be aware of. Your awareness of the sensation as located is itself a form of bodily awareness—a form of awareness of your body, or at least some part of it, 'from the inside', as it is sometimes put.[3]

---

[2] For example, O'Shaughnessy (1980) claims to find it 'all but impossible to comprehend a claim concerning sensation position that detaches it from actual or seeming limb, e.g. "A pain to the right of my shoulder and not even in a seeming body part"' (162). Martin (1995) on phantom limb cases: 'it is not as if it feels to the subject as if there is a pain at some place in midair. Instead it feels to her as if her body is located at that place, even though the relevant body part no longer exists . . . in having bodily sensations, it appears to one as if whatever one is aware of through having such sensation is a part of one's body' (269). Smith (2002) on phantom limb cases: 'although the subject feels a mere sensation to be at a point in space that is in fact beyond his body, it is not felt to be beyond his body; it is, rather, that the body itself is felt to be beyond a point at which it objectively terminates' (136). Brewer 1995: 'That the pain is in a phantom foot is not derived from the fact that there is pain that seems to be at a place where the foot would have been if it were still there. It is given directly in the experience of pain-in-the-foot-there' (299).

[3] The respect in which you are aware of your body 'from the inside' in feeling such sensations will be discussed in Chapter 5.

However, your awareness of a bodily sensation like pain isn't *simply* an awareness of some part of your body 'from the inside'. For example, if you are suffering from a severe migraine headache it doesn't simply seem to you as though you are aware of your head, or some part of it. You seem to be aware of something else as well—i.e. the pain you feel to be there. So if we accept that your awareness of the sensation as located is itself a form of bodily awareness—a form of awareness of your body, or some part of it—we should add at least the following: when you are aware of the sensation as located you are not just aware of some part of your body, you are also aware of some occurrence at that part of the body, or some condition of that body part. The migraine sufferer isn't simply aware of his head, but also the headache that he feels to be there.

So what can be said about the occurrence/condition that one seems to feel in one's head when one has a headache? One thing that I think it is at least intuitive to claim is the following. The occurrence/condition that you feel to be in your head strikes you as being an occurrence/condition whose existence entails phenomenal consciousness. That is to say, if the occurrence/condition is thought of as a bodily event or a bodily condition, then that bodily event/condition strikes one as being of a sort that could not occur/obtain in the body of a subject who was not phenomenally conscious.

We might speculate about the various ways in which a subject who lacks phenomenal consciousness might nonetheless retain some form of perceptual awareness of her environment. Such speculation invites us to compare and contrast phenomenally conscious versus non-phenomenally conscious ways of being perceptually aware of things, which in turn invites us to speculate about what is distinctive of a phenomenally conscious way of being perceptually aware of something—what it adds to one's mental life that would otherwise be lacking, and perhaps what distinctive functional role that form of awareness might play. In the case of a severe, throbbing migraine headache, I think it is counterintuitive to say that what you seem to be aware of in feeling that sensation is something that it might, in principle, be possible for you to be aware of in a non-phenomenally conscious way. Perhaps it is possible for you to be aware of your head in a non-phenomenally conscious way, but it is counterintuitive to think that the sort of severe, throbbing headache you feel to be in your head is the kind of thing that it might be possible for you to be aware of in a non-phenomenally conscious way. So in the case of a located bodily sensation such as a headache, if we think of the apparent object of awareness as a bodily event/condition, then it's intuitive to think that the relevant bodily event/condition is something that it is not possible for one to be aware of in a non-phenomenally conscious way.

A connected claim is this. One feature of the phenomenology of the experience of located bodily sensation is the apparent mind-dependence of some aspect of what you seem to be aware of in feeling the sensation. That is to say, when feeling a bodily sensation (say, a stabbing pain in your knee), it seems to you that some aspect of what you are aware of is the kind of thing that couldn't exist independently of your awareness of it. Although your knee seems to you to be the kind of thing that can exist independently of your awareness of it, the stabbing pain that you feel to be there does not.[4] Moreover, but connected with this, in feeling such a bodily sensation, it seems to you that there is an aspect of what you seem to be aware of that isn't publicly observable. Other subjects may come to know that you are feeling a stabbing sensation in your knee, but there is something odd in the idea that they might come to know this through feeling it. The particular painful, stabbing sensation that you feel to be in your knee seems to you to be something that others could not be sensing, and this appears to be somehow reflected in the phenomenology of the experience itself. Something that doesn't appear to be in tension with the phenomenology of the experience of your sensation is that other subjects might be feeling painful, stabbing sensations *of the same kind* in *their* knees, but what does appear to be somehow in tension with the phenomenology of your experience is that other subjects might be sensing the particular stabbing sensation that *you* are aware of in *your* knee. This, in turn, appears to be connected with the idea that a significant aspect of the phenomenology of your experience of the bodily sensation is the fact that the knee where you feel the stabbing sensation to be seems to you to be *yours*.[5]

A further, and connected, claim is this. There seems to be something rather counter-intuitive about the idea that it might be possible for one to have a veridical hallucination of this sort of located bodily sensation. In discussions of perception—e.g. vision—a suggestion that is sometimes made is that it may be possible in principle for a neuroscientist to induce in a subject a visual hallucination, through suitable stimulation of the subject's sensory cortices, and possible manipulation of the subject's psychological condition, despite the fact that the experience induced matches the scene before the subject—i.e. despite the fact that the scene before the subject really does contain the sorts of objects and features her perceptual experience suggests.[6] The subject is having a hallucination, and so isn't aware of the scene before her, despite the fact that her experience 'matches' that scene. In the case of vision, there doesn't appear to be anything particularly counterintuitive about this suggestion. However, by contrast, there does seem to be something counterintuitive in the following suggestion: a subject is having an experience as of a throbbing migraine headache, and what she seems to be aware of is indeed occurring—i.e. a throbbing pain is occurring in her head—but the subject's experience is a hallucination, and so the subject isn't aware of the throbbing pain in her head. While there might not be anything especially counterintuitive about the idea that one can have a veridical hallucination of one's limb (e.g. its extent, position, and movement), there does seem to be something counterintuitive about the suggestion that one might have a veridical hallucination of a pain that is actually occurring there.

---

[4] Note that I am not here assuming that this is equivalent to the claim that the stabbing pain in your knee seems to you to be something that cannot exist when you are not *attending* to it.

[5] If it were the case that some other subject and I shared the same body, would it follow that when I feel a stabbing pain in my knee it would seem to me that *we* were aware of a stabbing pain in *our* knee? If not, then even though my body is the other subject's body, the notion that the other subject may be aware of the stabbing sensation I feel to be in my knee may still be in tension with the phenomenology of my experience of the sensation.

[6] See Grice 1961.

To summarize, so far I have suggested that there are good reasons to hold that in feeling a sensation as located one thereby senses (or at least seems to sense) some part of one's body—the part of the body where the sensation is located. So there are good reasons to hold that your awareness of the sensation as located is itself a form of bodily awareness—a form of awareness of your body, or at least some part of it, 'from the inside'. Furthermore, when you are aware of the sensation as located, you are not just aware of some part of your body; you are also aware of some occurrence at that part of the body (e.g. the throbbing sensation in your head), and/or some condition of that body part (e.g. your headache). However, I've also suggested that if the occurrence/condition is thought of as a bodily event or a bodily condition, then that bodily event/condition strikes one as being of a sort that could not occur/obtain in the body of a subject who was not phenomenally conscious. It's intuitive to think that the relevant bodily event/ condition is something that it is not possible for a subject to be aware of in a non-phenomenally conscious way. A connected point is that a feature of the phenomenology of the experience of located bodily sensation is the apparent mind-dependence of some aspect of what you seem to be aware of in feeling the sensation. When feeling a bodily sensation, it seems to you that some aspect of what you are aware of is the kind of thing that couldn't exist independently of your awareness of it. Moreover, in feeling such a bodily sensation, it seems to you that there is an aspect of what you seem to be aware of that is private to you as subject of the experience, in so far as it seems to you that there is an aspect of what you seem to be aware of that isn't publicly observable. And finally, I've suggested that there seems to be something rather counterintuitive about the idea that it might be possible for one to have a veridical hallucination of this sort of located bodily sensation.

3.2 A phenomenological puzzle

One puzzle to which this combination of claims gives rise is the following. If we retain the suggestion that the experience of bodily sensation is a form of bodily awareness (a form of awareness of your body, or some part of it), then given that your body is a mind-independent, publicly observable object, how are we to accommodate the apparent mind-dependency and privacy of what you seem to be aware of in feeling the sensation?

If we rest with the suggestion that the object one seems to be aware of in feeling such bodily sensations is a publicly observable, space-occupying object (i.e. one's body and its parts), it seems that the apparent privacy of this form of conscious awareness cannot be accounted for simply in terms of its object. And yet to say that the 'privacy' in question concerns the distinctive *manner* in which the subject is aware of that publicly observable object, rather than the privacy of the object of awareness itself, leaves unexplained the question of why others cannot be aware of this publicly observable object in that same 'private' manner. The *particular* experience I have when I feel a bodily sensation may not be one that you can have, but why can't you have a distinct particular experience of the same kind? And if the particular object I am aware of in having that kind of experience is a publicly observable object, then why can't you too be aware of that same particular object in having that kind of experience? Furthermore, how are we to accommodate the intuition that the relevant bodily event/condition that one seems to be aware of in feeling a located bodily sensation is of a sort that it would not be possible for a subject to be aware of in a non-phenomenally conscious way?

One might think that the simplest way to accommodate the idea that the experience of bodily sensation provides us with a 'private' awareness of a publicly observable object is to say that when one feels such a sensation the apparent object of experience is a mind-independent object with a mind-dependent/subjective property.[7] However, there are three reasons for thinking that this simple proposal doesn't suit our purposes as it stands. Firstly, accounts of what it is for a property to be mind-dependent/subjective are usually consistent with the idea that when one experiences such a property it doesn't positively seem to one that the object ceases to have that property when one ceases to be aware of it—consider, for example, certain views on which secondary qualities, such as colours, are mind-dependent, subjective qualities. Secondly, to say that some property you are aware of is mind-dependent/subjective is not in itself to say that the property in question seems to you to be one that *only you* can be aware of—i.e. the fact that a property is mind-dependent/subjective seems not to entail its privacy. Thirdly, if we do say that the property you seem to be aware of in feeling a bodily sensation seems to you to be a property that only you can be aware of, we thereby appear to commit ourselves to something that is too strong—i.e. the claim that the *property* you seem to be aware of in feeling a bodily sensation seems to you to be of a kind that no other subject could sense, so it seems to you that no other subject could experience the *kinds* of bodily sensations you do.

Continuing on the theme of the first difficulty for this simple proposal, the *seeming* mind-dependence of an aspect of what one experiences when one feels a bodily sensation is what is in need of explanation here, and it is far from clear that we provide such an explanation by simply appealing to the *actual* mind-dependence of some thing we experience. For example, it is noteworthy that although sense-datum theorists often introduce sense-data as objects of awareness on phenomenological grounds, the status of these sense-data as mind-dependent is something that they tend only to argue for subsequently, by inference to the best explanation. The mind-dependence of sense-data is usually introduced as a theoretical commitment. So it is not at all obvious that one would be accounting for the *apparent* mind-dependence of some aspect of what one is aware of in feeling a bodily sensation by simply citing sense-data, which actually happen to be mind-dependent, among the entities one is aware of in feeling a sensation.

---

[7] For discussion of this general approach, see Stephens and Graham 1987 and Newton 1989.

Aydede, while not endorsing a sense-datum theory of bodily sensation, makes the following remark about the view:[8]

Whatever merits sense-datum theories might have with respect to genuine perception and mis-perception, its attraction seems undeniable when it comes to its treatment of pains...According to many sense-datum theorists, pains are paradigm examples of phenomenal individuals, mental objects with phenomenal qualities whose existence depends on their being sensed or felt, and thus are logically private to their owners who feel them. (Aydede 2007: section 2.1)

Aydede talks here of sense-data as 'mental objects', and such talk is common, but what does it mean? Does it mean that mental predicates are true of such objects? If so, what mental predicates? Presumably we're not to take such talk as implying that sense-data have psychological states. Perhaps we should just take such talk to be another way of say-ing that these entities are mind-dependent. This raises further questions concerning the kind of commitment involved in thinking of sense-data as 'mind-dependent' in the first place. Is the claim that such objects exist only when sensed to be taken as contingently true, or necessarily true? One view might be that a nomologically necessary condition for the existence of a sense-datum is its being sensed by a subject. But this would be to allow for the metaphysical possibility of unsensed sense-data, and wouldn't be sufficient to account for the *seeming* mind-dependence of a 'pain' sense-datum. Alternatively, one might take the view that it is necessarily true that sense-data only exist when sensed, but it is not at all obvious what explanation might be given of this metaphysical fact. Saying that these entities are 'mental' just seems to be a way of relabelling the view.

Philosophers often focus on the question of whether and how experience presents its objects *as* mind-*independent*. For example, they ask: is it part of the phenomenal charac-ter of perceptual (e.g. visual) experience that such experience is as of entities that can exist independently of our awareness of them, and if so, what might account for this? However, it seems that there is also a question to be asked about how an experience might present its object as mind-*dependent*. How can it present its object as something that *cannot* exist independently of one's awareness of it? Providing an answer to this question is far from straightforward. And a further point we can add is this. In accom-modating the respect in which located bodily sensations are experienced as mind-dependent/experience-dependent we presumably don't want our account to commit to the idea that a creature can only be the subject of an experience with that sort of phe-nomenology if that creature possesses a concept of mind or experience.

One response to these difficulties is to say that it is our talk about pain that is confused and which can lead to philosophical confusion. We have various ways of talking about pain. We talk in terms of (a) pain as object of awareness (there is a burning sensation in my hand); (b) pain as awareness of sensation (the feeling of a burning sensation in my hand); (c) pain as a condition of some part of one's body (my hand hurts); and (d) we

---

[8] For defence of a sense-datum approach, see Jackson 1977. See also Addis 1986.

often talk of pain as a psychological state of the subject (I am *in* pain). According to one kind of approach, talk that locates sensations of pain in parts of one's body (as in (a)) is not to be taken at face value. The pain is to be identified with an experience/feeling as of something at some bodily location (as in (b)), but where the thing one feels to be at that location is a condition of some part of one's body (as in (c)). Pitcher, for example, writes:

[T]he criterion for the identity of a pain is not the identity of the bodily part whose disordered state is felt, but rather the identity of the act (or state) of feeling it. Pains, then, are not interestingly private: I mean, they are private because they are particulars enjoying a special nonphysical status. They are boringly private, because their privacy really amounts only to the following triviality: each person can perform only his own acts of feeling something (or can be only in his own states of feeling something). (1970: 378)[9]

This line of response seems unsatisfying. Talk of mind-dependent sensations located in body parts is driven by the phenomenology of having such experiences. If our talk about pain is confused, this is because the phenomenal character of such experiences is confusing, and this line of response seems simply to be ignoring the confusing and inconvenient aspects of the phenomenology of such experiences. It appears to ignore those distinctive claims that it is intuitive to make about the experience of located bodily sensations, which are quite unlike the claims that it is natural to make about other conscious experiences (e.g. visual experiences). For example, the intuition that it is not possible to have a veridical hallucination of this sort of located bodily sensation, and the intuition that the bodily event/condition that one seems to be aware of in feeling a located bodily sensation is not of a sort that it would be possible for a subject to be aware of in a non-phenomenally conscious way.

In the next section I will suggest how the general proposal about the ontology of conscious sensory experience that I outlined in the previous chapter can be used to accommodate the various distinctive aspects of the phenomenology of the experience of located bodily sensation that I have highlighted, and I will suggest how it can resolve the puzzles to which that distinctive phenomenology gives rise. It can serve as an account of the ontology of the experience of the bodily sensation of pain that fits the phenomenology.

3.3 An ontology that fits the phenomenology

Aydede talks of sense-data as mental objects that are 'phenomenal individuals' with 'phenomenal qualities'. While it may have fallen out of fashion to posit mental objects like sense-data, many now talk of perceptual experiences as mental *events* that have phenomenal qualities, and presumably many would be happy to regard such events as phenomenal individuals with phenomenal qualities. On one view, what makes it appropriate

---

[9] See also Armstrong 1962, McKenzie 1968, Fleming 1976, Tye 1997 and 2006, and Hill 2006.

to regard the event in question as mental is the relation it bears to a psychological state or property of a subject. For example, we can regard as mental an event that is the acquisition of a psychological state of a subject. However, there are other ways in which event and state may be related. There can be cases where a state obtains in virtue of the occurrence of an event, and where that event is not to be thought of as the causal antecedent of the state, nor simply the event that is the acquisition of the state. There can be cases in which the state obtains over a given period of time only if certain kinds of events are occurring *during* that period of time.

In the non-mental domain, it seems we can make sense of the idea that an event (or series of events) involving an object can amount to that object being modified in some way or other. In such a case, the object is in its modified state while, and because, the event occurs, hence the idea that some state of the object (the way in which it is modified) obtains in virtue of, and for the duration of, the occurrence of the event. For example, we think that the temperature of a liquid (a state of the liquid) depends upon the motion of the molecules of the liquid (occurrence).[10] So too in the mental domain, there seems to be no reason to deny that the occurrence of an event (or series of events) involving a subject can amount to the subject being modified in some way or other. In such a case, the subject is in her modified state while, and because, the event occurs, hence the idea that some psychological state of the subject (the way in which she is psychologically modified) obtains in virtue of, and for the duration of, the occurrence of the event. Here the relation between the event and the psychological state isn't simply causal, but constitutive. The obtaining of the psychological state of the subject depends constitutively on the occurrence of the event.

The view of the ontology of conscious sensory experience that I outlined in the previous chapter—the interdependence thesis—can be seen as an instance of this sort of relation between state and occurrence. According to that proposal, conscious sensory experience involves the occurrence of mental events/processes, and when such mental events/processes occur, the subject undergoing them is in psychological states that wouldn't otherwise obtain. Moreover, the nature of the mental event/process is to be specified in terms of the sort of psychological state of the subject that obtains when the mental event/process occurs; and at a certain level of abstraction, the nature of this psychological state is to be specified in terms of the kind of event/process in virtue of whose occurrence it obtains.

Under this sort of view, one can say that what makes an event a phenomenal one—an event with phenomenal qualities—is that its nature is to be specified in terms of the kind of phenomenally conscious state of the subject that obtains in virtue of its occurrence, which is in line with the idea that what makes the event a phenomenal one is the fact that there is something it is like *for the subject* to be undergoing it, and also in line

---

[10] For discussion of this example, see Steward 1997: 72.

with the idea that to be concerned with the event's phenomenal properties is to be concerned with *what it is like* for the subject to be undergoing it. The fact that the nature of the event is to be specified in terms of the kind of psychological state of a subject that obtains in virtue of its occurrence is what makes it appropriate to regard such an occurrence as a mental individual with phenomenal properties, rather than an independently specifiable event upon which a mental state of the subject merely supervenes.

This understanding of what it is for an individual event to have phenomenal qualities can be used to help resolve the earlier puzzle that was raised about the phenomenology of a bodily sensation of pain. Recall, the puzzle, crudely formulated, was the following: if we retain the suggestion that the experience of bodily sensation is a form of bodily awareness (a form of awareness of your body, or some part of it), then given that your body is a mind-independent, publicly observable, one-among-many, how are we to accommodate the apparent mind-dependency and privacy of what you seem to be aware of in feeling the bodily sensation? I suggested that an adequate resolution of the puzzle won't be forthcoming if we adopt the proposal that when one feels such a sensation the apparent object of experience is simply a mind-independent object (one's body part) with a mind-dependent/subjective property. I also suggested that it doesn't help matters to posit sense-data as mind-dependent objects of awareness. The puzzle here primarily concerns how we should characterize what it is that one is apparently aware of in feeling a bodily sensation. If body part and its properties alone won't do the explanatory work, and adding sense-data doesn't help, what is missing? The missing piece of the puzzle, which needs to be introduced onto the scene as object of awareness, is, I suggest, an *event*, and the discussion of what is involved in thinking of an event as an individual that has phenomenal qualities can help us to see why.

Let's now think of a bodily sensation that one seems to feel at some bodily location as an *event* that seems to one to be occurring *at that bodily location*. I suggested that your awareness of the spatial location of the sensation isn't, and doesn't seem to you to be, simply a matter of your awareness of something occupying a spatial location that just happens to be coincident with the spatial location of some part of your body that you also happen to be aware of. Your awareness of the sensation as located is itself a form of bodily awareness—a form of awareness of your body, or at least of some part of it. So how is this aspect of the phenomenology to be accommodated?

The located event one seems to be aware of in feeling a sensation, such as the throbbing pain in the head experienced by the migraine sufferer, can be regarded as a bodily occurrence if that event seems to constitute a modification of the body part at which it occurs.[11] What I have in mind is the following picture: when a sensation of pain seems

---

[11] Again, note that in talking of how things 'seem' in this context, I am attempting to articulate, with 'conceptual tweezers', so to speak, aspects of the phenomenology of experiencing a bodily sensation. But I am not thereby assuming that these claims characterize the intentional contents of mental states that inevitably obtain when one experiences a bodily sensation.

to occur at some part of one's body (e.g. the throbbing sensation in one's temple), it seems to one as if a bodily condition/state (e.g. a headache) obtains in virtue of the occurrence of that event. The way in which that part of the body is affected is the bodily condition that obtains in virtue of (i.e. because of and for the duration of) the occurrence of the sensation *at that part of the body*. The sensation-event is not to be thought of simply as the causal antecedent of the bodily state in question, and neither is it to be thought of as an event that is the mere acquisition of that bodily state. The bodily condition (e.g. the headache) obtains because of and for the duration of the occurrence of the event (e.g. the throbbing sensation in your temple), as the bodily condition (i.e. the headache) depends *constitutively* on the occurrence of the event. Moreover, the nature of the event is to be specified, at least in part, in terms of the way in which it modifies the body part when it occurs.

The suggestion so far, then, is that when one feels a located bodily sensation, one seems to be aware of an event occurring at some bodily location. The occurrence of the event seems to constitute a modification of the body part at which it occurs, and it seems to be an event whose nature is to be specified, at least in part, in terms of the way in which it modifies the body part at which it occurs. For that reason it can be regarded as a bodily event, and awareness of the event can be regarded as a form of bodily awareness. However, saying this much is not yet to accommodate the apparent mind-dependency and privacy of what one seems to be aware of in feeling a bodily sensation, so how is this to be accounted for?

I suggested that what makes an event a phenomenal one—an event with phenomenal qualities—is that its nature is to be specified in terms of the kind of phenomenally conscious *state of the subject* that obtains in virtue of its occurrence—a state that is constitutively dependent on the occurrence of that event. Applying this idea to the case at hand, the suggestion is that your bodily sensation not only seems to you to be an event whose occurrence seems to constitute a modification of the body part at which it occurs, but it also seems to you to be an occurrence whose nature can only be fully specified in terms of some phenomenally conscious state of yours that obtains in virtue of its occurrence. It seems to you to be an event whose nature is to be specified, in part, in terms of what it is like for you when such an event occurs. Hence the occurrence seems to you to be an event with phenomenal qualities. There is a sense, then, in which the occurrence you seem to be aware of in feeling a bodily sensation seems to you to be both bodily and mental. It seems to you to be an event whose nature can only be specified in terms of the way in which its occurrence modifies *both* your body part *and* you as psychological subject.

The suggestion being made here is that the event you seem to be aware of in feeling a located bodily sensation is an event that constitutes, at one and the same time, a modification of your body part and your mental life, and *necessarily* so. That is to say, it is not that the event simply seems to you to be one that *causes* something bodily and something mental. The event you seem to be aware of is of a kind whose nature can only be specified in terms of the kinds of bodily *and* mental states that depend *constitutively* upon its occurrence. It is not possible for such an event to occur without such states obtaining in virtue of, and for the duration of, its occurrence.[12]

In what way does the sensation modify you psychologically when it occurs? In the case of a phenomenally conscious visual experience, the phenomenally conscious state of the subject that obtains in virtue of, and for the duration of, the occurrence of the phenomenally conscious perceptual event, and in terms of which the nature of the event is to be specified, is one that is intentionally directed upon the mind-independent environment of the subject. The phenomenally conscious event is not itself, and does not seem to the subject to be, an object of her conscious visual state. By contrast, in the case of bodily sensation, the phenomenally conscious state of the subject that obtains in virtue of, and for the duration of, the occurrence of the sensation, and in terms of which the nature of the sensation is to be specified, is intentionally directed upon the sensation itself, occurring at some bodily location.

This accounts for the apparent mind-dependency of the sensation. The sensation seems to one to be an event whose nature can only be fully specified in terms of a phenomenally conscious state that is an awareness of it. The sensation cannot occur without the obtaining of a psychological state, and the psychological state in question is intentionally directed on that very sensation. This also accounts for the apparent privacy of some aspect of what one seems to be aware of in feeling the sensation. Again, comparing the case of a phenomenally conscious visual experience: the nature of the particular phenomenally conscious visual experience *I* have is to be specified in terms of what it is like for *me* to be undergoing that experience. Another subject may be undergoing an experience of the same phenomenal kind, but this will be a distinct particular occurrence. Likewise, the nature of the particular bodily sensation *I* feel is to be specified in terms of what it is like for *me* to be undergoing it. Another subject may be undergoing a bodily sensation of the same kind, but this will be a distinct particular occurrence, and not the particular bodily sensation that I am aware of. This last point is, I take it, relevant to at least one respect in which the body you seem to be aware of in feeling bodily sensations seems to you to be yours. The bodily events that you seem to be aware of in feeling bodily sensations seem to you to be *bodily* events that *only you* can be aware of, and in that respect the body that you seem to be aware of in feeling such sensations seems to you to be your own.

Given that the proposal accounts for the apparent mind-dependency of the located sensation, it also accommodates the intuition that it is not possible to have a veridical hallucination of a located sensation. If the located sensation seems to one to be

---

[12] Compare here the discussion in the previous chapter of what one might say about a phenomenally conscious perceptual, say visual, event: it is not possible for there to occur such a phenomenally conscious perceptual event without there being something it is like *for the subject* undergoing it, and the nature of the phenomenally conscious event is specified in terms of *what* it is like for the subject to be undergoing it. So such a phenomenally conscious visual event cannot occur without the obtaining of a phenomenally conscious visual state of the subject that depends constitutively on its occurrence, and in terms of which the nature of the visual occurrence is to be specified.

mind-dependent, then the idea of a veridical hallucination of that sensation will seem counterintuitive, as it will involve the idea of the occurrence of a sensation in some part of your body that you are not aware of, because you are hallucinating, which in turn involves the idea of the occurrence of a located sensation whose existence is not dependent on your awareness of it.

What about the intuition that the bodily event/condition that one seems to be aware of in feeling a located bodily sensation is not of a sort that it would be possible for a subject to be aware of in a non-phenomenally conscious way? The proposal I've outlined has the resources to accommodate that intuition as well. According to the proposal I'm making, a located bodily sensation can be regarded as a bodily event because its nature it is to be specified, at least in part, in terms of the way in which it modifies the body part at which it occurs. However, the sort of bodily event that you seem to be aware of in feeling a located bodily sensation is an event whose nature can only be *fully* specified in terms of the way in which it modifies you both bodily *and* psychologically when it occurs. It is an event that constitutes, at one and the same time, a modification of your body part and your mental life, and *necessarily* so. I have suggested that when the sensation occurs, you are psychologically modified in the following way: a phenomenally conscious state of yours obtains in virtue of, and for the duration of, the occurrence of the sensation, and that phenomenally conscious state is intentionally directed upon the sensation itself occurring at some bodily location. If the bodily event you seem to be aware of in feeling a sensation is to be specified, at least in part, in terms of some phenomenally conscious state of yours that is an awareness of it, then it will seem to you that that sort of bodily event is not of a sort that it would be possible for a subject to be aware of in a non-phenomenally conscious way.

So far I've suggested that a bodily sensation is an event whose nature can only be fully specified in terms of the way in which its occurrence modifies both your body part and you as psychological subject, and I have suggested a way in which the sensation modifies you psychologically when it occurs: a phenomenally conscious state of yours obtains in virtue of, and for the duration of, the occurrence of the sensation, and that phenomenally conscious state is intentionally directed upon the sensation itself occurring at some bodily location. There may, however, be other ways in which the occurrence of the sensation modifies you psychologically. Other psychological states may obtain in virtue of the occurrence of the sensation, and the nature of the sensation may need to be specified, at least in part, in terms of these other psychological states.

I said earlier that we have various ways of talking about pain, one of which is in terms of the subject's *being in pain*. The painfulness of a pain sensation seems to depend on the notion that the subject of the sensation is *in pain* when the sensation occurs. So we can add that when a sensation of pain occurs, the subject of the sensation is, standardly, thereby in the affective psychological state of *being in pain* (a psychological state that is likely to have emotional and behavioural components).[13] Again, we should say that this

---

[13] Standardly, but perhaps not invariably. For discussion of pain asymbolia, see Grahek 2001.

psychological state of the subject, her being in pain, is constitutively dependent on the occurrence of the sensation, and the nature of the painful occurrence can only be fully specified in terms of the psychological state of her *being in pain* that obtains in virtue of, and for the duration of, its occurrence.

So to summarize, according to the proposal being made here, when a subject feels the throbbing pain of a migraine in her head, she not only seems to be aware of her head (a mind-independent body part), she also seems to be aware of a *mind-dependent bodily event* occurring at that body part. There is a constitutive, and not merely causal, relation between the occurrence of the sensation-event and the bodily and mental states that obtain in virtue of, and for the duration of, its occurrence; and the psychological states of the subject that obtain in virtue of and for the duration of the occurrence of the sensation include her awareness of the event itself, and, we might add, (standardly at least) the affective state of her *being in pain*.

At the beginning of the chapter I suggested that some of the remarks that Moore makes about the diaphanousness of the sensation of blue do not seem to apply straightforwardly to our experience of located bodily sensations. I now want to return to those remarks in light of the proposal about the ontology of the experience of located bodily sensation that I've just outlined.

3.4 Bodily sensation, transparency, and intentionality

Moore (1903) suggests that 'when we try to introspect the sensation of blue, all we can see is the blue: the other element is as if it were diaphanous' (41). Moore (1925) also claims:

Although I know for certain both that I have had many experiences, and that I have had experiences of many different kinds, I feel very doubtful whether to say the first is the same thing as to say that there have been many events, each of which was an experience and an experience of mine . . . I cannot satisfy myself that I am acquainted with any events of the supposed kind. (1925: 123)

Here is one way of articulating what Moore may be getting at: when you have a conscious sensory experience, what the experience seems to put you in a position to attend to directly is what the experience is an experience of. If your experience is a conscious experience of something blue, you seem to be presented with, to be confronted with, a blue thing and its blue colour, and your experience seems to put you in a position to attend directly to the blue thing and its blue colour. You don't in the same way seem to be presented with, confronted with, a conscious *event* that is your *experience* of the blue thing. If you try to attend to such a conscious event, all you find is the blue thing; and its blueness does not strike you as being a property of some conscious event that you are directly aware of. In that sense, when you have the conscious experience, you don't seem to be in a position to attend directly to the conscious properties of an event that is your conscious experience.

I suggested that Moore's remarks do not seem to apply straightforwardly to the experience of located bodily sensation, because when you feel a stabbing pain in your knee, say, it seems as though you *are* directly aware of/presented with/confronted with a phenomenal event that you can attend to directly—i.e. the stabbing sensation that you feel to be *in your knee*. And it seems as though you can attend directly to its phenomenal qualities. So should we hold that when you feel a located bodily sensation you are directly aware of/presented with/confronted with a conscious event that is your *experience*? Well, it's not obvious that the painful occurrence that you feel to be in your knee, and to which you can directly attend, is intentionally directed on anything. It's not obvious that it is about, or represents, anything. So if one identifies the phenomenal event that one seems to be directly aware of when one feels a sensation of pain with one's conscious experience, one might be led to accept that one's experience of pain lacks intentionality.

I think we find something like this line of thought in the following passage from Broad:

A sensation of red seems clearly to mean a state of mind with a red object, and *not to mean a red state of mind* . . . [But] [i]t is by no means obvious that a sensation of headache involves an act of sensing and a 'headachey' object; on the contrary, *it seems on the whole more plausible to describe the whole experience as a 'headachy' state of mind* . . . it seems plausible to hold that a sensation of headache is an unanalysable mental fact, within which no distinction of act and object can be found. (1923: 255)

One might interpret Broad as reasoning in the following way: a sensation of red isn't itself red. So we shouldn't think of it as a red state of mind. We should think of it as a state of mind directed upon a red thing; and for Broad, this is to be given an 'act-object' analysis. However, a sensation of a headache is itself headachy. In this case there is no distinction to be drawn between the sensation and what the sensation is a sensation of.[14] So we can regard it as a headachy state of mind. There's no distinction between 'act and object' to be found, and so we should regard the experience as one which lacks intentionality.

This line of reasoning leads to an unsatisfactory conclusion. For, as a number of philosophers have pointed out, there are good reasons for denying that our experiences of bodily sensations lack intentionality. When you have a headache, you are having an experience that is intentionally directed upon some part of your body—i.e. your head, or some part of it—and you seem to be aware of something going on there. I think the correct thing to say here is the following. Broad is right to point out that there is a significant difference to highlight between an experience of red and an experience of a headache. For in the case of the experience of a headache, you seem to be directly aware of/presented with/confronted with a phenomenal event whose phenomenal properties you can attend to directly; and in the case of an experience of red, this doesn't seem to be

---

[14] This line of thought can lead to the labelling of located sensations of pain as 'intransitive'. See Armstrong 1962.

the case. According to the proposal I've outlined, this is because in the case of a phenom-enally conscious visual experience, the phenomenally conscious state that obtains in virtue of, and for the duration of, the occurrence of the phenomenally conscious event that occurs, and in terms of which the nature of the event is to be specified, is one that is intentionally directed upon a red thing, and not the phenomenally conscious visual event itself. The phenomenally conscious visual event is not itself, and does not seem to you to be, an object of your conscious visual state. By contrast, in the case of bodily sen-sation, the phenomenally conscious state that obtains in virtue of, and for the duration of, the occurrence of the sensation, and in terms of which the nature of the sensation is to be specified, *is* intentionally directed upon the sensation itself, occurring at some bodily location.

So according to this proposal, when you experience a located bodily sensation of pain, you are directly aware of a phenomenal event. However, the phenomenal event you are aware of isn't your experience. It is, rather, what your experience is an experi-ence of. It is an event whose occurrence entails your experience of it; and it is an event whose nature is to be specified in terms of the kind of phenomenally conscious state that obtains when it occurs, and which is intentionally directed on it. But this phenom-enal event is not itself an experience of anything.

So although there is an important difference between a visual experience of blue and the experience of located bodily sensation, a certain reading of Moore's claims about the sensation of blue also applies to the case of the experience of located bodily sensation. I suggested that in his discussion of the sensation of blue, Moore can be interpreted as making the following claim: when your experience is a conscious experience of some-thing blue, you seem to be presented with, to be confronted with, a blue thing and its blue colour, and your experience seems to put you in a position to attend directly to the blue thing and its blue colour. You don't in the same way seem to be presented with, confronted with, a conscious *event* that is your *experience* of the blue thing. We can now see that there are reasons for thinking that similar remarks apply to your experience of a headache. When you have a headache, you have an experience that puts you in a posi-tion to attend directly to a phenomenal event. You seem to be directly aware of, to be confronted with, a phenomenal event. However, the phenomenal event that you are directly aware of is not to be identified with a conscious event that is your experience. It is, rather, what your experience is an experience of—i.e. a *bodily* event with phenomenal properties that seems to be occurring in your head.

One might think that the phenomenal qualities of the located sensation of pain one seems to be directly aware of—qualities one seems to be in a position to attend to directly—are qualities of one's experience, which in turn may lead one to think that the phenomenal event one is aware of *is* one's experience. However, the temptation to iden-tify the located sensation's qualities with qualities of one's experience of it can be explained by the form of explanatory circularity to which this account of the ontology of the experience of bodily sensation gives rise. The nature of the located sensation one seems to be aware of is to be specified, at least in part, in terms of the sort of phenomenally conscious state that obtains when it occurs, and the nature of that phenomenally conscious state is to be specified in terms of the kind of phenomenal event in virtue of whose occurrence it obtains, namely the located sensation it is intentionally directed upon. So one must appeal to qualities of the located sensation in specifying qualities of one's experience of it, and one must appeal to one's experience when specifying the qualities of the located sensation.

To summarize, according to the proposal I've been outlining, when you have an experience of a located bodily sensation of pain, the object of experience, the object of your awareness, is a mind-dependent bodily occurrence with phenomenal properties. But that phenomenal occurrence is not itself your experience. It is what your experience is an experience of. We can regard the object of your experience as an occurrence with phenomenal properties, because there is something it is like for you when it occurs. Its nature is to be specified in terms of what it is like for you when it occurs. That is to say, its nature is to be specified in terms of the sort of phenomenally conscious mental state that obtains when it occurs—a phenomenally conscious mental state that is intentionally directed upon it.

This is to emphasize the respect in which the object of your awareness when you feel a located bodily sensation is a mind-dependent occurrence with phenomenal properties. However, according to the account of bodily sensation I'm proposing, the object of awareness has a *dual* nature. The occurrence you seem to be aware of when you're aware of a bodily sensation seems to you to be both mental *and bodily*. The sort of event that you seem to be aware of in feeling a located bodily sensation is an event whose nature can only be fully specified in terms of the way in which it modifies you both psychologically *and bodily* when it occurs. It is an event that seems to you to constitute, at one and the same time, a modification of your mental life and your body part, and necessarily so. In the next section I shall be discussing in more detail the bodily nature of the occurrence you seem to be aware of in feeling a bodily sensation of pain.

3.5 Mind-dependent bodily events and the biological function of pain

I suggested that the located event one seems to be aware of in feeling a sensation of pain can be regarded as a bodily event, as that event seems to constitute a modification of the bodily part at which it occurs. When a sensation of pain seems to occur at some part of one's body, it seems to one as if a bodily condition/state obtains in virtue of the occurrence of that event—the part of the body where the sensation occurs being thereby affected. The way in which that part of the body is affected is the bodily condition that obtains in virtue of (i.e. because of and for the duration of) the occurrence of the sensation at that part of the body. The sensation-event is not to be thought of simply as the causal antecedent of the bodily state in question, and neither is it to be thought of as an event that is the mere acquisition of that bodily state. Moreover, the nature of the event is to be specified, at least in part, in terms of the way in which it modifies the body part when it occurs.

In the case of a located sensation of pain, what, if anything, does the occurrence of that sort of event, considered as a bodily occurrence, entail about the *physical* condition of the body part at which it occurs? On one view, in experiencing a bodily sensation of pain, one is thereby having an experience as of some sort of physical damage to some part of one's body. If this view is correct, then we might expect that the actual occurrence of the bodily event that you seem to be aware of in feeling a bodily sensation of pain should entail something about the physical condition of the body part at which it occurs. It should entail that there is damage to that body part. Is this a suggestion we should accept? What, for example, should we say about cases in which it feels to the subject as though there is some painful sensation-event occurring in some body part, she has the relevant body part, there is no reason to think that she is not aware, through bodily awareness, of that body part, but where there is no physical damage at that body part? Should we regard such an experience as illusory?[15]

Whether we think of such experiences as illusory/hallucinatory may depend on whether we should think of a pain experience as being as of/representing some physical condition of/damage to the body part, where the obtaining of the physical condition/damage in question is something that we could in principle rule out by inspection of the physical condition of the body part—what we might call an *objective* physical condition of the body. If we do think that pain experiences are as of/represent some such objective physical condition of the body, then presumably we should say that in such cases where the relevant objective physical condition of the body does not obtain, the subject's pain experience is illusory/hallucinatory. However, the suggestion that pain experience represents some *objective* physical condition of the body (the obtaining of which is something that could in principle be ruled out by inspection of the physical condition of the body part) would seem to be in tension with the proposal that in feeling a located pain one is simply aware of a located *mind-dependent* bodily occurrence. The issue I now want to address is whether it is appropriate to regard the kind of pain experience just described as illusory, and if so whether this creates a difficulty for the proposed account of the ontology of pain.

According to Tye, pain experiences do represent bodily damage. It is a commitment of Tye's view that we should regard the cases I've just described as ones in which the pain experience misrepresents, and so as ones in which the pain experience is illusory or hallucinatory, given that in such cases there is no bodily damage. Tye writes:

---

[15] A connected question is this: suppose we have two subjects whose legs, say, are in the same kind of physical condition. One of these subjects seems to feel a sensation of pain in her leg, the other does not. Should we say that one subject is hallucinating the occurrence of a pain-sensation in her leg and the other is not, or perhaps that one of these subjects fails to perceive something that is occurring in her leg whereas the other succeeds in perceiving the occurrence in her leg?

Which quality (or type) is represented? Pain experiences normally track tissue damage. So, tissue damage is the obvious naturalistic candidate for the relevant quality. (2006: 101)

Pains . . . are sensory representations of tissue damage. To feel a pain, one need not have the resources to conceptualize what the pain represents . . . One need not be able to say or think that such-and-such tissue damage is occurring. Still, the content of the pertinent sensory representation is what gives the pain its representational character. . . . A twinge of pain is a pain that represents a mild, brief disturbance. A throbbing pain is one that represents a rapidly pulsing disturbance. Aches represent disorders that occur inside the body, rather than on the surface. (1997: 333)

The first issue I want to address is whether Tye is right to claim that 'Pain experiences normally track tissue damage.' The biological function/significance of pain certainly seems to have something to do with bodily damage, but it may not be quite right to say that its function is simply to inform the subject of damage to her body.

Grahek (2001) suggests that we regard pain as a biological self-defence mechanism. It is an alarm mechanism that warns an organism about harmful and potentially harmful features of its environment. It monitors the extent of damage inflicted, and induces the organism to take evasive action, or refrain from doing anything that might exacerbate the damage. More specifically, according to Grahek, we can think of pain as involving an avoidance system, and a restorative/repair system, where such systems differ in their function, targets, and underlying structures and mechanisms, and characteristic behaviour produced. The avoidance system has a preventative capacity that can reliably detect *potentially* harmful stimuli and induce immediate withdrawal,[16] whereas the restorative system is sensitive to changes produced by damage that has been inflicted to joints, muscles, and nerves.[17] In the case of the latter system, tenderness spreads around the damaged part of the joint or nerves, making it sensitive to *innocuous* stimuli. In doing so it inhibits movements and manipulation of the affected area, thereby preventing the organism from inflicting further injury to the already damaged area of the body.

What this suggests is that the biological function of pain isn't simply to inform the subject of damage that has been inflicted to her body—its location, nature, extent, etc. It also serves to induce the subject to avoid *potential* damage to her body and to inhibit the subject from doing things that might *exacerbate* (or prolong the obtaining of) damage that has already been inflicted to her body. For this reason, it doesn't seem right to say that the located pain a subject might feel when the avoidance system is at work, but where no actual bodily damage has been inflicted, *misrepresents* the obtaining of damage to her body, and equally it doesn't seem right to say that an increase in the intensity of

---

[16] For example, this system appears to respond preferentially to temperatures just below 48°C, the threshold above which nerve damage occurs. Associated with this avoidance system is the activity of A-Δ nociceptive fibres, the activity of which is related to fast, sharp, pricking pain. For discussion, see Grahek 2001: 11 ff.

[17] Associated with this restorative/repair system is the activity of C-nociceptive chemi-fibres that react to chemicals released after injury has been inflicted, the activity of which is related to slow, dull, or burning pain. Grahek: 'The system is slow but is of lasting and steady influence' (2001: 14).

located pain a subject might feel when the restorative system is at work, but where no further damage has been inflicted, *misrepresents* the obtaining of such further bodily damage.

This, however, is not out of line with what appears to be the spirit of Tye's suggestion, something that common sense would suggest, that the biological function of pain is to track changes to the *objective physical* condition of the body, where the physical condition in question will either be actual damage to the body, or a physical condition that is relevant to potential damage to the body. So, for example, in the case of a subject suffering from some chronic pain syndrome in which the subject continues to feel located pain in a particular region of the body long after that body part has healed, we can say that the subject's pain system, at least in this particular instance, is failing to serve its biological function. In this respect we can say that there is a sense in which such experiences are misleading. However, in conceding that such experiences can, in this sense, be regarded as misleading, we need not deny that in having such an experience the subject is indeed aware of a mind-dependent bodily occurrence—the located sensation-event that she seems to be aware of in having the experience. Indeed, I think we can go further than this. Not only is the account of the ontology of pain that I have proposed consistent with what we may want to say about the biological function of pain, its features may be relevant to explaining the distinctive way in which the experience of pain serves that biological function.

Something that is emphasized in Grahek's discussion of the biological function of pain is the importance of the affective, 'emotional-cognitive', and behavioural components of pain experience. Just as the pain experience of the subject suffering from chronic pain syndrome, whose pain experience is no longer tracking any relevant objective physical condition of the body, is failing to serve the biological function of pain, so too is the experience of the subject suffering from pain asymbolia. There is a sense in which the asymbolic's experience is successfully tracking the relevant objective physical conditions of the body—actual damage to the body, or physical conditions that are relevant to potential damage to the body—for when such physical conditions obtain the subject will usually feel an appropriately located bodily sensation whose quality, intensity, and extent varies with variations in relevant physical conditions of the body part. However, in the case of the asymbolic subject, such experience does not induce any avoidance or protective reactions, nor does it induce the usual affective emotional reactions. Despite the fact that the subject's experience is reliably tracking the objective physical bodily conditions that it is the biological function of pain to track, in having such experience the subject is not thereby *in pain*. In consequence, according to Grahek (2001), such pain experience 'is no longer a signal of threat or damage and no longer moves one's mind or body in any way. It becomes a blunt, inert sensation, with no power to galvanize the mind and body for fight or flight. Such pain no longer serves its primary biological function' (73).

As a way of illustrating the crucial importance of the affective dimension of pain experience to the biological function of the pain system, Grahek describes a failed attempt made by Paul Brand to devise a prosthetic pain system. The project known as 'A Practical Substitute for Pain' was devised and executed by Brand to compensate for the defective pain perception of leprosy patients, congenital painlessness, diabetic neuropathy, and other nerve disorders. This attempt involved the use of specialized transducers at the extremities, sensitive to damaging or potentially damaging stimuli, which would trigger a device like a hearing aid, emitting a piercing sound when potentially threatening stimuli were detected. Here is Brand's description of the failure of this attempt:

> We had grandly talked of "retaining the good parts of the pain without the bad", which meant designing a warning system that would not hurt ... But when a patient with a damaged hand turned a screwdriver too hard, and the loud warning signal went off, he would simply override it . . . Blinking lights failed for the same reason. (Brand and Yancey 1993: 194, quoted in Grahek)

> The sobering realization dawned on us that unless we built in a quality of compulsion, our substitute pain system would never work. (1993: 194, quoted in Grahek)

The prosthetic pain system failed even when it was modified so that the effect of appropriate stimulation of the transducers was to induce a painful but harmless electric shock in an area of the body in which the subject could still feel pain (often under the armpits in those suffering from leprosy). Of this modification to the prosthetic pain system, Brand and Yancey write:

> They viewed pain from our artificial sensors in a different way than pain from natural sources. They tended to see the electric shocks as punishments for breaking rules, not as messages from an endangered body part. They responded with resentment, not an instinct of self-preservation. (1993: 195)

> We found no way around the fundamental weakness in our system: it remained under the patient's control. If the patient did not want to heed the warning from our sensors, he could always find a way to bypass the whole system . . . Any system that allowed our patients freedom of choice was doomed. (1993: 195)

For Grahek, the failure of this project is an illustration of the fact that the affective dimension of pain experience (what he calls its 'emotional-cognitive' dimensions) is of crucial importance to the way in which the pain system serves its biological function. To understand the way in which the pain system standardly serves its biological function, we should not simply focus on the fact that a subject's pain experience involves the sensory discrimination of, and tracking of, damage, or potential damage, to the body, for the following reasons: (a) this would not be enough to capture the fact that it's usually the case that when a subject has a pain experience, she is *in pain*; and (b) the fact that the subject is standardly *in pain* when she has such experience is of crucial importance to the way in which the pain system serves its biological function.

One could regard the modification made by Brand to his prosthetic pain system as an attempt to accommodate the crucial importance of the affective dimension of pain— the relevance of the fact that a subject is usually *in pain* when she has a pain experience. But this was in effect achieved by causing the subject to feel 'normal' pain in some other part of his body. That is to say, the prosthetic pain system was set up to cause the subject to feel a painful sensation in a part of the body other than the body part that the prosthetic pain system was designed to protect. What conclusions might we draw from the failure of this modification to the substitute pain system?

The failure of the modified version of Brand's prosthetic pain system suggests that the fact that a subject is aware that the occurrence of some event in some part of his body is causing him to be in pain is not in itself sufficient to make him naturally inclined to be protective of that body part. The subject's natural inclination was to protect the part of the body where he felt the sensation-event to occur. Although the subject was aware that it was damage to his hand, say, that was causing him to be in pain, his natural inclination was to protect not his hand, but his armpit—the body part where he felt the sensation to occur. This needs explaining.

The account of the distinctive relation between the occurrence of the located sensation-event and the subject's being in pain that is part of the account of the ontology of pain that I have been proposing is, I think, relevant to this explanation. According to that account, when a located sensation of pain occurs, the subject of the sensation is, standardly, thereby in the affective psychological state of *being in pain*. This psychological state of the subject, her being in pain, is *constitutively* dependent on the occurrence of the sensation, and the nature of the located painful occurrence can only be fully specified in terms of the psychological state of her being in pain that obtains in virtue of, and for the duration of, its occurrence. For this reason, although it doesn't make sense to say that the subject's psychological state of *being in pain* is located in some body part, there's nonetheless a sense in which the painfulness of the subject's pain does seem to her to be located in some part of her body—the part of the body where she feels the sensation-event to occur.

From the subject's point of view, it is not simply as though some event occurring in some part of her body is causing her to be in pain, where an event of the same kind could in principle occur in that body part without its having that effect.[18] The kind of located sensation-event that is occurring feels to the subject to be one that couldn't occur without her being aware of it and without her being in pain—without that part of her body hurting. So it feels to the subject as though it is not possible to stop the unpleasant effect of the occurrence of the located sensation-event without stopping the occurrence of that located sensation-event. Therefore, the subject won't simply be inclined to avoid the unpleasant *effects* of the occurrence of the sensation-event by protecting herself *from* the located sensation-event. The subject's natural inclination will be to protect herself from whatever it is that is *causing* the occurrence of the located sensation-event, and this will often require protecting the body part where she feels the sensation-event to occur.

The phenomenology of the subject's pain experience is such that it seems to her as though in order to stop the unpleasant *experience* of the located sensation-event it is

---

[18] This is one of the reasons the phenomenon of pain asymbolia can appear so puzzling.

necessary to stop the occurrence of the *located sensation-event*. The subject will therefore be naturally inclined to prevent the cause of the located sensation-event from having its effect, so she will thereby be naturally inclined to protect the body part where she feels the sensation-event to occur. This, I take it, is of relevance to explaining why it is that the subjects of Brand's modified prosthetic pain system were naturally inclined to be protective *of* the body part where they felt the sensation-event to occur, which inclined them to protect themselves *from* the events at their extremities that they knew to be causally responsible for the occurrence of these located sensation-events. This explanation crucially depends on the apparent mind-dependence of the located sensation-event. If the pain system is to perform its biological function successfully, it must track changes to the *objective physical* condition of the body. However, the effective way in which it performs this biological function is for such physical conditions to cause the subject to be aware of *mind-dependent, located* bodily occurrences, which induce the subject to protect the *body parts* at which such mind-dependent bodily occurrences are felt to occur. From the subject's point of view, there is no obvious way to prevent her awareness of a painful located sensation-event without stopping the occurrence of that located sensation-event. And stopping the experience of the sensation-event will usually require protecting the body part at which the sensation-event is felt to occur.

3.6 Explanatory circularity and physicalism

According to the account of located pain sensation that I have proposed, when you feel a sensation of pain in some part of your body, you are aware of a *mind-dependent* bodily occurrence. However, I suggested that this account is consistent with what we may want to say about the biological function of pain—that its biological function is to track changes to the objective, physical condition of the body, where the physical condition in question may be either actual damage to the body, or a physical condition that is relevant to potential damage to the body. Moreover, I have suggested that the account of the ontology I have proposed may be relevant to explaining the distinctive way in which pain experience serves this function.

Having said that, it is far from clear that all experiences of pain serve some biological function. For example, it's far from clear what should be said about the biological function of a migraine headache, just as it's far from clear what should be said about the biological function of a migraine aura that may precede or accompany that headache. And when a pain experience isn't serving a particular biological function, I don't think we should automatically conclude that the subject of that experience is not aware of some bodily event occurring at the location where she feels the pain sensation to be. For it may be that the subject is simply aware of some mind-dependent bodily occurrence at that bodily location.[19]

---

[19] In this chapter I have been focusing on the bodily sensation of pain. There may be rather different things to be said about different kinds of bodily sensation. In some cases we may want to say that the

What makes the bodily event that the subject is aware of mind-dependent is the fact that its nature is to be specified, at least in part, in terms of the kind of phenomenally conscious state of the subject that obtains in virtue of its occurrence and which is intentionally directed on it. What makes that mind-dependent event a bodily occurrence is the fact that its nature can only be fully specified in terms of the kind of bodily condition that obtains when it occurs—a bodily condition whose obtaining depends constitutively on its occurrence. The nature of the bodily condition is to be specified in terms of the kind of occurrence on which it constitutively depends, which in turn is an occurrence whose nature is to be specified in terms of the kind of phenomenally conscious state that obtains in virtue of that occurrence and which is intentionally directed on it and the bodily condition. So in that sense the bodily condition that obtains in virtue of the occurrence of the sensation is itself mind-dependent.

This proposal, then, gives rise to a form of explanatory circularity when it comes to specifying the kind of bodily condition that obtains, and which you are aware of, when you feel a sensation of pain in some part of your body. The nature of the bodily condition cannot be specified independently of the kind of located sensation-event that it constitutively depends upon. The nature of that located sensation-event cannot be specified independently of the kind of bodily condition that obtains in virtue of its occurrence, and moreover, the nature of that located sensation-event cannot be specified independently of the kind of phenomenally conscious mental state that obtains when it occurs—a phenomenally conscious mental state that is intentionally directed on the located sensation-event and the bodily condition that obtains in virtue of the occurrence of that located sensation-event. In order to know the nature of the bodily condition that obtains when a subject feels a sensation in some part of her body one needs to know what it would be like to be aware of it. And knowing what it would be like to be aware of it requires knowing what kind of bodily condition it is.

As I mentioned in the previous chapter, at a certain level of abstraction one may be able to type the kind of state that obtains when a phenomenal event occurs without making essential reference to the nature of that phenomenal event. So at a certain level of abstraction one could type the mental and bodily states that obtain when a subject feels a sensation in some part of her body without making reference to the phenomenal properties of the sensation-event. One could thereby avoid this sort of explanatory circularity. So, for example, certain ways of characterizing the experience of the bodily sensation of pain in functional terms could avoid this form of explanatory circularity.

experience of the located mind-dependent bodily sensation is also an experience of some mind-*independent* bodily event/condition/property, and/or some mind-independent object/event beyond the body. The obvious candidate for the latter sort of experience is the experience of tactile sensations. Indeed, in certain cases of pain experience one might want to hold that the experience of the located mind-dependent bodily sensation of pain is also an experience of some mind-independent object/property/event. For example, the sort of pain experience one feels at the surface of one's body when one touches a hot stove, or the sort of pain experience one feels when being cut by a sharp object.

However, in typing the relevant states at this level of abstraction, one would be omitting something, for one would not be characterizing as such the sorts of phenomenal events and states that occur and obtain when the subject feels the sensation in her body. And typing as such the sort of phenomenal events and states that occur and obtain will involve the form of explanatory circularity that I've outlined.

The account of the bodily sensation of pain that I've outlined involves the idea that when you feel a pain sensation in some part of your body you are aware of a mind-dependent entity—a mind-dependent individual that has phenomenal properties. One might think that it therefore has something in common with certain versions of sense-datum theories that posit mind-dependent objects of awareness. As I mentioned in Chapter 1, it is sometimes suggested that these sense-datum theories are inconsistent with physicalism. So is the account I've outlined one that a physicalist should reject?

According to this account of bodily sensation, the phenomenal mind-dependent object of awareness can only occur if there obtains a phenomenally conscious state that is intentionally directed on it, and the nature of the phenomenal event and state are to be specified in terms of one another. So in accepting this account one will be accepting that there are events and states that have this sort of interdependent status. However, accepting that there are events and states that have this sort of interdependent status does not in itself commit one to denying that the occurrence and obtaining of these interdependent events and states supervenes on the physical. For all that has been said, acceptance of the proposal I've outlined may be consistent with accepting the idea that there is a set of physical conditions the obtaining of which is sufficient for both the occurrence of an event and the obtaining of a state that have this interdependent status. However, the account I have proposed does suggest that simply knowing that those physical conditions obtain won't in itself inform one about the nature of the interdependent event and state that supervene on those physical conditions. In order to acquire knowledge of the nature of the event and state one needs to break into the explanatory circle. In order to acquire knowledge of the nature of the event one needs to know what it would be like to be aware of it. And in order to know what it would be like to be aware of the event, one needs to know the nature of that event.

There is a further point to make about the dual status of the sensation-event that is the object of awareness when you feel a sensation of pain in some part of your body—i.e. its dual status as both mind-dependent phenomenal event and as bodily event. Given that one's body is a mind-independent thing, certain mind-independent conditions must obtain if this sort of mind-dependent event is to occur; and so certain mind-independent conditions must obtain in order for one to be aware of its occurrence. For example, in order for you to be aware of this sort of mind-dependent bodily occurrence you must be aware of the body part that the occurrence modifies, and so you must have the relevant body part. A consequence of this is that if a subject is having an experience as of a located pain sensation in some part of her body but she lacks the relevant body part, then she is hallucinating the occurrence of that mind-dependent bodily

occurrence.[20] It is for the subject as though she is aware of a phenomenal event occurring in some part of her body, but she isn't. We need not deny that the subject is *in pain*
in such circumstances, but we need to deny that the mind-dependent event that seems
to her to occur, does in fact occur. This consequence of the account introduces some
further questions and puzzles that I shall touch on in the final section of this chapter.
But we won't be in a position to address these issues fully until the end of Part I.

3.7 Hallucinating phenomenal events

According to the account of located bodily sensation that I have proposed, when you
are aware of a located sensation of pain in some part of your body, the relation between
the located mind-dependent bodily event that you seem to be aware of and the
phenomenally conscious state of yours that is intentionally directed upon it, is *constitutive*, and not merely causal. A commitment to this claim arose out of the attempt to
accommodate an aspect of the phenomenology of the experience of located bodily
sensation—i.e. the fact that one seems to be aware of a *mind-dependent* bodily occurrence when one experiences such a bodily sensation.

If we accept that the phenomenology of the experience of located bodily sensation is
consistent with the obtaining of a merely causal, and not constitutive, connection
between the object of awareness and one's experience of it, then we seem thereby to
allow not only that one can have the experience without the occurrence of its object,
but also that the object of experience can occur without the experience of it. For on
such a view it becomes unclear why there cannot occur in one's body a located bodily
sensation that fails to cause an experience of it.

Given that it is part of the phenomenology of the experience of a located bodily sensation that some aspect of what one seems to be aware of in having the experience is
mind-dependent, we should deny that the phenomenology of the experience is consistent with the obtaining of a merely causal, and not constitutive, connection between the
object of awareness and one's experience of it—hence the proposal that an aspect of the
phenomenology of the experience is to be accounted for by appeal to the obtaining of a
constitutive, and not merely causal, connection between (a) the occurrence of the
located bodily sensation and (b) the obtaining of a phenomenally conscious state that is
intentionally directed on it.

I suggested that we should hold that if a subject is having an experience as of a located
pain sensation in some part of her body but she lacks the relevant body part, then she is
hallucinating the occurrence of a mind-dependent bodily event. If the subject is hallucinating the occurrence of a mind-dependent bodily event, then no such mind-dependent

---

[20] A subject might have an experience that misrepresents the location of a body part that seems to be
modified by the occurrence of a sensation-event. And we might regard this as a case of illusion, rather than
hallucination. However, here I am considering a case in which a subject doesn't merely misrepresent the
location of part of her body. I am considering a case in which she hallucinates the body part in question.

bodily event is occurring. In which case, the phenomenology of her experience cannot be accounted for by appeal to the obtaining of a constitutive connection between (a) the mind-dependent bodily event, and (b) her experience of it. So if such hallucinations are possible, what account of their phenomenology should we give?

One proposal might be that we should say that when a subject has such hallucinations, the subject is having an experience that merely represents the occurrence of a mind-dependent bodily event that has phenomenal properties. According to this proposal, the subject is having an experience with an intentional content that has veridicality conditions, and the intentional content of the subject's experience is veridical just in case the subject is undergoing a mind-dependent bodily event that has phenomenal properties. As no such event is occurring, the content of the subject's experience is non-veridical. On this view, when a subject hallucinates a located bodily sensation, it seems to the subject as though she is undergoing a phenomenal event of a kind that is not in fact occurring.

If one thinks that this sort of proposal adequately accounts for hallucinations of located bodily sensation, one might think that it should also be able to account for *all* experiences of located bodily sensation. In which case, one may be led to the view that in *all* cases of the experience of located bodily sensation one is having an experience with an intentional content that represents the occurrence of a mind-dependent phenomenal event in some part of one's body. According to this view, one provides the same account of the experience of located bodily sensation, irrespective of whether or not the experience is a hallucination. So according to this view, as there isn't a constitutive connection between the object of experience and one's experience of it in the case of hallucination, the same should be said of the non-hallucinatory cases as well.

I have suggested that the sort of phenomenal bodily occurrence that you seem to be aware of in experiencing a located bodily sensation seems to you to be mind-dependent. It seems to be an event whose occurrence entails your phenomenally conscious awareness of it. And I suggested that for this reason, we should deny that the phenomenology of the experience is consistent with the obtaining of a merely causal, and not constitutive, connection between (a) the occurrence you seem to be aware of, and (b) your experience of it. So if there isn't a constitutive connection between (a) and (b), then the following is true: it seems to you as though you are undergoing a phenomenal event of a kind that you are not in fact undergoing.

I suggest that all should accept that when you have a hallucination of a sensation of pain in some part of your body, it seems to you as though you are undergoing a phenomenal event of a kind that you are not in fact undergoing. It seems to you as though you are undergoing a *bodily* event with phenomenal properties that modifies the body part at which it seems to occur; and since you are hallucinating the body part, no such event is occurring. However, those who accept that there *never* obtains a constitutive connection between your experience of a located bodily sensation of pain and your experience of it, will be committed to the further claim that *whenever* you experience a located sensation of pain, you seem to be undergoing a phenomenal event of a kind that you are not in fact undergoing. Does this consequence provide us with a reason to give *different* accounts of hallucinatory and non-hallucinatory experiences of located bodily sensations? That is, should we accept that when you are *not* hallucinating the relevant body part, there *is* a constitutive connection between (a) the occurrence you seem to be aware of, and (b) your experience of it, even though the same cannot be said of hallucinations of located bodily sensations?

This is an issue that I shall return to at the end of Part I. For now I just want to highlight some puzzling aspects of the phenomenology of hallucinations of located bodily sensations: (i) it is intuitive to think that hallucinations of located bodily sensations are phenomenally conscious experiences—i.e. there is something it is like for you when you hallucinate a located bodily sensation; (ii) when you hallucinate a located bodily sensation you seem to be undergoing a phenomenal event of a kind that you are not in fact undergoing; and (iii) it is intuitive to think that if you hallucinate a located bodily sensation, you are, ceteris paribus, in a position to know what it is like to undergo the sort of phenomenal event that you seem to be undergoing, but which you are not in fact undergoing.

A challenge that all accounts of the hallucination of bodily sensation will need to address is how to account for the conjunction of claims (i)–(iii). This is a challenge one will need to address even if one holds that hallucinations of bodily sensations are experiences that have intentional contents with veridicality conditions.

At the end of Chapter 2 I said that the discussion of bodily sensation would give rise to issues that begin to re-engage with a question that I introduced and left hanging in Chapter 1—the question of whether we need to appeal to the obtaining of a distinctive kind of psychological relation when characterizing the manifest image of conscious sensory experience. I shall be considering the question of whether there are reasons for favouring a relationalist view of conscious sensory experience in the next chapter. That discussion will connect with the points I have just made about hallucinations of bodily sensations, for as we shall see, certain versions of the relationalist view involve claims about visual hallucination that are analogues of claims (i)–(iii). They involve the claims that (i)★ it is intuitive to think that visual hallucinations are phenomenally conscious experiences; (ii)★ when you have a visual hallucination you seem to be undergoing a phenomenally conscious experience of a kind that you are not in fact undergoing; and (iii)★ it is intuitive to think that if you have a visual hallucination, you are, ceteris paribus, in a position to know what it is like to have a successful visual perception of the world.

4

Temporal Transparency and Perceptual Acquaintance

The general proposal about the ontology of conscious sensory experience that I've been making so far—the interdependence thesis—is the following: conscious sensory experience involves the occurrence of mental events/processes, and when such mental events/processes occur, the subject undergoing them is in psychological states that wouldn't otherwise obtain; the nature of the mental event/process is to be specified in terms of the sort of psychological state of the subject that obtains when the mental event/process occurs; and at a certain level of abstraction, the nature of this psychological state is to be specified in terms of the kind of event/process in virtue of whose occurrence it obtains. So the occurrence and state in question have an interdependent status. I put this proposal to work in the previous chapter, by making use of it to outline an account of the experience of located bodily sensation that is able to accommodate the distinctive phenomenology of such sensations.

I noted that there seems to be a significant difference between the phenomenology of the experience of a located bodily sensation on the one hand, and our visual experience of the world on the other. In the case of the experience of a located bodily sensation, you seem to be presented with a phenomenal event whose phenomenal properties you can attend to directly, and in the case of a visual experience of the world, this doesn't seem to be the case. However, I suggested that despite this difference, the same general proposal about the ontology of conscious sensory experience might apply in the both cases. The suggestion was that we can accommodate this difference in the phenomenology by saying that in the case of a phenomenally conscious visual experience, the phenomenally conscious state that obtains in virtue of, and for the duration of, the occurrence of the phenomenal event that occurs, and in terms of which the nature of the event is to be specified, is one that is intentionally directed upon the subject's mind-independent environment, and not the phenomenal event itself. That is to say, the phenomenal event is not itself, and does not seem to one to be, an object of one's conscious visual state. By contrast, in the case of bodily sensation, the phenomenally conscious state that obtains in virtue of, and for the duration of, the occurrence of the sensation, and in terms of which the nature of the sensation is to be specified, *is* intentionally directed upon the sensation itself, occurring at some bodily location.

In certain cases, we may also want to say that the phenomenally conscious state that obtains in virtue of, and for the duration of, the occurrence of the phenomenal event that occurs is one that is intentionally directed upon (a) the phenomenal event itself, occurring at some bodily location, *and* (b) some mind-independent condition of the subject's body (or some mind-independent event involving the subject's body), *and* (c) the subject's mind-independent environment. This is a proposal that we might want to make about tactual conscious sensory awareness. In so far as such phenomenally conscious states are directed on a mind-dependent bodily event, they can be regarded as experiences of located bodily sensations, but in so far as such phenomenally conscious states are also directed on mind-independent events and conditions, including objects/events/features in the subject's mind-independent environment, they also have something in common with visual experiences.

Part of the general proposal is that in all these different cases there obtains a phenomenally conscious state that is intentionally directed on something. In this chapter I want to focus on the *manner* in which conscious sensory experiences are intentionally directed on their objects.

4.1 Representation and the perceptual relation: what is in dispute?

In Chapter 1 I contrasted two opposing views on the general shape of the manifest image of conscious sensory experience—a view according to which we need to appeal to a distinctive psychological relation that obtains when we have conscious sensory experience, and a view according to which we should just be appealing to distinctive properties of mental states/events. I noted that with the decline in popularity of sense-datum approaches to sensory experience one finds that debates about the sensuous character of conscious sensory experience are generally no longer framed in terms of the question of what is distinctive of a particular kind of psychological relation that obtains when one has conscious sensory experience, but rather in terms of the question of what properties conscious sensory events/states have; and disagreements about the sensuous character of conscious sensory experience are usually thought of as disagreements about the properties of mental events/states. Conscious sensory experiences are thought to be personal-level mental states/events that have representational properties (where such representational properties are to be understood in terms of the idea that sensory experiences have intentional contents with veridicality conditions), and for some, non-representational properties as well.

However, I also suggested that the recent re-emergence of relational views of sensory experience can be seen as a challenge to this consensus on the general shape of the manifest image of conscious sensory experience. These relationalists endorse the idea that we need to appeal to the obtaining of a distinctive kind of psychological relation when characterizing the manifest image of conscious sensory experience, but they claim that the relevant psychological relation is one that subjects bear to material objects and their features, and not to the sorts of entities posited by sense-datum theorists. Given that this psychological relation to material objects and their features cannot plausibly be held to obtain when a subject hallucinates, these relationalists maintain that when a subject hallucinates, although it may seem to that subject as though she is having a conscious sensory experience that involves the obtaining of a distinctive psychological relation to material objects and their features, she isn't. And so the sort of conscious sensuous character that seems to the subject of the hallucination to be introspectively accessible to her, is not in fact introspectively accessible to her.

This new relationalist proposal reintroduces the idea that the sensuous character of conscious sensory experience that is manifest to one when one has a conscious sensory experience is to be articulated (at least in part) by appeal to a distinctive psychological *relation* that obtains when one has conscious sensory experience, and not simply by appeal to the occurrence/obtaining of a mental event/state that has certain distinctive properties. This rather different claim about the general shape of the manifest image of conscious sensory experience intersects with a view about self-knowledge—a view about what a subject is in a position to know about her conscious sensory experience when she has it, and what puts her in a position to know it. It involves the idea that an account of what one can know about the sensuous character of the conscious sensory experience one has when one perceives the world, and one's account of what puts one in a position to know it, cannot be straightforwardly and symmetrically applied to the case of hallucination.

In what follows I will be introducing considerations that speak in favour of this relationalist view of the manifest image of conscious sensory experience; and I will be doing so by discussing some puzzles that concern the conscious character of our perceptions of events. First though, I shall say a bit more about where the disagreement between the relationalist and the representationalist lies. This will help clarify what kind of argument might speak in favour of a relationalist view rather than a representationalist one.

A feature of the phenomenology of conscious sensory experience that these relationalists highlight is the phenomenal presence of mind-independent objects and their features; and relationalists place emphasis on the claim that when we perceive the world we are *directly* aware *of* mind-independent objects and their features—we are *perceptually acquainted* with such objects and their properties—and this perceptual relation doesn't obtain when a subject hallucinates, even though it may seem to the subject of hallucination that it does. However, these are all claims that a representationalist might accept. A representationalist can say that the intentional content of experience concerns material objects and their features, hence the apparent presence to mind of such entities; and they can maintain that when a subject's experience is appropriately caused by what it represents, the subject is directly aware *of* those objects and features. In that sense, the subject is *perceptually acquainted* with those objects and features; and this is a perceptual relation that doesn't obtain in the case of hallucination. So where does the real disagreement between the relationalist and the representationalist lie?

A common way of articulating what is really at issue between them is in terms of a disagreement over whether successful perceptions and hallucinations are experiences of the same kind. It is suggested that the representationalist accepts, whereas the relationalist rejects, the claim that they are experiences of the same kind, and so the representationalist accepts, whereas the relationalist rejects, the claim that the kind of experience a subject has when she perceives the world is one the subject could be having if she were hallucinating. However, there are a number of reasons for thinking that this way of expressing what's at issue between them fails to engage with what is at the heart of the relationalist's proposal. Given that we can type mental events and states in a variety of different ways, for a variety of different purposes, it is open to a representationalist to accept that the terms 'veridical perception' and 'hallucination' mark useful distinctions between perceptual experiences that may, in certain contexts, be of explanatory significance. So the representationalist may agree that there is a sense in which veridical perceptions and hallucinations can be thought of as perceptual experiences of different kinds. And as the relationalist need not deny that successful perceptions and hallucinations have anything in common, she can accept that there are features that they share, and so she can agree that there is a sense in which successful perceptions and hallucinations can be thought of as experiences of the same kind.[1]

Furthermore, simply expressing the difference between the relationalist and the representationalist in these terms leaves open the possibility that they simply disagree over the question of whether the intentional content of a successful perception should be regarded as object-dependent;[2] and it also leaves open the possibility that their disagreement is over the question of whether *seeing that p* should be regarded as a factive mental state that is not to be given a conjunctive analysis.[3] Neither of these debates engages directly with what is at the heart of the relationalist's proposal about the conscious sensory experience involved in successful perception, for at the heart of that proposal is a view of the conscious character of successful perception that denies that the conscious character of that sort of experience is simply determined by the obtaining of a mental state which has an intentional content with veridicality conditions—irrespective of

---

[1] One formulation of the disagreement between the relationalist and her opponent might invoke the notion of a *fundamental* kind. (This formulation is principally due to Martin 2002, 2004, and 2006, but see also Snowdon 2005.) According to this formulation, the relationalist is committed to denying that successful perceptions and hallucinations are mental events/states of the same *fundamental* kind. This formulation obviously depends on further questions about what it is that makes a kind 'fundamental'.

[2] The sort of view I have in mind here is one according to which (i) a particular experience E that is a veridical perception of a particular mind-independent object O will have an intentional content with a demonstrative element that successfully refers to O and a distinct particular experience E* will have an intentional content with the same veridicality conditions only if its intentional content contains a demonstrative element that also refers to O, and (ii) if two experiences have intentional contents which differ in their veridicality conditions, then this is not just a respect in which these mental events differ; it also amounts to a difference in their mental kinds.

[3] I have in mind a view that regards the state of *seeing that p* in the same sort of way that Williamson (2000) regards the state of knowing that *p* (whether or not the view commits one to the claim that seeing that *p* is a way of knowing that *p*).

whether one thinks of the intentional content of the mental state as object-dependent, and irrespective of whether one thinks of the mental state as factive.

The idea that the conscious character of experience is not simply determined by its representational properties is a familiar one. Some hold that conscious experiences have non-representational, phenomenal qualities—psychological properties that contribute to what it is like for the subject to have the experience but which are not simply determined by the experience's possession of an intentional content with veridicality conditions. The relationalist can be understood as making a similar claim. But rather than simply appealing to psychological but non-representational properties, the relationalist appeals to a psychological but non-representational relation—a psychological relation whose obtaining contributes to what it is like for the subject to be having the experience, but which is not simply determined by the experience's possession of an intentional content with veridicality conditions.

Those who advocate the claim that experience has non-representational phenomenal properties assert that it is the fact that experience actually possesses such properties that contributes to the conscious character of experience. The mere representation of such properties, they claim, doesn't adequately account for the phenomenology. Likewise, the relationalist asserts that it is the actual obtaining of the relevant psychological but non-representational relation that contributes to the conscious character of successful perception, and the mere representation of such a relation doesn't adequately account for the phenomenology.[4] Furthermore, those who appeal to non-representational properties in their account of the conscious character of experience need not deny that experiences have intentional contents with veridicality conditions, and likewise, a relationalist need not deny that when a subject succeeds in perceiving the world, that subject is in mental states that can be regarded as perceptual and which have intentional contents with veridicality conditions. They might hold that the obtaining of the relevant psychological but non-representational relation is an *element* of the conscious character of successful perception.[5]

Given this understanding of what is distinctive of the relationalist proposal, considerations motivating this sort of account of successful perception should be considerations motivating an appeal to the obtaining of a non-representational psychological relation to objects and features in an account of the conscious character of successful perception (and not just the representation of one); and the claim that the relevant psychological relation is non-representational should be understood in terms of the idea that the obtaining of the relation isn't simply determined by the obtaining of a mental state that has an intentional content with veridicality conditions—irrespective of whether the mental state in question is a factive one, and irrespective of whether the content of the

---

[4] Just as those who claim that conscious sensory experience possesses non-representational phenomenal properties needn't be committed to denying the supervenience of the mental on the physical, the same can be true of the relationalist.

[5] Compare here the way in which the sense-datum theorist Price (1932) claims that the relation of acquaintance is an 'element' of perceptual consciousness.

state is object-involving. In what follows I shall be suggesting that there are considerations relating to the conscious character of our perception of events that can be appealed to in motivating this sort of relationalist view.

4.2 The temporal transparency of our experience of events

I have talked about the way in which Moore appeals to the idea that conscious sensory experience seems to be 'diaphanous'. The suggestion is that when one tries to focus in introspection on one's experience and its properties it seems to one as though one cannot help but 'see right through' the experience, so that what one seems to be attending to are the objects and qualities the experience is an experience of—objects and properties that are distinct from the experience itself and its properties. One also finds appeals to the 'transparency' of sensory experience being made by those defending representationalist accounts of sensory experience. They too claim that sensory experience seems to one to be transparent, or diaphanous, to the objects and properties one is apparently perceptually aware of in having that experience.[6]

This idea is sometimes expressed in terms of the claim that introspection of one's perceptual experience seems to one to reveal *only* the objects, qualities, and relations one is apparently perceptually aware of in having that experience, and not qualities of the experience itself. A weaker version of the claim is that when one attempts to attend introspectively to what it is like for one to be having a perceptual experience, it seems to one as though one can only do so through attending to the sorts of objects, qualities, and relations one is apparently *perceptually* aware of in having the experience. That is, when one tries to introspect one's visual experience and its qualities, it seems to one as though one can only do so by *looking at* the objects, qualities, and relations one seems to be aware of in having that experience.

The transparency claim that representationalists appeal to is also sometimes summarized in terms of the idea that introspection of one's experience seems to support certain positive and negative claims concerned with what one does and doesn't discover when introspecting—e.g. the positive claim that one does seem to discover mind-independent objects and their properties, and the negative claim that one doesn't seem to discover the qualia or sense-data posited by certain accounts of the conscious character of experience.[7] The representationalist argues that the appropriate way to accommodate these positive and negative claims is to hold that such sensory experience is a mental

---

[6] See e.g. Harman 1990, Tye 1992, 2000, and 2010, Siewert 2004, and Stoljar 2004. For further discussion of the way representationalists appeal to the transparency of experience, see Martin 2002 and Crane 2006.

[7] Not all of those who appeal to the 'transparency' of experience agree on the details of the positive and negative claims, and some of those who appeal to the transparency of experience are not attempting to highlight the claim that we seem to be directly aware of mind-independent material objects—e.g. Moore 1903.

state/event with an intentional content that has veridicality conditions, and which concerns mind-independent objects and features in the environment of the subject.

I want to suggest that an appeal to what it is like to introspect one's experience can be used to support other positive and negative claims that are relevant to an account of the conscious character of our experience of *events*. For example, a positive claim that can be made is that introspection of one's experience seems to reveal (at least often) not only objects and their properties, but also events. In certain cases, one's introspection of the conscious character of one's experience seems to one to require attending to the occurrence of events and/or processes that are distinct from the experience itself. Furthermore, in such cases, the occurrences one thereby seems to be attending to seem to one to have temporal extension. In a given case, it may be that it doesn't seem to one as though one is thereby attending to all of the temporal parts of that occurrence; however, it seems to one as though one cannot attend to the occurrence without attending to *some* temporal part of it and, moreover, some temporal part of the occurrence that has temporal extension. If one tries just to attend to an instantaneous temporal part of the occurrence, without attending to a temporal part of the occurrence that has temporal extension, then one will fail. An analogous claim that can be made about one's experience of the spatial objects one seems to be attending to in introspecting the conscious character of one's experience is that it does not seem to one as though one is attending to all of the spatial parts of the object; however, it seems to one as though one cannot attend to the object without attending to *some* spatial part of the object, and, moreover, some spatial part of the object that has spatial extension. It might be suggested that instantaneous events also feature in the conscious character of experience (e.g. the event of an object *starting* to move), but if they do, it seems to one as though one cannot attend to them without thereby attending to something that has temporal extension (e.g. the object moving). An analogous claim that can be made about the spatial phenomenology of experience is that it seems to one as though one cannot attend to the spatial boundary of an object of experience without thereby attending to some spatial part of the object that has spatial extension.[8]

These remarks are concerned with some of the positive claims that introspection of one's experience seems to support—claims concerned with what one does seem to discover when one introspects. There are also certain negative claims that can be made. When one introspects one's experience, the temporal location of one's perceptual experience seems to one to be transparent to the temporal location of whatever it is that one is aware of in having that experience. Introspectively, it doesn't seem to one as though one can mark out the temporal location of one's perceptual experience as distinct from the temporal location of whatever it is that one seems to be perceptually aware of. Furthermore, it seems to one as though the temporal location of one's experience

---

[8] Compare here Sorabji 1983 on an 'instant' as the boundary of a period of time: 'An instant is not a very short period, but rather the beginning or end (the boundary) of a period. It therefore has no size, for it is not a very short line, but rather the boundary of a line. The idea that there are sizeless instants should be no more controversial than the idea that periods have beginnings and ends' (8). (See also Moore 1990: 158.)

depends on, and is determined by, the temporal location of whatever it is that one's experience is an experience of.

In this, perception is quite unlike episodic recollection. Introspectively, it does not seem to one as though the temporal location of one's act of episodic recollection is, in the same way, transparent to the temporal location of the event one is recollecting, for one can mark out the temporal location of one's act of recollecting as distinct from the temporal location of whatever it is one is recollecting. Introspectively, an episode of apparent episodic recollection does not strike one as being the kind of event that depends on the temporal presence of its object. Indeed, it is arguable that an aspect of the phenomenology of such an episode is the current absence of the event recollected. Similar remarks apply to the objects of perceptual imagination. For the temporal location of an act of perceptual imagination doesn't seem to one to depend on, and be determined by, the temporal location of the object perceptually imagined. This is connected with a distinctive respect in which perception seems to one to be passive and not subject to the will. Even when perception involves agential perceptual activity, such as looking and watching, it seems to one as though the inception and course of one's perception depend upon the temporal location of the object perceived.

When one perceives an unfolding occurrence (e.g. the movement of an object across space), it seems to one as though one's perceptual experience has the temporal location and duration of its object, and it seems to one as though the temporal location and duration of each temporal part of one's experience is transparent to the temporal location and duration of each temporal part of the unfolding occurrence one seems to perceive. In this respect, perception is also quite unlike a present-tensed conscious act of judging—e.g. an act of judging that 'The hurricane is now passing over Cuba'. In the case of the judgement, it does not seem to one as though the duration of one's act of judging depends on, and is determined by, the duration of whatever it is that one's present-tensed judgement represents.

Providing an account of experience that can accommodate both these positive and negative phenomenological claims is far from straightforward. I shall be outlining what the general difficulty involves and offering a diagnosis of it. But first I want to focus on the question of how a representationalist might attempt to accommodate these phenomenological claims. According to the representationalist, the conscious character of experience is largely determined by the representational content of that experience. So how might representationalists attempt to accommodate the positive and negative phenomenological claims in their accounts of the content of experience?

4.3 Representationalism and the temporal transparency of experience

The most natural way for the representationalist to accommodate the positive phenomenological claim, concerning what one does discover when one introspects, is for her to say that the content of experience represents non-instantaneous occurrences—it represents, as such, events, or temporal parts of events, that have temporal extension. The most natural way for the representationalist to accommodate the negative phenomenological claim that pertains to the temporal transparency of experience is for her to say that the content of experience includes a temporal indexical element. So according to such a view, the content of experience represents, as such, events (or temporal parts of events) that have temporal extension as occurring '*now*'.

One question we can raise about such an account is the following. Let us label the occurrence with temporal extension that is represented, as such, by the content of experience 'O'. As O seems to S (the subject of experience) to have temporal extension, O seems to S to have earlier and later temporal parts—call them X and Y respectively. X is not represented as having the temporal extension of O, and neither is Y. X and Y are represented as occurring at different times. Given that X and Y are represented as occurring at different times, how can both X and Y be represented as occurring 'now' within the same representational content?

A simple reply here is that there is nothing incoherent in the idea of a temporal indexical element picking out an interval of time within which both X and Y are represented as occurring, for there is nothing incoherent in the idea that the indexical 'now' picks out an *interval* of time that *includes* the time at which the experience occurs. The content of the experience is correct only if both X and Y occur during the interval of time that the indexical thereby refers to, but the correctness of that content does not require that X and Y occur at the same time, so X and Y can also be represented as occurring at different times.

Although this suggestion doesn't suffer from any kind of incoherence, the difficulty with it is that it doesn't seem to capture adequately the sort of phenomenological datum that lies behind the claim of temporal transparency. The negative claim of temporal transparency is that the temporal location and duration of one's experience seems to one to be transparent to the temporal location and duration of the occurrence one seems to perceive. And so it seems to one as though the temporal location and duration of each temporal part of one's experience is transparent to the temporal location and duration of each temporal part of the unfolding occurrence one seems to perceive. When one attends to what it is like to experience the perceived occurrence, and in so doing attends to the perceived occurrence itself, one does not discover any temporal part of the perceived occurrence that does not seem to be concurrent with one's awareness of it. If one holds a view according to which the indexical 'now' that is contained within the content of experience picks out an interval of time that merely *includes* the time at which the experience occurs, then one doesn't capture the fact that the experience seems to have the temporal location and duration of the occurrence it represents, for one allows that the experience does not seem to one to have the duration of the occurrence it represents. By analogy, consider a judgement with a content that contains the indexical 'today'. The episode of judging does not seem to one to have the temporal duration of the day one thereby refers to.

This suggests that in the case of the content of experience, the interval of time picked out by the indexical 'now' just is the interval of time that is occupied by the experience that represents it. However, this leads us back to the puzzle. If O is represented as occurring 'now', then O is represented as filling the interval of time that is occupied by the experience that represents it. In which case X (the earlier temporal part of O) and Y (the later temporal part of O) cannot be represented as occurring 'now', for then they too would be represented as filling the interval of time that is occupied by that experience—an interval of time that O seems to fill. In which case it would seem to the subject of experience that X and Y each have the temporal extension of O.

Why not say that when one has an experience as of O, one has an experience with a content that contains distinct temporal indexical elements—e.g. why not say that the content contains an indexical 'now 1' that picks out the time at which X occurs and a distinct indexical element 'now 2' that picks out the distinct time at which Y occurs? The difficulty facing this suggestion is the following. For the representationalist, the basic unit of phenomenological explanation should be a content with veridicality conditions. An indexical element that is a constituent of the content of an experience cannot pick out an instant or interval of time independently of the content with veridicality conditions of which it is a constituent. Recall the discussion in Chapter 2 of the relation between the content of experience and the temporal profile of the experience which that content characterizes: perhaps contents with veridicality conditions can be used to specify the kind of experience undergone by a subject over an interval of time, but such intervals are not to be thought of as intervals that can be broken down into sub-intervals in each of which the subject undergoes an experience that is to be specified in terms of some part of the content experienced, where such parts lack veridicality conditions. Each temporal indexical that picks out an instant or interval of time is an element of a representational content with veridicality conditions. In the case of experience, the time picked out by a temporal indexical n is the time at which there occurs (or obtains) a mental event (or state) e with a representational content C that has n as a constituent. If n1 and n2 are constituents of the same content C, then the time picked out by n1 is the time at which e occurs (or obtains) and the time picked out by n2 is also the time at which e occurs (or obtains), for each indexical element picks out the interval of time occupied by the experience with the content that contains that indexical element; and since each indexical is an element of the same content, they are elements of the content of the same experience, and so pick out the same interval of time.

4.4 The ontological challenge

It is not just the representationalist who faces difficulties in providing an account of experience that can accommodate both the positive and negative phenomenological claims about our experience of events. In discussions of temporal experience, so-called 'specious present' theories have been criticized by some for the way in which they attempt to accommodate both positive and negative phenomenological claims.

According to certain versions of such theories, the subject of experience seems to be perceptually aware of things that fill an interval of time, where all of the temporal parts of that which seems to fill that interval of time seem to the subject to be temporally 'present'. Some have accused such theories of being incoherent in committing to the idea that it can seem to a subject as though something has earlier and later temporal parts while all such temporal parts seem to the subject to be, at one and the same time, temporally present.[9]

I think there need be no incoherence in the view, if we think of 'temporal presence' as picking out an *interval* of time which *includes* the time at which the subject is having that experience. However, as mentioned earlier, the difficulty with this suggestion is that it doesn't seem to capture adequately the sort of phenomenological datum that lies behind the claim of temporal transparency. If one holds a view according to which 'temporal presence' picks out an interval of time that merely *includes* the time at which the experience occurs, then one doesn't capture the fact that the experience seems to have the temporal location and duration of the perceived occurrence, for one allows that the experience does not seem to one to have the duration of the perceived occurrence.

So-called 'retention' theories have been proposed as alternatives to specious present accounts. According to such theories, the positive phenomenological claim is accommodated, as it seems to the subject as though she is perceptually aware of things with temporal extent—things that fill an interval of time. However, such theories suggest that it is a mistake to think that the whole occurrence thus perceived is presented to the subject as temporally present. An instantaneous temporal part of the perceived occurrence is presented as concurrent with one's awareness of it, and the rest of the perceived occurrence experienced is presented as just past.[10] However, such accounts seem just to reject the negative phenomenological claim that when one introspects one's experience, one cannot discover any occurrence that does not seem to be concurrent with one's awareness of it. If the retention theories were correct, one would expect to be able to discover introspectively events, or temporal parts of events, that seem to one to have temporal locations that are earlier than one's experience of them.[11]

Some general observations on the ontology of experience may help provide a diagnosis of the general difficulty one faces in providing an account of experience that can accommodate both positive and negative phenomenological claims. One might think the best way of providing an account of experience that can accommodate the negative phenomenological claim, concerning the temporal transparency of experience, is to think of experience as an occurrence that unfolds over time. On such a view one can say that an experience E of an occurrence O that unfolds over an interval of time t1–tn

---

[9] See e.g. Kelly 2005.

[10] But see Husserl 1905 for a view that appeals to 'protensions' as well as retentions.

[11] Alternatively, it could be said that certain versions of the retention view fail to accommodate the positive phenomenological claim, in so far as they imply that if one attempts to attend to the temporal part of an occurrence that is concurrent with one's awareness of it, one will only discover an instantaneous temporal part of that occurrence.

itself unfolds over that interval of time t1–tn. One can then hold that each temporal part of E is concurrent with some temporal part of O, of which it is an experience. However, if we want to provide an account that accommodates what it is like for a subject S to undergo E, then we need to say something about the properties of E, and, moreover, we need to say something about the psychological properties of the subject S that obtain when S undergoes an experience E with such properties. The difficulty that this presents is that such properties, of E and of S, do not themselves unfold over time. A psychological property of a subject can be regarded as a mental state of that subject, and the same can be said of mental states: mental states are not the kinds of things that unfold over time. They obtain over intervals of time. Given that they obtain, and do not unfold over time, one might think that mental states with temporal extension *continue* to obtain *throughout* the interval of time over which they obtain.

So suppose that we want our account of the experience E to accommodate the positive phenomenological claim concerning what the subject does seem to discover when she introspects—i.e. events, or temporal parts of events that have temporal extension. One option is to say that the experiential occurrence E, which unfolds over t1–tn, has the property of being as of an occurrence O with temporal extension. We can then say something about the psychological state of S that obtains over the interval of time during which the experience E occurs. We can say that over the interval of time during which experience E occurred it seemed to S as though she was aware of O, where O is an occurrence with temporal extension. However, even though the experiential occurrence E may be something that unfolds over time, the properties of that occurrence, and the psychological state of the subject that obtains when it occurs, do not themselves unfold over time. Since the psychological state of the subject—its seeming to her as though she is aware of an occurrence O—is not something that unfolds over that interval of time, one might think that that perceptual state *continues* to obtain *throughout* that interval of time. In which case, we do not then capture the idea that what seemed to the subject to be the case during sub-intervals of that interval of time was different. So it looks as though we do not capture the idea that during the sub-interval t1–t2 it seemed to S as though she was merely aware of a temporal part of O, during the sub-interval t2–t3 it seemed to S as though she was aware of a different temporal part of O, and so on. In which case it looks as though we do not capture the temporal transparency of experience.

Suppose now we say instead that the experiential occurrence E that occurs over t1–tn has different properties during its different phases—e.g. during the sub-interval t1–t2 it has the property of being as of a temporal part of O, during the sub-interval t3–t4 it has the property of being as of a different temporal part of O, and so on. We can then say that what seemed to S to be the case when she underwent her experience E changed. S's psychological states changed over that interval of time, and so she was in a series of different perceptual states during that interval of time—i.e. during the sub-interval t1–t2 it seemed to S as though she was aware of a temporal part of O, during t3–t4 it seemed to S as though she was aware of a different temporal part of O, and so on. But then the problem is that if the psychological states of the subject are changing in this way during the interval t1–tn—if what seems to her to be the case changes during each sub-interval of t1–tn—then it looks as though we fail to capture the fact that over that interval of time t1–tn she has a psychological property that accounts for the positive phenomenological claim—namely its seeming to her as though she is aware of an occurrence with the temporal extension of O.[12]

The general difficulty here is one of providing an account of experience that can attribute to the subject a psychological property/state that accounts for the fact that it seems to her as though she is perceptually aware of an occurrence with temporal extension, while at the same time accommodating the idea that each temporal part of that occurrence seems to the subject to be concurrent with her awareness of it. And the obstacle to success seems to reside in the fact that mental states are not the kinds of things that can unfold over time.

4.5 The ontological challenge illustrated: two puzzles

The general difficulty that I've just outlined can be illustrated by raising couple of puzzles about our perception of events. One such puzzle concerns the perception of instantaneous events. Suppose you are staring intently at an object that is in full view, when suddenly the object vanishes into thin air, and suppose too that you see the object disappear. The event of the object disappearing happens at a time, but does not take time. It marks the boundary of an interval of time over which the object is visible. If you really did see the object disappear, what account can we give of your perception of the event?

Your perception of the object is not, in itself, a perception of the event of the object's disappearance, and neither is your perception of the absence of the object. For in general,

---

[12] The idea that it is not enough simply to say that experience unfolds over the interval of time that is occupied by the occurrence of which it is an experience can lead to an endorsement of what has been called the 'principle of simultaneous awareness'—the idea that in experience we are simultaneously aware of (or represent) different temporal parts of an occurrence (see Miller 1984). The thought here is that even if we accept that the experiential occurrence unfolds over the interval of time occupied by the occurrence of which it is an experience, we still need to appeal to properties of that experiential occurrence, and properties of the subject that obtain when he undergoes it, in order to account for the phenomenology of the experience of that occurrence. We may then say that the subject is aware of/seems to be aware of O (or the experience is as of O). But although such properties may be possessed for intervals of time, they do not unfold over time. So we then should accept, it is suggested, that different temporal parts of O are experienced/represented together at, or over, the same instant, or interval, of time. The principle of simultaneous awareness is then thought to be in tension with what has been called the 'principle presentational concurrence': 'the duration of a *content* being presented is *concurrent* with the *act* of presenting it . . . the time interval occupied by a content which is before the mind is the very same interval which is occupied by the act of presenting that content' (Miller 1984: 107). Attempts to resolve this tension one way or another can lead to different versions of specious present theories and retention theories. Dainton (2000) appeals to the phenomenal relation of 'co-consciousness' in his account. However, one might again think that if the obtaining of this relation between phases of experience is to make a difference to what it is like for the subject to have an experience in which this relation obtains, then this ought to be reflected in the psychological properties/states of the subject that obtain when the subject undergoes experience in which such a relation obtains. So arguably, for Dainton's account too, the problem re-emerges.

the fact that you see that an object has disappeared doesn't in itself entail that you saw the event of its disappearance.[13] Furthermore, the event that is the acquisition of your perception of the scene without the object is also not a perception of the event of the object disappearing, for the event of the acquisition of a perception is not itself the perception of an event. The perception of the event of the instantaneous disappearance of an object appears to entail the perception of both the object, and its absence—one's perception of the object prior to its disappearance, and the scene after the object's disappearance. For if you don't see the object, then you can't see it disappear; and if you don't see the scene without the object, then you won't yet have seen it disappear. If you perceive the instantaneous event of the disappearance of the object, then your perception of that event must also have been a perception of the object *and* its absence, and so your perception of the instantaneous event requires the perception of something that isn't instantaneous—it requires the perception of something, in this case the scene before you, enduring for an *interval* of time, an interval of time that spans both the presence of the object and its absence. You might say that this is why the event of the disappearance of an object can be videoed, but not photographed, despite the fact that it happens at a time.[14]

We can now introduce a couple of assumptions that generate a puzzle about this case. Suppose that (a) if you successfully perceive something enduring for an interval of time, t1 to tn, then you are aware *of* that thing *for* an interval of time, t1 to tn. This assumption may be motivated by what I called the temporal transparency of experience. Let's also suppose that (b) if a subject is in a given state over a given period of time, then this is determined by, and hence explained by, the fact that she is in that state at each of the instants that make up that period of time. So according to this assumption, if a subject is in a given perceptual state over a given period of time, then this is determined by, and

---

[13] We can contrast the example of the kind of perception of an instantaneous event that we are considering here with a case in which you can perceive that change has occurred, but without having been able to perceive any event of change—e.g. a case in which a series of imperceptibly slight changes over long periods of time eventually results in a perceptible difference—say the changing position of the hour hand. (For discussion of the suggestion that we simply fail to *notice* such change, see Graff 2001.)

[14] According to Kelly's (2005) characterization of retention theories of our experience of time, the retention theorist accepts, whereas the specious present theorist denies, the claim that we start with (what at least seems to be) a sequence of independent and static 'snapshots' of the world at a time. According to the retention theorist, these snapshots are supplemented with retentions and maybe also protensions—memories and anticipations. However, in the example we are considering here, it seems that successive 'snapshots' will reveal that the object has disappeared, but there won't be a 'snapshot' of the object's disappearance. So on the retention view, although we may have a snapshot of the present and the retention of a snapshot of the past, neither will itself be a snapshot of the event, and it can seem puzzling as to how a combination of both can itself amount to a perception of the event, as opposed to a perception of the fact that the event has occurred. The same general line of reasoning can be applied to other examples of what Vendler (1957) calls 'achievements'—e.g. the appearance of an object, starting, stopping, and instantaneous change in colour. The example of the event of the disappearance of an object perhaps brings out the point more clearly, as in these other cases the *object* that instantaneously appears, starts, stops, changes in colour, at a time, can be photographed at that time, and one might then be misled into thinking that this establishes that one can photograph the instantaneous event it undergoes at a time. (For a discussion of the influence of the 'snapshot' on our understanding of the perception of events, see Gombrich 1964.)

hence explained by, the fact that she is in that perceptual state at each of the instants that make up that period of time. This assumption may be motivated by the idea that states obtain, and do not unfold over time, which might lead one to think that mental states with temporal extension *continue* to obtain *throughout* the interval of time over which they obtain.

Now let's consider again your perception of the disappearance of the object. We have said that in order to perceive the instantaneous event of the object's disappearance, you must perceive the scene before you enduring for an interval of time, t1 to tn. On the first assumption, this entails that you are aware of the scene before you for an interval of time, t1 to tn. It seems plausible to hold that there is no instant of time during this interval at which you are aware of both the scene with the object present and also the scene without the object present. Rather, it seems plausible to think that at any instant during this interval, you are *either* aware of the scene with the object present *or* the scene without the object present. But then, on the second assumption, it would seem to follow that there can be no interval of time *over* which you are aware of the scene before you enduring for an interval that spans *both* the presence of the object *and* its absence, an interval of time that includes the instant at which the object disappeared, in which case you can't have been aware of the event of the object's disappearance.

A related puzzle concerns our perception of events or processes that aren't instantaneous, for example the perception of the movement of an object across space. Arguably, non-instantaneous events and processes don't, strictly speaking, 'endure' for periods of time, but rather *take* certain amounts of time to occur, or *go on* for periods of time. So perhaps we should say that the successful perception of a non-instantaneous event or process is a perception as of something *unfolding* over time, rather than a perception as of something *enduring* for a period of time. It's not clear, then, that our first assumption, (a), can be straightforwardly applied to a case in which one perceives a non-instantaneous event or process. However, we can apply a related assumption, (a)⋆: If you successfully perceive an occurrence unfolding over some interval of time, t1 to tn, then there are sub-intervals of an interval of time, t1 to tn, *over* which you are aware *of* temporal parts of that unfolding occurrence. For example, if you successfully perceive the event of an object moving from location L1 to location L10 over some interval of time, t1 to t10, then there is some sub-interval of time, e.g. from t1 to t5, over which you are aware of some temporal part of that occurrence, e.g. the object moving from L1 to L5. It would appear to follow from this assumption that your awareness of an occurrence unfolding over time cannot be instantaneous. An occurrence that unfolds over time is something that you can only be aware of, as such, over time.[15] Again, this assumption might be motivated by the temporal transparency of experience.

---

[15] Note that if assumption (a)⋆ is accepted, it should also apply to any of the occurrence's non-instantaneous temporal parts.

Now let's apply our second assumption, (b), and again suppose that if a subject is in a given perceptual state over a given period of time, then this is determined by, and hence explained by, the fact that she is in that perceptual state at each of the instants that make up that period of time. So, for example, if over an interval of time, t1 to t10, a subject is aware of the movement of an object from location L1 to location L10 happening over some interval of time, t1 to t10, then this is explained by the fact that at t1 she was in that state of awareness, at t2 she was in that state of awareness, and so on. And yet it seems intuitively plausible to think that at any instant of time within the interval t1 to t10, the subject can only have been aware of some temporal part of the unfolding occurrence. For example, it seems intuitively plausible to think that over the interval t1 to t5 the subject will have been aware of the movement of the object from, say, L1 to L5, but not yet aware of the movement of the object from L1 to L10, in which case at t5 it won't yet be true of the subject that she is aware of the movement of the object from L1 to L10. At any instant of time within the interval t1 to t10, the subject won't yet have been aware of the movement of the object from L1 to L10, so, given assumption (b), there cannot be an interval of time, t1 to 10, *over* which the subject is aware of the movement of the object from L1 to L10. The same reasoning can be applied to any of the event's non-instantaneous temporal parts.[16]

These puzzles about our perception of events (both instantaneous and non-instantaneous) emerge when we hold on to assumptions (a)/(a*) and (b). But it is natural to think that we need to hold on to assumptions (a)/(a*) and (b) if we are to provide an account of our conscious experience of events that accommodates both the positive and negative phenomenological claims that I've outlined. The puzzles appear to be symptoms of the general difficulty of providing an account of experience that can attribute to the subject a psychological property/state that accounts for the fact that it seems to the subject as though she is perceptually aware of an occurrence with temporal extension, while at the same time accommodating the idea that each temporal part of that occurrence seems to the subject to be concurrent with her awareness of it. And the obstacle to success seems to reside in the fact that mental states are not the kinds of things that can unfold over time, which in turn leads to the claim that they are the kinds of things that *continue* to obtain *throughout* the interval of time over which they obtain. In the next section I shall outline what puts the relationalist in a position to respond to this general difficulty.

---

[16] One might think that assumption (a)* is in tension with a certain interpretation of the claim that our powers of perceptual discrimination are finite—e.g. see one of the interpretations of the claim that is considered by Graff (2001): for some sufficiently slight amount of change, we cannot perceive an object as having changed by less than that amount unless we perceive it as not having changed at all (as having changed by a zero amount). However, acceptance of (a)* may be consistent with the claim that some temporal part, x, of an occurrence that occurs over some interval of time, t, is something one can be aware of only if one is aware of an occurrence, y, that unfolds over an interval of time that is greater than t, and x is a temporal part of y (which may capture what Graff takes to be behind this interpretation of the claim that our powers of perceptual discrimination are finite, namely that there is a limit to how slight an apparent change can be.)

4.6 A relationalist proposal

Relationalists and representationalists can agree that when S succeeds in perceiving the world, then some kind of relation of perceptual acquaintance obtains—S is perceptually *aware of* mind-independent objects and events and their features. All should agree that when a subject is perceptually aware of objects and events in the world, this makes a difference to the subject's psychological properties—i.e. whenever a subject stands in that perceptual relation to objects and events in the world, certain perceptual psychological states of the subject must obtain.[17] Let us now focus just on the phenomenally conscious perceptual states that obtain when a subject stands in that relation of perceptual acquaintance to objects and events in the world.

Some will hold that the obtaining of those phenomenally conscious states does not depend on the obtaining of the relation of perceptual acquaintance—the subject could be in the same phenomenally conscious state without the obtaining of that relation of perceptual acquaintance. Others may hold that there are phenomenally conscious states that only obtain when the relation of perceptual acquaintance obtains, because the obtaining of these phenomenally conscious states entails the obtaining of the relation of perceptual acquaintance, but they may hold that the phenomenally conscious states in question can be specified independently of the relation of perceptual acquaintance.[18] According to the relationalist view I am focusing on here, there are phenomenally conscious states whose obtaining requires the obtaining of a relation of perceptual acquaintance, but which *cannot* be specified independently of that relation.

This sort of relationalist account may accommodate the positive phenomenological claim I outlined earlier concerning our conscious perception of events. According to the relationalist, the phenomenally conscious state that obtains when one perceives an event is to be specified, at least in part, in terms of a psychological relation of perceptual acquaintance that obtains when one perceives such events. So the relationalist can allow that occurrences with temporal extension are among the entities to which we stand in that psychological relation of perceptual acquaintance, and the relationalist can also

---

[17] This need not involve denying that when the relation obtains, perceptual *events* and *processes* also occur, and it need not involve denying that the perceptual events and processes that occur are phenomenally conscious. But the phenomenally conscious properties of such events will be ones that make a difference to the *subject's* psychological properties. So when such events occur the subject will be in phenomenally conscious states that would not otherwise obtain, and here I am focusing on the question of what to say about such phenomenally conscious states.

[18] For example, consider a position according to which there is a phenomenally conscious mental state of seeing that *p*, the obtaining of which entails awareness of objects and their features, but according to which this phenomenally conscious state of seeing that *p* can be specified independently of the relation of awareness of. Or consider a position according to which the phenomenal character of a conscious experience is determined by the intentional content of that experience, but according to which the content in question contains demonstrative elements that are object-dependent. On one such view, one has an experience with such content only if the demonstrative elements have referents, and if they have referents then the subject of experience is aware of objects and features, but that which determines the referents of those demonstrative elements can be specified independently of the relation of awareness of—e.g. perhaps an appropriate causal relation.

allow that when we stand in that psychological relation to an event, we also stand in that relation to temporal parts of the event that have temporal extent. When a subject introspects her perceptual experience, she discovers occurrences with temporal extension, as these are among the entities to which she stands in the psychological relation of perceptual acquaintance in undergoing such experience.

The relationalist can also say that over an extended interval of time a series of different such phenomenally conscious states will obtain. For example, suppose a subject continuously watches an occurrence for several minutes. The relationalist can say that the subject will be in a series of different phenomenally conscious states over the course of those several minutes, each of which spans some sub-interval of that time, but each of which is to be specified (at least in part) in terms of the relation of perceptual acquaintance. In other words, the relationalist need have no reason to attribute to the subject a *single* phenomenally conscious state that spans the whole of the several minutes that make up that interval of time.[19]

But what about the negative phenomenological claim? How is the relationalist supposed to accommodate that aspect of the phenomenology of the conscious perception of events that I have labelled 'temporal transparency'? I suggested that the general difficulty in accommodating both positive and negative phenomenological claims is that of providing an account of experience that can attribute to the subject a psychological state that accounts for the fact that it seems to the subject as though she is perceptually aware of an occurrence with temporal extension, while at the same time accommodating the idea that each temporal part of that occurrence seems to the subject to be concurrent with her awareness of it. And I suggested that the obstacle to success seems to reside in the fact that mental states are not the kinds of things that can unfold over time. For given that mental states obtain over time, and do not unfold over time, one might think that mental states with temporal extension *continue* to obtain *throughout* the interval of time over which they obtain.

I said that the relationalist holds that when a subject successfully perceives the world, the subject is in a phenomenally conscious state whose obtaining depends on the obtaining of a relation of perceptual acquaintance, and the nature of that phenomenally conscious state is to be specified, at least in part, in terms of that psychological relation. The relationalist can say that when a subject consciously perceives an event, the relation in question, in terms of which the subject's phenomenally conscious state is to be specified, seems to the subject to have the following features: the relation is a relation to the event, and the relation to the event obtains only if the event occurs; moreover, the temporal location of the obtaining of the relation to the event seems to the subject to depend on, and be determined by, the temporal location of the event—in particular, the relation to the event is one that seems to the subject to obtain only *when* the event occurs.

Now consider what a relationalist can say about a case in which a subject perceives the movement of an object across space—e.g. a case in which the subject perceives the

---

[19]   I shall be discussing this point in more detail in Chapter 6.

object moving from location L1 to location L5 over an interval of time t1 to t5. Given that the obtaining of the subject's phenomenally conscious state seems to her to depend on the obtaining of the relation of perceptual acquaintance, and given that the relation obtains only when the event occurs, the obtaining of the subject's phenomenally conscious state seems to her to depend on the occurrence of the event. Given that the event in question is something that *takes* an interval of time to occur, the obtaining of the phenomenally conscious state over that interval of time seems to the subject to depend on the occurrence of something that *takes* that interval of time to occur.

States obtain over intervals of time and do not happen/occur/unfold over intervals of time, and so are not thought to *take* intervals of time. As I mentioned earlier, this might lead one to think that if a state obtains over an interval of time, this is because it *continues* to obtain *throughout* that interval of time. However, we've seen that although states obtain over time, and do not occur/unfold over time, some states are such that their obtaining can depend constitutively on the occurrence of events and processes, which do unfold over time and which can take intervals of time to occur. Given that the obtaining of such states depends on the occurrence of events that take intervals of time to occur, there is something misleading in the claim that such states *continue* to obtain *throughout* the intervals of time over which they obtain.

According to the relationalist, the phenomenally conscious state that obtains when one perceives the movement of the object from location L1 to L5, is one whose obtaining over an interval of time seems to the subject to depend on the occurrence of something that *takes* that interval of time. For that reason, the phenomenally conscious state doesn't seem to its subject to be one that *continues* to obtain *throughout* that interval of time. So the phenomenology is therefore that of being aware of something that fills an interval of time *over* that interval of time; and being aware of something that fills a sub-interval of that interval of time *over* that sub-interval of time. In other words, it doesn't seem to the subject as though she is aware of something that fills an interval of time from a point in time that is distinct from that interval of time—e.g. from a point of time that falls within that interval of time. And given that the relation in question is one that seems to the subject to obtain only when the event occurs, the subject's awareness of the event will seem to her to have the temporal location of the event she perceives, and so too will the phenomenally conscious state that obtains when she stands in that relation to it. This fits in with that aspect of the phenomenology of the experience of events that I've labelled 'temporal transparency': when one perceives an unfolding occurrence (e.g. the movement of an object across space), it seems to one as though one's perceptual experience has the temporal location and duration of its object, and it seems to one as though the temporal location and duration of each temporal part of one's experience is transparent to the temporal location and duration of each temporal part of the unfolding occurrence one seems to perceive.

In light of this relationalist proposal, let's now return to the two puzzles that I raised earlier about our perception of events. One puzzle concerned our perception of instantaneous events, and the other our perception of non-instantaneous events. Both puzzles depended on acceptance of assumption (b): the assumption that the question of what state a subject is in *at* a time is explanatorily prior to the question of what state a subject is in *over* a given period of time. We are now in a position to diagnose what is wrong with assumption (b) and explain why we should reject it.

4.7 An ontological resolution

Assumption (b) is, I think, related to a certain understanding of the notion that states are 'homogeneous down to instants', a claim that is sometimes made in discussions of Vendler's (1957) classifications of verbs into the categories of state, achievement, activity, and accomplishment. Rothstein (2004) offers the following rough approximation of the distinctions Vendler draws between these categories of verbs:

Crudely, states are non-dynamic situations, such as *be happy* or *believe*; activities are open-ended processes, such as *run*; achievements are near-instantaneous events which are over as soon as they have begun, such as *notice*; and accomplishments are processes which have a natural endpoint, such as *read the book*. (2004: 6)

Neither states (believes, loves) nor achievements (recognize, notice) usually occur in the progressive, whereas activities (walking, eating) and accomplishments (building a house, walking to the shops) do. The latter pair can be answers to the question 'what are you doing?', whereas the former pair cannot. Verb predicates that fall under the category of state do not usually occur in the progressive, as the situations they signify do not unfold over time in the way that activities and accomplishments do. Achievements do not usually take the progressive either. This is not because they signify situations that occupy time in the way that states do, but rather because they relate to things that happen instantaneously. Things one might have done or will do, but not things one can be in the process of doing. Although accomplishments are like activities, in so far as they take the progressive, they are unlike activities, in so far as they have a terminus. Accomplishments are movements towards an end point.

Rothstein offers the following characterization of the notion of homogeneity, which is of interest to us here: if a predicate is homogeneous, then *x Φ-ed for y time* entails that at any time during y, *x Φ-ed* was true. It has been suggested that activities, unlike accomplishments, are homogeneous, and this is why accomplishments, unlike activities, are subject to what has been called 'the imperfective paradox'. If Φ-ing is an accomplishment (e.g. walking to the shop), then the truth of 'S was Φing from t1 to t10' does not entail that at t5 S Φ-ed (e.g. walked to the shop). The suggestion has been that in this respect accomplishments can be contrasted with activities. Where Φ-ing is an activity, if it is true that S was Φ-ing from t1 to t10 (e.g. walking, as opposed to walking to the shop), then at every point during that interval it is true that that S Φ-ed (e.g. walked). Taylor (1977) and Dowty (1979) have raised the following objection to this claim. In the case of activities, the truth of 'S was Φ-ing from t1 to t10' need not entail that at t2 S Φ-ed. For it to be true that S Φ-ed there must have occurred some 'minimal' event relevant to that activity. For example, the fact that a subject moved his foot from the ground does not in itself make it true that the subject walked. Perhaps two steps are required for it to be true that walking occurred.[20]

This leads Rothstein to claim that only *states* are unqualifiedly homogeneous as only states are homogeneous down to instants: 'If John loved Mary for twenty years then he loved her at each instant during that twenty-year period' (2004: 14). Perhaps what lies behind this idea is the following line of thought. Since states *obtain* over time, and do not unfold/occur/happen over time, they do not have temporal parts. One might think that in this respect they are like continuants—they *endure* through intervals of time.[21]

If a continuant, o, exists for an interval of time t1 to tn, then one might argue that it automatically follows that o has temporal extension, for it occupies an interval of time, from which one might argue it automatically follows that there is a sense in which the continuant has temporal parts.[22] However, in the case of a continuant it seems intuitive to accept the following: even if things had turned out very differently after any instant within that interval (e.g. after t2) o (i.e. that particular continuant which in fact existed over the interval t1 to tn) would still have existed.[23] At t2 the continuant o has existed already—in a sense, its existence has already been guaranteed—and it is because of this that it can be said to *continue* to exist after t2.[24]

In thinking of states as like continuants in this respect one might similarly think that if a state obtains over an interval of time t1 to tn, then at any instant within the interval of time t1 to tn (e.g. at t2) the state will have obtained already—in a sense, the obtaining of the state has already been guaranteed by t2—and it is because of this that the state can be

---

[20] It is not obvious that this need entail that it isn't true of the subject that she *was walking* prior to the completion of the minimal event. In which case we may be able to generate something like the imperfective paradox for such activities. Note also that to deny that an activity or accomplishment is homogenous (in the sense specified by Rothstein) need not involve denying that the process or event is dense and continuous. For example, consistent with the non-homogeneity of an activity that occurs over an interval of time t1 to tn, it may be true that between any two instants of time within the interval t1 to tn the process is occurring, and it may be true that there are no sub-intervals of time or instants of time within the interval t1 to t10 when the process is not occurring.

[21] For this claim, see Steward 1997: 78.

[22] For discussion of this idea, see Hofweber and Velleman 2011.

[23] Note that this need not involve any commitment to the idea that the existence of the continuant can be duration-less.

[24] Here we might contrast what can be said of an event. In the case of a particular event, e, that occurs over the interval of time, t1 to 10, arguably it won't be true to say that e (the particular event that in fact occurred over the interval t1 to t10) would have existed even if things had turned out very differently after t2. In the case of the event, e, there is a sense in which it isn't true that at t2 the event had existed already, for at t2 the event hadn't yet occurred—part of the process that constitutes the event will have occurred, but not the particular event, e, itself. At t2 it won't yet be true of the event that it has happened—and so in that sense, its existence won't yet have been guaranteed. (For the distinction between event and process, see Mourelatos 1978.)

said to *continue* to obtain after t2. And so for this reason one might think that states must be homogeneous down to instants.[25]

Now apply the claim that states are homogeneous down to instants to what appears to be a stative: 'be aware of'.[26] If over the interval of time, t1 to tn, S was aware of o, then it should be true that at each instant within that interval of time that state of awareness obtained. The thought that the state of 'awareness of' is homogeneous down to instants can then lead to the following assumption, an instance of assumption (b): if a subject is in a given state of 'awareness of' over a given period of time, then this is determined by, and hence explained by, the fact that she is in that state at each of the instants that make up that period of time. But, as we have seen, this assumption can lead to puzzlement as to how we can be aware of events, whether they are instantaneous or non-instantaneous.

Rothstein (2004) makes the following two claims about states: (i) we cannot identify stages in the development of a state, and (ii) no change necessarily takes place while a state holds. The intuition behind the first claim, I take it, is that states, unlike activities and accomplishments, are non-dynamic. They do not unfold over time; rather they obtain, or hold, over periods of time. Accepting this, however, we might still question whether the second claim follows. As I mentioned in the previous chapter, there appear to be states whose obtaining necessarily requires the occurrence of events *while* the state holds—states that obtain for a given period of time only if certain kinds of events occur *during* that period of time. The obtaining of the state is *constitutively* dependent on the occurrence of those events. The fact that the obtaining of certain states can be constitutively dependent on the occurrence of certain events or processes shows why (ii) doesn't follow from (i), and it can also be used to show why Rothstein is wrong to claim that all states, unlike activities and accomplishments, have the distinctive feature of being homogeneous down to instants.

Now let's focus on our perception of non-instantaneous events and processes, and in particular let's focus on what to say about the state of *being aware of* the event or process

---

[25] Is it only states that are homogeneous down to instants? Although walking is an activity that may not be homogeneous down to instants, it is not obvious that there can be *no* activities that are homogeneous down to instants—e.g. an object moving. Furthermore, it doesn't appear as if there is anything obviously wrong in saying that an activity can *continue to occur*, just as we can say that a state can continue to obtain. However, in spite of this one might think that two important differences between states and activities remain—differences that preserve the idea that states are more like continuants than activities: (a) An activity is something that can, in a sense, *continue to occur*, but arguably this should be understood in terms of the idea that *more* of the activity can occur—e.g. if over an interval of time walking continued to occur, this is because during that interval of time *more* walking occurred. (Compare Mourelatos 1978 on the distinction between process and event.) It is not clear that analogous claims apply to the continuing existence of a continuant and the continuing obtaining of a state. (b) One might think that in the case of an activity like moving, whether the activity *is occurring* at a time depends on what happens *after* that time—the thought here being that what happens after that time determines whether the object is moving at that time or comes to rest at that time. Whereas in the case of a state, one might think, whether a state obtains at a time is not dependent on what happens after that time. (Although in what follows I shall be offering reasons to be sceptical of this latter claim.)

[26] Compare here Price on acquaintance: 'Acquaintance just is, and there is no passage in it. We might describe it as a *standing* awareness, whereas other kinds of awareness are, so to speak, fluent' (1932: 125).

of x Φ-ing, where this Φ-ing is an activity or accomplishment, rather than an achievement. This state, according to the relationalist, is a phenomenally conscious state that obtains when a subject perceives an occurrence with temporal extension. The state of being aware of x Φ-ing appears to be a further counterexample to (ii), for it's intuitive to think that such a state can obtain only if x *is* Φ-ing. So this is a state that obtains only if there occurs some event or process, the event or process that the subject is aware of. From the fact that S was aware of x Φ-ing over the interval t1 to t10, it does not follow that at t2 that state of awareness already obtained. It may be that at t2 the accomplishment/activity of Φ-ing had not yet occurred. So although the subject was aware of x Φ-ing over the interval t1 to t10, it is not true that at t2 her state of awareness obtained. If the state of being aware of x Φ-ing is not homogeneous down to instants, it is a mistake to think that a subject's awareness of x Φ-ing over an interval of time is to be explained by the fact that the subject is in that state of awareness at each of the instants that make up that interval of time. This needn't involve a rejection of the claim that there are times at which such states of awareness obtain, but it does require holding that the fact that there is a time at which the state obtains is explained by the fact that there is an interval of time, which includes that instant, over which the state obtains.

The relationalist's rejection of assumption (b) allows us to resolve our puzzle concerning the perception of non-instantaneous events. We can now deny that the subject's awareness over time of the occurrence unfolding over time is to be explained by the fact that the subject was in such a state of awareness at each of the instants within that interval of time. At any instant within the interval of time t1 to t10, the subject's awareness of the movement of the object from L1 to L10 had not yet obtained, but it doesn't follow from this that the subject wasn't aware of the movement of the object from L1 to L10 *over* that interval of time.

Can we accept the claim that there was a time *at* which the subject was aware of the movement of the object from L1 to L10? If we don't, it might be objected, we'll have to say that at no time was the subject aware of such an event, a claim that appears to entail that the subject can't have perceived the event.[27] We can accept such a claim, but only in

---

[27] This simple thought can motivate certain versions of 'specious present' accounts of our experience of time. According to such accounts, at a time one is aware of an interval of time, or something occupying or taking up an interval of time. If we deny that at a time a subject can be aware of something that takes time, it seems as though we are committed to claiming that at no time is a subject aware of something that takes time, which in turn appears to commit one to the view that the kind of thing that necessarily takes time, i.e. the occurrence of a non-instantaneous event, cannot be an object of awareness. Such a claim appears to conflict with what many think is a phenomenological datum. However, this version of the specious present account appears to be in tension with another phenomenological datum, namely that what one is aware of is concurrent with one's awareness of it (i.e. assumption (a)★). The puzzle this generates for the specious present theorist is the following: how can something be given as *earlier* than something one is aware of, and at the same time as *concurrent* with one's awareness of it? If one's awareness of something is to be concurrent with the thing it is an awareness of, then one's awareness of the earlier thing must be earlier than one's awareness of the later thing. However, accepting such a claim then seems to lead to the idea that there occurs a succession of states of awareness—first an awareness of the earlier thing, and then of the later thing, and so on. (Even if one was tempted to accept an at-at theory of motion, according to which motion is a functional relation between time and position (e.g. see Russell 1903: 347 and Salmon 2001: 23), an at-at theory of the

so far as we understand the claim as asserting that there are instants of time that fall within an interval of time over which the subject was aware of the movement of the object from L1 to L10.[28] This in turn suggests that in certain cases the answer we give to the question of what state a subject is in at a time may be determined by the answer we give to the question of what state the subject is in over an interval of time that includes that instant. Furthermore, the answer we give to the question of what state a subject is in over an interval of time that includes that instant may be, to a certain extent, contextually dependent on the interval of time we have in mind.

Now let's return to the puzzle concerning the perception of the instantaneous event of an object's disappearance. It was argued that your successful perception of such an event requires the perception of something, the scene before you, *enduring* for an interval of time, an interval of time that spans both the object's presence and its absence. The scene before you cannot endure *for* an interval of time *at* an instant of time, so although your awareness over time of the scene may be homogeneous down to instants, your awareness over time of the scene *enduring for an interval of time* cannot be. So the fact that there is an interval of time over which you are aware of the scene before you enduring for an interval of time is not to be explained by the fact that you were in such a state of awareness at each of the instants that make up that interval of time. Your awareness of the scene enduring for an interval of time spanning both the presence and absence of the object is not to be explained by the fact that there is a time *at* which you are aware of both the presence and absence of the object.

With this in mind we can now say that from t1–n to t1 you were aware of the presence of the object, and from t1 to t1+n you were aware of the absence of the object, and yet consistent with this we can say that at t1 you were aware of the event of the object's disappearance. For as I said earlier, if a state is not homogeneous down to instants, then the answer we give to the question of what state a subject is in *at* a time may be determined by the answer we give to the question of what state the subject is in over an interval of time that includes that instant, and the answer we give to the question of what state a subject is in over an interval of time that includes that instant may be, to a certain extent, contextually dependent on the interval of time we have in mind. Hence we can say that over the interval of time t1–n to t1 you were aware of the presence of the object,

awareness of motion, according to which awareness of motion consists in a functional relation between time and state of awareness, seems far less tempting.) Resting with such a view, it might be thought, then leads us back to the claim that at no time is a subject aware of something that takes time, which in turn suggests that a non-instantaneous event cannot be an object of awareness. It can then seem that the two phenomenological claims are somehow in tension with one another. The problematic assumption that leads to this impasse, I suggest, is the assumption that the fact that we are aware of non-instantaneous events is to be *explained* by the fact that there are times *at* which we are aware of such events.

[28] Compare here Bergson's (1911) discussion of Zeno's arrow, in which he is perhaps arguing for something stronger: 'But the arrow never *is* in any point of its course. The most we can say is that it might be there, in this sense, that it passes there and might stop there. It is true that if it did stop there, it would be at rest there, and at this point it is no longer movement that we should have to do with. The truth is that if the arrow leaves the point A to fall down at point B, its movement AB is as simple, as indecomposable, in so far as it is movement, as the tension of the bow that moves it' (in Salmon 2001: 63).

over the interval of time t1 to t1+n you were aware of the absence of the object, and over the interval of time t1−n to t1+n you were aware of the presence of the object, its absence, and the event of its disappearance.

4.8 The problem of hallucination

At the beginning of the chapter I suggested that considerations motivating the relationalist's proposal about successful perception should be considerations motivating an appeal to the obtaining of a non-representational psychological relation in an account of the conscious character of successful perception (and not just the representation of one)—where the claim that the relevant psychological relation is non-representational should be understood in terms of the idea that the obtaining of the relation isn't simply determined by the obtaining of a mental state that has an intentional content with veridicality conditions, irrespective of whether the mental state in question is a factive one, and irrespective of whether the content of the state is object-involving. I have pointed to difficulties one faces in accommodating aspects of the temporal phenomenology of our experience of events if one restricts oneself to explaining the phenomenal character of such experience in terms of the obtaining (or occurrence) of a perceptual state (or event) that has an intentional content with veridicality conditions (section 4.3). It is not clear that one can overcome these difficulties by simply holding that the intentional content of such experience is object-dependent, or by holding that the mental state with those veridicality conditions is a factive one that cannot be given a conjunctive analysis. For the difficulties I raised did not depend on denying these claims. Furthermore, it is not clear that one is helped in accommodating this aspect of the phenomenology of experience if one simply appeals to the idea that experience has non-representational qualia in addition to having an intentional content with veridicality conditions.

I have suggested a way in which one might accommodate the relevant aspect of the temporal phenomenology of the conscious perception of events by appealing to the obtaining of a psychological, but non-representational, relation. According to this relationalist proposal, when characterizing the conscious character of the perception of an event we need to appeal to a psychological relation of perceptual acquaintance that obtains when the subject has that experience. When the subject has the experience, it seems to her as though she stands in that relation. However, we should not understand this claim in terms of the idea that the subject is in some state with an intentional content that represents the obtaining of that perceptual relation. For then the problem of specifying the temporal content of the state that represents the obtaining of the perceptual relation just re-emerges. So according to the account just outlined, it is the actual obtaining of some non-representational psychological relation between the subject and entities in the world that is doing some work in explaining the phenomenology. An aspect of the temporal phenomenology is determined by the obtaining of a non-representational psychological relation of perceptual acquaintance, and not simply the temporal content of a state that represents it. This account need not deny that a subject is in perceptual states with representational content when she has such experience, but the claim is that one misses out some aspect of the phenomenology of the experience if one does not appeal to the obtaining of a non-representational psychological relation between subject and entities in the world when it comes to fully characterizing the phenomenology of the experience undergone.

The obvious difficulty facing this account is that most philosophers now want to say that it is possible for a subject to undergo an experience which is a complete hallucination, during whose occurrence the subject is not perceptually aware of anything. So if a hallucination can have the same conscious character as a successful perception, then we should not need to appeal to the obtaining of a psychological relation of perceptual acquaintance when providing an account of the conscious character of a successful perception. The relationalist, then, is committed to denying that a complete hallucination has the same conscious character as a successful perception.

As I said earlier, the relationalist's proposal about the general shape of the manifest image of conscious sensory experience intersects with a view about self-knowledge—a view about what a subject is in a position to know about her conscious sensory experience when she has it, and what puts her in a position to know it. It involves the idea that an account of what one can know about the conscious character of the conscious sensory experience one has when one successfully perceives the world, and one's account of what puts one in a position to know it, cannot be straightforwardly and symmetrically applied to the case of hallucination.

At the end of Chapter 3 I highlighted some puzzling aspects of the phenomenology of hallucinations of located bodily sensations: (i) it is intuitive to think that hallucinations of located bodily sensations are phenomenally conscious experiences—i.e. there is something it is like for you when you hallucinate a located bodily sensation; (ii) when you hallucinate a located bodily sensation you seem to be undergoing a phenomenal event (i.e. a phenomenal *bodily* event) of a kind that you are not in fact undergoing; and (iii) it is intuitive to think that if you hallucinate a located bodily sensation, you are, ceteris paribus, in a position to know what it is like to undergo the sort of phenomenal event that you seem to be undergoing, but which you are not in fact undergoing. According to the sort of relationalist view I have been trying to motivate in this chapter, the sort of conscious character that seems to the subject of hallucination to be introspectively accessible to her is not in fact introspectively accessible to her. So this relationalist view gives rise to similar claims about other perceptual hallucinations (e.g. visual hallucinations): the claims that (i)★ it is intuitive to think that visual hallucinations are phenomenally conscious experiences; (ii)★ when you have a visual hallucination you seem to be undergoing a phenomenally conscious experience of a kind that you are not in fact undergoing; and (iii)★ it is intuitive to think that if you have a visual hallucination, you are, ceteris paribus, in a position to know what it is like to have a successful visual perception of the world.

In order to address the issues raised by claims (i)–(iii) and (i)⋆–(iii)⋆, we'll need to examine issues in the epistemology of mind. In particular, we'll need to address the following questions: what account should be given of our knowledge of the conscious character of our conscious sensory experiences, and what account should be given of that which puts one in a position to have such knowledge—for example, what is the role of 'introspection' in such accounts? I'll be discussing these matters further in the final chapter of Part I. For now though, there are further questions to be asked about the sort of relationalist view that I have been proposing in this chapter.

In Chapter 1 I suggested that a question that can be raised for relationalist views is the following: how should one go about trying to articulate what is distinctive of the sort of psychological relation that obtains when one has a conscious sensory experience? I said that one of the tasks undertaken by sense-datum theorists, who took seriously the idea that conscious sensory experience involves a fundamental psychological relation of perceptual acquaintance, was to say more about the nature of that relation. For example, I mentioned the way in which both Russell and Broad attached importance to the idea that this psychological relation appears to reveal its objects as temporally present. So what more can the new relationalist say about the distinctive sort of psychological relation that obtains when one has conscious sensory experience? Should the relationalist be seeking to describe certain general features of the relation? Should the relationalist hold that there are different things to be said about different features of the relations that obtain in different modalities of sense perception? In Chapter 1 I mentioned that the sense-datum theorist Price denied that there are different kinds of sensing. He held that the difference between the senses seems to be wholly on the side of the data that are sensed. Is this something that the new relationalist should accept? I turn to these issues in the next chapter.

5

Structural Features of Perceptual Acquaintance

In his discussion of our attempts to introspect the *conscious* element of a sensation of blue, Moore (1903) writes that 'When we try to introspect the sensation of blue, all we can see is the blue: the other element is as if it were diaphanous.' But as I mentioned in Chapter 1, Moore goes on to add 'Yet it *can* be distinguished if we look attentively enough, and if we know that there is something to look for' (1903: 41). Is Moore right about this? When one has a conscious sensory experience of blue, what more is there to discern introspectively, other than the blue? Do we only find other objects, events, features, and relations that are all to be thought of as what the conscious experience is an experience of?

In the previous chapter I mentioned that one finds appeals to the 'transparency' of sensory experience being made by some of those defending representationalist accounts of sensory experience. They too claim that sensory experience seems to one to be transparent, or diaphanous, to the objects and properties one is apparently perceptually aware of in having that experience. I said that this idea is sometimes expressed in terms of the claim that introspection of one's perceptual experience seems to one to reveal *only* the objects, qualities, and relations one is apparently perceptually aware of in having that experience, and not qualities of the experience itself; but I also mentioned that there is a weaker version of the claim, according to which, when one attempts to attend introspectively to what it is like for one to be having a perceptual experience, it seems to one as though one can only do so through attending to the sorts of objects, qualities, and relations one's experience is an experience of. The advocate of the weaker version of the transparency claim asserts that it doesn't seem as though one can focus solely on the conscious character of one's experience without attending to the objects one's experience is an experience of. However, the weaker version of the claim is consistent with the proposal that when one has a conscious sensory experience, there are things one can discern introspectively about one's experience other than what one's experience is an experience of, for it just commits one to the claim that if there are such further things to discern introspectively, it seems to one as though one cannot discern these things introspectively *without* focusing on the objects that one's experience is an experience of.

For some, the question of whether or not we should accept the stronger version of the transparency claim becomes the question of whether or not we should accept that the conscious character of conscious experience is solely determined by the representational content of experience—whether or not it is solely determined by what one's experience represents as being the case. So, for example, some have tried to argue that the phenomenology of blurry vision gives us reason to think that there are aspects of the conscious character of some experiences that are not solely determined by the representational contents of such experiences, on the grounds that it wouldn't be true to the phenomenology of blurry vision to say that such experience represents the existence of objects as having the feature of being blurry.[1] The suggestion is that the blurriness of the experience seems to one to be a feature of the visual experience itself, and not a feature of what one's visual experience is an experience of, and so not something that is solely determined by what one's experience represents to be the case.

Once we have in play the idea that we need to appeal to the obtaining of a psychological relation of perceptual acquaintance in characterizing the phenomenology of conscious sensory experience, we need not think of the issue of whether or not we should accept the stronger transparency claim in quite these terms. That is, we need not think that the issue is simply one of whether or not we should accept that the conscious character of conscious sensory experience is solely determined by the representational content of experience. For if one holds that it is necessary to appeal to the obtaining of a psychological relation of perceptual acquaintance in characterizing the phenomenology of conscious sensory experience, one can raise the following questions about its conscious character. Is the conscious character of a conscious sensory experience determined solely by the entities to which one is psychologically related in having the experience, or is it also determined by the manner in which one is psychologically related to those entities? And if it is determined, at least in part, by the manner in which one is psychologically related to those entities, can introspection of one's conscious sensory experience reveal something about the manner in which one is psychologically related to the entities one is aware of, in addition to revealing what one is psychologically related to?

These questions are related to an issue I mentioned in Chapter 1, when I was outlining sense-datum approaches to sensory experience. I said that one of the tasks undertaken by sense-datum theorists, who took seriously the idea that conscious sensory experience involves a fundamental psychological relation, was to say more about the nature of that relation. A question that can be raised for those relationalists who reject sense-datum theories, is whether they too think it important to say more about the nature of the psychological relation that they appeal to in characterizing the conscious character of experience. Can more be said about the manner in which one is psychologically related to the entities one is perceptually aware of when having a conscious sensory experience, and is the conscious character of such experience determined, in

---

[1] For discussion of this idea, see Smith 2008 and Allen 2011.

part, by the manner in which one is psychologically related to those entities? Are there things about the nature of the relation that one can discern introspectively?

Something that a relationalist might seek to do is articulate aspects of the conscious character of conscious sensory experience that are relatively fixed and invariant—aspects of the conscious character of sensory experience that are common to different sensory experiences that have different objects. The thought here being that when explaining the way in which the conscious characters of such experiences differ, we may need to appeal to differences in the objects of awareness, and when explaining the respect in which aspects of the conscious characters of such experiences are the same, we may need to appeal to the common manner in which subjects are aware of the different entities they are aware of.

Consider, for example, the way in which both Russell and Broad appeal to the idea that the psychological relation that obtains when one has conscious sensory experience appears to reveal its objects as temporally present. In Chapter 1 I suggested that we can see this as an attempt to say something about the nature of the distinctive psychological relation that obtains when one has a conscious sensory experience. I mentioned that Russell claims: 'It is not a definition of sensation that it is acquaintance with an object which is in fact simultaneous with the subject: the simultaneity must be not merely a fact, but must be deducible from the nature of the experience involved in the sensation' (1992: 63). In a similar vein, Broad claims that 'it is the *essence* of the perceptual situation that it claims to reveal its object as it is at the time when the situation is going on' (1925: 145).

In the previous chapter I presented a claim about the phenomenology of our conscious sensory experience that is, in certain respects, similar to the claims that Russell and Broad were invoking. I suggested that when one has a conscious sensory experience it seems to one as though the temporal location and duration of one's experience is transparent to the temporal location and duration of whatever it is that one is experiencing. This is an aspect of the conscious character of conscious sensory experience that seems to be fixed and invariant—it is an aspect of the conscious character of sensory experience that appears to be common to different sensory experiences that have different objects. So it may be an aspect of the conscious character of conscious sensory experience that is not simply to be explained in terms of the natures of the entities one is aware of when having a conscious sensory experience, but, rather, in terms of the *manner* in which one is aware of those entities when having a conscious sensory experience. So the thought here might be that if one were to undergo a conscious mental occurrence for which the temporal transparency claim didn't hold (e.g. if one were to undergo a conscious mental occurrence that presented its object as being earlier than one's awareness of it), then the way in which the conscious character of that conscious occurrence would differ from typical conscious sensory experience would be due to a difference in the manner in which one was aware of the entity to which one was psychologically related, and not simply due to a difference in the entity to which one was psychologically related.

Once we mark a distinction between (a) the contribution made to the conscious character of one's experience by entities one is psychologically related to, and (b) the contribution made to the conscious character of one's experience by the manner in which one is psychologically related to those entities, we might consider the following possibility: there may be different ways in which the conscious characters of one's conscious sensory experiences may vary—some differences may be due to differences in the sorts of entities one is psychologically related to, and some differences may be due to the different ways in which one is psychologically related to them. I mentioned that the sense-datum theorist Price (1932) denied that there are different kinds of sensing. He held that the differences between the senses seem to be wholly on the side of the data that are sensed. A relationalist might disagree with Price on this point, and hold instead that there are differences between the senses—differences in the conscious characters of the experiences we have in different sense modalities—that are not simply due to differences in the entities one is psychologically related to, but which are due to differences in the manner in which one is psychologically related to them.

Consistent with this, a relationalist may want to maintain that there are aspects of the manner in which one is psychologically related to the entities one is aware of when one has conscious sensory experience that are common to *all* the modalities of sense perception. For example, she might maintain that (i) the phenomenological claim of temporal transparency is true of the conscious sensory experiences one has in all the modalities of sense perception, and (ii) this is to be explained by something common to the manner in which one is psychologically related to the entities one is aware of when one has conscious sensory experience in all the modalities of sense perception. Someone holding this sort of view might agree with Broad, as well as Russell, that it is of the '*essence*' of a 'perceptual situation', as Broad calls it, that 'it claims to reveal its object as it is at the time when the situation is going on'. Alternatively, someone holding this sort of view might claim that it is just a contingent fact about us that all the modalities of sense perception that we happen to possess share this common feature, and they might maintain that it would be in principle possible for a subject to stand in a *perceptual* psychological relation to entities that did not present those entities as temporally present.

In this chapter I shall be exploring these issues in more detail. I start by considering the suggestion that there may be differences between the senses—differences in the conscious characters of the experiences we have in different sense modalities—that are not simply due to differences in the entities one is psychologically related to, but which are due to differences in the ways in which one is psychologically related to them. In Chapter 3 I mentioned that the experience of located bodily sensation seems to involve a form of awareness of one's body, or some part of it, 'from the inside'. In what respect are you aware of your body 'from the inside' when you feel such sensations? Is this something that is to be explained by the *manner* in which you are psychologically related to your body in feeling a sensation, in contrast to the manner in which you are psychologically related to your body when you perceive your body in other modalities of perception—e.g. in vision?

5.1 Bodily awareness, vision, and the spatial sensory field

Consider a case in which you feel a stabbing pain in your left hand and at the same time a stabbing pain in your right hand. The sensations have different felt locations. That is, there's a sense in which they're felt to be located in different places. While these sensations are felt to be located in different places, it wouldn't be right to say that there is a particular point, or place, from which, and relative to which, these sensations are felt to be. Something present in, say, vision, but lacking in the case of feeling bodily sensations is what A.D. Smith calls spatial *over-againstness*: 'an over-againstness which involves a part of our body functioning as a sense organ' (Smith 2002: 134).

A bodily sensation such as a headache is experienced as *in* your head; it is not perceived as an object *with* your head. When, by contrast, you look at your hand, although the object seen is not spatially separated from you (since it is part of you), it is, nevertheless, spatially separate from the eye with which (and from where) you see it. (2002: 134)

We can attend more fully to a sensation, but we cannot turn it over and contemplate its different aspects–not even in our mind's eye. A sensation has no hidden sides because we are not aware of it through the exercise of a sense organ spatially distinct from it. (2002: 134)

Another important aspect of the phenomenology of these bodily sensations that I mentioned in Chapter 3 is that it does not seem to one as though one feels these sensations to be in space but not in a body. Furthermore, it does not seem to one as though one feels these sensations to be in different bodies. Rather, it seems to one as though one feels the sensations to be in different parts of *one* body.

Following M.G.F Martin, I shall be suggesting that these aspects of the phenomenology of the experience of located bodily sensations are to be explained, in part, by appeal to certain *structural* features of our awareness of the locations of our bodily sensations;[2] and I shall be suggesting that we think of these structural features of one's awareness of the location of one's bodily sensations as aspects of the *manner* in which one is psychologically related to one's own body when one is aware of one's body in feeling bodily sensations. Martin's suggestion that certain aspects of the phenomenology of our experiences of located bodily sensations are to be explained by appeal to structural features of our awareness of our bodily sensations is connected with his suggestion that bodily awareness lacks a spatial sensory field. My first aim is to begin to clarify the relevant notion of a spatial sensory field.

In work comparing sight and touch, Martin invokes a notion of the 'visual field' that he takes to be a phenomenological feature of visual experience. In articulating the notion he has in mind, Martin writes:

We can think of normal visual experience as experience not only of objects which are located in some space, but as of a space within which they are located. The space is part of the experience in as much as one is aware of the region as a potential location for objects of vision. (1992: 189)

---

[2] See Martin 1992, 1995, 1997, and 1999.

One is aware of the location of visual objects not only relative to other visually experienced objects, but also to other regions of the spatial array–regions where nothing is experienced, but where something potentially could be. (1992: 188)

To help clarify the suggestion being made here, consider first the Kantian thought that when looking straight ahead, any region of space in front of you that you are thereby aware of is presented as a sub-region of a region of space that has that sub-region as part.[3] As the relevant spatial region is presented as a *sub*-region of space, it might be said that when you are visually aware of a region of space in front of you there's a sense in which it thereby seems to you as though there are *other* regions of space that are potential locations for objects of vision—'regions where nothing is experienced but where something potentially could be'. Yet these other regions of space—e.g. regions of space behind your head—are not regions of space that you are visually aware of, in the relevant sense. So what more can be said about the way in which you are aware of the region of space in front of you, which isn't a way in which you are aware of these other regions of space—e.g. a region of space behind you?

When Martin says that in normal visual perception one is aware of 'regions where nothing is experienced, but where something potentially could be', we should understand this, not in terms of the idea of there being an absence of the experience of things, but rather in terms of there being the experience of the absence of things.[4] When looking straight ahead you may be aware of regions of *empty* space—i.e. regions of space that are empty of visible objects. When looking straight ahead you are not aware of a region of space behind your head in that way—i.e. as empty of visible objects. There may be a sense in which it is correct to say that when looking straight ahead you are thereby aware of the existence of other spatial regions as spatial regions within which things can be experienced but which are not experienced; however, this is not to be explained by the fact that you are aware of those regions as *empty* of objects that could potentially be experienced.

One might then think that a crucial component of the right characterization of the way in which we are visually aware of regions of space, when we are aware through vision of the spatial locations of objects, should accommodate the idea that this can involve the visual registration of an absence—one's perception of regions of space as *empty of visible objects*. However, further clarification is needed concerning the kind of perception of absence involved. One might question whether the notion of perception of absence in play here should be construed as equivalent to a certain variety of negative perception—a perception that something isn't the case—e.g. my perception that the blue book in front me is not red.

---

[3] A number of claims that I shall be making in this chapter echo remarks that Kant (1998) makes in the metaphysical expositions of space and time in the Transcendental Aesthetic, where Kant marks a distinction between the 'matter' and 'form' of appearances, and argues that space and time are 'pure forms of sensible intuition'.

[4] See especially Martin 1999 and Richardson 2009.

O'Shaughnessy claims that 'There is no perceiving an absence that is not a cognition.' According to O'Shaughnessy, a cognitive attitude—in particular a belief that something isn't the case—is a necessary condition of the perception of absence. 'The experience of seeing the absence of X is the experience of coming to know of the absence of X (directly given as arising out of a present visual experience of what shows no X)' (2000: 330). He adds: 'while the object is undoubtedly experienced as privative in a certain respect, it is thus experienced only because of one's presently occurrent *negative belief*. And that negative belief arises out of one's seeing what is *there* . . . There is no intuition of absence' (2000: 304).[5] O'Shaughnessy claims that 'Real perceiving is invariably of the concrete . . . It is of phenomenal realities. And thus invariably of what one might call "positivities" ' (2000: 333). 'Perception is of "positivity" all the way' (2000: 304).

However, it's often the case that when we perceive such 'positivities', we also seem to perceive some of their boundaries (e.g. some of their spatial boundaries); and our perception of the spatial boundaries of such positivities may in certain circumstances require, in a certain sense, the perception of absence as well—the perception of where things are not. C.B Martin claims that absences are needed as much as entities for the edges, limits, or bounds of entities. For example, he writes:

The concept of an edge is the concept of a limit of where something is and where something isn't...The reference of the referring term 'world' is divided into presences whose limits are drawn by absences. (1996: 60)

This suggests that there are certain varieties of the experience of absence which are not of marginal significance, and which are fairly ubiquitous. This in turn might lead one to think that there are varieties of the experience of absence that do not depend on the subject of experience having a negative belief that something isn't the case. The fact that we can be aware, in vision, of regions of space within which the boundaries of objects are perceived, and the fact that we can be aware, in vision, of sub-regions of that region of space as empty of visible objects, should not be thought to depend on one's coming to have a negative belief to the effect that something isn't case. So should we insist, *contra* O'Shaughnessy, that our visual *experiences* usually have negative representational contents, without accompanying negative beliefs?

I suggest that it would be a mistake to think that in order to accommodate the idea that we can be aware, in vision, of regions of space that are empty of visible of objects we need to assume that visual experience has a negative representational content—i.e. a content that explicitly represents the fact that there are regions of space within which there are no visible objects. The key to avoiding the mistake is to note that the conscious character of a normal visual experience is not *solely* determined by the sorts of objects and events one is apparently aware of in having that experience. For it is also determined, in part, by the way in which one's visual awareness of those objects and events

---

[5] For defence of the claim that we can perceive absence, see Taylor 1952, Martin 1996, Kukso 2006, and Sorensen 2008. For criticism of the claim, see Molnar 2000.

seems to be structured, and we should appeal to these structural features of visual awareness when accounting for the sense in which it seems to one as though one is visually aware of regions of space that are empty of visible objects. The notion of a 'visual field'—and in particular, the *spatial* sensory field of vision—can be invoked to mark the relevant *structural* feature of normal visual experience.

Consider again the idea that when looking straight ahead, any region of space in front of you that you are thereby aware of is presented as a *sub*-region of a region of space that has that sub-region as part. The region of space in front of you that you are aware of does not strike you as being some object or thing that has boundaries you are visually aware of. There may be a sense in which there are boundaries to be identified in your visual awareness of the region of space in front of you, for it may be said that you are visually aware of something like a cone of physical space in front of you, and we might think of the boundaries of this cone as the boundaries of your visual field—boundaries of the spatial sensory field of vision. But the boundaries of this spatial sensory field do not seem to you to be the boundaries of some thing you are visually aware of that happens to move around with you; and changes in the boundaries of this spatial sensory field (e.g. when you close one eye) do not seem to you to amount to changes in the boundaries of some thing that you are visually aware of—some thing that you are visually aware of as changing size and shape.

Rather than thinking of the boundaries of the spatial sensory field of vision as boundaries of some thing one is sensing, like the frame of a painting, we should think of its boundaries in terms of one's sensory limitations. That there are limits to what can now be sensed that are due to one's sensory limitations, rather than due to the limits of whatever it is that one is now sensing, brings with it the idea that there is more to be sensed beyond those sensory limits, hence the idea that your visual awareness of the region of space in front of you is in some sense an awareness of the region *as* a sub-region of a region of space that has that sub-region as part.[6] That you visually experience a region of space in front of you in this way is an important part of the conscious character of visual experience. The existence of some kind of sensory limitation features as an aspect of the conscious character of the visual experience.

Earlier I distinguished a stronger and weaker version of the claim that the conscious character of perceptual experience is transparent to its objects. According to the stronger version, introspection of one's perceptual experience reveals *only* the mind-independent objects, qualities, and relations one is apparently aware of in having the experience. According to the weaker version, when one introspectively attends to what it is like for one to be having a perceptual experience, it seems to one as though one can only do so by attending to the sorts of objects, qualities, and relations one is apparently

---

[6] In characterizing Kant's view of the way in which we experience space as unbounded, Melnick (1973) writes: 'We do not perceive spatial regions . . . that are limitless or without bounds. Rather, we perceive space under the pre-conception (or better, under the "*pre-intuition*") that the bounded spatial extents we do perceive are parts of a limitless or unbounded space' (11). According to Kant, we arrive at the notion of such bounded sub-regions of space through the 'introduction of limitations' to the all-embracing space.

perceptually aware of in having that experience. The fact that the spatial sensory field of vision is a phenomenological feature of visual experience gives us reason to reject the stronger version of the claim. The boundaries of this spatial sensory field are not features of some object one is visually aware of in having a visual experience. One cannot directly attend to them in the way in which one can directly attend to the objects and features that fall within them. But they do nonetheless feature in the conscious character of one's visual experience, and one can become aware of them when attending to the objects that fall within them. For in attending directly to the objects of visual awareness, one can reflect on the way in which one's visual awareness of those objects seems to one to be structured.

In saying that an aspect of the conscious character of normal visual experience is to be accounted for by appeal to some structural feature of the experience, I am suggesting that there is an aspect of the conscious character of the experience that can be common to various visual experiences but which isn't to be accounted for by appeal to the fact that these experiences are as of the same kinds of objects and features. As these aspects of the conscious character of experience are relatively invariant, and as one cannot directly attend to them in the way in which one can directly attend to the objects one is apparently perceptually aware of in having that experience, they go largely unnoticed. However, we can, nonetheless, introspectively reflect on these relatively invariant aspects of the conscious character of visual experience, common to one's conscious visual experience of all sorts of different objects, which are determined by the ways in which one's conscious visual awareness of those objects seems to be structured. These are aspects of the conscious character of experience which, to quote Moore again, '*can* be distinguished if we look attentively enough, and if we know that there is something to look for' (1903: 41). The relatively invariant structural feature of the conscious character of visual experience that is of relevance here is the fact that this form of conscious awareness involves a spatial sensory field. It is this feature of this form of conscious awareness that accounts for the fact that when one has a visual experience of the spatial locations of objects, it seems to one as though one is visually aware of a region of space within which those objects are located, where the boundaries of the relevant region of space are determined by one's sensory limitations, rather than the limits of some thing one is sensing.

When one has a visual experience as of objects, parts of objects, and their features, one is aware of those objects, parts of objects, and their features, because they fall within one's sensory limits. The sensory limits we are concerned with here are to be characterized in spatial terms: in having a visual experience one is aware of objects, or parts of objects, and their features, because they fall within a region of space one is aware of in having the experience. As these sensory limits are reflected in the conscious character of one's experience, when one has a visual experience there is a sense in which it seems to one as though one is aware of a region of space, whose bounds are determined by one's sensory limits, within which objects can be experienced and rearranged, and which may be presented as including sub-regions that are empty of visible objects. As the relevant spatial region is experienced as a region whose bounds are determined by one's sensory limitations, there is a sense in which one visually experiences a spatial region, delimited by one's sensory limitations, as a region within which objects must fall if they are to be seen. In consequence, there is a sense in which one experiences a spatial region as a region within which objects *can* be seen. This is what accounts for the sense in which, in vision, one can be consciously aware of a region of space as a region within which there are no objects to be seen, but within which objects potentially can be seen. The suggestion being made here is that these aspects of the conscious character of visual experience are a reflection of the way in which such conscious awareness is structured. So the correct explanation of the respect in which we can be consciously aware, in vision, of absence—e.g. of regions of space as empty of visible objects—will sometimes need to appeal to relatively invariant structural features of such conscious awareness.

Not all modes of conscious awareness have the same structure. For example, the structural feature of normal visual experience that accounts for the existence of its spatial sensory field is lacking in the form of bodily awareness involved when one feels a located bodily sensation. When you have a visual experience, you seem to be aware of objects that fall within a region of space that you are aware of in having that experience, where the bounds of that region of space seem to you to be determined by your sensory limitations, rather than by the limits of some thing you are sensing. In contrast, in the case of the experience of located bodily sensation, the boundaries of any spatial region you are aware of, within which things are experienced to be, *do* seem to you to be set by the limits of some *thing* you are sensing that moves around with you (i.e. your body), rather than by your sensory limitations. The fact that the experience of located bodily sensation lacks the structural feature of visual experience that provides visual experience with its spatial sensory field, is connected with the fact that when bodily sensations are felt to be located, it seems to one that one is aware of a region of space within which they are located only in so far as one is aware of some *thing* occupying that region of space. Hence the fact that one does not feel these sensations to be in space but not in a body.[7]

Furthermore, the fact that one is aware of the thing (i.e. one's body) occupying the region of space within which sensations are experienced to be does not seem to one to be something that is to be explained by the fact that *it* (i.e. one's body) falls within a region of space one is aware of in having the experience, where the extent of that region of space is determined by one's sensory limitations. When one feels located bodily sensations there is a sense in which it seems to one that one is aware of a space within which one's body is located, but this is simply because one is aware of one's body as a space-occupying object. That is to say, that there is a sense in which one is aware of a space within which one's body falls is simply entailed by the fact that one is aware of one's body as a spatial object. The body one seems to be aware of in feeling bodily sensations does not seem to one to fall within some spatial sensory field, within which some *distinct*

---

[7] This discussion follows Martin 1995.

object can also be experienced (through bodily awareness) to be. Hence the idea that it does not seem to one as though one feels sensations to be in different bodies; rather, it seems to one as though one feels the sensations to be in different parts of one body. Any bodily parts that it seems to one that one is aware of in feeling bodily sensations seem to one to be part of one object.[8]

This is connected with Martin's claim that in the case of bodily sensation, there is no distinct point of view that the subject possesses independent of the object, her body, which she is aware of in this way.[9] It is often said that in feeling bodily sensations one is aware of one's body 'from the inside', but we should not understand this in terms of there being some point in space from which and relative to which one is aware of one's body, from which and relative to which other objects could also be sensed in this way. The sense in which one is aware of one's body 'from the inside' in feeling a located bodily sensation is to be understood in terms of the idea that when one feels a bodily sensation there is no point of view one has on one's body, in so far as there is no point of view under which some other spatial object could also potentially fall.

To summarize, I have suggested that some of the differences between the conscious characters of visual awareness and bodily awareness are to be explained in terms of the different ways in which one's conscious awareness is structured in these different modalities. There are differences in the conscious characters of the experiences one has in these different modalities that are not simply determined by differences in the entities one is aware of in having such experiences, but rather in terms of differences in the ways in which one is aware of those entities. One such difference is the fact that in the case of normal vision, but not in the case of the experience of located bodily sensation, when one experiences the spatial locations of entities, it seems to one as though one is aware of a region of space within which those entities are located, where the boundaries of the spatial region one is aware of seem to one to be determined by one's sensory limitations, rather than the limits of some thing that one is sensing. This aspect of the conscious character of visual experience—its possession of a spatial sensory field—should be thought of as a relatively invariant structural feature of this form of conscious awareness. The fact that this form of conscious awareness is structured in this way accounts for the respect in which one can be aware, in vision, of regions of space that are empty of visible objects, and the respect in which one can be aware, in vision, of regions of space within which the spatial boundaries of objects can be perceived.

The form of bodily awareness involved in the experience of located bodily sensation lacks this structural feature—it lacks the sort of spatial sensory field that vision has. In the case of the experience of located bodily sensation, the boundaries of any spatial region that one is aware of, within which things are experienced to be, seem to one to be set by the limits of some thing that one is sensing (i.e. one's body), rather than by one's sensory limitations. This is what accounts for various aspects of the phenomenology of the

---

[8] Again, this discussion follows Martin 1995.
[9] See Martin 1995.

experience of located bodily sensation: the fact that it doesn't seem right to say that there is some point or place from which and relative to which one's bodily sensations are felt to be, the fact that one doesn't feel sensations to be in space but not in a body, and the fact that one doesn't feel these sensations to be in different bodies but rather it seems to one as though one feels the sensations to be in different parts of one body.

The fact that the form of bodily awareness involved in the experience of located bodily sensation is structured in this way accounts for the fact that the phenomenology of such experience is such that it seems to one as though a precondition of feeling such sensation is that the sensation should occur *within an object* (namely, one's body), rather than within a region of space whose bounds are determined by one's sensory limitations. Furthermore, the object one is aware of in this way—one's body—does not seem to one to be something that one is aware of because *it* falls within one's spatial sensory field. So one distinctive aspect of the conscious character of the experience of located bodily sensation, in contrast to vision, is the absence of apparent spatial enabling conditions. That is to say, in contrast to the case of visual awareness of objects and their features, in the case of the experience of located bodily sensation it doesn't seem to you as though you and/or the bodily occurrence you are aware of have to be in the right place at the right time in order for you to be aware of that bodily occurrence. There is no sense that one can prevent one's awareness of the bodily occurrence by altering one's spatial relation to it, and there is no sense that one can prevent one's awareness of the bodily occurrence by affecting some organ with which one senses it.[10] These points are, I take it, important to the way in which the pain system performs the sort of biological function that I mentioned in Chapter 3. From the subject's point of view, there is no obvious way to prevent her awareness of a painful located sensation-event without stopping the occurrence of that located sensation-event. She cannot simply move away from it, or shut her eyes to it. And stopping the experience of the sensation-event will usually require protecting the body part at which the sensation-event is felt to occur.

In this section I have argued that the relationalist should accept that we can mark a distinction between (a) the contribution made to the conscious character of one's experience by the entities one is psychologically related to, and (b) the contribution made to the conscious character of one's conscious experience by the manner in which one is psychologically related to those entities. I have suggested that there are different ways in which the conscious characters of one's conscious sensory experiences can vary: some differences will be due to differences in the sorts of entities one is psychologically related to, and some differences will be due to differences in the manner in which one is psychologically related to them. By comparing and contrasting vision and the experience of located bodily sensation, we can see that there are differences between the conscious characters of the experiences one has in these different sense modalities that are not simply due to differences in the entities one is psychologically related to, but which are due to differences in the ways in which one is psychologically related to them.

---

[10] For discussion of this idea, see Langsam 1995.

The respect in which you are aware of your body 'from the inside' when you experience a located bodily sensation is something to be explained, in part, by the *manner* in which you are psychologically related to your body when feeling a located sensation, in contrast to the manner in which you are psychologically related to your body when you perceive your body in other modalities of perception, such as vision.

As I mentioned earlier, adopting this stance is consistent with maintaining that there are aspects of the manner in which you are psychologically related to the entities you are aware of when you have conscious sensory experience that are common to *all* the modalities of sense perception. For example, as I said earlier, one might maintain that (i) the phenomenological claim of temporal transparency is true of the conscious sensory experience one has in all the modalities of sense perception, and (ii) this is to be explained by something common to the manner in which one is psychologically related to the entities one is aware of when one has conscious sensory experience in all the modalities of sense perception. I shall begin considering this proposal in the next section. One of the claims I have made so far is that in contrasting the ways in which the forms of conscious awareness involved in vision and the experience of bodily sensation are structured, we can invoke the notion of a *spatial sensory field* that vision has and which the experience of located bodily sensation lacks. In what follows I will be suggesting that there is reason to invoke the notion of a *temporal sensory field* in our characterization of the temporal structure of the form of conscious awareness that we have in all the modalities of sense perception.

5.2 Hearing silence and the temporal sensory field

The spatial sensory field of vision was invoked to characterize the respect in which one can be aware, in vision, of a region of space within which space-occupying objects can be seen. One can be aware, in vision, of a region of space within which (some of) the spatial boundaries of space-occupying entities can be seen, and one can be aware, in vision, of sub-regions of that region of space as empty of visible objects. The boundaries of such a region of space do not seem to one to be the boundaries of some *thing* one is visually aware of that happens to move around with one. I suggested that we should think of these boundaries as boundaries of the *spatial sensory field* of vision, and that we think of the boundaries of the spatial sensory field in terms of one's sensory limitations.

Just as there is reason to think that we seem to be aware in vision of a region of space within which (some of) the spatial boundaries of space-occupying entities can be seen, there is also reason to think that we seem to be aware in vision of a temporal region/interval within which the temporal boundaries of time-occupying entities can be seen. In the previous chapter I made some positive phenomenological claims concerning the conscious character of our experience of events. I said that in certain cases one's introspection of the conscious character of one's experience seems to one to require attending to the occurrence of events and/or processes that are distinct from the experience itself, and furthermore, in such cases, the occurrences one thereby seems to be attending to seem to one to have temporal extension. In a given case, it may be that it doesn't seem to one as though one is thereby attending to all of the temporal parts of that occurrence; however, it seems to one as though one cannot attend to the occurrence without attending to *some* temporal part of it and, moreover, some temporal part of the occurrence that has temporal extension. I suggested that instantaneous events may also feature in the conscious character of experience, for example the event of an object starting to move, but when they do, it seems to one as though one cannot attend to them without thereby attending to something that has temporal extension, for example the object moving.

We can add that your experience of the event of an object starting to move appears to entail both your experience of the object moving and your experience of the object at rest. If you don't experience the object at rest, then you can't experience it starting to move, and if you don't experience the object moving you won't yet have experienced it starting to move. If you experience the instantaneous event of an object starting to move, then your experience of that event must also have been an experience of the object at rest *and* in motion, and so your experience of the instantaneous event requires the experience of something that isn't instantaneous—it requires the experience of something occupying an *interval* of time, an interval of time that spans both a time at which the object is at rest and a time at which the object is moving.

We can think of this sort of instantaneous event as marking a temporal boundary of a time-occupying entity—i.e. a temporal boundary of the time-occupying occurrence that is the movement of the object. Similar remarks apply to the instantaneous event that marks the point at which the object comes to rest. We can regard instantaneous events of starting and stopping as marking the temporal boundaries of time-occupying entities. In vision we seem to be aware of the temporal boundaries of time-occupying entities through being aware of intervals of time that span these relevant temporal boundaries. We seem to be aware in vision of a temporal interval within which such instantaneous events can occur—an interval of time within which the temporal boundaries of time-occupying entities can be experienced.

In discussing the spatial sensory field of vision I suggested that one can be aware, in vision, of a region of space within which (some of) the spatial boundaries of space-occupying entities can be seen, and that one can be aware, in vision, of sub-regions of that region of space as *empty of visible of objects*. I have suggested that there is a sense in which we seem to be sensorily aware of intervals of time within which the temporal boundaries of time-occupying entities can be experienced. Is there also reason to think that we can be consciously aware of sub-intervals of such an interval of time as *empty of perceptible objects*? I want to suggest that we should think of the phenomenon of hearing silence in something like these terms. We should invoke a *temporal sensory field* of audition, analogous to the spatial sensory field of vision, to explain the respect in which we can hear silence.

Sorensen claims that hearing silence is the most negative of perceptions, for when one hears silence 'there is nothing positive being sensed, and no positive sensation representing absence' (2008: 272). According to Sorensen, there is no sensation of silence to introspect. You instead introspect the absence of auditory sensation. This observation might lead one to deny that a positive auditory experiential event occurs when a subject perceives silence. It might lead one to think that we should rather hold that a subject can be said to hear silence when the subject doesn't have any auditory experiences despite the fact that she is perceptually sensitive to sounds. When it comes to explaining why a subject perceives silence when she does, we should be seeking to explain why the subject doesn't have any auditory experiences at that time despite the fact that she is perceptually sensitive to sounds at that time, and here we can cite the absence of audible events in the subject's surroundings at that time. However, I think that as it stands, this proposal does not provide us with an adequate account of hearing silence, for the following reason. We are reluctant to say that a subject hears the silence that surrounds her when she is asleep, even if it is true that were sounds to occur during that time she would wake up and have auditory experiences of them. Is it possible to refine this proposal about hearing silence in a suitable way by simply adding to it?

O'Shaughnessy's account of what is involved in hearing silence might be regarded as just such a modified proposal. O'Shaughnessy (2000) thinks that no auditory experience occurs when one hears silence. He accepts that there is a distinction to be drawn between hearing silence and simply not hearing anything. However, O'Shaughnessy thinks that a *cognitive* attitude, with silence figuring in its content, is a necessary condition for hearing silence. On O'Shaughnessy's view, hearing silence is logically equivalent to, and identical with, a variety of hearing *that* it is silent. It is a special case of coming to know that it is silent which arises out of an absence of auditory experience: 'Whereas there is both a hearing-of a whistle and a hearing that the whistle sounds, there is only hearing that it is silent. There is no such thing as the hearing-of silence: there is merely the absence of hearing-of anything, occurring in a self-conscious setting which is such that a cognitive experience occurs whose content refers to the prevailing silence' (2000: 333).

O'Shaughnessy's account of what is involved in hearing silence is rather different from Sorensen's. Sorensen argues that one can non-epistemically hear silence. According to Sorensen, hearing silence isn't a matter of inferring an absence of sound from one's failure to hear a sound, for one can hear silence while being neutral about whether one is hearing silence—e.g. when wondering whether or not one has gone deaf. He suggests that there can be creatures that hear silence despite their inability to introspect. Just as animals stop and orient to an unexpected sound, they sometimes stop and orient to an unexpected silence. Should we accept O'Shaughnessy's proposal and hold, against Sorensen, that a cognitive attitude with silence featuring in its content is a necessary condition for hearing silence?

O'Shaughnessy's discussion of hearing silence arises in the context of a discussion of whether negation features in the content of experience. Once one thinks of the issue in such terms, one might think that one can strengthen the case for thinking that (a) no auditory experience actually occurs when one hears silence, and (b) a cognitive attitude with silence featuring in its content is necessary for hearing silence. One might reason as follows. Either we accept that when a subject hears silence, a positive auditory experience occurs with negation featuring in its content (e.g. 'it's not the case that there are sounds'), or we accept that no such event occurs, and hold instead that negation features in the content of a cognitive attitude. Silence is the absence of sound. Our perceptual system is incapable of speaking to the question of whether there is an absence of sound everywhere. It can only speak to the question of whether there is an absence of sound within a certain region. But within which region? Is this something that our auditory system really specifies? Shouldn't we rather say that one's auditory system simply speaks to the question of whether there are sounds near enough and loud enough for one to hear? And doesn't this simply amount to the idea that one's auditory system simply speaks to the question of whether one is currently hearing anything? So if a positive auditory experience occurs when one hears silence, with negation featuring in its content, 'hearing' will also need to feature in its content—e.g. 'it's not the case that a sound is heard'. But it's more plausible to hold that no such positive perceptual event occurs, and instead hold that negation and hearing feature in the content of a cognitive attitude. When one hears silence, one becomes cognitively aware that one isn't *hearing* anything, and one assumes that this is because there are no sounds near enough and loud enough for one to hear.

I want to suggest that there is reason to be dissatisfied with the conclusion of this line of reasoning, and that this should lead us to question certain assumptions on which the line of reasoning depends. Although Sorensen claims that there is an absence of auditory *sensation* when one hears silence, he does appear to be committed to the claim that a positive auditory experience occurs when one hears silence. For he suggests that it is possible for one to hallucinate silence. It is difficult for one to make sense of this suggestion without assuming that there is such a thing as a positive auditory occurrence as of silence. Here is Sorensen's example of the veridical hallucination of silence.

Consider a man who experiences auditory hallucinations as he drifts off to sleep. He "hears" his mother call out his name, then wait for a response, and then call again. The cycle of calls and silence repeats itself eerily. As it turns out, his mother has unexpectedly paid a late-night visit and is indeed calling out in a manner that coincidentally matches the spooky hallucination. The hallucinator is not hearing the calls and silence of his mother. (2008: 269)

A significant feature of the example is the fact that the silences are gaps between *positivities*—sounds—that the subject hallucinates. Let's assume that when a subject hears a sequence of sounds with silent gaps between them, the subject has a positive auditory experience of the positivities sensed—i.e. the sounds he hears. Should we also assume that the subject has a positive auditory experience of the silences between the sounds?

If the subject doesn't have an auditory experience of the silences between the sounds, then arguably the subject doesn't hear the temporal boundaries of the sounds—i.e. the starting and stopping of the sounds. For the subject will need to experience the silence before a sound starts and after the sound stops in order to hear its stopping and starting.

Compare here Smith's discussion of the experience of hearing the tone of a melody begin sounding:

Starting to experience in a certain way does not obviously entail experiencing something of a certain sort starting. I need to have now, as the first note begins to sound, an awareness that just before now I was aware of silence. (2003: 88)

On the auditory experience of a series of discrete pips, he writes:

such pips are presented to us as discrete only in virtue of each one being preceded and followed by a relevant silence. We have to be aware of this silence, this non-sounding, as such if we are to be aware of the discrete sounding pips. And the pips will be perceived as further apart or closer together in time depending on how long these silences are. Perceiving silence is not the absence of any awareness, but is itself an intentional achievement. (2003: 88)

If a subject doesn't have an auditory experience of the silences between such sounds, then the subject doesn't hear the temporal boundaries of the sounds—i.e. the starting and stopping of the sounds. For the subject will need to experience the silence before a sound starts and after the sound stops in order to hear its stopping and starting.[11]

By invoking the idea that auditory experience has a temporal sensory field, analogous to the spatial sensory field of vision, we can say that our auditory experience is not only of sounds that are located in time, but also of a temporal interval within which they are located. The claim that in auditory perception we hear a sound as having a temporal location within an interval of time that we are consciously aware of can accommodate the fact that we can hear the temporal boundaries of a sound—the stopping and starting of the sound. For it can accommodate the idea that one can be consciously aware, in having auditory experience, of the temporal locations of sounds relative to other experienced sounds, and also to other regions of time where no sounds are experienced, but where other sounds potentially could be experienced.

That we are consciously aware, in auditory experience, of intervals of time within which sounds can be heard, is an invariant feature of the way in which such conscious awareness is structured. In this respect, auditory awareness has a temporal sensory field analogous to the spatial sensory field in vision. In accounting for the sense in which we can be consciously aware of silence, we should appeal to this invariant, structural feature of auditory awareness. In the case of auditory perception, one can be consciously aware of an interval of time as an interval within which sounds can potentially be heard, even if no sounds can actually be heard to fill that temporal interval, just as in vision one can be consciously aware of a region of space as a region within which objects can potentially be seen, even if no objects can actually be seen to occupy that region. When we hear silence we hear an interval of time as empty of audible sounds, just as in vision we can see regions of space as empty of visible objects.

---

[11] Consider Sorensen's remark that animals can stop and orient themselves to an unexpected silence. Presumably here they hear the sudden stopping of sounds.

To summarize, I am proposing that the perception of silence involves a positive experiential occurrence, and it doesn't require the acquisition of a cognitive attitude with silence featuring in its content. Furthermore, when one hears silence, something positive is experienced—namely an interval of time within which no sounds are heard. We do not need to commit ourselves to the idea that the positive experiential occurrence involved has a negative representational content, explicitly representing the fact that there are no sounds to be heard during that interval of time. In explaining the sense in which one can have conscious auditory contact with an interval of time during which no sounds are heard, we should, rather, appeal to relatively invariant structural features of conscious auditory awareness—its possession of a temporal sensory field. In the case of auditory perception, in virtue of its possession of a temporal sensory field, we can have conscious contact with intervals of time within which sounds can be heard *or potentially heard*. Just as in the case of visual perception, in virtue of its possession of a spatial sensory field, we can have conscious contact with a region of space, of limited extent, within which objects can be seen *or potentially seen*.

Our conscious auditory contact with an interval of time within which sounds can potentially be heard does not depend on our actually hearing some sound filling that temporal interval. And so it does not depend on our being causally affected by some sound that falls within that temporal interval. If no sounds are heard to fall within such a temporal interval, then we can hear the silence that fills that interval of time. And analogous remarks can be made in the case of vision. In virtue of its possession of a spatial sensory field, in vision our conscious visual contact with a region of space, of limited extent, within which objects can potentially be seen, does not depend on our actually seeing some object occupy that spatial region. And arguably, it does not depend on our seeing light fall within that spatial region either. And so it does not depend on our being causally affected by objects, or light, that fall within that spatial region. If no objects and no light are seen to fall within such a spatial region, we see the darkness that fills that limited region of space.[12] When one hears silence and sees darkness one has a positive perceptual experience of some positivity. When one hears silence one perceives some positivity—namely an interval of time, of limited extent, within which no sounds can be heard. And likewise when one sees darkness one also perceives some positivity— namely a region of space, of limited extent, within which no light or objects are seen.[13]

This account accommodates the respect in which hearing silence isn't simply a matter of absence by omission—i.e. the fact that hearing silence isn't simply a matter of a case in which an absence of auditory experience is to be explained by an absence of sound. It accommodates the fact that one cannot hear silence when asleep, despite the

---

[12] For defence of the claim that we can see darkness, see Sorensen 2008.

[13] Sorensen (2008) writes: 'There is a reliable connection between each portion of one's visual field being black and there being an absence of light in the corresponding region of the environment' (257–8). 'If the universe goes dark the observer sees the darkness of the universe. He does not see all of the darkness because his range of vision is limited. The limit is not imposed by an obstruction. The observer has limited acuity, like a man amid the vast expanse of the ocean' (263).

fact that there may be a sense in which one's auditory system is sensitive to sounds in one's environment when one is asleep.[14] In order to hear silence one must have conscious perceptual contact with an interval of time, of limited extent, within which sounds potentially can be heard. This form of conscious perceptual contact with time is one that human subjects tend not to have when asleep.[15] The idea that there is a form of conscious perceptual contact with intervals of time which we have when awake, but which we don't have when asleep, is a point to which I'll return in the next chapter.

I am invoking the notion of a temporal sensory field to mark a relatively invariant structural feature of our conscious sensory awareness—an aspect of the *manner* in which we are psychologically related to the entities we are consciously aware of in having sensory experience, and which contributes to the conscious character of our sensory experience. I think there is reason to hold that our conscious sensory experience in all the modalities of sense perception has a temporal sensory field that is, in certain respects, analogous to the spatial sensory field of vision.

There are reasons to think that the things we perceive are perceived as filling, occupying, or having some location within, an interval of time, and there is also reason to think that the temporal interval that we can perceive something as filling, or occupying, is of limited extent—even when we continue to perceive that thing for an indefinite period of time. Sometimes, no matter how carefully we attend to a continuously moving object we fail to perceive the event of it moving, even if we continue to scrutinize it for hours (e.g. the movement of the hour hand of a clock). We may be able to see that it has moved, but we never see it moving. Our finite capacity to perceive the spatial location of an object is insensitive to very slight variations in the object's spatial location, so the movement of an object across a very a short distance may be imperceptible to us. A continual series of such imperceptible movements may constitute the movement of the object across a much greater distance, and yet still we may be unable to perceive the object moving across that greater distance, no matter how carefully we continue to scrutinize it, and no matter for how long. This suggests that in certain cases the continual movement of an object may be imperceptible to us not simply because that movement is too slight (or even too fast) to be perceived, but, rather, because it is too slow. And this in turn

[14] I have argued that hearing silence isn't simply a matter of absence by omission, and there are similar reasons for thinking that seeing darkness isn't simply a matter of absence by omission either. That is, seeing darkness isn't simply a matter of a case in which an absence of visual experience is to be explained by the fact that there is an absence of suitably placed illuminated items in the environment of the perceiver. Consider a subject who can only sleep with her eyes open in a dark room. Suppose that if there were illuminated items suitably placed in the environment of the perceiver, then she would wake up and perceive them. In this case we would not say that the subject could see the darkness surrounding her when she was asleep.

[15] When you are awake and you have conscious perceptual contact with a silent interval of time, what makes it appropriate to regard your perceptual experience of that interval of time as an auditory one? There may be reason to think that it is only appropriate to regard the perceptual experience involved as an auditory one if the following counterfactual is true: if sounds were to have occurred during that interval, one would have heard them. For instance, I suspect that there are no distinctively auditory phenomenal properties that the experience has that would allow one to differentiate a case in which one is temporarily deaf from a putative case of the occurrence of a hallucinatory experience of silence. For further discussion of the hallucination of silence, see Phillips (forthcoming).

can be explained by the idea that the temporal interval that we can perceive something as filling, or occupying, is of limited extent. For over that limited temporal interval the movement of the object may be too slight to be perceived. In which case, we will be unable to perceive any of the temporal parts of the event of the object moving. And if we can't perceive any of the temporal parts of the event of an object moving, then the motion of the object will be imperceptible to us, no matter how long we continue to observe the object.

So we have reason to think that (a) the things we perceive are perceived as filling, occupying, or having some location within, an interval of time, and (b) the temporal interval that we can perceive something as filling, or occupying, is of limited extent. I have suggested that we should understand this aspect of the conscious character of conscious perceptual experience in terms of an invariant structural feature of conscious perceptual awareness. Up until now I have been treating the spatial and temporal cases as analogous. However, there are some significant *disanalogies* between the cases that are worth noting, and I'll briefly mention some in the next, and final, section of this chapter.

5.3 Perceptual perspectives on space and time: a structural difference

Let us return to the suggestion that there is a respect in which in vision, any region of space you are aware of is presented as a sub-region of a region of space that has that sub-region as part. I suggested that when you are visually aware of a region of space in front of you, that region of space does not strike you as being some object or thing that has boundaries that you are aware of. I suggested that there is, nonetheless, a sense in which there are boundaries to be identified in your visual awareness of that region of space. It seems to you as though you are aware of something like a cone of space. We can think of the boundaries of this cone as the boundaries of the spatial sensory field of vision. I suggested that as the boundaries of this spatial sensory field do not seem to you to be the boundaries of some thing that you are visually aware of, we should think of these boundaries in terms of your sensory limitations. In vision, the region of space in front of you is experienced as a region whose bounds are determined, or delimited, by your sensory limitations. That there are limits to what can be sensed that are due to one's sensory limitations, rather than due to the limits of whatever it is that one is sensing, brings with it the idea that there is more to be sensed beyond those sensory limitations (i.e. other regions of space, even if there are no objects to be perceived as falling within those other regions of space). Hence the idea that there is a sense in which your visual awareness of the region of space in front of you is an awareness of the region as a sub-region of space.

The boundaries of the spatial sensory field of vision do not seem to one to be features of some object that one is visually aware of, but they do nonetheless feature in the conscious character of one's visual experience. I suggested that although one cannot directly attend to them in the way in which one can directly attend to the objects and features that fall within them, one can become aware of them when attending to the objects that fall within them, through reflecting on the way on which one's conscious awareness of those objects seems to one to be structured. We are to think of this aspect of the conscious character of visual experience as a reflection of the way in which such conscious awareness is structured. Because one's conscious visual experience has such invariant structural features, implicit in the phenomenology of visual experience is the idea that whatever region of space you visually experience will be experienced as a sub-region of a region of space that has that sub-region as part. Arguably, as this region of space is experienced as the sub-region of a region of space whose full extent you are not visually aware of, also implicit in the phenomenology of visual experience is the notion that the relevant sub-region of space is independent of your awareness of it.[16]

In the case of spatial visual awareness one can say something, at least very roughly, about the extent and shape of the region of space (delimited by one's sensory limitations) that one is visually aware of. One has the impression that it remains relatively fixed over time, and so one has the impression that one can take one's time in attending to it. One can also notice that it seems to shrink when one closes an eye. Our conscious perceptual awareness of time is somewhat different.

Firstly, there doesn't appear to be any temporal equivalent of the act of closing of one eye that one can perform which makes a discernible difference to the extent of the temporal interval one is consciously aware of. Secondly, and more importantly, when we are consciously aware of an interval of time, of limited extent, within which we seem to perceive objects and events, it doesn't seem to us as though we are aware of that interval of time from a point in time that is distinct from it—e.g. from a point in time that falls within that interval of time. This is something I remarked upon in the previous chapter, when I suggested that the temporal location and duration of one's perceptual experience seems to one to be transparent to the temporal location and duration of the objects of perception.

Introspectively, it doesn't seem to one as though one can mark out one's own temporal location as distinct from the temporal location of whatever it is that one is perceptually aware of. It doesn't seem to one as though one is perceptually aware of an entity occupying some temporal location that is distinct from the temporal location *from* which one is perceptually aware of it. Since the temporal location and duration of perceptual awareness seems to one to be transparent to the temporal location and duration of what one perceives, the temporal phenomenology is that of being aware of an interval of time over that interval of time. In consequence, there is a sense in which one's perceptual access to an interval of time doesn't seem to one to be perspectival—for it doesn't seem to one as though one has a perceptual point of view on an interval of time from a

---

[16] Of course, even if such notions are implicit in the phenomenology of experience, what it may take to grasp them in thought may be a further matter.

temporal location that is distinct from it. As the phenomenology of conscious temporal awareness lacks this perspectival aspect, it doesn't seem to one as though one can identify, in conscious experience, a perceptual temporal point of view on an interval of time—a perceptual temporal point of view with manifest boundaries that one can discern, and which seem to be delimited by one's sensory limitations.

It remains true that there are reasons to think that we are perceptually aware of intervals of time, of limited extent, within which objects and events are perceived. But the extent of the temporal interval one is aware of doesn't seem to one to be determined by one's sensory limitations. In this respect, one's conscious perceptual experience of limited temporal intervals is quite unlike one's visual experience of bounded regions of space.[17] This difference in the phenomenology of temporal and spatial perceptual awareness might have some role to play in explaining some of the ways in which our intuitions about time can differ from our intuitions about space. For example, while it is intuitive to think that the fact that one cannot see a larger region of space from one's spatial location is something that is to be explained, at least in part, by one's sensory limitations, it is less intuitive to think that the fact that one cannot hear the whole one-hour symphony from one's current temporal location is something that is to be explained by one's sensory limitations.

The phenomenological fact that it doesn't seem to one as though the extent of the temporal interval that one can have perceptual access to is something that is determined by one's sensory limitations might make intuitive the thought that the extent of the temporal interval that one can have perceptual access to is something that is determined by facts about that temporal interval that are independent of one's sensory limitations. Whether entities are perceptually accessible to one depends in part on whether those entities fall within an interval of time that one is perceptually aware of. The phenomenological fact that it doesn't seem to one as though one's sensory limitations determine whether entities fall within an interval of time that one is perceptually aware of might make intuitive the thought that whether entities are perceptually accessible to one depends in part on temporal facts about those entities that are independent of one's sensory limitations. This in turn might make intuitive the thought that whether entities are perceptually accessible to one depends in part on whether they fall within an interval of time that is temporally present, where this is thought to be a non-perspectival temporal fact about those entities that is independent of one's sensory limitations.

---

[17] One could add that it is also quite unlike one's experience of the spatial region within which one experiences one's bodily sensations to be located. I said that in the case of one's experience of located bodily sensations, the region of space within which one experiences such sensations to be located seems to one to be determined not by one's sensory limitations but rather by the spatial limits of some thing one is sensing—i.e. one's body. So the region of space within which one can experience sensations to be located seems to one to be determined by the contingencies of the size of one's body. In contrast, the extent of the temporal interval one can be perceptually aware of does not seem to one to be determined by the contingencies of the temporal extent of some entity one is perceptually aware of.

In this chapter I have been suggesting that relatively invariant structural features of conscious perceptual awareness contribute to the conscious character of sensory experience. I have just been suggesting that the way in which our conscious perceptual awareness of time seems to be structured is not quite the same as the way in which our conscious perceptual awareness of space seems to be structured. In particular, in the case of our conscious perceptual awareness of time there do not appear to be any introspectively discernible manifest boundaries that delimit the extent of any temporal interval that we have perceptual access to—neither boundaries that seem to be determined by our sensory limitations, nor boundaries that seem to be determined by the temporal size of some entity that we are perceptually aware of. I have suggested that this structural difference between our conscious awareness of space and our conscious awareness of time might have some role to play in explaining some of the ways in which our intuitions about time can differ from our intuitions about space. However, I should note that to accept this much leaves open the further question of whether these relatively invariant structural features of conscious sensory awareness reflect the real nature of space and time themselves, and that is an issue I won't be engaging with.

There are, however, further issues connected with our conscious sensory awareness of intervals of time that I do want to address. Earlier I alluded to the idea that there is a form of conscious sensory contact with time that we have when we are awake but which we seem to lack when we are asleep. I shall be discussing this idea in the next chapter. In that chapter I shall also be suggesting that there is a distinctive form of conscious contact with intervals of time that is made available to phenomenally conscious subjects. In outlining this proposal I shall be invoking, once again, the general proposal that I have been making about the ontology of conscious sensory experience—the interdependence thesis.

This discussion will give us reason to posit the occurrence of phenomenally conscious mental events and processes when one has conscious sensory experience, even in cases where that phenomenally conscious occurrence is not *directly* introspectively accessible to one in the way in which a phenomenally conscious bodily sensation is introspectively accessible to one.

6

Conscious Contact with Time and the Continuity of Consciousness

One of the claims that I argued for in the previous chapter is that hearing silence isn't simply a matter of absence by omission. That is, hearing silence isn't simply a matter of a case in which an absence of auditory experience is to be explained by an absence of sound. A subject does not hear the silence that surrounds him when he is asleep, even in a case in which it is true that were sounds to occur during that time, he would wake up and have auditory experiences of them. In order to hear silence one must have conscious perceptual contact with an interval of time, of limited extent, within which sounds can potentially be heard, and this form of conscious perceptual contact with time is one that human subjects tend not to have when asleep. What is absent in the case of the sleeping subject who fails to hear the silence that surrounds him is a conscious sensory experience with a temporal sensory field.

In this chapter I shall be saying more about the distinctive form of conscious contact with time that our conscious sensory experiences provide us with. The general proposal I have been making about the ontology of conscious sensory experience—the interdependence thesis—will be put to work in outlining the account I shall be offering. I shall be suggesting that the distinctive form of conscious contact with time that we are provided with when we have conscious sensory experience gives us reason to hold that conscious sensory experience involves the occurrence of phenomenally conscious events/processes, even in cases in which the phenomenally conscious event/process in question is not directly introspectively accessible to one in the way in which a phenomenally conscious bodily sensation is directly introspectively accessible to one. I shall go on to draw out some further consequences of this account of the ontology of conscious sensory experience, pertaining to the 'continuity' of conscious sensory experience.

6.1 Conscious contact with time in the state of wakeful consciousness

What is distinctive of the form of conscious contact with time that a conscious sensory experience with a temporal sensory field provides one with? To make progress on this issue I want to examine O'Shaughnessy's (2000) illuminating discussion of his proposal that 'the experiencing subject stands in a special relation to time not discoverable in those not experiencing' (2000: 50). O'Shaughnessy tries to bring that 'special relation to time' into view by addressing the following question: 'what, in the way of a relation to time, is inaccessible to non-experiencing subjects?' (50). O'Shaughnessy pursues this question by first considering the sort of temporal knowledge that *can* be possessed by a subject who is not having conscious sensory experience—e.g. the sort of temporal knowledge that a subject can have during dreamless sleep.

As O'Shaughnessy points out, there seems to be no reason to deny that a subject can be in mental states with temporal contents during dreamless sleep. For example, there seems to be no reason to deny that a subject can retain knowledge of temporal facts during dreamless sleep—e.g. the knowledge that Descartes was born in 1596. Moreover, there seems to be no reason to deny that during dreamless sleep a subject can be in a mental state with a content that contains a temporal indexical. Consider a subject who takes an afternoon nap of ten minutes knowing that 'Today is Tuesday'. We can imagine that if you were to wake that subject during that ten-minute interval and ask him what day it was, he would answer 'Tuesday', and that answer would express knowledge, and not knowledge that is newly acquired on waking up. We can also imagine that if the subject were to continue to sleep for a much longer period of time, say several hours, then after that longer period of time he might no longer be automatically disposed to give that answer. This suggests that the continued obtaining of a certain kind of *dispositional* state that is specified in terms of an intentional content with a temporal indexical is not in itself enough to provide one with the sort of contact with time that is available to one when one is awake and having conscious sensory experience.

Suppose that our afternoon napper is not in deep sleep. Suppose that if, at any time during his ten-minute sleep, one were to address him and ask him 'what is going on now?', then the subject would wake up and be able to answer. The coherence of this scenario suggests an additional point. During dreamless sleep a subject can retain his capacity to refer indexically to distinct sub-intervals of the period of time during which he sleeps. So there is an attenuated sense in which it may be correct to claim that during his ten-minute sleep the subject is in a position to refer to distinct sub-intervals of that ten-minute period as 'now' and make knowledgeable claims about what is going on in his environment in doing so.

However, there is a sense in which the following also seems to be true: during that ten-minute sleep distinct sub-intervals of that ten-minute period of time are not presented to the subject as temporally present. We can bring out this point by comparing a dreamless sleep situation in which a subject continues to be in a dispositional mental state that is specified in terms of a temporal indexical content, with a situation in which the subject continues to have an experience of the same general type and character for a period of time of the same length—e.g. the continuous auditory experience of a humming sound. Over the period of time during which the subject has conscious sensory experience, even if that conscious sensory experience does not change in general type and character, the subject is aware of distinct sub-intervals of that period of time—distinct sub-intervals of that period of time each of which is presented to the subject as temporally present, and which the subject can refer to as 'now'.

Over a period of time that a subject is having conscious sensory experience (even if that experience does not change in general type and character, and even if that experience is as negative as that of hearing silence), the subject has a form of conscious contact with distinct sub-intervals of that period of time that presents those sub-intervals as temporally present, and this is not true of the subject who is in dreamless sleep and not having conscious sensory experience. So the respect in which the experiencing subject has conscious contact with distinct sub-intervals of that period of time is not simply a matter of his retaining the capacity to refer indexically to sub-intervals of that period of time as 'now'.

O'Shaughnessy suggests that 'something in the way of "now" must surely be inaccessible to non-experiencers'; and he claims that 'What that is, seems to be a direct consequence of their incapacity to experience the passage of time' (2000: 50). In what follows I shall be trying to articulate the sense in which O'Shaughnessy is correct to claim that conscious sensory experience appears to make us conscious of 'the passage of time'. I shall be connecting this idea with a further proposal that O'Shaughnessy makes—the proposal that the continuity of conscious sensory experience is *processive* in character.

I mentioned O'Shaughnessy's endorsement of this claim in Chapter 2, when I was seeking to identify the assumptions that Geach may have been making about the temporal profile of continuities in the stream of consciousness. In that discussion I quoted O'Shaughnessy's claim that,

Even when experience does not change in type or content it still changes in another respect: it is constantly renewed, a new sector of itself is then and there taking place. This is because experiences are events or processes, and each momentary new element of any given experience is a further happening or occurrence. (2000: 42)

According to O'Shaughnessy,

Even in the situation of total lack of change in the objects of perception, change continues—within. However frozen the perceptible world may in fact be, the internal clock of consciousness ticks on... Heracliteanism is true in the domain of experience. (2000: 61)

Even the unchanging perception of a fixed and immobilized world conceals a processive continuity, that of the perceiving itself, which is occurrently renewed in each instant, defining itself through that change as it proceeds. (2000: 63)

In the next section I shall be linking O'Shaughnessy's proposal that occurrence is 'the very stuff' of experience (2000: 48) with his proposal that 'experience guarantees a direct confrontation with the passage of time' (51). I shall be arguing that we need to appeal to the respect in which the continuity of conscious sensory experience is *processive* in character in order to accommodate the respect in which the subject of conscious sensory experience has a distinctive form of conscious contact with sub-intervals of the period of time over which he has conscious sensory experience—a form of conscious contact with those sub-intervals of time that presents each sub-interval as temporally present, even when the subject's experience does not change in type and character, and even when the subject's gaze is fixed upon a static scene.

However, I shall also be arguing that the appeal to processive perceptual occurrence alone is not in itself sufficient to explain the distinctive form of conscious contact with time that our conscious sensory experience provides us with. We also need to appeal to the obtaining of perceptual *states*. Not the merely dispositional mental states that can be possessed by the dreamless sleeper, but also what I shall call 'occurrent' perceptual states—perceptual states whose obtaining *constitutively* depends on the occurrence of phenomenally conscious events/processes in the stream of conscious sensory experience. If we do not appeal to the obtaining of these 'occurrent' perceptual states, we may be able to accommodate passage *within* experience, but we will not be able to accommodate the distinctive experience *of* passage that is available to the phenomenally conscious subject.

Later on in the chapter I shall also be discussing how this account of the ontology of conscious sensory experience may be relevant to certain debates that fall under the headings of 'the continuity of consciousness' and 'the diachronic unity of consciousness'.

6.2 'Occurrent' perceptual states and experiencing the 'passage' of time

In what respect might it be true to say that conscious sensory experience 'guarantees a direct confrontation with the passage of time', and how might this be connected with the idea that conscious sensory experience presents as temporally present distinct sub-intervals of the period of time over which one has the experience? It will help us to answer this question if we first consider a more general question: what is the connection between the idea of the 'passage of time' and the idea of the 'presentness' of moments of time?

In his discussion of the more general question, Kit Fine (2005) argues that even if one is a realist about the present and one thinks that reality itself is tensed, the idea of the passage of time cannot simply rest on the notion that a given time is present and other times are earlier and later than it. For, as Fine puts it, 'the passage of time requires that the moments of time be *successively* present and this appears to require more than the presentness of a single moment of time' (2005: 287).

Even if presentness is allowed to shed its light upon the world there is nothing in [this] metaphysics to prevent that light from being 'frozen' on a particular moment of time. (287)

Fine goes on to point out that the idea that there are *distinct* moments of time that are 'present' is also not in itself sufficient to account for the notion of the passage of time.

The idea of an equitable distribution of presentness across moments of time does not in itself entail the passage of time, 'just as an equitable distribution of me-ness applied across the board to everyone does not in itself secure a moving me!' (288). What's missing in the view on which there are distinct moments of time that are present is the idea that these moments of time are *successively* present.

Fine's discussion suggests that if one were trying to account for experience of the passage of time, then the idea that one experiences a particular moment as present would not in itself be enough, and neither would the idea that one experiences distinct moments of time as present. For what would be needed is the idea that one experiences moments of time *as successively present.*

In Chapter 4 I made some claims about our conscious experience of events that are relevant to an account of our conscious experience of succession. I now want to suggest that the account of our conscious experience of events that I offered can be used to explain the respect in which conscious experience appears to make us conscious of the 'passage of time', by explaining the respect in which our conscious sensory experience appears to make us aware of sub-intervals of intervals of time that we are consciously aware of as 'successively present'. The proposal I shall be making will support O'Shaughnessy's claim that the continuity of conscious sensory experience is processive in character, and so support the thesis that the distinctive form of the conscious contact with time that we have when we have conscious sensory experience gives us reason to hold that conscious sensory experience involves the occurrence of phenomenally conscious events/processes, even in cases in which the phenomenally conscious event/process in question is not directly introspectively accessible to one in the way in which a phenomenal bodily sensation is directly introspectively accessible to one. First I shall briefly summarize some of the points that arose in my earlier discussion of the conscious character of our experience of events.

In Chapter 4 I suggested that there is a general difficulty that one appears to face in providing an account of experience that can (a) attribute to a subject a psychological property/state that accounts for the fact that it seems to the subject as though she is perceptually aware of an occurrence with temporal extension, while at the same time accommodating the idea that (b) each temporal part of that occurrence seems to the subject to be concurrent with her awareness of it. And the obstacle to success, I suggested, seems to reside in the fact that mental states are not the kinds of things that can unfold over time. For given that mental states obtain over time, and do not unfold over time, one might think that mental states with temporal extension *continue* to obtain *throughout* the intervals of time over which they obtain. I argued that the notion that our perceptual states *continue* to obtain *throughout* the intervals of time over which they obtain presents an obstacle to the attempt to provide an account of our experience of events that accommodates a negative phenomenological claim that can be made about our conscious sensory experience of events: when one introspects one's experience, the temporal location of one's perceptual experience seems to one to be transparent to the temporal location of whatever it is that one is aware of in having that experience.

Introspectively, it doesn't seem to one as though one can mark out the temporal location of one's perceptual experience as distinct from the temporal location of whatever it is that one seems to be perceptually aware of.

The solution, I suggested, is to accept a relationalist account of our conscious sensory experience of events, according to which the phenomenally conscious state that obtains when a subject has conscious sensory experience seems to the subject to depend on the obtaining of a relation of perceptual acquaintance. This psychological relation is a relation to the event perceived, and it is a relation that obtains only when the event occurs. According to this view, given that the event perceived is something that *takes* an interval of time to occur, the obtaining of the subject's phenomenally conscious state over that interval of time seems to the subject to depend on the occurrence of something that takes that interval of time to occur. For example, the phenomenally conscious state that obtains when one perceives the movement of an object from location L1 to L5 is one whose obtaining over an interval of time seems to one to depend on the occurrence of something that *takes* that interval of time. For this reason, the phenomenally conscious state doesn't seem to its subject to be one that *continues* to obtain *throughout* that interval of time. So the phenomenology is therefore that of being aware of something that fills an interval of time *over* that interval of time. In other words, it doesn't seem to the subject as though she is aware of something that fills an interval of time from a point in time that is distinct from that interval of time—e.g. from a point of time that falls within that interval of time. Given that the psychological relation in question is one that seems to the subject to obtain only when the event occurs, the subject's awareness of the event will seem to her to have the temporal location of the event she perceives, and so too will the phenomenally conscious state that obtains when she stands in that relation to it.

An important element of the account is the suggestion that we need to appeal to the obtaining of perceptual states that are not homogeneous down to instants. The obtaining of these perceptual states over an interval of time depends constitutively on the occurrence of perceived events—events that *take* that interval of time to occur. I now want to propose that we should also appeal to the obtaining of perceptual states that are not homogeneous down to instants when providing an account of our conscious sensory experience of an unchanging static scene over some interval of time. I shall label such states 'occurrent' perceptual states. This proposal I shall offer will bring out the respect in which our conscious sensory experience appears to make us aware of the 'passage of time'.

According to the proposal I want to make, when one has a conscious sensory experience of an unchanging static scene, one is in a phenomenally conscious state that is to be characterized, at least in part, in terms of the obtaining of a psychological relation of perceptual acquaintance. A structural feature of this psychological relation is its possession of a temporal sensory field. The entities one is perceptually aware of are perceived as occupying an interval of time, which coincides with, or falls within, the temporal sensory field of one's conscious experience. In the case of one's conscious experience of events, I suggested that the phenomenally conscious state that obtains is constitutively dependent on the occurrence of the perceived event. In the case of our conscious experience of a static scene, I also want to suggest that the phenomenally conscious state that obtains is constitutively dependent on the occurrence of an event/process. This is where the general proposal I have been making about the ontology of conscious sensory experience can be put to work.

When one perceives a static scene, the phenomenally conscious state that obtains is an 'occurrent' state whose obtaining over an interval of time is constitutively dependent on the occurrence of an event/process that takes that interval of time to occur. The event/process in question is not an event/process one is perceptually aware of—for in the case imagined one is aware of a static scene. The event/process in question is, rather, a phenomenally conscious event/process that occurs during the time over which the phenomenally conscious state obtains. The 'occurrent' phenomenally conscious state obtains in virtue of, and for the duration of, the occurrence of the phenomenally conscious event/process. The nature of the phenomenally conscious event/process is to be specified in terms of the kind of phenomenally conscious state that obtains when it occurs, and the nature of the phenomenally conscious state is to be characterized, in part, in terms of the kind of event/process upon which the obtaining of that state constitutively depends.

The phenomenally conscious state that obtains in virtue of the occurrence of the phenomenally conscious event/process is not intentionally directed on that phenomenally conscious event/process. It is, rather, intentionally directed on the mind-independent static scene. However, there is a sense in which the subject's awareness of the static scene as occupying an interval of time seems to the subject to take that interval of time. This is because the obtaining of the state of awareness depends on the occurrence of something that takes that interval of time to occur, namely the phenomenally conscious event/process upon which the obtaining of the subject's phenomenally conscious state constitutively depends.

We can now bring out the respect in which such phenomenally conscious 'occurrent' states appear to make us conscious of the 'passage of time', taking as our example a case in which a subject seems to be aware of a static scene. The entities the subject is perceptually aware of are experienced as occupying an interval of time. Everything that the subject is perceptually aware of seems to her to be concurrent with her awareness of it. So in that sense, everything that the subject is perceptually aware of is experienced as occupying an interval of time that is temporally 'present'. Each sub-interval of that interval of time seems to the subject to be concurrent with her awareness of it, and so in that sense, each sub-interval of time seems to the subject to be temporally 'present'. Those sub-intervals of time seem to the subject to be successive, in so far as it seems to *take* time to be perceptually aware of their sum—i.e. the interval of time that is determined by the extent of the subject's temporal sensory field, and which those sub-intervals of time together constitute. So there is a sense in which the interval of time that falls within the subject's temporal sensory field seems to the subject to be made up of

successively present times. As a result, the phenomenology is something like the successive unfolding of present times.[1]

I suggested earlier that during the period of time that he sleeps, the dreamless sleeper
can continue to be in a dispositional mental state that is specified in terms of a temporal
indexical content. I also suggested that the dreamless sleeper can retain his capacity to
refer indexically to distinct sub-intervals of the period of time during which he sleeps.
So there is an attenuated sense in which it may be correct to claim that during his
dreamless sleep the subject is in a position to refer to distinct sub-intervals of the period
of time during which he sleeps as 'now', and make knowledgeable claims about what is
going on in his environment in doing so. However, I also suggested that the following is
true: during a period of dreamless sleep, distinct sub-intervals of that period of time are
not presented to the subject as temporally present; whereas, over a period of time during
which a subject has conscious sensory experience, even if that experience does not
change in general type and character, the subject of experience is aware of distinct sub-
intervals of that period of time—distinct sub-intervals of that period of time each of
which is presented to the subject as temporally present. I am now proposing that we
explain this difference between the situation of the dreamless sleeper and the subject of
conscious sensory experience in terms of the idea that the subject of conscious experience is in 'occurrent' perceptual states whose obtaining constitutively depends on the
occurrence of phenomenally conscious events/processes whose continuity is processive
in character.

This proposal accommodates the respect in which the subject of conscious sensory
experience seems to be made aware of the 'passage of time' in a way that the dreamless
sleeper is not. For it accommodates the respect in which the subject of conscious sensory experience seems to be made aware of 'successively present' times in having that
experience, even when the experience does not change in general type and character,
and even if the subject's gaze is fixed upon a static scene. (Even, one could add, if the
conscious sensory experience is as negative as that of hearing silence.)

In the proposal I have been making I have suggested that we need to appeal to the
obtaining of perceptual *states* when it comes to accommodating the distinctive form of
conscious contact with time that phenomenally conscious experience provides us with.
However, I have suggested that the states in question are 'occurrent' perceptual states—
and not merely dispositional mental states. These 'occurrent' perceptual states are ones
whose obtaining *constitutively* depends on the occurrence of phenomenally conscious
events/processes—events whose nature is to be specified, at least in part, in terms of the

---

[1] In the previous chapter I made some suggestions about how aspects of the temporal phenomenology
of conscious sensory experience might make intuitive the following thought: whether entities are perceptually accessible to one depends in part on whether those entities fall within an interval of time that is temporally present, where this is thought to be a non-perspectival temporal fact about those entities that is
independent of one's sensory limitations. Conjoining that suggestion with the suggestion that I have just
made about the respect in which we seem to be aware of the passage of time in having conscious sensory
experience might, in turn, make intuitive the thought that time itself seems to unfold over time.

kind of state that obtains when they occur. So although the proposal I have offered appeals to the obtaining of perceptual *states*, it also appeals to the occurrence of phenomenally conscious events/processes whose continuity is processive in character. In that respect, there is a measure of agreement with O'Shaughnessy's claim that 'Even the unchanging perception of a fixed and immobilized world conceals a processive continuity, that of the perceiving itself, which is occurrently renewed in each instant, defining itself through that change as it proceeds' (2000: 63), and his claim that 'Even in the situation of total lack of change in the objects of perception, change continues—within. However frozen the perceptible world may in fact be, the internal clock of consciousness ticks on' (2000: 61).

The 'occurrent renewal' of conscious sensory experience is an ingredient of the account we need to appeal to in order to accommodate the distinctive form of conscious contact with the 'passage of time' that our conscious sensory experience appears to provide us with. But so too are the 'occurrent' perceptual *states* that obtain when they occur. While it is often thought that states with temporal extension *continue* to obtain *throughout* the intervals of time over which they obtain, this is not true of the 'occurrent' perceptual states that obtain when we have conscious sensory experience. This has some further consequences, which I discuss in the next section.

6.3 Occurrent perceptual states and Dennett's 'multiple drafts'

States *obtain* over time, and do not *unfold* over time. However, if the obtaining of a state depends constitutively on the occurrence of an event, then the obtaining of that state over an interval of time may depend on the occurrence of something that *takes* an interval of time to occur. And so the obtaining of that state will not be homogeneous down to instants. In the case of such 'occurrent' states, we should not assume that if a subject is in such a state over a period of time, then this is determined by, and hence explained by, the fact that the state obtains at each of the instants that make up that period of time. For in the case of such 'occurrent' states, it may be that the fact that a subject is in such a state at a particular instant of time is determined by, and hence explained by, the fact that the state obtains over an interval of time that includes that instant. The subject may be in that state at a particular instant only in so far as she is in that state over an interval that includes that instant.

In the case of the occurrent perceptual states that I have been discussing, there is a further consequence to note. I have suggested that the nature of the phenomenally conscious occurrence upon which the obtaining of the phenomenally conscious occurrent perceptual state constitutively depends is to be specified in terms of the kind of phenomenally conscious occurrent state that obtains when the phenomenally conscious event/process occurs. We specify the kind of phenomenally conscious event/process that occurs at a particular instant in terms of the kind of phenomenally conscious occurrent state that obtains at that instant. However, since this occurrent perceptual state obtains at a particular instant only in so far as that instant falls within an interval of time over which the state obtains, we must specify the kind of phenomenally conscious event/process that occurs at a particular instant in terms of a phenomenally conscious occurrent state that obtains over an interval of time that includes that instant.

In Chapter 4 I argued that an aspect of the temporal phenomenology of conscious sensory experience is determined by the obtaining of a non-representational psychological relation of perceptual acquaintance, and not simply the obtaining of a state with a representational content. I argued that one misses out some aspect of the temporal phenomenology if one does not appeal to the obtaining of a non-representational psychological relation between the subject and entities in the world when it comes to fully specifying the phenomenology of the sensory experience undergone. However, I also suggested that someone who accepts this proposal need not deny that subjects are in perceptual states with representational contents when they have such experiences. I now want to discuss briefly how the account of the ontology of occurrent perceptual states that I have just outlined may bear on one's specification of the representational contents of such states.

An assumption sometimes made in representationalist accounts of experience is that we can refer to a subject's perceptual experience in such a way that we can then ask after *the* content of *that* experience. In particular, the assumption seems to be that if we specify the particular time, subject, and perceptual modality we have in mind, we can then ask after *the* content of *the* perceptual experience of the subject, within that perceptual modality, at that time—e.g. 'what is the content of the visual experience you are having now?'. One complication that arises for the assumption is the following. It seems reasonable to assume that the content of a perceptual state can represent change. Since such change can take time (e.g. in the case of the movement of an object), a question we might then ask is, what determines what kind of change is represented at a time, and what determines when there is, rather, a change in representational content at that time? Did there obtain at time tn a perceptual state with a content representing change, or did there, rather, occur at that time a change in representational content? It is not obvious that there is a non-arbitrary way of settling this question. So such cases might be used to put pressure on the assumption that it is always the case that there is some fact of the matter that determines *the* content of *the* perceptual state a subject is in at a given time.

It is here that our discussion of the ontology of occurrent perceptual states becomes relevant. Given that such states are not homogeneous down to instants, we can reject the assumption that the question of what perceptual representational state a subject is in at an instant is explanatorily prior to the question of what perceptual representational state a subject is in over a given period of time. The result will be the following: a subject will be in a given representational state at a time in virtue of being in that representational state over a period of time that includes that instant. As there will be many different periods of time that any instant will part of, it may be true to say that S was in state P from t1 to t4, but also true to say that S was in state Q from t2 to t6, and state R from t3 to t7, and so on. Given this account, it will be a mistake to think that we can identify *the* perceptual representational state a subject is in by simply specifying the time *at* which it obtains and then ask after *the* content of *that* state. For example, we can no longer simply ask what perceptual representational state S was in at t3. So acknowledging that perceptual states with representational content obtain in virtue of the occurrence of events and processes might then explain what is wrong in thinking that there must be some way of determining whether, at a given time, there occurs a change in representational content rather than a content that represents change.

A consequence of this account of the ontology of occurrent perceptual states that is worth noting is that there is some measure of agreement with some of the claims that Dennett (1991) makes when outlining his 'Multiple Drafts' model of consciousness.[2] According to the Multiple Drafts model, information entering the nervous system is 'under continuous "editorial revision"'. 'These editorial processes occur over large fractions of a second during which time various additions, incorporations, emendations, and overwritings of content can occur, in various orders' (1991: 136). Dennett holds that although the brain events involved, which can be thought of as feature detections and discriminations, are precisely locatable in both space and time, it is a mistake to think that their onsets mark the onset of the consciousness of their content. He claims that 'It is always an open question whether any particular content thus discriminated will eventually appear as an element in conscious experience, and it is a confusion . . . to ask *when it becomes conscious*' (136). For on this view, the subject's experiential point of view is 'spread over' a temporal interval. When we descend to a level at which a sequence of brain events occur within such a temporal interval, it is a mistake to assume that it should be possible to identify some *one* of these brain events as marking the onset of consciousness of some stimulus. Moreover, how any one of these brain events contributes to, and what effects it has on, the prevailing brain state, and thus awareness, 'can change from moment to moment depending on what else is going on in the brain' (1991: 136). So probing and interrupting this stream of 'content-fixations' at different times can produce different effects, precipitating different narratives from the subject; and it is a mistake to think there is some 'optimal' time of probing which precipitates what the subject is *really* consciously experiencing.

According to the account of the ontology of occurrent perceptual states that I have been outlining, such states are not homogeneous down to instants. What conscious perceptual state a subject is in at a particular instant is determined by what conscious perceptual state obtains over an interval of time that includes that instant. So this account of the ontology is in agreement with Dennett's claim that the subject's experiential point of view is 'spread over' a temporal interval. There is therefore a measure of agreement with Dennett's suggestion that when we descend to a level at which a sequence of brain events occur within such a temporal interval, it is a mistake to assume that it

---

[2] See also Dennett and Kinsbourne 1992. For critical discussion of the Multiple Drafts theory, see Rosenthal 1993, W.S. Robinson 1994, Van Gulick 1995, Brook 2000.

should be possible to identify some *one* of these brain events as marking the onset of consciousness of some stimulus. According to this account of the ontology of conscious sensory experience, what conscious perceptual state you are in at a particular instant depends on what happens before *and after* that instant, so there is also a measure of agreement with Dennett's suggestion that how any one of these brain events contributes to, and what effects it has on, the prevailing brain state, and thus awareness, 'can change from moment to moment', and it is a mistake to assume that there is an optimal time at which this sequence of brain events can be probed or interrupted to determine what the subject is really experiencing.[3]

Dennett holds that 'conscious experience is a succession of states constituted by various processes occurring in the brain, and not something over and above these processes that is caused by them' (1991:136). On his view, the events that perceptual states are constituted by, rather than caused by, are brain events, or *sub-personal* mental events with content, and not phenomenally conscious events/processes in the stream of conscious sensory experience. Dennett's objections to the notion of a stream of phenomenally conscious experience appear to be premised on the idea that the relevant notion of a stream of conscious experience should be understood on the model of a successive series of events with determinate personal-level contents, according to which it is possible to identify, at a time, *the* content of a particular mental occurrence in the stream of conscious experience that occurs at that time. The account of the ontology of conscious sensory experience that I have offered allows one to acknowledge that there is something right in Dennett's objection; for it *is* a mistake to think that there is something that determines what *the* content of the occurrence in the stream of conscious experience is at any given time. Given that the nature of an occurrence in the stream of conscious experience is to be specified by making reference to the personal-level perceptual states that obtain in virtue of it, we can say that just as it is a mistake to ask after *the* content of *the* perceptual state that obtains at a given time, it is also a mistake to ask after *the* content of an occurrence in the stream of conscious experience at a given time.

Why does Dennett assume that the notion of a stream of conscious experience should be understood on a model according to which it is possible to identify, at a time, *the* content of a particular mental occurrence in the stream of conscious experience that occurs at that time? The alternative is a view according to which (i) what the content of an occurrence in the stream of conscious experience is at a time may be affected by what happens after that time, and according to which (ii) the answer we give to the question of what the content of the occurrence is at a time may be determined by the answer we

---

[3] Someone accepting this account of the ontology of conscious perceptual states can concur with Dennett in rejecting the assumption that the sequence of brain events that determine the content of conscious perception can only be those that occur *prior* to the onset of the conscious perceptual state, and not those occurring during the time over which the state obtains. So they can accept Dennett's proposal that we reject the assumption that we either need to appeal to a 'Stalinesque show trial', or an 'Orwellian revision', when it comes to explaining the perceptual illusions that Dennett discusses—e.g. colour phi illusions and flash-lag illusions.

give to the question of what the content of the occurrence is over an interval of time that includes that instant, where the answer we give to this question may be, to a certain extent, contextually dependent on the interval of time we have in mind. (i) and (ii) may be thought to be in tension with the notion that the phenomenal character of an experience a subject is having at a time must be accessible to the subject *at that time*. Surely, it might be thought, any defensible account of a *phenomenally conscious* stream of experience will have to accommodate the idea that the subject of such experience should, ceteris paribus, be in a position to know, at a time, what the phenomenal character of her experience is at that time, and so what the content of an occurrence in the stream of her conscious experience is at that time. However, if we think of the subject's state of knowledge of the phenomenal character of an occurrence in the stream of conscious experience as *itself* a state that is constitutively dependent on the occurrence of events and processes in the conscious stream, and hence a state that is not homogenous down to instants, then this difficulty can be resolved.

On this view, just as it is a mistake to ask after *the* content of *the* perceptual state that obtains at a given time, it is a mistake to ask after *the* content of one's knowledge of the character of the stream of conscious sensory experience at that time. I shall be saying more about our knowledge of the phenomenal character of our conscious sensory experiences in Chapters 7 and 8. In the next section of this chapter I want to discuss briefly how this account of the ontology of conscious sensory experience bears on certain debates that fall under the headings of 'the continuity of consciousness' and 'the diachronic unity of consciousness'.

6.4 The diachronic unity and continuity of consciousness

In Chapter 2 I outlined Geach's argument designed to 'call...attention to the discontinuous character of thought', and 'the complete inappropriateness of James' expression "the stream of thought"' (1969: 34). William James claimed that 'Consciousness...does not appear to itself chopped up in bits...It is nothing jointed: it flows. A "river" or a "stream" are the metaphors by which it is most naturally described' (1890: 233). According to Geach, although sensory aspects of mind may be 'stream-like', acts of thinking thoughts are not; and this becomes clear, according to Geach, once we attain a correct understanding of the way in which acts of thinking are to be individuated in terms of their propositional contents.

Geach argued that we should reject a certain mistaken picture of what is involved in thinking a thought that is individuated in terms of a propositional content. According to that mistaken picture, a mental act of, say, judging that *p* is thought of as filling an interval of time that can be broken down into sub-intervals of time in each of which there occurs a temporal part of that mental act that is to be specified in terms of a part of the propositional content that *p* that is judged. Geach claimed that when a subject judges that p there is no sequence of successive thinkings of different parts of the content that p, for although a propositional content may be complex and have parts, there can be no question of the *temporal order* of the parts of the propositional content in terms of which we individuate an act of thinking. So the parts of the propositional content judged do not occur 'separately and successively'. For this reason he denied that there can be any succession within such an act of thinking that p.

For the same reason, he denied that such thoughts 'pass into one another by gradual transition' (1969: 35). Consider again the illustration that I gave of this point in Chapter 2. Suppose that a subject successively thinks two thoughts that are individuated in terms of their propositional contents. The first act of thinking is a judging that p and the second act of thinking is a judging that q. Suppose that the propositional content that p and the propositional content that q have a part in common—suppose that both judgements are about John. If one held that the parts of the propositional content judged occur separately and successively one might think it possible for the judgement that p and the judgement that q to share a *temporal* part—the part that is about John—and so in that sense there could be a gradual transition from one act of judging to the next. However, Geach argued that given that the parts of the propositional content judged are not temporally ordered, it is a mistake to think that when the propositional contents of two judgements have a part in common it is possible for them to have a temporal part in common. So, in that sense, there can be no gradual transition from one thought to another. This leads Geach to claim:

Thinking consists in having a series of thoughts which can be counted off discretely–the first, the second, the third, . . .—; which, if complex, must occur with all their elements present simultaneously; which do not pass into one another by gradual transition. (1969: 35)

I'll be saying more about Geach's view of thinking in Part II. For now I just want to focus on those aspects of mind that Geach *contrasted* with this view of thinking—sensory aspects of mind. As I mentioned in Chapter 2, it is intuitive to think that when conscious sensory experience fills an interval of time, that interval of time can be thought of as an interval that can be broken down into sub-intervals in each of which there occurs some successive phase of the sensory experience. And it's intuitive to think that one's experience of A can share a temporal part with one's subsequent experience of B, which can share a temporal part with one's subsequent experience of C, and so on. (For example, suppose one is watching the movement of the seconds hand of a clock for some period of time. It's intuitive to think that one's experience of the seconds hand moving from location L1 to location L5 can share a temporal part with one's experience of the seconds hand moving from L5 to L10, which in turn can share a temporal part with one's experience of the seconds hand moving from L10 to L15, and so on.) For this reason one might think it a mistake to hold that conscious sensory experience is 'discontinuous'. For example, one might think it a mistake to hold that the conscious visual experience one has when one continuously watches something over an extended period of time consists in a series of distinct and separate conscious sensory episodes that can be counted off discretely—the first, the second, then the third.

Considerations of this kind emerge in Tye's (2003) discussion of the diachronic unity of consciousness. As I mentioned in Chapter 2, Tye suggests that over a period of time during which one is awake one has just one temporally extended experience. He claims that this 'one experience hypothesis' finds support in the general difficulty we face in individuating experiences through time:

Consider an ordinary visual experience and suppose that it is exclusively visual. When did it begin? When will it end? As I write now, I am sitting in a library. Looking ahead, and holding my line of sight fixed, I can see many books, tables, people in the distance walking across the room, a woman nearby opening some bags as she sits down. Is this a single temporally extended visual experience? If not, why not?

...These difficulties of individuation arise once it is assumed that the stream of consciousness divides into different token experiences...that come and go. The difficulties disappear if it is held instead that each stream of consciousness is itself just one temporally extended experience. (2003: 97)

According to Tye, 'A stream of consciousness is just one temporally extended experience that represents a flow of things in the world. It has no shorter experiences as parts. Indeed it has no experiences as proper parts at all' (2003: 106).

This 'one experience' view becomes implausible if we regard this one experience as a perceptual state of the subject that continues to obtain throughout the period of time during which the subject is awake. Moreover, during a period of time that a subject is awake, there won't usually obtain just one perceptual state over that period of time. This is a point I made in Chapter 2. Over the course of the day, a subject's psychological properties change a great deal. Some of her beliefs, desires, and intentions may be retained over the course of the day, but she will undergo a series of changes to her *perceptual* psychological states.

Suppose we want to accommodate the idea that during the period of time that a conscious subject is awake there obtains a series of successive and distinct perceptual states. Can we still retain something of the 'one experience hypothesis' by holding that these perceptual states are just distinct temporal parts of one experience? In a case in which a subject believes that p from t1 to t10, and then believes that q from t10 to t20, we do not regard these belief states as temporal parts of some further belief that obtains from t1 to t20. For example, we do not regard this as a case in which the subject has a belief that p & q from t1 to t20. Similar considerations may lead us to think that the distinct, successive perceptual states that obtain during a period of time that a conscious subject is awake should not be thought of as different temporal parts of one perceptual experience.

The proposal I've been making about the ontology of conscious sensory experience can again be put to explanatory work here. It can accommodate the idea that a series of distinct perceptual states obtain during the period of time a subject is awake and having conscious sensory experience, but it can also accommodate the idea that one's experience of A can share a temporal part with one's subsequent experience of B, which in turn can share a temporal part with one's subsequent experience of C, and so on. The 'occurrent' perceptual state that obtains when a subject wakes does not obtain for the whole of the period of time over which the subject remains awake. The subject will be in a series of distinct occurrent perceptual states during that period of consciousness. But the conscious perceptual occurrence upon which an occurrent perceptual state constitutively depends can share a temporal part with the conscious perceptual occurrence upon which a subsequent occurrent perceptual state constitutively depends.

This view accommodates the idea that one is in a series of distinct, successive, albeit overlapping, perceptual states when one undergoes conscious sensory experience over an extended period of time, and it also accommodates the idea that one's experience of A can share a temporal part with a subsequent experience of B, which can share a temporal part with a subsequent experience of C, and so on. But it does so without needing to invoke the idea that the distinct and successive perceptual states that obtain when one undergoes conscious sensory experience over an extended period of time are temporal parts of some perceptual state that obtains over the whole of that extended period of time.

Note that this is also a proposal one could apply to perceptual states with representational contents that obtain in virtue of the occurrence of one's conscious sensory experience. One can hold that the conscious perceptual occurrence one undergoes when one is in a perceptual state with the representational content that p can share a temporal part with the subsequent conscious perceptual occurrence one undergoes when one is in a perceptual state with a representational content that q. One can thereby accommodate the idea that there is a temporal part common to the experience one undergoes when one is in these perceptual states with these distinct representational contents, but without needing to think that the parts of the representational contents of these perceptual states are temporally ordered, and so without needing to think that the representational content that p shares a temporal part with the representational content that q.

Earlier I was emphasizing the following consequence of the account of the ontology of conscious sensory experience that I am proposing: the fact that a subject is in a given occurrent perceptual state at a particular time is determined by, and explained by, the fact that that occurrent perceptual state obtains over an interval of time that includes that instant. So what a subject is aware of at a particular time is determined by, and explained by, what the subject is aware of over an interval of time that includes that instant. But we should also hold that when a subject continues to be perceptually aware of her environment over an extended period of time, distinct perceptual states obtain during that extended period of time. It isn't the case that the same occurrent perceptual state obtains over the whole of that extended period of time. So we also need to accommodate the idea that what a subject is perceptually aware of over an extended period of time is determined by, and explained by, what the subject is aware of during subintervals of that extended period of time. The proposal I've been making allows one to do this, but while also accommodating the respect in which one's conscious sensory experience over that extended period of time is continuous; for it accommodates the respect in which during that extended period of time, one's conscious experience of A can share a temporal part with one's subsequent conscious experience of B, which in turn can share a temporal part with one's subsequent conscious experience of C, and so on.

This proposal about the ontology of conscious sensory experience can accommodate a respect in which there can be continuity in the stream of conscious sensory experience over time. The claim that our conscious sensory experience is in fact continuous is controversial, so I just want to make some further, brief clarificatory remarks on this issue. The first, very general remark that can be made is that one might question whether there is anything in the phenomenology of conscious sensory experience that speaks to the question of whether one's conscious sensory experience seems to one to be strictly continuous, or dense. It may be the case that the conscious sensory experience one has over an interval of time does not seem to one to be discontinuous, but this isn't equivalent to the claim that one's conscious sensory experience seems to one *not* to be discontinuous. There are further general remarks that can be made. Suppose that the sub-personal perceptual processing that is involved when one has conscious sensory experience consists in a series of discrete events with brief temporal gaps between them. Is this inconsistent with the idea that sensory experience is a 'continuous' process? One thing to note here is that there is a respect in which one can regard a process as continuous despite the fact that that process is constituted by a series of discrete events with temporal gaps between those events. For example, a subject can be said to be continually tapping her fingers on the table despite the fact that there are temporal gaps between the discrete taps that make up the process of her tapping. The fact that the subject's finger does not make contact with the table at t5 does not in itself entail that a continuous process of tapping did not occur from t1 to t10. So whatever position one favours on the relation between sub-personal perceptual processes and conscious sensory experience, it is not obvious that establishing that a sub-personal perceptual process consists in a series of discrete events separated by temporal gaps would in itself establish that it would be a mistake to regard these sub-personal occurrences as involving a continuous process.[4]

In the case of the conscious sensory occurrence that I have been suggesting should be an ingredient in the right account of the ontology of conscious sensory experience, there is an added complication to note. I have suggested that the nature of the conscious sensory occurrence in question is to be specified in terms of the kind of occurrent perceptual state that obtains when it occurs. So an answer to the question of whether a certain kind of conscious sensory experience occurs at a particular time will depend on an answer to the question of whether a certain kind of occurrent perceptual state obtains at that time. Establishing that there are times at which such conscious sensory occurrence does not occur would involve establishing that an occurrent perceptual state does not obtain at those times. And note too that I have said that the fact that a subject is in an occurrent perceptual state at a time is determined by the fact that that occurrent perceptual state obtains over an interval of time that includes that instant. So

---

[4] Much the same could be said of the neural events and brain oscillations that may be involved in having conscious sensory experience. For discussion, see Rashbrook 2011.

establishing that the occurrent perceptual state does not obtain at a given instant would involve establishing that the state in question does not obtain over an interval of time that includes that instant.

Although these remarks apply to the issue of whether conscious sensory experience is 'continuous', similar remarks may apply to the more general question of the continuity of 'consciousness'. Earlier I said that it would be a mistake to hold that the same occurrent perceptual state obtains over the whole period of time that a subject is awake and having conscious sensory experience. During that extended period of time a series of distinct and successive occurrent perceptual states will obtain. However, one could maintain that there is an occurrent mental state that obtains throughout that extended period of time—namely, the state of wakeful consciousness. We might regard this state of wakeful consciousness—the state of being awake—as a state whose obtaining constitutively depends on the occurrence of conscious events. The state of wakeful consciousness is not itself a perceptual state, and although its obtaining may depend on the occurrence of mental events/processes that have intentionality, the state of wakeful consciousness is not itself a mental state with an intentional content, as O'Shaughnessy (2000) has pointed out. So the idea that this state of consciousness continues to obtain throughout the period of time that one is awake does not involve the idea that one continues to be in a mental state with a certain intentional content throughout that extended period of time.

As this state of consciousness is an occurrent mental state, the fact that this state of consciousness obtains at a particular time will be determined by the fact that the state obtains over an interval of time that includes that instant. So establishing that this state of consciousness does not obtain at a particular time will involve establishing that this state of consciousness does not obtain over an interval of time that includes that instant. Of course, there may be good reason to think that there can be cases in which a subject's state of wakeful consciousness does not obtain over certain intervals of time despite the fact that the subject in question does not realize that there have been discontinuities in her state of wakeful consciousness. For example, there are reasons to think that the sleep-deprived can have 'micro sleeps' for brief intervals of time without realizing that this has happened. In such cases it doesn't seem to the subject as though there have been discontinuities in her consciousness. But as mentioned earlier, this isn't equivalent to saying that it positively seems to the subject as though there are no discontinuities in her consciousness.

6.5 The ontology of the manifest image of conscious sensory experience

In Chapter 1 I suggested that appropriate articulation of the manifest image of conscious sensory experience will depend on finding an ontology that fits the phenomenology and the knowledge that we have of that phenomenology. Of crucial importance to this enterprise, I have been suggesting, are various ontological distinctions that are to be marked between different aspects of mind that are determined by the different ways in which those aspects of mind fill time. The particular proposal I have been defending is that conscious sensory experience involves the occurrence of mental events/processes, and when such a mental event/process occurs the subject undergoing it is in a psychological state that wouldn't otherwise obtain; the nature of the mental event/process is to be specified in terms of the kind of 'occurrent' mental state that obtains when that mental event/process occurs, and the nature of the occurrent mental state that obtains is to be specified in terms of the kind of mental event/process upon which its obtaining constitutively depends. The occurrent mental state, and the occurrence on which the obtaining of that state constitutively depends, have an interdependent status.

This interdependence thesis has been put to work in various ways. I have suggested that this account of the ontology of conscious sensory experience gives rise to a form of explanatory circularity, and that this consequence of the account may help to diagnose certain intuitions that arise in debates about the phenomenal character of experience. I have outlined how this account of the ontology of conscious sensory experience can inform our account of the phenomenology of bodily sensations—those aspects of mind that are generally thought to be paradigmatic of those mental events/states that only a phenomenally conscious subject can be the subject of. And I have also been developing the idea that this account of the ontology of conscious sensory experience can help to illuminate a distinctive form of conscious contact with time that phenomenally conscious subjects have, as well as suggesting how the account bears on issues relating to the continuity of conscious sensory experience over time.

In Chapter 2 I also suggested that this account of the ontology can help illuminate the respect in which there are certain things that only phenomenally conscious subjects can do—e.g. engage in acts of perceptual imagining—and that it can help provide an account of a variety of knowledge that only phenomenally conscious subjects can have—e.g. knowing what it is like to have a conscious sensory experience. These proposals are the topic of the next chapter.

7

Perceptual Imagination and Perceptual Recollection

Just as it is intuitive to think that a bodily sensation of pain is something that only a phenomenally conscious subject can feel, it is also intuitive to think that perceptually imagining something is an activity that only a phenomenally conscious subject can engage in. Under the category of perceptual imagination I have in mind acts of visualizing, hearing in one's mind's ear, and so on, as well as acts of imagining (from the inside, as one might put it) feeling a sensation and performing an action. In particular, I think it is natural to hold the following: one couldn't be engaged in the activity of perceptually imagining something without the occurrence of phenomenally conscious events, and the phenomenal character of the mental events involved determine, at least in part, and in some important way, the kind of mental activity one is engaged in. Furthermore, it is intuitive to think that the phenomenology of an act of perceptual imagination has something in common with the sensuous character of a conscious sensory experience. The phenomenology of such an act seems to have some significant connection with the phenomenology of some corresponding conscious sensory experience—e.g. the phenomenology of an act of visualizing a red square seems to have some significant connection with the phenomenology of having a conscious visual experience of a red square.

I have been defending the idea that various ontological distinctions between aspects of mind that are marked by the different ways in which those aspects of mind fill time are relevant to an account of the phenomenology of conscious sensory experience, and when I discussed how Geach contrasts the way in which acts of thinking fill time with the way in which sensory aspects of mind fill time I mentioned that Geach includes under the heading of sensory aspects of mind acts of perceptual imagining, as well as sensations and sensory experiences. I noted that it is intuitive to hold that when an act of perceptual imagining fills an interval of time, that interval of time can be thought of as an interval that can be broken down into sub-intervals in each of which there occurs some successive phase of that act of imagining. For example, when one imagines saying 'John is tall' in inner speech, it is intuitive to think that there is a temporal phase of the overall episode that involves saying 'is' in inner speech, where that phase of the episode can be thought of as being a temporal part that is common to the earlier phase of saying

'John is' in inner speech and the later phase of saying 'is tall' in inner speech. In that respect there appears to be a parallel between the temporal profile of an act of perceptual imagining and the temporal profile of conscious sensory experience.

Given these similarities and correspondences between the phenomenology of acts of perceptual imagination and the phenomenology of conscious sensory experience, and given the similarities between the ways in which these aspects of mind fill time, is there reason to think that the account of the ontology of conscious sensory experience that I have been proposing can be straightforwardly applied to the ontology of acts of perceptual imagination?

7.1 Perceptual imagination and perceptual experience: the 'same but different' puzzle

The account of the ontology of conscious sensory experience that I have been proposing has a relational component. According to that account, when a subject successfully perceives the world, an 'occurrent' phenomenally conscious perceptual state obtains, and the nature of that phenomenally conscious state is to be specified, at least in part, in terms of a psychological relation of perceptual acquaintance that obtains between the subject and the mind-independent entities that the subject perceives. Given that we are capable of *successfully* perceptually imagining mind-independent entities without there being any such mind-independent entities that we are thereby psychologically related to, it seems implausible, on the face of it, to think that the ontology of acts of perceptual imagining will involve this sort of relational component.

The argument I offered for the relational component in conscious sensory experience depended on an appeal to the phenomenological claim of temporal transparency. This was the claim that the temporal location of one's perceptual experience seems to one to be transparent to the temporal location of whatever it is that one is aware of in having that experience. Introspectively, it doesn't seem to one as though one can mark out the temporal location of one's perceptual experience as distinct from the temporal location of whatever it is that one is perceptually aware of. Moreover, it seems to one as though the temporal location of one's perceptual experience depends on, and is determined by, the temporal location of whatever it is that one's experience is an experience of. The phenomenological claim of temporal transparency is not true of acts of perceptual imagination, unless one is projectively perceptually imagining an object occupying a location within a scene that one is currently perceiving. Nor is the phenomenological claim of temporal transparency true of acts of perceptual recollection. So the argument I offered for the relational component in the ontology of conscious sensory experience cannot be straightforwardly applied to the cases of perceptual imagination and perceptual recollection.

The fact that the temporal location of one's perceptual experience seems to one to be determined by the temporal location of its object is connected with a distinctive respect in which perceptual experience is *receptive*, and not subject to the will. Even when successful perception involves agential perceptual activity, such as looking, watching etc., one's successful perception depends upon the occurrence of perceptual experience whose inception and course is determined by the temporal location of the object perceived. One might regard cases of so-called 'unbidden' mental imagery, for example a case in which the perceptual recollection of some past event pops up in one's mind unbidden, as passive mental events of which one is not an agent. But even such cases are not truly 'receptive' in the way that conscious sensory experience is. In the case of successful episodic recollection, we can say the following: the fact that a past event is successfully recollected entails that that past event actually occurred, and occurred at a time earlier than the time at which one recollects it; and one might also hold that some kind of causal connection between the past event recollected and the event of recollecting it determines that it is that particular past event that is recollected rather than any other. However, when it comes to explaining why the event of recollecting occurred *when* it occurred, one cannot simply cite the temporal location of the past event recollected. There might be any number of different explanations that could be offered as to why a particular episode of apparent recollection occurred when it occurred that are consistent with that episode being a genuine case of recollection, and there is no reason to think that an explanation of the particular temporal location of an episode of recollection should appeal to the temporal location of the event recollected. In that sense, the temporal location of the act of recollecting is not passive with respect to the temporal location of the event recollected in the way that the temporal location of perception is passive with respect to the items perceived; and in that sense, even when an act of recollecting is 'unbidden', this is not an exercise of a 'receptive' faculty.

There are further reasons for thinking that the account that I've offered of the ontology of conscious sensory experience cannot be straightforwardly applied to acts of perceptual imagination and recollection. As Martin points out, although it seems that there is a significant correspondence between the phenomenology of an act of perceptual imagination and the phenomenology of a conscious sensory experience, there are also important differences between them, and there is an intuition that these differences are differences in kind, and not just in degree. Martin makes this point by appealing to a case in which one imagines (from the inside) feeling a bodily sensation, such as an itch.

One can not only feel itches but also imagine them and such imagining can be experiential ... It does not seem right to say that one is still feeling an itch, albeit one that is less intense in character than itches not brought about through imagining. Nor does it seem right to suppose that in imagining an itch one is aware of anything other than the quality of itchiness itself. So, we seem to be caught both saying that we should think of imagining an itch as experiential and like a sensation of an itch and hence the same, and yet denying that they are the same, since in having a sensation of an itch there is an actual itch of which one is aware, while in imagining an itch there is no such actual itch. (Martin 2002: 406)[1]

---

[1] See also the discussion in Martin 2001: 271–2.

As Martin notes, when one imagines an itch in one's thigh one does not actually feel an itch—an itch that is just less intense and itchy than a non-imagined one. This appears to give us reason to think that an act of imagining an itch in one's thigh does not have the same sort of phenomenal properties as the actual bodily sensation, albeit to a lesser degree. For it is intuitive to think that if an event actually has the same sort of phenomenal properties as a bodily sensation, then one is aware of, and feels, a bodily sensation. Indeed, this was a claim I defended in the account of the phenomenology of bodily sensation that I outlined in Chapter 3.

Generalizing, then, it seems to be a mistake to insist that an act of perceptual imagining actually has the same sort of phenomenal properties as a corresponding conscious sensory experience. However, it also seems inadequate simply to say that an act of perceptually imagining a sensation has its phenomenal character in virtue of the fact that its *object*—i.e. *what is imagined*—is a phenomenally conscious sensation. Usually, being told what a subject is thinking about does not in itself tell one anything about the phenomenal character of the activity of her thinking. So why should the fact that one is told that the object of an episode of imagining is a phenomenally conscious mental event in itself tell one anything about the phenomenal character of that episode of imagining?

It seems that if one is to be informed about the phenomenal character of the event of imagining, one must not only be told what is being imagined, but also the *way* in which it is being imagined. Hence, in the case of imagining an itch, the stress on the idea that one is imagining the itch 'from the inside'. The problem is that this talk of the *way* in which one is imagining might then tempt one back into thinking that this, in turn, is determined by the phenomenal properties of the event of imagining, and if we are to capture the connection between the phenomenology of perceptual imagination and its corresponding perceptual experience or sensation, we'll have to say that the event of perceptual imagining actually has some of the phenomenal properties of the corresponding perceptual experience or sensation. So, for example, what it is to visualize something—to imagine something in a *visual* way—is for the event of imagining to have the same sort of phenomenal character as a visual experience; and what it is for the event of imagining to have the same sort of phenomenal character as a visual experience is for it to have some of the actual phenomenal properties of a visual experience.

This gives rise to what we might call a 'same but different' puzzle. As McGinn (2004) remarks, 'When we think about our mental images we should be struck by two things: (1) how *similar* they are to regular perceptions, and (2) how *different* they are from regular perceptions...The philosophical task—by no means an easy one—is to explain precisely in what way images and percepts are alike and precisely how they differ' (2004: 2). The puzzle is that, on the one hand, any claim that falls short of committing to the idea that an episode of perceptual imagination actually has some of the phenomenal properties of its corresponding perceptual experience or sensation seems too weak to capture the distinctively sensuous aspect of its phenomenology and its connection with that corresponding experience or sensation. On the other hand, we have reason to think that the claim that an episode of perceptual imagination actually has some of the phenomenal properties of its corresponding perceptual experience or sensation is too strong. In what follows, I shall be offering what I take to be the correct resolution of this 'same but different' puzzle, and central to the proposal I shall be making is an account of the ontology of these mental acts.

7.2 The dependency thesis

It has been argued by Martin, Peacocke, Foster, and Vendler that to visualize an object or event is to imagine visually experiencing it.[2] More generally, according to Martin,

To imagine sensorily a Φ is to imagine experiencing a Φ. (2002: 403)

Following Martin, I shall label this view the 'Dependency Thesis'.

On this view, one kind of phenomenally conscious state, an event of imagining, takes as its object another type of conscious state of mind, a sensory experience. (2002: 404)

Peacocke (1985) claims:

To imagine something is always at least to imagine, from the inside, being in some conscious state. (21)

To imagine being Φ . . . is always at least to imagine from the inside an experience as of being Φ. (22)

And according to Vendler,

The material *ex qua* of all imagination is imagined experience and other sensations, feelings and sentiments–subjective things. These are the atoms out of which the world of imagination, subjective and objective is constructed. (1984: 34)

I said earlier that it seems that one can't adequately account for the phenomenal character of an act of perceptual imagination by simply appealing to the fact that its *object*—i.e. *what is imagined*—is a phenomenally conscious perceptual experience or sensation. For it seems that if one is to be informed about the phenomenal character of the event of imagining, one must not only be told what is being imagined, but also the *way* in which one is imagining it. Hence, in the case of imagining an itch, the stress on the idea that one is imagining the itch 'from the inside'. And one might suspect that all the important explanatory work here is being left to a notion which itself remains obscure and unexplained—i.e. the notion of imagining something *from the inside*. However, accepting this line of thought need not lead one to dismiss the dependency thesis as incorrect. For in accepting this line of thought one is merely acknowledging the limitations that an appeal to the dependency thesis might have when it comes to accounting for the phenomenal character of perceptual imagining, and the respects in which its phenomenal

---

[2] Foster 1982, Vendler 1984, Peacocke 1985, Martin 2001 and 2002.

character is similar to its corresponding perceptual experience or sensation. But why think the dependency thesis is true?

In arguing for the dependency thesis, Martin appeals to certain perspectival aspects of visualizing that appear to correspond with certain perspectival features of visual experience. He notes that one often visualizes from a point of view, and gives as an example a case in which one visualizes a red light to the left and a green light to the right. He claims that if you now visualize the reverse—a green light to the left and a red one to the right—how you are visualizing is different from the first case, and furthermore, what is visualized is different. The two situations that are visualized can only count as different if there is a point of view relative to which the one light is to the left and the other is to the right. But is this point of view itself imagined?

If the point of view relative to which the lights are imagined as being to the left and right is not itself imagined, then one will be imagining the lights to be to one's *actual* left and to one's *actual* right. This is something one could do—one might imaginatively project the imagined lights onto locations to the left and right in one's actual environment—but, says Martin, this is not necessary, and nor is it the simplest case of visualizing. In the simplest case, one is not imagining the lights to be to one's *actual* left and to one's *actual* right, occupying locations in one's actual environment. In the simplest case, the point of view relative to which the objects are imagined as being to the left and right is itself imagined. What is represented is not the actual position of the imagined lights relative to oneself. Rather, what is represented is the point of view from which the lights are imagined as being to the left and right.

[W]hat difference need there be in the imagined scene in order for what has been imagined to be different in the two cases? . . . The two situations count as different only where there is a point of view relative to which the one object is to the left and the other to the right, or *vice versa*. So, if we absent a point of view from the imagined scene, then what appears in visualising to be a difference in the scene imagined, and not just a difference in one's state of mind, cannot be so . . . if one does have to imagine a point of view within the scene, then one thereby must be imagining an experience within the scene. (2002: 408–9)

According to Martin, one visualizes the lights as being to the left and right through imagining a point of view relative to which they are to the left and right, and one imagines this point of view through imagining an experience with the appropriate perspectival feature—i.e. one in which lights are experienced to the left and right. So in certain central cases of visualizing, one visualizes objects through imagining an experience of them.

One of Vendler's (1984) arguments also appeals to perspectival features of perceptual imagining, although Vendler appeals to linguistic considerations rather than phenomenological ones. Vendler claims that when we talk of imagining x, where x is some object or event, there is a suppressed perceptual verb: imagining x is elliptical for 'imagining *seeing/hearing* x', for example. He argues that the suppressed perceptual verb can be demonstrated by considering certain adverbs such sentences can take. He invites us to consider the following sentences:

> Imagine the battlefield from above.
> Imagine the statue sideways.
> Imagine the music coming from a distance.

He argues that in contrast to an adverb like 'vividly', which can modify the verb imagine itself, these adverbs modify suppressed perceptual verbs—seeing and hearing in these cases. If these adverbs were to modify the verb imagine itself, rather than the deleted perceptual verbs, then nothing would prevent the formulation of such sentences as:

> Imagine a thunderbolt from the side.
> Imagine the taste of lemon from above.

These arguments for the dependency thesis appeal to certain spatial perspectival aspects of perceptual imagining, but one might also appeal to temporal aspects of the phenomenology of perceptual imagining in support of the thesis. For example, when one perceptually imagines the occurrence of a temporally extended event, there is a respect in which one perceptually imagines the occurrence of the different temporal parts of the event as 'successively present'. When one imagines the successive unfolding of the temporally extended occurrence (e.g. the utterance of a speech), it seems to one as though one is successively imagining different temporal parts of that unfolding occurrence, and there is a sense in which each successive phase of the act of imagining represents each temporal part of the imagined event as being temporally present. However, one needn't be imagining that the event is occurring at the time at which one is engaged in the act of perceptual imagining. One could be imagining a future event; and when one is imagining a future event, one is not thereby imagining that one's act of imagining is occurring in the future. The dependency thesis accommodates the respect in which one imagines the occurrence of the different temporal parts of the event as being successively present without involving the idea that one is imagining the event to occur at the time of imagining. For in imagining an experience of an event, one will thereby be imagining a temporal perspective on that event—the temporal perspective of an experience that presents each temporal part of the event as temporally present—but one needn't be imagining that the experience of the event is occurring at the time at which the act of perceptual imagining is actually occurring.

However, one might object to the dependency thesis on the grounds that often when we visualize objects or events, imagining an experience of those objects and events is no part of our imaginative project.[3] The thought here is that the dependency thesis mistakenly commits to the idea that we are doing more than we are actually doing in most cases of perceptual imagination. When one visualizes an object, one need not be, thereby, imagining a visual experience of the object. The dependency thesis commits to the idea

---

[3] See Williams 1973a. See also Currie and Ravenscroft 2002 and Noordhof 2002.

that in many cases of perceptual imagining we are overpopulating our imaginary worlds.

In support of this line of objection one might argue that the case of imagining a bodily sensation, like an itch or pain, is exceptional and so can be misleading. If, as I argued in Chapter 3, such bodily sensations are mind-dependent bodily events, then one cannot imagine the occurrence of such a bodily sensation without thereby imagining an experience of it. Imagining the occurrence of such a bodily event entails imagining the experience of such a bodily event. So, arguably, in the case of imagining a bodily sensation of pain, the dependency thesis holds, inasmuch as one kind of conscious mental act, one's perceptually imagining the bodily sensation, takes as its object a phenomenal bodily event whose occurrence entails a conscious experience of it. However, when it comes to perceptually imagining mind-independent objects and events (e.g. visualizing a red square), the same line of reasoning does not apply.

A further and related concern about the dependency thesis is this. If visualizing a red square involves imagining a visual experience of a red square, what kind of imagining is involved in imagining the visual experience of a red square? It seems that a defender of the dependency thesis should not maintain that one *perceptually* imagines the visual experience of the red square, for according to the dependency thesis this would involve imagining an experience of a visual experience of a red square. The problem with this proposal is not just that it is controversial to hold that we experience our perceptual experiences, but also that it raises the further question of what kind of imagining is involved in imagining the experience of a visual experience of a red square. If the defender of the dependency thesis claims that when one visualizes a red square one doesn't *perceptually* imagine a red square, but imagines *that* (perhaps supposes that) there is a visual experience of a red square, then this makes even more pressing the objection that when visualizing a red square, supposing that there is a visual experience of the square need be no part of one's imaginative project.

This point also connects with the respect in which one might think that an appeal to the dependency thesis can have only limited explanatory value when it comes to accounting for the phenomenal character of perceptual imagining and for accounting for the way in which its phenomenal character is similar to a corresponding perceptual experience or sensation. I said earlier that it seems inadequate simply to say that an act of perceptually imagining a sensation has its phenomenal character in virtue of the fact that its *object*—i.e. *what is imagined*—is a phenomenally conscious sensation, for usually being told what a subject is thinking about does not in itself tell one anything about the phenomenal character of the activity of her thinking. And being told that a subject is *supposing* that there is a visual experience of a red square does not tell us anything much about the phenomenology of her act of imagination. Indeed, it is consistent with her failing to visualize a red square. I said that if one is to be informed about the phenomenal character of an event of imagining, one must not only be told what is being imagined, but also the *way* in which it is being imagined.

The plausibility of the dependency thesis (for example, the resources that it has at its disposal to respond to the 'overpopulation' objection that I just outlined) and the explanatory value of the dependency thesis in accounting for the phenomenology of acts of perceptual imagining will depend in large part on the account that is given of the way in which visual experiences are imagined when one visualizes an object. This issue is the focus of the next section of the chapter, where I shall be making some proposals about the ontology of perceptual imagination

7.3 The ontology of perceptual imagination

According to the dependency thesis, when one perceptually imagines a Φ, one imagines experiencing a Φ. But if the dependency thesis is true, what sort of imagining takes as its object an experience of a Φ when one perceptually imagines a Φ? There are reasons for thinking that the form of imagining involved isn't that of perceptually imagining an experience of a Φ and there are reasons for thinking that the imagining involved isn't that of supposing that there is an experience of a Φ. My proposal is that the form of imagining involved is that of imagining what it would be like to experience a Φ.

'Imagine what it would be like to experience a Φ' can be issued as an instruction. In complying with the instruction, what is one doing? The instruction contains an embedded question: 'what would it be like to experience a Φ?' In attempting to comply with the instruction, one is attempting to do something that answers the question. We should think of imagining what it would be like to experience a Φ as doing something that attempts to answer the question 'what would it be like to experience a Φ?', and my suggestion is that when one perceptually imagines a Φ one is doing something that answers that question.

Suppose one thinks of the answer to the question as being propositional in form— e.g. 'this is what it would be like to experience a Φ'—and so thinks of one's perceptual imagining as having an intentional content. The intentional content of the perceptual imagining, so construed, is not a content one is taking an imagining attitude towards. That is, in doing something that answers the question 'what would it be like to experience a Φ?', one is not *imagining that* 'this is what it would be like to experience a Φ'. For in taking an imagining attitude towards a proposition, one treats the proposition as true irrespective of whether it is true, whereas one's aim in imagining what it would be like to experience a Φ is to do something that gives a *correct* answer to the question 'what would it be like to experience a Φ?' So if we think of the answer as the content of the imagining, then the content of the act of imagining, so construed, aims at truth. My suggestion is that we should think of the content of perceptual imagination, so construed, as the content of a mental *state* that aims at truth and that represents what it would be like to experience a Φ. If we regard a case of imagining what it would be like to experience a Φ as one's doing something that answers the question, then we can regard a case of one's imagining what it would be like to experience a Φ as an episode that manifests a mental state that represents the phenomenal character of the experience one would be having if one were experiencing a Φ.

Of course, more needs to be said about what is distinctive of the way in which an episode of perceptual imagining gives an answer to the question 'what would it be like to experience a Φ?' For there are answers one can give to the question that do not involve any episode of perceptual imagining—e.g. one can give the answer 'it would be awful/wonderful', etc. In such a case, one's answer is the content of a judgement or assertion. The judgement or assertion is a manifestation of a belief, and the content of the judgement or assertion is the content of the belief of which it is a manifestation. In the case of perceptual imagination, although the content that is one's answer to the question is the content of a mental state that aims at truth, it is not the content of an act of judging or assertion. When one perceptually imagines a Φ, one does something that answers the question 'what would it be like to experience a Φ?', in so far as one's episode of perceptual imagining is to be thought of as an episode that manifests a mental state that represents what it would be like to experience a Φ. The content of the *state* manifested in the episode of perceptual imagining represents what it would be like to experience a Φ, but the *episode* of perceptual imagining that manifests that mental state is not itself an episode of judging the content of that mental state. So how should we think of the relation between the episode of perceptual imagining and the mental state of which it is a manifestation?

Central to the answer I want to offer to this question is an account of the ontology of perceptual imagining that parallels in some significant ways the account I have been proposing about the ontology of conscious sensory experience. I have been arguing that conscious sensory experience involves the occurrence of phenomenally conscious events/processes and the obtaining of phenomenally conscious 'occurrent' states. When such a phenomenally conscious event/process occurs, a phenomenally conscious 'occurrent' state obtains, and the obtaining of that state is constitutively dependent on the occurrence of the phenomenally conscious event/process. The occurrence and state in question have an interdependent status, in so far as the nature of the occurrence is to be specified, at least in part, in terms of the kind of state that obtains when it occurs, and the nature of the state is to be specified, at least in part, in terms of the kind of occurrence that its obtaining is constitutively dependent on. The account of the ontology of perceptual imagining that I want to offer also invokes the general idea that we need to appeal both to the occurrence of a phenomenally conscious episode and the obtaining of a conscious state, and that the state and occurrence in question have an interdependent status.

In skeletal form the proposal is this. When a subject perceptually imagines a Φ, a phenomenally conscious episode occurs. Unlike the case of conscious sensory experience, the state that obtains when such an episode occurs is not a perceptual state that is intentionally directed on the subject's environment, but rather a mental state that aims at truth and that represents the phenomenal character of an experience of a Φ. The mental state that obtains when the phenomenally conscious episode of imagining occurs is an 'occurrent' state whose obtaining is constitutively dependent on the phenomenally conscious episode of imagining. The nature of the phenomenally conscious episode that occurs when one perceptually imagines a Φ is to be specified, at least in part, in terms of the kind of occurrent mental state that obtains when that episode occurs, and the nature of the mental state that obtains when the phenomenally conscious episode of imagining occurs is to be specified, at least in part, in terms of the kind of phenomenally conscious episode that it is constitutively dependent on. So again we have a case in which a phenomenally conscious occurrence and a conscious mental state have an interdependent status. When it comes to specifying the phenomenal character of a phenomenally conscious episode of perceptually imagining a Φ we do so by appeal to the obtaining of a state that represents the phenomenal character of an experience of a Φ, and when it comes to specifying the content of that mental state we do so by appealing to the phenomenal character of the episode of perceptually imagining a Φ.

I have said that the mental state that obtains when one perceptually imagines a Φ is an 'occurrent' one whose obtaining constitutively depends on the occurrence of the episode of perceptual imagining. But can't one retain in memory a mental state that represents what it would be like to experience a Φ when one isn't actually engaged in an episode of perceptual imagining? According to the account I am proposing, such a mental state is retained in memory only in so far as one retains the capacity to engage in appropriate episodes of perceptual imagining. If one loses the capacity to engage in such episodes, then one no longer retains that mental state in memory. Given that there is a sense in which the mental state that represents what it would be like to experience a Φ can be retained when one isn't actually engaged in an episode of perceptual imagining a Φ, we can think of the episode of perceptual imagining as an episode that *manifests* a mental state that represents what it would be like to experience a Φ, but the content of the mental state that one retains when one retains the capacity to engage in episodes of perceptually imagining a Φ is determined by the phenomenal character of the episodes of perceptual imagining that one retains the capacity to engage in; for the content of the mental state that is retained when one isn't actually engaged in an episode of perceptual imagining is determined by the content of the *occurrent* mental state that obtains when one is actually engaged in such an episode of perceptual imagining, which in turn is determined, at least in part, by the phenomenal character of the episode of perceptual imagining.

How does this account of perceptual imagination bear on the dependency thesis? Martin's endorsement of the dependency thesis is accompanied by an endorsement of Sartre's rejection of the background assumption made in much philosophical work on imagery that 'imagistic experience or consciousness is a neutral core common to perception and imagery' (Martin 2001: 271).[4] The dependency thesis is appealed to in an explanation of why Sartre is right to reject this assumption. Martin claims we should

---

[4] See Sartre 1948: 261.

think of perceptual experience and imagery 'as being phenomenologically the same not in terms of literally sharing experiential properties, but in virtue of a representational or intentional connection between them—imagery is experientially the same as perception through being the representation of such a perceptually experiential event' (2001: 270). This claim is in line with the account of perceptual imagination I have just outlined. The phenomenological connection between an episode of perceptual imagining and its corresponding perceptual experience or sensation is explained by a 'representational or intentional connection between them'. For under my account, the phenomenal character of one's episode of perceptual imagining should be thought of as determining the content of a mental state that aims at truth and which the episode manifests; and the intentional object of this mental state is the phenomenal character of the perceptual experience one would be having if one were perceptually aware of the entity one is perceptually imagining. However, under my account, the intentional connection between an episode of perceptual imagining a Φ and its corresponding perceptual experience does not hold in virtue of the fact that a perceptual experience of a Φ is *perceptually* imagined; and it does not hold in virtue of the fact that one *supposes* that there is a perceptual experience of a Φ either. For the state that represents the phenomenal character of an experience when one engages in an episode of perceptual imagination is a mental state that aims at truth. This point is relevant to the 'overpopulation' objection to the dependency thesis I mentioned earlier.

When one visualizes a red square, so the objection runs, surely one can simply imagine the red square, without having to imagine a visual experience of it as well. As it is sometimes put, in visualizing the red square, one need not populate one's imaginary world with a visual experience of the red square. Although the square is part of the imagined scene, a visual experience of it need not be. We can now see that there is a sense in which this objection is quite right. When one visualizes an object or event, one need not, thereby, be *perceptually* imagining an experience of it, and one need not be *supposing* that there is an experience of it. So if what it is for something to populate one's imaginary world—to be part of the scene imagined—is for it to be perceptually imagined, or for one to suppose that it exists, then when one visualizes one need not be, thereby, overpopulating one's imaginary world with experiences of objects, as well as the objects themselves. So although I think the dependency thesis is correct, inasmuch as when one perceptually imagines an object one imagines being perceptually aware of it, the gloss that is sometimes put on what this claim commits one to can be misleading. While I think it is true that when one visualizes an object, one imagines experiencing that object, we should unpack the claim that one imagines experiencing the object as the claim that one *imagines what it would be like* to experience the object, and I have suggested an account of what this claim amounts to. It involves engaging in an episode that manifests a mental state that aims at truth and that represents what it would be like to experience the object.

A further concern one might have with the dependency thesis is the worry that it commits one to a view on which one somehow *under*populates the imagined world when one visualizes. The objection runs as follows. According to the account I've proposed, when one visualizes a Φ there obtains a mental state that represents the phenomenal character of a visual experience of a Φ. But the occurrence of a phenomenally conscious visual experience of a Φ doesn't entail the existence of a Φ. And when one visualizes a red square, doesn't one thereby represent a red square, and not just an experience of a red square? So doesn't an adherent of the dependency thesis commit to a view which somehow underpopulates the perceptually imagined world through failing to capture the fact that when one visualizes a Φ one's episode of visualizing is not neutral as to whether the imagined scene contains a Φ?

The relational component of the account of the ontology of conscious sensory experience that I have argued for can provide a response to this line of objection. According to that account, when a subject successfully perceives the world, an 'occurrent' phenomenally conscious perceptual state obtains, and the nature of that phenomenally conscious state is to be specified, at least in part, in terms of a non-representational psychological relation of perceptual acquaintance that obtains between the subject and the mind-independent entities that the subject perceives. So according to this relational view of the phenomenal character of conscious sensory experience, when one represents the phenomenal character of a conscious visual experience of a Φ one thereby represents the obtaining of a psychological relation to a Φ—the non-representational psychological relation of perceptual acquaintance. So when one visualizes a Φ there obtains an occurrent mental state that represents the phenomenal character of a visual experience of a Φ, which involves representing a non-representational visual awareness of a Φ, and which thereby involves representing a Φ.[5]

This aspect of the account is also relevant to the way in which an episode of perceptual imagination can be thought of as a form of non-propositional imagining. There are varieties of imagining that one can engage in that take propositional objects. That is to say, when engaged in some imaginative project one may be imagining or supposing *that* such and such is the case. I shall be saying more about such propositional forms of imagining, and in particular supposition, in Part II. The point I want to make for now is this. While it doesn't make sense to say 'suppose an x', where x is some object or event, it does make sense to say 'imagine an x'. The psychological verb 'imagine' can take a non-propositional object, in so far as it can be followed by a noun-phrase that refers to some object, event, or feature; and when the verb 'imagine' takes a non-propositional object in this way, the sort of imagining picked out is that of perceptual imagining. The account of perceptual imagining I've offered can explain why this should be so.

According to the account of the ontology of perceptual imagining that I've outlined, when a phenomenally conscious episode of perceptually imagining a Φ occurs, there obtains an 'occurrent' mental state that represents the phenomenal character of an experience of a Φ. But although the act of perceptual imagining is an episode that manifests

---

[5] Such considerations are appealed to by Martin in his 2002 argument for a naïve realist account of perception.

a mental state that represents the phenomenal character of an experience of a Φ, the episode of imagining is not itself one of judging, or even supposing, the content of the occurrent mental state that it manifests. It's rather that the conscious character of the episode of imagining determines the content of the occurrent mental state that obtains when the conscious episode of imagining occurs. This occurrent mental state represents a phenomenally conscious experience of a Φ, and thereby represents a non-representational awareness of a Φ. In the episode of perceptual imagining, a Φ is thereby represented. The Φ represented in the act of imagining need not be an actually existing Φ, and when it isn't, an imaginary Φ—i.e. non-existent Φ—is represented in the episode of imagining. But although one represents an imaginary Φ in the episode of perceptual imagination without thereby believing that such a Φ exists, this does not amount to one's *supposing that* a Φ exists. For according to the account I've offered, an imaginary Φ is represented in the act of perceptual imagination without one's taking a suppositional attitude towards a propositional content that concerns a Φ. In that sense, the act of perceptual imagination can be regarded as a case of the non-propositional imagining of a Φ.

Let us briefly summarize some of the main points covered so far. I started the chapter by suggesting that it is natural to think that (a) one couldn't be engaged in the activity of perceptually imagining something without the occurrence of phenomenally conscious events, and (b) the phenomenal character of the events involved determine, at least in part, and in some important way, the kind of activity one is engaged in. I noted that the phenomenology of an act of perceptual imagining seems to have some significant connection with the phenomenology of some corresponding conscious sensory experience. However, I also noted that there is reason to think that although it seems that there is a significant correspondence between the phenomenology of an act of perceptual imagination and the phenomenology of a conscious sensory experience, there are also important differences between them, and there is reason to think that these differences are differences in kind, and not just in degree. The account of the ontology of perceptual imagination that I've been outlining accommodates each of these points.

This account is in line with Martin's suggestion that imagination relates to perception 'not through replicating the sensational or imagistic component of perception, but through being a form of representing such experiential encounter with the world' (2001: 273–4). This is what makes the difference between the phenomenal character of an act of imagination and the phenomenal character of conscious sensory experience a difference in kind, and not just in degree. However, the way in which conscious sensory experience is represented in perceptual imagination necessarily involves the occurrence of a phenomenally conscious episode. For when one perceptually imagines something, it is the phenomenal character of the episode of perceptual imagining that determines the content of a state that represents a conscious sensory experience of that thing. In determining the content of a state that represents the phenomenal character of a conscious sensory experience, the phenomenal character of the episode of imagining thereby determines what objects, events, and features are perceptually imagined. So the phenomenal character of the episode of perceptual imagining determines, at least in part, and in some important way, the kind of activity one is engaged in. The conscious character of the episode of perceptual imagining is to be specified, at least in part, in terms of the occurrent mental state that obtains when it occurs, and this mental state, which aims at truth, represents the phenomenal character of a conscious sensory experience. So specification of the phenomenal character of the episode of perceptual imagining will necessarily involve reference to the conscious character of a conscious sensory experience. This aspect of the account accommodates the fact that the phenomenology of an act of perceptual imagining seems to have some significant connection with the phenomenology of some corresponding conscious sensory experience.

I also noted at the outset that there appears to be a parallel between the temporal profile of an act of perceptual imagining and the temporal profile of conscious sensory experience. In outlining my account of the ontology of perceptual imagination I noted some parallels with the account I've been offering of the ontology of conscious sensory experience. In both cases we need to appeal to the occurrence of phenomenally conscious events/processes as well as the obtaining of 'occurrent' conscious states. In both cases the phenomenally conscious occurrences and states in question have an interdependent status. This similarity in the accounts of the ontology of each accommodates the fact that these different aspects of mind fill time in similar ways. Finally, I have also suggested that the account of perceptual imagination that I have offered can accommodate and explain the respect in which perceptual imagination can be thought of as a form of non-propositional imagining. In the next section I shall be suggesting how this general proposal about perceptual imagination can be applied in an account of perceptual recollection.

7.4 Perceptual memory and episodic recollection

A very natural thought is that perceptual imagination exploits perceptual memory. For example, when I perceptually imagine an acquaintance of mine playing the opening bars of Beethoven's Fifth on a harmonica, although I may be imagining an event of a kind that I have never witnessed, in doing so I am exploiting perceptual memories of things that I have witnessed—e.g. a perceptual memory of the appearance of my acquaintance, a perceptual memory of the sound of a harmonica, a perceptual memory of the sound of the opening bars of Beethoven's Fifth, and so on.

When it comes to considering the notion of memory in general, a natural starting point is the thought that to say that a subject remembers something is to assume that some knowledge the subject has, or had, has been preserved or retained. So, for instance, to say that a subject remembers some fact is to assume that the subject's knowledge of that fact has been retained. To say that a subject remembers a person or place is to assume that the subject's knowledge of that person or place (or the knowledge she had of that person or place) has been retained. And to say that a subject remembers how to do something is to assume that the subject's knowledge of how to do that thing has been retained. If one holds that perceptual imagination exploits a form of memory—perceptual memory—then one might think that perceptual imagination exploits a form of knowledge that one has that has been retained over time.

In his *Psychology of the Imagination*, Sartre claims that 'Nothing can be learnt from an image that is not already known . . . I shall never find anything in the image but what I put there' (1948: 11). This claim is perhaps an overstatement, as it seems that we can discover new things about objects through imagining them.[6] However, if perceptual imagination exploits perceptual memory and perceptual memory involves a form of retained knowledge, then there might be something to Sartre's claim that 'An image could not exist without a knowledge that constitutes it' (1948: 11). But if perceptual memory involves a form of retained knowledge, what account should be given of this variety of knowledge? I'll address this question by first focusing on a sub-variety of perceptual memory—that of episodic recollection.

In the case of episodic recollection, that which is recollected is a particular past event that one has witnessed or performed. Earlier I said that there is a sense in which perceptual recollection, of which episodic recollection is a sub-variety, is not truly receptive in the way that perception is. When one successfully perceives some entity, one can explain why the perceptual experience involved occurs when it occurs by citing the temporal location of events involving the item perceived. But this form of explanation is not available in the case of episodic recollection. One cannot explain why such an episode of recollection occurs when it occurs by citing the temporal location of events involving the entity recollected. In that sense, episodic recollection is not passive, or receptive, in the way that perception is, for the temporal location of an event of episodic recollection is not passive with respect to the temporal location of its object in the way that successful perception is.

When one tries to recollect some past event, and one mentally reaches for some patch of the past, that past episode cannot causally sustain some *current* episode of one's recollecting what happened (although it did in the past causally sustain the past perceptual experience of it, and this may be crucial to explaining the nature of the episode of recollection).[7] This may then suggest that *I* am causally responsible for my current episode of recollecting. That is to say, when I mentally reach for the past with a question, no past event will causally sustain some current mental episode that provides me with an answer to the question. Only *I* can provide an answer to my question, and my act of recollection is my act of providing such an answer. So in this respect one might think that an act of episodic recollection is like an act of judging.

---

[6] For a seminal discussion of this issue, see Kosslyn 1996.

[7] One aspect of the phenomenology of episodic recollection is the current absence of its object. Although the event may strike one as the kind of event that cannot occur without the past occurrence of its object, it does not strike one as the kind of event that cannot occur without the *current presence* of its object. Furthermore, if the object of the act of recollection is a past occurrence, it cannot be the kind of thing that one conjures into existence in order to causally sustain the current episode of recollection. So although the *act* of episodic recollection may strike one as something one has conjured into existence, its *object* does not.

However, if there are certain respects in which an act of episodic recollection is some-what like an act of judging, there are also significant respects in which it is quite unlike an act of judging. To think of an act of episodic recollection as like an act of judging about the past suggests an account that assimilates episodic recollection to a variety of factual, or semantic, recollection, and a number of philosophers have argued that such assimilation is a mistake. Earlier I said that one might think of perceptual imagining as a form of non-propositional imagining, and there are similar reasons for thinking of episodic recollection as a form of non-propositional recollection. The verb 'remember' (or 'recollect') can be followed by the propositional complement 'that' and a proposition that concerns a partic-ular past event—e.g. I can remember *that* John dropped the precious vase—but it can also be followed by a noun-phrase that refers to a particular past event—e.g. I can remember John dropping the precious vase. There are reasons for thinking that this verbal difference reflects a genuine difference in the nature of the acts of recollection that are picked out. In the case of an act of episodic recollection, in contrast to an act of semantic recollection, it is much more intuitive to think that the phenomenal character of the episode of recollecting determines, at least in part, and in an important way, what event is recollected. Moreover, an act of episodic recollection appears to have a temporal profile that is significantly similar to one's original experience of the event recollected. One's episodic recollection of a past event unfolds over time in a way that is similar to the experience one had of that event, and this isn't true of an act of the semantic recollection of some fact about that event.

In the case of perceptually imagining the occurrence of some event with temporal extension, I suggested that there is a respect in which one perceptually imagines the occurrence of the different temporal parts of the event as 'successively present'. When one imagines the successive unfolding of the temporally extended occurrence (e.g. the utterance of a speech), it seems to one as though one is successively imagining different temporal parts of that unfolding occurrence, and there is a sense in which each succes-sive phase of the act of imagining represents each temporal part of the imagined event as being temporally present. Similar remarks apply in the case of episodic recollection. When one episodically recollects some temporally extended past event, there is a respect in which one recollects the occurrence of the different temporal parts of the event as 'successively present'. When one recollects the successive unfolding of that temporally extended event, it seems to one as though one is successively recollecting the different temporal parts of that unfolding occurrence, and there is a sense in which each succes-sive phase of the act of recollection represents each temporal part of the event recol-lected as being temporally present. It remains true that the event recollected is presented as past. However, there is a sense in which that past event is relived in the act of recollect-ing it. This connects with the way in which some have argued that episodic recollection is like a form of 'mental time-travel', a case of revisiting, or reacquaintance with, some past episode.[8] And for those who claim that an act of episodic recollection is a form of

---

[8] See, Russell 1912: 26 and 1992: 70 ff. and 171 ff., McDowell 1978: 306, Tulving 1982: 331, Campbell 2001: 171–4, Hoerl 2001: 329, Martin 2001: 259.

reacquaintance with some past episode, part of the idea is to emphasize the respects in which an act of recollection is not like one of judging some proposition about that past event.

If the nature of an act of episodic recollection is quite unlike an act of semantic recollection, does this reflect a difference in what is retained in memory in each case? In the case of semantic recollection, it seems clear that that which is retained in memory, and which underlies one's capacity to recollect facts, is propositional knowledge. But what is retained in memory in the case of episodic recollection?

In his discussion of episodic recollection, Martin argues that 'we cannot conceive of such remembering as the preservation of *knowledge*, for one cannot know what one now recollects in episodic memory' (2001: 264). That which is recollected is a particular past event.

In such cases as 'Mary remembers John falling asleep in the talk', where the derived nominal here picks out an event or episode which is being recalled, there is no well-formed substitution using a term for knowledge. 'Mary knows/knew John falling asleep in the talk' is simply not English. (2001: 264)

As Martin remarks, we are reluctant to talk of knowing events or episodes. He offers the following explanation of why this is so:

Apprehension is episodic: seeing, feeling, tasting something are all events or occurrences. Knowledge itself is a standing condition–although one can know something at a particular time, knowledge itself is not episodic. Nevertheless, the state of knowledge is closely linked to episodes of apprehension: one must have apprehended an individual at some time to know them, and to continue knowing them one must have the possibility of further apprehensions of them. Now, while we can apprehend events through perceiving them, in general we do not take ourselves to be in a position to re-apprehend them. Hence, apprehension of an event is not a precursor to a standing condition of cognitive contact with what is apprehended, and so does not lead to knowing the event, although one will, of course, tend to acquire knowledge of the event. (2001: 267)

Martin goes on to suggest that this gives us reason to think of apprehension and knowledge as closely connected—the former being the episodic counterpart of the latter standing condition—and both involving forms of cognitive contact with an object. Martin then proposes that we state a general condition on memory as that of preserving *either* knowledge *or* past apprehension:

When we turn to episodic memory, if we are to ask what it is that is retained in such memory, the answer would seem to be past apprehension of the event now recalled. One's memory of the episode is simply the retained apprehension or acquaintance with a past happening. (2001: 267)

A general concern one might have with this proposal is how we are to make sense of the idea of *retained* apprehension. Martin claims that an apprehension is 'episodic'—an 'event or occurrence'. However, it is not clear how a past apprehension can be retained if it is an occurrence—something episodic. Occurrences that have duration are not 'retained', or 'preserved'. Although it seems right to claim that mental states can be preserved or retained, it doesn't seem right to say that mental events can be preserved or retained. But then if we deny that past apprehensions can be retained, and only allow that mental states can be retained, aren't we back with the suggestion that what is retained in episodic memory is a mental state—a standing condition? And so why not a standing condition of knowledge?

Let us return to one of the examples Martin uses to argue that in the case of episodic memory we cannot conceive of such remembering as the preservation of knowledge: 'Mary remembers John falling asleep in the talk.' In this case, Martin suggests, there is no well-formed substitution for what is remembered using a term for knowledge. This would seem to be a prime example of non-propositional recollection. Mary non-propositionally recollects a particular past event. The sentence does not report that Mary remembers that *p*, where *p* is some proposition about the event of John's falling asleep. In the earlier discussion of non-propositional imagining, the suggestion was that to non-propositionally imagine an object or event is to perceptually imagine that object or event; and to perceptually imagine that object or event is, in turn, to imagine being perceptually aware of it. So if we consider a sentence of the form 'Mary *imagines* John falling asleep in the talk', Vendler's suggestion was that there is a deleted perceptual verb here, and so the sentence is elliptical for, e.g. 'Mary imagines *hearing* John falling asleep in the talk.' Let us apply this idea to Martin's example of non-propositional recollection.

The idea here is that just as in the case of the sentence about Mary's non-propositional imagining, there is a deleted perceptual verb here. 'Mary remembers John falling asleep in the talk' is elliptical for, e.g. 'Mary remembers *hearing* John falling asleep in the talk.' Does this help us with our attempt to find a well-formed substitution for what is remembered using a term for knowledge? Again, let us go back to the case of perceptual imagination. There I suggested that 'S imagines seeing x' should be unpacked as 'S imagines what it would be like to see x'. So the analogous unpacking of 'Mary remembers hearing John falling asleep in the talk' would be 'Mary remembers *what it was like to hear* John falling asleep in the talk.' This unpacking of the original sentence does, after all, seem to give us a sentence in which we can make a well-formed substitution for what is remembered using a term for knowledge—i.e. 'Mary knows what it was like to hear John falling asleep in the talk.' I suggest that what is retained in the case of episodic memory is knowledge of an apprehension, i.e. a perception, of a past event, and in particular, knowledge of what it was like to apprehend the particular event now recollected. Is this to assimilate episodic memory to semantic memory?

If one's knowledge of what it was like to apprehend some event is simply propositional knowledge—knowledge that *p*—then this suggests that the acts of recollection that this knowledge underlies are acts of semantic recollection—acts of recollecting that *p*. So if we wish to maintain that acts of episodic recollection should not be assimilated to a variety of semantic recollection, then it seems we have reason to deny that the preserved knowledge that underlies one's ability to recollect past events should be thought of as propositional knowledge. But there are reasons for thinking that 'knowing what' is a form of propositional knowledge. So does this undermine the suggestion that what is retained in the case of episodic recollection is knowledge of what it was like to perceive a past event?

I think it may help to compare the case of 'know how'. It has been argued that 'know how', like 'know what', should be thought of as a variety of propositional knowledge. 'S knows how to Φ' contains an embedded question: 'how does one Φ?', just as 'S knows what to do' contains an embedded question: 'what should one do?'. In each case, to ascribe such knowledge to a subject is to ascribe to the subject knowledge of an answer to the question, and in each case the answer the subject knows is propositional in form. So the idea is that in the case of know how, what one knows when one knows how to Φ is propositional in form, e.g. 'This is a way of Φ-ing', where the way of Φ-ing is presented under a practical mode of presentation.[9] Many, I think, share the intuition that there is something unsatisfactory in assimilating know how to straightforward propositional knowledge. Remembering how to do something should not be assimilated to semantic memory—remembering some fact. What is retained in the case of remembering how to do something should not be assimilated to retained propositional knowledge. Procedural memory is to be contrasted with semantic memory.

In the case of 'know how', is the proposition that is an answer to the question 'how does one Φ?' (i.e. the proposition 'this is a way to Φ') the propositional content of a state of knowledge that is retained over time? As the way of Φ-ing is presented under a practical mode of presentation, one might argue that this state of propositional knowledge is an 'occurrent' state of knowledge that lasts only so long as one's act of Φ-ing. So what then is retained over time? As long as one is able to Φ (or perhaps recollect Φ-ing), one has an ability to do something that puts one in an occurrent state of knowledge whose propositional content is a distinctive kind of answer to the question 'how does one Φ?'. For one's ability to Φ makes possible one's knowing a way of Φ-ing under a practical mode of presentation. So in the case of know how, that which is retained over time is an ability to do something that can put one in an occurrent state of knowledge whose propositional content is a distinctive kind of answer to the question, 'how does one Φ?'.

I suggest that there is something similar going on in the case of episodic memory. One knows what it was like to apprehend some past event in the sense that one has an ability to do something that can put oneself in an occurrent state of knowledge whose propositional content is a distinctive kind of answer to the question, 'what was it like to apprehend that event?'. The occurrent state of knowledge whose content is an answer to the question (the propositional knowledge that 'this is what it was like to apprehend that event') obtains in virtue of the occurrence of a phenomenally conscious mental episode of recollecting the event and lasts only so long as the phenomenally conscious mental episode of recollecting. The obtaining of this occurrent state of propositional knowledge requires the occurrence of the event of recollecting.

---

[9] See Stanley and Williamson 2001, and see also Snowdon 2003.

Although I have argued that episodic recollection is not to be assimilated to a variety of semantic recollection, and so is not a case of judging a proposition about some past event, the account accommodates a sense in which it is true to say that I cannot recollect what I don't already know. For an act of episodic recollection manifests my knowledge of what it was like to apprehend a particular past occurrence, and this knowledge is retained in memory prior to the act of recollection. However, this retained knowledge is not to be thought of as retained propositional knowledge, but rather as a retained ability to do something that puts one in an occurrent state of propositional knowledge whose propositional content is a distinctive kind of answer to the question 'what was it like to apprehend that particular?'. Although the answer may be propositional in form, the episode of recollecting is not an episode of recollecting that p. It is, rather, an episode the occurrence of which is required for the obtaining of the occurrent state of knowing that p.

The parallels with the account of perceptual imagination that I've outlined should be clear. In both cases the occurrence of a phenomenally conscious episode manifests an occurrent mental state that represents the phenomenal character of a conscious sensory experience. In both cases the phenomenally conscious mental episode that occurs and the occurrent conscious mental state that obtains when it occurs have an interdependent status. The obtaining of the occurrent mental state depends constitutively on the occurrence of the phenomenally conscious mental episode, and the phenomenal character of that mental episode determines, at least in part, the content of that occurrent mental state. Furthermore, the phenomenal character of the mental episode is to be specified, at least in part, in terms of the kind of occurrent mental state that obtains when it occurs.

In the case of perceptually imagining a Φ, the occurrent mental state that the phenomenally conscious mental episode manifests is a mental state that represents what it would be like to have a conscious sensory experience of a Φ. In the case of episodic recollection, the occurrent mental state that the phenomenally conscious mental episode manifests is knowledge concerning what it was like to experience a particular past event. In outlining my account of perceptual imagination, I suggested that the relevant mental state that represents what it would be like to have a conscious sensory experience is retained by a subject in so far as she retains the capacity to engage in episodes of perceptual imagination that manifest that mental state. If the subject loses the capacity to engage in such episodes of perceptual imagining, then she has no longer retained the relevant mental state. I said that the content of the mental state that one retains when one retains the capacity to engage in episodes of perceptually imagining a Φ is determined by the phenomenal character of the episodes of perceptual imagining that one retains the capacity to engage in; for the content of the mental state that is retained when one isn't actually engaged in an episode of perceptual imagining is determined by the content of the occurrent mental state that obtains when one is actually engaged in such an episode of perceptual imagining. Much the same is true of the knowledge that one retains in the case of episodic recollection. The relevant knowledge that a subject retains about what it was like to perceive a particular past event is retained in so far as she retains the capacity to engage in the relevant phenomenally conscious episodes of recollection. If the subject loses the capacity to engage in such phenomenally conscious episodes of recollection, then she loses that knowledge. The content of the knowledge that is retained is determined by the content of the occurrent state of knowledge that obtains when the subject is engaged in such an episode, which in turn is determined, at least in part, by the phenomenal character of the episode of recollection.

This account of what is retained in memory in the case of episodic recollection accommodates the various ways in which an act of episodic recollection is quite unlike an act of semantic recollection, for it accommodates the following distinctive features of an act of episodic recollection: (a) Episodic recollection can be thought of as a form of non-propositional recollection. (b) The phenomenal character of the act of recollecting determines, at least in part, and in some significant way, what event is thereby recollected. (c) The act of episodic recollection has a phenomenal character that corresponds in some significant way to the phenomenal character of a past experience of the event recollected. (d) The temporal profile of the act of recollection is similar to the temporal profile of one's original experience of the event recollected. (e) Episodic recollection can be thought of as a form of 'mental time-travel'—a way of reliving the past event recollected. I shall comment briefly on these points in turn.

(a) Although the act of episodic recollection involves an episode that manifests one's knowledge of the phenomenal character of a past experience of a particular past event, the episode of recollecting is not itself one of judging the content of the occurrent state of knowledge that obtains when it occurs. That is to say, the episode of recollecting is not an act of judging that 'This is what it was like to experience that event.' It's rather that the conscious character of the episode of recollecting determines, in part, the content of the occurrent state of knowledge that obtains. The occurrent state of knowledge that the episode of recollection manifests, represents a past phenomenally conscious experience of an event, and thereby represents a non-representational awareness of that event. So although the episode of recollecting does not have a propositional content that concerns a past event, in the act of episodic recollection a past event is thereby represented.

(b) When a subject episodically recollects some past event, it is the phenomenal character of the episode of recollecting that determines, at least in part, the content of the occurrent state of knowledge that obtains and that represents the phenomenal character of a conscious experience of the past event. In determining the content of this occurrent state of knowledge, the phenomenal character of the episode of recollecting determines, at least in part, what is recollected. So the phenomenal character of the episode of recollecting determines, at least in part, what event is thereby recollected.

(c) The phenomenal character of the episode of recollecting is to be specified, at least in part, in terms of the occurrent state of knowledge that obtains when it occurs, and this occurrent state of knowledge represents the phenomenal character of a past conscious experience of an event. So specification of the phenomenal character of the episode of recollection will necessarily involve reference to the conscious character of a conscious sensory experience of that past event.

(d) This account of the ontology of episodic recollection has some significant parallels with the account I've offered of the ontology of conscious sensory experience. In both cases we need to appeal to the occurrence of phenomenally conscious events as well as the obtaining of occurrent conscious states. In both cases the phenomenally conscious occurrences and states in question have an interdependent status. This similarity in the accounts of the ontology of each accommodates the fact that these different aspects of mind fill time in similar ways.

(e) In the case of episodic recollection, that which is recollected is a particular, past event—an unrepeatable occurrence—and so something one cannot re-apprehend.[10] The mental episode of recollection manifests knowledge of the phenomenal character of a particular, past, unrepeatable apprehension of the event, and not simply knowledge of the phenomenal character of a kind of apprehension—i.e. it does not simply manifest knowledge of the phenomenal character of the sort of thing that is repeatable. A mental episode that simply manifests one's knowledge of the phenomenal character of a kind of apprehension will be an episode that manifests one's knowledge that 'this is what it is like to apprehend an event of that kind'. Therefore, in the case of an act of episodic recollection, a particular, past, unrepeatable apprehension of an event is represented by the state of knowledge that the episode manifests. This state of knowledge represents one's past experience of that past, unrepeatable event, and thereby represents the temporal perspective of that past experience—an experience that presented each temporal part of the past event as 'successively present'. An episode that manifests such knowledge will therefore have the phenomenology of an episode of reliving a particular, past, unrepeatable apprehension. This gives us the notion of mental time-travel. The phenomenology of the current episode of recollecting is one of now reliving an unrepeatable past episode of apprehending.

---

[10] There are two types of potential counterexample to this claim: (i) one can re-apprehend an event by, for example, watching it on video, and (ii) one can re-apprehend an event with mirrors suitably placed. In the first case one is not re-apprehending the event. One is, rather, apprehending a distinct event that represents the earlier event. So there is nothing illusory about one's apprehension. It doesn't seem to one as if the event one is watching is occurring at a time at which it did not, in fact, occur. In the second kind of case, there is an illusion. It seems to one as if the event one is watching is occurring at the time of apprehension, which it is not. Just as mirrors can give one an illusory experience of the spatial position of an object or event, they can give one an illusory experience of the temporal position of an event.

I said earlier that it is natural to think that perceptual imagination exploits perceptual memory. When I perceptually imagine an acquaintance of mine playing the opening bars of Beethoven's Fifth on a harmonica, although I may be imagining an event of a kind that I have never witnessed, in doing so I am exploiting perceptual memories of things that I have witnessed. The form of perceptual memory exploited here is not 'episodic memory', in the technical sense of that term—I am not recollecting a particular past event that I have witnessed. So what sort of perceptual memory is exploited in this sort of case?

In perceptually imagining an acquaintance of mine playing the opening bars of Beethoven's Fifth on a harmonica, I am engaged in a mental episode that manifests a mental state that represents what it *would* be like to experience such an event. In performing the episode I am thereby exploiting knowledge that I have concerning what it *is* like to perceive my friend, what it *is* like to experience the sound of a harmonica, and so on. Although the knowledge that I manifest in performing this mental episode is not knowledge of what it *was* like to experience a particular past event, the knowledge I have of what it *is* like to experience certain objects, features, and kinds of events is manifested in the episode of perceptual imagination. It is such knowledge that is retained in perceptual memory and exploited in the act of perceptual imagination.

7.5 Perceptual imagination and knowing what it's like

At the start of the chapter I suggested that just as it is intuitive to think that a bodily sensation of pain is something that only a phenomenally conscious subject can feel, it is also intuitive to think that perceptually imagining something is an activity that only a phenomenally conscious subject can engage in. The account I've offered of perceptual imagination confirms and explains this. Episodes of perceptual imagination and episodes of perceptual recollection manifest mental states that represent the phenomenal characters of conscious sensory experiences. One might think that the fact that a mental event or state represents a conscious sensory experience need not in itself entail that the mental event or state doing the representing is a phenomenally conscious one. However, in the case of perceptual imagination and perceptual recollection, the phenomenal character of the mental episode that occurs determines, at least in part, the content of a mental state that represents a conscious sensory experience. So the way in which a conscious sensory experience is represented in perceptual imagination and perceptual recollection necessarily involves the occurrence of phenomenally conscious mental episodes. This is a way of representing conscious sensory experience that is only available to phenomenally conscious subjects.

Central to the account I've offered is an account of the ontology of perceptual imagination and perceptual recollection. I have noted that this account of the ontology parallels in some significant ways the account of the ontology of conscious sensory experience that I've been proposing. In both cases we need to appeal to the occurrence of phenomenally conscious events as well as the obtaining of occurrent conscious states. In both cases the phenomenally conscious occurrences and states in question have an interdependent status, and in both cases this gives rise to a form of explanatory circularity. In the case of perceptual imagination and recollection, the form of explanatory circularity that arises is this. When one perceptually imagines or recollects something, the content of the occurrent conscious state that obtains is determined, at least in part, by the phenomenal character of the mental episode of imagining or recollecting. But the phenomenal character of the mental episode of imagining or recollecting is to be specified in terms of the content of the occurrent mental state that the episode manifests.

This account of perceptual imagination and perceptual recollection invokes a form of knowledge that only a phenomenally conscious subject can possess—a certain kind of knowledge of what it is (or was) like to have conscious sensory experience. There is a respect in which such knowledge can be retained when no phenomenally conscious episodes are occurring. For example, one may want to hold that this form of knowledge (knowledge of what it is/was like to have a given conscious sensory experience) can be retained in dreamless sleep. However, the relevant knowledge that the subject retains is retained only in so far as the subject retains the capacity to engage in phenomenally conscious episodes of perceptual imagination or recollection. If the subject loses the capacity to engage in such phenomenally conscious episodes of perceptual imagination or recollection, then she loses that knowledge. And the content of the knowledge that is retained is determined by the content of the occurrent state of knowledge that obtains when the subject is engaged in such an episode, which in turn is determined, at least in part, by the phenomenal character of the episode of perceptual imagination or recollection that she thereby engages in.

In Chapter 1 I said that an appropriate articulation of the manifest image of conscious sensory experience should provide an account of the ontology of conscious sensory experience that fits the phenomenology as well as the knowledge that we have of that phenomenology. The account of perceptual imagination/memory that I have offered in this chapter is an important element of the account of our knowledge of the phenomenology of conscious sensory experience that I want to propose. These issues in the epistemology of mind will be explored further in the next chapter.

In Chapter 1 I also suggested that an account of the manifest image of conscious sensory experience is likely to intersect with views on self-knowledge. I noted that the relationalists' distinctive claim about the general shape of the manifest image of conscious sensory experience intersects with a view about self-knowledge—a view about what a subject is in a position to know about her conscious sensory experience when she has it, and what puts her in a position to know it. For it involves the idea that an account of what one can know about the sensuous character of the conscious sensory experience one has when one successfully perceives the world, and one's account of what puts one in a position to know it, cannot be straightforwardly and symmetrically applied to the case of hallucination. In the next chapter I shall also be discussing how the relationalist view of conscious sensory experience that I have been arguing for intersects with these issues in the epistemology of mind.

8

Introspection and Knowing What It's Like

In the previous chapter I argued that when a subject episodically recollects a past event, the subject represents a past experience of that past event. In particular, I argued that the episode of recollection manifests the subject's knowledge of what it was like to experience that past event. An occurrent state of knowledge that concerns the conscious character of a past experience of a past event obtains when the subject engages in a phenomenally conscious episode of recollecting a past event; and the phenomenal character of the episode of recollection determines, at least in part, the content of that occurrent state of knowledge. So according to this view, episodic recollection involves a form of self-knowledge—one's knowledge of the conscious character of one's past experience.

I argued that acts of perceptual imagination also involve the representation of experience. When one perceptually imagines a φ, one is in an occurrent mental state that represents an experience of a φ. The phenomenal character of the episode of perceptual imagination determines, in part, the content of an occurrent mental state that represents the conscious character of an experience of a φ. These acts of perceptual imagination usually exploit perceptual memory. They manifest one's knowledge of what it is like to experience objects, features, and events. So acts of perceptual imagination also involve a form of self-knowledge—they involve one's knowledge of the conscious characters of one's experiences of objects, object-kinds, event-kinds, features, and relations.

There are a couple of points that I want to emphasize about the sort of self-knowledge that I have invoked in this account of perceptual imagination and perceptual recollection. The first point to emphasize is the significance of ontological considerations to the account I've offered. The ontology of 'occurrent state' is a crucial component of my characterization of this form of self-knowledge. These occurrent states are states of knowledge whose obtaining is constitutively dependent on the occurrence of phenomenally conscious episodes. The subject's knowledge of the conscious characters of her experiences can be retained when these phenomenally conscious episodes do not occur, but this knowledge is retained only in so far as the subject retains the capacity to engage in certain kinds of phenomenally conscious mental episodes. The conscious characters of these phenomenally conscious mental episodes determine, in part, the content of the knowledge she possesses. This is why this form of knowledge is only available to the phenomenally conscious.

The second point to emphasize is that in this account of this form of self-knowledge, no appeal has been made to conscious mental acts of judging. The conscious mental episodes invoked are phenomenally conscious episodes of perceptual imagination and perceptual recollection, and these phenomenally conscious mental episodes are not episodes of judging the contents of the occurrent states that obtain when they occur; so they are not to be regarded as knowledgeable judgements about the conscious character of experience. Moreover, the occurrent states of knowledge that obtain when these phenomenally conscious episodes occur are not themselves conscious mental acts of judging. They are not episodes in the stream of consciousness. These occurrent *states* of self-knowledge are the 'silent partners'[1] of phenomenally conscious *episodes* (episodes of imagining and recollecting) in the stream of consciousness.

So the account of perceptual imagination and perceptual recollection that I've offered invokes a form of self-knowledge—knowledge of one's own experience, and in particular knowledge of the phenomenal character of one's experience—but in the account of self-knowledge that I invoked, no appeal was made to the idea that the subject of such knowledge must be capable of making conscious judgements or assertions about her experience. There was no assumption that the subject of such knowledge must be capable of thinking about, reasoning about, and drawing inferences about, her experience. So in that sense, there is no clear reason to hold that the subject of such knowledge must possess a concept of her own experience—a concept that can figure in the contents of judgements about her own experience. To possess this variety of self-knowledge, the subject simply has to have the capacity to engage in episodes of perceptual imagination and/or acts of perceptual recollection. For this reason, it is not clear that we need be committed to the claim that the contents of the occurrent states of knowledge that obtain when a subject perceptually imagines or recollects must be conceptual contents.

I have suggested that in the case of episodic recollection, the self-knowledge that is retained in perceptual memory and manifested in episodes of recollecting past events is knowledge of what it was like to have a past experience of a past event. This is knowledge one acquired in experiencing that past event. But so far I have said very little about the account that should be given of the knowledge one can have of conscious sensory experience when one undergoes that sensory experience. Addressing this issue raises further questions about the ontological ingredients that should be appealed to in an account of one's knowledge of one's experience and its conscious character.

The self-knowledge invoked in my account of perceptual recollection and imagination appealed to *occurrent states* of knowledge, as well as the *dispositional capacity* to engage in phenomenally conscious *episodes* that determine the content of those occurrent states. When it comes to providing an account of the knowledge one can have of a conscious sensory experience when one undergoes that sensory experience, should we also appeal

---

[1] This phrase is borrowed from O'Shaughnessy 2000: 106.

to further ontological ingredients? For example, should we appeal to an *activity* of *introspecting* one's own experience? Is such activity the epistemic source of *conscious judgements* that can be made about one's experience? And is such activity made possible by a *relation of acquaintance* that one has with one's experience? Addressing these questions will once again connect with the question of the extent to which one's conscious sensory experience is 'transparent', for as we shall see, the claim that experience is transparent appears to pose a challenge to the idea that we are acquainted with the experiences we undergo, which in turn raises questions about what is involved in introspecting them.

8.1 Introspecting 'transparent' experience

In Chapter 6 I said that an assumption that is sometimes made in representationalist accounts of experience is that we can refer to a subject's perceptual experience in such a way that we can then ask after *the* content of *that* experience. In particular, the assumption seems to be that if we specify the particular time, subject, and perceptual modality we have in mind, we can then ask after *the* content of *the* perceptual experience of the subject, within that perceptual modality, at that time—e.g. 'what is the content of the visual experience you are having now?'. This, I think, is symptomatic of a more general tendency to assume that it is possible to learn something about the experience one is having by first attending to it and then determining its nature. That is to say, the assumption seems be that one can first pick out introspectively, and home in on, some experiential event or state *prior* to making a judgement about its nature, and as a result of engaging in this activity one can then form some judgement about the kind of experience one is having, and thereby acquire knowledge about it. Under its representationalist guise, the assumption is that one can introspectively pick out, and home in on, some experiential event or state and then come to some judgement about the representational content of that experiential event or state.

We can contrast this sort of assumption about experience with the sort of assumptions we tend to make about belief. We don't tend to think that it makes sense to ask after *the* content of *the* belief you have at a time. At a time you not only believe many different things, you have many different beliefs, and so it doesn't seem right to ask after, say, *the* content of *the* belief you have now. We specify beliefs in terms of their contents, and the question, 'what is the content of your belief that *p*?' answers itself. We can of course ask *whether* you now believe that *p*, and we can also ask for your opinion about x, but the point is that in answering such questions you would not then be characterizing the content of a mental state that had been picked out and identified prior to some specification of its content, for which we could then ask, 'is that really the content of *that* belief?' We could of course say, 'do you really believe that?', but again, we would not be questioning whether you had given a correct account of the content of a mental state that you already identified prior to some specification of its content. In other words, it doesn't seem right to think that a subject can check what the content of a particular belief of hers is, by introspectively homing in on that target belief and *then* determining its content.[2]

Is experience unlike belief in this respect? Should we accept the assumption that it is possible for one to pick out introspectively, and home in on, some experiential event or state *prior* to making a judgement about it, and as a result of engaging in this activity form some judgement about its features? Someone who is sceptical about this assumption need not be sceptical about the idea that there are things one can know about an experience one is undergoing. They may just be sceptical about a model on which such knowledge is grounded in a pre-judgemental activity of introspectively attending to that experience. Consider again the comparison I made with the case of belief. I suggested that there isn't the same tendency to assume that it is possible for one to engage in the activity of picking out introspectively, of homing in on and attending to, some belief one has *prior* to making a judgement about it—e.g. prior to reaching a belief about its content. But nonetheless the standard assumption is that we can, and often do, know what we believe.

In what follows I want to consider how the claim that experience is 'transparent' might be brought to bear on the assumption that one can engage in the pre-judgemental activity of introspectively attending to an experience one is undergoing. Is there reason to think that the transparency claim undermines this assumption? In Chapter 2 I quoted a passage from Moore in which he warns against the quick and easy importation of metaphysical assumptions when characterizing sensory experience, and I connected this with Moore's claim that experience is transparent, or 'diaphanous'. Moore says:

Although I know for certain both that I have had many experiences, and that I have had experiences of many different kinds, I feel very doubtful whether to say the first is the same thing as to say that there have been many events, each of which was an experience and an experience of mine ... The proposition that I have had experiences does not necessarily entail the proposition that there have been many events which were experiences; and I cannot satisfy myself that I am acquainted with any events of the supposed kind. (1925: 123)

A defender of the claim that experience is transparent might assert that when one has a conscious sensory experience it often seems to one as though one is directly aware of particulars—objects and events—that one can attend to and that one can shift one's attention across, but these particulars that one is confronted with, and which one seems to be able to shift one's attention across and focus on, appear to one to be the particulars that one is experiencing, and the particular event that is one's experience of them doesn't seem to be among them. So, for example, although it seems to one as though one can shift one's attention from one experienced event to another, it doesn't seem to one as though one can shift one's attention in the same way from some particular event that

---

[2] We may of course believe that we believe that *q* when we rather believe that *p*, but that is not the same thing as taking one's belief that *p* to be the belief that *q*—i.e. in such cases one doesn't 'misidentify' one's belief.

one is experiencing to the particular event that is one's experience of it. In that sense, it is not clear that one is acquainted with any such experiential event.

In Chapter 3 I mentioned that Moore's remarks do not seem to apply straightforwardly to the case of located bodily sensation, because when you feel a stabbing pain in your knee, say, it seems as though you *are* directly aware of/presented with/confronted with a phenomenal event that you can attend to directly; and it seems as though you can attend directly to its phenomenal qualities. However, I went on to argue that although you are directly aware of a phenomenal event when you experience a located bodily sensation of pain, the phenomenal event you are aware of isn't your experience. It is, rather, what your experience is an experience of. It is an event whose occurrence entails your experience of it, and it is an event whose nature is to be specified in terms of the kind of phenomenally conscious state that obtains when it occurs, and which is intentionally directed on it. But this phenomenal event is not itself an experience of anything. It is a mind-dependent, phenomenal, *bodily* event that you are *experiencing*. When you experience a stabbing pain in your knee, you have an experience that puts you in a position to attend directly to a phenomenal event. You seem to be directly aware of, to be confronted with, a phenomenal event. However, the phenomenal event that you are directly aware of, and which you can attend to, is not to be identified with a conscious event that is your experience. It is, rather, a bodily event that your experience is an experience of. And again, when you experience such a bodily sensation, it is not clear that you are acquainted with the particular event that is your experience of it.

How do these general claims bear on the assumption that when one undergoes a sensory experience one can engage in the pre-judgemental activity of introspectively attending to that experience? A proponent of the transparency claim might contend that those who assume that it is possible for one to engage in the pre-judgemental activity of introspectively attending to one's experience are confusing this putative activity with the activity of perceptually attending to a particular that one is experiencing. They might contend that when one has a conscious sensory experience, one can engage in the activity of perceptually attending to the particulars that one's experience is an experience of—for example, in the case of vision one can look at, and watch, the particulars one is experiencing. One can look at and attend to their properties and as a result of engaging in this activity one can thereby reach judgements about the particulars that one is looking at; but one isn't thereby introspectively attending to a particular that is one's experience. One is, rather, *perceptually* attending to a particular that one is experiencing.

Does this line of thought establish that it is a mistake to assume that we can engage in the pre-judgemental activity of introspectively attending to an experience one is undergoing? Well, for those who insist that one can engage in the pre-judgemental activity of introspectively attending to some experience one is having, it at least poses the following challenge, or question: what is the difference between, and relation between, (a) introspectively attending to an experience one is having, and (b) perceptually attending to an object of that experience?

I propose to address this question by first considering the question of what is involved in perceptually attending to an object of experience. I shall take as my examples the visual activities of looking at and watching something.[3] I shall then go on to consider what further activity may be involved in putative cases of introspectively attending to the experience itself.

8.2   Noticing, looking at, and watching

Looking at, and watching, something are activities one can be engaged in. When one engages in these activities, perceptual states obtain and conscious sensory experience occurs. But the activities of looking at and watching are not themselves identical with the obtaining of perceptual states, and nor are they identical with the occurrence of the conscious sensory experience that merely happens to one as one looks at and watches. Looking at and watching something can be *agential* activities that one can choose to engage in.

The objects of the psychological verbs 'look at' and 'watch' are not propositional in form. Looking at, and watching, are activities directed at particulars, their properties, and the relations they stand in to one another. Furthermore, these activities are relational in the following sense: the truth of 'S is looking at/watching an x' entails that there is an x that S is looking at/watching. In this, looking at and watching can be contrasted with looking for. The truth of 'S is looking for an x' doesn't entail that there is an x that S is looking for, just as the truth of 'S is thinking about an x' does not entail that there is an x that S is thinking about. In order to be looking at (or watching) something, that thing must exist, for in order to look at (or watch) something one must stand in a perceptual relation to it—one must be perceptually aware of it.

Although the perceptual activity of looking at something presupposes perceptual awareness of that thing, it is not equivalent to the obtaining of that perceptual relation; for one can now begin to look at (or watch) something that one was previously perceptually aware of. So what changes when one begins to look at (or watch) something that one was previously perceptually aware of? Not simply the position of that thing in one's visual field. One can be looking at something 'out of the corner of one's eye'. Moreover, something can be in the centre of one's visual field and one can fail to notice it; and if one fails to notice it, although one's eye's may be directed towards it, one isn't yet engaged in the agential activity of looking at it. One can only be looking at x, in the sense I'm interested here, if one has noticed x. Given this connection between looking at/watching and noticing, it will be helpful to consider what is involved in perceptually noticing something.

---

[3] Here I am concerned with agential perceptual activities that are attributable to a subject at a personal level, rather than the psychological processes involved in 'attention'. For philosophical discussions of the latter issue, as well as the former, see Mole, Smithies, and Wu 2011.

I have said that one can be perceptually aware of something without noticing it. One can, for example, be perceptually aware of something prior to noticing it. What changes when one notices the perceived item? 'Notice' is a perceptual achievement (as is 'spot'), so one might think that this perceptual verb is used to mark the acquisition or onset of something. But what? The most obvious answer is that it marks the acquisition of a belief about the item that is noticed—a belief that is caused by one's experience of that item. For when one notices the perceived item, one has a certain kind of cognitive and epistemic contact with that item that was absent during one's prior, purely perceptual, and ignorant encounter with it. This much appears to be captured by the suggestion that when one notices the perceived item one acquires a belief about it.

However, this suggestion is perhaps too simple as it stands. For a belief that one acquires about a perceived item when one notices it (even a present-tensed one) can be retained beyond one's perceptual encounter with it, whereas one's noticing something also appears to mark the onset of a more distinctive kind of cognitive and epistemic contact with that thing—a form of cognitive and epistemic contact with a perceived item which can continue as one continues to look at it attentively and watch it, but which does not outlast one's perceptual encounter with it. I want to suggest that in order to get clearer on what is involved in noticing, looking at, and watching something, we need to get clearer on what form this distinctive cognitive contact with perceived items takes. For my proposal is going to be that (a) perceptual noticing marks the onset of this distinctive form of cognitive contact with a perceived item, and (b) when one looks at and watches a perceived item one engages in the activity of *maintaining* this distinctive form of cognitive contact with that perceived item.

Our perceptual experience of the world appears to afford us the opportunity to have a form of cognitive, and not merely experiential, contact with what is happening in the world, *as it happens*. When one notices and then watches attentively the movement of an object, one's encounter with the movement of that object need not be purely experiential. One can have a form of knowledge of the movement of the object *as that movement unfolds*. In such a case one knows what the object is doing because one is watching the object, and one can see what it is doing.

As one continues to watch a continuously moving object, there is a respect in which one's epistemic contact with the perceived object itself seems to be continuous. For example, it is intuitive to think that one's epistemic contact with an object as it moves from, say, location L1 to L10 shares a temporal part with one's epistemic contact with the object as it moves from location L5 to L15. We fail to accommodate this idea if we simply say that one's knowledge of the movement of the object is constituted by some mental state (i.e. some belief) that continues to obtain *throughout* the interval of time that one watches the object. For this fails to respect the fact that what one knows of the movement of the object changes as that movement unfolds. We should be able to accommodate the idea that one's knowledge of the movement of the object keeps up with one's experience of the movement of the object.

However, it doesn't seem right to hold that when one continuously watches a moving object, one's epistemic contact with the object—one's knowledge of what the object is doing—is constituted by a series of successive judgements that one makes about that object. One's knowledge of the movement of the object is not simply constituted by some state that continues to obtain throughout the interval of time that one watches the object, but neither is one's knowledge of the movement constituted by a series of successive 'episodes' of knowing. That is to say, we want our account of this variety of perceptual knowledge to be able to accommodate the idea that knowledge is stative and not episodic. When a subject attentively watches the continuous movement of an object, we are loathe to posit the occurrence of an extended event of knowing. We are also loathe to posit the obtaining of a series of successive but instantaneous states of knowing. It is unclear what explanatory work can be done by positing the obtaining of a state of knowledge that lacks any temporal duration. The states of knowledge involved must be ones that obtain over intervals of time. However, in the case of this variety of knowledge we also want to be able to accommodate the idea that the obtaining of such states of knowledge depends on something occurrent and processive. They depend on the occurrence of the perceptual experience one undergoes. This is not simply to say that the obtaining of such a state of knowledge is the causal upshot of some temporally prior experiential event. For we need to accommodate the idea that what a subject knows of the movement of an object over the interval of time that she watches it is determined, at least in part, by the perceptual experience of the object that she undergoes *during* that interval of time; and the same remark applies to any of the sub-intervals of the interval of time over which she watches the object.

The proposal I have made about the ontology of perceptual experience offers us an appropriate model of the ontology of the cognitive states that obtain when one knows what an object is doing through watching it and seeing what it is doing. The cognitive states in question are, I suggest, *occurrent* cognitive states whose obtaining over an interval of time depend constitutively on the occurrence of the conscious experience one undergoes during that interval of time. Under the right circumstances, when conscious perceptual events and processes occur, there obtain, in virtue of their occurrence, not just conscious perceptual states, but also concurrent states of knowledge of the mind-independent phenomena that those perceptual states concern. In particular, these occurrent states of knowledge concern those aspects of the experienced mind-independent scene that one notices. Such states of world-directed perceptual knowledge may not be homogeneous down to instants. It may be that they do not continue to obtain throughout the interval of time over which they obtain; for their obtaining over an interval of time may depend on the occurrence of something that takes that interval of time to occur. In which case, at a time, a subject has such world-directed perceptual knowledge in virtue of the fact that there is an interval of time over which she has such knowledge.

This proposal respects the idea that knowledge is stative, and not episodic, while accommodating the intuition that in the case of this variety of knowledge what one knows over any interval of time is determined, at least in part, by what happens during that interval of time. It also accommodates the respect in which one's perceptual knowledge of a perceived item over an interval of time can be continuous despite the fact that such knowledge involves a series of successive and distinct cognitive states. For according to this view of the ontology, the conscious perceptual occurrence upon which an occurrent cognitive state constitutively depends can share a temporal part with the conscious perceptual occurrence upon which a subsequent occurrent cognitive state constitutively depends.

This account of the ontology of this variety of perceptual belief also accommodates the intuition that the sort of conscious contact with the passage of time that we have when we are awake and having conscious perceptual experience can be cognitive and not merely experiential. Consider, for example, a situation in which one notices the absence of a sound that one had previously been experiencing. One listens carefully for that particular sound over an extended interval of time. Over that period of time one continues to register the absence of that sound. Not just experientially, but cognitively and epistemically. Over that extended interval of time one continues to believe that the sound cannot be heard. But the continued obtaining of this cognitive state is unlike the continued obtaining of a present-tensed belief during an interval of dreamless sleep. As one listens out for the sound, there is a sense in which one's cognitive registration of the absence of the sound is 'occurrently renewed'. The 'occurrent renewal' of conscious sensory experience is an ingredient of the account we need to appeal to in order to accommodate the distinctive form of conscious *cognitive* contact with the 'passage of time' that our conscious sensory experience appears to provide us with.

This view of the ontology of this variety of perceptual belief has a bearing on our understanding of the relation between perceptual experience and perceptual belief. According to one view, the relation between perceptual experience and perceptual belief is merely causal. On this view, what makes a belief a perceptual one simply has to do with its causal origin, and the same kind of belief could have had a different causal origin. Some want to add that the relation between perceptual experience and perceptual belief is not merely causal but also epistemic. That is to say, perceptual experiences not only cause, but also warrant/justify perceptual beliefs. But on such views there appears to be no obvious reason why the same kind of belief couldn't have lacked that perceptual epistemic ground and cause. One might add to this view the suggestion that perceptual belief inherits and shares some aspect of the content of the perceptual experience that causes it. But this seems to amount to no more than the claim that perceptual belief and perceptual experience can have some property in common—the possession of a certain kind of intentional content—and it is not obvious why a belief that has the same property as a perceptual experience couldn't have had a very different causal origin.

According to the account I have proposed, there is a variety of perceptual belief that is *constitutively* dependent upon the occurrence of perceptual experience, and not merely causally dependent on perceptual experience. This account does not identify perceptual experience with a variety of perceptual belief. It allows that one can have perceptual experience without perceptual belief. But it posits a variety of perceptual belief that is itself experiential. For it posits a variety of 'occurrent' cognitive state whose obtaining over an interval of time depends constitutively, and not merely causally, on the manner in which an experiential occurrence unfolds over that interval of time. In the case of this variety of perceptual belief, one might say that the experiential source of the belief is a constituent of it. So there is no question that this variety of perceptual belief might have had a different source.

One's perceptual noticing of something, I suggest, marks the onset of this form of cognitive contact with a perceived item. It marks the onset of an occurrent cognitive state that concerns the perceived entity that one notices. When one notices a perceived entity, one can acquire perceptual memories of, and non-occurrent beliefs about, that perceived entity—perceptual memories and non-occurrent beliefs that can outlast one's perceptual encounter with that entity. But one's perceptual noticing of the perceived entity also marks the onset of an occurrent cognitive state that can obtain only when one perceives the entity one notices—an occurrent cognitive state whose obtaining depends constitutively on the occurrence of one's experience of that entity.

I said earlier that when one engages in the activities of looking at and watching something, perceptual states obtain and conscious sensory experience occurs, but the activities of looking at and watching are not themselves identical with the obtaining of perceptual states, and nor are they identical with the occurrence of the conscious sensory experience that merely happens to one as one looks at and watches. We can now add that the activities of looking at and watching are not identical with the sort of occurrent cognitive state that obtains when one notices something. However, the sort of cognitive contact with a perceived item that one has when one notices it, when one is in an occurrent cognitive state directed upon it, is of crucial importance to an account of looking at and watching. For the agential activity of looking at and watching something is, I suggest, the activity of *maintaining* this form of cognitive contact with the thing that is looked at and watched.[4] When one is agentially looking at something, or watching it, one is actively and intentionally maintaining the sort of cognitive contact with something that one has when one notices it—the sort of cognitive contact with a perceived item that involves the obtaining of occurrent cognitive states which are directed upon that item, and which constitutively depend for their obtaining on the occurrence of experience of that item. One's engagement in this sort of activity affects the way in which one's conscious sensory experience unfolds—it affects the course taken by that conscious sensory occurrence. It thereby affects the sorts of occurrent perceptual states that obtain in virtue of the occurrence of that conscious sensory experience. Moreover, it affects the way in which one is cognitively modified by the occurrence of that conscious sensory experience, for it has an effect on the sort of occurrent cognitive states that obtain in virtue of the occurrence of that conscious sensory occurrence. During

---

[4]   Compare Crowther's discussion of agential perceptual activity in his 2009a, 2009b, and 2010.

the activity of looking at, and watching, something one continues to be in occurrent cognitive states directed at that thing, and this *because* one is looking at and watching that thing.

The activity of looking at something and watching it can lead one to make a conscious perceptual judgement about that thing. But the activity of looking at and watching something is not itself a matter of a making a judgement about that thing. The sort of occurrent cognitive state that obtains when one perceptually notices something is not a perceptual judgement either. That is to say, it is not identical with a conscious *episode* of judging. The event of noticing which marks the onset of this occurrent cognitive state is also not an act of making a perceptual judgement. So what is the relation between a conscious perceptual judgement that one might make about a perceived item and the sort of occurrent cognitive state that obtains when one notices it and continues to look at it? A given conscious perceptual judgement that one makes may be an articulation in conscious, conceptual thought of some aspect of the content of an occurrent cognitive state that obtains when one notices something—the sort of conscious articulation of what one occurrently believes that may serve as an initial step in some reasoning that one engages in. And such acts of judging can be grounded in one's occurrent perceptual beliefs and result from the activity of looking at and watching something.

There are various ontological ingredients to be uncovered and distinguished in an account of the epistemology of conscious perception. As well as the occurrence of conscious sensory processes and the occurrent perceptual states whose obtaining depends constitutively upon the occurrence of those conscious sensory processes, I have suggested that we can distinguish the following: (i) the achievement of perceptual noticing, which marks the onset of (ii) an occurrent cognitive state whose obtaining is constitutively dependent on the occurrence of conscious sensory experience; (iii) the non-occurrent perceptual beliefs that can be acquired on noticing a perceived item, and which can outlast one's perceptual encounter with that object; (iv) the perceptual memories that one can acquire when one perceives something, where this involves acquiring the capacity to engage in phenomenally conscious episodes that put one in occurrent states of knowledge representing the conscious character of one's experience of that thing; (v) conscious acts of perceptual judgement; (vi) the agential activities of looking at and watching, which involve the activity of maintaining the sort of cognitive contact with a perceived item that one has when one notices it. And to this list we might add a further epistemic ingredient—that of knowing what one is doing when one is intentionally looking at and/or watching something.

My aim in discussing these issues has been that of trying to get clearer on what is involved in perceptually attending to (e.g. looking at and watching) a particular that one is experiencing; and this endeavour has been a first step in an attempt to address a more general question to which the claim that experience is 'transparent' gives rise: what is the difference between, and relation between, (a) introspectively attending to an experience one is having, and (b) perceptually attending to an object of that experience? With this discussion of looking at and watching in mind, in the next section I shall consider what further activity may be involved in putative cases of introspectively attending to one's experience.

8.3 The introspective perspective on experience and our perceptual perspective on the world

In earlier discussions of the transparency of experience I distinguished stronger and weaker versions of the claim that experience is transparent, and I argued that there is reason to reject the stronger version. According to the stronger version, introspection of one's perceptual experience seems to one to reveal *only* the objects, qualities, and relations one is apparently perceptually aware of in having that experience, and not qualities of the experience itself. I argued that the fact that one can introspectively discern relatively invariant structural features of conscious sensory awareness gives us reason to reject the stronger version of the claim. For example, the boundaries of the spatial sensory field of vision are not features of some object one is visually aware of, but even though one cannot directly attend to them in the way in which one can directly attend to the objects and features that fall within them, they do nonetheless feature in the conscious character of one's visual experience, and one can become aware of them when attending to the objects that fall within them. For in attending directly to the objects of visual awareness, one can reflect on the way in which one's visual awareness of those objects seems to one to be structured. These are aspects of the conscious character of experience which, to quote Moore again, 'can be distinguished if we look attentively enough, and if we know that there is something to look for' (1903: 41).

The advocate of the weaker version of the transparency claim asserts that it doesn't seem as though one can focus solely on the conscious character of one's experience without attending to the objects one's experience is an experience of. However, the weaker version of transparency is consistent with the claim that when one has a conscious sensory experience, there are things one can discern introspectively about one's experience other than what one's experience is an experience of, for it just commits one to the claim that if there are such further things to discern introspectively, it seems to one as though one cannot discern these things introspectively *without* focusing on the objects that one's experience is an experience of.

If the weaker version of the transparency claim is correct, what, if anything, does this establish about the relation between perceptually attending to a particular that one is aware of, and introspectively attending to one's experience of it? Let us start with the following question: given the proposal about looking at and watching outlined in the previous section, should we accept that one cannot introspectively attend to some visual experience one is undergoing without looking at/watching something that one is visually aware of?

Sense-datum theorists might deny that one can introspectively attend to an experience one is undergoing without perceptually attending to objects of that experience—

without attending to objects and features that one is actually *perceptually aware of* in having that experience. But those who reject sense-datum theories, and who also think that it is possible for one to engage in the pre-judgemental activity of introspectively attending to one's experience, are likely to hold that one can engage in such activity without perceptually attending to anything—e.g. without looking at anything in the visual case. For they are likely to hold that (a) one can introspectively attend to a hallucinatory experience, and (b) when one is hallucinating one cannot be looking at anything, for (c) when one is hallucinating one isn't perceptually aware of anything. We will need to consider what should be said of such cases in due course, but first I want to consider what should be said of the experience one undergoes when one genuinely perceives one's environment. For example, when one successfully sees one's environment, can one engage in the pre-judgemental activity of introspectively attending to the visual experience one undergoes without engaging in the activity of looking at/watching something that one is visually aware of?

Let us first consider the attempt to introspectively attend to representational properties of a visual experience one is undergoing, or more generally, those properties, whatever they are, that determine what one's visual experience is an experience *as of*. Can one engage in the activity of introspectively attending to such properties without engaging in the activity of looking at, or watching, something that one is visually aware of? In the case of veridical perception it appears that one cannot. In the case of veridical visual perception it appears to be impossible to comply with the following request: introspect those properties that determine what your experience is an experience *as of*, but make sure you don't look at anything.

What about the attempt to introspectively attend to what I have been calling 'structural features' of visual awareness? Again, in the case of veridical visual perception it appears to be impossible to engage in the activity of attending to such features without engaging in the activity of looking at something that one is visually aware of. For example, one cannot introspectively attend to the boundaries of one's spatial visual field without looking, 'out of the corners of one's eyes', at peripheral sectors of the perceived scene.

According to the account of looking at and watching that I proposed in the previous section, this means that in the case of veridical visual perception, when one engages in the activity of introspectively attending to one's visual experience one is inevitably engaged in the activity of maintaining cognitive contact with some aspect of the visually perceived scene. One is unavoidably engaged in the activity of maintaining the sort of cognitive contact that one has with something when one perceptually notices it. This, in turn, entails that when one engages in the activity of introspecting one's visual experience, one will be in occurrent cognitive states that are directed upon those aspects of the perceived scene that are looked at/watched.

But when one is introspecting some visual experience one is undergoing, one is not *merely* looking at/watching something that one is visually aware of. So what distinguishes the introspective case? The first point to note concerns the distinctive *aim* and *outcome* of the activity one engages in when one introspectively attends to one's experience. One's aim in engaging in such activity won't simply be that of acquiring world-directed perceptual knowledge, for one's aim will include that of discovering something about the experience one is having. And the outcome of one's introspective activity will include judgements about one's experience—e.g. about what perceptually seems to one to be the case—and not simply judgements about the objects one perceives. But how does one go about achieving the distinctive epistemic aim that one has in the introspective case? What does one do to put oneself in a position to discern features of, and make judgements about, the visual experience one is undergoing, as opposed to features of the entities one sees? In the case of veridical visual perception, although the aim of one's introspective activity may differ from the aim of the activity one engages in when one is simply concerned to discover/discern something about the environment one perceives, the means one employs in order to achieve that aim are much the same. One looks at/watches entities one perceives. One maintains cognitive contact with them.

In order to have the capacity to engage in an activity the epistemic aim of which is to discern something about the experience one is undergoing, one must have the ability to frame thoughts about one's experience. This capacity isn't possessed by all of those subjects who are capable of looking at, and watching, the entities they perceive. It is not possessed by those subjects who lack the concept of experience. But those subjects who do possess the concept of experience, and who are thereby capable of framing thoughts about their experience, can look at an entity that they perceive with the *intention* of discerning something about the experience they undergo. The subject who frames such an intention will be in an epistemic and cognitive condition that is unlike that of the subject who is merely concerned to find out something about the environment she perceives. This difference will affect the way in which the subject is cognitively modified by the occurrence of the conscious sensory experience she subsequently undergoes, and it will thereby have an effect on the sorts of occurrent cognitive states that subsequently obtain as that conscious sensory experience unfolds. The subject will be poised to discern things about her experience, and she will find out things about her experience. But, I suggest, the judgements the subject makes about her experience will ultimately be grounded in occurrent cognitive states that are directed upon entities that she perceptually notices, looks at, and watches.

But what of the situation in which one is under the misapprehension that one isn't perceptually aware of anything—e.g. a situation in which one has the false belief that one is hallucinating? In this sort of situation, when one introspectively attends to one's experience in order to determine what one's experience is an experience *as of*, the fact that one doesn't believe that one is perceptually aware of anything will not alter the fact that one will inevitably notice some of the things one is perceptually aware of—certain objects and/or events, and certain of their properties. It won't alter the fact that one will inevitably be engaged in the activity of looking at/watching such entities, and thereby maintaining cognitive contact with those entities. So one's ignorance of the existence of those entities will not be due to the fact that one fails to notice them. One may not believe that one is perceptually aware of anything, and so one may not believe that one is looking at anything. But nonetheless, in introspectively attending to one's experience one will perceptually notice entities that one is perceptually aware of, and one *will* be looking at entities that one is perceptually aware of; so one will inevitably be in occurrent cognitive states that are directed upon entities one is perceptually aware of.

If a subject falsely believes that she is hallucinating, then the occurrent cognitive states that obtain when she perceptually notices, looks at, and watches entities that she is perceptually aware of, should not be regarded as beliefs that those entities exist. For the subject who is under the misapprehension that she is hallucinating will reason on the assumption that she isn't aware of entities in her environment. She may refrain from making judgements about what is actually going on in her environment, and she will restrict her perceptual judgements to those concerned with what perceptually *seems* to her to be the case. Given that such a subject will be so disposed, there may be reason for thinking that the occurrent cognitive states that obtain as she introspects her experience should be regarded as occurrent beliefs about what perceptually *seems* to be the case— e.g. the occurrent belief that 'It *seems* that that F is G.' But such occurrent cognitive states will, nonetheless, still be directed on, and hence be about, objects (and/or events) and properties that the subject perceptually notices, looks at, and watches—entities with which she maintains cognitive contact, as she introspects her experience. The subject may even judge of the entities that she notices and looks at—of the entities that she maintains cognitive contact with—that they do not exist—e.g. '*That F* does not exist.' But her ability to do so will depend on the fact that, as she introspects her experience, she will be in occurrent cognitive states that are directed on those entities.

In my discussion of looking at and watching in the previous section I suggested that there are various ontological and epistemic ingredients to be uncovered in an account of the epistemology of conscious perception. One of the epistemic ingredients I mentioned was that of one's knowledge of what one is doing when one is intentionally engaged in the activity of looking at and/or watching something. If a subject believes that she is hallucinating, then this will have an effect on how she regards what she is up to when she looks at and watches entities that she is perceptually aware of. If the subject believes that she is hallucinating, then she won't believe that she is actually looking at material objects in her environment. She may believe that she is looking at some non-material object—e.g. some sense-datum and its properties. Or she may believe that it merely seems as if she is looking at something. But in one way or another she will treat as false the premise that she is actually looking at material objects in her environment. She may do this by reasoning on the assumption that she isn't aware of entities in her environment, by refraining from making judgements about what is actually going on in her environment, and by restricting her perceptual judgements to those concerned with what perceptually seems to her to be the case. However, the fact that she believes that she is not in a position to look at anything, because she believes that she is hallucinating, will not prevent her from behaving as though she is looking at something as she introspects her experience. And if her belief that she is hallucinating is false, it will not prevent her from actually looking at something that she is perceptually aware of.

So even when a subject believes that she is hallucinating, she cannot engage in the activity of introspecting her experience without behaving as she would behave if she were perceptually aware of something. Indeed, I suggest that the intentional introspective behaviour that the subject engages in cannot be adequately characterized independently of the kind of behaviour that she can only engage in when she is perceptually aware of something. In engaging in the activity of introspecting her experience, the subject behaves *as though* she is in a position to look at (and watch)—i.e. maintain cognitive contact with—entities that she is perceptually aware of. And if her belief that she is hallucinating is false, she will *actually* be looking at (and watching)—maintaining cognitive contact with—entities that she is perceptually aware of. Moreover, she behaves in this way intentionally and with a distinctive epistemic aim in mind—i.e. with the intention of discerning something about the experience she is undergoing.

At the beginning of this chapter I suggested that the claim that experience is 'transparent' appears to pose a challenge to the idea that we are *acquainted* with the conscious sensory experiences we undergo, which in turn raises questions about what is involved in putative cases of introspecting one's experience. Let us now reconsider this issue in light of the proposals I have so far made in my attempt to address the question of the difference between, and relation between, (a) introspectively attending to an experience one is having, and (b) perceptually attending to an object of that experience.

There is a respect in which it is correct to claim that we are not acquainted with the conscious sensory experiences we undergo: we are not acquainted with the experiences we undergo in so far as we do not experience those experiences in the way in which we experience the entities that we are perceptually acquainted with. This is why, although it seems to one as though one can shift one's perceptual attention from one experienced event to another, it doesn't seem to one as though one can shift one's attention, in the same way, from some particular event that one is experiencing to the particular event that is one's experience of it. But this doesn't establish that it is not possible for one to engage in the pre-judgemental activity of introspectively attending to one's experience. It merely reveals something about what that activity involves.

I have suggested that what is right about the claim that experience is transparent—in particular, what's right about the weaker version of that claim—is the fact that one engages in the activity of introspectively attending to one's visual experience by looking at (and watching) entities that one is perceptually aware of, or by behaving *as if* that is what one is doing. When one introspects one's experience one looks at (or behaves as if one is looking at) something, with the intention of discovering something about the experience one is undergoing. When one introspects one's experience one isn't thereby acquainted with one's experience in the way in which one is perceptually acquainted with the objects of one's experience. This introspective activity doesn't initiate an experience of one's experience. But as one introspects, one has a form of pre-judgemental, but cognitive, awareness of the experience one is undergoing—a form of cognitive awareness of one's experience that is constitutively dependent on the occurrence of that experience. One is in occurrent cognitive states that depend constitutively for their obtaining on the occurrence of the conscious sensory experience one undergoes. And these occurrent cognitive states ground the judgements one is poised to make about one's experience as one looks at (or merely behaves as if one is looking at) something with the intention of discerning something about the experience one is undergoing.

I have suggested that although the weaker version of the transparency claim is consistent with the idea that we can engage in the pre-judgemental activity of introspectively attending to our experiences, it shows that the sort of intentional behaviour one thereby engages in cannot be characterized independently of the sort of behaviour one can only engage in when one is perceptually aware of something. For example, when one introspectively attends to one's visual experience, even if one believes that one is hallucinating, one behaves *as though* one is *looking at* and/or *watching* something. And one can only be engaged in the activity of looking at or watching something if one is perceptually aware of something. If one's belief that one is hallucinating is true, then one is not in a position to look at/watch entities one is perceptually aware of, but it remains the case that in introspecting one's experience one behaves as though one is looking at/watching entities that one is perceptually aware of.

Consideration of the kind of intentional behaviour that we engage in when we introspectively attend to our experience intimates something about the kind of introspective access to our experience that we *seem* to have. The sort of intentional behaviour one engages in when one introspects one's experience reveals that it seems to one as though one doesn't have available to one a form of introspective access to one's experience that is independent of one's perceptual access to the objects of that experience. It's a perceptual perspective on the world that seems to provide one with an introspective perspective on one's experience.[5]

If a subject is hallucinating—if she isn't perceptually aware of anything—then her epistemic position with respect to her environment isn't all it seems to be. She doesn't have the kind of perceptual access to her environment that she seems to have—she isn't able to engage in the activities of looking at and watching (maintaining cognitive contact with) things that she seems to be perceptually aware of. But there is also a sense in which her epistemic position with respect to her experience isn't all that it seems to be. For if she isn't perceptually aware of anything, then she doesn't have available to her the kind of introspective access to her experience that she seems to have. When one hallucinates, one seems to have available to one the kind of introspective access to one's experience that is made possible by having perceptual access to the objects of one's experience—the kind of perceptual access to those objects that makes it possible for one to look at and watch those objects in the visual case. There is a sense, then, in which we need to characterize in *derivative* terms the kind of introspective access to one's experience that one seems to have when one is hallucinating. When one hallucinates, it seems to one as though one has the kind of introspective access to one's experience that

---

[5] Compare Martin's (2006) proposal that a subject's introspective perspective on her experience coincides with, and is not independent of, her experiential perspective on the world.

one has when one is *perceptually* aware *of* something. In the next section I shall be discussing how this conclusion bears on the relationalist account of conscious sensory experience that I have argued for.

8.4 A relationalist response to the problem of hallucination

According to the sort of relational view of conscious sensory experience that I have argued for, we need to appeal to the obtaining of a distinctive kind of psychological, but non-representational, relation when articulating the distinctive sensuous character that is manifest to one when one has a conscious sensory experience. The relevant psychological relation is the relation of perceptual acquaintance, and according to the view I have proposed, when a subject succeeds in perceiving her environment she stands in this perceptual relation to material objects (and events) and their features, and not to the sorts of entities posited by sense-datum theorists. I have argued that it is the actual obtaining of this non-representational psychological relation between the subject of experience and entities in the world that is doing some work in accounting for the conscious character of successful perception. According to this proposal, one misses out some aspect of the phenomenology of the experience if one does not appeal to the obtaining of this relation when it comes to fully characterizing the phenomenology of the experience undergone.

The obvious difficulty facing this account is that this psychological relation to material objects (and events) cannot plausibly be held to obtain in the case of hallucination. So if we accept that a hallucination can have the same conscious character as a successful perception, then we should either accept that (a) we do not, after all, need to appeal to the obtaining of this perceptual relation when providing an account of the conscious character of a successful perception, or (b) in the case of hallucination the relation of perceptual acquaintance is one that obtains between the subject of experience and non-material objects and their features—i.e. sense-data.

The relationalist response to this dilemma that I think should be endorsed is one that rejects the assumption upon which it depends—i.e. the response that denies that a complete hallucination has the same conscious character as a successful perception. According to this relationalist proposal, when a subject hallucinates, although it may seem to that subject as though she is having a conscious sensory experience that involves the obtaining of this distinctive psychological relation, she is not. In Chapter 1 I said that questions about self-knowledge lie right at the heart of questions about what I called the 'manifest image' of conscious sensory experience. Disagreements about the manifest image of conscious sensory experience intersect with disagreements in the epistemology of mind—e.g. disagreements about what one can and cannot know about the conscious character of a conscious sensory experience one is undergoing; and disagreements about what puts one in a position to know what one can know of such experience. Here we have an instance of that general idea. For the relationalist holds that the right account of what one can know of the conscious character of the conscious sensory experience one undergoes when one perceives the world, and one's account of what puts one in a position to know it, cannot be straightforwardly and symmetrically applied to the case of hallucination.

A proper assessment of this relationalist view will depend, in part, on an assessment of its commitments in the epistemology of mind. In what follows I want to reconsider this relationalist view of the conscious character of experience in light of the proposals that I have so far made about the activity of introspection and the ontology of self-knowledge. First, though, I want to consider why this relationalist stance on hallucination can seem such a counterintuitive position to be committed to.

Many find counterintuitive the claim that a hallucination cannot have the same conscious character as a successful perception. For it is plausible to hold that it is in principle possible for one to have a hallucination that is introspectively indiscriminable from a successful perception, and it is intuitive to think that if a hallucination is introspectively indiscriminable from a successful perception then this is to be explained by the fact that it has the same conscious character as a successful perception. Those who hold the sort of relationalist position that I'm suggesting we should endorse need to reject the assumption that introspectively indiscriminable experiences must have the same conscious, phenomenal, character. One way they might do this is by arguing that we are not infallible when it comes to making judgements about the phenomenal characters of our own experiences. We need to accept a more modest view of the extent to which we can know our own minds and mental lives. Not even the phenomenal properties of our own mental events are luminous.[6] So from the fact that two conscious experiences are introspectively indiscriminable, it does not follow that they have the same phenomenal character.

While I think that this more modest view of the extent to which we can know our own minds and mental lives is correct, I suggest that this response does not seem to engage adequately with the intuitions that lie behind opposition to the relationalist stance on hallucination. One can accept that we are not infallible when it comes to making judgements about the phenomenal characters of our experiences, one can accept that not even the phenomenal properties of our experiences are luminous, yet still one can feel that the relationalist's commitment—that a genuine perception and an introspectively indiscriminable hallucination have different phenomenal characters— must somehow lack warrant.

I shall return to this suggestion shortly, but before doing so I want to mention another standard argument against the relationalist stance on hallucination—the causal argument. One version of the argument presents the relationalist with the following

---

[6] For an influential argument against the luminosity of the mental, see Williamson 2000, especially chapter 4. For a discussion of the claim that the anti-disjunctivist common-kind assumption depends on an immodest view of the extent to which we can know our own minds, see Martin 2004. For a critical discussion of Martin's argument, see Siegel 2003.

problem.[7] Whatever account the relationalist gives of the phenomenal character of hallucinatory experience, she has a problem when it comes to explaining why the proximate cause of a genuine perception is not sufficient to produce an experience of that phenomenal kind; for presumably the specified type of proximate cause *is* sufficient to produce an experience of that phenomenal kind when an appropriate event involving the apparent object of perception does *not* occur prior to the proximate cause. So is there some kind of action at a distance when we successfully perceive the world, which alters the phenomenal character of a genuine perception? Surely this would saddle the relationalist with an implausible commitment. If the proximate cause of a genuine perception *is* sufficient to produce an experience of a given phenomenal kind, an experience with the phenomenal character of a hallucination, then surely when it comes to articulating the phenomenal character of a genuine perception we should not need to appeal to the obtaining of a perceptual relation between the subject of experience and material objects/events in her environment, given that this relation doesn't obtain in the case of hallucination.

Here it seems that the relationalist must reject the assumption that it is possible to provide a positive, non-derivative account of the kind of conscious sensory experience involved when a subject hallucinates—at least in the case of a causally matching hallucination.[8] This is why this relationalist should reject the claim that in the case of hallucination the relation of perceptual acquaintance is one that obtains between the subject of experience and non-material entities and their features—i.e. sense-data. So according to this relationalist, it is not just that the phenomenal character of the experience a subject has when she perceives the world is different in kind from the phenomenal character of an introspectively indiscriminable hallucination. As it turns out, according to this relationalist, it is not possible to provide a positive, non-derivative account of the phenomenal character of a hallucination. Surely hallucinations do have a phenomenal character—surely they do have phenomenal properties—but when it comes to specifying, in a positive, non-derivative way, the phenomenal character of such an experience, the relationalist must remain mysteriously silent. The best one can do is to describe the kind of phenomenal character from which it cannot be introspectively discriminated.

This move naturally strikes many as ad hoc and counterintuitive. Are we being asked to accept that hallucinations have phenomenal properties that are somehow strangely inaccessible, and necessarily so?[9] And are we being asked to swallow this counterintuitive claim simply to avoid what seems to be a reasonable argument against the relationalist view of successful perception? I suggest that in order to answer this question we need

---

[7] A version of the causal argument against disjunctivism is put forward by Robinson 1985 and 1994. Johnston 2004 also appeals to a version of the causal argument in outlining his opposition to the disjunctive theory. For a defence of disjunctivism against the causal argument, see Martin 2004 and 2006.

[8] For a discussion and defence of the claim, see Martin 1997, 2004, and 2006, where Martin rejects Dancy's (1995) suggestion that the disjunctivist can allow that there may be available a direct characterization of the kind of experience involved when a subject hallucinates (in the case of causally matching hallucination).

[9] For an objection along these lines, see Johnston 2004.

to re-examine the opposition to the relationalist stance on hallucination that is motivated by intuitions concerning introspective indiscriminability and sameness of
phenomenal character. The explanation of why the relationalist does not adequately
address intuitions behind such opposition by simply appealing to the fallibility of the
judgements we make about the phenomenal character of our own experiences can
actually throw some light on her response to the causal argument. It is not simply the
immodest assumption of infallibility that is driving intuitions here. It is something else.
And identifying what this is can help make sense of the relationalist's position with
regard to the causal argument.

I suggest that the arguments against the relationalist stance on hallucination that are
based on the claim that hallucinations can be introspectively indiscriminable from genuine perceptions get their intuitive force from an assumption about the *source* of the
warrant of our judgements about phenomenal character, rather than an intuition about
their infallibility. It is the same intuition that lies behind the thought that Mary, before
she leaves her black and white room, cannot know what it is like to see red.[10] The intuition is that Mary cannot acquire knowledge of the phenomenal character of an experience of seeing red in, what we might call, a *purely third-personal* way. By this I mean that if
she is to acquire such knowledge, she must be, or have been, in a position to *introspect* an
experience as of something red, or at least she must have the capacity to imagine *from the
inside*, an experience as of something red.

If we accept this intuitive idea, then according to the proposals I have so far made
about introspection, perceptual memory, and perceptual imagination, this means that
one's knowledge of what it is like to have an experience depends on one's being in, or
having the capacity to put oneself in, occurrent cognitive states that depend constitutively for their obtaining on the occurrence of phenomenally conscious events/proc-
esses—i.e. the sorts of occurrent cognitive states that I have suggested obtain as one
introspects one's experience, and the sorts of occurrent cognitive states that I have suggested obtain when one perceptually recollects or imagines something.

If one accepts the general intuition about the possible sources of knowledge of the
phenomenal character of an experience (i.e. the intuition that one cannot acquire such
knowledge in a purely third-personal way), then one might find intuitive the idea that if
a judgement or claim about the phenomenal character of an experience is to be warranted, then it must ultimately be grounded in such sources. It must ultimately be
grounded in what we might broadly call 'introspective' evidence—i.e. the evidence that
is made available to one through being in such occurrent cognitive states.[11] Note that

---

[10] See Jackson 1982.

[11] I suggest that the same intuition lies behind the thought that we cannot know what it is like to be a
bat. (See Nagel 1974 and 1986.) Even the knowledge we can have of the phenomenal character of the
experiences of other creatures must ultimately be grounded in the knowledge we have of the phenomenal
character of our own experiences, which is ultimately grounded in what I have called 'introspective' evidence. Knowledge of the phenomenal character of an experience cannot simply be grounded in *non*-
introspective evidence.

this intuition does not seem to depend upon an immodest view of the knowledge we have of our own minds. The intuition that lies behind the Mary thought experiment persists for many who agree that we are not infallible when it comes to making judgements about the phenomenal character of our experiences.

Let us try to articulate an argument against the relationalist stance on hallucination that makes explicit this assumption, and which uses it as a premise:

(1) The knowledge we have of the phenomenal character of our experiences must ultimately be grounded in 'introspective' evidence. It cannot be grounded in purely third-personal, non-introspective evidence. Positive claims about the phenomenal character of experience, if they are to be warranted, must ultimately be grounded in introspective evidence.

(2) Since any positive claims about the phenomenal character of experience must ultimately be grounded in introspective evidence if they are to be warranted, then one can be warranted in claiming that one's experience A has some phenomenal character ϕ and one's experience B has a different phenomenal character ϕ only if this claim is warranted by some introspective evidence.

(3) If a veridical perception and a hallucination are genuinely introspectively indiscriminable, then there can be no introspective evidence to warrant the claim that the veridical perception has some phenomenal character ϕ and the hallucination has some different phenomenal character ϕ. For to concede that there may, after all, be some introspective evidence to warrant the claim that they have different phenomenal characters is to concede that they are not, after all, genuinely introspectively indiscriminable. Therefore,

(4) Any claim of the form that the phenomenal character that veridical perception has is different from the phenomenal character that an introspectively indiscriminable hallucination has must ultimately be unwarranted. The introspective evidence does not warrant the claim (as they are introspectively indiscriminable), and the non-introspective evidence *cannot* warrant the claim (given premise (1)).

This line of argument suggests that the relationalist's claim that veridical perceptions and hallucinations do not have the same conscious character must ultimately be unwarranted. The argument stops short of asserting that the relationalist's claim is false, but it does seem to put the relationalist in an awkward position. So how should she respond? Should the relationalist reject premise (1)? I think that there is no need for the relationalist to reject premise (1)—the claim about the special role of introspective evidence in grounding claims we make about the phenomenal character of our experiences. For still the anti-relationalist conclusion does not automatically follow, and understanding why the conclusion does not automatically follow gives us a clearer view of what the relationalist must be committed to, and helps to make sense of her response to the causal argument.

Even if we accept that positive claims about the phenomenal character of experience can only be warranted by what I have called 'introspective' evidence, the anti-relationalist conclusion does not follow if *non*-introspective evidence can, in principle, *defeat* the warrant of claims about the phenomenal character of experience that is provided by one's introspective evidence. Positive claims about the phenomenal character of experience cannot be warranted by purely third-personal, non-introspective evidence. So if the positive claims about the phenomenal character of an experience that are warranted by introspective evidence are defeated by non-introspective evidence, then we cannot be warranted in making positive, non-derivative claims about the phenomenal character of the experience. The introspective evidence does not warrant any such claims, as they are defeated by non-introspective evidence, and the non-introspective evidence *cannot* warrant any such claims. So the best we can do is to characterize the phenomenal character of such experiences derivatively, in terms of the kind of phenomenal character they are introspectively indiscriminable from. A defence of the relationalist stance on hallucination will therefore depend on the idea that the positive claims about the phenomenal characters of hallucinatory experiences that are warranted by introspective evidence are defeated by non-introspective evidence, whereas the positive claims about the phenomenal characters of veridical perceptions that are warranted by introspective evidence are *not* defeated by non-introspective evidence. This idea is, I suggest, in line with the proposals that I have so far made about what is involved in introspectively attending to an experience one is undergoing.

One might think that when one hallucinates, although one's epistemic position with respect to one's environment may be disadvantaged, one's epistemic position with respect to the conscious character of one's own experience is not. That is to say, some might think that one is no better placed, epistemically speaking, to make judgements about the conscious character of one's experience when one perceives the world than when one hallucinates. For although one's environment may not be perceptually accessible to one when one hallucinates, one's experience is still introspectively accessible to one, and in the same way in which it is introspectively accessible to one in cases of successful perception. On one such view, what grounds one's judgements about the conscious character of one's conscious experience is one's introspective access to the experience (the sort of introspective access to experience one can have whether or not the experience is a successful perception), where introspection might be thought of as a capacity to alight on, and attend to, phenomenal properties that the experience possesses (whether or not the judgements one makes as a result of so introspecting are true). This picture lends plausibility to the idea that what grounds judgements of introspective indiscriminability in the case of hallucination is the fact that introspection is alighting on phenomenal properties of the experience that it actually possesses, and which it shares with successful perception.

This is a picture of introspection that I have suggested we have reason to reject. I suggested that consideration of the kind of intentional behaviour that we engage in when we introspectively attend to our experience reveals that it seems to one as though one doesn't have available to one a form of introspective access to one's experience that is independent of one's perceptual access to the objects of that experience. When one hallucinates, one seems to have available to one the kind of introspective access to one's experience that is made possible by having perceptual access to the objects of one's experience—the kind of perceptual access to those objects that makes it possible for one to look at and watch those objects in the visual case. So, I suggested, we need to characterize in *derivative* terms the kind of *introspective* access to one's experience that one seems to have when one is hallucinating. When one hallucinates, it seems to one as though one has the kind of introspective access to one's experience that one has when one is perceptually aware *of* something.

Even if a subject is aware that she is hallucinating, the kind of intentional behaviour that she engages in as she introspects her experience cannot be adequately characterized independently of the kind of intentional behaviour that she can only engage in when she is perceptually aware of something. In engaging in the activity of introspecting her experience she behaves *as though* she is in a position to *look at (and watch)*—i.e. maintain cognitive contact with—entities that she is perceptually aware of. So in the case of the subject who knows that she is hallucinating, there is a sense in which the following is true. The subject's introspective access to her experience seems to her to be made possible by her perceptual access to the world. If a subject is hallucinating, then it is not just her epistemic position with respect to her environment that is compromised. Her epistemic position with respect to her own experience is also compromised; for given that she isn't perceptually aware of anything, and so given that she doesn't have the kind of perceptual access to the world that she seems to have, she doesn't have the kind of introspective access to her experience that she seems to have.

What can one know about the experience one undergoes in such circumstances? As self-conscious subjects we can qualify the perceptual judgements we make about the world—the judgements we make on the basis of the occurrent cognitive states that obtain when we undergo conscious sensory experience. We can restrict our perceptual judgements to those concerned with the kind of perceptual access to, and perspective on, the world that we *seem* to have. But equally, we can qualify the introspective judgements we make about our experience—the introspective judgements we make on the basis of the occurrent cognitive states that obtain when we undergo conscious sensory experience. We can restrict our judgements to those concerned with the kind of introspective access to our experience that we *seem* to have. In the case of hallucination, just as one is in a position to know what *perceptually* seems to one to be the case, one can know what *introspectively* seems to one to be the case.

In the case of hallucination, the conscious character of the conscious sensory experience one undergoes needs to be characterized in derivative terms, and this is because the kind of introspective access to one's experience that one seems to have needs to be characterized in derivative terms; and this, in turn, is because the kind of intentional behaviour one engages in when one introspects one's experience needs to be characterized in derivative terms. What one can know of the conscious character of the conscious sensory experience one undergoes when one hallucinates is that it *introspectively seems* to one to have the conscious character of a genuine perceptual *awareness of* some entity or entities.

The subject's epistemic position with respect to the conscious character of the conscious sensory experience that she undergoes when she successfully perceives the world is somewhat different. In the case of successful perception the subject has available to her the kind of introspective access to her experience that she seems to have, because she has available to her the kind of perceptual access to objects of experience that she seems to have. The objective commitments of the sort of intentional behaviour that she engages in as she introspects her experience are not (objectively) defeated by non-introspective evidence. The subject is in a position to acquire knowledge of the conscious character that the experience actually has, and not just knowledge of the conscious character that it introspectively seems to have. It is for this reason that the relationalist holds that the right account of what one can know of the conscious character of the conscious sensory experience one undergoes when one perceives the world, and one's account of what puts one in a position to know it, cannot be straightforwardly and symmetrically applied to the case of hallucination.

In light of this discussion I now want to return to some remarks I made in Chapter 3 on the hallucination of bodily sensation. According to the account I proposed, when you have a hallucination of a sensation of pain in some part of your body, it seems to you as though you are undergoing a phenomenal event of a kind that you are not in fact undergoing. It seems to you as though you are undergoing a phenomenal *bodily* event that modifies the body part at which it seems to occur; and since you are hallucinating the body part, no such event is occurring. I went on to highlight some puzzling aspects of the phenomenology of such experiences: (i) it is intuitive to think that hallucinations of located bodily sensations are phenomenally conscious—i.e. there is something it is like for you when you hallucinate a located bodily sensation; (ii) when you hallucinate a located bodily sensation you seem to be undergoing a phenomenal event of a kind that you are not in fact undergoing; and (iii) it is intuitive to think that if you hallucinate a located bodily sensation, you are, ceteris paribus, in a position to know what it is like to undergo the sort of phenomenal bodily event that you seem to be undergoing, but which you are not in fact undergoing.

Regarding claims (i)–(iii) we can now say the following. When you hallucinate a sensation of pain in some part of your body, you seem to be in a position to attend to a phenomenal bodily event. But you are not. For no such event is occurring. However, although you are not undergoing a phenomenal bodily event, as you lack the relevant body part, you are undergoing a phenomenally conscious *experience as of* such a phenomenal bodily event. The conscious character of that phenomenally conscious experience needs to be specified in derivative terms. This is because the kind of introspective access to that experience that you seem to have needs to be characterized in derivative terms, and this because the kind of intentional behaviour you engage in when you introspect that experience needs to be characterized in derivative terms. What you can know of the conscious character of the conscious sensory experience you undergo in such circumstances is that it introspectively *seems* to you to have the conscious character of a genuine perceptual *awareness of* some phenomenal bodily event.

When you undergo such an experience you are not in fact perceptually aware of the kind of phenomenal bodily event that you seem to be perceptually aware of, and for this reason you are not in fact introspectively aware of the kind of phenomenally conscious experience that you seem to be introspectively aware of. However, in undergoing such an experience you can acquire knowledge of what it *would* be like to attend perceptually to such a bodily occurrence, and you can acquire knowledge of what it *would* be like to attend introspectively to an experience that was a perceptual awareness of such a bodily occurrence. And moreover, in acts of perceptual imagination and memory you can manifest knowledge of what it *is* like to be perceptually aware of such a bodily occurrence. So when you hallucinate a located bodily sensation, you are, ceteris paribus, in a position to know what it is like to undergo the sort of phenomenal bodily event that you seem to be undergoing, but which you are not in fact undergoing.

Similar remarks apply to other conscious sensory hallucinations—e.g. visual hallucinations. For in the case of visual hallucinations, analogues of claims (i)–(iii) apply: (i)★ it is intuitive to think that visual hallucinations are phenomenally conscious experiences; (ii)★ when you have a visual hallucination you seem to be undergoing a phenomenally conscious experience of a kind that you are not in fact undergoing; and (iii)★ it is intuitive to think that if you have a visual hallucination, you are, ceteris paribus, in a position to know what it is like to have a successful visual perception of the world. The relationalist should accept that visual hallucinations are phenomenally conscious occurrences. But she should hold that the conscious character of such a phenomenally conscious experience needs to be specified in derivative terms. What you can know of the conscious character of the conscious sensory experience you undergo in such circumstances is that it *introspectively seems* to you to have the conscious character of a genuine perceptual *awareness of* some entity.

When you undergo such an experience you are not in fact perceptually aware of the entities that you seem to be perceptually aware of, and for this reason you are not in fact introspectively aware of the kind of phenomenally conscious experience that you seem to be introspectively aware of. However, in undergoing such an experience you can acquire knowledge of what it would be like to attend perceptually to such entities, and you can acquire knowledge of what it would be like to attend introspectively to an experience that is a perceptual awareness of such entities. And moreover, in acts of perceptual imagination and memory you can manifest knowledge of what it is like to be perceptually aware of such entities. So when you experience such a visual hallucination you are, ceteris paribus, in a position to know what it is like to undergo the sort of phenomenally conscious event that you seem to be undergoing, but which you are not in fact undergoing—i.e. a visual awareness of some entity.

8.5 The ontology of knowing the phenomenology

In much of Part I of this book, I have been focusing on claims that concern what I have been calling the 'manifest image' of sensory consciousness; and I have discussed how these claims intersect with views about the kind of knowledge we can have of our conscious sensory experiences as self-conscious subjects of them. I noted that disagreements about how to articulate the manifest image of conscious sensory experience can be quite basic and fundamental. There can be disagreements over the *general shape* of the manifest image of conscious sensory experience, and not just disagreements over the fine details.

I have defended the claim that when articulating the general shape of the manifest image of conscious sensory experience we need to invoke a relationalist framework that appeals to structural features of perceptual awareness. But I have also argued that there are further important ontological distinctions to keep in mind—ontological distinctions that are determined by the different ways in which different aspects of mind fill time. I have suggested that appropriate articulation of the manifest image of sensory consciousness will depend on finding an ontology that fits the phenomenology and the knowledge that we have of that phenomenology; and in this enterprise the ontological distinctions between event, process, and state are important, and so too is the role played by the ontological category of 'occurrent' state.

I have tried to show how these ontological proposals can contribute to our philosophical understanding of sensory consciousness, by putting them to explanatory work in a variety of ways: (i) I have suggested how the proposal I have made about the ontology of conscious sensory experience can give rise to a certain kind of explanatory circularity, and I have suggested how the existence of this form of explanatory circularity can be used to diagnose certain intuitions that arise in debates about the phenomenal character of experience (Chapter 2). (ii) I have argued that this general view of the ontology of conscious sensory experience can be used to inform our account of the phenomenology of bodily sensations—aspects of mind that are generally thought to be paradigmatic of those mental occurrences/states that only a phenomenally conscious subject can be the subject of (Chapter 3). (iii) I have argued that this view of the ontology can be used to resolve certain puzzles about the temporal phenomenology of experience and our experience of events (Chapter 4). (iv) I have suggested that it can be used to help illuminate a distinctive form of conscious contact with time that phenomenally conscious subjects have, and I have outlined how this proposal bears on debates concerned with the 'continuity' of conscious sensory experience (Chapters 5 and 6). (v) I also invoked these ontological proposals in accommodating and explaining the notion that there are certain activities that only a phenomenally conscious subject can engage in— i.e. the activities of perceptually imagining and perceptually recollecting (Chapter 7). And finally, (vi) I have suggested that these ontological considerations can be used to provide an account of a variety of knowledge that only phenomenally conscious subjects can have—knowledge of what it is like to have conscious sensory experience (Chapters 7 and 8).

At the outset I suggested that an account of the ontology of sensory consciousness that fits the phenomenology and the knowledge we can have of that phenomenology, should ideally be one that can accommodate the existence of disagreement about that phenomenology; for as I have said, disagreements about conscious sensory experience are not restricted to those that fall under the purview of the 'scientific' image of mind. Disagreements about the *manifest* image of conscious sensory experience can be quite basic and fundamental. So I want now to end Part I with some brief remarks on that point.

I have suggested that one's knowledge of what it is like to have an experience depends on one's being in, or having the capacity to put oneself in, occurrent cognitive states that depend constitutively for their obtaining on the occurrence of phenomenally conscious events/processes. These are the sorts of occurrent cognitive states that obtain as one introspects one's experience, and the sorts of occurrent cognitive states that obtain when one perceptually recollects or imagines something. These occurrent cognitive states account for a variety of knowledge of the conscious character of conscious sensory experience that is made available to one simply in virtue of having the capacity to introspectively attend to an experience one is undergoing; and they account for a variety of knowledge of the conscious character of conscious sensory experience that one can manifest in acts of perceptual imagination and recollection.

Although the knowledgeable judgements we can make about the conscious character of conscious sensory experience must ultimately be grounded in the 'introspective' evidence that is made available to us through being in such occurrent cognitive states, these occurrent cognitive states are not themselves judgements. So the fact that we, as self-conscious subjects, can be in such occurrent cognitive states, and thereby have this variety of knowledge of the conscious character of conscious sensory experience, is no guarantee that we will inevitably agree in the *judgements* we reach about the ontology of the manifest image of sensory consciousness.

I have proposed accounts of (a) the activity of introspecting one's experience and (b) the sort of self-knowledge involved in perceptual imagination and perceptual recollection, which are in line with a relationalist view of conscious sensory experience. I have suggested that some form of commitment to the relationalist view is revealed in, and implicit in, the sort of intentional behaviour we engage in when we introspectively attend to an experience we are undergoing. But this activity is not equivalent to that of judging something about the conscious character of one's experience. Moreover, I have suggested that the sort of knowledge of the conscious character of conscious sensory experience that we manifest in acts of perceptual imagination and recollection also supports the relationalist view. But these are not acts of judging something about the conscious character of experience either. This is why, even though there is a variety of knowledge of the conscious character of experience that is made available to one simply in virtue of being the sort of self-conscious subject who can introspect her experiences and engage in acts of perceptual imagination and recollection, when it comes to uncovering an ontology of sensory consciousness that fits the phenomenology and the knowledge we have of that phenomenology, we need to resort to use of the appropriate 'conceptual tweezers aided and abetted by argumentation', and not just the use of our 'attentional tweezers' (O'Shaughnessy 2000: 452). And with the adoption of such an approach agreement is by no means guaranteed.

PART II

Conscious Thinking

9

The Place of Mental Action in the Metaphysics of Mind

In Part I, I tried to show how issues in the ontology of mind can contribute to our philosophical understanding of sensory consciousness. In Part II the focus of enquiry will shift, from sensory consciousness to conscious thinking; but the ontological considerations that I raised in Part I will continue to have a significant role to play. In Part I, I introduced Geach's argument for the claim that there is no 'stream of conscious thought'. According to Geach, although sensory aspects of mind are 'stream-like', acts of thinking thoughts are not. As we saw, the question of whether an aspect of mind is stream-like connects with the ontological question of the manner in which that aspect of mind fills time. So what we find in Geach's argument is the suggestion that our conscious mental acts of thinking thoughts do not fill time in the same manner as our conscious sensory experiences. We will need to reconsider Geach's proposal about conscious thought in due course, and I shall begin to do so in the next chapter. In this chapter I want to introduce one of the other main themes of the second part of this book: the question of the place of mental action in an account of mind. This concern will connect with the enquiry into conscious thinking, for I shall be arguing that a consideration of the agency that we are able to exercise over our mental lives should be central to an account of conscious thinking and the form of self-conscious consciousness that we have as subjects capable of engaging in such activity.

One finds little mention of mental action in most of the current philosophical discussions of consciousness and self-consciousness. Indeed the topic is not often discussed in accounts of mentality (or 'the mind') in general, and it does not feature prominently in accounts of action and agency. In what follows I shall start by outlining some of the background to this apparent neglect of the topic in accounts of consciousness, mentality, and action. I shall then go on to introduce some of the main questions about mental action that I shall be addressing in the rest of Part II.

9.1 'Cartesian' and 'anti-Cartesian' approaches

Much of the current literature on consciousness is vexed with the task of understanding the nature of phenomenal consciousness—a task that has been labelled the 'hard problem'.[1] These discussions often focus on sensory aspects of mind—e.g. perceptual experiences and sensations. As I noted in Chapter 1, there has been a persistent and prevalent tendency among philosophers to assume that the knowledge we have, or can have, of our sensory experiences when we have them has a special and significant role to play when it comes to offering a philosophical account of conscious sensory experience, and that an appeal to introspection and phenomenology is legitimate when theorizing about the nature of such experience in a way it perhaps isn't when theorizing about thought. The underlying assumption is that one's conscious sensory experiences have a sensuous character that is characteristic of them, and moreover, this sensuous character that they have is somehow manifest to one as a self-conscious subject when one has them.

As I discussed in Part I, this assumption is now intimately bound up with the claim that these conscious sensory aspects of mind have phenomenal/what-it-is-like properties. The idea is that there is *something it is like* for the subject of them when they occur/ obtain. For example, there is something it is like for a subject when she feels a sensation of pain. The experience has a *phenomenal* character. This phenomenal character is thought to be determined by the phenomenal properties that the experience possesses, where such phenomenal properties are thought to be introspectively accessible to the subject of experience.

The sorts of 'hard' questions that dominate discussions of consciousness now get framed in terms of the place of such properties in an account of mind. For example: what is the relation between the phenomenal properties of an experience and its representational properties? What should we make of the place and role of such properties in functionalist accounts of the mind? Does the fact that our conscious sensory experiences possess such properties make problems for a physicalist view of the mind? The conscious sensory aspects of mind that are thought to be the most striking examples of mental states/events that have such phenomenal properties (e.g. perceptual experiences and sensations) are ones we tend to think of as non-agential. In consequence there has been very little discussion of the relevance that the topic of mental action might have to our understanding of phenomenal consciousness, and as a result there has been little discussion of the relevance that the topic of mental action might have to our understanding of consciousness in general.

Recently there has been some discussion of the suggestion that cognitive aspects of mind may also have phenomenal, what-it-is-like properties.[2] For example, just as there is something it is like to experience a sensation of pain, perhaps there is also something it is like to consciously judge an arithmetical proposition. But as considerations regarding mental agency are not thought to be of much help in resolving the questions and problems that arise in the case of conscious sensory experience, this assumption is inherited

---

[1] For the idea that phenomenal consciousness presents the 'hard' problem of consciousness, see Chalmers 1996.

[2] See e.g. Bayne and Montague 2011.

in many of the discussions of the phenomenology of cognitive aspects of mind, such as conscious thought.

We can contrast the set of assumptions guiding current philosophical discussions of consciousness and mind with those influencing the earlier Cartesian approach. One might think that there is some common ground to be identified here, for Descartes presumably thought that there is something about certain conscious aspects of mind that presents a 'hard problem' for materialism, just as some philosophers now think that phenomenal consciousness presents the hard problem for physicalism. Indeed, Descartes is sometimes criticized for focusing exclusively on conscious aspects of mind. However, it is noteworthy that the conscious aspects of mind that philosophers now tend to suggest create a hard problem for physicalism are not the aspects of mind that Descartes focused on, and the sorts of problems that now get raised for physicalism are not the ones that Descartes raised for materialism. While a number of philosophers now think that sensory consciousness presents the hard problem for physicalism, Descartes seemed to think that it is a consideration of conscious thinking, and the sort of self-conscious consciousness that enables us to engage in that kind of activity, that should lead us to reject materialism; and for Descartes, conscious thinking crucially involves 'the will'. For Descartes, then, the agency that we can exercise over our mental lives appears to be central to his conception of consciousness.

This difference is no doubt connected with the differences between the kind of metaphysical dualism that Descartes was concerned to argue for, and the kind of metaphysical dualism that philosophers are now more concerned to consider and address—i.e. the differences between substance dualism and property dualism. In discussions of the latter we find considered the conceivability and metaphysical possibility of the physical world without phenomenal properties. In Descartes' discussion of the former we find considered the conceivability and metaphysical possibility of disembodied existence. In his attempt to protect the coherence of the notion of disembodied existence Descartes was concerned to protect the coherence of the notion of a disembodied agent—an agent capable of action but incapable of bodily action. Under such an approach, the agency that we can exercise over our mental lives becomes of paramount concern. For Descartes, sensory consciousness is a form of consciousness that is only available to the embodied subject, whereas conscious thinking is an activity that the disembodied agent can engage in. So it is the latter, and not the former, that occupies a central place in his argument against materialism. Concerns that arise in connection with the former—i.e. sensory consciousness—seem, for Descartes, to have more to do with embodiment—the distinctive way in which distinct substances are united in the embodied, conscious, human subject.

The sort of mind–body problems that now receive attention in the philosophy of mind are no longer framed in terms of questions about the distinctions between, and relations between, substances. Mind–body problems are now more often framed in terms of an attempt to understand how the workings of the mind relate to the workings of the body—that is, in terms of questions concerned with the distinctions between, and relations between, mental and bodily *events*, *states*, and *properties*. Under this framework, questions regarding agency are, of course, still of concern. Just as we can raise questions about how the workings of the mind relate to the workings of the body, we can raise questions about how the workings of the mind relate to the activity of an agent. Under this sort of approach, one might then identify two distinct problems to be addressed: a mind–body problem (how do the workings of the mind relate to the workings of the body?) and an agent–mind problem (how do the workings of the mind relate to the activity of an agent?). These two problems can be combined to yield an agent–body problem (how do the workings of the body relate to the activity of an agent?), but one might think that the best strategy is to start by pursuing each independently—the former problem falling under the purview of the philosophy of mind, and the latter problem falling under the purview of the philosophy of action.[3] With this sort of division of labour in place, the questions concerning consciousness that are of primary concern are usually thought to fall under the mind–body problem, and so in contrast to the Cartesian approach, considerations regarding agency are not thought of as central to our understanding of consciousness—or at least not to our understanding of the 'hard' problem of phenomenal consciousness that dominates so much of the current theorizing about consciousness.

Although discussions of mental agency do not often feature prominently in current discussions of consciousness, a case can be made for thinking that action is now right at the heart of the current orthodox understanding of mentality in general, in so far as emphasis is now placed on the notion of psychological subject as *bodily agent*. Under this approach, the notion of psychological subject as agent of bodily action is emphasized, and the notion of psychological subject as agent of mental action is downplayed. This might be seen as a legacy of a shift in the philosophical terrain that occurred in the twentieth century, when there was a reaction against a 'Cartesian' approach to mind. In this context, the label 'Cartesian' is used to refer to a cluster of related views, rather than a particular thesis that Descartes endorsed, but this cluster of views is commonly thought of as a legacy of Descartes' way of thinking about the mental. One key strand in this 'Cartesian' approach is the idea that there is a merely *contingent* connection between one's mental life and the expression of one's mental life in the publicly observable realm that one's bodily actions inhabit. This metaphysical view is connected with an epistemological proposal. The suggestion is that even when a subject's epistemic access to the material world is compromised, her epistemic access to her own mind and mental life remains intact.

The metaphysical thesis and the epistemological thesis can be seen as natural allies. The subject's epistemic access to her own mind and mental life does not depend on a secure epistemic route to the material world, for the connections between the mental and material realms are merely causal and contingent, and not constitutive. Under this

---

[3] I owe this way of summarizing such an approach to David Velleman's seminars on action, previously published on his website (<https://files.nyu.edu/dv26/public/>).

approach, there is a significant difference between one's knowledge of one's own mind and one's knowledge of the material world—the former is secure in a way that the latter is not. And this brings with it a significant difference between one's knowledge of one's own mind and one's knowledge of the minds of others, on the assumption that the primary evidential mediators of one's knowledge of the minds of others are the publicly observable bodily manifestations of their interior mental lives. In its most extreme and radical form, this 'hoarding of interiority', as O'Shaughnessy (2008: 13) describes it, results in a picture according to which each subject has *infallible* access to her own *private* mental realm. As O'Shaughnessy remarks, the inhabitants of this mental realm 'stand in no binding need of manifesting their existence in bodily extremities in any way: metaphysical hermits!' (2008: 13)

The twentieth-century reaction against this 'Cartesian' conception of the mental, and against the postulation of such 'metaphysical hermits', emerges under various guises, and develops in a variety of ways. The earlier contributors to this general trend include Wittgenstein (1953) (e.g. in his attack on private language and his invocation of non-contingent links between the mental and bodily criteria), Ryle (1949) (e.g. his critique of the 'ghost in the machine'), Sellars (1963) (e.g. in his attack on the 'myth of the given' and in his critique of the 'classical view' of thought), and Strawson (1959) (in his critique of the Cartesian conception of self). A common thread is the rejection of an epistemic view that would make a subject's mental life both private to that subject and infallibly accessible to her. A connected thread is the idea that it is a mistake to regard as merely contingent the connections between one's mental life and publicly observable bodily manifestations of one's mental life; and this development puts bodily action right at the heart of this new approach to, and understanding of, mentality. Under this approach, some accord a central place to those bodily actions that *successfully* engage with the environment. And for some, when it comes to providing an account of thought, and in particular an account of the kind of thoughts that we as self-conscious subjects are capable of entertaining, a special significance is attached to a species of bodily action that we perform when we engage in a distinctive social practice, namely our publicly observable linguistic acts, which make publicly accessible and shareable the thoughts that they express.[4]

One of the earliest, and perhaps crudest, forms of this reaction against the Cartesian view of the mental is the behaviourist one. This is now seen by many as a flawed attempt to squeeze out altogether a subject's inner mental life, by reducing mentality to its publicly observable, bodily manifestations. But we have since seen a number of more sophisticated and subtle developments of the idea that the relation between mentality and bodily behaviour should not be thought of as merely contingent. Proponents of these more subtle approaches do not deny the reality of a subject's inner mental life, but they hold that a subject's inner mental life will necessarily be anchored in publicly observable bodily behaviour that expresses, and that is an effect of, that subject's mentality. For

---

[4] For the latter two points, see especially Davidson 2001a and 2001b.

example, a number of functionalist and interpretationist accounts of the mental incorporate this idea in different ways.

While the more subtle versions of this conception of mentality accommodate the existence of an inner mental life, a worry that is often raised is that they do not successfully incorporate the introspectively accessible phenomenal properties that are exemplified by our conscious sensory experiences and sensations. For it is suggested that the publicly observable bodily manifestations of our mentality and agency can be explained without essential recourse to them. So an upshot of opposition to the Cartesian conception of mentality is that conceptual space is created for a notion of mentality and agency that doesn't require phenomenal consciousness.[5] The suggestion is that were we to strip mentality of these phenomenal properties we would still have mentality and agency. We would still have a psychological subject, and an agent no less autonomous than a phenomenally conscious subject. The assumption, then, is that accounts of mentality and agency can proceed without a solution to the 'hard problem' of consciousness, which requires its own special and separate treatment.

With the advent of the anti-Cartesian notion of psychological subject as bodily agent, the agency that we exercise over our mental lives is not thought central to our understanding of mentality, and it is not thought central to our understanding of consciousness. So we find a considerable downgrading of the significance that had previously been attached to the notion of mental action. So what then is the place of mental action in these anti-Cartesian accounts of mentality? This question is rarely addressed explicitly, but we can try to identify some implicit assumptions that often seem to be in place. The functionalist approaches to mind that take the individuation of a mental state to be determined by its causal relations to sensory stimulations, other mental states, and behaviour, are usually confined to treating the relevant behaviour in question as bodily behaviour. This doesn't mean that such accounts are incompatible with the idea that we can perform mental as well as bodily actions, but the implicit assumption often seems to be that agential mental behaviour is to be explained and characterized in terms of the prior notions of sensory stimulation, bodily behaviour, mental states, and the events that are transitions between such states that contribute to the causal explanation of bodily behaviour. Similarly, under interpretationist approaches to the mental, the focus is invariably on mental state attributions that rationalize and causally explain *bodily* behaviour. The implicit assumption is that although bodily behaviour is to be taken as basic, mental behaviour is not. That is to say, the assumption seems to be that mental action is to be analysed as a variety of mental activity involving transitions between mental states that enable, rationalize, and causally explain *bodily* behaviour.

Again, we can contrast here the Cartesian conception of mental agency. As I mentioned, a major and obvious difference between the Cartesian approach and the current approach is that Descartes was interested in the possibility of disembodied existence in a way that most of those now participating in the current debate are not. Arguably, in

---

[5] For critical discussion of this approach to consciousness, see Eilan 2000.

order to make sense of the notion of disembodied existence we need to be able to make sense of the notion of disembodied agency, and in order to make sense of disembodied agency we need to think of the disembodied agent as capable of engaging in mental action. But the very idea of disembodied agency, and hence disembodied existence, seems to unravel if we conceive of mental actions as reducible to mental processes that enable and explain overt bodily actions.[6] So Descartes obviously had a motive to reject such a conception of mental action. Those who reject Descartes' substance dualism won't have the same motivation; but are there other reasons for thinking that this reductive understanding of mental action is problematic? This is a question I shall return to in later chapters. For now I just want to note how an implicit commitment to this conception of mental action can affect the way in which discussions of consciousness and phenomenal consciousness are framed.

Consider, for example, the way in which debates about phenomenal consciousness are sometimes set up in terms of the notion of functional equivalence. The following question is posed: is it possible for there to be two subjects who are functionally equivalent, but only one of whom is phenomenally conscious? This thought experiment calls into question the functional roles of the phenomenal properties of our phenomenally conscious mental states and events. In order to assess whether this is a genuine metaphysical possibility we need to know the criteria for assessing functional equivalence. Are two subjects functionally equivalent just in case they are in psychological states that play the same functional roles, and if so, how are we to determine what sameness of functional role consists in? Are two subjects functionally equivalent only if they are able to perform the same kinds of actions? So must they be capable of performing the same kinds of mental actions?

As I have already mentioned, functionalist approaches to mind that take the identity of a mental state to be determined by its causal relations to sensory stimulations, other mental states, and behaviour, are usually confined to treating the relevant behaviour in question as bodily behaviour. So, for example, mental events with phenomenal properties are not usually regarded as constituting mental *behaviour* that is the *output* of the functional roles that mental states characteristically play; nor are they regarded as occurrences constituting mental behaviour that needs to be rationalized and explained by mental state attributions. There is an implicit commitment to the idea that the notion of agential mental behaviour is to be analysed in terms of the prior notions of sensory stimulation, mental state, and *bodily* behaviour. In consequence, it is often assumed that the subject who is not phenomenally conscious will be capable of doing whatever the phenomenally conscious subject is capable of doing—the implicit assumption being that phenomenal consciousness is not only inessential to bodily action, it is also inessential to mental action. This helps to reinforce the assumption that considerations regarding mental action can at best be of marginal significance to a philosophical account of consciousness.

[6] See Shoemaker 1976.

9.2 The place of mental action in accounts of agency

Just as one finds that the topic of mental action is not often discussed in current accounts of mentality and consciousness, one also finds that the topic is not often accorded a prominent role in current accounts of action and agency. A central concern in the philosophy of action has been that of attempting to address what I earlier called the 'agent–mind problem'—how do the workings of the mind relate to the activity of an agent? According to one standard approach to this issue, we should be seeking to identify the appropriate *ingredients* of action. That is, we should be seeking to identify ingredients that are not themselves agential but whose appropriate combination can yield something agential—e.g. an appropriate combination of belief, desire, intention, bodily movement, and the relation of causation. When it comes to such an enterprise, an appeal to mental action is obviously inappropriate, for this presupposes agency—the notion to be accounted for and explained. Just as we ask, 'what is it that makes a bodily event a bodily action of an agent?', we might also ask, 'what is it that makes a mental event a mental action of an agent?' But the assumption is that the mental ingredients that we would need to appeal to in answering the latter question will not be significantly different from the mental ingredients that we would need to appeal to in answering the former question. So the assumption is that there is no special pay-off to be gained by focusing on the case of mental action when one's interest is in providing a general account of action and agency.

One might also regard the relative neglect of the topic of mental action in accounts of action as a natural reflection of our pre-philosophical interests in, and intuitions about, action. For the common-sense notion of action is one we most naturally associate with bodily action. Perhaps this has something to do with the associations we tend to make between the notions of inactivity and immobility, or perhaps it is a reflection of our tendency to think that, as O'Shaughnessy puts it, it is what we end up doing in the 'public physical realm' that really matters to us.

Think how one might ruminate for days in making a decision that issues in a simple but momentous act of signing one's name. Then it is the outcome in the public physical world that ultimately matters to one's life. More: it is the *active* outcome. A life is something which is almost in its entirety assessed in terms of physical action in situation. Man may not actually *be* the sum total of his intentional physical deeds: not much slips through the net however. (2000: 101)

On this latter point, given that discussions of moral psychology play such a central role in the philosophy of action, and given that our public deeds are the primary focus of moral interest, it should come as no surprise that it is an account of bodily action that should be of primary concern. However, it is also worth noting that there is a line of thought that takes questions of *mental* agency to be crucial to moral psychology, and in particular to an account of the respect in which we are morally responsible and culpable for our bodily actions. For example, it has been argued by some (e.g. by Pink 2009) that the right account of moral responsibility should accommodate the idea that free agency begins at the will, and is exercised in and through what we *decide*. According to this approach, we need to provide an account of action that can accommodate the idea that our decisions are mental *actions*.

This line of thought can be seen as a challenge to the idea that there is no particular pay-off to be gained by focusing on mental action when it comes to providing an account of agency—particularly if one's interest is in providing an account of the sort of autonomous agency that is available to a self-conscious subject. If, contrary to orthodox expectations, the topic of mental action also turns out to be important to an under-standing of consciousness (and in particular, consciousness in the self-conscious), then it may turn out to serve as an important connecting thread that needs to be woven through interlocking accounts of consciousness, self-consciousness, and autonomy.

O'Shaughnessy is probably the philosopher who has done the most to buck the current trend, in making a case for thinking that mental action should be accorded a prominent place in an account of consciousness, and in particular, in an account of consciousness in the self-conscious. On the one hand, O'Shaughnessy falls firmly into the anti-Cartesian camp in his approach to mind. He emphasizes the notion of 'man's mind as vital and animal, and tied in its essence to a sustaining world' (2008: 29), which leads him to emphasize the 'functional primacy of purposive bodily action . . . even in the case of a complicated rational creature like man' (2008: 23). On the other hand, there are certain parallels between his approach to consciousness and the Cartesian approach. For a consideration of conscious thinking, and the sort of self-conscious consciousness that enables us to engage in that kind of activity, is accorded a central and significant place in O'Shaughnessy's treatment of conscious-ness. And like Descartes, O'Shaughnessy holds that conscious thinking crucially involves 'the will'. 'The will . . . in a certain sense actually *invades* the domain of con-sciousness and epistemology' (2008: 29). In the next section I shall briefly outline some of the distinctive features of O'Shaughnessy's approach, which will serve to introduce some of the main questions about mental agency and conscious thinking that I shall be addressing in the rest of this book.

9.3 O'Shaughnessy on consciousness and mental action

One of O'Shaughnessy's main aims in *Consciousness and the World* is to provide an analysis of *wakeful* consciousness—'that vastly familiar light that appears in the head when a person surfaces from sleep or anaesthetic or dream' (2000: 68). According to O'Shaughnessy, we can mark distinctions between 'states of consciousness'. Wakeful consciousness is the pre-eminent parent variety with which, for example, unconscious sleep and dreaming can be compared and contrasted. O'Shaughnessy argues that these other states of con-sciousness are to be characterized derivatively, in terms of the state of wakeful conscious-ness. When one is in one of these other states of consciousness, one is deprived of certain functions that hang together in the fully awake.

Central to O'Shaughnessy's discussion of the state of wakeful consciousness is his discussion of the *stream of consciousness,* which he calls 'the experience'. In Part I, I discussed O'Shaughnessy's claim that continuities in the stream of consciousness are processive in character, and I discussed how he links this with his claim that the experiencing subject stands in a special relation to the passage of time that does not obtain in those who are not experiencing—e.g. those in dreamless sleep. Another important strand in O'Shaughnessy's analysis of the state of wakeful consciousness is his attempt to articulate 'the contribution made to consciousness, not by the bodily will (for we can be fully conscious though supine in a hammock, and even if totally paralysed), but by the mental will', which, O'Shaughnessy claims, 'cannot in the conscious be analogously incapacitated' (2000: 226). O'Shaughnessy suggests that with the imposition of what he calls a 'will freeze' upon one's conscious mental life, 'one cannot but replace the prevailing state of consciousness, waking, with another state of consciousness, perhaps sleep' (2000: 229). So mental action plays a crucial role in O'Shaughnessy's account of the state of wakeful consciousness, and in particular, in his account of the state of wakeful consciousness in the self-conscious subject. He argues that in the case of the self-conscious subject, 'The mind of one who is conscious [i.e. awake] is necessarily a mind actively governing the movement of its own attention and thinking processes...In general the direction taken by our thoughts and attention is in the conscious actively self-determined' (2000: 89).

In the previous chapter I touched upon the way in which agency is implicated in perceptual activities such as looking at and watching. I suggested that these activities involve the active maintenance of the sort of cognitive contact that one has with a perceived item when one perceptually notices it. The agency involved in perceptual activities such as looking and listening is something that O'Shaughnessy discusses at length, and his account of 'activeness' in perceptual function plays an important role in his account of the role of the 'mental will' in consciousness. I won't be going into that particular aspect of his discussion of the state of wakeful consciousness here. For I want to focus primarily on some claims that O'Shaughnessy makes about a connection between mental agency, *conscious thinking,* and the state of wakeful consciousness in the self-conscious subject.

For O'Shaughnessy, the importance of mental agency to his account of consciousness depends, in part, on the link he sees between 'operations of the mental will' and the form of self-knowledge, and rationality of state, that he claims is distinctive of wakeful consciousness in the self-conscious. O'Shaughnessy's view, very roughly, is that in the awake, self-conscious subject the progression of the stream of their conscious thought and imagination is distinctive. The respect in which it is distinctive is connected with the variety of self-knowledge that accompanies it, and the relevant form of self-knowledge is linked with the idea that the 'mental will' is operative. Roughly speaking, the idea appears to be that the awake, self-conscious subject is able to make sense of what is happening in a certain domain of her mental life in so far as she is able to make sense of what she is up to, and the variety of self-knowledge involved here is importantly linked with the idea that the perspective she has on this aspect of her mental life is that of its agent.

When one isn't awake, events may occur in the stream of consciousness, as when one dreams, but in such a state of consciousness there is a respect in which one is deprived of the operation of one's 'mental will'.

Dreaming precisely is the stream of consciousness when the guiding hands are taken off the reins controlling that phenomenon... Lacking the active control of a governing mind, the dream is a pure work of Nature. It is a kind of mental flower, and in any case no sort of intentional psychic artefact. But conversely, the thinking process precisely is what happens to the dream when the mind comes under the guiding hand of its owner. (2008: 30)

O'Shaughnessy connects the proposal that one lacks a form of active control of events in the stream of consciousness when one dreams, with the idea that one thereby lacks a distinctive form of self-knowledge regarding the progression of events in one's stream of consciousness.

Only a mind steering its own cognitive path through a wider cognitive scene, a self-causing which is furthered by rational steps, can introduce pellucidity into the flow of experience. (2000: 227)

Another important strand in O'Shaughnessy's treatment of consciousness in the self-conscious is the connection he sees between the distinctive sort of self-knowledge that is available to a self-conscious subject and what he calls 'mental freedom'. He suggests that our capacity to know that we have a thought, 'together with the capacity to contemplate its denial as a possibility that is here not in fact realized' (2000: 111), provides us with a form of mental freedom that allows us to 'transcend the condition of animal immersion' (2000: 112):

the animal merely has its beliefs, which are produced in it through sense, regularities in experience, desire, innate factors, etc. It does not know it has them, it has no hand in their installation, and it cannot compare them to the world. All it can do is harbour them and act upon them. (2000: 112)

In this special sense animals may be said to be *immersed* in the world in a way thinking beings are not... there can in their case be no *working towards* a belief, no believing through *cogitation*, no form of *responsibility* for belief, and in consequence no kind of *mental freedom*. (2000: 111)

one of the primary uses of self-awareness in thinking creatures is in self-determination and mental freedom. (2000: 110)

Korsgaard is another philosopher who connects the human capacity for self-awareness with the idea that 'the human mind is active in some way that the minds of the other animals are not' (2009b: 23), which, in turn, she claims, provides us with a form of epistemic autonomy. She connects the idea that we have a distinctive capacity for *active* reasoning with the idea that we have a form of 'reflective' consciousness that allows us to engage in self-critical reflection.

A lower animal's attention is fixed on the world... It is engaged in conscious activities, but it is not conscious of them... They are not the objects of its attention... Our capacity to turn our attention on to our own mental activities is also a capacity to distance ourselves from them, and call them into question. (1996a: 93)

According to Korsgaard, as self-conscious subjects we have reflective awareness of our own mental states and activities as such, and this self-conscious form of consciousness opens up what she calls 'a space of reflective distance', hence her suggestion that our capacity to turn our attention onto our own mental activities 'is also a capacity to distance ourselves from them, and to call them into question'. Korsgaard then claims that this space of reflective distance ensures that 'we are, or can be, active, self-directing, with respect to our beliefs'. It 'presents us with the possibility and the necessity of exerting a kind of control over our beliefs'.[7] This is similar to O'Shaughnessy's suggestion that as self-conscious subjects we have a form of 'mental freedom' that gives us a form of 'responsibility' for our beliefs, by allowing us 'to have a hand in their installation'.

One difficulty with the sort of view that both O'Shaughnessy and Korsgaard appear to endorse is that it leaves unclear how the mere capacity to become conscious of one's own beliefs, and their grounds, can provide one with the ability to 'have a hand in their installation'. How is the 'space of reflective distance' that Korsgaard cites supposed to allow us to 'exert control over our beliefs'? As Moran puts it, it is not as though, glancing inwards, we can simply manipulate our attitudes as so much mental furniture.[8] So how does agency figure in the exercise of self-critical reflection that is made possible by 'the space of reflective distance'? Some of Korsgaard's critics have objected to the idea that our ability to reflect on our own beliefs somehow allows belief formation to be governable by such reflection. They argue that it is a mistake to think that we have 'reflective *control*' over belief acquisition and revision. The fact that we have a reflective form of consciousness (e.g. the fact that we know what we think), they object, does not thereby allow the notion of freedom to get a grip in the realm of belief, and so does not thereby provide us with a form of epistemic autonomy.[9]

This line of thought calls into question the connection that O'Shaughnessy and Korsgaard are concerned to forge between conscious reasoning, mental agency, and the sort of self-knowledge that is available to the self-conscious subject. It suggests that the role of mental agency in conscious reasoning (including self-critical reflection) can at best be rather limited. And if the role of mental action in conscious reasoning can at best be rather limited, one might wonder whether mental action does, after all, have an *essential* role to play in an account of the sort of conscious reasoning and conscious thinking that can go on in the mind of a self-conscious subject.

We can contrast O'Shaughnessy's proposal about the centrality of mental agency to conscious thinking, self-consciousness, and self-critical reflection, with the rather different view that Galen Strawson defends. According to Strawson, a reasoning, thinking, judging, self-conscious creature need not be an agent at all, for such mental activity, he

---

[7] Korsgaard 2009b: 32. See also Korsgaard 2009a: 115–16.
[8] See Moran 1999 and 2001.
[9] For this line of objection to Korsgaard, see Owens 2000.

suggests, need not involve any mental action. So Strawson suggests that there is no inco-herence in the idea of what he calls a 'Pure Observer': 'a motionless, cognitively well-equipped, highly receptive, self-conscious, rational, subtle creature that is well-informed about its surroundings and has, perhaps, a full and vivid sense of itself as an observer although it has no capacity for any sort of intentional action, nor even any conception of the possibility of intentional action' (2003: 228).

To sketch briefly the line of thought that lies behind Strawson's very different posi-tion, he claims that thinking about something involves the occurrence of mental acts individuated, in part, by their propositional contents, and he argues that these mental acts can be mental actions only if the particular contents that individuate them are ones that the subject intends to think. However, in the case of many such mental acts it seems that the content of the mental act cannot figure in the content of one's prior intention. Strawson has argued that no thinking of a particular thought-content is ever an action. This is because one's thinking of the particular content can only amount to an action if the content thought is already there, 'available for consideration and adoption for inten-tional production', in which case 'it must already have "just come" at some previous time in order to be so available' (2003: 235).[10] Here we might contrast thinking with talking. For example, although some have suggested that judging should be understood as the interiorization of the act of asserting, one might think that the analogies between these acts break down when we consider the role that intention can play with respect to each.[11] Having judged that *p*, one might choose to assert that *p*. Having formed the intention to Φ, one might choose to express that intention. But the mental acts of judg-ing that *p* and deciding to Φ cannot themselves be intended.

It should be said that on this latter point there is wide agreement. In saying that the awake, self-conscious subject takes active charge of her own thoughts and attendings, O'Shaughnessy remarks, 'I do not mean actively determines their *content*, which would be at once omnipotent, barren, self-refuting and logically impossible' (2000: 89).[12] How-ever, for O'Shaughnessy this still leaves intention with a significant role to play in con-scious thinking. O'Shaughnessy claims that the intentions involved when one is engaged in such activity select 'the content of the governing enterprise', 'stir one's mental machinery', and constrain, 'under definite description', the advance of one's thinking.[13]

---

[10] Strawson does not deny that mental actions do occur, but on his view, 'Mental action in thinking is restricted to the fostering of conditions hospitable to contents' coming to mind' (2003: 234).

[11] For the idea of understanding judging as the interiorization of an act of asserting, rather than under-standing asserting as the exteriorization of an act of judging, see Dummett 1973: 362. See also Geach 1957, Kenny 1963: chapter 10, Sellars 1963: section 50.

[12] Peacocke concedes that 'when you think a particular thought, there is of course no intention in advance to think that particular thought' (Peacocke 1999: 209). According to Peacocke, for a mental event to be a mental action, it must consist of an event which either is, or constitutively involves, a trying, and Peacocke has argued that tryings should be distinguished from prior intentions.

[13] See O'Shaughnessy 2000: 89 and 221. Compare Peacocke's claim that directed, as opposed to idle, thought involves 'the intention to think a thought which stands in a certain relation to other thoughts or contents' (Peaocke 1999: 210).

9.4 Questions and issues

One of the aims in Part II of this book is to explore whether O'Shaughnessy is right to hold, *contra* Strawson, that mental action should be accorded a central place in an account of conscious thinking, and as part of this endeavour we will need to consider disputes about the putative role of mental agency in conscious reasoning and self-critical reflection. Progress on this issue will depend in part on addressing questions about the scope of mental agency. How much of our mental lives is genuinely agential? A striking feature of recent work on mental action is the extent to which opinions appear to diverge on this issue. As I have already mentioned, Pink argues that our decisions are mental actions, whereas Galen Strawson argues that although there is such a thing as mental action, most of our thoughts, including our decisions, 'just happen' and 'action and intention need have little or nothing to do with their occurrence'. Peacocke goes further than Pink (1996 and 2009) in holding that judgings, as well as decidings, are mental actions; and he holds that acceptings, attendings to something or other, calculatings, reasonings, and tryings can all be instances of mental action.[14] The position one takes on the scope of mental agency is obviously going to depend on the answers one thinks should be given to the following questions: (i) What makes a mental action a *mental* action, as opposed to a bodily action? And (ii) what makes a mental action a mental *action*, as opposed to some non-agential mental event?

The answer one gives to the second question will depend, in part, on one's general view of agency and action; and what the requirements are for something to be a genuine action is, of course, itself a contested matter. Some have argued that an adequate account of agency should be able to recognize and accommodate the idea that there can be significant differences between varieties of behaviour that fall under a broad category of the agential. For example, consider the sort of case that I quoted from O'Shaughnessy earlier: a momentous act of signing one's name that issues from a decision one eventually reaches after days of rumination. One might think of this as a paradigm case of 'full-blooded' autonomous action. But one might also think that we need a much broader notion of the agential that can encompass behaviour that departs from this paradigm in significant ways—for example, absent-minded and habitual actions, the idle tapping of one's fingers on a table, compulsive behaviour, and the purposive bodily behaviour of a relatively primitive animal.

This sort of approach to action and agency may bear on a consideration of mental action in at least a couple of ways. Firstly, it may be that we need to recognize examples of agential mental behaviour that depart from the paradigm of full-blooded autonomous action in various ways, just as we may need to recognize examples of agential bodily behaviour that depart from that paradigm. So, for example, perhaps we need a notion of the agential that is broad enough to encompass compulsive mental behaviour, and habitual mental behaviour. Perhaps there can be a mental equivalent of the absent-minded, but

---

[14] See Peacocke 2007 and 2009.

nonetheless agential, tapping of one's fingers on the table. Secondly, it may turn out that one needs to appeal to mental action in an account of what is distinctive of the so-called 'full-blooded' examples of autonomous agency. It is natural to think that the agent who is capable of exercising full-blooded autonomous agency is the subject capable of engaging in practical deliberation and making decisions, and as I have already mentioned, some have argued that decisions are themselves mental actions. These issues, and in particular the second set of issues, will surface in the discussion of mental action in Part II. For one of the questions I shall be exploring is whether there is a connection between (a) self-conscious consciousness, (b) having the capacity to engage in certain kinds of mental action, and (c) having the capacity to exercise the full-blooded variety of autonomous agency.

Another issue I shall be exploring is the way in which a consideration of mental action can inform debates in the epistemology of mind. Earlier I said that a key aspect of O'Shaughnessy's proposal is the suggestion that there is a distinctive variety of self-knowledge that accompanies the activity of conscious thinking in the awake, self-conscious subject, and the respect in which this form of self-knowledge is distinctive is importantly linked with the idea that the perspective that the subject has on this aspect of her mental life is that of its agent.[15] It is often said that it is a mistake to think of oneself as merely the spectator of one's own actions, just as it is a mistake to think of one's intentions as merely predictions concerning what is going to happen. One's involvement in the action as its author makes one more than a spectator and more than a predictor. In certain cases, one's knowledge of one's own mental life may be a matter of knowing that one is doing something and knowing what one is doing, and an account of such knowledge may involve epistemic considerations that are importantly distinct from those relevant to accounts of our knowledge of our standing attitudes and our knowledge of our perceptual experiences and sensations.

In the discussion of sensory consciousness in Part I, ontological considerations played a key role in the account I offered of a variety of knowledge that is only available to the phenomenally conscious subject. Issues in the ontology of mind will once again re-emerge as significant in my discussion of the epistemology of mental action in Part II. These ontological issues will play a prominent role in an attempt to address the following two questions: (i) is there a distinctive form of self-knowledge that accompanies mental action?, and (ii) is this form of self-knowledge only available to the phenomenally conscious subject?

This discussion will connect with the general questions I raised earlier about the place of mental action in an account of mind and consciousness. Is it wrong to assume that a subject who is not phenomenally conscious is capable of doing whatever a phenomenally conscious subject can do? Are there mental actions that the latter can perform that the former cannot? And if so, is it wrong to assume that mental action is to be

---

[15] O'Brien (2007) also emphasizes the importance of the agential awareness that one has of one's own mental life both to issues in the epistemology of mind and to an account of self-conscious consciousness.

reductively analysed as a variety of mental activity involving transitions between mental states that enable, rationalize, and causally explain *bodily* behaviour?

I shall be starting with some of these ontological concerns in the next chapter. I said that central to O'Shaughnessy's account of consciousness is the notion of a 'stream of consciousness', and I also noted how he appeals to mental agency in his account of what is distinctive of the progression of the stream of conscious thought and imagination in the awake, self-conscious subject. As I discussed in Part I, according to Geach, although sensory aspects of mind are stream-like, acts of thinking thoughts are not. There is no stream of conscious thought. To think otherwise is to make the mistake of thinking that 'to think certain thoughts is to have certain mental images, feelings, unspoken words etc., passing through one's mind' (1969: 34). In the next chapter I shall be examining in more detail Geach's argument for this claim, and I shall be connecting the issues it raises with the question of the role of mental agency in conscious thinking.

10

The Ontology of Conscious Thinking

The subtitle of a paper that Ryle once wrote on thinking thoughts is 'What is "Le Penseur" Doing?'[1] The assumption behind the question is that in portraying a man thinking, Rodin portrayed a man *doing* something. Arguably, not everything one does counts as an action one performs, but whether or not it is appropriate to regard consciously thinking about something as a mental action performed by an agent, we can perhaps at least agree to the less committal assumption behind Ryle's question: that when a subject is consciously thinking about something (e.g. deliberating about what to do, or trying to figure out some puzzle or problem), that subject is thereby *doing* something. According to what we might call our 'common-sense ontology' of conscious thinking, consciously thinking about something is an activity one can be engaged in. Moreover, it's intuitive to think that this sort of temporally extended activity can involve *episodes* of conscious thinking. So, for example, it's natural to think that in the case of conscious deliberation or calculation, one's train of thought can involve a series of conscious cognitive episodes, such as conscious judgement and decision.

My primary aim in this chapter is to address questions about the ontology of the conscious mental acts involved in the temporally extended activity of consciously thinking about something, and in particular the conscious mental act of judging, which in turn will lead to a reconsideration of Geach's argument for the claim that there is no stream of conscious thought. Later on I shall be suggesting that these ontological issues are relevant to the general question of the place of mental action in an account of mind. In particular, I shall try to show how a consideration of these ontological issues can help uncover connections between the notions of conscious thinking and mental action.

First though, I want to consider an epistemic dimension of the activity of conscious thinking that can potentially affect the account one gives of its metaphysics. It's intuitive to think that the conscious thoughts that are involved in the temporally extended activity of consciously thinking about some matter can be, in some sense, private to the

---

[1] Ryle 1968.

subject who is thinking them. But in what sense? And can this idea be accommodated by the sort of anti-Cartesian approach to mentality that I mentioned in the previous chapter?

10.1 The privacy of conscious thinking

Presumably we should grant that one can see someone engaging in the activity of think-ing about something, and one can see *that* they are engaging in that activity. This is, after all, something that Rodin exploited in his depiction, in a *visual* medium, of the subject of 'Le Penseur'. It could also be said that one can sometimes discern, by perceptual (e.g. visual) means, *what* someone is thinking about—e.g. one can see that the chess player is trying work out what move she should make next. However, from the fact that one sees someone A-ing, and sees that they are A-ing, it's not clear that it follows that one sees the event that is their A-ing.[2] From the fact that one can see the chess player attempting to work out what move she should make, and one can see *that* she is attempting to work out what move she should make, it's not clear that it follows that one can see the mental events that constitute her attempt to work out what move she should make. Indeed, there seems to be something off-key in the suggestion that one can see the chess player's *attempt* to work this out. The thinking behind the chess player's next move is something that her opponent can only guess at.

A related point is this. One can sometimes see *that* someone is thinking, without knowing what he or she is thinking, and equally, one can sometimes see *that* someone is performing some 'overt' bodily activity without knowing exactly what he or she is doing. But even here there is still an important distinction to be made—a distinction that can perhaps be brought out by considering the differences between the question, 'what are you doing?' asked of each. In the case of the overt bodily activity, one may be able to observe the agent's bodily behaviour as agential and wonder about the intention with which it is being performed.[3] In the case in which one sees that someone seems to be thinking about something, one is not similarly able to observe the agent's mental events, as such, and then wonder about the intention with which they are being per-formed. When one is given an answer to the question, 'what are you doing?' asked of the overt bodily action, then perhaps the observable bodily behaviour can start to make sense in a way that it didn't before, or perhaps, given what one is able to observe, one can point out to the agent of the action that what they are doing may not be the most effec-tive way of achieving that aim. These points do not seem to apply in the same way to the case of the activity of conscious thinking when one is simply told of the agent's aim in engaging in that mental activity.

---

[2] Compare here O'Shaughnessy's discussion of the idea that 'that which is invisible may at the same time be eminently detectable by visual means' (2008: 394).

[3] On the observability of agential aspects of bodily behaviour, see Marcel 2003: 55. See also Hornsby 1997: essay 6.

Note that this line of thought, regarding the respect in which episodes of conscious thinking are private to the subject thinking them, need not be in tension with the suggestion that these conscious episodes are identical with physical, perhaps neural, events that can in principle be observed. Suppose, for example, that some form of physicalist supervenience thesis is true. Suppose that the mental supervenes on the physical, and in the case of at least certain kinds of mental events—i.e. conscious episodes of *thinking*—each such mental event is token identical, and not type identical, with some neural event. Suppose too that we have some means of observing the neural events that occur when a subject is consciously thinking about something. Although we may be in a position to observe the particular neural events that are her conscious thoughts, it's not clear that we are thereby in a position to discern what she is thinking about. For even in this situation, it's not clear that one would be in a position to observe *as such* the particular kinds of cognitive episodes that make up the activity of the subject's conscious thinking. So this suggestion about the respect in which the activity of conscious thinking can be private to its subject seems to be consistent with certain forms of physicalism. But is it in tension with the anti-Cartesian approach to mentality that I mentioned in the previous chapter?

That anti-Cartesian view, as I characterized it, places emphasis on the notion of psychological subject as bodily agent—that is to say, it places emphasis on the notion of psychological subject as an agent that performs bodily actions. For according to this anti-Cartesian approach, it is a mistake to regard as merely contingent the connections between a subject's mental life and the publicly observable bodily behaviour that manifests that subject's mental life. It rejects the idea that our mental states, events, and processes are what O'Shaughnessy dubbed 'metaphysical hermits'—entities that 'stand in no binding need of manifesting their existence in bodily extremities in any way' (2008: 13).

The sort of anti-Cartesian approach to mentality that I have in mind is not simply distinguished by a rejection of dualism and a commitment to physicalism. To place emphasis on the notion of psychological subject as an agent capable of bodily action, as I am understanding this idea, is not equivalent to being committed to the idea that each psychological subject is a material entity. As a way of illustrating this point we might imagine a physicalist view that holds that the mental supervenes on the physical but which allows that it is possible for there to be psychological subjects that have never performed, and that cannot perform, bodily actions—e.g. perhaps an envatted brain that has experiences, beliefs, desires, and intentions, and engages in conscious thinking, but which has never performed a bodily action.

To the suggestion that this sort of brain-in-vat subject does not perform bodily actions, we might envisage the following line of objection. Perhaps this subject performs certain mental actions—e.g. perhaps attempting to work out an arithmetical problem is an action performed by that subject; and if each of this subject's mental events is token identical with some brain event, then why not grant that there is a sense in which that subject can perform bodily actions, in so far as these brain events are, in some sense, bodily events that are intentional under some description?

Note that this way of characterizing the case would appear to collapse any distinction between mental action and bodily action. It suggests that if all our mental events are in fact identical with bodily events, then all our mental actions are in fact bodily actions, in so far as they are bodily events that are intentional under some description. Specifying what it is that distinguishes mental actions from bodily actions is a far from straightforward matter, but we can note a couple of salient points about this case that make it odd to describe such a subject as performing bodily actions.

(a) From the first-person point of view—i.e. from the point of view of the agent of the action—given the description under which these events are intentional (e.g. attempting to work out some arithmetical problem), the subject may be completely unaware of what sorts of bodily events the action involves, and indeed she might be completely unaware that these actions involve any kind of bodily event at all. And a related point is this. (b) From the third-person point of view—i.e. from the point of view of another subject observing the action—although the neural events involved may be ones that can in principle be perceived, it is not clear that the conscious episodes of thinking, with which these neural events are identical, can be perceived *as such*. So it's not clear that an observer of these actions could be in a position to know what the agent was thinking about, hence it's not clear that an observer of the action could be in a position to know what kind of action was being performed.

These points give us reason to think that in the case of a subject who is only capable of performing actions that involve the activity of conscious thinking, there won't be the kind of connection between the subject's mental life and observable bodily behaviour that is characteristic of the anti-Cartesian approach to mentality as I am construing it—even though each of this subject's conscious thoughts may be identical with some bodily (i.e. neural) event. So do these sorts of consideration give us reason to think that the sense in which the activity of conscious thinking is private to its subject is in tension with the anti-Cartesian approach to mentality?

As I mentioned in the previous chapter, those who adopt an anti-Cartesian approach to mentality need not be committed to the idea that it is possible to reduce mentality to its publicly observable bodily manifestations. That is, they need not be committed to a strong form of behaviourism that would appear to squeeze out altogether a subject's 'inner' mental life. Ryle, in his later writings on thinking[4] (including the aforementioned essay, 'What is *Le Penseur* doing?'), appears to reject a reductive behaviourist approach to mentality, but we should not conclude from this that he is no longer committed to an anti-Cartesian approach to mentality. For those who adopt the anti-Cartesian approach need not deny the reality of a subject's 'inner' mental life. They can hold instead that a subject's inner mental life will necessarily be anchored in publicly observable bodily behaviour that expresses, and is an effect of, that subject's mentality.

---

[4] See e.g. Ryle 1967–8 and 1968.

A number of functionalist and interpretationist accounts of mind incorporate this idea, and such views appear to be able to accommodate a respect in which episodes of conscious thinking are private to the subject thinking them. According to such views, we not only attribute mental states (e.g. beliefs, desires, and intentions) in order to explain and rationalize overt bodily behaviour, we also attribute or posit 'inner' episodes—mental events and processes—that involve changes to, and transitions between, these mental states, in order to explain and rationalize the overt bodily behaviour that is our primary data. We not only attribute mental states that are to be functionally characterized, in part, in terms of output that includes bodily behaviour, we also posit mental events and processes that are changes to and transitions between these mental states. On such views, there appears to be no reason to think that these sorts of transitions should be observable *as such* from a third-person point of view—even if such transitions are identical with neural events that can, in principle, be observed.

According to this sort of view, what is it for such a mental process to be an instance of *conscious* thinking as opposed to a non-conscious mental process? There are reasons for thinking that conscious thinking cannot simply be a matter of there being a process that results in the acquisition of a personal-level mental state (a belief, desire, or intention, say). Such aspects of mind—personal-level mental states—can be non-conscious states, which are sometimes labelled as 'non-occurrent'. We think of them as being the kinds of features of mind that can persist during dreamless sleep. And there seems to be no reason to deny that an event that is the *acquisition* of such a non-conscious state can also be non-conscious.[5] This suggests that there is no reason to think that we cannot make sense of the existence of a *non*-conscious process constituted by series of non-conscious events that are simply changes to, or acquisitions of, non-conscious, personal-level mental states.[6] Although such processes would affect an agent's personal-level mental states, that would not suffice for them being instances of conscious thinking. This may suggest that we should go for some sort of higher-order account of what it is for the mental episodes or acts that constitute one's conscious thinking to be conscious.[7]

In what follows I want to consider the tenability of a particular kind of higher-order account of conscious thinking. It's what we might call a 'bottom-up' approach. According to this bottom-up approach, conscious mental acts of thinking thoughts, such as the conscious mental act of judging, involve the occurrence of a certain kind of independently specifiable mental event—i.e. one that can be specified independently of the event being a conscious one—plus awareness of the occurrence of the event.

---

[5] Compare the discussion of experiences, states, and processes in O'Shaughnessy 2000: chapter 1.

[6] Compare Carruthers' (2005) criticism of first-order accounts of conscious thinking. See also Carruthers 2000: chapter 6. For a discussion of the idea that we are *always* dreaming while asleep, see Flanagan 2000: 68.

[7] As I am using the term, in committing to a 'higher-order' account of conscious thinking one need not thereby commit oneself to a higher-order *representationlist* account of conscious thinking. The latter involves the claim that higher-order representations are necessary for conscious thinking together with the claim that phenomenal character supervenes on representational content, whereas the former simply involves the claim that higher-order representations are necessary for conscious thinking and is consistent with (what has been called) a 'phenomenist' account of phenomenal character. See Byrne 2004.

10.2 A 'bottom-up' approach to conscious thinking, and the temporal profile of the conscious act of judging

Let us start by focusing on the conscious mental act of judging that p. If we do go for some sort of higher-order account of the mental act of consciously judging that p, then what should we say about the object of the higher-order awareness, other than its being an aspect of mind with the propositional content that p? In particular, what should we say about the ontological category to which it belongs?

There are problems involved in the suggestion that when one consciously judges that p one is simply in a higher-order state that represents the fact that one believes that p—e.g. the suggestion that to consciously judge that p just is to believe that one believes that p. Even if it is true that when one consciously judges that p one believes that one believes that p, there is no reason to think that such a belief about what one believes ceases to obtain when one isn't consciously judging that p, any more than there is reason to think that one's belief that p ceases to obtain when one isn't consciously judging that p. It might be thought that this problem can be resolved if we hold that the object of the higher-order awareness is not the mental state of belief, but rather something event-like or episodic. Accepting this much, however, leaves unanswered a number of questions about the ontological category of the object of the higher-order awareness. For example, when one consciously judges that p, is the object of the higher-order awareness an event with temporal extension—an event that unfolds over time?

In addressing this question it will be helpful to reconsider some of the points raised by Geach in his argument against William James' suggestion that there is a *stream* of conscious thought. In Part I we saw that Geach argued that 'thoughts occur not in a Jamesian stream, but . . . as a series in which certain thought-contents successively occur, with no succession within any one thought and no gradual transition from one thought to another' (1969: 35–6). Central to Geach's argument is the claim that our mental acts of thinking thoughts should be individuated in terms of their propositional contents, and the claim that the propositional content in terms of which we individuate any given act of thinking is a 'non-successive unity'. According to Geach, proper acknowledgement of this point should lead us to reject a certain mistaken picture of those acts of thinking that are individuated in terms of propositional contents. According to that mistaken picture, a mental act of judging that p is thought of as filling an interval of time that can be broken down into sub-intervals of time in each of which there occurs a temporal part of that mental act that is to be specified in terms of a part of the propositional content that p that is judged—e.g. when one judges that 'John is tall', one first judges 'John' and then judges 'is tall'. When Geach claims that there is no succession within any one act of thinking a thought, he appears to mean us to reject this mistaken picture of what is involved in an act of thinking a thought.

What bearing do such considerations have on the question of whether an act of judging that p should be regarded as a mental event with temporal extension? One might think that the main conclusion to be drawn from Geach's argument is simply that if we are individuating an aspect of mind in terms of a propositional content, then the fact that that aspect of mind may have temporal extension and successive phases cannot be captured in the propositional content (a 'non-successive unity') that we use to individuate it. But this does not in itself show that the aspect of mind individuated by reference to that propositional content is not a mental event with temporal extension and successive phases. However, in his discussion of these issues, Geach raises further considerations that appear to give us reason to think that a mental act of judging that p is not a mental event with temporal extension and successive phases. In his essay 'What do we think with?', Geach writes:

I think Norman Malcolm was right when he said that a mental image could be before one's mind's eye for just as long as a beetle took to crawl across a table...but I think it would be nonsense to say that I 'was thinking' a given thought for the period of a beetle's crawl–the continuous past of 'think' has no such use. (The White Knight 'was thinking' of a plan in that he thought certain thoughts successively; and for each individual thought 'was thinking' would have no application.) (1969: 64)

Why should a consideration as to whether the continuous past of the verb has any such use be relevant to the question of whether the mental act of judging is an event with temporal extension? Discussions concerning linguistic aspect, largely influenced by Vendler's classifications of verbs into the categories of state, achievement, activity, and accomplishment, are useful in unpacking this part of the argument. I mentioned these distinctions in Chapter 4. Let me briefly summarize once again the way in which these distinctions are usually drawn. Recall the following summary of the distinctions Vendler draws between these categories of verbs, offered by Rothstein (2004): 'Crudely, states are non-dynamic situations, such as be happy or believe; activities are open ended processes, such as run; achievements are near-instantaneous events which are over as soon as they have begun, such as notice; and accomplishments are processes which have a natural endpoint, such as read the book' (6). Neither states (believes, loves) nor achievements (recognize, notice) usually occur in the progressive, whereas activities (walking, eating) and accomplishments (building a house, walking to the shops) do. The latter pair can be answers to the question 'what are you doing?', whereas the former pair cannot. Verb predicates that fall under the category of state do not usually occur in the progressive, as the situations they signify do not unfold over time in the way that activities and accomplishments do. States obtain over periods of time. Achievements do not usually take the progressive either. This is not because they signify situations that occupy time in the way that states do, but rather because they relate to things that happen instantaneously. Things one can have done or will do, but not things one can be in the process of doing. Although accomplishments are like activities, in so far as they take the progressive, they are unlike activities, in so far as they have a terminus. Accomplishments are movements towards an end point. If Geach is right to claim that 'think that p', and 'judge that p', do not usually occur in the progressive, this would then suggest that the phrases pick out a state or an achievement. There is a use of the verb 'judge' (and 'think') that picks out the mental state of belief ('S judges/thinks that p'). So where the verb is used to pick out a mental event, the indications are that we should regard it as picking out an achievement—an instantaneous event that lacks duration.

Why not regard 'judging that p' as an accomplishment? Accomplishments are events that have internal structure, which have temporal parts, but which have a terminus. So what would be wrong in thinking of an act of judging as an event with internal temporal structure that has a terminus? One reason for thinking that a subject is in the process of A-ing, where A-ing is an accomplishment, is the fact that the subject is doing something X with the intention of reaching a certain kind of terminus. In this respect, the process can have started but not yet reached its terminus. But it seems that this explanation can-not apply to the case of judging. If judging were an accomplishment, it should be possible to stop S halfway through her act of judging. It should be possible for there to be a situation in which it was not yet true that the subject had judged that p, but in which it was true that she had already begun her act of judging that p. However, here we might ask, what could the subject have done that counted as having already started the act of judg-ing, and what else would she have needed to do in order to finish it? If we think of the content of the act of judging as having parts that signify the temporal parts of the act, then this would perhaps provide us with an answer—e.g. the subject had already started her act of judging that John is tall because she had already judged John, a temporal part of the accomplishment of judging John is tall. But Geach's observation is that we should not regard the propositional content of an aspect of mind in this way. Considerations of this kind lead Mouton, in his paper 'Thinking and Time', to claim that, 'It is impossible for one to get half way through a thought and stop. This is because thoughts are individuated by their content and every such content which comes before one's mind is a complete thought. There is, therefore, no such thing as a partial thought' (1969: 65). We can think of the propositional content of an act of thinking as having structure, and so as having struc-tural parts, but these structural parts do not signify temporal parts of the aspect of mind they individuate. To borrow O'Shaughnessy's analogy, an act of judging is not like putting together the discrete parts of a jigsaw, and neither is it like an artist making preliminary sketches of the final work. The act of judging does not appear to be an activity either—i.e. an open-ended process with duration, such that it would make sense to think of a sub-ject's act of judging that p as something that she had already been doing for some period of time and which she could continue to do more of.[8]

All of this points to the conclusion that 'judge that p' is an achievement—i.e. when the phrase is used to refer to an event, as opposed to the state of belief, it is used to refer to an instantaneous event. And the most natural way to think of this achievement is as an event that is the acquisition of a mental state. According to this view, an act of judging is an instantaneous event with no internal structure, but where the state it is the acquisition of is individuated by something that has structure—namely its propositional content.

---

[8] The same considerations appear to apply to the case of the mental act of deciding to φ.

And we should not be misled into thinking that the structure of the propositional content of the state that is referred to in individuating this instantaneous event has anything to do with the event's internal temporal structure.

According to the 'bottom-up' approach currently being considered, the activity of conscious thinking involves the occurrence of events of a kind that can be non-conscious together with higher-order states of awareness whose obtaining makes those events conscious. We have seen that in the case of the mental act of judging there are reasons for thinking that the event in question lacks temporal extension and is an event that is the acquisition of a mental state. This suggests a picture on which an activity such as conscious calculation involves (a) the occurrence of a series of instantaneous events that are acquisitions of (and transitions between) mental states with content, together with (b) higher-order states that represent those events. Note that this bottom-up approach is one according to which the ontology of conscious calculation is reducible to, and analysable in terms of, mental states and events/processes that are changes in those states. I mentioned this sort of view of the ontology of the activity of thinking in Chapter 2, when I was attempting to unpack the assumptions behind Geach's argument for the claim that there is no stream of conscious thought. On this view, we are to regard the temporal boundaries of the obtaining of a mental state as marked by the occurrence of events—namely the event of the mental state's acquisition and the event of its extinction. A mental process can be constituted by a series of such events—e.g. the event of the acquisition of mental state M1 at t1 and the event of its extinction at t5, the event of the acquisition of mental state M2 at t5 and the event of its extinction at t10, and so on. We can think of this as a process constituted by a series of transitions between mental states. According to the bottom-up, higher-order approach to conscious calculation, the mental states in question include higher-order states that represent the events that are the acquisitions of the first-order states; and this account does not invoke mental occurrences that are processive in character but which are not reducible to events/processes that are changes in mental states.

Let's now consider this proposal in more detail. If we agree that the mental act of judging lacks duration, then how might this affect the idea that the mental act of *consciously* judging that *p* involves a higher-order state that takes the mental act of judging as its object? Suppose we regard the higher-order state as a belief and the mental event that is its object as an event that is the acquisition of an intentional mental state with content—e.g. an event that is the acquisition of a belief. If the higher-order belief has a present-tensed content and simply concerns a mental event that lacks temporal extension, then one might think that the higher-order belief would have to lack temporal extension as well, and it's not clear that we can make sense of the idea that a belief, as opposed to an event of judging, can lack temporal extension. It doesn't help to hold that the higher-order awareness is an instantaneous act of judging, for on the present understanding this is just an event that is the acquisition of a mental state (e.g. a belief), and so on this proposal we would still be left with the difficulty of accommodating the idea that this acquired higher-order state has a present-tensed content that concerns an instantaneous event. On the other hand, if we say that the higher-order belief doesn't have a present-tensed content, and is rather the belief that one has just acquired the belief that *p*, then it looks as though we end up with a view according to which what makes an event of judging *conscious* is the fact that one has the belief that the event has just occurred. And so one ends up with a view according to which one is never aware of these conscious events occurring, one only comes to believe that they have occurred.

Can these sorts of problems be overcome if we say that the higher-order state is a belief-independent state of awareness? Peacocke (2009) has offered an account of conscious judging that appeals to a belief-independent state of awareness of the act of judging, and he seems to agree with the idea that the act of judging lacks duration. So we might consider his view as an example of such an approach.

Peacocke's account of how we standardly know our own actions appeals to the occurrence of belief-independent events of 'action awareness' that have a first-personal, present-tensed content of the form 'I am doing such-and-such now'. According to Peacocke, this action awareness is standardly brought about by an event of trying that causes the action that the action awareness represents, and the distinctive way in which a subject comes to know of her own actions is by taking such an apparent action awareness at face value. Peacocke suggests that action awareness makes available demonstrative ways of thinking of actions given in one's action awareness. He argues that this distinctive action awareness exists for mental actions, as well as for bodily actions, and he holds that one's mental actions include judgings and decidings. So for Peacocke, the distinctive way in which a subject comes to know that she is judging that *p* is by taking at face value an action awareness with the content 'I am judging that *p*'. He says, in a footnote:

I use the notation 'φ-ing' to formulate these generalizations, but this should not be taken to imply that it is only continuing events of which one can have action awareness...Judging and deciding are...not temporally extended processes, but the subject can have action awareness of them too. (2009: 199)

Are there any problems involved in thinking of conscious judging as involving a belief-independent state of awareness with an instantaneous event as its object? I think any difficulty that might arise here can't simply be due to the idea that instantaneous events are over too quickly for us to be aware of them as occurring. For example, it can be argued that we can perceive instantaneous events—e.g. the event of something starting, stopping, or disappearing, as I discussed in Chapter 4. But I think the comparison with perception can prove instructive, and uncover further difficulties for this account of conscious judging.

Consider once again some of the remarks made in Chapter 4 about our perception of instantaneous events. I gave as an example a case in which you are staring intently at an object that is in full view, when suddenly the object vanishes into thin air. You see the object disappear. The event of the object disappearing happens at a time, but does not take time. The perception of the event of the instantaneous disappearance of an object appears to entail both the perception of the object, and its absence—one's perception of the object prior to its disappearance, and one's perception of the scene after the object's disappearance.

For if you don't see the object, then you can't see it disappear, and if you don't see the scene without the object, then you won't yet have seen it disappear. If you perceive the instantaneous event of the disappearance of the object, then your perception of that event must also have been a perception of the object *and* its absence, and so your perception of the instantaneous event requires the perception of something that isn't instantaneous—it requires the perception of something, in this case the scene before you, enduring for an *interval* of time, an interval of time that spans both the presence of the object and its absence.

In general, perceptual awareness of an instantaneous event requires awareness of an interval of time during which some instantaneous change occurs, for it requires awareness of how things are before and after the change occurs. Should we likewise hold that when one consciously judges that p one is in a belief-independent state of awareness that represents how things are before and after some instantaneous event of change occurs? If so, what is the relevant event of change? Is it the acquisition of a belief? This would lead to the proposal that when one consciously judges that p one is in a belief-independent state of awareness that represents one's not having the belief that p and then one's having the belief that p, and one might worry about positing a belief-independent state of awareness that represents the absence of a belief as well as its obtaining.

There are further problems with the sort of approach to conscious judging we've been considering so far. The idea behind the sort of bottom-up approach being considered is that a conscious act of judging involves a higher-order state of awareness of an event of a kind that can occur whether or not it is conscious. There are reasons for thinking that the event in question is an achievement—i.e. an event that is the acquisition of a mental state—and the most obvious candidate for such an event is the acquisition of a belief. However, not all acts of consciously judging that p need involve an event of acquiring the belief that p. For when one attempts to determine the truth value of a proposition by some active process of thinking, that process is constituted, in part, by conscious judgements one makes which are themselves manifestations of beliefs *already held*. Indeed it is unclear how one could engage in an attempt to determine whether a proposition is true via some active process of thinking if one could not avail oneself of conscious judgements that are simply manifestations of beliefs already held.[9]

There are, then, problems facing the sort of 'bottom-up' approach to conscious thinking that we have been considering. To summarize, one difficulty facing such a view is that it is unclear that it can accommodate adequately the idea that we can be aware of the occurrence of the conscious mental events that constitute the activity of conscious thinking. The view may be able to accommodate the idea that one can come to believe that such events *have occurred*, but it even faces difficulties in accommodating the idea that it can *seem* to one as though one can be aware of the occurrence of these conscious events. A further difficulty with the view is that it leaves unclear what sort of mental states are acquired when such instantaneous events occur. For example, while it might seem reasonable to hold that an instantaneous event of judging that p is an event that is

---

[9] Similar considerations apply to the conscious judgements involved in conscious deliberation.

the acquisition of a belief that p, there are reasons for thinking that this suggestion cannot apply to all acts of consciously judging that p, for in certain cases a conscious act of judging that p can be a manifestation of a belief that p that one already holds.

These are difficulties that appear to face any account of conscious thinking that commits to the idea that the activity of conscious thinking is reducible to, and analysable in terms of, mental states and events/processes that are simply changes in those states (e.g. acquisitions of, and transitions between, those states). The alternative would be to invoke in one's account of conscious thinking conscious occurrences that are not reducible to changes in mental states. These would be mental occurrences with the ontological profile of those aspects of mind that O'Shaughnessy labels 'experiences'—i.e. mental occurrences with the ontological profile of aspects of mind that feature in the stream of consciousness. We have seen that there are problems facing an account of conscious thinking that does not invoke these sorts of temporally extended mental occurrences; but there are also problems facing an account of conscious thinking that does invoke them. If one were to invoke such mental occurrences in an account of conscious thinking, then one would need a response to Geach's argument for the claim that there is no stream of conscious thought. One would need to respond to the arguments for thinking that conscious mental acts of thinking thoughts—e.g. conscious mental acts of judging—fall under the category of achievement. And one would also need to respond to Geach's suggestion that those who think that there is such a stream of conscious thought are making the mistake of thinking that 'to think certain thoughts is to have certain mental images, feelings, unspoken words etc., passing through one's mind' (1969: 34). In the next section I shall begin to make some proposals about how these challenges can be met. The first step will involve a consideration of the activity of thinking out loud.

10.3 Thinking out loud

In his argument against the notion of a stream of conscious thought, Geach discusses the difference between speech and thought as regards temporal duration. In *Mental Acts*, he writes:

Spoken words last so long in physical time...–one could sensibly say that the utterance of the words was simultaneous with the movement of a body...from one place to another. The same would go for the duration of mental images of words, or any other mental images...

With a thought it is quite different. Even if we accepted the view...that a judgement is a complex of Ideas, we could hardly suppose that in a thought the Ideas occur successively, as the words do in a sentence; it seems reasonable to say that unless the whole complex content is grasped all together–unless the Ideas...are all simultaneously present–the thought or judgement just does not exist at all. (Geach 1957: 104)

When one utters something in speech (e.g. 'John is tall'), the spoken words one utters can occur separately and successively. The spoken words uttered are temporally ordered. But, Geach argues, the parts of the propositional content in terms of which we individuate an act of judging are not temporally ordered. One cannot simply judge 'John', and one cannot first judge 'John', and then judge 'is tall'. These claims seem to me to be correct. However, it should also be noted that similar remarks appear to apply in the case of an *utterance* that is individuated in terms of a propositional content—e.g. an assertion that *p*.

In the case of an assertion, the utterance is an action that we characterize in terms of a propositional content. Certain properties of the utterance, e.g. the kinds of sounds that are uttered and the order in which those sounds occur, are relevant to the question of the kind of assertion that is performed when the utterance is made. Those properties of the utterance (e.g. the kinds of sounds that are uttered and the order in which they occur) contribute to determining, at least in part, the propositional content that is expressed by that utterance. However, it does not follow from this that the temporal parts of the utterance signify temporal parts of the propositional content expressed by that utterance. Although the action of asserting has temporal parts and successive phases, and although the temporal order of those successive phases contributes to determining the propositional content expressed by that action, it does not follow from this that the propositional content in terms of which we individuate that action must itself have temporal parts and successive phases.

We might think of the utterance as an event that is a vehicle of representation. We specify representational properties of that vehicle in terms of a propositional content with truth conditions. We are familiar with the idea that the same representational properties can be possessed by vehicles with rather different non-representational properties, and we are also familiar with the idea that we should not confuse and conflate properties of the vehicle of representation with the properties represented by that vehicle. However, we should also note that we should not conflate properties of the vehicle of representation with properties of the propositional content that we invoke in specifying the representational properties of that vehicle. In particular, we should not conflate the temporal profile of the vehicle of representation with the temporal profile of the propositional content expressed by that vehicle.

So suppose that over an interval of time t1–t5 S asserted that John is tall. At t2 an event of uttering the word 'John' may have occurred, and that may be a temporal part of the event of asserting that 'John is tall', but it does not follow from this that what has occurred is an event of asserting 'John'; for one might maintain that contents with truth conditions are asserted, but not the parts of those contents that lack truth conditions. So one might maintain that in the case of an utterance that is an assertion that *p*, although the utterance has temporal parts and successive phases, the propositional content in terms of which we individuate it does not. Although the words uttered occur successively, the parts of the propositional content that they express do not.

This point about assertion is an instance of a general remark I made earlier. We might accept that the propositional content that we invoke in individuating a given event does not have temporal parts and successive phases; but it does not follow from this that the event that we thereby individuate does not have temporal parts and successive phases. So establishing that an event of judging is individuated in terms of such a propositional content does not in itself suffice to show that the event of judging lacks temporal parts and successive phases. However, I also noted that Geach provides further reasons for thinking that the event of judging is an achievement, and not an accomplishment or activity. In the case of assertion, it makes sense to say that a subject has started but not yet finished her act of asserting that p (which, note, is not equivalent to saying that she has asserted part of the content that p), but arguably, in the case of an act of judging it does not make sense to say that the subject has started but not yet finished her act of judging that p. An act of asserting is an accomplishment, but an act of judging is not.

But now let us consider what should be said about a case in which a subject is thinking out loud. It seems reasonable to think that the activity of out-loud thinking can involve out-loud judging. Is an out-loud judging an achievement? If so, how is this to be made consistent with the idea that the act involves an out-loud utterance, which is not an achievement? Should we say that so-called cases of judging out loud are really cases in which an act of judging, which is an achievement, precedes an event of uttering words out loud? Or should we perhaps say that the act of judging, which is an achievement, occurs at some instant during the time that the out-loud utterance occurs?

In the case of thinking out loud (e.g. calculating whether p out loud), it seems wrong to regard the out-loud utterances as overt actions that merely accompany, and that are separate from, the real mental activity of calculating whether p. For then we would not seem to have a genuine case of calculating whether p *out loud*, but rather a case of the agent reporting out loud what he or she had just done, or simply being engaged in two distinct activities that happen to be going on at the same time.[10] One can be tempted into regarding thinking out loud as involving the conjunction of two separate activities— bodily activity *plus* a distinct and separate mental activity—for the following reason: saying various things out loud is not, in itself, sufficient for thinking out loud, and one doesn't need to say anything out loud in order to calculate whether p. So this can make it seem as though the mental activity of calculating must be constituted by something other than the overt bodily action—a distinct 'inner' process, separate from it. So we have two separate activities accompanying each other. But this, I think, is a mistake, and a mistake we can avoid if we hold instead that the activity of thinking out loud is a non-reducible basic activity—an activity of a basic, non-reducible type, that we might call *mental activity with an overt-bodily-action vehicle* (in this case, calculating whether p out loud).[11]

<hr>

[10] Compare Wittgenstein: 'There are important accompanying phenomena of talking which are often missing when we talk without thinking, and this is a characteristic of talking without thinking. But *they* are not thinking' (1953:: 218).

[11] This proposal connects, I think, with Ryle's discussion of what 'le Penseur' is doing (Ryle 1968). There Ryle writes: 'It is often supposed by philosophers and psychologists that thinking is saying things to oneself, so that what *le Penseur* is doing on his rock is saying things to himself. But, apart from other big defects in this view, it fails because it stops just where it ought to begin. Very likely *le Penseur* was just now murmuring something under his breath or saying it in his head. But the question is, "What is the thick description of what he was essaying or intending in murmuring those words to himself?" The thin description "murmuring syllables under his breath", though true, is the thinnest possible description of what he was engaged in. The important question is "But what is the correct and thickest possible description of what *le Penseur* was trying for in murmuring those syllables?"' (in Ryle 2009: 501).

According to this way of regarding the case, the verbal utterance instantiates two kinds of activity—overt bodily (talking out loud), and mental (calculating whether p)—in virtue of the fact that it instantiates a third, basic, non-reducible kind of activity, namely a mental activity with an overt-bodily-action vehicle (in this case, calculating whether p out loud). On this view, an event of one's verbal utterance can instantiate two types of act, one's saying something out loud and one's judging that p, *because* it instantiates a third, basic, non-reducible type of act, namely one's judging that p out loud.

How should this affect our view of the temporal profile of the out-loud act of judging that p? Is it an achievement, an accomplishment, or an activity? Since an out-loud utterance has temporal extension, then judging out loud must have temporal extension too. But then how is this consistent with the idea that judging isn't something one can have started but not yet finished doing (unlike crossing the street), and the idea that it isn't something one can have been doing and can continue doing more of (unlike walking)?

We might think of the case of judging out loud as a case in which an agent performs an act that we think of as an achievement *in*, or *by*, φ-ing, where φ-ing is not an achievement. According to this way of regarding the case, although an event with some temporal extension must occur if there is to be an event that is an out-loud judging, and so we can describe the subject as continuing to utter words over that interval of time, it doesn't follow that the subject can be described as continuing to judge over that interval of time. There is a distinction to be drawn between the temporal profile of the occurrence that is the vehicle of the act of judging, and the temporal profile of the act of which it is a vehicle. Failure to mark this distinction is what leads to questions that appear to be nonsensical—e.g. 'At which particular instant (during her utterance) did the subject judge that p out loud?', 'For how long did the subject continue to judge that p?', 'How long did it take the subject to finish judging that p?' Here we might compare a case in which one starts a race by firing a gun. The sound of the gun shot has temporal extension, but starting is usually thought of as an achievement. The sound of the gunshot continues to occur over an interval of time, but it doesn't make sense to ask 'for how long did the race continue to start?', any more than it makes sense to ask 'how long did it take for the race to finish starting'?

As has already been noted, saying various things out loud is not in itself sufficient for judging that p out loud, and in general, saying various things is not sufficient for thinking out loud. So if this proposal is to work, more needs to be said about what it is that makes a given utterance an instance of the kind *judging that p out loud*. A reasonable starting point is the idea that a subject counts as thinking out loud only if certain *cognitive* changes to that subject are involved. So what sort of cognitive changes? In particular, what sort of cognitive change must be involved if a subject's utterance is to count as a case of judging that p out loud? Recall that we have already seen reason to think that a subject's act of judging that p need not always involve the acquisition of the belief that p, for a subject's act of judging that p can be a manifestation of a belief that p that she already holds. Given that the cognitive change involved in judging that p out loud will not always involve the acquisition of the belief that p, what other cognitive changes might we cite?

The proposal I want to offer is that a subject's out-loud utterance counts as a case of judging that p out loud only if the subject believes that she is judging that p. In the case of the act of asserting that p, it is not obvious that an equivalent claim holds—i.e. the claim that a subject's utterance counts as an assertion that p only if the subject believes that she is asserting that p. For some might argue that the facts that determine which particular content is asserted by a subject in making a given utterance include facts about the conventional significance of the sounds uttered, and in a way that allows for the possibility that a subject can be asserting that p in making an utterance despite the fact that she takes herself to be asserting that q. However, in the case of the act of judging that p out loud, it seems safe to assume that if the subject does not believe that she is judging that p when she makes the out-loud utterance, then there is no good reason to regard her utterance as a case of judging that p out loud.

More still needs to be said about the relation between the subject's belief that she is judging that p and the out-loud utterance she makes in judging that p out loud, and I will return to this issue in due course. But now let us consider how we might apply these ideas regarding out-loud judging to the case of the conscious act of judging that does not involve any out-loud utterance. Recall that at the end of the previous section I argued that there are difficulties that appear to face any account of conscious thinking that commits to the idea that the activity of conscious thinking is reducible to, and ana- lysable in terms of, mental states and events/processes that are changes in those mental states. An alternative is to invoke in one's account of conscious thinking mental occur- rences with temporal extension but which are not reducible to changes in mental states. However, I said that if one were to defend this alternative, one would need to respond to the arguments for thinking that conscious mental acts of thinking thoughts—e.g. the mental act of consciously judging that p—fall under the category of achievement. For if the mental act of consciously judging that p does fall under the category of achieve- ment, that would appear to suggest that it is not an occurrence with temporal extension. Our discussion of the case of out-loud judging now opens up the following line of response.

We might think of the conscious mental act of judging as involving the occurrence of a conscious event that has temporal extension—a conscious event that is not reducible to an event/process that is a change in mental states. This would be a conscious mental occurrence with the temporal profile of those aspects of mind that O'Shaughnessy labels 'experiences'—i.e. mental occurrences with the temporal profile of aspects of mind that feature in the stream of consciousness. We can regard this conscious event with temporal extension as the *vehicle* of the mental act of judging, just as, in the case of thinking out loud, the bodily action of one's saying something is the vehicle of one's judging that p out loud. On this proposal, conscious mental activity, such as conscious calculation (in one's head), involves the occurrence of conscious events with temporal extension that serve as *vehicles* of acts of thinking thoughts.

On this view, the conscious event that is the vehicle of the conscious mental act of judging has temporal extension and hence temporal parts—but the temporal parts of that conscious event do not signify temporal parts of the content judged. When a subject consciously judges that p, that agent does something that we think of as an achievement *in*, or *by*, φ-ing, where φ-ing is not an achievement. According to this way of regarding the case, although a mental event with some temporal extension must occur if there is to be an event that is a *conscious* judging, it doesn't follow that the subject can be described as continuing to judge during the interval of time that the conscious event occurs. For there is a distinction to be drawn between the temporal profile of the conscious occurrence that is the vehicle of the act of judging and the temporal profile of the act of which it is a vehicle. Failure to mark this distinction is what leads to questions that appear to be nonsensical—e.g. 'For how long did the subject continue to judge that p?', 'How long did the subject take to finish judging that p?'

At one point, Geach himself considers and rejects a view of conscious thinking that is similar, in certain respects, to the one I've just outlined. He considers the idea that thinking is what he calls a 'non-basic' activity. This is the suggestion that thinking that p (e.g. judging that p) is something one does in, or by, doing something else—φ-ing, where φ-ing is the 'basic' activity relative to which the act of thinking that p is 'non-basic'. In response to this suggestion, Geach makes the following remark: 'If thinking were shown to be a less basic activity in relation to certain clockable activities, we might perhaps cease to be puzzled by the fact that some questions about time relations of thinking to physical events are in principle unanswerable...This, I think, is the point at which my argument should be most closely scrutinised. But so far as I can see, thinking is a basic activity' (1969: 37).

In the next section I shall try to make explicit a critical line of thought that may lie behind Geach's dismissal of the idea that thinking is a 'non-basic' activity, and I shall develop this line of thought into a series of objections to the account of conscious judging that I have just proposed—objections that centre on the criticism that the proposal pushes too far an analogy between thinking and talking. The response that I shall go on to offer to these objections will help to elaborate and clarify the account of the ontology of conscious judging that I want to defend; and I shall try to show how this account of the ontology can be used to respond to Geach's suggestion that those who think that there is a stream of conscious thought are making the mistake of thinking that 'to think certain thoughts is to have certain mental images, feelings, unspoken words etc., passing through one's mind' (1969: 34).

10.4 Thinking and talking

The following objection to the account of conscious judgement that I've just outlined is based on a development of Budd's (1989) reading of some remarks of Wittgenstein on inner speech in the *Philosophical Investigations*. The tenor of the objection is that although it may be tempting to model calculation in one's head on calculation out loud, it is a mistake to push too far the analogy between these activities, for the account of the 'inner' process involved in the activity of conscious thinking that one thereby ends up with is ultimately untenable.

Calculation out loud or on paper requires a vehicle: the concept demands that the calculation is embodied in a process that begins when the subject begins to calculate and terminates when she reaches the conclusion. The process has an independently specifiable nature as well as satisfying a description in terms of what is calculated. One might think that there are similarities here with calculation in the head, for the concept is of something that occurs within a stretch of time and that can be said to consist of stages or steps. This encourages the following picture. In the case of calculation in the head, the role of the vehicle of the calculation is played by an inner process, e.g. inner speech (which has an independently specifiable nature), rather than an outward process.[12] So in modelling calculation in the head on calculation out loud, we are tempted into accepting that when you calculate in your head:

  (a) something happens in you,
  (b) which you bring about,
  (c) which is the internal analogue of what happens and is brought about by you when you speak or calculate overtly.

And to this picture one might be tempted to add the following:

  (d) That which occurs in you, and which you bring about, when you calculate in your head is something that you have direct and infallible concurrent awareness of.

But there are reasons for thinking that this picture pushes too far the analogy between calculation out loud and calculation in the head, principally because it pushes too far an analogy between thinking and talking.

Let us start by focusing on some disanalogies between the act of asserting that p and the act of judging that p. The notion of assertion is constitutively linked with the notion of communication in a way that the mental act of judging is not. There are reasons for thinking that an act of asserting that p must involve a vehicle of representation in so far as it requires a vehicle of communication. That is to say, the act of assertion seems to require the *production* of something that can potentially serve as a vehicle of communication. This is what makes room for the possibility of having an intention to assert that p. In intending to assert that p, one intends to do something (to perform some act) that thereby serves as a vehicle of representation, in so far as one intends to do something (to perform some act) that can potentially serve as a vehicle of communication. One can fail to fulfil this intention through failing to perform the act that can potentially serve as a vehicle of communication.

There are reasons for thinking that these points do not apply in the case of the conscious mental act of judging that p. The act of judging that p does not require the

---

[12] See Wittgenstein 1953: 366.

production of something to serve as a potential vehicle of communication. One way of putting this is to say that the mental act of judging is not to be understood as an inner assertion, where this is a matter of communicating something to oneself. That is why although one can intend to assert that p one can't intend to judge that p; and so in contrast to the case of assertion, one cannot intend to judge that p and fail to do the thing (perform the act) required for fulfilling that intention. When you judge that p you don't need to produce inner sounds that you hear with your inner ear in order to understand and know what you are judging. In that sense, although the act of assertion requires the production of something that can potentially serve as a vehicle of communication, the mental act of judging doesn't seem to require the production of anything. In which case, what use have we for the notion that the mental act of judging involves a conscious mental act with temporal extension that serves as a *vehicle* of representation?

Concerns along these lines are expressed by Travis (2008) in the following remarks:

Both thinking and saying represent something as so. Saying relies on means for representing to others. Thinking–representing to oneself–does not . . . So saying needs vehicles–incarnations of visible, audible, forms, recognisably doing what they do. Representing to myself works otherwise. One *chooses* what to say; not what to think. I judge *just* where I can judge no other. It need not be made recognisable to me what I am judging for me to do so . . . Judging needs no vehicles in *such* roles. Does it need vehicles at all? (4)

Vendler also expresses similar concerns about making too much of the analogy between speech and thought:

Whereas speech is the expression of thought in a code—that is by means of a language— thought is not an expression of anything and is not conceived in or via a code. It is inconceivable that I might fail to understand what I think. Hearing the speaker's voice, or seeing his writing, is indispensable for getting at what he said, but what do I have to see or hear, externally or in my mind, to get at my own thoughts? [In the case of thinking] there is no message to encode and no private language to use for the encoding. (1972: 42)

Encoding and decoding can be correct or incorrect—misunderstanding, and slips of the tongue etc. are possible. If thinking needed a code, consisting of words or other symbols, then on the one hand the thinker might know what he wanted to 'say' to himself, and on the other he could be mistaken about what he did 'say'. In other words it would be possible for him to know and not know what he thinks at the same time. This is absurd. (1972: 44)

Considerations of this kind lead Vendler to hold that mental acts of thinking thoughts are not to be identified with 'the flux of words and images we perceive with the imagination', which is similar to Geach's dismissal of the idea that 'to think certain thoughts is to have certain mental images, feelings, unspoken words etc., passing through one's mind' (1969: 34).

These points can provide reasons for thinking that it is a mistake to push too far an analogy between calculation out loud and calculation in one's head. Let us reconsider the case of thinking out loud that I discussed earlier. Consider again the case of judging that p out loud. Here it seems that the following counterfactual is true: such a subject would have known that she was judging that *p* even if she failed to produce any sounds at all. So shouldn't we likewise say that in a case of consciously judging that *p* that doesn't involve an out-loud utterance, one can know that one is judging that *p*, even if no conscious vehicle of the act of judging occurs—e.g. even if one doesn't actually say anything in inner speech?

One might argue that the event of acquisition of one's knowledge of the content of one's mental act of judging must be instantaneous. And if the event of acquisition of one's knowledge is instantaneous, then the unfolding of the conscious mental event that is supposed to serve as the vehicle of one's conscious mental act of judging is either redundant, or what one must interpret and understand in order to acquire the knowledge. For example, if an event of one's silently saying something in inner speech is supposed to be the conscious vehicle of a given mental act of judging that *p*, then either one already knows what one is doing as one starts silently saying that thing, or one must silently say it in order to know what one is doing. The former option suggests that the unfolding of the conscious event of one's silently saying something is inessential to one's consciously judging that *p*, since it suggests that one can know what one is doing in judging that *p* without having to say anything silently. And the latter option suggests that one must wait for the completion of this conscious event, and interpret it, in order to know what one thinks.

In what follows I shall be suggesting that the appropriate response to these objections will need to focus on the question of the relation between the *occurrence* that is supposed to serve as a vehicle of representation in a conscious mental act of judging that *p*, and a mental *state* of the subject—namely the subject's belief that she is judging that *p*. In particular, my suggestion is going to be that the correct account of conscious judgement will, once again, need to appeal to a notion of 'occurrent mental state'.

10.5 The ontology of conscious judgement

Let us start with the dilemma posed at the end of the previous section. One horn of the dilemma is this. Suppose one holds that when a subject consciously judges that *p*, the occurrence of a conscious event with temporal extension must serve as a vehicle of the conscious mental act of judging. Presumably, those taking this stance must think that one cannot know that one is judging that *p* if no such conscious event occurs. In which case, they must hold that in order for one to know what one is thinking one needs to interpret and understand the conscious event involved—i.e. the conscious event that serves as a the vehicle of representing the content that *p*. The idea that the character of some conscious event serves as *evidence* for one when it comes to knowing what one is thinking in judging that *p* looks very close to the view of conscious thinking that Travis objects to in the quote given earlier: 'It need not be made recognisable to me what I am judging for me to do so…Judging needs no vehicles in *such* roles' (2008: 4). So one might think that embracing this horn of the dilemma will commit one to some kind of version of the view of conscious thinking that Vendler suggests is absurd:

Hearing the speaker's voice, or seeing his writing, is indispensable for getting at what he said, but what do I have to see or hear, externally or in my mind, to get at my own thoughts? [In the case of thinking] there is no message to encode and no private language to use for the encoding...If thinking needed a code, consisting of words or other symbols, then on the one hand the thinker might know what he wanted to 'say' to himself, and on the other he could be mistaken about what he did 'say'. In other words it would be possible for him to know and not know what he thinks at the same time. (1972: 42)

The other horn of the dilemma is this. Suppose that one denies that in order to know what one is thinking one needs to interpret and understand some conscious occurrence that serves as a vehicle of the mental act of judging that p. Then this suggests a picture on which the actual occurrence of a conscious event with temporal extension is not needed if one is to know that one is judging that p, which in turn suggests that the actual occurrence of a conscious event with temporal extension is not required if one is to be consciously judging that p.

Now let us consider what sort of response to this dilemma is made possible by an appeal to the notion of an occurrent mental state. Recall that an 'occurrent' mental state, as I have been characterizing that notion, is a mental state whose obtaining is constitutively dependent on the occurrence of some mental event with temporal extension. The mental state and event in question have an interdependent status, and the mental event in question is not to be thought of as an antecedent, temporally prior, cause of the obtaining of the mental state. The mental state obtains *while* and because the event with temporal extension occurs. This notion of an occurrent mental state makes available the following general form of response to this dilemma. The belief that one is judging that p is an occurrent mental state. The obtaining of this state is constitutively dependent on the occurrence of a conscious mental event with temporal extension. So the occurrence of a conscious mental event with temporal extension is necessary for one to know that one is judging that p, given that it is necessary for the obtaining of a belief that one is judging that p. Hence the second horn of the dilemma is avoided. Moreover, the conscious event with temporal extension is a vehicle of a mental act of judging that p only if the belief that one is judging that p obtains when that event occurs. So the belief that one is judging that p is not a belief one acquires *after* the occurrence of the conscious event, as a result of interpreting that one is thinking (i.e. judging) that p. Hence the first horn of the dilemma is avoided. This is to reintroduce into the account of conscious judging a higher-order state of belief that concerns an act of judging. But although higher-order beliefs play a role in this account of conscious judging, note that it is not a version of a 'bottom-up' approach to conscious thought. For it does not hold that such conscious mental acts involve events of a kind that can occur without being conscious and which simply require further higher-order states to represent them in order for them to be conscious.

That, in general outline, is the form of response made available by the proposal that an account of the ontology of conscious judging should appeal to the notion of occurrent mental state. In what follows I shall try to elaborate the view and in doing so I shall draw out some important differences between the kind of occurrent mental state that is involved in conscious judgement, and the kind of occurrent mental states that I invoked in Part I, when discussing aspects of *sensory* consciousness.

First it will be helpful to recap on how we arrived at the current proposal. I suggested that there are problems facing any account of conscious thinking that commits to the idea that the activity of conscious thinking is reducible to, and analysable in terms of, mental states and events (or processes) that are simply changes in those states (e.g. acquisitions of, and transitions between, those states). I have been trying to make defensible an alternative proposal about conscious thinking—one that invokes mental occurrences with temporal extension that are not reducible to changes in mental states.

A problem facing this alternative proposal is the following: given that there are reasons for thinking that a mental act of consciously judging that p is an achievement, rather than an activity or accomplishment, it looks as though there are reasons for denying that we should appeal to an occurrence with temporal extension in an account of the conscious mental act of judging that p. The response offered to this problem was that we can make sense of the idea that a mental event with temporal extension must occur if there is to be an event that is a conscious judging that p, despite the fact that we think of judging that p as an achievement, if we accept the following view. The conscious mental act of judging that p involves the occurrence of a conscious event with temporal extension that is to be thought of as a *vehicle* of the conscious mental act of judging. That conscious occurrence has temporal extension and hence temporal parts, but the temporal parts of that conscious event do not signify temporal parts of the content judged. When a subject consciously judges that p, that agent does something that we think of as an achievement *in*, or *by*, φ-ing, where φ-ing is not an achievement. This is what explains why it doesn't make sense to ask: 'for how long did the subject continue to judge that p?' and 'How long did it take the subject to finish judging that p?'

A natural question to ask of this proposal is the following: what makes it the case that the relevant act of φ-ing is the vehicle of a mental act of judging that p? We cannot answer that it is the subject's intention to judge that p in, or by, φ-ing; for the subject who judges that p does not intend to judge that p. This is where there is a significant disanalogy between asserting and judging. In contrast to the case of assertion, in the case of judging that p one doesn't make use of some vehicle (e.g. perform some act of φ-ing that can serve as a vehicle of representation) with the aim/intention of representing something to someone.

The account of conscious judging that appeals to an occurrent mental state of belief makes available the following alternative answer: what makes it the case that the relevant act of φ-ing is the vehicle of a mental act of judging that p is the fact that the state that obtains when the act of φ-ing occurs is one of believing that one is judging that p. On this view, the occurrence of an event of the kind *conscious judging that p* depends upon the *concurrent* obtaining of some mental state of the subject—namely her belief that she is judging that p. The conscious mental act of judging involves the occurrence of a conscious event with temporal extension—the event of φ-ing; but if the subject's belief that she is judging that p does not obtain when the act of φ-ing occurs, then that act of φ-ing doesn't count as an instance of judging that p.

Now let's consider in more detail how to understand, in this context, talk of a *vehicle* of representation. In the case of assertion that p, an act of φ-ing (e.g. saying things out loud) counts as a vehicle of representation in the following sense: the occurrence of an event of the kind φ-ing doesn't in itself entail that an act of the kind asserting that p has occurred. Moreover, an act of the kind asserting that p can have a vehicle with very different properties (e.g. one can assert that p in, or by, saying very different things out loud on different occasions). Let's apply this idea to the proposal that some conscious event with temporal extension is to be thought of as the vehicle of the conscious mental act of judging. We should presumably say the following: suppose that in a given case a conscious event of kind φ serves as a vehicle of a conscious act of judging that p. Then, (i) the mere occurrence of an event of that kind φ doesn't in itself entail the occurrence of an event of the kind judging that p; and (ii) numerically distinct episodes of judging that p can involve the occurrence of conscious events with very different properties. But now note that the following seems to be a consequence of this way of conceiving of the idea that a conscious event with temporal extension can serve as a vehicle of the mental act of judging that p: the mere occurrence of a conscious event of that phenomenal kind φ doesn't in itself entail the obtaining of belief that one is judging that p. This means that if the belief that one is judging that p is an occurrent mental state, it is unlike the other sorts of occurrent mental states that were introduced in Part I, in our discussion of sensory aspects of mind.

In Part I, I argued that we should appeal to occurrent perceptual states in an account of the ontology of conscious perceptual experience. I said that the occurrence and state in question have an interdependent status, in so far as the nature of the occurrence is to be specified, at least in part, in terms of the kind of state that obtains when it occurs, and the nature of the state is to be specified, at least in part, in terms of the kind of occurrence that its obtaining is constitutively dependent on. I suggested that the fact that the occurrence and state in question have this interdependent status is what gives rise to a form of explanatory circularity. I also argued that we need to appeal to occurrent mental states in an account of perceptual imagination and recollection, and that in this case too the state and event in question have an interdependent status that gives rise to a form of explanatory circularity. In the case of perceptual imagination and perceptual recollection, the phenomenal character of the mental episode that occurs determines, at least in part, the content of an occurrent mental state that represents a conscious sensory experience. So the way in which a conscious sensory experience is represented in perceptual imagination and perceptual recollection necessarily involves the occurrence of phenomenally conscious mental episodes. Moreover, the phenomenal character of the mental episode of imagining or recollecting is to be specified in terms of the content of the occurrent mental state that obtains when that episode occurs. Hence, the interdependent status of occurrence and state, and the form of explanatory circularity to which it gives rise.

The proposal about the conscious act of judging currently under consideration is that the mental act of judging that p involves the occurrence of a conscious event that serves as a *vehicle* of representation, and in having the status of a *vehicle* of representation, that conscious occurrence has an independently specifiable nature. That is to say, a conscious event of that independently specifiable kind can occur without being the vehicle of an act of judging that p. This allows that the conscious event that serves as a vehicle of the act of judging that p could be an occurrence of kind φ, whilst also allowing that there can be cases where the occurrence of an event of kind φ does not entail the obtaining of a mental state of belief that one is judging that p. Moreover, the obtaining of the mental state that is one's belief that one is judging that p doesn't in itself require the occurrence of an event of the *specific* kind φ, given that numerically distinct episodes of judging that p can involve the occurrence of conscious events with very different properties. So according to this proposal, the belief that one is judging that p and the conscious event that is the vehicle of the mental act of judging don't have the sort of interdependent status exemplified by the phenomenal events and states invoked in the accounts of perceptual experience and perceptual imagination that I proposed. In particular, this proposal allows that we can specify the kind of mental state that obtains when one believes that one is judging that p *independently* of any *specific* kind of phenomenally conscious event that its obtaining may be constitutively dependent on.

However, according to this account, the belief that one is judging that p is a state that can only obtain if there does occur some mental event with temporal extension that serves as the vehicle of one's act of judging that p.[13] The mental state that is one's belief that one is judging that p is a mental state whose obtaining is constitutively dependent on the occurrence of a conscious event with temporal extension that is the vehicle of one's act of judging that p. Without the occurrence of some such event to serve as the vehicle of the act of judging that p, the belief that one is judging that p cannot obtain. The belief that one has just *judged* that p can obtain. But this is not equivalent to the belief that one is judging that p. This proposal provides us with a way of addressing a concern raised earlier—namely the problem of identifying a role for a vehicle of representation in the case of conscious judging, given that it is not that of serving as a vehicle of communication. A conscious mental act of judging requires a conscious occurrence to serve as its vehicle, for the form of *self-knowledge* that accompanies a conscious act of judging can only obtain if such an event occurs. Without the occurrence of a conscious mental event that unfolds over time and that serves as a vehicle of representation, there is no belief that one is judging that p. At most, there is simply a higher-order mental state

---

[13] So the occurrent mental state that is one's belief that one is judging that p has temporal extension. But as it is an occurrent state, it does not automatically follow that it is homogeneous down to instants. So although one's belief that one is judging that p obtains over an interval of time, it may not be correct to claim that it continues to obtain throughout the interval of time over which it obtains. So it may not be correct to claim that one *continues* to believe that one is judging that p *throughout* an interval of time. Note that this is in keeping with the suggestion that we think of the act of judging as falling under the category of achievement, and not under the category of activity.

with another mental state as its object (e.g. the belief that one believes that *p*), and not a mental act; or there may be a belief that one has just judged that *p*.

The view according to which conscious thinking is reducible to, and analysable in terms of, mental states and events/processes that are changes in those mental states can accommodate the idea that a subject can know that she believes that *p*. It can accommodate the idea that a subject can know that she has just acquired the belief that *p*. And it can also accommodate the idea that at certain times the subject will be poised to express her belief that *p* in overt verbal behaviour. However, it cannot adequately accommodate the distinctive form of self-knowledge that accompanies the conscious mental act of judging. This distinctive form of self-knowledge is not equivalent to knowing that one believes that *p*, it's not equivalent to knowing that one has just acquired the belief that *p*, and it isn't simply a matter of being poised to express one's belief that *p* in an overt bodily action. This distinctive form of self-knowledge involves the obtaining of an occurrent mental state—a mental state whose obtaining is constitutively dependent on the occurrence of a conscious mental event with temporal extension—and so a form of self-knowledge that is only available to the subject whose mental life includes a stream of consciousness. In the next section I shall offer some further clarification of this proposal by discussing how it impacts on the question of whether there is a *stream of conscious thought*.

10.6 Is there a stream of conscious thought?

In *Res Cogitans*, Vendler offers an account of thinking that involves an analysis of propositional verbs of the categories 'mental act' and 'mental state'. He imagines an objector to his account arguing in the following way:

By focusing exclusively on the sense of the word *thought*, which denotes the content or product of the mental processes, I ignore these processes themselves, or worse...I create the impression that...I have exhausted the topic of thinking altogether. (1972: 40)

The hypothetical objector continues:

Thinking is an activity, a process, something that goes on, which we can pursue, and of which we are aware throughout our conscious life. Thinking is the stream of consciousness, the buzzing, blooming confusion of images, sounds, feelings, and emotions; interspersed, it is true, by words or even sentences dimly 'heard', sub-vocally 'pronounced', or 'glanced at' with the mind's eye...We ask in the progressive tense 'what are you thinking about?'...Moreover the philosophically interesting sense of thinking is this process sense; the process of thinking constitutes our 'inner life'. (40)

In replying to this objection, Vendler writes:

In thinking about something one goes through a series of mental acts often involving some changes of mental states; one may guess, assume, realise, or conclude that something is the case; regard, consider or view a certain thing in many ways; contemplate, plan, and decide to do one thing or another; and wonder about consequences. The idea that one might be thinking about something without performing any of these or similar acts is as incomprehensible as the idea of talking about something without saying anything at all. (41)

According to Vendler, these mental acts and states are individuated, in part, by their propositional contents, and they are not to be identified with 'the flux of words and images we perceive with the imagination'. As we have seen, Geach, in a similar vein, rejects the idea that 'to think certain thoughts is to have certain mental images, feelings, unspoken words etc., passing through one's mind' (1969: 34). The message from both Geach and Vendler seems to be that the activity of thinking is to be distinguished from the kind of sensory activity that makes up the *stream* of one's conscious mental life. So should we accept the conclusion that there is no stream of conscious *thought*?

In Chapter 2, I suggested that we can individuate at different levels of abstraction a mental state that obtains in virtue of the occurrence of a phenomenally conscious mental event or process. For example, we can individuate such a state at a level of abstraction that makes no reference to the kind of event in virtue of whose occurrence it obtains. In individuating a mental state at this level of abstraction we do not individuate it in terms of its phenomenal character. Individuating a mental state at this level of abstraction can be useful, for it allows us to pick out important commonalities between phenomenally conscious mental states and states that are not phenomenally conscious, and it also allows us to pick out important commonalities between mental states that obtain in virtue of phenomenally conscious mental events of different kinds.

We can also make sense of the idea of individuating phenomenally conscious mental *events* at different levels of abstraction. We can individuate a phenomenally conscious mental event at a level of abstraction that does not make any reference to its phenomenal character. For example, if the occurrence of a phenomenally conscious mental event involves the acquisition of a mental state that is not phenomenally conscious, then in individuating the event *as such* (i.e. as an event that involves the acquisition of such a state), we need make no reference to the phenomenal features of the event. Individuating mental events at this level of abstraction may also allow us to pick out important commonalities between mental events of different phenomenally conscious kinds.

Mental events that we think of as cognitive, rather than sensory, are generally mental events that are individuated at this level of abstraction—i.e. without making reference to phenomenal features of the event in question. The mental act of judging is just such an example. This then suggests the following possibility. A subject's mental act of judging that *p* may involve the occurrence of a phenomenally conscious mental act, for example the subject's saying something in inner speech, but when this mental event is individuated as one of judging, the phenomenal character of the mental event drops out of the picture, for we want to allow that a mental act of the same kind—'judging that *p*'— could occur even if it did not have the same phenomenal character. This is because in the case of conscious mental acts of judging, any phenomenally conscious occurrence can at best be seen as a *vehicle* of that act of judging. This marks an important difference between the cognitive and the sensory (i.e. conscious thinking and sensory consciousness) that is reflected in a difference between the sorts of occurrent mental states that I invoked in my account of sensory aspects of mind (perceptual experiences and perceptual imagination) and the occurrent mental state that I have invoked in my account of the conscious act of judging. The occurrent mental state that is one's belief that one is judging that p and the phenomenally conscious event that may serve as the vehicle of the act of judging do not have the sort of interdependent status exemplified by the phenomenal events and states invoked in the accounts of perceptual experience and perceptual imagination that I proposed.

The result is that when one individuates a phenomenally conscious mental act as one of judging, the kind of event one individuates it as, makes no reference to its phenomenal character. So although the event has temporal extension, as it is a phenomenally conscious one, the kind of event one individuates it as, makes no reference to its being the kind of event that has temporal extension. So a mental event that is an element in the Jamesian stream of consciousness—a phenomenally conscious occurrence—is individuated as a mental event of a kind that makes no reference to the features of it that make it suited to be an element in the stream of consciousness. This can then lead to the conclusion that there is no stream of *thought*. There can only be a stream of processes of a *sensory* nature—where this includes acts of perceptual imagination.

The temptation, then, is to think that an account of the activity of conscious thinking (e.g. conscious calculation) need not involve mental occurrences with the ontological profile of those aspects of mind that feature in the stream of consciousness—mental continuities that are processive in character but which are not reducible to mental events/processes that are changes in mental states. That is to say, the temptation is to think that the mental activity of conscious thinking is reducible to, and analysable in terms of, mental states and events/processes that are changes to or in those states. Much of what goes on when one is engaged in the activity of conscious thinking (e.g. the activity of conscious calculation) can be captured by such an account. For example, the account can capture the idea that when one engages in such activity one acquires new beliefs—including beliefs about what one believes, and including beliefs that one has just acquired new beliefs. The account can also accommodate the idea that when one engages in such activity one is poised to express in overt verbal behaviour beliefs about the activity one is engaged in. However, I have suggested that a difficulty facing such an account is that it cannot accommodate adequately the idea that we can be aware of (or even seem to be aware of) the occurrence of the conscious events that constitute the activity of conscious thinking *when they occur*. In particular, it cannot adequately accommodate the distinctive form of self-knowledge that accompanies the conscious mental act of judging—one's knowledge that one is judging that p. This distinctive form of self-knowledge is not equivalent to knowing that one believes that p. It's not equivalent to knowing that one has just acquired the belief that p. And it isn't simply a matter of being poised to express one's belief that p in an overt bodily action. This distinctive form of self-knowledge involves the obtaining of an occurrent mental state—a mental state whose obtaining is constitutively dependent on the occurrence of a conscious mental event with temporal extension; it is a form of self-knowledge that is only available to the subject whose mental life includes a stream of consciousness.

So what distinctive role does this distinctive form of self-knowledge play, which can't be played by the other forms of self-knowledge that I listed? What would be lost if our mental lives did not include a stream of consciousness and we didn't have this distinctive form of self-knowledge? What would be lost, I suggest, is the ability to engage in mental actions, such as conscious calculation and deliberation, that don't require the performance of an overt bodily action to serve as their vehicle. Although the account of conscious judging being proposed here doesn't commit one to the idea that such mental acts are mental actions, part of what's being suggested is that the right account of the conscious mental act of judging must be given in terms of the distinctive form of self-knowledge that accompanies it, and I now want to add to that the suggestion that the role of this distinctive form of self-knowledge is to be understood in terms of its role in agential mental activity, e.g. working out a problem, or deliberating about what to do—mental activities that one can choose to engage in.

This is in line with a suggestion once made by A.C. Ewing. He said that 'With cognition . . . we should distinguish a continuous process of thinking from particular "cognitive acts". The former should . . . be regarded as basic rather than the latter, and the process of thinking out a problem should not be reduced to a mere series of such acts' (1948: 217). In a similar vein, my suggestion is that there is a sense in which we get at the notion of a conscious mental act (e.g. the conscious mental act of judging) by subtracting from the notion of mental action. For we need to think of the kind of mental events involved in conscious thinking in terms of the idea that a sequence of these events can amount to a mental activity that has an *agential* explanation—i.e. in terms of the idea that an appropriate sequence of them can constitute an activity that is attributable to the agent, as opposed to some part of her.

I will be expanding on this suggestion in later chapters. Further elucidation of the idea will depend on a view about what it is that makes a mental activity an *agential* activity, and this is something I haven't yet made any proposals about. But to review: in this chapter I have made a proposal about the ontology of the activity of conscious thinking. I have argued that such activity is not reducible to, and analysable in terms of, mental states and events (and processes) that are simply changes in or to those mental states. I have argued that the bottom-up approach to conscious thinking should be rejected, and that an account of the ontology of conscious thinking should invoke occurrent mental states—states whose obtaining constitutively depends on the occurrence of conscious occurrences with temporal extension. However, I have also noted differences between these occurrent mental states and the varieties of occurrent mental state that I invoked in Part I, when discussing aspects of sensory consciousness. These differences, I have suggested, are relevant to differences between the sensory and the cognitive—between sensory consciousness and conscious thinking. I have also argued that the occurrent mental states invoked in this account of conscious thinking provide us with a distinctive form of self-knowledge—a form of self-knowledge that is only available to those whose mental lives include a stream of consciousness. And finally, I have made the tentative suggestion that the significance of this distinctive form of self-knowledge is to be understood in terms of its role in agential mental activity (e.g. working out a problem, or deliberating about what to do), mental activities that one can choose to engage in. In order to make good the suggestion that this account of the ontology of conscious thinking is relevant to uncovering a connection between conscious thinking and mental action, more needs to be said about what it is that makes a mental activity an *agential* activity. I shall be considering this issue in the next chapter.

11

'The Mind Uses Its Own Freedom': Suppositional Reasoning and Self-Critical Reflection

A conclusion reached in the previous chapter is that we need to invoke *occurrent* mental states in our account of the ontology of conscious thinking. These occurrent mental states, I argued, provide us with a distinctive form of self-knowledge—e.g. knowledge that one is judging that *p*, which is neither equivalent to the knowledge that one believes that *p*, nor the knowledge that one has just acquired the belief that *p*. The activity of consciously thinking about something involves a distinctive form of self-knowledge that is only available to those in whom such occurrent mental states obtain, and these occurrent mental states can only obtain in subjects whose mental lives include a stream of consciousness.

I ended the chapter by tentatively suggesting that the significance of this form of self-knowledge is to be understood in terms of its role in agential mental activity. I suggested that there is a sense in which we get at the notion of a conscious cognitive mental act (such as the conscious mental act of judging) by subtracting from the notion of mental action. For we need to think of the kind of mental events involved in conscious thinking in terms of the idea that a sequence of these events can amount to a mental activity that has an *agential* explanation. In that respect there is a connection between the notions of conscious thinking and mental action, albeit an indirect one.

This suggestion is rather vague as it stands, and further clarification and defence of the idea will, amongst other things, require saying a lot more about what it is that makes a mental activity an *agential* activity. As I have already mentioned, some deny that there is *any* connection between the notions of mental action and conscious thinking. For example, although Galen Strawson does not deny that there is such a thing as mental action, he denies that mental agency has any essential role to play in an account of the sort of conscious reasoning and conscious thinking that can go on in the mind of a self-conscious subject. Indeed he goes so far as to suggest that a self-conscious thinking subject need not be an agent at all. He suggests that there is no incoherence in the idea of what he calls a 'Pure Observer': 'a motionless, cognitively well-equipped, highly receptive, self-conscious, rational, subtle creature that is well-informed about its surroundings and has, perhaps, a full and vivid sense of itself as an observer although it has no capacity for any sort of intentional action, nor even any conception of the possibility of intentional action' (2003: 228). According to Strawson, even in the mental lives of agents such as ourselves, most conscious thoughts 'just happen' and 'action and intention need have little or nothing to do with their occurrence' (2003: 228). When mental action is involved in conscious thinking, its role can at best be 'merely catalytic' and 'indirect' (2003: 231).

Defence of the idea that the agency we can exercise over our mental lives should be accorded a central place in an account of conscious thinking will need to explain what is wrong in the alternative picture that Strawson proposes. In this chapter I shall try to meet that challenge by focusing on the question of the role of agency in suppositional reasoning and self-critical reflection.

As I mentioned in Chapter 9, some have suggested that there is an important connection between a distinctive form of self-knowledge that is available to the self-conscious subject and the agency that such a subject can exercise over her mental life. For example, O'Shaughnessy suggests that a distinctive form of self-knowledge available to the self-conscious subject makes possible a certain kind of 'mental freedom'. He suggests that our capacity to know that we have thought, 'together with the capacity to contemplate its denial as a possibility that is here not in fact realized' (2000: 111), provides us with a form of mental freedom that allows us to 'transcend the condition of animal immersion' (2000: 112):

the animal merely has its beliefs, which are produced in it through sense, regularities in experience, desire, innate factors, etc. It does not know it has them, it has no hand in their installation, and it cannot compare them to the world. All it can do is harbour them and act upon them. (2000: 112)

In this special sense animals may be said to be *immersed* in the world in a way thinking beings are not... there can in their case be no *working towards* a belief, no believing through *cogitation*, no form of *responsibility* for belief, and in consequence no kind of *mental freedom*. (2000: 111)

Korsgaard makes what looks to be a similar proposal. She claims that as self-conscious subjects, we have reflective awareness of our own mental states and activities as such, and this self-conscious form of consciousness opens up what she calls 'a space of reflective distance'. Korsgaard argues that this space of reflective distance ensures that 'we are, or can be, active, self-directing, with respect to our beliefs'. It 'presents us with the possibility and the necessity of exerting a kind of control over our beliefs' (2009b: 32).

As I also noted in Chapter 9, a difficulty with this proposal, as it stands, is that it leaves unclear how the 'space of reflective distance' that Korsgaard cites is supposed to allow us to 'exert control over our beliefs'. Why should we accept that our ability to reflect on our own beliefs somehow allows belief formation to be governable by such reflection? How, exactly, is agency supposed to figure in the exercise of the sort of self-critical reflection that is made possible by 'the space of reflective distance'? If we concede that a subject doesn't decide or intend to judge that p, even when such a judgement occurs during self-critical reflection, then shouldn't we agree with Strawson that the role of agency in self-critical reflection can at best be 'merely catalytic' and 'indirect'? In which case, doesn't this call into question the connection that O'Shaughnessy and Korsgaard are concerned to forge between conscious reasoning, mental agency, and the sort of self-knowledge that is available to the self-conscious subject? These are among the questions I aim to address in this chapter.

11.1 Suppositional reasoning

Korsgaard notes that there is a venerable philosophical tradition that holds that 'reason is what distinguishes us from other animals, and that reason is in some special way the active dimension of mind' (2009b: 23). Under this view, 'the human mind is active in some way that the minds of the other animals are not, and…this activity is the essence of rationality' (2009b: 23). Korsgaard cites as examples of philosophers belonging to this tradition Kant, in his association of reason with the mind's spontaneity, and Aristotle, in his doctrine of the active intellect, or *nous*. To this list I think we can also add Descartes.

Descartes is notorious for the way in which he downgrades the psychology of non-human animals, going so far as to deny them a mind in denying them a rational soul; and he also often places emphasis upon, and attaches significance to, active, agential aspects of the rational human mind. As I mentioned in Chapter 9, while a number of philosophers now think that sensory consciousness presents the hard problem for physicalism, Descartes seemed to think that it is a consideration of conscious thinking, and the sort of self-conscious consciousness that enables us to engage in that kind of activity, that should lead us to reject materialism; and for Descartes, conscious thinking crucially involves 'the will'. In his attempt to protect the coherence of the notion of disembodied existence, Descartes was concerned to protect the coherence of the notion of a disembodied agent—an agent capable of action but incapable of bodily action. Under such an approach, the agency that we can exercise over our mental lives becomes of paramount concern. For Descartes, sensory consciousness is a form of consciousness that is only available to the embodied subject, whereas conscious thinking is an activity that the disembodied agent can engage in. So it is the latter, and not the former, that occupies a central place in his argument against materialism. Concerns that arise in connection with sensory consciousness seem, for Descartes, to have more to do with the distinctive way in which distinct substances are united in the embodied, conscious, human subject.

The activity of self-critical reflection obviously plays a central role in the arguments that Descartes presents in the *Meditations*, and in that work he alludes to the way in which the mind 'uses its own freedom' when engaged in the method of doubt. In the *Principles of Philosophy*, Descartes is explicit that it is our free will that allows us to withhold our assent in doubtful matters.[1] And the Fourth Meditation is largely devoted to

---

[1] For discussion of the role of the mind's freedom in the method of doubt, see *Principles of Philosophy*, Pt. I: 6 and 39.

arguing that the act of judgement involves not only the intellect but also the will.[2] Although my principal aim here isn't that of defending a particular interpretation of Descartes' texts, I do want to consider some remarks that Descartes makes in the *Meditations* as a springboard for a discussion of the role of agency in our conscious thinking—and in particular, the extent to which self-determination may be involved in conscious reasoning and self-critical reflection. In the Synopsis of the *Meditations*, when summarizing the Second Meditation, Descartes writes:

> In the Second Meditation, the mind uses its own freedom and supposes the non-existence of all the things about whose existence it can have even the slightest doubt; and in so doing the mind notices that it is impossible that it should not exist during this time. This exercise is also of the greatest benefit, since it enables the mind to distinguish without difficulty what belongs to itself, i.e. to an intellectual nature, from what belongs to the body.

Descartes claims here that the mind 'uses its own freedom' in supposing something. The first question I want to address is the following. In what respect, if any, does the mind 'use its own freedom' when engaged in supposition? In particular, what is the role of agency in supposing something for the sake of argument? The specific description that Descartes offers of the mind's aim in the Second Meditation is that of supposing the non-existence of all the things 'about whose existence it can have even the slightest doubt'. Identifying the propositions one believes, whose veracity there can be the slightest reason to doubt is an exercise in self-critical reflection. So how are we to understand the role of agency in self-critical reflection? Is this related to the role of agency in suppositional reasoning? And if so, in what way?

Let's start with the question about suppositional reasoning. First we need to narrow down the notion of supposition that is our concern. The phrase 'S supposes that *p*' is sometimes used to attribute to S the belief or opinion that *p*, or an unacknowledged commitment to the truth of *p*, whereas the sort of supposition I want to focus on is more like an exercise of the imagination. However, we shouldn't simply equate 'supposing that *p*' with 'imagining that *p*', for to do so might invite the following line of thought. A way of imagining that *p* is to imagine a situation in which *p* is true, and a way of imagining a situation in which *p* is true is by imagining (e.g. visualizing) a scene in which *p* is true. Indeed, whenever one visualizes a scene one thereby imagines a situation in which certain propositions are true. So whenever one visualizes a scene one thereby imagines that such and such is the case; and since supposing that *p* *is* imagining that *p*, whenever one visualizes a scene one thereby supposes that such and such is the case.

The problem with the conclusion of this line of thought is that visualizing a scene isn't in itself sufficient for engaging in the kind of supposition that is our concern. For the notion of supposition that I want to focus on is the kind of supposition that is involved in assuming something for the sake of argument; and intuitively, visualizing

---

[2] In *Principles of Philosophy*, Descartes also claims that 'the supreme perfection of man' is that he acts freely, and in the Fourth Meditation Descartes writes, 'it is above all in virtue of the will that I understand myself to bear in some way the image and likeness of God'.

something doesn't in itself amount to assuming something for the sake of argument. So what is involved in assuming something for the sake of argument? Perhaps just putting forth, or introducing, p as a premise in one's reasoning, or treating p as a premise in one's reasoning? But these descriptions can also apply to judging that p (and also to asserting that p). So what is the difference between judging that p and supposing that p?

Judging that p involves representing p *as true*. Representing p as true isn't simply equivalent to entertaining in thought the proposition that p is true, for one can entertain in thought the proposition that p is true without representing p *as true*, as when one judges that 'either p is true or it isn't'. But for the same reason, entertaining in thought the proposition that p is true isn't sufficient for supposing that p, for entertaining in thought the proposition that p is true is something that one can do when one supposes for the sake of argument that '*either p* is true or q is true'.

If we hold that judging that p involves representing p as true, a temptation may be to think that supposing that p for the sake of argument is a matter of acting *as if* one is representing p as true—perhaps imagining or pretending to represent p as true. However, a problem with this proposal is that it suggests that supposing that p can be a stand-alone mental act—i.e. it suggests that it might be possible for one to suppose that p for the sake of argument, without doing anything else. If judging (or asserting) that p can be a stand-alone act, it should be possible for pretending or imagining that one is judging (or asserting) that p to be a stand-alone act too. However, supposing that p for the sake of argument is not a stand-alone mental act—it is not something one can do without doing anything else. And this is relevant to why visualizing something cannot in itself be sufficient for assuming something for the sake of argument.

The idea that supposing that p is not a stand-alone act is something that is touched upon by Dummett in his chapter on assertion in *Frege: Philosophy of Language*. There Dummett considers the question of whether there is a force that attaches to the proposition that p when one supposes that p, which is distinct from the force that attaches to the proposition that p when one asserts that p. At one point Dummett makes the following remark:

In supposition a thought is expressed but not asserted: 'Suppose . . .' must be taken as a sign of the force (in our sense) with which a sentence is uttered. (Certainly it is not logically an imperative: I could, having said, 'Think of a number', ask 'Have you done so yet?', but it would be a joke if I asked that question having said 'Suppose the witness is telling the truth'.) (1973: 309)

If 'suppose the witness is telling the truth' is understood as 'suppose *for the sake of argument* that the witness is telling the truth', then there is an oddity in the question, 'Have you done so yet?' As Dummett remarks, the oddity of the question wouldn't apply if one had said, 'Think of a number'. And we can add, neither would the oddity apply if one had said 'imagine a bowl of cherries', or 'imagine asserting that the witness is telling the truth'. This is connected, I suggest, with the idea that the latter can be, what I have been calling, stand-alone mental acts, whereas supposing that p for the sake of argument cannot.

The idea that supposing that *p* for the sake of argument cannot be a stand-alone mental act is also connected, I think, with Frege's stance on supposition.[3] Frege denies that in the case of supposing that *p* a force that is distinct from that of assertion attaches to the proposition that *p*. He holds instead that the force of assertion attaches to a sentence that has *p* as a constituent.[4] On Frege's view, in the case of supposition that *p*, '*p*' does not appear as a complete sentence at all, but only as a constituent in a more complex sentence—in particular, it features as the antecedent of a conditional that is asserted. So Frege does not make use of a distinct force of supposition in formalizing logic.

Gentzen later went on to do so.[5] As Dummett notes,

[Gentzen] had the idea of formalizing inference so as to leave a place for the introduction of hypotheses in a manner analogous to that in which in everyday reasoning we say 'suppose...' We require no warrant for introducing any new hypothesis, and we reason from it with just the same rules as those governing inferences from premises which we assert outright: the point of the procedure being that from the fact that certain consequences follow from some hypothesis, we can draw a conclusion that no longer depends on that hypothesis. (1973: 309)

This looks like an improvement on Frege's proposal. As Gentzen observed, it is closer to the modes of inference that occur in informal reasoning.[6] For our purposes, a point that might be made against Frege's view is that it fails to mark adequately the distinction between (a) a part, or constituent, of a thought one judges, and (b) a step taken in reasoning.[7] However, Dummett suggests that there does seem to be *something* right in what Frege says, and here I agree with Dummett. He writes:

Although we may, contrary to Frege's view, regard suppositions as complete sentences, still supposition is different from other linguistic acts in that it is possible only as a preparation for further acts of the same speaker: namely for a series of utterances not themselves assertions (but consequences of the supposition), which culminate in an assertion. I could not just say, 'Suppose 2 has a rational square root', and then stop... I must go on to discharge the original supposition. (1973: 313)

The idea here, I take it, is that one can only genuinely be said to have introduced a supposition into one's reasoning if one does things that count as discharging that supposition (or starting to discharge that supposition);[8] and furthermore, one can only discharge

---

[3] See Frege 1906, 1918, and 1923.

[4] An issue that is also relevant to Frege's view of supposition, which I don't discuss here, is the suggestion that he commits to the view that one can make inferences only from *true* premises, and hence not from a mere hypothesis. On this issue, see Anscombe 1959. For a diagnosis of Frege's commitment to this claim, different from that offered by Anscombe, see Dummett 1973; and for scepticism about the claim that Frege should be interpreted as committing to this view, see Stoothoff 1963.

[5] See also the system developed by Fitch (1952), discussed by Green (2000).

[6] Gentzen 1969: 78.

[7] See also Bell 1979: 90–2.

[8] One can of course express one's intention to suppose that *p* without discharging that supposition, and one can also issue an invitation to others to engage in that supposition, but an expression of an intention to suppose that *p* isn't in itself sufficient for supposing that *p*, and neither is the issuing of such an invitation. It might be held that in the case of a speech act, an utterance of 'suppose that *p*' can be regarded as having the force of supposition,

the supposition if it has been introduced. Frege captures this idea by holding that when one supposes that p, a single force (i.e. assertion) attaches to a complex hypothetical sentence that has p as a constituent. If we hold instead that when one supposes that p, a distinct force attaches to the proposition that p, we should hold that the force that attaches to the proposition that p and the force that attaches to propositions one infers from p are, in a certain sense, interdependent. That is to say, the fact that the force of supposition attaches to a proposition that p depends upon the occurrence of acts that count as discharging that supposition. And furthermore, when one infers q from p, the force that attaches to one's inference that q depends upon the fact that it is made under the scope of a supposition.

This is a reflection of the idea that we do not capture adequately the attitudinative aspect of a subject's mental condition when she supposes that p if we allow that supposing that p can be a stand-alone mental act—i.e. if we allow that a subject can be said to be supposing that p for the sake of argument without doing anything else. The fact that a subject has adopted a suppositional attitude toward the content that p depends upon the occurrence of acts that count as discharging (or starting to discharge) the supposition. This is why we fail to capture adequately the attitudinative aspect of a subject's mental condition when she supposes that p if we say that the subject is merely pretending or imagining that she is representing p as true. When one supposes that p and infers q from p, one isn't imagining or pretending that one is representing those propositions as true; and this is connected with the fact that when one is engaged in supposition, one is engaged in *actual* reasoning, not pretend or imagined reasoning.[9]

We can capture the idea that supposing that p for the sake of argument is not a stand-alone mental act if we say that the subject who supposes that p for the sake of argument represents p as true *by* reasoning on the assumption that p (where reasoning on the assumption that p is genuine reasoning, not pretend or imagined reasoning). Not just any old reasoning counts as reasoning on the assumption that p. When one reasons on the assumption that p, one reasons with certain constraints in play—e.g. one reasons on the assumption that p by drawing inferences from p and/or by introducing other propositions as premises in one's reasoning that are not inconsistent with p (unless entailed by p). Of course, these constraints on one's reasoning are also in play when one

whether or not one successfully begins to discharge that supposition, as long as the utterance is understood as carrying the normative requirement that one should attempt to discharge it. One might argue that in the case of thought, where this doesn't involve any overt speech acts, the decision to suppose that p brings with it a similar normative commitment. For example, in deciding to suppose that p one commits oneself to discharging that supposition. However, deciding to suppose that p isn't equivalent to supposing that p; and once a decision to suppose that p has been made, I suggest, one doesn't genuinely start supposing that p until one begins to discharge that supposition. It is thought, and not speech acts, that I am principally concerned with here.

[9] Compare Anscombe's remark: 'Aristotle rightly says that a conclusion is reached in just the same way in a "demonstrative" and a "dialectical" syllogism: if you say "suppose p, and suppose q, then r"; or if, being given "p", you say: "suppose q, then r"; you are just as much inferring, and essentially in the same way, as if you are given "p" and "q" as true and say "*therefore* r"' (1959: 116).

introduces p as a premise in one's reasoning by *judging* that p. So what is the difference between these cases?

When one reasons on the *supposition* that p, the relevant constraints on one's reasoning are self-imposed. They are not simply constraints on one's reasoning that are imposed by facts in the world whose obtaining one acknowledges. And furthermore, when one reasons on the supposition that p, one *treats* the relevant constraints on one's reasoning as self-imposed. When one reasons on the supposition that p, one recognizes that the constraint of treating p as true is a constraint on one's reasoning that one has imposed on oneself. One manifests this recognition in the way in which one reasons—e.g. by discharging the supposition with an outright conditional judgement or assertion that is outside the scope of the supposition.

So when one supposes that p for the sake of argument, one imposes a constraint on one's reasoning *by* reasoning in recognition of it. For the subject who supposes that p for the sake of argument represents p as true by reasoning on the assumption that p, where this involves reasoning in recognition of the *self-imposed constraint* of treating p as true. This is related to the respect in which the introduction of a supposition into one's reasoning and the occurrence of acts that count as discharging that supposition are interdependent—i.e. the idea that one can only genuinely be said to have introduced a supposition into one's reasoning if one does things that count as discharging that supposition, and one can only discharge the supposition if it has been introduced.

We are now in a position to turn to the question of the role of agency and self-determination in suppositional reasoning. When one acts in recognition of a self-imposed constraint, one treats oneself as a source of constraint over that activity. This is one way of thinking of what is going on in cases of self-governed behaviour. Metaphorically speaking, there's a sense in which the self-governing agent must simultaneously occupy the role of legislator and legislatee. Her authority as self-governing legislator depends upon her own recognition of that authority as legislatee. In fact it is necessary and sufficient for it. If she doesn't recognize the authority of her own legislations, then she cannot be self-governing, for she will have no authority over herself; but if she does recognize the authority of her own legislations, then she has that authority, and so is self-governing. So all an agent needs to do in order to authoritatively legislate with respect to her own conduct is to recognize the authority of that self-imposed legislation. In particular, all she needs to do is act in a way that manifests her recognition of that self-imposed legislation.

The self-governing agent takes herself to have authority over herself, and she manifests this stance towards herself in the way that she acts. That is to say, the self-governing agent can impose constraints on herself by simply behaving in a way that manifests her recognition of constraints that she has imposed on herself. She imposes a constraint on herself by behaving as though she has. In this way she acts 'under the idea of freedom'. Acting as if one has imposed a constraint on oneself, one thereby imposes the constraint on oneself. One treats oneself as a source of constraint on oneself, and thereby governs oneself.[10] I shall be saying more about the notion of self-governance in the next chapter, but the point I want to highlight for now is this. The suggestion that has been made is that when one supposes that *p* for the sake of argument, one imposes on one's reasoning the constraint of treating *p* as true *by* reasoning in recognition of that self-imposed constraint. There is, then, a sense in which 'the mind uses its own freedom' when engaged in suppositional reasoning. For the mental activity involved is self-determined, in the following respect: one treats oneself as a source of constraint over one's own thinking, and one thereby makes oneself a source of constraint over one's own thinking.

The suggestion here is that the mental activity one engages in when supposing that *p* is activity that manifests an attitude towards oneself—an attitude of treating oneself as the source of that activity. The mental activity one engages in is, in this respect, *self-conscious* mental activity. When this kind of activity occurs, something imposes a constraint on itself by acting in recognition of it. The source of the constraint on the activity is that which is acting in a constrained manner. In acting in this way, that which is acting is aware of itself as imposing a constraint on its activity in so acting. So that which is acting is presented to itself, in so acting, under a reflexive mode of presentation.[11] The subject of the activity is presented, under reflexive guise, as that which is imposing constraints on the activity by acting in recognition of them—that which determines the activity by performing it. In this respect, when such reasoning occurs, the subject of that reasoning is presented, under reflexive guise, as locus of mental autonomy—as that which determines one's thinking and reasoning when it is self-determined.

I have tried to identify a respect in which Descartes is right to claim that the 'mind uses its own freedom' when engaged in supposition. Descartes' more specific description of the mind's aim in the Second Meditation is that of supposing 'the non-existence of all the things about whose existence it can have even the slightest doubt'. Identifying the propositions one believes, whose veracity there can be the slightest reason to doubt is an exercise in self-critical reflection. To what extent is agency implicated in self-critical reflection? Is the kind of suppositional reasoning we have just been concerned with necessarily involved in self-critical reflection? I turn to these questions in the next section.

11.2 Self-critical reflection and bracketing belief

Self-critical reflection can potentially result in a variety of belief loss that is subject to epistemic evaluation—i.e. the withdrawal of assent. Not all belief loss is subject to epistemic evaluation, and not all belief loss that is subject to epistemic evaluation need be the result of self-critical reflection. Belief is always subject to epistemic evaluation, no

---

[10] These remarks on the notion of self-governance obviously ignore a number of important and substantive questions—e.g. the question of the constraints that the *truly* self-governing should impose on themselves when determining which constraints to impose on themselves.

[11] For a discussion of the notion of a 'reflexive mode of presentation' that has influenced my thinking here, see Velleman 2005b.

matter what its causal origin, but the same is not true of belief loss. The fact that one forgets things that one used to believe is not generally thought of as subject to epistemic evaluation.[12] So whether or not an *event* of belief loss is subject to epistemic evaluation cannot be solely determined by the epistemic status of the subject's beliefs prior to and after the belief loss. Belief loss is subject to epistemic evaluation only if it is somehow guided by the aim of avoiding error, where belief loss that is aimed at error-avoidance can either be guided by a conscious intention to avoid error, or by a sub-personal cognitive system that has that function. Belief loss that is aimed at avoiding error need not be guided by error-avoiding mechanisms alone; and we can make sense of belief loss that is *mis*directed at error avoidance.[13] This seems to allow us to make sense of there being instances of belief loss that are subject to epistemic evaluation but which we regard as epistemically inappropriate.

Not all instances of belief loss aimed at avoiding error, so construed, are instances of a subject withdrawing assent from some proposition as a result of self-critical reflection. Belief revision that results from the acquisition of, and updating of, evidence need not involve anything as reflective as self-critical reflection. Self-critical reflection, as I am understanding that notion here, occurs only when a subject engages with the question of whether p with the aim of avoiding error when she already believes that p. We can regard withdrawal of assent that results from self-critical reflection as a variety of the more general notion of belief revision, and we can regard belief revision as a variety of the more general notion of belief loss.

One question that can be raised about this notion of self-critical reflection is the following: how are we to make sense of the idea of a subject being consciously engaged with the question of whether p when she already believes that p? One might think that when one believes that p one regards the question of whether p as settled, whereas the subject who raises the question of whether p, and attempts to answer it, does not regard the question of whether p as settled.[14] So as soon as one raises the question of whether p and attempts to answer it, hasn't one ceased to regard the question of whether p as settled, and so hasn't one surrendered one's belief that p? In which case, how is self-critical reflection possible?[15]

Consider a related case in which one attempts to come up with a proof for a proposition that one already knows to be true (e.g. an arithmetical theorem that one knows, via testimony, to be true). It doesn't seem right to say that a subject engaged in such activity is attempting to determine whether p is true, for she already knows that p is true. Nonetheless, there is an important sense in which the activity the subject is engaged in is epistemic

---

[12] Compare Harman 1984, 1986, and 1999. See also Williamson 2000: 219.

[13] Compare Velleman's discussion, in 'On the Aim of Belief', of what makes an 'acceptance' a belief (Velleman 2000a: 252–4).

[14] Compare the discussions of Levi 1980 in Adler 2002: chapter 11, and in Roorda 1997.

[15] Compare Adler 2002 on, what Adler calls, the 'blindness problem': 'The normal workings of belief is to "blind" us to what might be described from the outside as clues to the contrary... The "blindness" problem is deep because to solve it we cannot just attempt to remove the blinders, since they are a facet of the good workings of belief' (286).

and truth-directed. The subject is engaged in actual (and not pretend or imagined) reasoning, where such reasoning is subject to epistemic evaluation. Steps taken in such reasoning may be epistemically unjustified, and indeed the conscious judgement 'therefore, p' that concludes such reasoning may be epistemically unjustified, despite the fact that the subject retains her knowledge (and hence justified belief) that p throughout such reasoning.

When one attempts to come up with a proof for the truth of p when one already believes (or knows) that p, one *brackets* one's belief that p. Importantly, to bracket one's belief that p is not to withdraw assent from p. The bracketing of one's belief that p is not something that is subject to epistemic evaluation and it is not something that requires epistemic grounds, whereas withdrawing assent from p (or suspending judgement over p) is subject to epistemic evaluation, and does require epistemic grounds.

When one brackets one's belief that p one does not use p as a premise in the reasoning one is engaged in. Of course, the fact that a subject engages in reasoning without using p as a premise in her reasoning does not in itself entail that the subject has bracketed a belief that p. Such a subject may not believe that p, and even if she does, the truth of p may not be relevant to the reasoning she is engaged in, and even if it is, she may not realize that it is. We have a case in which a subject is bracketing her belief that p only when the fact that the subject is not using p as a premise in the reasoning she is engaged in is a constraint on that reasoning that the subject has imposed on herself, and one which the subject treats as a constraint that she has imposed on herself.

What we have here is akin to the account of supposing that p for the sake of argument outlined in the previous section. One brackets one's belief that p *by* reasoning in recognition of a self-imposed constraint—where the relevant constraint in this case is that of *not* using p as a premise in one's reasoning. Agency is implicated in the bracketing of one's belief in just the same way in which it is implicated in suppositional reasoning. When one brackets one's belief that p, one imposes a constraint on one's reasoning by reasoning in recognition of it. The mental activity involved is self-determined, in the following respect: one treats oneself as a source of constraint over one's own thinking, and thereby makes oneself a source of constraint over one's own thinking. The mental activity one engages in is *self-conscious* mental activity. The subject of the activity is presented, under reflexive guise, as that which determines the activity by performing it—that which is imposing constraints on the activity by acting in recognition of them. In this respect, when such reasoning occurs, the subject of that reasoning is presented, under reflexive guise, as locus of mental autonomy.

The suggestion here is that one brackets one's belief by reasoning in recognition of a self-imposed constraint; and importantly, the reasoning one thereby engages in is actual (and not pretend or imagined) reasoning—reasoning that is epistemic, that is truth-directed, and subject to epistemic evaluation, just as suppositional reasoning is. In the case of self-critical reflection, one brackets one's belief that p and attempts to rule out not-p, with the aim of avoiding error. This involves mental activity that is self-conscious and self-determined, but which is also epistemic, truth-directed, and subject to epistemic evaluation.

This leaves unspecified the conditions under which one is epistemically justified in suspending judgement over *p* (and hence epistemically justified in withdrawing assent from *p*) as a result of such self-critical reflection. That is an issue I shall return to in Chapter 15. What is important for our purposes now is the claim that the sort of self-critical reflection involved in searching for epistemic grounds for doubting propositions one believes to be true does involve a form a conscious reasoning very much like that involved in suppositional reasoning. It involves reasoning that is self-conscious and self-determined.

As I said earlier, my aim here isn't to offer a particular interpretation of Descartes' thinking on these matters; but as an aside we can note a way in which this discussion of self-critical reflection may be relevant to claims that Descartes makes in the rest of the passage from the Synopsis of the *Meditations* that I quoted earlier:

the mind uses its own freedom and supposes the non-existence of all the things about whose existence it can have even the slightest doubt; and in so doing the mind notices that it is impossible that it should not exist during this time. This exercise is also of the greatest benefit, since it enables the mind to distinguish without difficulty what belongs to itself, i.e. to an intellectual nature, from what belongs to the body.

I have argued that when one engages in self-critical reflection, an aspect of oneself is presented, under reflexive guise, as locus of mental and epistemic autonomy—i.e. as that which determines one's reasoning *by* reasoning, where the aim of such reasoning is to determine what to believe. When one engages in self-critical reflection, there is a sense in which that aspect of oneself that is presented under reflexive guise is an aspect of oneself from which one cannot dissociate oneself. For example, when one considers the question 'what am I?', and one questions one's beliefs about what one thinks one is, it is hard to conceive of how one might dissociate oneself from that which is presented under a reflexive guise in considering that question. Indeed, this aspect of oneself will necessarily be presented under reflexive guise whenever one engages in self-critical reflection in an attempt to dissociate or distance oneself from some aspect of oneself.

We can compare here some comments that Velleman makes about Aristotle's claim that each person seems to be his 'Intellect' (sometimes translated as 'Understanding'). Aristotle describes the Intellect as 'that whereby the soul thinks and supposes'.[16] Its activity is 'reflective', and it is that element which is 'naturally to rule and guide'.[17] In the *Nicomachean Ethics*, he claims of the Intellect that, 'Each of us would seem actually to *be* this, given that each is his authoritative and better element', and 'man is this most of all'.[18] Commenting on this claim, Velleman writes:

This part of your personality constitutes your essential self in the sense that it invariably presents a reflexive aspect to your thinking: it invariably appears to you as "me" from any perspective,

---

[16] *De Anima* III. 4, 429a.
[17] *NE* X. 7, 1177a.
[18] *NE* X. 7, 1178a.

however self-critical or detached. That's what Aristotle means, I think, when he says that each person seems to be his understanding. You can dissociate yourself from other springs of action within you by reflecting on them from a critical or contemplative distance. But you cannot attain a similar distance from your understanding, because it is something that you must take along, so to speak, no matter how far you retreat in seeking a perspective on yourself. You must take your understanding along, because you must continue to exercise it in adopting a perspective, where it remains identified with you as the subject of that perspective, no matter how far off it appears to you as an object... It's your inescapable self, and so its contribution to producing your behaviour is, inescapably, your contribution. (2000: 30)

Now let us consider Descartes' claim that in supposing the non-existence of all things about whose existence it can have the slightest doubt, 'the mind notices that it is impossible that it should not exist during this time'. According to the account of suppositional reasoning outlined in the previous section, one makes such a supposition *by* reasoning on that assumption, and when one reasons on that assumption one thereby engages in self-conscious mental activity that presents an aspect of oneself under reflexive guise. One can of course reason on the assumption that one does not exist, but it is impossible to reason on the assumption that one does not exist without thereby engaging in mental activity that presents an aspect of oneself under reflexive guise during the time that one is engaged in such reasoning. And that which is presented under reflexive guise is presented as locus of mental autonomy—as that which determines one's thinking when it is self-determined.

Furthermore, when one engages in self-critical reflection and considers what one can have the slightest grounds to doubt, one may bracket one's belief that one exists, but when one does so, one thereby engages in self-conscious mental activity that presents an aspect of oneself under reflexive guise. In particular, one engages in self-conscious mental activity that presents an aspect of oneself, under reflexive guise, as locus of mental and epistemic autonomy. And furthermore, I have suggested, that which is thereby presented under reflexive guise is an aspect of oneself from which one cannot dissociate oneself. In that respect we might agree with Descartes that one cannot dissociate oneself from one's 'intellectual nature' when engaged in such an exercise.

In the rest of the quote from the Synopsis of the *Meditations*, Descartes goes on to claim, 'this exercise... enables the mind to distinguish without difficulty what belongs to itself, i.e. to an intellectual nature, *from what belongs to the body*'. On one reconstruction of Descartes' thinking, Descartes is alluding here to an epistemological criterion that enables the mind to distinguish what belongs to itself 'from what belongs to the body'. According to this interpretation, for Descartes the application of this epistemological criterion is supposed to help protect the coherence of the notion of disembodied existence, which in turn is used as a step in an argument for substance dualism.

If we assume that, for Descartes, the application of such an epistemological criterion is supposed to help protect the coherence of the notion of disembodied existence, we should look to Descartes' conception of disembodied existence in order to get a clearer view of how the application of the epistemological criterion is to be understood. It is worth noting in this context that according to Descartes, the disembodied soul has the faculty of the intellect, but lacks the faculties of sensory perception and imagination.[19] Moreover, a point that is perhaps obvious, but one which I think is worth emphasizing, is that for Descartes the disembodied soul is a disembodied *agent*. Making coherent the notion of a disembodied intellectual *agent* would require making sense of the notion of an agent capable of action but incapable of bodily action. One might then wonder whether an epistemological criterion can be applied to mark a distinction between mental action and bodily action.[20] Can the latter be the subject of sceptical attack in a way in which the former cannot?[21] And if so, can this be used to make coherent the notion of such a disembodied agent? It would take us too far afield to address these issues here, as Descartes' thinking isn't our principal concern, but in Chapter 13 I shall be returning to questions that concern the epistemology of mental action and comparing the epistemology of bodily action. In the rest of this chapter I want to remain focused on the question of the role of agency in self-critical reflection.

Earlier I cited Korsgaard's recent discussion of the claim that 'reason is what distinguishes us from other animals, and that reason is in some special way the active dimension of mind' (2009b: 23). Korsgaard connects the idea that we have a distinctive capacity for *active* reasoning with the idea that we have a form of 'reflective' consciousness that allows us to engage in self-critical reflection. As I mentioned, some of Korsgaard's critics have objected to the idea (which they take to be part of her proposal) that our ability to reflect on our own beliefs somehow allows belief formation to be governable by such reflection. They argue that it is a mistake to think that we have 'reflective *control*' over belief acquisition and revision. The fact that we have a reflective form of consciousness (e.g. the fact that we know what we think), they object, does not thereby allow the notion of freedom to get a grip in the realm of belief, and so does not thereby provide us with a form of epistemic autonomy.[22]

The view I have been outlining is similar to Korsgaard's, in so far as I too have been suggesting that there is a form of reasoning implicated in our capacity to engage in self-critical reflection that is both self-conscious and self-determined. However, central to

---

[19] In the Sixth Meditation, the faculty of the intellect is distinguished from the faculties of sensory perception and imagination. There Descartes claims that the faculty of the intellect can exist without the latter two faculties, but these latter two faculties cannot exist without the faculty of intellect. See also *Principles of Philosophy*, pt. II: 3 and the letter to Gibieuf, 19 January 1642, where Descartes is explicit that the faculties of sensory perception and imagination belong to the soul only in so far as it is joined to the body.

[20] For a brief discussion of this idea, see Soteriou 2009.

[21] It seems clear that in the First Meditation, in attempting to undermine by sceptical argument the putative knowledge we acquire via the senses, Descartes takes himself to be undermining the knowledge we have of our own bodily actions: 'I shake my head and it is not asleep; as I stretch out and feel my hand I do so deliberately and I know what I am doing...Suppose then that I am dreaming, and that these particulars—that my eyes are open, that I am moving my head and stretching out my hands—are not true.' So one relevant consideration here is whether sceptical arguments that target the putative knowledge we acquire via the senses can be used to undermine our putative knowledge of our own bodily actions, in a way in which they cannot be used to undermine our putative knowledge of our own mental actions.

[22] For this line of objection to Korsgaard, see Owens 2000.

that view is the claim that the role of mental autonomy in self-critical reflection is to be understood in terms of our capacity to *bracket* our beliefs, and not merely in our capacity to know what we believe. I have suggested that our capacity to bracket beliefs is related to our capacity to engage in suppositional reasoning, which involves reasoning in recognition of a self-imposed constraint. In the next section I want to clarify further how I think we should conceive of the role of agency in self-critical reflection, given this emphasis on the notion of bracketing. In particular, I want to do so by contrasting my proposal with Strawson's (2003) view, according to which the role of agency in such reasoning (and indeed, all conscious reasoning) can at best be 'merely catalytic' and 'indirect' (2003: 231).

11.3 Locating the agency in suppositional reasoning and self-critical reflection

Korsgaard connects the human capacity for self-awareness with the idea that 'the human mind is active in some way that the minds of the other animals are not' (2009b: 23), which, in turn, she claims, provides us with a form of epistemic autonomy. O'Shaughnessy (2000) expresses a similar line of thought when he suggests that our capacity to know that we have thought, 'together with the capacity to contemplate its denial as a possibility that is not in fact realized' (2000: 110), provides us with a form of mental freedom that allows us to 'transcend the condition of animal immersion' (2000: 111). One difficulty with this sort of view, one might think, is that it leaves unclear how the mere capacity to become conscious of one's own beliefs, and their grounds, can provide one with the ability to 'have a hand in their installation'. How is this 'space of reflective distance' supposed to allow us to 'exert control over our beliefs'? As Moran puts it, it is not as though, glancing inwards, we can simply manipulate our attitudes as so much mental furniture.[23] So how does agency figure in the exercise of self-critical reflection that is made possible by 'the space of reflective distance'?

According to one way of regarding this issue, the role of mental agency in self-critical reflection can at best be rather limited. Consider again Galen Strawson's scepticism about the extent of the role of agency over our thinking and reasoning. Thinking about something involves the occurrence of mental acts individuated, in part, by their propositional contents, and Strawson claims that these mental acts can be mental actions only if the particular contents that individuate them are ones that the subject intends to think. However, in the case of many such mental acts, it seems that the content of the mental act cannot figure in the content of one's prior intention. Strawson has argued that no thinking of a particular thought-content is ever an action. This is because one's thinking of the particular content can only amount to an action if the content thought is already there, 'available for consideration and adoption for intentional production', in

---

[23] See Moran 1999 and 2001.

which case 'it must already have "just come" at some previous time in order to be so available' (2003: 235). One way of putting this point is to say that when conscious reasoning occurs, there is no *attempt* to think a thought with a given content. In the case of the sort of thinking that occurs when one reasons, what is important is that relevant changes to one's mind occur. Perhaps sometimes one also knows that such changes occur, but arguably the acquisition of such knowledge is itself simply a further change to one's mind. So agency is not, after all, implicated in the thinking of the particular thoughts that occur when one reasons. Strawson does not deny that mental actions do occur, but on his view, 'Mental action in thinking is restricted to the fostering of conditions hospitable to contents' coming to mind' (2003: 234).

Strawson claims that 'the role of genuine action in thought is at best indirect. It is entirely prefatory, it is essentially—merely—catalytic' (2003: 231). It 'is restricted to the fostering of conditions hospitable to contents' coming to mind' (234), for according to Strawson, the component of agency in thinking and reasoning is restricted to that of setting the mind at a given topic, aiming or tilting the mind in a given direction, and waiting for contentful thoughts to occur—waiting 'for the "natural causality of reason" to operate in one' (231). Once one has taken mental aim at a given topic, 'the rest is a matter of ballistics, mental ballistics'—'as ballistic as the motion of the ball after it has ceased to be in contact with one's foot' (239). Strawson writes: 'There is I believe no action at all in reasoning...considered independently of the preparatory, catalytic phenomena just mentioned' (232).[24] On this view, the mental events involved in conscious reasoning are not in themselves agential; rather, they can (sometimes) be the effects of something agential.

I have offered a rather different proposal as to how we should conceive of the role of mental agency in the sort of conscious reasoning that occurs when one engages in self-critical reflection. On my view, the notion of bracketing one's beliefs has a key role to play. I have argued that self-critical reflection involves a capacity to bracket one's beliefs, and agency is implicated in the bracketing of one's belief in just the same way in which it is implicated in suppositional reasoning.[25] In both cases the mental activity involved is self-determined, in the following respect: one treats oneself as a source of constraint over one's own thinking, and thereby makes oneself a source of constraint over one's own thinking. For in both cases one imposes a constraint on one's reasoning *by* reasoning in

---

[24] Strawson's view is criticized by Buckareff 2005, and discussed in Mele 2009. Compare also Dorsch's (2009) notion of the 'mediated' agency involved in certain varieties of thinking: we ' "trigger" ' some process (epistemic or merely causal) with some goal in mind, but recognize, and instrumentally rely on, the capacity of such a process to lead, *by itself*, to the desired outcome. For a rather different view of the role of agency in reasoning, see Gibbons 2009.

[25] O'Shaughnessy seems to acknowledge the significance to our 'mental freedom' of our ability to bracket our beliefs and engage in suppositional reasoning, although he doesn't put this in quite the terms I do. He writes: 'cogitation entertains propositions under the heading "not yet to be used", or "may be rejected", it "puts them on ice for the time being", whereas the "practical immersion" of animals only entertains propositions as "to be used here and now" '; and 'Transcending the condition of "animal immersion" is achieved through the linguistically assisted capacity to think in the modalities of the possible and the hypothetical, which is an exercise of the imaginative power' (2000: 110).

recognition of it. This leads to a rather different view of how we should conceive of the extent of the role of mental agency in such reasoning.

First, we can contrast the picture I have offered of the way in which agency is implicated in suppositional reasoning and self-critical reflection, with the conception of action that Frankfurt criticizes in his paper 'The Problem of Action'. In that paper, Frankfurt targets a view of action that holds that the 'essential difference between actions and mere happenings lies in their prior causal histories', and which thereby implies that 'actions and mere happenings do not differ essentially in themselves at all' (1978: 69).[26] According to the account of action that Frankfurt objects to, actions and mere happenings are 'differentiated by nothing that exists or that is going on at the time those events occur, but by something quite extrinsic to them—a difference at an earlier time among another set of events entirely... they locate the distinctively essential features of action exclusively in states of affairs which may be past by the time the action is supposed to occur' (1978: 70).

According to the accounts of suppositional reasoning and self-critical reflection I have been recommending, agency is implicated in the conscious mental events that constitute a subject's suppositional reasoning and self-critical reflection, in so far as such events manifest the subject's recognition of a self-imposed constraint. For example, when a subject supposes that p for the sake of argument, the constraint of treating p as true is a constraint that the subject imposes on herself *by* reasoning in recognition of it. The constraint she imposes on herself is *sustained* by the occurrence of conscious mental events that manifest her recognition of that self-imposed constraint. So the agency that is implicated in such reasoning does not simply reside in its prior causal history—i.e. in the fact that some appropriate, temporally prior, intention or belief/desire pair initiated it.

For this reason, the picture that I am suggesting of the way in which agency is implicated in suppositional reasoning and self-critical reflection can also be contrasted with Strawson's characterization of the role of agency in thinking and reasoning. Strawson's view suggests that the conscious mental events involved in suppositional reasoning, and the sort of reasoning that occurs when one engages in self-critical reflection, can in principle lack appropriate, agential, causal antecedents and thereby lack any aspect of agency whatsoever. In contrast, I have argued that in the cases of suppositional reasoning and self-critical reflection, the conscious reasoning one engages in manifests an attitude towards oneself—an attitude of treating oneself as the source of that activity. Acting as if one has imposed a constraint on oneself, one thereby imposes the constraint on oneself. One treats oneself as a source of constraint on oneself, and in doing so one thereby determines one's own behaviour. So the forms of reasoning involved in suppositional reasoning and self-critical reflection—the forms of reasoning that allow us to 'transcend the condition of animal immersion'—are *necessarily* self-conscious *and* self-determined.

---

[26] Page references are to the paper as it appears in Frankfurt 1988.

In the next chapter I shall have more to say about this notion of self-determination, where I shall be exploring in more detail connections between mental agency, self-consciousness, and notions of self-determination and self-governance. One of the central issues I shall be addressing is the following. Does the self-conscious subject who is able to 'transcend the condition of animal immersion' possess a distinctive form of *autonomous* agency—a distinctive form of autonomy that is made possible by her capacity to engage in mental action?

12

Mental Action, Autonomy, and the Perspective of Practical Reason

In the previous chapter I argued that the agency that is implicated in suppositional reasoning and self-critical reflection does not simply reside in the prior causal history of such reasoning—i.e. in the fact that some appropriate, temporally prior, intention or belief/desire pair initiated it. According to the account I proposed, when a subject engages in such reasoning that subject imposes a constraint on her reasoning *by* reasoning in recognition of that constraint. Agency is implicated in the conscious mental events that constitute a subject's suppositional reasoning and self-critical reflection, in so far as such events manifest the subject's recognition of a self-imposed constraint. The constraint that the subject imposes on her reasoning is *sustained* by the occurrence of the conscious mental events that constitute her reasoning and that manifest her recognition of that self-imposed constraint. So, *contra* Strawson, in the case of these forms of conscious reasoning the role of agency is not 'merely catalytic' (2003: 231).

This kind of conscious mental activity can be thought of as *self*-conscious activity in at least the following two respects. Firstly, the conscious mental acts that constitute this kind of mental activity are accompanied by a certain form of self-knowledge— knowledge of what one is thinking. These states of knowledge are the occurrent mental states that I have argued one needs to invoke in an account of the ontology of the activity of conscious thinking. And secondly, when one engages in this kind of conscious reasoning, an aspect of oneself is presented under reflexive guise as that which determines the activity by engaging in it—that which imposes a constraint on the reasoning by reasoning in recognition of that constraint. So this kind of self-conscious mental activity crucially involves not only a form of self-knowledge, but also a form of self-determination.

My aim in this chapter is to explore in more detail connections between self-determination, self-knowledge, and mental agency. In particular, I shall be addressing the question of whether the self-conscious subject possesses a distinctive form of autonomous agency that is made possible by her capacity to engage in certain kinds of mental action.

12.1 Agential activity, autonomous action, and mental action

In Chapter 9 I remarked on the fact that the topic of mental action is not often accorded a prominent role in general accounts of action and agency, and I offered the following suggestion as to why this might be so. A central concern in the philosophy of action has been that of attempting to address an 'agent–mind problem'—the question of how the workings of the mind relate to the activity of an agent. According to one standard approach to this issue, we should be seeking to identify the appropriate *ingredients* of action. We should be seeking to identify ingredients that are not themselves agential but whose appropriate combination can yield something agential. On this approach, an appeal to mental action is inappropriate, for this presupposes agency—the notion to be accounted for. Just as we ask, 'what is it that makes a bodily event a bodily action of an agent?', we might also ask, 'what is it that makes a mental event a mental action of an agent?' But the assumption is that the kind of ingredients that we would need to appeal to in answering the latter question will not be significantly different from the ingredients that we would need to appeal to in answering the former question. So the assumption is that there is no special pay-off to be gained by focusing on the case of mental action when one's interest is in providing a general account of action and agency.

As I also mentioned, according to one strand of thinking about action, an adequate account of agency should be able to recognize and accommodate the idea that there can be significant differences between varieties of behaviour that fall under a broad category of the agential. According to this line of thought, this broad category of the agential should of course cover intentional actions that result from decisions to act, decisions which themselves may result from careful practical deliberation, but it should also be broad enough to encompass other varieties of 'active' behaviour, such as habitual behaviour, absent-minded behaviour, compulsive behaviour, and the purposive behaviour of relatively primitive animals. In marking distinctions between these different forms of agential behaviour we might thereby make room for the idea that there is a distinctive form of *autonomous* agency that a self-conscious agent is able to exhibit, even if we concede that not all of the agential behaviour that such an agent engages in should be regarded as an instance of the fully autonomous kind. We might then raise the question of whether mental action should have a significant role to play in an account of this distinctive form of autonomous agency.

The idea that an account of agency should be able to accommodate significant differences between varieties of behaviour that can fall under a broad category of the agential is one that Frankfurt underlines in his approach to the philosophy of action. In 'The Problem of Action', Frankfurt warns that 'we must be careful that the ways in which we construe agency and define its nature do not conceal a parochial bias, which causes us to neglect the extent to which the concept of human action is no more than a special case of another concept whose range is much wider' (1978: 79). He introduces a notion of 'activity', of 'being active', that is intended to be broader than the category of 'action'.

Frankfurt notes that although behaviour such as the idle, inattentive tapping of one's fingers on a table might not be thought of as an intentional 'action' that one performs, it is 'surely not a case of passivity: the movements in question do not occur without one's making them' (1978: 58). Although this sort of behaviour might not be thought of as an action, it is not a 'mere happening', and it can be regarded as an instance of the broader category of 'activity'.

Frankfurt goes on to suggest:

The contrast between activity and passivity is readily discernible at levels of existence where we are disinclined to suppose that there are actions. Thus, a spider is passive with respect to the movements of its legs when its legs move because the spider received an electric shock. On the other hand the spider is active with respect to the movements of its legs–though it performs no action–when it moves its legs in making its way along the ground. We should not find it unnatural that we are capable, without lapsing into mere passivity, of behaving as mindlessly as the spider. (1978: 58)

In outlining the respect in which 'the concept of human action is no more than a special case of another concept whose range is much wider', Frankfurt first introduces a notion of purposive/'guided' behaviour. This is simply behaviour whose course is subject to adjustments that compensate for the effects of forces which would otherwise interfere with the course of the behaviour. Not all 'guided' behaviour, so characterized, should be regarded as agential behaviour. Such guided behaviour will count as agential only when the guidance of the behaviour is attributable to the agent, as opposed to being merely attributable to some control mechanism within the agent; and importantly, according to Frankfurt, our answer to the question of whether the guidance of the behaviour is attributable to the agent, as opposed to some control mechanism within her, will turn, in part, on the kind of agent in question. So, as Velleman has put it, Frankfurt's shift to the question of agential guidance thereby results in 'a further shift to the question of agential identity—or the self'.[1]

This approach allows Frankfurt to hold that the concept of human action is just a special case of another concept whose range is much broader, while accepting that an account of human agency may need to invoke distinctive notions and concerns that are inapplicable to the varieties of agential behaviour that more primitive creatures exhibit. He writes:

The conditions for attributing the guidance of bodily movements to a whole creature, rather than only to some local mechanism within a creature, evidently obtain outside of human life. Hence they cannot be satisfactorily understood by relying upon concepts which are inapplicable to spiders and their ilk. This does not mean that it must be illegitimate for an analysis of human agency to invoke concepts of more limited scope. While the general conditions of agency are unclear, it may well be that the satisfaction of these conditions by human beings depends upon

---

[1] From David Velleman's seminars on action (Seminar 7: Frankfurt), previously published on his website <https://files.nyu.edu/dv26/public/>.

the occurrence of events or states which do not occur in the histories of other creatures. (1978: 78–9)

According to Frankfurt, distinctive issues and concerns arise when it comes to providing an account of the forms of agency that can be exhibited by self-conscious agents. For example, the self-conscious agent is able to reflect on her motives, and in doing so she may dissociate herself from some of them.[2] She may feel alienated from some of them. So from the agent's own point of view, there is a respect in which such motives may be thought of as external influences to be resisted, obstacles to be overcome. In consequence, actions which spring from such motives might be regarded as less than fully autonomous.

This approach to agency makes room for the idea that there can be varieties of human behaviour that are agential and yet which are less than fully autonomous, and under such an approach a central task becomes that of specifying what it is that makes certain forms of agential behaviour 'full-blooded', *autonomous* actions. Many of those undertaking this task conform to what I earlier called an 'ingredients' approach to the philosophy of action—i.e. they attempt to identify ingredients of action that are not themselves agential but whose appropriate combination can yield something agential. Under this sort of approach, one might try to specify the appropriate non-agential ingredients that together yield agential human behaviour, and then simply cite further non-agential ingredients when it comes to providing an account of the narrower category of 'full-blooded' *autonomous* action. For example, one of Frankfurt's early suggestions was that an agent's action is autonomous when an agent identifies herself with a motive that actuates her behaviour, and he suggested that an agent identifies herself with such a motive when she has the second-order volition that her behaviour be actuated by that motive.[3]

A number of difficulties with this particular suggestion have since been raised, and a number of alternative 'hierarchical' variations have since been proposed. I don't intend to go into the details of that debate here. The main points I want to highlight at this stage are simply the following. This sort of approach to action does accommodate the idea that there can be significant differences between varieties of behaviour that fall under a broad category of the agential. It accommodates the idea that the concept of human action is 'no more than a special case of another concept whose range is much wider', and it accommodates the idea that self-conscious agents are able to exercise a distinctive form of *autonomous* agency. But if the 'ingredients' approach to action is still in play, it's not clear that the notion of mental action can have a significant role to play in an account of this distinctive form of autonomous agency. If one's concern is to specify what it is that makes a subject's agential behaviour a case of 'full-blooded' autonomous action, one might seek to identify the distinctive additional ingredients that yield

---

[2] 'No animal other than man...appears to have the capacity for reflective self-evaluation that is manifested in the formation of second-order desires' (1971: 12).

[3] See Frankfurt 1971 for the distinction between second-order desires and second-order volitions.

full-blooded autonomous forms of agency. But just as human bodily behaviour can be agential but less than fully autonomous, one might also think that human mental behaviour can be agential but less than fully autonomous, so it's not clear how citing mental action as a further ingredient is supposed to help with this enterprise. Moreover, with the ingredients approach in place, an appeal to mental action would in any case need ultimately to be cashed out in further terms, as such an appeal to mental action, without such further unpacking, appears to presuppose agency—the notion to be accounted for and explained. So again, the assumption often appears to be that there is no special pay-off to be gained by focusing on the case of mental action, even when one's interest is in providing an account of a distinctive form of autonomous agency that can be exercised by a self-conscious subject.

There are accounts of autonomous action that take a rather different line. According to one such account, we need to invoke a certain kind of mental action in an account of the kind of autonomous agency that can make a self-conscious agent morally responsible for their actions. The line of thought here is, roughly, as follows. If we are to account adequately for the way in which an autonomous agent can be morally responsible and culpable for their actions, we need to be able to accommodate the idea that free agency begins at the will, and is exercised in and through what that agent *decides* to do. So we need to provide an account of action that can accommodate the idea that our decisions are mental actions.

There is something intuitive in the thought that in having the capacity to engage in practical deliberation and make decisions the self-conscious subject is thereby able to exercise a distinctive form of autonomous agency. Such an agent is able to govern her own behaviour in a way that more primitive agents are not. And this capacity for self-governance appears to be importantly linked with the idea that such an agent can be morally responsible for what she does in a way that other more primitive agents cannot. But if we maintain an ingredients approach to action, then we appear to face difficulties in accommodating the idea that this is to be explained, in part, by the fact that a decision to φ can be an agent's action. What might the relevant ingredients be? Should they include some belief/desire pair, and/or an intention, that concerns that act of deciding to φ?

Decisions don't seem to fit the standard accounts of what it is that makes an event an agent's action. Our decisions are not preceded by decisions or intentions to so decide, and moreover, if anything moves one to decide to φ on a given occasion, it seems that it is some reason for acting as decided—i.e. some reason for φ-ing—rather than some reason or desire that concerns the event of deciding itself. This might lead one to doubt whether our decisions are mental actions that we are motivated to perform. And if our decisions are not themselves mental actions, in what sense can we be said to be exercising our agency in deciding to act? This difficulty gives rise to a further question. If we accept that decisions to act are not themselves actions of an agent, then what role does this leave for mental action in an account of practical deliberation? One might think that mental action can at best have a 'merely catalytic', initiating role to play, which might lead one to think that the activity of practical deliberation thus initiated can in principle occur in the absence of that kind of initiating cause. This might lead one to think that mental action does not have an essential role to play in an account of practical deliberation, which in turn might lead one to conclude that mental action cannot have an essential role to play in an account of the autonomous agency that a self-conscious agent is able to exercise in simply having the capacity to engage in practical deliberation and make decisions.

There are two key questions here, which I shall be addressing in what follows. (i) How should we understand the agency that is exercised by a self-conscious subject when that subject makes a decision about what to do? And (ii) what account should be given of the distinctive form of self-governance and autonomous agency that a self-conscious agent is able to exercise in having the capacity to engage in practical deliberation and make decisions? I shall consider the second question at the end of this chapter. But before getting there I shall be making a proposal about what decisions are and how we should understand the agency that a subject exercises in deciding to act. I'll now briefly sketch the form that this proposal will take.

We will, I think, continue to face difficulties in accommodating the idea that we exercise agency in deciding to act if we assume that the agency in question is to be accounted for by simply looking to the psychological causes of the mental event of deciding—psychological causes that can explain why it is correct to think of that mental event as an action of its agent. In what follows I shall be proposing an alternative. I shall be suggesting that when it comes to accommodating and explaining the respect in which we exercise agency and self-determination in making a decision, we need to look to the result of this mental act, rather than its causes. It is what happens after one's decision to act that makes it the case that one has exercised agency and self-determination in making that decision.[4]

In this chapter I shall be focusing on the decisions that we make about our future actions, rather than the decisions we make to act now. I'll be considering decisions of the latter kind in the next chapter. On the view I shall be proposing, a decision you now make to act in the future just is the event of acquiring a distinctive kind of mental state, and so an account of what is involved in making such a decision should seek to clarify what is distinctive of the kind of mental state that you acquire when you decide to act. It is often noted that the intention you form when you decide to act is directed toward your future—i.e. directed toward your future action, or the future completion of your current action. But the intention you form when you decide to act also involves an orientation towards your past as well. This is reflected in the fact that just as you can express your current intention to act by talking about your future—'I am going to φ'—you can

---

[4] Pink (1996 and 2009) presents an important defence of the claim that our decisions are mental actions. Peacocke (2007 and 2009) also holds that decisions can be mental actions, but for rather different reasons. Gibbons (2009) and Hieronymi (2009) have also offered accounts that accommodate, in different ways, a role for agency in decision and intention. These accounts differ from the one I shall be proposing in this chapter.

also express your current intention to act by talking about your past—'I have decided to φ'. This, I shall be arguing, is because the mental state that you acquire when you decide to act is to be characterized, at least in part, but essentially, in terms of how you are disposed to regard and treat your prior act of deciding; and this is connected with a way in which the continued obtaining of the mental state that you acquire when you decide to act involves a feat of memory. I shall be proposing that this feature of the mental state that you acquire when you decide to act plays a crucial role in accounting for the agency and self-determination that is exercised in making a decision. When this mental state obtains you are disposed to engage in a form of mental activity that is both self-conscious and self-determined and which involves treating your prior act of deciding as agential and self-determined. And your being so disposed makes it the case that your prior act of deciding is both agential and self-determined.

I shall also be arguing that the particular way in which mental agency is implicated in the obtaining of the mental state that you acquire when you decide to act can accommodate and explain a way in which this mental state embodies an epistemic perspective on your future action that is significantly different from the epistemic perspective embodied in your ordinary beliefs about your future. This can account for a difference between, on the one hand, the epistemic perspective that you have on your future from the standpoint of practical reason and, on the other hand, the epistemic perspective that you have on your future from the standpoint of theoretical reason. And this in turn can account for a distinctive respect in which your future can seem to you to be open from the standpoint of practical reason.

I shall start by considering this future-oriented aspect of the mental state that you acquire when you decide to act. In particular I want to start by focusing on the question of whether it is right to hold that when you decide to act in the future you thereby believe that you will perform the action that you have decided upon. As a way of setting the stage for that discussion I shall outline, in the next section, an objection that David Velleman has raised against Michael Bratman's rejection of a cognitivist view of intention.

12.2 Bratman and Velleman on intention

According to Bratman, the capacity to form intentions is supplementary to the capacity for belief/desire motivation.[5] Not all agents who are capable of acting with a goal/aim that is attributable to them have the capacity to form intentions in Bratman's sense. Bratman suggests that our capacity to form intentions allows us to deliberate in advance of action, when time and resources are more plentiful, and arrive at plans for future conduct. On this view, our future-directed intentions are typically elements in larger plans for future conduct that help us to coordinate and project our agency in an organized

---

[5] See Bratman 1987, 1999, and 2006.

way over time. The exercise of this capacity allows for interpersonal and intra-personal coordination, for it helps us to coordinate our future actions by committing us to future actions that we, and others, can rely on.

So according to Bratman, in providing an account of intention we should be focusing on the role of intention in future-directed planning. In explicating the mental state of intention, Bratman attempts to characterize its distinctive functional role, and in outlining the functional role of intention Bratman suggests that this mental state has both volitional and reason-centred dimensions. Intention, he argues, is conduct-controlling, in contrast to desire, which is conduct-influencing, as intention settles an issue and resists reconsideration of it. It involves dispositions towards further practical reasoning: a disposition to reason about means to intended ends, and a disposition not to form incompatible intentions.

On Bratman's view, the coordinating role of intention requires that one's plans should be internally consistent, consistent with one's beliefs about the world, and means-end coherent. One's intention to φ will normally support one's expectation that one will φ. However, Bratman denies that one's intention to φ entails the belief that one will φ, for he thinks it is possible for there to be cases in which one intends to φ although one is agnostic about whether one will succeed in φ-ing, and indeed he thinks there can be cases in which one intends to φ despite the fact that one is agnostic about whether one will even try to φ. According to Bratman, we can accommodate the role of intention in our planning agency and the norms that are associated with its playing that role, without having to commit to cognitivism—the view that the intention to φ involves the belief that one will φ.

In this he is in disagreement with David Velleman, who argues that intention is itself a distinctive kind of belief.[6] Velleman claims that when a subject decides to act, the intention to act she thereby acquires has the same direction of fit as belief and not desire. Deciding to act does not simply consist in regarding something as *to be* arranged, for once a subject has chosen to act, a question has been settled in her mind. As far as the subject is concerned, she is going to act. Things have been arranged. The proposition that she is going to act is represented by her as true. Velleman argues that although intention has the same direction of fit as ordinary belief, it differs in its direction of guidance. According to Velleman, an attitude's direction of guidance 'consists in whether the attitude causes or is caused by what it represents' (2000b: 25). There can be two ways of accepting something as true: 'accepting so as to reflect the truth, and accepting so as to create the truth' (Velleman 1996; in Velleman 2000b: 194). And so an attitude's direction of guidance can be either 'passive', or 'directive'. Ordinary belief has a passive direction of guidance, whereas intention is directive.

So although Velleman thinks that both intention and ordinary belief have the same direction of fit, he does identify a difference between these mental states, namely the fact that they differ in their directions of guidance. What is more, according to Velleman this

<hr>

[6] See Velleman 1989a, 2000b, and 2009.

difference between an intention and ordinary belief is reflected in the propositional contents of these states. According to Velleman, an intention to φ is not only self-fulfilling, it is also self-reflective. That is, an intention to φ is a self-fulfilling expectation that one will φ that *represents itself as such*.

On this view, your intention to φ moves you to φ, and so the expectation that you will φ is self-fulfilling, according to Velleman, because knowing what you are doing is a sub-agential aim regulating your behaviour. You may have a number of motives for doing various things on a particular occasion, but as your behaviour is guided by this sub-agential aim of knowing what you are doing, in the standard case you will be inhibited from doing anything that you do not expect you are going to do, and so your expectation that you are going to do one of them—resulting from your intending to φ—will result in an additional inclination to φ rather than anything else.

A problem that Velleman raises for Bratman's account of intention is the frequency with which we form immediate intentions to act now, without any prior planning. The difficulty for Bratman's account, as he sees it, is to explain why we bother to form intentions when there is no opportunity for them to play the functional roles that Bratman specifies. For Velleman, in contrast to Bratman, the motivational role of intention is not to be explained in terms of its coordinating role in future-directed plans. It is, rather, simply to be explained in terms of the standing desire an agent has to understand what she does. In contrast to Bratman, Velleman suggests that our capacity to form intentions 'emerges as a byproduct of curiosity plus self-awareness, which are fundamental endowments of human nature, designed for purposes far more general than scheduling deliberation and facilitating coordination' (2007: 211).

In due course, I shall be arguing that the mental state that you acquire when you decide to do something does embody an epistemic perspective on your action. On this point I will be agreeing with Velleman. However, I also think that our understanding of the relevant mental state can be illuminated by following Bratman's lead, and focusing on the role that this mental state plays in planning and coordinating future action. So I don't agree with Velleman's suggestion that the focus on planning results in a distorted view of the nature of intention. Although I shall be suggesting that the mental state that you acquire when you decide to do something embodies an epistemic perspective on your future action, I shall also be suggesting that the kind of epistemic perspective that is in question differs in important ways from the kind that can be embodied in your beliefs about your future; and I shall be outlining ways in which this is related to a significant difference between the perspective one has on oneself and one's future from the standpoint of theoretical reason, and the perspective one has on oneself and one's future from the standpoint of practical reason. These points are best brought out, I think, by focusing on the role that is played by this mental state in future-directed planning. So for now, I want to remain focused on cases in which one makes relatively long-term decisions to act in the future, rather than decisions to act now, and consider the bearing that such decisions have on the further planning one subsequently engages in. In particular, I want to start by considering an objection that Velleman raises for

Bratman's account of the role of intention in planning, which arises out of Bratman's rejection of cognitivism.

Velleman argues, *contra* Bratman, that if my intention to φ doesn't involve the belief that I will φ, then my intention won't be able to play the coordinating roles that Bratman identifies, and it won't be subject to the rational requirements that Bratman specifies. The thought here is that if I don't believe that I'll do what I intend, then my intention to φ is no longer sufficient as a basis for planning on the assumption that I will φ, and what is more, if I don't believe that I'll do what I intend, it becomes unclear why I should limit myself to intentions that can jointly be satisfied in the world as I believe it to be, given that I needn't believe that I will satisfy all of them.

In what follows I shall try to unpack in stages some of the issues that lie behind this objection. This discussion will eventually lead us back to the question of how we should understand the role and place of mental agency in making a decision.

12.3 Decision, planning, and assumption

Let us start by considering the suggestion that when a subject makes a *decision* about what to do in the future, the further planning she subsequently engages in will be based on the background assumption that she will do that thing—i.e. the suggestion that once a subject has decided to φ, she will reason on the background assumption 'I will φ', when she engages in further planning and practical deliberation. What reasons are there for accepting this claim?

If a subject doesn't assume that she will φ when she engages in further planning and practical deliberation, then the way in which that subject makes plans for future action may be consistent with her keeping open, as a possible course of action, the option of φ-ing, but arguably the planning of a subject who is merely keeping open the option of φ-ing is the planning of a subject who hasn't yet reached a decision as to whether to φ—it is the planning of a subject who hasn't yet settled in her own mind the question of whether to φ. Both Bratman and Velleman connect the notion of intention with the idea that an issue or question has been 'settled' for the subject of intention. Bratman suggests that a subject's intention to φ settles an issue for the subject of intention and resists reconsideration of it; and Velleman claims that when a subject has decided to φ 'a question has been settled in his mind'. So how should we understand what is involved in 'settling' the relevant issue in making a decision to φ? It doesn't seem to be simply a matter of reaching a conclusion about what one will end up doing; nor does it seem to be simply a matter of arriving at a judgement about what one ought to do. Arriving at a decision to φ is not equivalent to a straightforward case of predicting that one will φ, for the fact that a subject has predicted, on the basis of the evidence available to her, that she will eventually end up φ-ing, does not entail that the subject has thereby decided to φ. Furthermore, arriving at a decision to φ is not equivalent to concluding that one ought to φ, for the fact that a subject judges that she ought to do something need not entail that the subject has thereby decided to do that thing. The subject who judges that she

ought to φ but who hasn't yet decided to φ, is a subject who hasn't yet committed herself to φ-ing—she hasn't yet committed herself to that particular course of action,
despite the fact that she thinks that it is something she ought to do. If deciding to act
involves settling an issue in one's own mind, then we should say that the relevant issue
has been settled for one only when one *commits* oneself to so acting. But then what is
involved in committing oneself to φ-ing in the relevant way?

The fact that one has committed oneself to φ-ing, in the relevant sense, is reflected, at
least in part, in the way in which one goes on to make further plans and decisions; and
planning on the background assumption that one will φ is the kind of planning that can
manifest one's commitment to that future course of action. So one might then think
that this gives us reason to endorse the suggestion introduced earlier—the suggestion
that when a subject makes a decision about what to do in the future, the further planning she engages in will be based on the background assumption that she will perform
that action. The thought here is that once a subject has decided to act, she has thereby
committed herself to that particular course of action, and being disposed to reason on
the background assumption that she will so act when she engages in further practical
reasoning is part of what is involved in being so committed.

An objection that might be raised against this line of argument is the following. Suppose that a subject's clear and definite aim is to φ on some future occasion. This subject
plans in determined pursuit of this definite aim, and in planning in this way the subject
isn't merely keeping open the option of φ-ing. Suppose too that when this subject plans,
she doesn't assume that she *will* φ, because she doesn't assume that her attempt at φ-ing
will be successful. Since this subject's clear and definite aim is to φ, when expressing
what she intends to do we might say that she intends to φ; but then we seem to have here
a case in which a subject intends to φ even though she doesn't assume that she will φ
when she makes further plans. So it can't be true to say that when a subject intends to
φ on some future occasion, the further planning she engages in will be based on the
background assumption that she will φ.

What this objection brings out is that it would be a mistake to say that if a subject
doesn't plan on the background assumption that she will φ, then she is at best merely
keeping open, as a possible course of action, the option of φ-ing. The subject who plans
her future conduct in determined pursuit of the goal of φ-ing might not assume that her
attempt at φ-ing will be successful, but she wouldn't be appropriately described as
merely keeping open the option of φ-ing. However, it's not clear that the objection provides us with a counterexample to the proposal about *decision* and assumption that is
under consideration. Although a subject's clear and definite aim may be that she φ on
some future occasion, and although she may plan her future conduct in pursuit of that
aim, it doesn't follow from this that she has decided to φ; and the proposal under consideration is that once a subject has *decided* to φ, she plans on the background assumption
that she will φ.

For example, suppose a subject's clear and definite goal is that of winning a particular
competition, and suppose she plans her future conduct in determined pursuit of that

goal. We might say that the subject intends to win the competition—she isn't just taking part in the competition for fun. And it doesn't seem appropriate to describe this subject's planning as that of a subject who is merely keeping open the option of winning the competition. However, it doesn't follow from this that the subject has *decided* to win the competition. The subject might not regard winning the competition as something that she can decide to do. The decision as to who wins the competition might lie in the hands of others—perhaps a panel of judges. In the case of this subject, it may be wrong to say that she has decided to win the competition. It may be more accurate to say that she has decided to do her best to win the competition. That is, she has decided to do things that she thinks will give her the best chance of achieving her goal of winning the competition. When the subject decides to do her best to win the competition, her goal/aim in making that decision is to win. In that sense, her intention is to win. But she hasn't decided to win the competition. We need to note here that when we express what a subject intends to do we may not be accurately specifying what the subject has decided to do, and I suggest that it is the mental state that a subject acquires when she *decides* to do something that we should be focusing on when our interest is in articulating the role played by a distinctive mental state in planning and coordinating future action.

The subject who doesn't plan on the background assumption that she will φ may be a subject who is planning on the background assumption that she will *attempt* to φ. But such planning indicates that this subject has *decided to attempt to* φ. This is what she has committed herself to doing. So the suggestion here is that we can, after all, identify a connection between what a subject decides to do, what she commits herself to doing, and the assumptions she makes about what she is going to do when she is engaged in further planning. This connection between decision, commitment, and the assumptions one makes in planning, gives us reason to endorse a claim that Velleman makes—the claim that when a subject decides to φ, that subject represents as true the proposition that she is going to φ. Given that assuming that *p* is a way of representing *p* as true, we can agree that when a subject decides to φ, that subject represents as true the proposition that she will φ.

However, establishing this much isn't yet to establish that when a subject decides to φ, that subject *believes* that she will φ. For it is not in general correct to claim that whenever a subject reasons on the assumption that *p*, that subject believes that *p*. For example, one can reason on the assumption that *p*, and thereby represent *p* as true, without believing that *p* when one engages in suppositional reasoning—when one assumes that *p* for the sake of argument. One might also assume that *p* in one's reasoning without believing that *p* in cases in which one believes that *p* is more likely true than not, and for practical purposes one makes the simplifying assumption that *p*. If we accept the claim that the subject who decides to φ assumes that she is going to φ when making further plans, should we also accept that this subject makes this assumption because she *believes* that she is going to φ? In addressing this question it will be helpful to focus first on cases in which a subject assumes that *p* when she engages in reasoning without believing that *p*.

Take the case of the kind suppositional reasoning that I considered in the previous chapter—e.g. the reasoning one engages in when one assumes that p for the sake of argument. I made the following claims about this form of reasoning. When one assumes that p for the sake of argument, one reasons with certain constraints in play—constraints that come with treating p as true. For example, one reasons on the assumption that p by drawing inferences from p and/or by introducing other propositions as premises in one's reasoning that are not inconsistent with p (unless entailed by p). These constraints on one's reasoning are also in play when one believes that p, but when one reasons on the *supposition* that p, the relevant constraints on one's reasoning are *self-imposed*. They are not simply constraints on one's reasoning that are imposed by facts in the world whose obtaining one acknowledges. And furthermore, when one reasons on the supposition that p one *treats* the relevant constraints on one's reasoning as self-imposed. When one reasons on the supposition that p one recognizes that the constraint of treating p as true is a constraint on one's reasoning that one has imposed on oneself, and one manifests this recognition in the way in which one reasons—e.g. by discharging the supposition with an outright conditional judgement that is outside the scope of the supposition.

We have said that the subject who decides to φ commits herself to φ-ing in making that decision, and her commitment to φ-ing is manifested, at least in part, in the way in which she makes her further plans on the assumption that she will φ. In assuming that she will φ, the subject treats as true the proposition that she will φ, and thereby plans with certain constraints in play. These constraints on the subject's planning are similar to the constraints that would be in play if the subject held the belief that she will φ. But there are reasons for thinking that the constraint of treating as true the proposition that she will φ is a constraint on the subject's planning that the subject regards as *self-imposed*. It is in this respect that it has something in common with the constraint of treating a proposition as true which is in play when one engages in suppositional reasoning.

In his account of intention, Velleman notes that when a subject decides to φ, and subsequently treats as true the proposition that she is going to φ, the subject regards her acceptance of that proposition as optional, in so far as she doesn't take herself to be *epistemically* obliged to accept that proposition.[7] Acceptance of the truth of the relevant proposition is not one that the subject takes to be grounded in evidence that she possess, in so far as she takes herself to be epistemically entitled, given her evidence, to make alternative decisions and hence to make any one of a number of other inconsistent assumptions about what she is going to do. So when a subject decides to φ, and then subsequently plans on the assumption that she is going to φ, the subject assumes something about her own future on the basis of evidence that, *from the subject's own point of view*, simultaneously licenses her to assume something about her future that contradicts it. Note that even *after* she decides to φ the subject still takes herself to be *epistemically* entitled, given her evidence, to make an alternative decision, and thereby assume something else about her future. In taking herself to be so entitled, the subject thereby treats this constraint on her planning as self-imposed. In that respect it has something in common with the constraint of treating a proposition as true which is in play when one engages in suppositional reasoning; and it is importantly different from the case in which a subject plans on the assumption that p because she has the ordinary belief that p.

There are, of course, important differences between one's planning assumptions and the assumptions one makes in suppositional reasoning. In the case of suppositional reasoning, when one reasons on the supposition that p one regards and treats the inferences one draws from p as inferences made under the scope of a supposition that is to be discharged by a conditional judgement that is outside the scope of the supposition. This doesn't seem to be true of the assumption one makes in planning. Moreover, in the case of planning, and not supposition, the range of assumptions one can make is rationally constrained by one's evidence, for there are rational constraints on the decisions one can make given one's evidence. It is irrational for one to decide to do something that one knows one is incapable of doing.

These two differences between one's planning assumptions and the assumptions one makes in suppositional reasoning are related, and can be explained as follows. When you assume that p for the sake of argument, you treat p as true, you regard and treat this constraint on your reasoning as self-imposed, and part of what is involved in treating the constraint as self-imposed is your treating the assumption as one that is to be discharged—e.g. with an outright conditional judgement that is outside the scope of the supposition. Likewise, when, having decided to φ, you plan on the assumption that you will φ, you regard and treat this constraint on your planning as self-imposed. And likewise, I want to suggest, part of what is involved in treating the constraint as self-imposed is your treating the assumption as one that is to be discharged. However, in the case of your planning assumption you don't treat the assumption as one that is to be discharged by an outright conditional judgement that is outside the scope of the assumption. Rather, you treat the assumption as one that is to be discharged by the performance of an action that makes that assumption true.[8] If you take yourself to be incapable of performing the action, then you take yourself to be incapable of making an assumption that is to be discharged in this way. This is why in the case of one's planning assumptions, the range of assumptions one can make is rationally constrained by one's evidence—in particular one's evidence about what one can and cannot do.

An important point to emphasize here is the following. I have said that when one decides to φ and one subsequently plans on the assumption that one will φ, one regards and treats that assumption as one that is to be discharged by an action that makes that assumption true. But this isn't equivalent to, or reducible to, the claim that one simply *predicts* that one will eventually perform an action that makes that assumption true. Compare the case of suppositional reasoning. When one assumes that p for the sake of

---

[8] It is in this sense that when the assumption is false the fault lies with the action and not the assumption. Compare here Anscombe 1963: 56–7: 'the mistake is not one of judgment but of performance'. See also Hampshire and Hart 1958.

argument, one regards and treats the inferences one draws from p as inferences made under the scope of a supposition that is to be discharged by a conditional judgement that is outside the scope of the supposition. But this isn't equivalent to, or reducible to, the claim that when one assumes that p for the sake of argument one simply *predicts* that one's reasoning will be followed by an appropriate conditional judgement.

This point is relevant to an important difference between ordinary belief and the mental state that you acquire when you decide to act, and it is connected with a suggestion I made earlier—the suggestion that there is a respect in which the mental state you acquire when you decide to act is both oriented towards your future and oriented towards your past. We can bring out this difference by noting a way in which a *distinctive* form of memory is involved in the continued obtaining of the mental state that you acquire when you decide to act.

12.4 Decision and memory

Although a subject's decision is usually thought to be an event, when one reports a past decision (e.g. 'I have decided to φ') one appears to be reporting something that entails the obtaining of a state, and we tend to think that the relevant state is one that can continue to obtain when the subject who has made the decision isn't acting on that decision—e.g. during dreamless sleep. There are reasons for thinking that the continuation of this state (unlike, say, the persistence of certain desires) involves, in part, a feat of memory. For it is not clear that we have reason to attribute to a subject the relevant state when that subject has forgotten about the decision she made. But the fact that a subject retains the knowledge that she decided to φ isn't in itself sufficient for the continuation of the relevant state, for one can retain the knowledge that one decided to φ when one no longer intends to φ—e.g. when one has changed one's mind about what to do. Should we say instead, then, that the continued obtaining of the subject's state depends on her retaining the belief that she will φ? This doesn't quite capture what is needed either, for as we have seen, this doesn't capture the idea that when a subject who has decided to φ subsequently plans on the assumption that she will φ, she regards this constraint on her planning as self-imposed.

When articulating the respect in which the continued obtaining of the state that one acquires when one decides to do something depends, in part, on a feat of memory, we need to recognize that the relevant feat of memory isn't simply a matter of remembering that something has happened ('I've decided to φ'), and it isn't simply a matter of remembering that something is going to happen ('I am going to φ'). For we need to accommodate the fact that the continued obtaining of the state depends on the kind of memory that we invoke when we talk of remembering/forgetting *to do* something. The suggestion I want to make here is that when a subject decides to do something in the future, that subject commits herself to that particular course of action, and behaviour that manifests that commitment is to be thought of as an instance of remembering. But the form of remembering involved is that of remembering *to do*, which isn't reducible to remembering *that*.

Just as there is something forward-looking in the commitment you make when you decide that you are going to φ in the future, there is a respect in which there is something backward-looking in the behaviour you engage in when you attempt to fulfil that commitment. When you attempt to fulfil that commitment, your behaviour manifests your *recognition* of the commitment you made *earlier*—the commitment you made when you decided that you would φ. A feat of memory connects a decision you made in the past, and the later behaviour you engage in when you attempt to fulfil the commitment you made in making that decision; for that behaviour manifests your recognition of that earlier decision. This is why that later behaviour can be thought of as an instance of remembering. But because that behaviour is an attempt to *fulfil* the commitment you made in making the decision, it is not equivalent to a case of remembering *that* you made the decision—i.e. the relevant behaviour isn't simply equivalent to a case of recollecting that you committed yourself to φ-ing. It is, rather, a case of remembering to *do* something.

Consider again the mental behaviour that you engage in when, having decided to φ, you subsequently plan on the assumption that you will φ. I noted that when you engage in such behaviour you do not regard the constraint of treating as true the proposition that you will φ as a constraint on your planning that is imposed by the evidence you possess. Rather, you regard this constraint on your planning as self-imposed. For this reason we shouldn't hold that the kind of memory that is implicated in such planning is reducible to a straightforward case of remembering *that* you will φ. The mental behaviour you engage in is a manifestation of your commitment to φ-ing, and this is part of what is involved in your attempting to fulfil that commitment. For in planning on the assumption that you will φ you are thereby taking measures to fulfil your commitment to φ-ing, by avoiding doing things, and avoiding committing yourself to doing things, that are incompatible with your future φ-ing, and perhaps also by reasoning about the required means for your φ-ing. And this in turn is part of what is involved in treating your assumption as one that is to be discharged by an action that makes true that assumption. For this reason we should say that in planning on the assumption that you will φ you are acting in recognition of the commitment you made earlier when you decided to φ, and in acting in recognition of that commitment you are thereby remembering *to do* something. You are remembering to impose on your planning the constraint of treating as true the proposition that you will φ, and you are remembering to treat that assumption as one that is to be discharged by an action that makes true that assumption. And this variety of remembering isn't reducible to that of remembering *that* something is the case.

Behaviour that manifests an ordinary belief that something has happened (or will happen) is not generally thought to be an instance of remembering to do something. Indeed, behaviour that manifests your belief that you intend to do something needn't be a case of remembering to do something. For example, when you manifest your belief that you intend to φ by telling someone of your intention, that behaviour is not generally thought to be a case of your remembering to do something, unless you made a prior decision to tell them of your intention. This is a respect in which ordinary belief differs from the state you acquire when you decide to do something. When you decide to do something in the future, the continued obtaining of the state you thereby acquire can be regarded as the continued obtaining of a dispositional state, and the continued obtaining of this dispositional state can be regarded as a feat of memory. But what makes it appropriate to regard the continued obtaining of this dispositional state as a feat of memory is the fact that the behaviour that is a manifestation of this dispositional state counts as a case of remembering *to do* something, and this distinguishes it from ordinary belief.

This is why it is a mistake to think one can assimilate this mental state to an ordinary belief by simply adding to, and filling out, the content of the relevant belief. Such a strategy fails to accommodate the fact that the behaviour that manifests the mental state that you acquire when you decide to φ is a case of remembering *to do* something, which isn't equivalent to remembering *that* something is the case. Moreover, it's not clear that one can remedy this lacuna by simply appealing to the idea that the kind of belief that you acquire when you decide to do something has a direction of fit that is active/directive, rather than passive. For the fact that a belief causes, and thereby makes true, what it represents needn't entail that what makes the content of that belief true is behaviour that can be regarded as the subject's remembering to do something.

Nonetheless, I want to suggest that there is a respect in which the mental state that you acquire when you decide to do something does embody an *epistemic* perspective on your future action—albeit one that is importantly different from the epistemic perspective that is embodied in your ordinary beliefs about your future. The distinctive epistemic perspective that is embodied in this mental state is related to a difference between, on the one hand, the epistemic perspective that you have on your future from the standpoint of theoretical reason, and, on the other hand, the epistemic perspective that you have on your future from the standpoint of practical reason. And this in turn is related to a respect in which your future seems to you to be open from the standpoint of practical reason

12.5 Epistemic freedom and the perspective of practical reason

According to the account I have proposed, when one decides to φ, one commits oneself to φ-ing, and being so committed involves being disposed to remember to do certain things. One of the things one is disposed to remember to do is to impose on one's subsequent planning the constraint of treating as true the proposition that one will φ. When one plans on the background assumption that one will φ one regards and treats this constraint on one's planning as self-imposed, and this is reflected in the way in which one takes oneself to be epistemically free in assuming 'I will φ'. That is to say, although the assumption is not entirely unconstrained by one's evidence, it is not an assumption that one takes to be *grounded* in evidence one has for the truth of the proposition assumed, in so far as one takes oneself to be epistemically entitled, given one's evidence, to make alternative decisions and thereby make any one of a number of other inconsistent assumptions about what one is going to do.

I have also said that the constraint you impose on your planning when you reason in this way is unlike the constraint you impose on your reasoning when you assume something for the sake of argument. For when you assume something for the sake of argument you regard and treat this assumption as one that is to be discharged by a conditional judgement made outside the scope of the supposition, whereas when you plan on the assumption that you are going to φ, you regard and treat this assumption as one that is to be discharged by an action that makes that assumption true. In treating the assumption that you will φ as an assumption that is to be discharged by an action that makes that assumption true you thereby regard and treat that assumption as one that entitles you to make outright non-conditional judgements that follow from that assumption. For in discharging the assumption you thereby make true the judgements that follow from that assumption. So on this proposal, an agent who makes a decision to act thereby takes herself to be entitled to make outright non-conditional judgements that follow from an assumption that she takes herself to be epistemically free to make.

The fact that the agent takes herself to be epistemically free to make such assumptions has a significant bearing on the epistemic perspective she has on her own future. This is something that Velleman has emphasized in his account of intention. From the agent's own point of view, there may be no *particular* way that she must assume the future to be in order for her assumption to be correct, in so far as there is no particular way that she is epistemically obliged to assume that the future will be in order for her assumption to be correct. The agent takes herself to be epistemically entitled to assume something about her own future on the basis of evidence that simultaneously licenses her to assume something that contradicts it.[9] She regards herself as epistemically free to make any one of a number of inconsistent assumptions about her future, and in that sense she regards her own future as epistemically open.

The respect in which such an agent regards her future as epistemically open is not equivalent to the idea that the agent is ignorant, and takes herself to be ignorant, about the course of future events. To bring out this point we can compare the case of one's ignorance of the past. When one is ignorant about what has happened in the past due to a lack of evidence, one might speculate about what happened in the past on the basis of the evidence that is available, but one does not thereby take oneself to be epistemically entitled to make any one of a number of *inconsistent* assumptions about the past—at least not assumptions that can ground non-conditional outright judgements about what actually did happen in the past. In that sense, one does not take oneself to be epistemically

---

[9] See Velleman 1989b: 'A person can know something on the basis of evidence that simultaneously licenses him to contradict it...Even if the future is going to turn out a particular way, we don't have to describe it as turning out that way in order to describe it correctly, since there are several other, incompatible ways in which we would be equally correct to describe it as turning out' (in Velleman 2000b: 34).

free to make assumptions about the past. In that sense, one does not regard the past as epistemically open, despite one's ignorance. But things are different in the case of the kind of assumption one makes about one's future conduct when one decides to do something.

I have suggested that once one has decided to φ, one subsequently plans on the assumption that one will φ, one regards and treats that constraint on one's planning as self-imposed, and one regards and treats that assumption as one that is to be discharged by an action that makes that assumption true. In so treating the assumption, one makes it more likely that one will perform that action, for so treating the assumption helps to prevent one from deviating from that course of action under the influence of other desires and inclinations, and what is more, it constrains one in a way that allows for means-end reasoning—reasoning which itself makes the performance of the action more likely. So when one decides to φ, one adds to whatever likelihood there was that one would end up φ-ing that obtained simply in virtue of one's prior motivational states. This suggests that when one decides to do something that one is capable of doing, the assumption that one will perform the action that one thereby makes has the direction of guidance that Velleman attributes to intention. The mental state you acquire when you decide to do something involves regarding as true a proposition that will be (or is usually) made true because you so regard it. The speculative hypotheses one might make about the past on the basis of the incomplete evidence available to one do not have this direction of guidance, and one does not take them to have this direction of guidance. This is why the distinctive epistemic perspective that the deciding agent has on her own future is not simply to be explained in terms of the agent's ignorance of the course of future events.

Note also that on the proposal being made here, the respect in which the deciding agent has a distinctive epistemic perspective on her own future is not simply to be explained in terms of the idea that such an agent has a distinctive form of epistemic access to a distinctive body of evidence that is relevant to her own future conduct—e.g. her distinctive first-person access to her own mental states together with evidence concerning the place and role of those mental states in effecting her future behaviour. To bring out this point we might compare a case in which one makes *predictions* about what is going to happen in the future on the basis of evidence concerning one's own mental states and events. In such a case, one is not epistemically entitled to make any one of a number of inconsistent *predictions* about what is going to happen on the basis of that evidence. From the perspective of *theoretical* reason, as we might put it, one does not regard oneself as epistemically free to make any one of a number of inconsistent predictions concerning what one is going to do. From the perspective of theoretical reason, one's future is not epistemically open. It is from the perspective of practical reason that one regards one's own future as epistemically open.

A number of philosophers have in the past appealed to the significance of a distinction between a perspective that we have on ourselves from the point of view of theoretical reason and a perspective we have on ourselves from the point of view of practical reason. For example, here is Korsgaard commenting on the use Kant makes of this sort of distinction.

Kant believed that as rational beings we may view ourselves from two different standpoints. We regard ourselves as objects of theoretical understanding, natural phenomena whose behaviour may be causally explained and predicted like any other. Or we may regard ourselves as agents, as thinkers of our thoughts and originators of our actions. These two standpoints cannot be completely assimilated to each other, and the way we view ourselves when we occupy one can appear incongruous with the way we view ourselves when we occupy the other. As objects of theoretical study, we see ourselves as wholly determined by natural forces, the mere undergoers of our experiences. Yet as agents, we view ourselves as free and responsible, as the authors of our actions and the leaders of our lives. The incongruity need not become a contradiction, so long as we keep in mind that the two views of ourselves spring from two different relations in which we stand to our actions. When we look at our actions from the theoretical standpoint our concern is with their explanation and prediction. When we view them from the practical standpoint our concern is with their justification and choice . . . Kant does not assert that it is a matter of theoretical fact that we are agents, that we are free, and that we are responsible. Rather, we must view ourselves in these ways when we occupy the stand point of practical reason—that is, when we are deciding what to do . . . This fundamental attitude is forced upon us by the necessity of making choices, regardless of the theoretical or metaphysical facts. (1996b: 377–8)

The account of deciding that I am proposing incorporates the idea that the perspective that one has on oneself from the standpoint of theoretical reason differs in an important way from the perspective that one has on oneself from the point of view of practical reason, in so far as it accommodates the idea that the epistemic perspective that one has on one's own future from the standpoint of theoretical reason can differ from the epistemic perspective one has on one's future from the standpoint of practical reason. Having said that, it should nonetheless be acknowledged that the subject who takes herself to occupy the one standpoint takes herself to be the subject who occupies the other. The epistemic perspective that one has on one's future conduct from the standpoint of practical reason cannot be isolated from, and needs to be integrated with, the deliverances of the standpoint of theoretical reason. This is why although one takes oneself to be epistemically free in assuming 'I will φ' when one decides to φ, that assumption is nonetheless rationally constrained by the evidence one possesses. If the outright judgements that follow from the assumption that one is going to φ are undermined by evidence that one possesses, then this ought rationally to have an effect on the way in which one plans one's future, and hence have an effect on the assumptions one makes when planning one's future. The deliverances of theoretical reason ought rationally to affect one's planning and thereby affect the assumptions one makes when planning.

If one concludes that as things stand one really can't count on one's being successful when attempting to φ, then it would seem reasonable to allow for this contingency in one's planning. For example, it would make sense to take further measures to improve one's chances of success where possible, and to plan for the contingency that one won't succeed. So what kind of assumption would one be making in one's practical reasoning in such cases? Well, arguably in planning for such contingencies one is still assuming that one will at least try to φ (or perhaps one is assuming that one will try to remember to φ).[10] When one makes a decision about what to do if one doesn't succeed in φ-ing (or if one doesn't succeed in remembering to φ), one imposes on oneself a conditional constraint—e.g. to ψ if one doesn't succeed in φ-ing. A constraint one thereby imposes on oneself is to assume that one will ψ if one fails to φ. In planning in this way one is still aiming to avoid doing things incompatible with φ-ing, and one still reasons about the means required for φ-ing, but in addition one is planning on the contingency that one won't succeed in φ-ing.

These changes in the assumptions one makes in one's planning reflect further *decisions* one has taken in light of the deliverances of theoretical reason. If one assumes that one is going to attempt to φ, then this is because one has decided to attempt to φ. If one assumes that one will ψ if one fails to φ, then this is because one has decided that one will ψ if one fails to φ. There is a sense in which one's intention may remain the same despite these further decisions, for one's goal in planning in this way may remain the same—i.e. to φ. But again, we need to note that when we express what a subject intends to do, we may not be accurately specifying what that subject has decided to do; and it is the state one acquires when one decides to do something that we should be looking to if our interest is in clarifying the role played by a distinctive mental state in planning and coordinating future action.

We preserve, then, a connection between what a subject decides to do and the assumptions that she makes about what she is going to do when she is engaged in further planning. We preserve the idea that when a subject decides to do something that subject thereby represents as true the proposition that she is going to do that thing. This mental state embodies a distinctive epistemic perspective on future action—one that is rationally constrained by the epistemic perspective delivered by theoretical reason, but one which is not reducible to the epistemic perspective delivered by theoretical reason.

The self-conscious agent cannot escape the distinctive epistemic perspective that she has on her own future from the standpoint of practical reason. As Korsgaard puts it, 'Human beings are condemned to choice and action...You have no choice but to choose and to act on your choice' (2009a: 1). And to choose in this way, I have argued, entails having a distinctive epistemic perspective on your own future. One has no choice but to regard one's own future as epistemically open. Even when one adopts what one might think of as the most detached theoretical perspective on oneself, and one questions whether one will end up doing what one has decided to do, there is still a respect in which one cannot escape the perspective of practical reason. When we question whether or not our commitment to φ-ing will result in our φ-ing, by adopting a detached perspective on ourselves, we do not treat the proposition 'I will Φ' as a premise in our reasoning—the truth value of the proposition is up for assessment—and in such cases we

---

[10] Note that this is not to say that the *aim* of performing the action is to try to φ. And so it is not to say that if one tries and fails to φ, then one's action has been successful.

bracket the assumption 'I will Φ', and consider the evidence for its truth value.[11] However, even when one adopts this 'detached' perspective on oneself and one's own mental states, and one seeks to explain and predict one's own mental states and behaviour from the standpoint of theoretical reason, one thereby engages in an exercise that presents an aspect of oneself to oneself as self-determining agent. For to adopt this perspective on oneself is to engage in a form of self-critical reflection, and as I argued in the previous chapter, when one engages in this kind of conscious reasoning an aspect of oneself is presented under reflexive guise as that which determines the activity by engaging in it—that which is imposing a constraint on the reasoning by reasoning in recognition of that constraint. An aspect of oneself is presented under reflexive guise as locus of mental autonomy.

I want now to return to the two questions that led us to embark on this discussion of decision. (i) How should we understand the agency that is exercised by a self-conscious subject when that subject makes a decision about what to do? And (ii) what account should be given of the distinctive form of self-governance and autonomous agency that a self-conscious agent is able to exercise in having the capacity to engage in practical deliberation and make decisions? We'll focus on the former question in the next section, and the latter question in the subsequent, final section of this chapter.

12.6 Decision and mental agency

I have suggested that the event of deciding to act just is the event of acquiring a certain kind of mental state, and so to understand the nature of the act of deciding we have to understand the nature of the kind of mental state that is acquired when one decides to act. When you decide to act you adopt an epistemic perspective on your future that isn't determined by, and which you don't regard as determined by, the evidence you have concerning what is going to happen, and in that respect you treat your future as epistemically open. Having decided to φ you subsequently plan on the assumption that you will φ and you treat this constraint on your planning as self-imposed. Moreover, you regard and treat the assumption as one that is to be discharged by an action that makes that assumption true. This is connected with the suggestion that when you impose this constraint on your planning you are thereby *remembering to do* something, for in so treating the assumption you are acting *in recognition* of a commitment you made when you decided to act. This is why reference to your perspective on *both* your future *and* your past is essential to a description of the mental state that you acquire when you decide to act.

---

[11] Implicit in this claim is the notion that we can bracket planning assumptions as well as beliefs, where bracketing a planning assumption or belief is not equivalent to giving up that assumption or belief. This marks an important distinction between the kinds of assumptions that I am claiming are involved when one decides to do something, and what Bratman (1992) labels 'acceptance in a context'. In the case of acceptance in a context, it seems there can be no bracketing of one's acceptance.

The subject who decides to φ commits herself to φ-ing, and in being so committed that subject is disposed to remember to do various things. For example, (a) the subject is disposed to remember to impose on her planning the constraint of treating as true the proposition that she is going to φ, and (b) the subject is disposed to treat this constraint on her planning *as* self-imposed. These two points are connected. When you plan on the assumption that you are going to φ, you regard and treat this constraint on your planning as self-imposed, and in doing so you thereby succeed in imposing that constraint on your planning. In acting as though *you* have imposed this constraint on your planning you thereby impose that constraint on your planning. For treating a constraint as self-imposed is sufficient for making it the case that you impose that constraint on yourself.

When this kind of mental activity occurs, the subject of the activity is presented, under reflexive guise, as that which imposes a constraint on the activity *by* acting in compliance with that constraint. The constraint that the subject imposes on her planning is constituted by the occurrence of conscious mental events that manifest her recognition of that self-imposed constraint. So when one is planning in this way, the planning one engages in manifests an attitude towards oneself—an attitude of treating oneself as a source of constraint over one's planning. As one plans, one treats oneself as a source of constraint over one's planning and one thereby determines the way in which one plans. In that respect, the form of conscious reasoning one engages in when one plans in this way is both self-conscious *and self-determined*.

I have said that when you plan in this way you are remembering to do something, for you are acting in recognition of a commitment you made when you decided to φ. So we can add that this kind of self-conscious mental activity manifests an attitude towards oneself *and* one's past decision to act. And this is relevant to the way in which agency and self-determination are implicated in the occurrence of that past decision. When you plan on the assumption that you will φ you are acting in recognition of a commitment you made when you decided to φ, and in acting in recognition of that commitment you are thereby recognizing the authority of your past decision over your present conduct. What is more, when you plan in this way you are not only recognizing the authority of your past decision over your present conduct, you are also thereby *granting* it that authority over your present conduct. That is to say, your past decision has authority over your present conduct only if, and only because, you now grant it that authority *by* acting as though it has authority over your present conduct. When you now grant authority to your past decision, by planning on the assumption that you will act as decided, you thereby make it the case that in so deciding your past self has succeeded in exercising authority over your present self. So the planning activity that now grants authority to your past decision is activity that thereby recognizes that authority. Your current behaviour—the way in which you now plan—at one and the same time both grants authority to, and recognizes the authority of, your past decision to act.

According to this proposal, your past decision is an act that determines your current behaviour, but only if, and only because, you grant authority to, and thereby recognize the authority of, that past decision in the way you now act. And the activity in question—the activity that both recognizes and grants this authority—is the self-conscious, *self-determined* mental activity that you engage in when you plan on the assumption that you will act as decided. If you are not disposed to engage in the self-conscious, self-determined behaviour that grants authority to your decision, then you haven't decided to act, and there is no authority to recognize. So your decision is an act that determines your behaviour, but it is also an act whose authority to so determine your behaviour is dependent on self-determined behaviour that grants it that authority. In that respect, your decision to act is a *self-determined*, self-determining act.

There is a familiar pre-philosophical distinction that we commonly draw between the things we actively do and the things that merely happen to us, and a familiar philosophical thought is that this difference is to be accounted for by citing appropriate causes of the relevant events. On this picture, when we actively do something, an event, of a kind which could have been a mere happening, is caused by certain psychological factors, and its being so caused makes it the case that the event counts as a self-determined action that the agent performs. On this approach, if one wanted to accommodate the idea that the psychological cause of an agent's behaviour is itself self-determined one would need to cite further, prior psychological causes of the relevant psychological states or events. These further, prior psychological causes are not themselves self-determined, unless caused by yet further, and prior, psychological causes. According to the account I have proposed, we should accept that a decision to act is a self-determining psychological act that is itself self-determined, but we shouldn't simply look to the psychological causes of the act of deciding in order to account for the respect in which this psychological act is self-determined. For the respect in which one's decision to act is self-determined is to be accounted for in terms of the self-determined behaviour that one is disposed to engage in once one has decided to act. And this is behaviour that one engages in after the act of deciding.

Having decided to act you are thereby disposed to regard and treat that past occurrence as an act of *your* determining your own behaviour. It is in that respect that you regard your decision as agential—as something you have done, rather than something that has merely happened to you. You don't regard that past event as a mere cause of your current mental condition—a mental condition that is a force within you which has the potential to influence your conduct by causing and determining your current and future behaviour.[12] In this case, being disposed to treat your past decision as an act of *your* determining your own behaviour thereby makes it the case that that past event *is* one of your determining your own behaviour. Since the event in question just is the acquisition of a mental state that involves being so disposed, it is not an event of a kind which, had it had a different causal origin, could have been a mere happening. In that respect, a decision to act is a self-determining psychological act that is *essentially* self-determined.

---

[12] Contrast here the acquisition of thirst or hunger.

12.7 Decision, practical deliberation, and autonomous agency

In light of this account of the agency that the self-conscious subject exercises in making a decision, what account should be given of the distinctive form of self-governance and autonomous agency that a self-conscious agent is able to exercise in having the capacity to engage in practical deliberation and make decisions? Can we identify a distinctive form of self-governance that is not only *available* to the self-conscious agent in having the capacity to engage in practical deliberation and make decisions, but which is actually *exercised* by the self-conscious agent when she engages in practical deliberation and makes decisions?

Recall that according to Frankfurt, the self-conscious agent is able to reflect on her motives, and in doing so she may feel alienated from some of them, and she may dissociate herself from them. So from the agent's own point of view, there is a respect in which such motives may be thought of as external influences to be resisted, and obstacles to be overcome. In consequence, actions which spring from such motives might be regarded as less than fully autonomous. On a Frankfurtian approach to self-governance, a question of concern then becomes that of providing some account of what it is that distinguishes those attitudes that 'speak for the subject' from those that do not. The aim is thereby to identify those attitudes whose role in action makes the action fully autonomous and self-governed.

We might think of this as an attempt to identify 'parts' of the agent whose appropriate role in the production of action makes that action an instance of 'full-blooded' autonomous action.[13] This sort of 'parts' approach to self-governance is consistent with what I earlier called an 'ingredients' approach to action and agency. It is consistent with the idea that some part, or element, of oneself, which is not itself agential, determines one's behaviour when one acts. Under such an approach, in seeking to explicate behaviour that is truly self-governed we should be seeking to identify the appropriate part, or ingredient, of one's psychology, whose appropriate role in the production of one's behaviour makes that behaviour an instance of self-governed action.

One can make decisions, and act on decisions, that are formed on the basis of motivations from which one feels alienated—motivations that are, even by one's own lights, the 'worse' elements of oneself. In consequence, not all of the actions that one performs that issue from decisions one has made will be regarded as fully autonomous, self-governed actions in Frankfurt's sense. But is there, nonetheless, a *form* of self-governance that is exercised in merely making a decision, whether or not that decision issues from a desire from which one feels alienated? That is, is there a notion of self-governance that applies

---

[13] This 'parts' approach to self-governance has an ancient precedent. In the *Republic*, Plato has Socrates saying: 'Isn't the phrase "self-mastery" absurd? I mean anyone who is his own master is also his own slave, of course, and vice versa, since it's the same person who is the subject in all these expressions' (430e). 'What this expression means, I think…is that there are better and worse elements in a person's mind, and when the part which is naturally better is in control of the worse part, then we use this phrase "self-mastery"'' (431a).

to the capacity exercised when an agent engages in practical deliberation and makes decisions, even in cases where one might think that the decisions formed, and the actions performed on the basis of those decisions, are less than fully autonomous in Frankfurt's sense?

I think we can identify a notion of *self-determination* that is in play when an agent acts on a decision she has made—a notion of self-determination that presupposes a certain kind of agential unity, and so which is slightly different from the 'parts' approach. On the view I have proposed, deciding to do something is itself a form of 'self-mastery' in so far as it is a form of self-binding. When one makes a decision, and acts on that decision, the course of one's future conduct is determined, at least in part, by oneself, and not simply some part of oneself. When one decides to do something, certain constraints on one's future conduct are *self*-imposed. One treats oneself as a source of constraint over oneself and in doing so one becomes a source of constraint over oneself. An aspect of oneself is presented under reflexive guise as that which is imposing a constraint on itself by acting in compliance with that constraint. One succeeds in imposing the constraint on oneself in making a decision only if one is subsequently disposed to engage in self-conscious, self-determined behaviour that both recognizes the authority of, and grants authority to, the imposition of that constraint. There is a sense, then, in which that which is acting in a constrained manner cannot disassociate itself from that which imposes the constraint, even though the actor may disassociate herself from the motive that led her to impose that constraint on herself. So while this is not to say that such an agent cannot feel alienated from some of her own motives, it is to suggest that when an agent decides to do something, even on the basis of such a motive, that which *imposes the constraint* on the agent's behaviour is something from which the actor cannot dissociate herself. This is what I mean when I say that there is a sense in which a certain kind of agential unity is involved in making a decision.

This now introduces an important distinction between decision and desire, as far as questions of self-determination are concerned. One might think of a desire that one has as a 'part', or 'element', of oneself from which one can feel alienated. But a decision that one takes should not be thought of in these terms. When a decision is made, that which the constraint is imposed upon cannot dissociate itself from that which imposes the constraint. The agent cannot dissociate herself from that aspect of herself that imposed the constraint on herself in making that decision. That aspect of herself is presented under reflexive guise, as self-determining agent—as that which determines her behaviour by engaging in it.

Choosing to do something (i.e. deciding to do something) is something over and above wanting to do that thing. A distinctive notion of self-determination applies in the case of decision, no matter what may have motivated that decision. This difference between decision and desire can affect how we should think of practical deliberation, given the role of decision in practical deliberation. This is connected with the following remark from Korsgaard:

From a third person point of view, outside the deliberative standpoint, it may look as if what happens when someone makes a choice is that the strongest of his conflicting desires wins. But that isn't the way it is *for you* when you deliberate. When you deliberate, it is as if there were something over and above all your desires, something which is *you*, and which *chooses* which desire to act upon. (1996a: 100)

Engaging in practical deliberation, from the point of view of the agent engaged in such deliberation, is not equivalent to simply waiting to see which desire wins. When one decides to do something, one imposes a constraint on oneself. The constraint is imposed on one (in the relevant sense) only if one is disposed to engage in self-conscious, self-determined behaviour that both recognizes the authority of, and grants authority to, that self-imposed constraint. So from the point of view of the deliberating agent, it's not simply some part of herself that determines her behaviour when she makes a decision to act.

There are some additional conclusions that Korsgaard goes on to draw from the difference she sees between desire and choice, and the bearing that this difference has on our understanding of practical deliberation.

The idea that you choose among your conflicting desires, rather than waiting to see which one wins, suggests that you have reasons for or against acting on them. And it is these reasons, rather than the desires themselves, which are expressive of your will. The strength of a desire may be counted *by you* as a reason for acting on it; but this is different from *its* simply winning. This means that there is some principle or way of choosing that you regard as expressive of *yourself,* and that provides reasons that regulate your choices among your desires. (1996b: 370)

There are two points that Korsgaard makes here which I want to highlight: (i) When decision is in play, it's not simply a case of the desire causing the behaviour. Rather, when your desire to do something leads you to decide to do that thing, the desire is counted *by you* as a *reason* for acting. (ii) When you engage in practical deliberation and make a decision, there is in play some principle or way of choosing that regulates your decisions and which you regard as expressive of *yourself.* What leads Korsgaard to make these additional claims?

Recall the discussion in the previous chapter of Korsgaard's notion of the 'space of reflective distance'. According to Korsgaard, we have reflective awareness of our own mental states and activities as such, and this self-conscious form of consciousness opens up 'a space of reflective distance'. Korsgaard argues that this space of reflective distance ensures that 'we are, or can be, active, self-directing, with respect to our beliefs'. It 'presents us with the possibility and the necessity of exerting a kind of control over our beliefs' (2009b: 32). She also makes a parallel claim with respect to the control that a self-conscious agent exercises over her actions:

Once the space of reflective awareness—reflective distance, as I like to call it—opens up between the potential ground of... action and the... action itself, we must step across that distance, and so must be able to endorse the operation of that ground, before we can act... What would have been the *cause* of our... action, had we still been operating under the control of instinctive or learned responses, now becomes something experienced as a consideration in favor of a certain...action instead, one we can endorse or reject. And when we can endorse the operation of a ground of...action on us *as a* ground, then we take that consideration for a reason. (2009b: 32)

What this means is that the space of reflective distance presents us with both the possibility and the necessity of exerting a kind of control over our...actions that the other animals do not have. We are, or can be, active, self-directing, with respect to our...actions to a greater extent than the other animals are, for we can accept or reject the grounds of...action that...desire offers to us. (2009b: 32)

I think we can agree with Korsgaard that the 'space of reflective distance' that is available to the self-conscious agent does add something of significance. Self-conscious agents are able to regard themselves as temporally extended agents, in the sense that they have the capacity to think of themselves as having different impulses and inclinations at different times.[14] As Velleman puts it, in the context of a discussion of Kantian ethics, when you have such a capacity you are able to attain 'a perspective that transcends that of your current momentary self' (2005a: 26).[15] You have the capacity to think of yourself as one and the same agent who once wanted to φ, but no longer does, as one and the same agent who now wants to φ, and who later won't want to φ, as one and the same agent who now wants to φ and who may later regret φ-ing. In that discussion of Kantian ethics, Velleman suggests that when you have the capacity to have this kind of perspective on yourself, you feel an impulse to find a constant perspective on the question of what to do when.

This impulse is unavoidable as soon as the more encompassing vantage point appears. As soon as you glimpse the possibility of attaining a constant perspective from which to reflect on and adjudicate among your shifting preferences, you are drawn toward that perspective, as you would be drawn toward the top of a hill that commanded a terrain through which you had been wandering. (2005a: 26–7)[16]

---

[14] Note that this capacity isn't simply to be understood as the capacity to do something now with the aim of getting something later. Compare here Elster's (1979) discussion of the difference between the capacity to employ indirect strategies and to enact behaviour that delays the attainment of a goal on the one hand, and the *generalized* capacity for global maximization on the other: 'The characteristic of man is not a programmed ability to use indirect strategies or adopt waiting behaviour in specific situations, but rather a *generalized* capacity for global maximization that applies even to qualitatively new situations' (15).

[15] See also Bratman 2000.

[16] I don't think that this in itself entails that one will thereby be drawn to make decisions concerning one's actions in a temporally neutral way. That is, the decisions one makes from such a perspective may still reflect a bias towards the present, a bias towards the near-in-time, and in some cases a bias towards the future. (See the discussion of these possibilities in Parfit 1984, Part II.) It might be argued that the subject who shows a preference for the present doesn't always fail to regard herself as an agent who occupies this encompassing perspective, for her current decision might in part be based on the fact that she trusts herself to make decisions from this encompassing perspective at a later time, in which case she thereby implicitly acknowledges her own ability to make decisions from this encompassing perspective. But whether the agent would be irrational in regarding things in this way is a further matter. For discussion of this issue, see Elster 1979 and 2000, Nagel 1979 and Parfit 1984.

The subject who attains this perspective on herself thereby regards herself as the kind of agent who can occupy such a perspective. So for such a subject, the question of what to do becomes the question of what she, as agent who occupies this encompassing perspective, should do, and so such a subject no longer *simply* has reason to do whatever she happens to feel like doing at the time. Such a subject can now have a reason not to be dictated to by her current impulse, as she regards herself as an agent whose perspective transcends that of her immediate felt impulse to act.

But why should this constitute a form of self-control and self-governance? As I discussed in the previous chapter, a potential problem with Korsgaard's proposal as applied to belief is that it leaves unclear how the 'space of reflective distance' that Korsgaard cites is supposed to allow us to 'exert control over our beliefs'. Why should we accept that our ability to reflect on our own beliefs somehow allows belief formation to be governable by such reflection? One might have similar worries about the supposed role of the space of reflective distance in the case of action. Why should the space of reflective distance entail that we can exercise a distinctive form of control over our actions?

Suppose we agree that the self-conscious agent who can attain this encompassing perspective on herself can appreciate reasons for acting as such, and make judgements about them. How does this enable the agent thereby to exercise control over her actions? Judging that one ought to do something is not equivalent to deciding to act for that reason. For one can, of course, judge that one ought to do something, and yet fail to decide to do that thing. One might think that in such cases the additional element that is required is a *desire* to so act—and one which is strong enough to countermand conflicting desires. That is to say, judging that one ought to φ for reason R does not in itself amount to exercising a form of control over one's actions, so one might think that the judgement will only result in one's φ-ing if one's desire to act on the reason articulated by such a judgement is strong enough. But then on this picture, in such cases, doesn't the relevant second-order desire 'just win'? That is to say, once this concession is made, the looming danger is that we are back with a view of practical deliberation that simply amounts to waiting to see which desire wins. On the one hand, it seems as though there is a kind of impotence in simply judging that one ought to do something, and yet on the other hand, it seems as though there is a kind of absence of control and self-governance (or self-mastery) in simply waiting to see which of one's desires wins. When the issue is put in these terms, the temptation may be to return to the 'parts' approach to self-governance—to concede that it *is* ultimately some part of yourself that determines your behaviour. So in specifying 'full-blooded' autonomous action, we should be seeking to identify the appropriate part.

However, there is, I think, an alternative way of responding to this difficulty. The first step lies in recognizing that practical deliberation is not reducible to a variety of theoretical reasoning—i.e. a variety of theoretical reasoning that includes normative judgements about one's actions and reasons for actions. The aim of practical deliberation is to reach decisions, and judgements about how one ought to act are not themselves decisions to act. That is to say, the aim of practical deliberation is to *govern* one's own conduct, and one fails to do this if one *simply* makes judgements about how one ought to act. Making judgements about how one ought to govern one's own conduct does not itself amount to governing one's own conduct.

So how, then, should we understand the transition from judging that one ought to φ to deciding to φ—the step from judging that one ought to φ for reason R to deciding to act for that reason? Here I think we should say that one effects this transition in the following way. One imposes a constraint on one's conduct for reason R by acting in recognition of a self-imposed constraint that was imposed for that reason. One can manifest one's recognition of the constraint one imposes on oneself in the way in which one acts, and one can also manifest one's recognition of the *reason* for which the constraint was imposed in the way in which one acts—e.g. by ceasing to act in recognition of the constraint if the reason no longer applies, or if it becomes outweighed by new considerations.

In summary, the present proposal is the following. The aim of practical deliberation is to govern one's own conduct, which involves governing the way in which one imposes constraints on oneself (i.e. governing the way in which one makes decisions), and this is not simply a matter of arriving at judgements as to how one ought to behave and how one ought to decide to behave. It is only by *making* decisions that one governs one's decision making. One governs the way in which one imposes constraints on oneself by imposing constraints on oneself. And one imposes those constraints on oneself by acting in recognition of them, and in recognition of the reasons for which they were imposed.

So the suggestion here is that when one imposes constraints on one's conduct, one *thereby* governs the way in which one imposes those constraints. When one acts in recognition of a self-imposed constraint, one thereby imposes the constraint on oneself, and one thereby governs the way in which one imposes the constraint. You are the source of the constraints you impose on yourself when you decide to act, and you are also, thereby, the source of the constraints imposed on the way in which you impose such constraints. That is to say, when you make decisions you determine the way in which you determine your own behaviour, and it is not simply some part of you that determines how you determine your own behaviour. You govern the way in which you govern yourself. This is what is right in Korsgaard's claim that when you choose to act, 'there is some principle or way of choosing that you regard as expressive of *yourself*, and that provides reasons that regulate your choices among your desires', which in turn accommodates her suggestion that when decision is in play, it's not simply a case of some desire of yours causing your behaviour. Rather, when your desire to do something leads you to decide to do that thing, the desire is counted *by you* as a *reason* for acting.

On the present account, we can, then, identify a notion of self-governance that is exercised in simply making decisions and engaging in practical deliberation, even if the actions that result from such decisions are less than fully autonomous in Frankfurt's sense. However, it does not follow from this that whenever you decide to act, you thereby govern your own conduct in the way that you think that you ought to. On the present proposal, there is an important respect in which you do govern your own conduct whenever you make a decision, but this does not mean that you thereby govern your conduct well, even by your own lights.

Suppose you judge that you ought to φ, but you don't decide to φ. You recognize that you are under some kind of obligation to φ, but you fail to make the decision to φ. You decide instead to take some other course of action. This looks like a failure of self-governance of some kind. Given that such cases can and do arise, it should be conceded that although we may be able to identify a distinctive notion of self-governance that is exercised by an agent when she engages in practical deliberation and makes decisions, there are further questions and issues concerning self-governance that are left open by the current proposal. I shan't be going into those further issues here, but I shall just make some very brief remarks on some of the directions in which they might proceed.

Governing one's own conduct involves imposing constraints on oneself, and one can always choose not to impose any given constraint on oneself by simply choosing to impose some other constraint on oneself instead. This perpetual possibility leads to further issues and problems regarding self-governance. How can the self-governing agent succeed in binding her future conduct given that she is aware that her future self is a self-governing agent who is at liberty to impose on herself whichever alternative constraints she chooses?[17] The Kantian response to this difficulty is to suggest that the self-governing agent should aspire to act for reasons that have a validity that is universally accessible to all reasoners. Under this conception, a reason for one is a reason for all, once and for all. Obligations that arise from reason as such are then inescapable. However, this cannot in itself solve the problem of self-governance. For such universal and objectively binding constraints can only succeed in constraining the way in which you act if you *impose them on yourself*. That is why, on the Kantian approach, true self-governance involves not only identifying obligations that are objectively binding, but also imposing those obligations on *oneself*, thereby making *oneself* the source of those objectively binding obligations. Here we have the notion that true self-governance involves 'willing the law', and not merely recognizing it.

Your recognizing that you are under an obligation to do something is not sufficient for imposing that obligation on yourself, and so it is not sufficient for governing your own conduct in the way that you think you should; and self-conscious agents can recognize this fact about themselves. The fact that self-conscious agents can recognize this fact about themselves can lead them to adopt the sorts of strategies that Elster discusses under the label of 'pre-commitment'. Elster (1979 and 2000) describes various ways in which agents can pre-commit themselves by choosing to set up some causal process in the external world with the intention of restricting their future freedom of choice, by 'removing certain options from the feasible set, by making them more costly or available only with delay, and from insulating themselves from knowledge of their existence' (2000: 1). Elster argues that since we are imperfectly rational, there are sometimes

---

[17] We might compare here the notion of a government rewriting its constitution in an attempt to prevent future governments from being able to rewrite their constitutions.

benefits from having fewer opportunities rather than more, and he has suggested that agents 'pre-commit' themselves in order to protect themselves against passion, preference change, and varieties of inconsistent time preference. Presumably, the agent who feels the need to 'pre-commit' herself, in Elster's sense, takes herself to be someone who can sometimes fail to act for the reasons she has as an agent who occupies the encompassing perspective that she has on herself. So there is a sense in which the agent who pre-commits herself feels the need to protect herself from herself. This is one kind of response to the distinctive problem faced by the self-governing agent who is capable of engaging in practical deliberation and making decisions. But there is a respect in which the agent who takes the sorts of measures that are involved in pre-commitment falls short of the ideal when it comes to exercising self-governance.

An alternative response to the difficulty is the Aristotelian one of developing a stable *hexis* from which one acts. And, it might be added, ideally a stable *hexis* from which one doesn't feel alienated. I won't pursue these issues further here. I merely want to signal that although I have tried to identify a form of self-governance that is exercised in simply engaging in practical deliberation and making decisions, there are, of course, a number of further questions and issues concerning self-governance to which this account can give rise.

According to the account of deciding that I have proposed, when one decides to do something one is in a mental state that implicates the capacity to engage in a certain kind of self-conscious, self-determined mental activity. That is to say, one cannot be in that kind of mental state if one lacks the capacity to engage in that kind of self-conscious, self-determined mental activity. That is not to say that one cannot be in that kind of mental state when one is not *actually engaging* in that self-conscious, self-determined mental activity. For example, when one decides to φ, the prior intention to φ that one thereby acquires can be a *dispositional* state that obtains when one isn't engaged in any kind of self-conscious activity at all—e.g. during sleep. But the preservation of that dispositional state is, in part, a feat of memory, and what makes it true that the state of prior intention is retained is the fact that one continues to be disposed to remember to act in recognition of the commitment one made when one decided to φ, where this includes being disposed to engage in self-conscious, self-determined mental activity that manifests one's recognition of self-imposed constraints. Where does this leave what I have been calling an 'ingredients' approach to the agency exercised by a self-conscious agent? This is a question I shall be returning to later. I'll close this chapter by briefly outlining some further issues we will need to address.

The account I have proposed of the mental state one acquires when one decides to do something has much in common with Bratman's planning theory of intention. On the view I have proposed, in having the capacity to decide to do something the self-conscious agent has the capacity to exercise a form of self-binding that enables her to govern her own conduct and project her agency in an organized way over time. She has the capacity to deliberate in advance of action, to engage in means-end reasoning, and to coordinate her future actions by arriving at future-directed plans. These are all points that Bratman emphasizes in his planning theory of intention. I have also argued that when one decides to φ, a constraint one imposes on oneself is to treat 'I will φ' as a premise in one's practical reasoning. In this respect, there is agreement with a claim that Velleman makes in his account of intention—i.e. when one decides to φ, one thereby regards as true the proposition 'I will φ'. Moreover, there is concord with claims that Velleman makes about the distinctive epistemic perspective that the deciding agent has on her own future conduct, as well as agreement with some claims he makes about the direction of fit of intention.

Velleman also proposes that intention plays a role in providing us with a distinctive form of knowledge of what we are doing when we *perform* our intended actions. Intended action on this view is behaviour that realizes the agent's knowledge of it— practical knowledge of the action that is embodied in the agent's intention. Should we agree with Velleman that intention can embody a form of practical self-knowledge of an action one intentionally performs? This is an issue I haven't yet discussed. Two further related issues are the following. So far I have focused on *prior* intention—future-directed intention—when discussing decision. But what account should be given of intention-in-action—present-directed intention? Moreover, as I mentioned earlier on in the chapter, a problem that Velleman raises for Bratman's account is the frequency with which we form immediate intentions to act now, without any prior planning. Why do we bother to decide to act when there is no opportunity for the mental state thus acquired to play the functional roles in planning that Bratman specifies? These are issues I shall be discussing in the next chapter, where I will be relating these concerns to the question of the significance of mental agency to our understanding of issues in the epistemology of mind.

13

Intention-in-Action and the Epistemology of Mind

In the previous chapter I argued that when one decides to φ, a constraint one imposes on oneself is to treat 'I will φ' as a premise in one's practical reasoning—to assume the truth of 'I will φ'. I also argued that the self-binding involved in deciding to do something makes it more likely that one will perform the action, for it helps to prevent one from deviating from that course of action under the influence of other desires and inclinations, and what is more, it constrains one in a way that allows for means-end reasoning—reasoning which itself makes the performance of the action more likely. So when one decides to φ, one adds to whatever likelihood there was that one would end up φ-ing that obtained simply in virtue of one's prior motivational states. In consequence, I suggested that some of the claims that Velleman makes about the direction of guidance of the mental state of intention can be understood in terms of the direction of guidance of the mental state one acquires when one decides to do something. When one decides to do something that one is capable of doing, the mental state one acquires involves regarding as true a proposition that will be (or is usually) made true because one so regards it.

Can such considerations be used to yield an account of how we know what we are doing when we are acting? Velleman has argued that intention plays a role in providing us with a distinctive form of knowledge of what we are doing when we *perform* our intended actions. Intended action on this view is behaviour that realizes the agent's knowledge of it—practical knowledge of the action that is embodied in the agent's intention. Should we agree with Velleman that intention can embody a form of practical knowledge of an action one intentionally performs? If so, how might this bear on an account of our knowledge of our own mental actions? These are among the questions I shall be addressing in this chapter. I shall go on to suggest various ways in which these issues can illuminate further central concerns in the epistemology of mind.

13.1 Intention-in-action and practical self-knowledge

Can the mental state one acquires when one decides to act play a role in providing one with a distinctive form of knowledge of what one is doing when one performs that intended action? In order to address this question, we first need to consider the notion of intention-in-action and its relation to prior intention. Central to the notion of committing oneself to φ-ing in deciding to φ is the idea of doing things, and being disposed to remember to do things, which manifest one's recognition of that commitment. One manifests one's recognition of one's commitment by imposing constraints on one's own conduct, and one imposes the relevant constraints on oneself by acting in recognition of them. In the case of a decision to φ, one of the things one does that manifests one's recognition of one's commitment to φ-ing is one's actual φ-ing. Me φ-ing today, or attempting to φ today, is itself part of what is involved in manifesting my recognition of the commitment I made yesterday when I decided that tomorrow I would φ. This is what makes that action count as a case of remembering to do something. One's φ-ing can only be a manifestation of one's recognition of one's commitment to φ-ing if one's commitment to φ-ing obtains while the action is being performed. If, when one φs, one no longer intends to φ, if one once was committed to φ-ing but no longer is, then the action cannot be regarded as behaviour that manifests one's recognition of the commitment one made when one decided to φ. So embedded in the notion of the kind of prior intention that makes planning for the future possible is a notion of intention-*in*-action—a state that obtains during the performance of the action. What then distinguishes intention-in-action from prior intention? Should we say that intention-in-action and the prior intention that precedes it have different objects?

If, when I decide to φ, I commit myself to φ-ing, then what I commit myself to, the object of my commitment, is doing that thing—that is, me φ-ing. If I commit myself to φ-ing tomorrow, then the object of my commitment is not 'I will φ tomorrow' but rather, me φ-ing tomorrow. When tomorrow arrives, me φ-ing on that day is what will discharge my commitment. In an important sense, when tomorrow arrives, the object of my commitment will not have changed. However, the temporal relation I stand to it will have, and so what I will need to do in order to manifest my recognition of the commitment I made in making the decision to φ tomorrow will have changed. For example, when tomorrow arrives, in order for me to manifest my recognition of the commitment I made in deciding to φ tomorrow, I will have to assume that 'I will φ *today*' when I engage in practical reasoning. So although the object of my commitment doesn't change as the time for action approaches, the propositional content I treat as true, the content of the assumption I make in having the intention to φ, does change as the time for the action approaches.[1] If the content of the assumption does not change, then I am failing to recognize and *keep track* of the commitment I made when I decided to φ. What then should be said about the content of the assumption when the prior intention evolves into an intention-in-action?

Suppose that we have a case in which although a subject starts φ-ing, from her perspective she has yet to start fulfilling her commitment to φ-ing. In such a case, although

---

[1] I am assuming here that the contents 'I will φ tomorrow' and 'I will today' are different propositional contents, even if 'today' and 'tomorrow' pick out the same date.

the subject is actually φ-ing, her φ-ing cannot be a manifestation of her *recognition* of her commitment to φ-ing. The subject isn't *remembering* to φ. So in such a case the subject's prior intention to φ has not evolved into an intention-in-action, for the prior intention to φ evolves into an intention-in-action only if the subject's φ-ing is a manifestation of her *recognition* of her commitment to φ-ing. When the subject's behaviour manifests her recognition of her commitment to φ-ing, she thereby knows why she is doing what she is doing, in so far as she is acting *in recognition* of that commitment. So if the subject's φ-ing is to be a manifestation of her recognition of the commitment she made when she made the decision to φ (i.e. if it is to be a manifestation of the mental state she acquired when she decided to φ), then the subject must think that she is φ-ing, or attempting to φ, when she is φ-ing. So at the point at which the subject's prior intention evolves into an intention-in-action, the subject stops assuming that she will start φ-ing and instead regards as true the proposition that she is φ-ing, or that she is attempting to φ.

But how should we understand the transition from the assumption 'I will start φ-ing' to acceptance of the proposition 'I am φ-ing' (or 'I am attempting to φ') as the prior intention evolves into an intention-in-action? Why does the subject stop assuming that she will start φ-ing? It isn't because the subject is no longer committed to φ-ing. So is it because the subject discovers that she has started φ-ing? Is it because she acquires a belief that she has started φ-ing that is grounded in some observational evidence she has acquired? Although one can discover via observational evidence that one is doing something that one committed oneself to doing, one can't discover via observational evidence that one is thereby manifesting one's recognition of that commitment. For if one's φ-ing really is a manifestation of one's own *recognition* of one's commitment to φ-ing, then one doesn't need to discover that this is so. So when a subject's prior intention to φ evolves into an intention-in-action, the subject regards as true the proposition that she is φ-ing (or that she is attempting to φ) and her doing so does not amount to a discovery that is grounded in observational evidence that she has acquired for the truth of the proposition that she has started φ-ing.

There is a further point we can add here. The intention-in-action obtains only if either there occurs the action that is its object, or there occurs an act that is an attempt to perform the action that is its object. If no such act occurs—if the agent doesn't even attempt to perform the intended action—then the intention-in-action does not obtain. If the agent doesn't attempt to perform the action, then either the prior intention, and not the intention-in-action, obtains (perhaps the subject has failed to keep track of the time) or neither the intention-in-action nor the prior intention obtains (perhaps the subject has changed her mind, or simply forgotten what she decided to do).[2]

If we accept that an intention-in-action cannot obtain if the agent doesn't even attempt to perform the relevant action, should we conclude that the intention-in-action is to be identified with the attempt to perform the action? A view along these lines is suggested by Searle. He proposes that an intention-in-action is to be identified with an

---

[2] See O'Shaughnessy 2008: 575–8.

experience of acting, and this experience of acting is to be identified with a trying. O'Shaughnessy (2008) objects to Searle's (1983) view with what I think are convincing arguments. O'Shaughnessy argues that intentions are states, whereas tryings are events. Intuitively, trying to φ (i.e. attempting to φ) is something an agent does, whereas an intention is a mental state of the subject. Furthermore, trying to φ can be the object of an intention, and in such a case it does not seem that one intends that one intend to φ. For example, one may decide to try to move a limb that is recovering from paralysis, uncertain that one will succeed in moving it, but hopeful that one will. One's attempt to move the limb will not succeed if one's limb does not move, so in that sense one's goal or aim in making the attempt is to move one's limb. But given that one was uncertain that one was able to move the limb, it could well be the case that one didn't decide that one *would* move the limb; rather, one decided to try to move the limb—one decided that now was the time to give it a go. Here the object of the mental state formed by that decision is one of attempting to move the limb. And the object of the state is not some further intention. Note too that when we talk of an agent trying hard to move a limb, or putting a great deal of effort into her attempt, although the content of the subject's intention may be directed onto an effortful attempt, it doesn't seem that we are saying that she was intending hard or with effort. Further evidence, one might think, that the trying is not to be identified with the agent's intention.

The conclusion we should draw here, I think, is that an intention-in-action is not to be identified with one's attempt to perform an action. The intention-in-action is a state, and one's attempt to perform the action is an occurrence. We should, rather, hold that the intention-in-action is an *occurrent state*. In this, an intention-in-action is unlike a prior intention. As I suggested in the previous chapter, when one decides to φ, the *prior* intention to φ that one thereby acquires can be a *dispositional* state that obtains when one isn't engaged in any kind of activity at all—e.g. during sleep. Whereas, in the case of intention-in-action we have a state whose obtaining requires the occurrence of some event—we have a state that only obtains while some occurrence manifests it, where that occurrence is its object or an attempt to perform the action that is its object. In recognizing that intention-in-action is an occurrent state we can note a certain kind of interdependence between the occurrence and state in question. A state of intention-in-action that is intentionally directed on one's φ-ing only obtains if there occurs an act that is a φ-ing, or an act that is an attempt to φ, where that act is an instance of the kind *acting in recognition of one's commitment to φ-ing*. And the occurrence of the φ-ing (or attempt at φ-ing) can only count as an instance of the kind *acting in recognition of one's commitment to φ-ing* if the state of intention-in-action obtains—a state which obtains only if the subject of the state regards as true the proposition 'I am φ-ing' (or 'I am attempting to φ').

The picture we then arrive at is the following. When one's φ-ing is a manifestation of the mental state one formed in deciding to φ one is in a state of intention-in-action, which is a state that can obtain only if (a) one is either φ-ing or attempting to φ, and (b) one regards as true the proposition that one is φ-ing (or that one is attempting to φ). So there are three components to keep in mind here: the state of intention-in-action, the action, and the acceptance of a present-tensed proposition that has an action as object. With this picture in mind, what conclusions can we draw about the epistemic role of the intention-in-action? In particular, what conclusions can we draw about the epistemic status of one's acceptance of the proposition that one is φ-ing?

The view I've outlined allows for the following possibility. One decides to φ, one attempts to φ but fails to φ, where this failed attempt at φ-ing is a manifestation of one's recognition of one's commitment to φ-ing, and during the attempt one thinks that one is φ-ing. So when one is in the state of intention-in-action, one's acceptance of the proposition that one is φ-ing can certainly fail to be knowledge, for it can be false. However, it doesn't follow from this that such an acceptance can never embody a form of knowledge. Suppose that an attempt at φ-ing that manifests one's recognition of one's commitment to φ-ing is successful. And suppose too that one's success is not accidental. One has the reliable ability to fulfil this kind of commitment and one has exercised that reliable ability on this occasion. Then it follows that one has a reliable ability to make true the proposition one accepts when fulfilling this commitment, and one has exercised that ability on this occasion. The concurrence of one's φ-ing and one's acceptance of the proposition that one is φ-ing is non-accidental. It is a reflection of one's reliable ability to fulfil this sort of commitment. Given that the concurrence of one's φ-ing and one's acceptance of the proposition that one is φ-ing is non-accidental, a case can be made for thinking that the intention-in-action thereby embodies a form of knowledge of the action it concerns. On this view, the state of intention-in-action is an occurrent state. When it embodies one's knowledge that one is φ-ing, one's φ-ing realizes one's knowledge of it.

It is often said that it is a mistake to think of oneself as merely the spectator of one's own actions, just as it is a mistake to think of one's intentions as merely predictions concerning what is going to happen. One's involvement in the action as its agent makes one more than a spectator and more than a predictor. This is a point stressed by, among others, David Velleman:

> What needs explaining in the case of practical self-awareness is that its crucial component seems to come without observation or inference. You do need to discover, or to have discovered in the past, what you're capable of doing. But among the many things that you're capable of doing, which one you're actually doing doesn't dawn on you as a further discovery. You don't find out what you're doing; in the normal case, you already know, because doing it was your idea to begin with. Your practical self-awareness therefore seems to constitute spontaneous knowledge, generated from within, not discovered from without. (1989a: 47)

The account I have proposed, on which intention-in-action can embody a form of self-knowledge, captures the intuitive thought that our knowledge of what we are doing is not usually a discovery, 'because doing it was our idea to begin with'. One's acceptance of the proposition that one is φ-ing, when one's φ-ing manifests one's recognition of one's commitment to φ-ing, is not grounded in observational evidence one possesses, and so in that sense one does not *discover* via observational evidence that one is φ-ing. However, I take this account to be consistent with the idea that perceptual experience can be a source of knowledge of what one is doing when one is performing an action; for there has been no suggestion that the sort of practical self-knowledge that an intention-in-action can embody is the only form of knowledge of one's action that one can have.[3] Moreover, although I have said that one's acceptance of a proposition about what one is doing when one is in the state of intention-in-action is not grounded in observational evidence, it can nonetheless be defeated by such evidence. When one acquires such defeating evidence, acceptance of the proposition 'I am now φ-ing' is undermined. So one's observational knowledge/evidence (including the evidence delivered by proprioception and kinaesthesia) is relevant to the epistemic status of one's acceptance of the proposition that one is φ-ing in so far as it can defeat acceptance of that proposition.

When one possesses observational evidence that undermines one's acceptance of the proposition that one is φ-ing, one ought not to accept the proposition that one is φ-ing. Should one then suspend judgement over what one is doing, and wait to find out? Recall that the state of intention-in-action cannot obtain without the occurrence of an event that is at least an attempt to perform the action, and what one is doing cannot be a manifestation of one's recognition of one's commitment to φ-ing unless one at least accepts the proposition that one is attempting to φ. So even if one possesses evidence that undermines an acceptance of the proposition that one is φ-ing, one is still entitled to accept the proposition that one is attempting to φ. It is always the case that the epistemic residue of this defeating evidence is knowledge that one is attempting to φ.[4]

To summarize, I have suggested that when one decides to do something, one commits oneself to doing that thing, and this commitment can be thought of as a form of self-binding. When one decides to do something, one is disposed to impose certain constraints on one's future conduct. One imposes the constraints on oneself by acting in recognition of them. One of the constraints one imposes on oneself is that of treating as true the proposition that one will φ when one engages in further practical deliberation. So the capacity to engage in the activities of practical deliberation and planning is central to the account, and this is something it has in common with Bratman's account of intention. However, although I introduced the account by focusing, as Bratman does, on the future-directed case, I have argued that the implications of the account have much in common with what Velleman says about the epistemic role of intention. For a consequence of this account is that when one's φ-ing manifests one's recognition of one's commitment to φ-ing, one accepts the proposition that one is φ-ing (or attempting to φ) and one's acceptance of this proposition can embody a form of practical knowledge of what one is doing.

---

[3] See Pickard 2004 and Roessler 2003 for further proposals about sources of our knowledge of our own actions.

[4] Note that this is not to commit to the claim that when one successfully φs, one's knowledge that one is φ-ing must be grounded in knowledge that one is trying/attempting to φ.

Recall that one problem that Velleman raises for Bratman's account is the frequency with which we form immediate intentions to act now without any prior planning for future conduct. The difficulty for Bratman's account, as he sees it, is to explain why we bother to form intentions when there is no opportunity for them to play the functional roles that Bratman specifies. This raises two questions for the account I have outlined. Firstly, if, when one decides to do something, one commits oneself to doing that thing, then why does one bother making *immediate* decisions do things now, as it seems we frequently do? We would perhaps have an answer to this question if it could be argued that such decisions can also provide us with this distinctive form of practical knowledge of what we are doing when we act. Making an immediate decision to act now would be a route to such self-knowledge. But then this leads to the second question, namely what might justify the claim that this form of practical self-knowledge can be attributed to a subject when there has been no prior deliberation or planning? What justifies the claim that a subject has committed herself to a particular course of action if there has been no opportunity for that commitment to be manifested in the subject's subsequent planning?

The answer to the second question, which thereby provides an answer to the first, is that, as I have argued, it is not just the subject's practical reasoning that can manifest her recognition of her commitment to φ-ing; for her φ-ing itself can manifest her recognition of that commitment. When a subject's φ-ing manifests her recognition of her commitment to φ-ing, the subject accepts the proposition that she is φ-ing (or attempting to φ). This acceptance is not grounded in observational evidence concerning what she is doing, and this acceptance can embody a form of practical knowledge of her action. So if we have a case where the subject has this form of knowledge of the action she is performing—a form of self-knowledge that involves the subject's acceptance of the proposition that she is φ-ing, where acceptance of the proposition is not grounded in observational evidence concerning what she is doing—then even if there is no deliberation and planning prior to the performance of the action, we still have reason to think that the other parts of the picture are in place. That is, the intention-in-action, and the prior, but immediate decision to now φ. However, we are still to regard this decision to φ as a case of the subject *committing herself* to φ-ing, as her φ-ing is a manifestation of her *recognition* of that commitment. So in forming the immediate decision to now φ, without any prior deliberation and planning, the agent is still exercising her capacity for self-determination. In which case, I suggest, although we can attribute this form of practical self-knowledge to a subject when she hasn't engaged in any prior deliberation or planning, we cannot attribute such self-knowledge to an agent who isn't capable of engaging in such prior deliberation and planning.

Note that no reason has been offered here for thinking that there cannot be action without a decision to perform the action. So no reason has been offered for thinking that there cannot be action without this form of self-knowledge. And as I mentioned earlier, I have not tried to suggest that the sort of practical self-knowledge that an intention-in-action can embody is the only form of knowledge of one's action that one can have. For all that has been said, there may be other forms of agential behaviour in which this form of self-knowledge is lacking. And in such cases there may well be other forms and sources of knowledge of the action available to the agent who is acting.

It should be emphasized that on the present proposal, the knowledge of one's action that is embodied in one's intention-in-action is only as specific as the content of the assumption one makes about what one is going to do when one decides to perform the action. The source of more detailed knowledge of what one is up to when acting must lie elsewhere. But having outlined at least *a variety* of practical self-knowledge—knowledge of one's own action that is embodied in an intention-in-action—I now want to consider the role and significance of this form of knowledge where the concern is with our knowledge of our own mental actions.

13.2 Intention-in-action and the epistemology of mental action

Let's first apply the above considerations to a very simple example of a case in which one decides to perform some mental act. One chooses to imagine an F, and one visualizes an F. In visualizing an F, one acts in recognition of a self-imposed constraint. One is thereby in a state of intention-in-action that involves regarding as true the proposition that one is imagining an F. This intention-in-action embodies a form of practical self-knowledge—knowledge that one is imagining an F.

I said that the knowledge of one's action that can be embodied in an intention-in-action is only as specific as the content of the assumption one makes about what one is going to do when one decides to act. The source of more detailed knowledge of what one is up to when acting must lie elsewhere. When one visualizes an F, there will typically be more detail in the act of imagining than is captured in the content of the assumption one makes about what one is going to do when one decides to imagine an F; and one is aware of this extra detail when visualizing. The practical self-knowledge that is embodied in one's intention-in-action does not explain this aspect of one's self-knowledge when visualizing, so what does?

An answer to this question lies in the account of perceptual imagination that I offered in Chapter 7. In that chapter I argued that acts of perceptual imagination involve the representation of experience. When one perceptually imagines an F, one is an occurrent mental state that represents an experience of an F. In particular, I argued that the phenomenal character of an episode of perceptual imagination determines the content of an occurrent mental state that represents the conscious character of an experience of an F. On the view I outlined, the obtaining of such an occurrent state is constitutively dependent on the occurrence of a phenomenally conscious episode. I also suggested that these episodes of perceptual imagination manifest one's knowledge of what it is like to experience objects, features, and events. So acts of perceptual imagination involve a form of self-knowledge—they involve one's knowledge of the conscious characters of one's experiences of objects, object-kinds, event-kinds, features, and relations. The conscious characters of these phenomenally conscious mental acts of imagining determine the content of the knowledge, and this is why this form of knowledge is only available to the phenomenally conscious.

The contents of these occurrent states, which are determined by the phenomenal characters of the episodes of imagining upon which they constitutively depend, can explain the respect in which one is aware of detail in one's visualizing when imagining an F—detail which is not captured in the content of the assumption one makes about what one is going to do when one decides to imagine an F. When one visualizes an F, one thereby manifests a mental state that represents what it is like to visually perceive an F. The extent to which there is detail in the phenomenal character of the act of visualizing is reflected in the content of the occurrent state of knowledge that obtains when it occurs—a state that represents what it is like to perceive an F.

But now given that this account of the ontology of perceptual imagination invokes a variety of self-knowledge—a variety of self-knowledge that can accommodate the respect in which one can be aware of detail in one's act of imagining that outstrips the content of a decision to imagine—one might think that the practical self-knowledge that is embodied in one's intention-in-action doesn't really add much that is of significance. One might think that it doesn't really provide one with much in the way of knowledge of what is going on in one's mind that one couldn't otherwise acquire—e.g. if, say, the act of visualizing an F had been a case of 'unbidden imagery'. That is, if there had been no decision to imagine an F, and an act of visualizing an F simply occurred unbidden, then arguably one would still know that one was imagining an F.

One response to this sort of downplaying of the significance of this kind of practical self-knowledge is the suggestion that an appeal to such practical self-knowledge can sometimes help explain how one can know whether one is imagining or recollecting something. Let us now explore that suggestion by focusing on a variety of perceptual recollection, namely episodic recollection. On the account of episodic recollection that I proposed in Chapter 7, the phenomenally conscious episode of recollecting a particular past occurrence should not be thought of as a kind of conscious judgement one makes about what happened in the past. The episode does manifest one's knowledge of a particular past event (namely knowledge of what it was like to perceive that past event), but the episode of recollecting is not itself an act of judging something about that past event, and, moreover, the occurrent state of knowledge that obtains when the episode of recollection occurs is also not itself an act of judging something about that past event. An act of episodic recollection can, however, ground judgements about what happened in the past. It can put one in a position to make warranted demonstrative judgements about past events. So what account should be given of this sort of epistemological role that acts of episodic recollection can play? Here I think we should appeal to a form of self-knowledge. An act of episodic recollection puts one in a position to make warranted judgements about the past when it is accompanied by knowledge *that one is recollecting*, as well as knowledge of what one is recollecting.

A kind of knowledge of *what* one is recollecting is embodied in the occurrent state of knowledge that obtains when the episode of recollection occurs. This is knowledge of what it was like to perceive a particular past event. In virtue of the occurrence of the episode of recollection there obtains an occurrent state of knowledge concerning what it was like to perceive that particular past event, and this occurrent state puts one in a position to make demonstrative judgements targeted on the particular event and individuals recollected. When one perceptually imagines an event, the act of perceptual imagination does not, in the same way, put one in a position to make demonstrative judgements about a particular past event. For the act of perceptual imagination does not manifest knowledge of what it *was* like to perceive a *particular* past event, rather it manifests knowledge of what it *is* like to perceive a certain *kind* of event. So when our concern is with providing an account of the epistemological role of episodic recollection, the following question is important. How does one know whether a given phenomenally conscious mental act manifests one's knowledge of what it was like to perceive a particular past event, or whether it simply manifests one's knowledge of what it *is* like to perceive an event of a given *kind*? When one episodically recollects a past event, one's knowledge that one is recollecting, and not simply imagining, plays an important role in grounding the knowledgeable judgements about the past that one makes on its basis. So what account should be given of this form of self-knowledge?

Appealing to the kind of practical self-knowledge that can be embodied in an intention-in-action can sometimes help provide a partial answer to this question. When one chooses to recollect some past event, or when one decides to recall what happened on some past occasion, if one can recollect the event, then in acting in recognition of that self-imposed constraint one is thereby in a state of intention-in-action that involves regarding as true the proposition that one is recollecting. This intention-in-action can embody a form of practical self-knowledge—knowledge that one is recollecting. This knowledge that one is recollecting, which accompanies the act of episodic recollection, can put one in a position to make warranted judgements about the past—in particular, demonstrative judgements about particular past occurrences and the individuals involved in them. This practical self-knowledge is not grounded in evidence, but it is rationally constrained by one's evidence. For example, one's acceptance of the proposition that one is recollecting can be undermined by counterevidence one may possess to the effect that no such event took place, or to the effect that one's memory on such matters is unreliable. If one's acceptance of the proposition that one is recollecting is undermined by such defeating evidence, then even if one does actually succeed in episodically recollecting a particular past event, and one is thereby in an occurrent state of knowledge that puts one in a position to demonstratively refer to that past event, one isn't in a position to make knowledgeable judgements about what happened in the past on the basis of that act of episodic recollection. But absent such defeating counterevidence, the practical self-knowledge embodied in an intention-in-action can play a role in an account of the epistemological role of episodic recollection.

This proposal about the epistemological role of episodic recollection rests on the idea that such acts can put one in a position to make warranted judgements about the past when accompanied by knowledge of what one is doing, and the suggestion I have made is that the practical self-knowledge that can be embodied in an intention-in-action can sometimes be appealed to in an account of one's knowledge of what one is doing when one knows that one is recollecting. However, no reason has been given for thinking that such phenomenally conscious mental acts cannot occur without a prior decision to recollect. So what should be said of one's epistemic state when an act of episodic recollection occurs 'unbidden'?

Compare the following two passages; in the first, William James describes the phenomenology of an intentional attempt to recollect, and in the second, Nabokov describes an episode of unbidden recollection:

Suppose we try to recall a forgotten name. The state of our consciousness is peculiar. There is a gap therein; but no mere gap. It is a gap that is intensely active. A sort of wraith of the name is in it, beckoning us in a given direction, making us at moments tingle with the sense of our closeness, and then letting us sink back without the longed-for term...Everyone must know the tantalizing effect of the blank rhythm of some forgotten verse, restlessly dancing in one's mind, striving to be filled out with words. (James 1890: 243–4)

In casual flash, for no reason at all, he recollected a way Olga had of lifting her left eyebrow when she looked at herself in the mirror. Do all people have that? A face, a phrase, a landscape, an air bubble from the past suddenly floating up as if released by the head warden's child from a cell in the brain while the mind is at work on some totally different matter? Something of the sort occurs just before falling asleep when what you think you are thinking is not at all what you think. Or two parallel passenger trains of thought, one overtaking the other. (Nabokov 1947: 179)

When an episodic recollection occurs unbidden ('an air bubble from the past suddenly floating up'), there is no attempt to recollect something, but a phenomenally conscious mental act nonetheless occurs, and in virtue of the occurrence of this mental act there obtains an occurrent state of knowledge of the phenomenal character of a perception of a particular past event. There is a sense in which the unbidden act of recollection offers a form of cognitive contact with the particular recollected, for in virtue of the occurrence of the episode of recollection there obtains an occurrent state of knowledge that puts one in a position to refer demonstratively to that particular. But one lacks practical self-knowledge of what it is that one is doing, at least initially, and perhaps only for a fraction of a second. So in such cases how does one know that the episode manifests one's knowledge of what it was like to perceive a particular past event, as opposed to manifesting merely one's knowledge of what it is like, or would be like, to perceive an event of a given kind?

This might be explained by the near-instantaneous occurrence of a certain kind of recognition of the event recollected. But if the act of recollection is not accompanied by this sort of recognition of the items recollected, the question of what one was doing might occur to one (was I recollecting or just imagining?). In attempting to answer the question, does one simply let one's mental activity continue and attend to what is going on? To quote James, this would be like trying to 'seize the spinning top to catch its motion', simultaneously adopting the attitude of both agent and observer of the mental act.[5] Attending more closely to the mental act is not a possible source of knowledge here. Furthermore, one cannot try to discover what one was doing by trying to do the same thing again. In order to attempt the same thing again, one will have to know already what it was that one was doing. One can intentionally recollect the content of the mental act, but this will not provide one with practical self-knowledge of whatever it was that one *was* doing. Rather, it provides one with practical self-knowledge concerning what one *is* doing, namely recollecting the content of one's prior mental act. This can provide one with a source of evidence about one's previous act of recollection. One can attempt to interpret that previous act and draw conclusions about what it was that one was doing. But in such a case, interpretation is ultimately the route to such knowledge.

Note too, that in the case described by James there is an *attempt* to recollect something, an attempt which *isn't* immediately successful, and which results in what James describes as a 'gap that is intensively active'. Arguably, in this sort of case the practical self-knowledge that is embodied in one's intention-in-action is simply knowledge that one is *attempting* to recollect. If and when one does succeed in recollecting, does one thereby have practical self-knowledge that one is recollecting? It could well be that one's knowledge that one is recollecting is, rather, explained by the near-instantaneous recognition of the items recollected. So we should be careful not to exaggerate the extent to which the practical self-knowledge that can be embodied in an intention-in-action can explain one's knowledge of whether one is recollecting or merely imagining in such cases. But once one knows that one was recollecting a past occurrence (no matter what the route to such self-knowledge may be), presumably one is then in a position to recollect intentionally that past occurrence at will. One thereby has a form of practical self-knowledge of what one is doing when subsequently recollecting—practical self-knowledge embodied in intention-in-action—and that practical self-knowledge can provide one with a distinctive form of warrant for one's judgements about the past that are based on those acts of episodic recollection.[6]

Let us now pause briefly to take stock of the suggestions that have so far been made about the explanatory role of the practical self-knowledge than can be embodied in

---

[5] William James (1890) makes the following remarks concerning the attempt to introspect the stream of one's conscious thoughts: 'If they are but flights to a conclusion, stopping them to look at them before the conclusion is reached is really annihilating them...The attempt at introspective analysis in these cases is in fact like seizing a spinning top to catch its motion, or trying to turn up the gas quickly enough to see how the darkness looks' (236–7).

[6] So, for instance, a sceptical argument targeted specifically at episodic recollection would have to challenge the idea that one really does know what one is doing when one takes oneself to be recollecting some past event. As such practical self-knowledge is not grounded in evidence, although rationally constrained by one's evidence, such an argument would have to take a rather different form from one targeted at perception as a source of knowledge.

intentions-in-action in cases of perceptual imagination and perceptual recollection. When one decides to imagine or recollect something and one acts in recognition of that self-imposed constraint, one has a form of practical self-knowledge of what one is doing that is embodied in the intention-in-action that thereby obtains. The content of this kind of practical self-knowledge is only as specific as the content of the assumption one makes about what one is going to do when one decides to imagine/recollect. The source of more detailed knowledge of what is going on as one imagines/recollects lies elsewhere. In particular, I have suggested that it lies in the content of an occurrent state that obtains when the act of perceptual imagination/recollection occurs, and the content of that state is determined by the phenomenal character of the episode of imagination/recollection.

The practical self-knowledge that can be embodied in an intention-in-action can have a significant explanatory role to play when it comes to accounting for how one knows of a given mental act whether it manifests one's knowledge of what it was like to perceive a particular past event, or whether it merely manifests one's knowledge of what it is like to perceive an event of a given kind—i.e. whether one is recollecting or merely imagining an event. I have acknowledged that acts of perceptual imagination and recollection can occur 'unbidden', in the absence of any decision to imagine/recollect; and when such acts occur unbidden they can still manifest a variety of self-knowledge—knowledge of what it is/was like to perceive something. I have also said that practical self-knowledge embodied in intention-in-action is not the only route to knowledge of whether a given mental act is an instance of perceptual recollection or perceptual imagination, for near-instantaneous recognition of the items recollected and self-interpretation are also possible routes to such self-knowledge. But the kind of practical self-knowledge that can be embodied in an intention-in-action standardly makes the route to self-knowledge which proceeds via self-interpretation unnecessary.

In a simple case of imagining (e.g. visualizing) an F, the fact that one has available to one a practical route to self-knowledge, which is made available to one through one's capacity to decide to imagine an F, may not seem especially significant. For in a case in which one is simply visualizing an F, the route to self-knowledge that proceeds via self-interpretation may well be quick and easy, and indeed near instantaneous. However, one's engagement in the activity of perceptual imagining can be far more complex than this simple example suggests. One's imaginative projects can be diverse and complicated—one can have all sorts of different aims, goals, and purposes in engaging in such mental behaviour over extended intervals of time. If your route to knowledge of what is going on in your own mental life in such cases were restricted to self-interpretation, then the achievement of self-knowledge would be a far more challenging task than it standardly is. For typically you have practical self-knowledge of what you are doing that is embodied in intention-in-action. Typically, you are apprised of much of what is going on in your mental life because it was your idea to begin with. Note too that the route to self-knowledge that proceeds via self-interpretation can itself involve practical self-knowledge embodied in intention-in-action. The activity of asking oneself questions about what is going on in one's own mental life and the activity of attempting to answer those questions can itself involve practical self-knowledge of one's aims and goals in asking and answering such questions—practical self-knowledge that is embodied in intention-in-action.

In this context it is also worth noting that the fact that one's knowledge of one's aims and goals in engaging in a given mental activity can be embodied in an intention-in-action is of relevance to the epistemology of another kind of mental activity that I discussed in Part I—namely the epistemology of the activity of introspecting one's perceptual experience. In Chapter 8 I argued that when one's visual experience is a successful perception of one's environment, in actively introspecting one's visual experience one is unavoidably engaged in the activity of looking at (and/or watching) items that one visually perceives. But when one is introspecting some visual experience one is undergoing, one is not *merely* looking at/watching something that one is visually aware of. I suggested that what distinguishes the introspective case lies, in part, in the distinctive *aim* of the activity one engages in when one introspects one's experience. One's aim in engaging in such activity isn't simply that of acquiring world-directed perceptual knowledge, for one's aim includes that of discovering something about the experience one is having. However, although the aim of one's introspective activity may differ from the aim of the activity one engages in when one is simply concerned to discover/discern something about the environment one perceives, the means one employs in order to achieve that aim are much the same. One looks at/watches entities one perceives. One maintains cognitive contact with them. We can now say that one's knowledge of one's distinctively introspective aim in engaging in such activity— one's knowledge that one is *introspecting* one's visual experience and not merely looking at/watching something—can be explained by appeal to the practical self-knowledge that can be embodied in intention-in-action. When one decides to introspect one's experience, one thereby has knowledge of what one is up to— knowledge that is embodied in one's intention-in-action.

In this section I have tried to make a case for thinking that the practical self-knowledge that can be embodied in intention-in-action can have a significant role to play in accounts of how we know what is going on in our own mental lives when we engage in various forms of mental activity. The account that I have offered of this form of self-knowledge accommodates the intuition that typically you are apprised of, and can make sense of, what is going on in your own active mental life in so far as engaging in that kind of mental activity was your idea to begin with. In the next section I want to explore further the kind of epistemic advantage that this form of self-knowledge affords us, by considering some of the claims O'Shaughnessy has made about the significance of the role of the 'mental will' in an account of the state of wakeful consciousness in the self-conscious subject.

13.3 States of consciousness, the 'mental will', and a hypothesis about dreams

As I outlined in Chapter 9, one of O'Shaughnessy's main aims in *Consciousness and the World* is to provide an analysis of the state of *wakeful* consciousness. According to O'Shaughnessy, we can mark distinctions between 'states of consciousness', and wakeful consciousness is the pre-eminent parent variety with which, for example, unconscious sleep and dreaming can be compared and contrasted. O'Shaughnessy argues that these other states of consciousness are to be characterized derivatively in terms of the state of wakeful consciousness. When one is in one of these other states of consciousness, one is deprived of certain functions that hang together in the fully awake. An important strand in O'Shaughnessy's analysis of the state of wakeful consciousness in the self-conscious is his attempt to articulate 'the contribution made to consciousness, not by the bodily will (for we can be fully conscious though supine in a hammock, and even if totally para-lysed), but by the mental will', which, O'Shaughnessy claims, 'cannot in the conscious be analogously incapacitated' (2000: 226).

O'Shaughnessy writes:

> Consciousness is a mental state that can exist when all occurrent interactive links to the environ-ment have been severed…Whereas one can stand in any old occurrent causal relation to one's surrounds and preserve the state of consciousness, we cannot extend a comparable license to the interior phenomena themselves. Decisive constraints operate within…that is to say the stream of consciousness of the conscious is both distinctive and inimitable. (2000: 213)

The thought here is that it is in principle possible for one to be conscious—i.e. awake—even in a situation in which (a) one doesn't successfully perceive one's environment and (b) one is incapable of performing any bodily actions. O'Shaughnessy argues that the fact that one is awake in such a situation cannot simply reside in the fact that one is the subject of conscious mental events, for the occurrence of conscious mental events in one's 'stream of consciousness' is consistent with one's being asleep and dreaming. This leads O'Shaughnessy to suggest that a 'special inner life is necessary for consciousness, one involving specific modes of thought, feeling and imagination' (2000: 212), and he attempts to identify and articulate its distinctive character. According to O'Shaughnessy, the 'operation of the men-tal will' plays a crucial role in explaining the way in which 'the stream of consciousness of the conscious is both distinctive and inimitable' (2000: 213)—the way in which, for exam-ple, the progression of thought and imagination in the awake, self-conscious subject has a distinctive, inimitable nature, which isn't instantiated when one dreams. So mental action plays a crucial role in O'Shaughnessy's account of the state of wakeful consciousness in the self-conscious subject. O'Shaughnessy suggests that with the imposition of what he calls a 'will freeze' upon one's conscious mental life, 'one cannot but replace the prevailing state of consciousness, waking, with another state of consciousness, perhaps sleep' (2000: 229).

My aim here isn't to assess the analysis that O'Shaughnessy offers of the state of wake-ful consciousness in the self-conscious subject, and I shall be avoiding committing to claims about the necessary constituents of that state. My more modest aim is simply to highlight, and draw on, what I think are some important insights in O'Shaughnessy's treatment of these issues. In particular, I want to focus on some remarks that O'Shaughnessy makes about a link that he sees between mental agency, a variety of self-knowledge, and the role that this variety of self-knowledge can play in our conscious mental lives when we are awake. In doing so I shall be drawing on and applying the account I have proposed of the practical self-knowledge that can be embodied in intention-in-action.

For O'Shaughnessy, the significance of mental agency to his account of consciousness in the self-conscious subject depends, in part, on the link he sees between 'operations of the mental will' and the form of self-knowledge and rationality of state that he claims is distinctive of waking consciousness. His view is that in the awake, self-conscious subject, the progression across time of the stream of conscious thought and imagination is distinctive, and the respect in which it is distinctive is connected with a variety of self-knowledge that accompanies it, where the relevant form of self-knowledge is linked with the idea that the 'mental will' is operative.

According to O'Shaughnessy, what makes the progression of one's conscious thought and imagination distinctive when one is awake is a respect in which the advance of one's thinking and imagining is not 'opaque' to one. When one is awake, the progression of one's thinking and imagining has a certain kind of 'explanatorial pellucidity', and according to O'Shaughnessy, it is the 'mental will' that imports 'internal intelligibility' and 'pellucidity' into the processive advance of the stream of one's conscious thought and imagination (2000: 226). O'Shaughnessy argues that in the mind of the awake, self-conscious subject there is a certain type of rationale governing the progression of the stream of their conscious thought and imagination. A certain kind of explanatory principle is at work—one that depends on an appeal to the agential mental activity of a self-conscious agent. The direction taken by a train of thought, or imagination, has, in the self-conscious subject who is fully conscious, a causal and rational explanation that is, at least in part, *agential*, and this is what makes the rationale of the progression, from moment to moment, openly accessible to that agent. The awake, self-conscious subject is able to make sense of what is happening in this domain of her mental life in so far as she is able to make sense of what she is up to, and the variety of self-knowledge involved here is importantly linked with the idea that the perspective she has on this aspect of her mental life is that of its agent. He claims that,

Only a mind steering its own cognitive path through a wider cognitive scene, a self-causing which is furthered by rational steps, can introduce pellucidity into the flow of experience. (2000: 227)

O'Shaughnessy is not claiming that each conscious thought of a fully awake, self-conscious subject is one that the subject intends to think. (The future is not 'already prefigured, so to say coiled up like a carpet in the subject's mind, merely awaiting the signal to unroll' (2000: 220).) In saying that such a subject takes active charge of her own thoughts and attendings, O'Shaughnessy remarks, 'I do not mean actively determines their *content*, which would be at once omnipotent, barren, self-refuting and logically impossible' (2000: 89). Rather, the subject 'selects the direction of their movement, which is to say the content of the governing enterprise' (2000: 89).

When one is awake one is 'master in one's own mental house'–a fact which is in no serious conflict with the unceasing spontaneity of thought, the continuing unanticipatedness of one's next thought. After all, to be a master in one's own mental house is not the same thing as being a tyrant!" (O'Shaughnessy 2000: 201)

So, despite the fact that many conscious mental occurrences in the conscious are not chosen, the flow of conscious thought and imagination is nonetheless 'active as a whole' (2000: 200).

Even in the case of what one might think of as a prime example of directed thinking––ratiocination––the causal explanation of the direction taken by the progression of thought is, according to O'Shaughnessy, only *in part* agential:

Ratiocinative exploratory thought shares this much with fishing, that one is in either case dependent upon whether anything of value lies within a given region and on whether any such item is accessible. In each case one engages in an activity in the hope that a desired entity 'surface' to cap one's efforts, something which is to this degree determined in advance: that it is singled out from the start under a definite description which unites the specificity of some desirable trait with an openness as to realization, in such a way as to leave scope for the unknown. (2000: 221)

O'Shaughnessy suggests that the intentions involved when one is engaged in such activity—ratiocination—'stir one's mental machinery' and constrain, 'under definite description', the advance of one's thinking. The account that I have offered of the practical self-knowledge that can be embodied in intention-in-action can explain the respect in which such intentions can provide one with a form of knowledge, under some description, of the mental activity one is engaged in; and while this sort of practical self-knowledge does not exhaustively account for one's knowledge of each conscious thought and its content, it can play a significant role in accommodating a respect in which the occurrence of such conscious thoughts makes sense to one given one's knowledge of one's aims and goals in engaging in such activity.

But what of the idle drift of thought involved in a daydream, when one is awake? O'Shaughnessy claims that one cannot intend to daydream—he says 'the process cannot be intentional under "daydream"', and adds, 'Mostly one slips into the state and discovers oneself adrift in the process a little later' (2000: 218). As he puts it, one cannot daydream with 'grit' and 'determination', and a certain frame of mind is required if daydreams are to occur. ('It is difficult to daydream with anxiety' 2000: 218.) Nonetheless, he claims, 'The mind remains intentionally active under headings at each point in that process' (2000: 217).

O'Shaughnessy compares the unfolding of a daydream to 'a young child wandering slowly across a field, his mind and its intentions drifting almost like a raft at the mercy of stray currents' (2000: 217–18). In daydreams, as opposed to ratiocination, 'Intention is continually giving way to successor intention...without realizing any single comprehensive intention...The connective tissue of these rapidly changing intentions is mere association and inclination' (2000: 217). Lacking an overarching goal and commitment one is aiming to fulfil, one is thereby deprived of a degree of self-knowledge when daydreaming. But on O'Shaughnessy's view, agency is nonetheless implicated in this activity.

At each point behind the scene lies an intention and its expression in the will. That causally active intention is at that very moment determining the next stage of the process, and so playing an explanatory role in relation to the advance of that process. And that is to say, that the subject himself is 'behind' it all. (2000: 224)

Thought of in this way, we might say that in the case of daydreaming, one imposes constraints on ensuing mental activity in a relatively unconstrained manner. But if O'Shaughnessy is right in his characterization of this activity, there is nonetheless a *degree* of practical self-knowledge here, and again, we can explain the degree to which there is such practical self-knowledge by appealing to the obtaining of a sequence of rapidly successive intentions-in-action that are connected by 'mere inclination and association'.

For O'Shaughnessy, the fact that a degree of agency is implicated in daydreaming is what accounts for the difference between daydreaming and dreaming. He observes that there may be a spectrum of cases falling between daydream and dream, giving as an example what he calls 'pre-sleep phantasy (that from which one sometimes "awakes" with a start!)' (2000: 218).

When this phase of the inner life looms up, the intentions have all but petered out, the objects of phantasy have acquired something of a life of their own, and it is less than clear why one imagined item gives way to its successor. (2000: 218)

O'Shaughnessy suggests that as one's capacity to exercise one's mental will deteriorates, so consciousness fades. He suggests that 'the lessening sway of intention and generally of active self-command within one's own mind' goes with a 'diminution of self-understanding', and the loss of this kind of 'internal intelligibility' is accompanied by a loss of consciousness. As he puts it, 'consciousness and transparency of rationale keep close company' (2000: 218). In the case of dreams (at least, in the case of those dreams that are not lucid), there is no rationale to the flow of the dream's progression that is accessible to the subject. The flow of experience does not have the 'pellucidity' that warrants rational, agential causal explanation—which is not to say that there is no *mental* causal explanation (e.g. memory is implicated).

Dreaming precisely is the stream of consciousness when the guiding hands are taken off the reins controlling that phenomenon...Lacking the active control of a governing mind, the dream is a pure work of Nature. It is a kind of mental flower, and in any case no sort of intentional psychic artefact. (2008: 30)

It seems to be part of O'Shaughnessy's proposal that when one is asleep and dreaming, it is not just that one isn't *actually engaging* in agential mental activity, one is also *deprived* (albeit temporarily) of the *ability to exercise* one's mental agency. This is a distinction that is important to mark, for those concerned to identify the necessary conditions of the state of wakeful consciousness in the self-conscious might argue that it is the *incapacitation* of one's mental will, rather than one's failure to exercise it, that truly marks the onset of sleep and the loss of consciousness—thereby allowing that there might be at least intervals of time during which agency isn't actually exercised in one's thinking, but during which one is nonetheless awake. This would potentially allow for a somewhat different characterization of daydreaming and the idle drift of thought. For example, it could be suggested that when one is in a daze and daydreaming, the guiding reigns of one's mental agency are requisitioned only at the point at which one '*discovers* oneself adrift in the process'. At that point, one begins to direct one's thinking and attain, once again, practical self-knowledge of one's mental behaviour—practical self-knowledge embodied in intentions-in-action. But to take this line would be consistent with accepting much of what O'Shaughnessy has to say about dreams—the suggestion that when one is dreaming, one's 'mental will' is incapacitated, and the suggestion that this deficit entails that an important avenue to self-knowledge is closed to one, an avenue to self-knowledge that only reopens when one wakes up.

One's assessment of a proposal about a respect in which we lack self-knowledge when dreaming will presumably turn, at least in part, on the stance one takes on the following two key issues: (a) the account that should be given of the kinds of conscious events that occur when we dream; and (b) the account that should be given of what we believe is happening when we dream. So, for example, under (a), when one dreams that one is in pain, does one actually experience a painful sensation? Is one really in pain? Or does one *merely* dream that one experiences such a sensation—does one *merely* dream that one is in pain? And if the latter, then is the mere dreaming of a sensation of pain to be understood as an act of imagining a sensation of pain—an act that manifests one's knowledge of what it is like to experience such a sensation? Likewise for other cases in which one dreams that one perceives something. Does one actually undergo a perceptual experience of the relevant kind—a hallucinatory experience—or does one merely imagine having such an experience?

Under (b): when one dreams that one experiences a sensation of pain, does one believe that one is experiencing a painful sensation, or does one merely dream that one believes that one is experiencing a painful sensation? Does one merely imagine that one believes that one is undergoing a sensation of pain? And when one dreams that one notices, judges, decides etc., does one actually notice, judge, decide, or does one merely dream that one does—where this is a matter of imagining noticing, judging, deciding etc.? On this latter point, Sosa argues that from the fact that things happen *in* one's dream it doesn't follow that they happen *while* one dreams, so even when in a dream one makes a conscious decision to do something one need not do so in actuality. Nor does one necessarily consciously affirm in reality what one consciously affirms in a dream.

Establishing what stance should be taken on these issues—(a) and (b)—is far from straightforward, for there are obvious difficulties associated with speculating, from a first-person point of view, about the extent of one's ignorance when dreaming. However, as a way of developing O'Shaughnessy's proposal I want to introduce a specific hypothesis about dreams in the hope that consideration of this hypothesis can help highlight some significant aspects of the role played in our conscious mental lives by practical self-knowledge of the sort embodied in intention-in-action.

The hypothesis I want to consider is the following. The conscious mental episodes that occur when we dream are acts of imagining. When one dreams, one lacks knowledge that these conscious mental events are acts of imagining. And the fact that one is ignorant that these conscious mental events are acts of imagining is to be explained by the fact that when one is asleep the following avenue to self-knowledge is closed to one: practical self-knowledge that is embodied in intention-in-action.

First, some clarificatory points about this hypothesis are in order. According to this hypothesis, when one dreams, one does not actually undergo conscious perceptual experiences that might tether the direction taken by one's thinking and imagining. Dreamt perceptual experiences are imagined perceptual experiences. They are episodes of perceptual imagination that manifest one's knowledge of what is (would be) like to have such experiences. Sosa (2007: chapter 1) suggests that the 'orthodox view' that dream states and waking states are intrinsically alike, and different only in their causes and effects, is 'deeply flawed'. He suggests that 'to dream is to imagine, not to hallucinate', and that dream states and waking states are 'constitutively different'. However, given that one can imagine various things when one is awake, the claim that 'to dream is to imagine' does not in itself explain the respect in which dream states are 'constitutively different' from waking states. This is where O'Shaughnessy's additional proposal can potentially play a significant explanatory role. O'Shaughnessy notes that one might be tempted to reject his proposal that the stream of consciousness in the awake, self-conscious subject is 'distinctive and inimitable' for the following reason. Given that one can dream that one is awake, one can presumably reproduce during sleep the contents of one's waking experiences. In response, he claims:

> Reproducing the *contents* of waking experience cannot reproduce the *causal rationale* of waking experience. And in fact not only is the rationale different, it is of a wholly different order . . . the flow of experience must be a radically different kind of phenomenon in the two cases. (2000: 214)

So O'Shaughnessy's proposal makes available the following line of thought. The conscious events that occur when one dreams are episodes of imagining, and events of this kind—imagining—can occur when one is awake. But when one is awake and imagining, there is a 'causal rationale' to the progression of one's imagining that is absent when one dreams.

For O'Shaughnessy, the kind of 'causal rationale' to one's imagining that is present when one is awake and absent when one dreams has to do with the role of mental agency in one's imagining when awake, and the kind of self-knowledge and self-understanding that he thinks accompanies the exercise of one's mental agency. The specific hypothesis about dreaming that I want to consider is that when one is asleep and dreaming, one lacks practical self-knowledge of a kind that can be embodied in intention-in-action. In particular, the hypothesis is that one lacks this form of self-knowledge because that avenue to self-knowledge is not *available* to you when you are dreaming. It has been knocked out. It's not just that you are failing to exercise your capacity to have this form of self-knowledge. The state, or condition, you are in is such that you are *unable* to exercise that capacity. Note that this hypothesis doesn't speak to the question of whether there might be *some* form of mental agency that can be exercised when one dreams, for it doesn't speak to the question of whether there are forms of mental agency that can be exercised in the absence of practical self-knowledge embodied in intention-in-action. Note too that this hypothesis doesn't commit one to the idea that some form of mental agency must always be exercised in one's acts of imagining when one is awake. For it simply commits one to the idea that an avenue to self-knowledge—practical self-knowledge embodied in intention-in-action—is *available* to one when awake, and *unavailable* to one when dreaming.

So according to this hypothesis, when you are dreaming—when you are in that state/condition—you are not in a position to make any decisions about the course of your thinking or imagining—not even decisions about the general direction the course of your thinking should take. When you are dreaming, any putative candidate for making a decision of any kind—whether or not that decision concerns the course of your thinking—is a case of *imagining* making that decision, where the occurrence of this imagining is itself an unbidden act of imagining that is not accompanied by any practical self-knowledge of a kind that can be embodied in intention-in-action.

Now let's consider this hypothesis in more detail. According to it, when one dreams, the fact that one is ignorant that one's conscious mental events are episodes of imagining is to be explained by the fact that the following avenue to self-knowledge is closed to one: practical self-knowledge that is embodied in intention-in-action. How might this explanation proceed? I have argued that when one decides to do something, one imposes constraints on oneself by acting *in recognition* of those self-imposed constraints. If one is unable to exercise one's capacity to make decisions, one cannot impose such constraints on the course taken by one's thinking and imagining. According to our hypothesis, when one is dreaming, one's condition is such that one cannot impose such constraints on one's own mental life, so it follows that when one is in this condition, one cannot act in recognition of the imposition of such constraints—for such behaviour would *constitute* imposing such constraints on oneself. In such a state, one might *imagine* imposing such constraints on oneself, but such imagining is not equivalent to acting in recognition of a self-imposed constraint. So now let us assume that when you are in this condition (dreaming) you cannot act in a way that manifests your recognition of constraints that you have imposed over your own mental life. You cannot engage in mental behaviour that amounts to treating yourself as a source of constraints over your own mental life.

If you are in such a condition, can you act in a way that manifests your recognition that an act of *imagining* deciding to φ is a *mere* imagining and not an instance of deciding to φ? Arguably, you cannot. For if you cannot engage in mental behaviour that amounts to treating yourself as a source of constraints over your own thinking and imagining, then you cannot act in a way that manifests your recognition of what constraints you have imposed on yourself and what constraints you haven't imposed on yourself. So you cannot act in a way that manifests your recognition that you haven't decided to φ. You therefore cannot act in a way that manifests your recognition that the act of imagining deciding to φ is mere imagining. You cannot engage in mental behaviour that amounts to treating that occurrence as a mere imagining—a departure from reality.

The more general conclusion we can draw here is the following. When you are in this condition, you are unable to exercise your capacity to engage in mental behaviour that manifests your recognition of the distinction between those constraints on your think-ing that are self-imposed, and those constraints on your thinking that are imposed by facts whose obtaining you acknowledge. You are thereby debilitated from exercising your capacity to act in a way that manifests your recognition of the distinction between what is and isn't imagined. So when you are in such a condition, not only can you not stop yourself from imagining, you are also not in a position to act in a way that manifests your recognition that these occurrences are mere imaginings. So this is unlike the situa-tion in which you daydream. When you daydream, you can at least 'discover yourself adrift in the process' and recognize that you are imagining; but when you are dreaming, this route to self-knowledge through self-interpretation is lost. If you are genuinely unable to impose constraints on your own thinking and imagining by acting in recogni-tion of them, any putative act of discovering that you are merely imagining, or merely dreaming, would itself be an act of imagining that discovery.[7]

In summary, the suggestion is that in being unable to exercise your capacity to impose constraints over your own thinking and imagining, you are thereby unable to exercise your capacity to engage in mental behaviour that manifests your recognition of the dis-tinction between those constraints on your thinking and imagining that are self-imposed and those constraints on your thinking and imagining that are imposed by facts whose obtaining you acknowledge. You are thereby unable to exercise your capacity to treat certain mental occurrences as mere imaginings, and thereby recognize them as depar-tures from reality. In consequence, this breakdown in your mental autonomy is accom-panied by an inability to exercise your capacity to act in a way that manifests your recognition of the distinction between the real and the imagined—i.e. the distinction between what is and what isn't imagined. So there is a respect in which the distinction between the real and the imagined is lost to you.

So does this mean that when one is in such a condition one believes that the imag-ined is real? If a subject's condition is such that she is unable to exercise her capacity to

---

[7] So-called 'lucid dreams' may then fall somewhere within the spectrum of cases that lie between dream and daydream.

manifest her recognition of the distinction between what is and isn't imagined, then we have no reason to attribute to that subject the belief that she is imagining. But for the same reason we also seem to have no reason to attribute to that subject the belief that she *isn't* imagining. If the subject's behaviour doesn't manifest her recognition of the distinction, and *cannot* manifest her recognition of the distinction, then it's not clear what would warrant the attribution of such a belief.

If this hypothesis about dreaming were correct, then we could, I think, also reach a further conclusion about dreams—one which points to a peculiar feature of the way in which time is represented in dreams. According to the hypothesis, when you dream that you perceive an event, you are not actually undergoing a perceptual experience as of an event of that kind. Rather, you are perceptually imagining an event of that kind. Applying the account of perceptual imagination that I argued for in Part I, we reach the conclusion that when you dream that a certain kind of event is happening, there occurs an episode of imagining that manifests a mental state that represents what it is (would be) like to experience that kind of event. When the episode of imagining occurs, there obtains an occurrent state that represents the conscious character of an experience of that kind of event. In Chapter 7, I argued that when one perceptually imagines an event, one thereby *represents* a temporal perspective on that event—the temporal perspective of an experience that presents each temporal part of the event as temporally present. But one needn't be thereby representing the imagined event as occurring at the time of the act of imagining. One could be imagining a future event. And when one is imagining a future event, one is not thereby imagining that one's act of imagining is occurring in the future. So if dreamt events are imagined events, then we have no reason to think that these imagined events are represented as occurring at the time of the act of imagining, any more than we have reason to think that these imagined events are represented as happening egocentrically from one's actual spatial location—e.g. from the actual spatial location that one occupies in one's bedroom when dreaming. So when in one's dream one imagines referring to the imagined event as happening 'now', one does not *thereby* refer to the time of one's imagining.

When one dreams, is one in a position to use the indexical 'now' to pick out the time of one's imagining? This would appear to require having a grip on a distinction between the temporal location of one's act of imagining and the temporal location represented in one's act of imagining. I have argued that if the hypothesis about dreaming is correct, then when one dreams one is unable to exercise one's capacity to treat certain mental occurrences as mere imaginings, and thereby recognize them as departures from reality. This suggests that when one dreams, one won't have a grip on a distinction between the temporal location of one's act of imagining and the temporal location represented in one's act of imagining; which in turn suggests that when one dreams, one isn't in a position to pick out the temporal location of one's dream using the indexical 'now'. When one dreams, there is a respect in which one is cut off from the present. Although one can imagine referring to the present, one cannot actually refer to the present as such.

In this section I have been drawing on some claims that O'Shaughnessy makes about a link that he sees between mental agency, a variety of self-knowledge, and the role that this variety of self-knowledge plays in the state of wakeful consciousness in the self-conscious subject. This led to a hypothesis about dreams—the suggestion that when one dreams the following avenue to self-knowledge is closed to one: practical self-knowledge that is embodied in intention-in-action. I have not tried to establish that this hypothesis about dreams is correct, and I have avoided committing to claims about the necessary ingredients of the state of wakeful consciousness in the self-conscious. However, I want to suggest that working through the consequences of this hypothesis about dreams can help to highlight some significant aspects of the role that can be played in our conscious mental lives by practical self-knowledge embodied in intention-in-action.

This variety of self-knowledge is not equivalent to knowledge of one's standing attitudes—e.g. knowledge of one's beliefs, desires, and intentions. It is plausible to hold that one's knowledge of one's standing attitudes can be retained during sleep, whether or not one is dreaming. This variety of self-knowledge is also not equivalent to the mere awareness of the occurrence of conscious mental events in the stream of one's conscious thought and imagination. According to the hypothesis about dreams, when one dreams, there is a sense in which one is aware of the occurrence of the conscious mental events that make up one's dream despite the fact that one lacks this form of practical self-knowledge, and there doesn't appear to be anything incoherent in that suggestion. The variety of self-knowledge in question provides one with a way of knowing what one is doing, under some description, when engaged in mental activity. And I have suggested that this avenue to self-knowledge comes with the capacity to impose constraints over one's own mental life by acting in recognition of them.

Through considering the hypothesis about dreams, I have tried to identify a connection between (a) exercising one's capacity to impose such constraints over one's own thinking and imagining (e.g. the general direction taken by one's thinking and imagining), and (b) exercising one's capacity to engage in mental behaviour that manifests one's recognition of the distinction between those constraints on one's thinking and imagining that are *self*-imposed, and those that are imposed by facts whose obtaining one acknowledges. I have suggested that given this link, a breakdown in this form of mental autonomy may debilitate one's capacity to act in a way that manifests one's recognition of what is and isn't imagined. This suggests that the availability of this avenue of self-knowledge may play a very central and significant role in the ordinary, awake, conscious mental life of a self-conscious subject.

In light of this discussion, in the next chapter I shall turn to more general concerns about the place and role of mental agency in an account of conscious thinking, which will lead to a reconsideration of the place of mental action in the metaphysics of mind.

14

Reconsidering the Place of Mental Action in the Metaphysics of Mind

In this chapter I shall be drawing together some of the lines of thought I have been developing over the previous five chapters with the aim of reconsidering the question of the place and role of mental action in an account of conscious thinking—and, more generally, the place of mental action in the metaphysics of mind. I shall be suggesting that mental action has an essential role to play in an account of issues in the epistemology of mind that are central to our understanding of the sort of conscious thinking that we, as self-conscious subjects, can engage in. I shall also be suggesting that in order to accommodate adequately these connections between mental action, the epistemology of mind, and conscious thinking, we need the right account of the ontology of conscious thinking, and that the right account of the ontology of conscious thinking should lead us to reject what often appears to be an implicit assumption in many of the standard current approaches to mind—the assumption that we can conceive of mental actions as reducible to mental processes (perhaps transitions between mental states) that enable and explain overt *bodily* action.

A key element in the proposal I shall be making is the position taken on the following question: should we adopt what I earlier called an 'ingredients' approach to mental action? I start by addressing that issue.

14.1 The place and role of mental agency in an account of conscious thinking

I characterized the 'ingredients' approach to action in the following way: in addressing the 'agent–mind' problem—the question of how the workings of the mind relate to the activity of an agent—we should be seeking to identify ingredients of action that are not themselves agential, but whose appropriate combination can yield something agential. In the case of bodily action, the typical ingredients appealed to, under this approach, are an appropriate combination of belief, desire, intention, bodily movement, and the relation of causation.

An assumption behind this approach is that in the case of bodily action we should be able to cite, as an ingredient of action, bodily behaviour that is, in itself, non-agential. The assumption is that there is a variety of bodily behaviour that we cite that can have both agential and non-agential instances—bodily behaviour of a kind that is a common factor to bodily action and a non-agential bodily occurrence that merely happens to its subject. This assumption is related to the idea that there is a question of Wittgensteinian arithmetic that we can address in the case of bodily action. Wittgenstein asked, 'What is left over if I subtract the fact that my arm goes up from the fact that I raise my arm?' (1953: section 621). The formula for applying the question more generally is to identify, in any given case of bodily action, an instance of non-agential, mere bodily behaviour, subtract that, and then identify the further ingredients that together make that instance of bodily behaviour a bodily action. According to one influential approach, when it comes to specifying what it is that makes such bodily behaviour a bodily action, we should be looking to the appropriate antecedent causes of that bodily behaviour.

In order to apply this approach to the case of mental action we would need to cite the mental equivalent of mere bodily behaviour. We would need to cite mere mental behaviour that is, in itself, non-agential—a variety of mental behaviour that can have both agential and non-agential instances; mental behaviour of a kind that is a common factor to mental action and a non-agential mental occurrence that merely happens to its subject. If we were then to adopt the causal approach to action that I just mentioned, in order to specify what it is that makes a given instance of that mental behaviour a mental action, we would need to look to the antecedent causes of that mental behaviour. This approach makes the following assumption appear reasonable: in the case of any given mental action, it is in principle possible for there to occur the same kind of conscious mental events but in the absence of the kind of initiating causes that make such mental behaviour a mental action; this, in turn, suggests that conscious thinking of the same basic kind could occur and yet be non-agential.

We should, I think, accept that there are conscious mental events of a kind that can be common to a mental action and a mere mental occurrence that isn't agential. To give just one example, I have suggested that there are acts of perceptual imagination and recollection that fit this description. However, I think we should resist the more general claim that in the case of *any* given mental action the following is true: conscious thinking of the same basic kind could occur and yet be non-agential. Some reasons for resisting the more general claim have already been given. In Chapter 11 I argued that the agency that is implicated in suppositional reasoning and self-critical reflection does not simply reside in the prior causal history of such reasoning—i.e. in the fact that some appropriate, temporally prior, intention or belief/desire pair initiated it. According to the account I proposed, when a subject engages in such reasoning, that subject imposes a constraint on her reasoning *by* reasoning in recognition of that constraint. Agency is implicated in the conscious mental events that constitute a subject's suppositional reasoning and self-critical reflection, in so far as such events manifest the subject's recognition of a self-imposed constraint. The constraint that the subject imposes on her reasoning is *sustained* by the occurrence of conscious mental events that constitute her reasoning and that manifest her recognition of that self-imposed constraint. When one engages in this kind of conscious reasoning, an aspect of oneself is presented under reflexive guise as that which determines the activity by engaging in it—that which is imposing a constraint on the reasoning by reasoning in recognition of that constraint. The conscious reasoning one engages in manifests an attitude towards oneself—an attitude of treating oneself as the source of that activity. Acting as if one has imposed a constraint on oneself, one thereby imposes the constraint on oneself. So the forms of conscious reasoning involved in suppositional reasoning and self-critical reflection are *necessarily* self-conscious and self-determined.

I also argued in Chapter 12 that when it comes to an understanding of the role of agency in making decisions and engaging in practical deliberation, it is a mistake simply to look to the distinctive antecedent causes of decisions and the distinctive antecedent causes of the mental events that constitute the activity of practical deliberation. According to the account I proposed, a decision to act is a self-determining psychological act that is itself self-determined, but we shouldn't simply look to the psychological causes of the act of deciding in order to account for the respect in which it is self-determined. For the respect in which one's decision to act is self-determined is to be accounted for in terms of the self-determined behaviour that one is disposed to engage in once one has decided to act. And this is behaviour that one engages in after the act of deciding. Mental agency is implicated in the *obtaining* of the kind of mental state one forms when one decides to do something. When one decides on some future course of action, one is in a mental state that implicates the capacity to engage in self-conscious, self-determined mental activity. One is disposed to remember to act in recognition of the commitment one made in making that decision, and this includes being disposed to engage in further practical deliberation and planning that is both self-conscious and self-determined. So this account of decision-making and practical deliberation crucially depends on an appeal to a variety of conscious thinking that is necessarily self-conscious and self-determined—a variety of conscious thinking that is to be characterized, at least in part, as mental behaviour that manifests recognition of a self-imposed constraint.

The general point here is the following. There is a variety of self-knowledge and a form of mental agency that *necessarily* accompany one another; and the obtaining of this variety of self-knowledge has an essential role to play in an account of certain forms of conscious thinking. This is why it is a mistake to think that in the case of *any* mental action, the following is true: conscious thinking of the same basic kind could occur and yet be non-agential.

Certain ontological considerations are relevant to understanding why this is so. In the previous chapter I focused on the kind of self-knowledge that can be embodied in intention-in-action. I argued that intention-in-action is an *occurrent* state. This is a state whose obtaining *constitutively* depends on the occurrence of a certain kind of event/activity. There is a certain kind of interdependence between the state and event/activity in question. The state of intention-in-action obtains only if there occurs an event/

activity of the kind *acting in recognition of a commitment*, and the event/activity in question counts as an instance of that kind only if the state of intention-in-action obtains when it occurs. So the variety of self-knowledge that can be embodied in intention-in-action obtains only when there occurs an event/activity in which a form of agency is exercised. This is why this variety of self-knowledge and a form of mental agency *necessarily* accompany one another when a state of intention-in-action is directed on mental activity.

This distinctive kind of self-knowledge plays a crucial role in various forms of conscious thinking—e.g. suppositional reasoning, self-critical reasoning, and practical deliberation. Moreover, at the end of the previous chapter I suggested that the availability of this avenue to self-knowledge may play a very central and significant role in the ordinary, awake, conscious mental life of a self-conscious subject. I argued that there is a connection between (a) the availability of this avenue to self-knowledge and (b) exercising one's capacity to act in a way that manifests one's recognition of which constraints on one's thinking and imagining are self-imposed and which are not; and I pointed to a connection between the exercise of this latter capacity and the ability to act in a way that manifests one's recognition of what is and isn't imagined.

In summary, it is far from clear that we can simply strip away certain mental ingredients that make our mental activity agential and yet still be left with a conscious mental life which is otherwise much the same. There is a distinctive variety of occurrent self-knowledge that plays an essential role in various forms of conscious thinking. The obtaining of this variety of self-knowledge constitutively depends upon the occurrence of conscious mental activity in which agency is exercised. This is why mental agency is essential to these forms of conscious thinking. So when we try to locate the place and role of mental agency in our conscious thinking, it is a mistake simply to look to a distinctive kind of initiating cause of that conscious mental activity.

I have said that a variety of self-knowledge and a form of mental agency necessarily accompany one another when a state of intention-in-action is directed on mental activity. So does this mean that one can't believe that one is engaged in a mental action when one isn't? It seems reasonable to assume that one can believe that one is performing a bodily action when one isn't. So is there reason to think that the epistemology of mental action and the epistemology of bodily action differ in this respect? I shall turn to this question in the next section, where I shall also comment on the relevance of this issue to scepticism directed at putative knowledge that one is thinking.

14.2 The epistemology of mental action and scepticism directed at conscious thinking

I have argued that intention-in-action is an occurrent state. If an intention-in-action is directed on an act of φ-ing, then the obtaining of that state constitutively depends upon the occurrence of an event that is either an act of φ-ing, or an act that is an attempt to φ.

This account allows that one can be in such a state, and think that one is φ-ing, when one isn't. Suppose, for example, that the φ-ing in question is a simple act of raising one's arm. One can decide to raise one's arm, the intention one thereby forms can evolve into an intention-in-action, at that point one can think one is raising one's arm, and yet consistent with this one's arm can fail to move. In the previous chapter I noted that the proposal I made about the epistemic role of intention-in-action is consistent with the idea that perceptual experience can serve as a source of evidence about what one is doing when one is acting, and in the case of bodily action one is usually constantly updated with such evidence. Such perceptual evidence can undermine one's acceptance of the proposition that one is φ-ing when one is in a state of intention-in-action directed on an act of φ-ing. In general, if φ-ing is some overt bodily action, such as an arm-raising, then one's belief that one is φ-ing is something that perceptual evidence can speak against. This enables us to make sense of the possibility of there being evidence that speaks against one's belief that one is φ-ing (e.g. raising one's arm) but which is inaccessible to one because one's senses fail to provide one with a source of knowledge. For example, it is possible to undergo an experience as of raising one's arm when one's arm isn't moving. So one can be ignorant of the fact that one's arm isn't moving despite the obtaining of an intention-in-action directed on an arm-raising, and despite the occurrence of perceptual experience that suggests that one is raising one's arm. This in turn makes it possible for us to conceive of a situation in which one believes one is performing a bodily action despite the fact that one is suffering from a form of bodily paralysis—i.e. despite the fact that one is unable to exercise agency over one's body.

Do analogous claims apply in situations in which an intention-in-action is directed on a mental action? We should, I think, accept that the following is possible. One's intention-in-action can be directed on a mental act of φ-ing, one can believe that one is φ-ing, and yet one can fail to φ. For example, one can decide to recollect some past event (under some description), the intention one thereby forms can evolve into an intention-in-action, at that point one can think one is recollecting some past event that one has perceived, and yet consistent with this one can fail to recollect. The obtaining of the intention-in-action constitutively depends on the occurrence of some mental act, but the act in question may be a failed attempt to recollect—e.g. it may be an act of mere imagining.

I have said that it is possible for us to conceive of a situation in which a subject's intention-in-action is directed on a bodily action in a case where that subject believes that she is performing that bodily action, despite the fact that she is suffering from a form of bodily paralysis. Can we make sense of an analogous possibility in the case of mental action? Can we conceive of a situation in which a subject's intention-in-action is directed on some mental action, and that subject believes that she is performing that mental action, despite the fact that she is suffering from a form of mental paralysis—i.e. despite the fact that she is unable to exercise agency over her mental life?

I suggested that the belief that one is exercising agency over one's body is something that perceptual evidence can speak against, and this allows us to make sense of the possibility of there being evidence that speaks against one's belief that one is exercising agency over one's body but which is inaccessible to one because one's senses fail to provide one with a source of knowledge. One can be ignorant of the fact that one is unable to exercise agency over one's body despite the obtaining of an intention-in-action directed on bodily action, and despite the occurrence of perceptual experience that suggests that one's body is moving. What might the mental equivalent of such a case be?

We could make sense of a mental equivalent if we could cite mental analogues of bodily movement and experience of bodily movement. A view of conscious thinking that I discussed in Chapter 10 would appear to offer the relevant mental analogues. This view of conscious thinking is what I called a 'bottom-up' approach to conscious thinking. According to that approach, conscious thinking involves the occurrence of mental events of a kind that can be non-conscious, together with higher-order states of awareness directed upon those mental events—higher-order states whose obtaining makes those events conscious. On the view I considered, an activity such as conscious calculation involves (a) the occurrence of a series of instantaneous events that are acquisitions of (and transitions between) mental states with content, together with (b) higher-order states that represent those events.

Under this sort of approach, we might think of the mental events mentioned in (a) as mental analogues of bodily movement, and the states mentioned in (b) as analogues of experiences of bodily movement. The mental events mentioned in (a) can in principle occur without one's having conscious awareness of them, just as bodily movements that are involved in a bodily action can occur without one's having conscious awareness of them. We might then suppose that mental events of this kind must occur if one is to exercise agency over one's conscious thinking, just as bodily movements must occur if one is to exercise agency over one's body. We might also suppose that the higher-order states mentioned in (b) can obtain in the absence of the occurrence of such mental events, just as an experience as of bodily movement can occur in the absence of actual bodily movement. So we might then envisage the following possibility. A subject is in a state of intention-in-action which is directed on, say, calculating whether p. The subject thereby believes that she is engaged in the activity of calculating whether p. It seems to the subject as though she is thinking conscious thoughts. This is because higher-order states represent the occurrence of such mental events. But in reality the subject is not thinking those conscious thoughts. The mental events represented by those higher-order states are not occurring. In reality, the subject is not calculating whether p. Despite appearances the subject is suffering from a form of mental paralysis—she is unable to exercise agency over her mental life.

This might appear to offer something like the mental equivalent of a situation in which a subject's intention-in-action is directed on a bodily action, and that subject believes that she is performing that bodily action despite the fact that she is suffering from a form of bodily paralysis. However, as I argued in Chapter 10, the 'bottom-up' approach to conscious thinking on which the imagined scenario depends is ultimately untenable. I argued that the mental activity of conscious thinking is not reducible to, and analysable in terms of, mental states and events (and processes) that are simply changes in those states. I argued that an account of the ontology of conscious thinking should invoke occurrent mental states—states whose obtaining constitutively depends on the occurrence of conscious events with temporal extension. On the account of conscious judging that I proposed, the conscious mental act of judging involves the occurrence of a conscious event with temporal extension that serves as a vehicle of representation. What makes it the case that the relevant conscious event is the vehicle of a mental act of judging that p is the fact that the state that obtains when the conscious event occurs is the belief that one is judging that p. And I argued that the belief that one is judging that p can only obtain if there occurs a mental event with temporal extension that serves as the vehicle of an act of judging that p. Under this account, we do not find, in the case of agential conscious thinking, mental analogues of the bodily movement and experience of bodily movement that we can cite in the case of bodily action. For according to this account, the activity of conscious thinking is not one that can be decomposed into the following separable elements: (a) occurrence of mental events of a kind that can in principle occur without one's having conscious awareness of them, together with (b) mental states that represent the occurrence of those kinds of mental events. On the account of conscious judging that I proposed, an act of judging that p is necessarily accompanied by the belief that one is judging that p, and the conscious mental act of judging that p is not decomposable in a way that would allow that one can believe that one is judging that p when one isn't.

Does this rule out the possibility of the illusion of mental agency, and does it rule out the possibility that it can merely appear to one as though one is engaged in the activity of conscious calculation or deliberation? One might think that the hypothesis about dreams that I considered at the end of previous chapter suggests otherwise. According to that hypothesis, when you are dreaming, you are not in a position to make any decisions about the course of your thinking or imagining. Any putative candidate for making a decision of any kind is a case of *imagining* making that decision, where the occurrence of this imagining is itself an unbidden act of imagining that is not accompanied by any practical self-knowledge of a kind that can be embodied in intention-in-action. Moreover, when you dream that you consciously judge something, you are merely imagining making that judgement. The suggestion was that in being unable to exercise your capacity to impose constraints over your own thinking and imagining, you are thereby unable to exercise your capacity to engage in mental behaviour that manifests your recognition of the distinction between those constraints on your thinking and imagining that are self-imposed and those constraints on your thinking and imagining that are imposed by facts whose obtaining you acknowledge; and you are thereby unable to exercise your capacity to treat these mental occurrences as mere imaginings, and thereby recognize them as departures from reality.

This hypothesis about dreams presents us with a way of conceiving of something like a form of mental paralysis that involves the illusion of mental agency and the mere appearance of being engaged in conscious calculation and deliberation. However, note that this does not serve as a counterexample to the claim that one can suffer a form of mental paralysis despite the obtaining of an intention-in-action directed on mental activity; and it does not serve as a counterexample to the claim that a variety of self-knowledge and a form of mental agency necessarily accompany one another when a state of intention-in-action is directed on mental activity. For according to this hypothesis about dreams, when one is dreaming no such state of intention-in-action obtains.

A point worth noting in passing here is the following. In the previous section I suggested that there is a variety of self-knowledge and a form of mental agency that *necessarily* accompany one another; and the obtaining of this variety of self-knowledge has an essential role to play in an account of certain forms of conscious thinking. So when we try to locate the place and role of mental agency in our conscious thinking, it is a mistake simply to look to a distinctive kind of initiating cause of that conscious mental activity. If our concern, then, is with the possibility of the illusion of mental agency in our conscious thinking, we should not suppose that this issue is simply determined by whether or not the activity of conscious thinking has a causal origin that makes such conscious thinking agential. For it may, rather, be determined by whether or not there obtains a variety of *self-knowledge* that accompanies the activity of conscious thinking.

Now if we accept that the hypothesis about dreaming presents us with a way of conceiving of something like a form of mental paralysis that involves the illusion of mental agency and the mere appearance of being engaged in conscious calculation and deliberation, can it serve as a sceptical hypothesis in an argument targeting putative knowledge that one is exercising mental agency over one's mental life and targeting putative knowledge that one is engaged in the activity of conscious calculation and deliberation? The prospects of mounting such a sceptical challenge look dim. For there is a clear epistemic asymmetry between the bad case (i.e. the sceptical hypothesis that one is dreaming) and the good case (i.e. the situation in which one is awake and engaging in conscious calculation/deliberation). In the bad case, intentions-in-action do not obtain. One isn't able to exercise a capacity to impose constraints on one's thinking by acting in recognition of them, and so an avenue to self-knowledge is thereby precluded. In the good case, intentions-in-action *do* obtain. One is able to impose constraints on one's thinking by acting in recognition of them and so this avenue to self-knowledge is not precluded. It is not as though the sceptic can cite a common evidential core to good and bad cases. A further point worth noting here, which is relevant to Descartes' Cogito argument, is the following. Suppositional reasoning and self-critical reflection are necessarily involved in engaging in Descartes' method of doubt, and the exercise of one's mental agency is necessarily involved in engaging in suppositional reasoning and self-critical reflection. So if one is engaged in the method of doubt, then one must be in the good case. Engaging in the method of doubt cannot provide one with a reason to doubt that one is in the good case.

Can the dreaming hypothesis be used to target putative knowledge that one is judging that *p*? Again, we don't have the kind of common core to good and bad cases that might potentially present a sceptical challenge. In the bad case, one is imagining judging that p and one isn't in a position to know that one is merely imagining. But if it is a mere imagining, and not a judging, then it is not accompanied by the belief that one is judging that p. For as I argued, the obtaining of the mental state that is one's belief that one is judging that p constitutively depends on the occurrence of a conscious event with temporal extension that serves as the vehicle of an act of judging that p. In the bad case, one does not believe that one is judging that p. In the good case, one does.

But now this response raises the following important question: what is the difference between (a) imagining judging that p and not being in a position to know that this is a mere imagining, and (b) the obtaining of the belief that one is judging that p? An answer to this question can help to illuminate our understanding of what it is to consciously judge something. In Chapter 10 I argued that the conscious act of judging that p is necessarily accompanied by a distinctive form of self-knowledge. This form of self-knowledge is not equivalent to the belief that one believes that p, it is not equivalent to the belief that one has just acquired the belief that p, and it is not a matter of being poised to express one's belief that p in an overt bodily action. An understanding of what it is to consciously judge something depends on an understanding of the nature and role of this distinctive form of self-knowledge. Our understanding of the nature and role of this distinctive form of self-knowledge can now be illuminated by considering the difference between (a) imagining judging that p and not being in a position to know that this is a mere imagining, and (b) the obtaining of the belief that one is judging that p. The belief that one is judging that p can play a role in mental action. The occurrence mentioned in (a) cannot play a role in mental action. This supports the suggestion I made in Chapter 10 that the significance of the distinctive form of self-knowledge that accompanies the conscious mental act of judging is to be understood in terms of its role in agential mental activity; e.g. working out a problem or deliberating about what to do—mental activities one can choose to engage in. This is not to commit to the claim that a conscious mental act of judging is a mental action, but it is to suggest that we cannot understand what it is to consciously judge something independently of the notion of mental action. With these considerations in mind, in the next section I turn to the more general question of the place of mental action in an account of the metaphysics of mind.

14.3 The place of mental action in the metaphysics of mind

In Chapter 9 I contrasted, at a very general level, what I called 'Cartesian' and 'anti-Cartesian' approaches to mind. I'll first recapitulate some of the remarks I made there. I said that one key strand in the 'Cartesian' approach is the idea that there is a merely *contingent* connection between one's mental life and the expression of one's mental life in overt bodily action. This metaphysical view is connected with an epistemological proposal, its natural ally: the suggestion that even when a subject's epistemic access to the material world is compromised, her epistemic access to her own mind and mental life remains intact.

A common thread to opposing, 'anti-Cartesian' approaches is the rejection of an epis-temic view that would make a subject's mental life both private to that subject and infal-libly accessible to her; and a connected thread is the idea that it is a mistake to regard as merely contingent the connections between one's mental life and publicly observable bodily manifestations of one's mental life. Proponents of an anti-Cartesian approach need not deny the reality of a subject's inner mental life, but they hold that a subject's inner mental life will necessarily be anchored in publicly observable bodily behaviour that expresses, and that is an effect of, that subject's mentality.

Under the anti-Cartesian approach, emphasis is placed on the notion of psychological subject as bodily agent, and with the advent of the anti-Cartesian notion of psychologi-cal subject as bodily agent, the agency that we exercise over our mental lives is not often thought central to our understanding of mentality, and it is not thought central to our understanding of consciousness. For example, functionalist approaches to mind that take the individuation of a mental state to be determined by its causal relations to sensory stimulations, other mental states, and behaviour, are usually confined to treating the rel-evant behaviour in question as bodily behaviour. This doesn't mean that such accounts are incompatible with the idea that we can perform mental as well as bodily actions; implicit is the assumption that agential mental behaviour is to be explained and charac-terized in terms of the prior notions of sensory stimulation, bodily behaviour, mental states, and the events that are transitions between such states that contribute to the causal explanation of bodily behaviour. Similarly, under interpretationist approaches to the mental, the focus is invariably on mental state attributions that rationalize and causally explain *bodily* behaviour. The implicit assumption is that although bodily behaviour is to be taken as basic, mental behaviour is not. That is to say, the assumption seems to be that mental action is to be analysed as a variety of mental activity involving transitions between mental states that enable, rationalize, and causally explain *bodily* behaviour.

Under such views, mental events with phenomenal properties are not usually regarded as constituting mental behaviour that is the output of the functional roles that mental states characteristically play; nor are they regarded as occurrences constituting mental behaviour that needs to be rationalized and explained by mental state attributions. Moreover, under such views it is not clear that we need to appeal to the phenomenal properties of mental events and states when it comes to explaining the publicly observ-able bodily manifestations of our mentality and agency. In consequence, under such views it is often assumed that the subject who is not phenomenally conscious will be capable of doing whatever the phenomenally conscious subject is capable of doing—the implicit assumption being that phenomenal consciousness is not only inessential to bodily action, it is also inessential to mental action. Implicit is the assumption that were we to strip mentality of phenomenal properties we would still have mentality and agency, and we would still have a psychological subject, and an agent no less autono-mous than a phenomenally conscious subject. The related methodological assumption is that accounts of mentality and agency can proceed without a solution to the 'hard problem' of consciousness, which requires its own special and separate treatment, and this helps to reinforce the assumption that considerations regarding mental action can at best be of marginal significance to a philosophical account of consciousness.

In Chapter 9 I noted that a major and obvious difference between the Cartesian approach and the now more prevalent anti-Cartesian approach is that Descartes was interested in the possibility of disembodied existence in a way that most of those participating in the current debate are not. Arguably, in order to make sense of the notion of disembodied existence we need to be able to make sense of the notion of disembodied agency, and in order to make sense of disembodied agency we need to think of the disembodied agent as capable of engaging in mental action. But the very idea of disembodied agency, and hence disembodied existence, is compromised if we conceive of mental actions as reducible to mental processes that enable and explain overt bodily actions. So Descartes obviously had a motivation to reject such a conception of mental action. But for those who reject Descartes' substance dualism, are there other reasons for thinking that this reductive understanding of mental action is problematic?

We are now in a position to see that we fail to accommodate adequately the place of mental action in an account of mind if we accept this reductive understanding of mental action, and proper acknowledgement of this point need not commit one to a 'Cartesian' conception of mentality. Two of the main points I have argued for so far are the following:

(A) When we try to locate the place and role of mental agency in our conscious thinking, it is a mistake simply to look to a distinctive kind of initiating cause of that conscious mental activity. For there is a variety of self-knowledge and a form of mental agency that *necessarily* accompany one another, and the obtaining of this variety of self-knowledge has an essential role to play in an account of certain forms of conscious thinking—e.g. suppositional reasoning, self-critical reflection, and practical deliberation. This is why it is a mistake to think that in the case of all mental actions, the following is true: conscious thinking of the same basic kind could occur and yet be non-agential.

(B) Although the individual conscious mental acts that constitute one's conscious thinking may not themselves be mental actions, we cannot understand their nature independently of the notion of mental action. For example, although the conscious mental act of judging that p may not be a mental action, we cannot understand what it is to consciously judge something independently of the notion of mental action. For the conscious act of judging that p is necessarily accompanied by a distinctive form of self-knowledge, and the significance of the distinctive form of self-knowledge that accompanies the conscious mental act of judging is to be understood in terms of its role in agential mental activity; e.g. working out a problem or deliberating about what to do—mental activities one can choose to engage in.

From these two points, it follows that mental action has an essential role to play in an account of those issues in the epistemology of mind that are central to our understanding of the kind of conscious thinking that a self-conscious subject can engage in. I have also argued that in order to accommodate adequately these connections between mental action, the epistemology of mind, and conscious thinking, we need to invoke *occurrent mental states* in our account of the ontology of conscious thinking. These are mental states whose obtaining constitutively depends on the occurrence of conscious events/ processes with temporal extension that serve as vehicles of conscious acts of thinking thoughts. They are mental states that can only obtain in the case of subjects whose mental lives include a stream of consciousness.

We fail to accommodate adequately the place of mental action in an account of conscious thinking if we hold that the activity of conscious thinking is reducible to, and analysable in terms of, mental states and events (and processes) that are simply changes to those mental states. This is why we fail to accommodate adequately the place of mental action in an account of mind if we conceive of mental actions as reducible to mental processes that simply enable and explain overt bodily actions. The view according to which conscious thinking is reducible to, and analysable in terms of, mental states and events/processes that are changes in those mental states can capture much of what goes on when one is engaged in the activity of conscious thinking—e.g. the activity of conscious calculation. For example, the account can capture the idea that when one engages in such activity, one acquires new beliefs—including beliefs about what one believes, and including beliefs that one has just acquired new beliefs. The account can also accommodate the idea that when one engages in such activity, one is poised to express in overt verbal behaviour beliefs about the activity one is engaged in. However, it cannot adequately accommodate the distinctive form of self-knowledge that accompanies the conscious mental acts that constitute the activity of conscious thinking. This distinctive form of self-knowledge is not equivalent to knowing that one believes that p. It's not equivalent to knowing that one has just acquired the belief that p. And it isn't simply a matter of being poised to express one's belief that p in an overt bodily action. This distinctive form of self-knowledge involves the obtaining of occurrent mental states— mental states whose obtaining is constitutively dependent on the occurrence of conscious mental events with temporal extension that serve as vehicles of conscious acts of thinking thoughts. This is a form of self-knowledge that is only available to the subject whose mental life includes a stream of consciousness. And the significance of this form of self-knowledge is to be understood in terms of its role in mental actions.

Nothing that I have said here is inconsistent with what I have been calling an 'anti-Cartesian' conception of mentality. For no reason has been given to deny that these occurrent mental states can only obtain in the case of an embodied subject capable of engaging in bodily action. However, there is a Cartesian insight that we need to reinstate. This Cartesian insight involves taking seriously the notion of agential mental activity, which is not simply to be thought of as a variety of mental process involving transitions between mental states that enables and explains overt bodily action. A consequence of reinstating what I am calling the 'Cartesian insight' is that various assumptions that usually frame debates about phenomenal consciousness may be undermined—for example, the assumption that the subject who is not phenomenally conscious can in principle perform all of the actions that the phenomenally conscious subject is capable of performing. Since we *are* embodied, when we perform mental actions there will occur mental processes involving transitions between mental states that enable and explain our overt bodily actions. But we overlook the Cartesian insight if we conceptualize our mental actions in this way, and we may thereby end up creating conceptual obstacles to a proper understanding of phenomenal consciousness.

In this and the previous chapter I have focused on the epistemic role of intention-in-action and its relevance to central concerns in the epistemology and metaphysics of mind. I have tried to outline various ways in which the avenue to practical self-knowledge that can be embodied in intention-in-action can play a very significant role in the ordinary, awake, conscious mental life of a self-conscious subject. One issue I haven't yet touched upon is the relevance of this variety of self-knowledge to questions concerning one's knowledge of one's standing attitudes. What connections can be made between (i) one's knowledge of what one is consciously thinking and (ii) one's knowledge of one's standing attitudes—e.g. one's beliefs? I shall be focusing on this issue in the final chapter of the book, where I shall also consider how this issue bears on the ethics of belief.

15

Thinking and Belief

The belief that one is judging that p is not equivalent to the belief that one believes that p. One can believe that one believes that p when one isn't consciously judging that p and when one doesn't believe that one is consciously judging that p. The belief that one has just judged that p is also not equivalent to the belief that one has just acquired the belief that p. One can consciously judge that p when one already believes that p and when one already believes that one already believes that p. More generally, one's beliefs concerning conscious mental activity one is engaged in are not equivalent to beliefs about one's standing attitudes. Beliefs about one's standing attitudes can obtain when one isn't engaged in any conscious mental activity and when one doesn't believe that one is engaged in conscious mental activity—e.g. during dreamless sleep. Given the non-equivalence of one's beliefs about what one is doing when engaged in conscious mental activity and one's beliefs about one's standing attitudes, how should we understand the connection between them? For example, can the former epistemically ground the latter?

It may well be the case that in answering this question we find that there are rather different things to say about the different standing attitudes. For example, the account that should be given of how beliefs about what one is doing when consciously thinking can ground beliefs about what one believes, may differ from the account that should be given of how beliefs about what one is doing when consciously thinking can ground beliefs about one's desires and intentions. In this chapter I shall narrow the focus of enquiry to the following issues: how should we understand the connections between one's beliefs about what one is doing when consciously thinking, and one's beliefs about what one believes? How should we understand the epistemic connections between such beliefs? Can one's beliefs about what one is doing when consciously thinking ground one's beliefs about what one believes? Can one's knowledge of what one is doing when consciously thinking provide one with a distinctive, first-personal way of knowing about one's beliefs? Later on in the chapter I shall go on to address some further epistemological questions about the connections between the activity of conscious thinking and the standing attitude of belief. In particular, I shall be exploring some of the ways in which the ethics of belief may be affected by the fact that we are, as self-conscious subjects, capable of engaging *agential epistemic* conscious mental activity, including self-critical reflection.

15.1 Knowing what you are thinking and knowing what you believe

Discussions of self-knowledge sometimes seek to clarify the respect in which we can know about our own minds in a distinctively first-personal way.[1] One can acquire knowledge of one's own mind in a third-personal way—in the kind of way that one might acquire knowledge of the mind of another—but each person seems also to have a distinctive kind of first-personal access to her own mind that no other can have. Some of the proposals that I have made about the epistemology of mental action, and the distinctive kind of self-knowledge that accompanies conscious mental acts of thinking thoughts, can contribute to an explanation of why this is so. The practical self-knowledge that one can have of one's own mental actions (practical self-knowledge embodied in intention-in-action) is not the kind of knowledge that one can have of the mental actions performed by another. Moreover, the distinctive kind of self-knowledge that accompanies one's conscious mental acts of thinking thoughts (such as the conscious mental act of judging) is not the kind of knowledge that one can have of the conscious thoughts of another. In Chapter 10 I discussed the respect in which it is intuitive to think that the conscious thoughts that are involved in the temporally extended activity of consciously thinking about some matter are, in some sense, private to the subject who is thinking them. The account that I have offered of the ontology of conscious thinking can accommodate and explain this idea.

However, this still leaves open the question of whether we have available to us a distinctive kind of first-personal way of knowing what we believe. Can the account that I have offered of the epistemology of mental action be used to explain a respect in which we have available to us a way of knowing about our own beliefs that is unlike the third-personal way in which we can know about the beliefs of another? Richard Moran (2001) has argued that there is an important link between the way in which a subject can know about her own mind from a distinctively first-personal perspective, and the perspective that each subject has on her own mind as agent.[2] Moran claims that 'Being the person whose mental life is brought to self-awareness involves a stance of agency beyond that of being a kind of expert witness' (2001: 4); and he suggests that in the epistemology of mind 'inadequate attention is given to the person as an epistemic agent, and hence to the mutual interaction between mental life and first-person awareness of it' (2001: 4). In what follows I want to explore the idea that when it comes to an account of how a self-conscious subject knows what she believes, it is important to pay attention to the role of the subject as epistemic agent—in particular, the perspective she has on her own mental life as an agent of epistemic mental action.

Let's start, though, by focusing on a much narrower question. How should we understand the connection between the belief that one is judging that p and the belief that

---

[1] For a seminal discussion of this topic, see Shoemaker 1996.
[2] For another development of this idea, see O'Brien 2007.

one believes that p? I have said that an act of consciously judging that p need not involve the acquisition of the belief that p, for one can consciously judge that p when one already believes that p. Moreover, an act of consciously judging that p need not involve the acquisition of the belief that one believes that p, for one can consciously judge that p when one already believes that one believes that p. But are there circumstances under which the belief that one is judging that p can epistemically ground the acquisition of the belief that one believes that p?

A straightforward answer could perhaps be given if it were not possible for a subject to judge that p without believing that p. However, it's not clear that there really is this kind of necessary connection between acts of judging and belief. At least some beliefs are dispositional states, and as such, they can be manifested in different ways. One's consciously judging that p is just one way in which one's belief that p can be manifested on a particular occasion. Given that a particular act of judging that p is not the only way in which the belief that p may be made manifest, it is not inconceivable that there may be instances where a subject judges that p when she considers the question of whether p, even though much of her behaviour appears to manifest the belief that not-p. In such cases one might think that the subject does not genuinely believe that p even though she consciously judges that p when she considers the question. Here is an example of such a case given by Peacocke:

Someone can make a judgement, and for good reasons, but it not have the effect that judgements normally do—in particular, it may not result in a stored belief which has the proper influence on other judgements and on action. A combination of prejudice and self-deception, amongst many other possibilities, can produce this state of affairs. Someone may judge that undergraduate degrees from countries other than her own are of an equal standard to her own, and excellent reasons may be operative in her assertions to that effect. All the same, it may be quite clear, in decisions she makes on hiring, or in making recommendations, that she does not really have this belief at all. (1999: 242–3)

If one can consciously judge that p when one doesn't believe that p, then what account should be given of the epistemic role of the belief that one is judging that p in grounding the belief that one believes that p?[3] If one can judge that p without believing that p, is the belief that one is judging that p to be thought of as mere evidence that one has for the belief that one believes that p—perhaps evidence of behaviour that indicates that one believes that p? The belief that one is judging that p is likely to result in the belief that one has just judged that p. How should we understand what is thereby believed? Does one simply believe that there occurred in one's conscious mental life some psychological episode that doesn't entail that one believes that p, but which is nonetheless a good indication that one does?

I have suggested that the distinctive kind of self-knowledge that accompanies the conscious mental act of judging that p is best understood in terms of the role that such

---

[3] For discussion of this question, see Cassam 2010, 2011a, and 2011b.

self-knowledge can play in mental actions, such as figuring out some problem or deliberating about what to do. This is important to bear in mind when it comes to an understanding of what one believes has just happened when one believes that one has just judged that *p*. For one's belief about what has just happened may sometimes be best understood in the context of one's beliefs about (a) what one set out to do, (b) what one did, and (c) how one did it. These considerations are, I suggest, relevant to an understanding of how one's beliefs about what one is doing when consciously thinking can ground one's beliefs about what one believes. To see why, let's start by comparing and contrasting the aim of practical deliberation and the aim of theoretical reasoning. In Chapter 12 I argued that the aim of practical deliberation is that of governing one's own conduct, which involves governing the way in which one imposes constraints on one's own conduct. This is not simply a matter of arriving at judgements as to how one ought to behave and how one ought to govern one's own conduct. For it is only by *making decisions* that one governs one's decision making. One governs the way in which one imposes constraints on oneself by imposing constraints on oneself—i.e. by deciding to act.

I have argued that in imposing constraints on oneself by making decisions, one thereby makes assumptions about one's own future conduct. But I also suggested that this involves an epistemic perspective on one's future that is unlike the perspective that one has on one's own future from the standpoint of theoretical reason. I suggested that from the standpoint of practical reason there is no particular way that one must assume the future to be in order for one's assumption to be correct, in so far as there is no particular way that one is epistemically obliged to assume the future to be in order for one's assumption to be correct. From the standpoint of practical reason, one takes oneself to be epistemically entitled to assume something about one's future on the basis of evidence that simultaneously licenses one to assume something that contradicts it. One regards oneself as epistemically free to make any one of a number of inconsistent assumptions about one's future, and in that sense one regards one's future as epistemically open. In contrast, from the perspective of theoretical reason, when one is engaged, say, in making *predictions* about one's future conduct, one does not regard one's future as epistemically open.

Of course, the epistemic perspective that one has on one's future from the standpoint of practical reason cannot be isolated from, and needs to be integrated with, the deliverances of the standpoint of theoretical reason, and the engagement of theoretical reasoning is crucially involved in, and can serve the aim of, practical deliberation. But there is, nonetheless, a sense in which the aim of practical deliberation is to be distinguished from the aim of theoretical reasoning. The aim of the former is self-governance, and this isn't the appropriate way to conceive of the aim of the latter. How then should we conceive of the aim of theoretical reasoning? Is it the acquisition of belief? Should we say that the aim of practical deliberation is making decisions, whereas the aim of theoretical reasoning is acquiring beliefs?

It is natural to think that theoretical reasoning has an epistemic aim, but it is not clear that this is best expressed in terms of the idea that the aim of such reasoning is the acquisition of belief. Standardly, when one is engaged in such reasoning one's aim is not that of acquiring a particular belief—that is, one's aim isn't that of forming the belief that p. One's aim will, rather, usually be that of working out/finding out/discovering/determining etc., whether..., or who..., or when..., or what..., or why..., or where..., or how...As Vendler (1972) pointed out, 'whether', 'who', 'when', 'what', 'why', 'where', and 'how' can introduce the verb-object of 'know', but this move in general fails with 'believe'. For example, whereas one can know where the treasure is hidden, one cannot believe where the treasure is hidden. This suggests that wanting to work out/determine whether p isn't a matter of wanting to believe whether p, but rather wanting to *know* whether p. As Vendler put it, 'S wants to know...' is normally followed by an indirect question—whether/who/where etc.—whereas 'S wants to believe...' normally requires a *that* clause, which, Vendler suggests, is reflected in the fact that 'wanting to know is a sign of curiosity, whereas wanting to believe is a sign of credulity, and the two things have nothing to do with one another' (1972: 118). There are reasons, then, for thinking that the aim of engaging in theoretical reasoning isn't the mere acquisition of belief. The fundamental ambition of engaging in theoretical reasoning is, rather, that of acquiring and sustaining knowledge.

It should also be noted that 'whether', 'who', 'what', etc., can also introduce the verb-object of 'guess'. One can attempt to guess whether/who/where, etc. But in general, when one is attempting to guess whether p, it isn't a requirement on fulfilling one's aim that one acquire a belief that has either p or not-p as its object. The term 'guess' can be used in different ways. It can, for example, be used as a success verb—e.g. the sense in which S managed to guess where the treasure is hidden only if the answer she gave was correct. Success here doesn't require the acquisition of knowledge that p or even the true belief that p. It doesn't require the acquisition of any particular standing attitude—just the correctness of an *episode* of guessing. The verb 'guess' can also be used to pick out cases of estimating. 'S estimates that p' need not simply report the occurrence of some episode of guessing an answer to the question of whether p. It can report a state. But 'S estimates that p' does not in general report the fact that S believes that p. It usually reports her belief that p is more likely true than not. If one estimates that p, one might then treat p as a premise in one's reasoning. But if one does so as a result of guessing, then there is a respect in which, from one's own point of view, one is assuming that p for practical purposes. In assuming that p in this way, one acts in recognition of a self-imposed constraint, rather than in recognition of a constraint on one's reasoning imposed by a fact whose obtaining one acknowledges. That is to say, in treating p as true in this way one isn't thereby acknowledging the fact that p. At most, one is acknowledging the fact that p is more likely true than not, and one's acknowledgement of this fact leads one to impose on oneself the constraint of treating p as true, for practical purposes. This again supports the claim that when one is attempting to guess whether p (whether or not 'guess' is understood as a success verb), it isn't a requirement on fulfilling one's aim that one acquires a belief as to whether or not p. In cases of theoretical reasoning in which it *is* a requirement on fulfilling one's aim that one acquire a belief as to whether or not p, this is because the more fundamental aim is that of acquiring *knowledge* of whether p.

Now let us return to my earlier suggestion that when it comes to an understanding of what one believes has just happened when one believes that one has just judged that p, this may sometimes be best understood in the context of one's beliefs about (a) what one set out to do, (b) what one did, and (c) how one did it. Suppose that one is engaged in the conscious activity of attempting to work out whether p, and suppose that one ends up concluding that p. One believes that what one set out to do was to work out whether p. If one believes that one has done what one set out to do, then one will believe that in concluding that p one has worked out that p. If one believes that one has worked out whether p, then one believes that one knows whether p. On the assumption that knowledge is a state, this means that one's belief about what just happened entails a belief about one's current state, and not simply a belief about some past event. And on the assumption that the obtaining of the state of knowing that p entails the obtaining of the state of belief that p, this makes plausible the claim that in acquiring this belief about what has just happened one has acquired the belief that one believes that p.

So in this sort of case, in believing that one has just judged that p, one doesn't simply believe that there occurred in one's conscious mental life some psychological episode that doesn't entail that one believes that p, but which is nonetheless a good indication that one believes that p. One's belief about what has just happened is a belief about what one has *done*, and this belief about what one has just done entails a belief about one's current beliefs. One believes that one believes that p, because one believes that one knows that p, and one believes that one knows that p, because one believes that one has just worked out that p.

A further point that Vendler makes in contrasting the verbs 'believe' and 'know' is that we say 'how do you know?' and not 'how do you believe?'; and we say 'why do you believe?' and we don't usually say 'why do you know?'[4] In the sort of case we are considering, one is likely to have beliefs about how one accomplished one's aim, which amounts to having beliefs about how one knows whether p. Although the question 'how do you know?' is not equivalent to the question 'why do you believe?', in having beliefs about how one knows, one thereby has beliefs about why one believes—i.e. beliefs about one's epistemic reasons for believing as one does. So one's beliefs about what just happened are likely to result not only in the belief that one believes that p but also in beliefs about why one believes that p. Note that one's beliefs about what epistemic reasons one has for believing as one does can include beliefs about facts that one takes oneself to *know*, given that the conscious mental activity one engages in can manifest one's recognition of the distinction between constraints on one's thinking and reasoning that are self-imposed, and constraints on one's thinking that are imposed by facts whose obtaining one *acknowledges*.

---

[4] For discussion of the significance of this difference, see Austin 1946.

In order to achieve the right understanding of how one's beliefs about what one is doing when consciously thinking can ground one's beliefs about what one believes, we need to appreciate the connections between one's beliefs about what one is doing when consciously thinking, and one's beliefs about what one *knows*. Failure to appreciate this point can invite the following line of thought. One's beliefs about what one is doing when consciously thinking are to be thought of as evidence one has that a certain kind of dispositional state obtains—a dispositional state that can be manifested by such conscious mental activity, but which can also be manifested in a number of other ways. According to this way of regarding matters, when it comes to checking whether one's belief about what one believes is correct, one should be considering what other evidence one has about how one behaves. The alternative that I am proposing is that one's beliefs about what one is doing when consciously thinking can ground one's beliefs about what one *knows*, and this can serve as a more basic way of acquiring beliefs about what one believes. If one believes that one believes that *p* because one believes that one has worked out whether *p*, then checking whether this higher-order belief is correct will involve checking whether one really has done what one thinks one has done; and this will involve checking whether one really knows whether *p*. The question of whether one really knows whether *p* does not amount to a question about whether one engages in behaviour that might be explained by the obtaining of a dispositional state. For the question of whether one really knows that *p* falls to the first-order question of whether *p*. Checking whether one really knows whether *p* involves reconsidering the question of whether *p*, rather than considering further evidence about one's behaviour.

This proposal can accommodate and explain what is right in a well-known remark made by Evans.

In making a self-ascription of a belief, one's eyes are, so to speak, or occasionally literally, directed outward–upon the world. If someone asks me, 'Do you think there is going to be a third world war?', I must attend in answering him, to precisely the same outward phenomena I would attend to if I were answering the question 'Will there be a third world war?' I get myself into a position to answer the question whether I believe that *p* by putting into operation whatever procedure I have for answering the question whether *p*. (1982: 225)

The most basic way of determining or checking what one believes about one's beliefs involves determining or checking what one knows. The question of whether one knows whether *p* depends on a question about the extra-mental facts—i.e. whether *p*. It doesn't simply depend on whether some psychological dispositional state obtains. This is why the question of whether one knows that *p* falls to the question of whether *p*; and this is why in making the self-ascription of belief one's 'eyes are directed outwards'. This proposal should alleviate any worries that might be had about how a proposition about the extra-mental world that one accepts can justify the proposition that one believes that *p*. It is not that the proposition *p*, which one judges, justifies the proposition 'I believe that *p*', which one subsequently judges. It is, rather, that when one concludes that *p* one has beliefs about what one set out to do, what one did, and how one did it. One believes that one has worked out whether p and one has beliefs about how one did this—which amounts to having the belief that one knows that p and having beliefs about how one knows that p. In consequence, one has the belief that one believes that p and one has beliefs about why one believes that p—i.e. beliefs about one's epistemic reasons for believing that p.

One has a distinctively first-personal way of knowing what one is doing when consciously thinking and this can provide one with a distinctively first-personal way of acquiring beliefs about what one believes. One's beliefs about what one is doing when consciously thinking can ground one's beliefs about what one knows, and thereby ground beliefs about what one believes. This first-personal way of acquiring beliefs about what one believes is not infallible. Obviously our beliefs about what we know are not infallible. One can believe that one knows that p when one doesn't know that p. In such cases, is one's belief that one believes that p nonetheless secure? If one takes oneself to know that p, then one's subsequent behaviour is likely to be that of someone who believes that p. But this may not be guaranteed, for the reasons illustrated by Peacocke's example, which I quoted earlier. So let us now reconsider such cases.

Some of our beliefs are not knowledge, and we know this fact about ourselves. We know that some of our beliefs are dispositional psychological states that explain the way we behave, but which do not constitute knowledge. Given the fact that we know this fact about ourselves, we might seek to determine what we believe by seeking to determine what belief ascriptions best explain our behaviour. Such an enterprise would amount to a third-personal way of ascribing beliefs to oneself—considering what evidence one has about one's behaviour and ascribing beliefs on that basis. A belief about what one believes reached in this third-personal way might potentially conflict with a belief about what one believes reached in the first-personal way. For example, when one considers the question of whether p, one might think that there is every good reason to judge that p and one might find oneself concluding that p. However, when one reflects on one's behaviour (e.g. how one reacts to certain situations), and when one listens to the opinions of others on this issue (e.g. an analyst), one might reach the conclusion that one believes that not-p after all. This doesn't mean that from then on one will judge that not-p when one considers the question of whether p. For one might still think that there is every good reason to think that p is true. In such cases, one cannot acquire knowledge of one's belief that not-p in the first-personal way. But then one might think that this marks such cases out as unusual—as cases of 'repressed' belief.

Here is an illustration of such a case, discussed by Moran.

The person who feels anger at the dead parent for having abandoned her, or who feels betrayed or deprived of something by another child, may only know of the attitude through the eliciting and interpreting of evidence of various kinds. She might become thoroughly convinced, both from the constructions of the analyst, as well as her own appreciation of the evidence, that this attitude must indeed be attributed to her. And yet, all the same, when she reflects on the world-directed question itself, whether she has indeed been betrayed by this person, she may find that the answer is no, or can't be settled one way or the other. So, transparency fails because she cannot learn of this attitude of hers by reflection on the object of that attitude. She can only learn of it in a fully theoretical manner, taking an empirical stance toward herself as a particular psychological subject. We might say that the analysand can *report* on such a belief, but she does not *express* it, since although she will describe herself as feeling betrayed she will not in her present state affirm the judgement that this person has in fact betrayed her. When the belief is described, it is kept within the brackets of the psychological operator 'believe'; that is, she will affirm the psychological judgement "I believe that P", but will not avow the embedded proposition itself. (2001: 85)

If a subject has a repressed belief that not-p, does it follow from this that it cannot be true of the subject that she really believes that p? This may not be a straightforward matter to determine. If the subject really does believe that she knows that p, then one might think that it follows from this that she believes that p, given that knowledge that p entails p and the subject knows this; in which case one might think that the subject has both the belief that p and the repressed belief that not-p.

What such examples bring out, however, is that there is a contrast to be drawn between differing ways of approaching the question of what one believes. One's concern might be with the question of whether there obtains a dispositional psychological state of a certain kind that plays a certain kind of explanatory role. Alternatively, one's concern might rather be with the question of what one knows. The former concern is perfectly legitimate, and in addressing this concern one may well regard the conscious mental activity that one engages in as part of the evidence one has of behaviour that bears on the question of what one believes. However, the latter concern—a concern with the question of what one knows—is also perfectly legitimate, and for us as self-conscious subjects, indispensable. In addressing this latter concern, one does not regard one's conscious mental activity as simply part of one's evidence which bears on the question of whether a certain kind of dispositional psychological state obtains. For one's perspective on such conscious mental activity can be that of an agent of epistemic mental action, an agent engaged in the activity of determining whether p and thereby determining what one knows. It is important to bear this in mind when considering the question of how one's beliefs about what one is doing when consciously thinking can ground one's beliefs about what one believes. This is to agree with Moran that in accounts of the first-personal ways we have available to us of knowing what we believe, attention should be given to the role of the subject as epistemic agent.

In the next section I shall begin to pursue further some of the connections and mutual interactions between the activity of conscious thinking and the standing attitude of belief that are brought to light by paying attention to the role of the subject as epistemic agent—i.e. the role of the subject as agent of epistemic mental action. In particular, I shall explore how such connections and mutual interactions bear on the ethics of belief.

15.2 Thinking, belief revision, and epistemic traps

Belief is the feature of the mental that has been the primary locus of attention in discussions of epistemic justification. This is understandable given that the main interest in the notion of epistemic justification has traditionally been in justification as a condition required for propositional knowledge, and the commonly held view is that justified *belief* is required for such knowledge. However, there are other aspects of mind that one might also think of as subject to epistemic evaluation, such as the mental act of consciously judging, withdrawing assent and suspending judgement, and mental actions and activities, such as coming up with a proof for a proposition that one already knows to be true. The fact that some of these aspects of mind are ontologically distinct may affect the account of epistemic evaluation appropriate to each. If this turns out to be the case, then we are faced with the question of how each of these various accounts of epistemic evaluation should be integrated with one another. For instance, how should the account we give of the justification of belief and judgement depend upon and affect the account we give of the justification of suspending judgement and withdrawing assent?

First let us consider ways in which the ontological differences between the standing attitude of belief and episodes of consciously judging might affect the accounts of epistemic evaluation that we think we should be given of each. A subject's belief that p, understood as standing attitude, is the kind of aspect of mind that can be retained over a period of time, whereas the mental episode of her judging that p is not. So if a particular act of judging that p is epistemically justified, then the justification that attaches to that mental act cannot be lost at a later time. However, this is not the case for belief. Given that a subject's belief can be retained over time, when giving an account of what justified belief consists in, we need to bear in mind that a subject's belief may be justified at one time and the same belief may have lost its status as justified at a later time. So we should accept that any account of what justified *belief* consists in that simply specifies the way in which a belief must be reached or acquired if it is to be justified will be incomplete. The causal origin of a belief is not something that changes over time, so if one claims that the fact that a subject's belief has a particular kind of causal origin is sufficient for that belief to be justified, then one is committed to the claim that as long as that belief is retained, its justification can never be lost. Any adequate account of justified belief needs to accommodate the fact that there are conditions that need to be satisfied if the justification of a belief is to be preserved.

As a mental act of consciously judging that p is a mental event, it does not make sense to say that a particular event of a subject judging that p can lose its status as justified over time. However, one might hold that the notion of preservation conditions for justification is still relevant to an account of what the justification of judging that p consists in, if one holds that the justification that attaches to an act of judging that p and the justification that attaches to a belief that p are related in important ways. For example, one might think that an act of judging that p is justified only if the belief that p one thereby acquires in so judging is justified. However, this particular view of the relation between the justification that attaches to an episode of judging that p and the justification that attaches to a belief that p seems oversimplified, for as I have already noted, one can consciously judge that p without that event resulting in the acquisition of a belief that p. One can consciously judge that p on a particular occasion even though one *already* believes that p.

For example, on an occasion when one recalls Hume's date of birth, one makes a conscious judgement about when he was born, but consistent with this, one already has a belief about when he was born. Such episodes of judging that *p* might be thought of as manifestations of the belief that *p*, and in such cases the justification that attaches to the act of judging might be understood derivatively in terms of the justification that attaches to the belief in a pretty straightforward way: the act of judging inherits its justificatory status from the corresponding belief. However, recollecting is just one of many ways in which one might consciously judge that *p* even though one already believes that *p*. For example, think of a case where one knows by testimony that a mathematical theorem is true, but one is trying to construct one's own proof for the theorem. In such a case, attempting to prove that *p* by the use of arithmetical reasoning is something one can choose to do even though one already knows that *p*. A subject can know that *p* and yet, consistent with this, she may make some kind of careless error in her reasoning when she engages in a particular attempt to prove, or check whether, *p*. So once we have properly distinguished the notions of having a belief that *p* and judging that *p*, and recognized that judging is an act and having a belief is not, we can make sense of the idea of a subject's belief that *p* being justified and yet at the same time the act of her judging *p* being unjustified.[5]

However, one still might think that the justification that attaches to an episode of judging is to be understood derivatively in terms of justified belief, for one might hold that an episode of judging that *p* is justified only if *either* the episode of judging that *p* is a manifestation of the subject's justified belief that *p*, *or* the belief that *p* which *would have been acquired* (were one acquired as a result of so judging) would have been a justified one.[6] If we understand the justification that attaches to an act of judging in this derivative way, then given that we can make sense of the idea of the event of a subject judging *p* being unjustified despite the fact that the subject has a justified belief that *p*, we need to distinguish the conditions required for *having* a justified belief and the conditions required for *acquiring* a justified belief. For in the case where the event of a subject's judging that *p* is unjustified despite the fact that she has a justified belief that *p*, what distinguishes an act of judging that is justified from one that is not is the fact that the *belief* which *would have been acquired* as a result of so judging would have been a justified one. So this suggests that there are both preservation and acquisition conditions that need to be satisfied if a belief is to be justified.

One of Bonjour's famous clairvoyance thought experiments, which he presents as counterexamples to certain externalist theories of justification, can be seen as a counterexample to any theory that fails to accommodate the fact that there are preservation

---

[5] Note also that it might turn out that one's previously acquired unjustified belief that *p* becomes justified as a result of one's consciously considering whether or not *p* and one's arriving at a justified conscious judgement that *p*.

[6] There is, perhaps, another way in which a conscious judgement that *p* might be justified. That is, if one is justified in judging that one's belief that *p* is justified, and this conscious judgement grounds one's conscious judgement that *p*.

conditions for justified belief. For it appears to target theories that hold that the fact that a belief has a particular kind of causal origin is sufficient for that belief to be justified. In Bonjour's example, a subject acquires a belief via a reliable method, but the subject has what we would regard as undermining counter-evidence against the belief.[7] We can explain why the subject's belief is unjustified at the point of acquisition in Bonjour's thought experiment by appealing to the idea that there are preservation conditions for justified belief. If a way of acquiring a belief is to result in justified belief, then the preservation conditions for justified belief must be satisfied at the point at which the belief is acquired. For if a way of reaching a belief results in a justified belief, then there is some period of time, no matter how short, during which the justification of the belief is not lost—so there is some period of time, no matter how short, during which the conditions required for preserving the justification of the belief are satisfied. So if absence of undermining counter-evidence is a condition required for preserving the justificatory status of a belief, then a way of acquiring a belief will result in justified belief only if this condition is satisfied at the point at which the belief is acquired. If absence of undermining counter-evidence is a condition required for preserving the justificatory status of a belief, then whether or not a belief is justified will depend, at least in part, on what other beliefs the subject has—it will depend, at least in part, upon its position in 'the logical space of reasons'.[8]

Accepting that there are acquisition as well as preservation conditions that need to be satisfied if a belief is to be justified is likely to lead to acceptance of the following claim: absence of undermining counter-evidence against one's belief is not a sufficient condition for justified belief. For the fact that there is no defeater against one's belief may be consistent with the fact that one's belief was acquired in an epistemically inappropriate way—making the belief an unjustified one.[9] If one allows that absence of undermining counter-evidence against one's belief is sufficient for justified belief, one seems, thereby, to be committed to the claim that the justificatory status of a subject's belief is simply determined by evidence that the subject possesses, and hence one thereby denies that there are acquisition conditions for justified belief.

I suggested that an act of consciously judging that p can be unjustified despite the fact that a subject has a justified belief that p. Just because a subject satisfies the conditions required for *having* a justified belief that p, it does not follow that any mental act of her consciously judging that p will be a justified one. The suggestion was that when a mental act of a subject consciously judging that p is an unjustified one despite the fact that the subject has a justified belief that p, that which determines that the act of the subject's consciously judging that p is unjustified is the fact that the belief the subject would have *acquired* in so judging would have been unjustified. So if we accept this suggestion, we

---

[7] See Bonjour 1980.

[8] The phrase is used by Sellars (1963). For a discussion and development of the notion, see McDowell 1995.

[9] For a seminal discussion of the notion of 'defeaters' for justified belief, see Pollock 1986: 37 ff. See also Plantinga 2000: 359 ff.

accept that there are acquisition conditions for the justification of belief. This, then, suggests we should accept the following claim:

(A) Absence of undermining counter-evidence against one's belief is a condition that is necessary but insufficient for justified belief.

Relevant to (A) is a distinction that Goldman has drawn between what he calls genetic/historical theories of justification on the one hand, and current time-slice theories of justification on the other.

A current time-slice theory makes the justificational status of a belief wholly a function of what is true of the cogniser at the time of belief. An historical theory makes the justificational status of belief depend on its prior history. (1979: 12)

If one accepts that there are acquisition as well as preservation conditions that need to be satisfied if a belief is to be justified, then one will be committed to a form of genetic theory of the justification of belief. If the justificatory status of a belief depends in part on how the belief was acquired, then whether a subject's belief that p is justified at time tn may depend on events that led to the acquisition of the belief at some earlier time, and so whether the belief is justified is not wholly determined by what is true of the cogniser at tn.

Goldman's version of a genetic theory of justification, his historical reliabilism, is usually classified as an externalist theory of justification,[10] but it is worth noting that those who are committed to a form of genetic theory may include those who hold theories that would usually be classified as internalist. For example, an evidentialist may hold a genetic theory of the justification of belief. She may hold that evidence accessible to the subject has to play the right kind of role in the acquisition of a belief if that belief is to be justified. Once the belief has been appropriately acquired, then evidence the subject possesses may play a role in satisfying preservation conditions for the justification of the belief. At a particular time, tn, the subject may possess evidence for her belief that p sufficient for satisfying these preservation conditions for justification, but her belief that p may nonetheless be unjustified because it failed to satisfy the appropriate (internalist, evidentialist) acquisition conditions for justification at some earlier time. Indeed, any evidentialist who is sensitive to the idea that the strength of evidence required for *reaching* a justified belief that p may be less than the strength of evidence required for *continuing* to believe that p may well be committed to a distinction between acquisition conditions for justification and preservation conditions for justification, and hence committed to a form of genetic theory of justification. They may thereby allow that although a subject's belief that p satisfies preservation conditions for justification, the subject is not justified in consciously judging that p. Her belief that p is unjustified because it was inappropriately acquired, and she does not have available to her evidence of sufficient strength for her to be justified in reaching the justified belief that p. One

---

[10] One might also regard a proper function account as a genetic externalist theory. See Plantinga 1993a, 1993b, and 2000. Note, however, that Plantinga claims he is giving an account of warrant, rather than justification.

reason an internalist, evidentialist might want to distinguish between the strength of evidence required to *reach* a justified belief that *p* on the one hand, and the strength of evidence required to *continue to hold* a justified belief that *p* on the other, may be Harman's claim that one cannot always be expected to remember one's initial grounds of belief and this fact should not affect the justificatory status of one's belief.[11]

If one accepts (A), should one also accept the following claim?

(B) If one believes that *p*, then presence of undermining counter-evidence against one's belief is necessary for one to be justified in suspending judgement over *p*.

If we accept both (A) and (B), then we seem to be allowing that there can be situations in which S's belief that *p* is unjustified even though she does not possess undermining counter-evidence (from (A)), and yet where the subject is not justified in suspending judgement (from (B)). In such a situation, the subject is not justified in judging that *p*, she is not justified in judging that not-*p*, and she is not justified in suspending judgement over *p*. She is epistemically trapped. In the case of an epistemic trap, there is no epistemically permissible option available to the subject with regard to the target proposition *p*. Whatever attitude she takes or does not take will be epistemically inappropriate. One might think this is simply a case where the subject is not in a position to know what rationality demands of her, and as Williamson argues, such cases can and do arise.[12] However, this is rather different. In the case of an epistemic trap, it is not just that the subject is not in a position to know what rationality demands of her; it is that the demands of rationality actually conflict.

One thing to note as an aside is that one way of thinking of the role of the 'proof' of God's existence in Descartes' *Meditations* is as a way of trying to establish that the demands of rationality cannot conflict in this way—i.e. as a way of trying to establish that epistemic traps are not possible. The proof of the existence of a benevolent God is supposed to establish that if it is epistemically impermissible for one to judge that not-*p* and it is also epistemically impermissible for one to suspend judgement over *p*, then *p*. So one way of thinking of Descartes' 'circular' argument in the *Meditations* is as follows. It is epistemically impermissible for one to believe that epistemic traps are possible and it is also epistemically impermissible for one to suspend judgement over the question. Therefore, epistemic traps are not possible. Should we agree with the Cartesian conclusion that epistemic traps are impossible?

There are accounts of epistemic justification that would appear to allow for the possibility of such epistemic traps. In 'What is justified belief?', Goldman attempts to explain the notion of justification in non-epistemic terms, and the notion of reliability is put to that explanatory purpose. Goldman is explicit that it is not only the causal origin of a belief that is relevant to its reliability, and hence its justificatory status, but also how the belief is causally sustained. This is what Goldman says when it comes to attempting to

---

[11] See Harman 1984, 1986, and 1999. For an internalist attempt to accommodate 'forgotten evidence', see Conee and Feldman 2001.
[12] See Williamson 2000: chapters 8 and 9.

accommodate the absence-of-undermining-counter-evidence condition for justification in non-epistemic, reliabilist terms. He specifies two conditions for justified belief. The notion of justified belief involves the idea that (i) S's belief that p at t results from a reliable cognitive process, and (ii) there is no reliable or conditionally reliable process available to S which, had it been used by S in addition to the process actually used, would have resulted in S's not believing p at t.[13]

Goldman wants to allow that there can be a reliable process available to a subject which would result in the suspension of judgement over p if used, even in a case where the subject's belief that p is in fact acquired by a reliable cognitive process—i.e. Goldman allows that (i) can be satisfied without (ii) being satisfied.[14] In such cases, according to Goldman, the subject's belief is unjustified. The implication of Goldman's account appears to be that S's undermining counter-evidence against p is that which can serve as input to a reliable process available to S, which would result in S suspending judgement over p if she had used it. On the assumption that without such counter-evidence there is no such reliable process available to the subject, and also assuming that without such a reliable process available to the subject she is not justified in suspending judgement over p, Goldman, then, seems to be committed to (B). Given that Goldman is also committed to (A), the account of the justification of belief offered in 'What is justified belief?' seems to allow for the possibility of epistemic traps.

In what follows, I shan't be trying to establish a priori that epistemic traps are impossible, but I shall be arguing that the correct account of the justification of suspending judgement and withdrawing assent explains why we should reject (B). To deny (B) is to allow that there can be cases where one believes that p, one's evidential situation is not sufficient to undermine the justificatory status of one's belief that p, and yet one is epistemically permitted to suspend judgement over p. The following is, I think, generally accepted: the fact that one possesses evidence sufficient to justify judging p does not epistemically oblige one to judge that p. The epistemic permissibility of judging that p does not entail the epistemic obligation to judge that p. To reject (B) is to claim that we should accept something similar in the case of withdrawing assent. That is, in rejecting

---

[13] It is interesting to note that under this account, whether or not a belief is justified is determined, at least in part, by what is 'available' to the subject. And for those of us who aren't clairvoyants, whether there is such a reliable process available to one is going to depend on what evidence is available to one. So there is some variety of accessibility requirement for justification—a requirement usually associated with internalist accounts. Also note that with this availability/accessibility requirement we seem to introduce a deontological aspect to justification—also usually associated with internalist accounts. Regarding a subject who acquires counter-evidence against a reliably acquired belief, we have Goldman saying that 'What we can say about James is that he fails to use a certain (conditionally) reliable process that he could and *should* have used. Admittedly, had he used this process, he would have "worsened" his doxastic states: he would have replaced some true beliefs with suspension of judgement. Still he couldn't have known this in the case in question. So he failed to do something which, epistemically, he *should* have done. The justificational status of a belief is not just a function of the cognitive processes actually employed in producing it, it is also a function of processes that could and *should* be employed' (1979: 351; my emphasis).

[14] In Goldman's example, a subject is told on fully reliable authority that a certain class of his memory beliefs are almost all mistaken. In actual fact the subject has been misinformed and his memory on these matters is fully reliable. See Goldman 1979: 350.

(B) we allow that the epistemic permissibility of withdrawing assent from p does not entail the epistemic obligation to withdraw assent from p.

If we reject (B), then we should deny that the epistemic impermissibility of continuing to believe that p is to be understood in terms of the notion of the epistemic permissibility of suspending judgement. The fact that Goldman's account allows for the possibility of epistemic traps is partly due to the fact that under his account the epistemic impermissibility of continuing to believe that p is understood in terms of the notion of the epistemic permissibility of suspending judgement—i.e. the availability to the subject of a reliable process that would result in her not believing that p if used.

To reject (B) is to allow that a subject can be justified in withdrawing assent from p despite the fact that she has a justified belief that p—indeed, despite the fact that she knows that p. I shall be arguing that as self-conscious agents capable of engaging in the epistemic mental action of self-critical reflection, we have available to us epistemically permissible routes to the loss of knowledge. In consequence, we have a certain degree of epistemic liberty when it comes to revising what we believe. There can be cases where we are both epistemically permitted to hold on to a belief that p and also epistemically permitted to withdraw assent from p. Both options can be epistemically available to one, and what one in fact ends up doing—how one makes use of this epistemic liberty—can be affected by practical considerations. This has some interesting implications. In any given evidential situation a subject may be in, the epistemically permissible options available to the subject are multiplied. And the path the subject takes through these epistemically permissible options in turn affects her evidential situation. The consequences that this has upon an account of the justification of belief and the ethics of belief will be discussed at the end of the chapter.

15.3 Losing knowledge through self-critical reflection

The fact that a subject does not believe that p does not in itself entail that the subject has suspended judgement over p. The question of whether p may never have occurred to her. In order for it to be true to say that a subject has suspended judgement over p, the subject must, at the very least, have considered the question of whether or not p. To consider whether p is to engage in a self-conscious activity. That is to say, when one considers whether or not p, one *does* something, and one knows what one is thereby doing. What a subject does in considering whether p, and her knowledge of what she is and isn't thereby doing, is relevant to the question of whether or not she is justified in suspending judgement over p.

Suppose, for example, one attempts to determine whether p, one knows what one is doing, and one knows that one's attempt has not been successful. That is, one would not be justified in judging whether or not p on the basis of what one has done, and one knows this—and as a result one suspends judgement over p. In such a case we would surely want to say that one's suspension of judgement over p is justified. We do not want to say that a subject who has attempted to determine whether p and who knows that she has not yet been successful in determining whether p, is unjustified in suspending judgement over p, and note that this seems to be true even when the subject happens to know something that entails p. Given this, we should be aware that the claim that 'S is justified in suspending judgement over p' can be interpreted as meaning different things: either (a) given S's evidential situation—i.e. given the evidence S does and does not possess—S ought to suspend judgement over p, or (b) S has attempted to determine whether p and she has not (yet) done anything that justifies her judging that p or judging that not-p. There are cases in which one considers whether p and then suspends judgement over p, where one hasn't formed a prior opinion as to whether or not p, but there are also cases in which the suspension of judgement over p results in belief revision. That is, there are cases in which the suspension of judgement over p amounts to the withdrawal of assent from p. What account should be given of the justification of withdrawing assent?

As I discussed in Chapter 11, belief is always subject to epistemic evaluation, no matter what its causal origin, but the same is not true of belief loss. The fact that one forgets things one used to believe is not generally thought of as subject to epistemic evaluation. So whether or not an *event* of belief loss is subject to epistemic evaluation cannot be solely determined by the epistemic status of the subject's beliefs prior to and after the belief loss. Belief loss is subject to epistemic evaluation only if it is somehow guided by the aim of avoiding error, where belief loss that is aimed at error avoidance can either be guided by a conscious intention to avoid error, or by a sub-personal cognitive system that has that function. Belief loss that is aimed at avoiding error need not be guided by error-avoiding mechanisms alone, and we can make sense of belief loss that is *misdirected* at error avoidance.[15] This seems to allow us to make sense of there being instances of belief loss that are subject to epistemic evaluation but which we regard as epistemically inappropriate.

As I also mentioned in Chapter 11, not all instances of belief loss aimed at avoiding error, so construed, are instances of a subject withdrawing assent from some proposition as a result of self-critical reflection. Belief revision that results from the acquisition of, and updating of, evidence need not involve anything as reflective as self-critical reflection. However, the withdrawal of assent can sometimes be the result of self-critical reflection. The notion of self-critical reflection I have in mind here is the notion I discussed in Chapter 11: self-critical reflection occurs when a subject engages with the question of whether p with the aim of avoiding error when she already believes that p. I argued that such activity involves the bracketing of one's belief that p. To bracket one's belief that p is not to withdraw assent from p. The bracketing of one's belief that p is not something that is subject to epistemic evaluation and it is not something that requires epistemic grounds, whereas withdrawing assent from p (or suspending judgement over p) is subject to epistemic evaluation, and does require epistemic grounds. When one brackets one's belief that p, one does not use p as a premise in the reasoning one is

---

[15] Compare Velleman's discussion, in 'On the Aim of Belief', of what makes an 'acceptance' a belief (Velleman 2000a: 252–4).

engaged in, and the fact that one does not use p as a premise in one's reasoning is a constraint on that reasoning that one imposes on oneself, and which one treats as a constraint that one has imposed on oneself. When one brackets one's belief that p one imposes a constraint on one's reasoning by reasoning in recognition of it. In the case of self-critical reflection, one brackets one's belief that p and attempts to rule out not-p, with the aim of avoiding error.

Here one might ask, why should the avoidance of error be of any concern to one if one already believes that p, and in particular, if one already knows that p? Relevant to this question is the dogmatism paradox: p implies that any evidence against p is misleading. So, by closure, whenever you know that p, you know that any evidence against p is misleading. And if you know that such evidence is misleading, you should pay it no heed. Whenever one knows, one should not heed any evidence suggesting one is wrong.[16] By applying this line of reasoning, one might argue that if one knows that p, then one knows that one should not heed any evidence suggesting that one is wrong. And if one knows that one should not heed any evidence suggesting one's belief is wrong, how can one do this without self-deception?[17]

There is a way in which this argument is question-begging. It *assumes* that if one knows that p, then one cannot withdraw assent from p without self-deception. For the explanation of why one cannot withdraw assent from p without self-deception when one knows that p simply involves an appeal to some further knowledge one has (i.e. that one knows that evidence against p is misleading). So this will not persuade us that one cannot withdraw assent from p without self-deception when one knows p, unless we already accept the claim being argued for. One can think that one knows that p because one thinks that one has previously worked out whether p, but consistent with this, as a self-conscious agent capable of engaging in mental action—an agent capable of imposing constraints on one's reasoning by reasoning in recognition of them—one can bracket one's belief that p and reconsider the question of whether p, and there need be no irrationality or self-deception in one's doing so. As O'Shaughnessy puts it, 'one cannot dump one's cognitive responsibilities on one's past self: it is not like signing a document in law' (2000: 261). As self-conscious agents capable of engaging in epistemic mental action, we have available to us what O'Shaughnessy describes as the 'permanent possibility of active thinking' (2000: 162), which implicates a certain kind of responsibility for belief.

Between insane hubristic choosing what shall be fact, and alienating invasiveness by fact, lies the possibility of coming to terms with fact. One absorbs fact into one's being in a way which confirms one's individuality, thanks to the power of rational judgement...The permanent

---

[16] The dogmatism paradox is discussed by Harman (1973), Ginet (1980), and Lewis (1996), where they attribute the paradox to Kripke. Kripke's discussion has since been published ('On Two Paradoxes of Knowledge') in Kripke 2011. My formulation of the paradox is taken from Lewis 1996. For an argument for the claim that a dogmatic attitude is required for knowledge, see Unger 1974.

[17] For a discussion of the issue of believing at will, see Williams 1973b. See also Winters 1979, Cook 1987, Scott-Kakures 1994, Radcliffe 1997, and Audi 1999.

possibility of active thinking, where one deems it necessary, is central to the speech form 'my reasons for believing _____'. It fills in what is meant by 'responsibility for belief'. (O'Shaughnessy 2000: 161–2)

The dogmatic refusal to bracket belief and reconsider questions formerly resolved suggests a certain kind of epistemic irresponsibility.

When one brackets one's belief that p, and one consciously considers the question of whether p, one may fail to uncover evidence that undermines the justificatory status of one's belief, but one might also know that one's consideration of whether p did not involve one's doing anything that would justify one's *acquiring* the belief that p. What are one's epistemic obligations in such circumstances? Is one epistemically obliged to suspend judgement? Is one epistemically permitted to suspend judgement?

Earlier I claimed that we should be aware that the claim that 'S is justified in suspending judgement over p' can be interpreted as meaning different things: either (a) given S's evidential situation—i.e. given the evidence S does and does not possess—S ought to suspend judgement over p, or (b) S has attempted to determine whether p and she has not (yet) done anything that justifies her judging that p or judging that not-p. If when one brackets one's belief that p and attempts to determine whether p, one knows that one's attempt has not been successful, then one is justified in suspending judgement in the second sense. But this does not entail that one does not know that p. For one's belief that p may have satisfied acquisition conditions for justified belief and it may satisfy preservation conditions for justified belief. In bracketing one's belief that p, one denies oneself a means of consciously judging that p which may in fact be epistemically permissible. That is to say, one denies oneself a means of making a justified conscious judgement that p—one that would have been available to one were one not attempting to determine whether p while bracketing one's belief that p.

To deny that a subject who knows that p can be epistemically permitted to suspend judgement over p once she makes this means of making the justified conscious judgement that p unavailable to herself, is to be committed to the following: a subject's belief that p has the kind of justification required for knowing that p only if the subject possesses evidence that makes her *epistemically obliged* to judge that p when she brackets her belief that p and attempts to determine whether or not p is true. This commitment will be rejected by anyone who holds that the strength of evidence required for satisfying the preservation conditions for justified belief is less than the strength of evidence required for satisfying the acquisition conditions for justified belief—and so anyone who holds that absence of a defeater against one's belief that p is a necessary but *insufficient* condition for one's belief that p to be justified.

The ability to engage in the mental action of self-critical reflection—to bracket one's belief that p and attempt to determine whether p is true—makes possible an epistemically permissible route to the loss of knowledge. A subject can be both justified in believing that p and justified in withdrawing assent from p. We are now in a position to see why assumption (B) should be rejected. It is not true that if one believes that p, the presence of an undermining defeater against one's belief that p is necessary for one to be justified in withdrawing assent from p. What are the consequences of rejecting (B)? What does this add to our understanding of the correct account of the justification of belief and knowledge?

15.4 Multiplying the epistemic options: epistemic liberty and the ethics of belief

There are situations in which it can be epistemically permissible for one to continue to believe that p and also epistemically permissible for one to withdraw assent from p, and what one in fact does will be affected by practical considerations. Firstly, the epistemically permissible route to withdrawing assent sometimes requires reflection—i.e. it can require the activity of bracketing one's beliefs and imposing constraints on one's reasoning by reasoning in recognition of them. Although bracketing one's beliefs is never epistemically impermissible, as the bracketing of one's beliefs is not subject to epistemic evaluation, there are occasions when, for purely practical reasons, it is obviously inappropriate to do so. This has been remarked upon by a number of different philosophers. Hookway, for example, writes:

> Reflection takes time and there will often not be time to carry out the required reflection in time to act upon its results... We can easily see that many of the questions that *could* be raised either need not, or should not, be considered within the context of a particular activity. (Hookway 2000: 63–4)[18]

Those who reflect on whether or not they know when they are unable to carry out the required reflection in time to act upon its results are not doing anything *epistemically* impermissible. They are doing something it is not practically rational to do. The distinction is important and can easily be obscured. Once we distinguish the notion of the *epistemic* liberty a subject has when more than one epistemically permissible option with regard to a proposition is available to her, we can accept that subjects have the epistemic liberty to behave in ways that we might regard as irrational.[19]

Secondly, there are occasions when the option of continuing to believe that p and the option of suspending judgement over p are both epistemically permissible, but for purely practical reasons it is more appropriate for one to take the latter option. For example,

---

[18] See also the discussion in Williams 1991: 181ff.

[19] For instance, we might regard those who insist on, and persist in, taking a detached, self-critical stance on their own beliefs and who persist in questioning the apparently obvious, as acting irrationally. Gaita (2000) suggests that 'Even in the best of worlds, the sane would be distinguished from the insane by the fact that they rule things out of consideration' (165). However, although we might regard those who persist in questioning the apparently obvious as acting irrationally, I suggest that we should not always think of what they are doing as being *epistemically impermissible*. The related issue of whether or not the sceptic can live her scepticism is, of course, an ancient one, and the discussion of the relevance of this issue to our assessment of sceptical arguments has been a recurrent theme. For a discussion of the ancient form of the question, see Burnyeat 1983.

where, given the subject's practical circumstances, the cost of error for the subject is greater than the cost of losing knowledge. Such cases are sometimes used in arguments for contextualist accounts of knowledge. We are presented with two situations, and although there are differences in the subject's circumstances in each situation, in both situations the subject has the same evidence available to her. Our intuition is that in one of the situations the subject is justified in judging that p and she is justified in judging that she knows that p, and in the other situation our intuition is that the subject is justified in suspending judgement over p and judging that she does not know that p.[20]

According to the contextualist, the explanation of our apparently conflicting intuitions here is that the truth values of knowledge ascriptions are sensitive to certain facts about the speakers and hearers of the context. For a particular subject S and proposition p, one speaker could truly say 'S knows p', while at the same time another speaker in a different context truly says 'S doesn't know that p'. According to one version of the theory, for each context of ascription there is a standard for how strong one's epistemic position with respect to a proposition must be in order for one to know it. When the contexts differ with respect to this standard, a speaker in one context may truly say 'S knows p' while a speaker in the other truly says 'S doesn't know that p'. If we accept a theory of this kind, we can explain how in the two situations the subject's contrary judgements as to whether or not she knows that p can both be warranted. In the first context, the epistemic standards required for ascribing knowledge that p are such that the subject is justified in judging that she knows that p. In the second context, the epistemic standards required for ascribing knowledge that p have shifted. So the subject has reason to believe that she does not know that p in the second situation, even though she has the same evidence available to her.

However, I suggest that we should not regard such cases as ones in which the epistemic standards required for knowledge have shifted. Rather, we should regard them as cases in which two options are epistemically available to the subject. Both suspending judgement over p and continuing to believe that p are epistemically permissible. The differences in practical circumstances between the two situations affect which epistemic option it is more *practically* rational for the subject to take.

Thirdly, just as the importance that a subject attaches to the cost of error can affect which of the two epistemic options available to her it is practically rational for her to take, the importance that the subject attaches to the cost of *losing* a particular item of knowledge can also affect which of the two epistemically available options it is practically rational for her to take. Consider, for example, the case of strongly held religious or moral beliefs. The importance that a subject attaches to 'knowing that God exists', or 'knowing that infanticide is morally wrong' may well affect the subject's resistance to apparent counter-evidence. And if a subject *does* know, for instance, that infanticide is morally wrong, then she is not only epistemically permitted to continue to hold that belief, it may be practically rational for her to do so. It might even be argued that she has

[20] See e.g. De Rose 1992.

a moral obligation to do so. Compare the following remarks by Adams (1995) on what he calls 'moral faith':

> Metaethics, the relevant branch of ethical theory, is a field in which philosophical experience suggests that no comprehensive or very complex theory is likely to attain a very high degree of certainty. Moral faith is therefore a stance we shall have to take, if we are reasonable, in the face of the recognition that any metaethical theory we hold *could* rather easily be mistaken. (84)
> When we resist refutation of an item of moral faith, we may, and should, be thinking of the danger of being misled into giving it up while it is true. From a moral point of view, that would be a worse mistake to make than the mistake of clinging to moral faith while it is false. (87)
> A moral person... will have a degree of commitment to some central ethical beliefs which is more than proportionate to the strength of the evidence or arguments supporting them. In that sense, morality requires a faith that goes beyond what we can establish by reasoning. It does not follow that the beliefs to which a moral person is committed cannot all be favoured by reason, in preference to alternatives. It is just that reason's support for them is not likely to be as solid as morality's. (91)[21]

I do not mean to suggest that these practical considerations affect the epistemic status of one's beliefs. They do not determine the epistemically permissible options available to one. They merely affect which of the epistemically permissible options available to one it is practically rational or 'reasonable' for one to take. For instance, just because a particular moral or religious belief plays an important role in the life of a subject, it does not follow that she is epistemically justified in continuing to hold on to it. The belief may be unjustified because the acquisition conditions required for justified belief are unsatisfied, and we should also allow that the belief might *become* unjustified because the preservation conditions for justification are no longer satisfied. Surely part of the point of introducing preservation conditions for the justification of belief in the first place is to accommodate the intuition that dogmatism in the face of counter-evidence is epistemically impermissible. So under what circumstances does one lose justification by acquiring counter-evidence? Under what circumstances does the acquisition of counter-evidence undermine the justification of one's belief and result in the loss of knowledge? Preservation conditions required for the justified belief that p fail when one is epistemically obliged to suspend judgement over p. So under what circumstances is one epistemically obliged to suspend judgement over p?[22]

Providing a non-question-begging answer is problematic once we reject assumption (B) and accept that there are circumstances under which losing one's knowledge through self-critical reflection is an epistemically permissible option. Even if, upon reflection, one realizes that one is justified in judging that one does not know that p, it does not

---

[21] Compare also Gaita 1991: chapter 17, and 'Forms of the Unthinkable', in his 2000, where Gaita discusses the moral implications of one's questioning the reality of evil.

[22] Note that an answer to this question is obviously going to affect the account that is given of the acquisition conditions for justified belief. For recall that a way of reaching a belief results in justified belief only if the conditions required for preserving the justificatory status of a belief are satisfied at the point at the which the belief is acquired.

follow that one does not know that p. For suspending judgement over q (when the evidence that q may have played a role in the reasoning leading to one's justified judgement that one does not know that p) may be an epistemically permissible option. This gives rise to a theoretical difficulty of being unable to specify in a non-circular, non-question-begging way the circumstances under which a subject has acquired undermining counter-evidence that results in the loss of justification. Given that there are circumstances under which it is both epistemically permissible to continue to believe that p and also epistemically permissible to withdraw assent from p, we cannot define the epistemic impermissibility of continuing to believe that p simply in terms of the epistemic permissibility of something else—i.e. the epistemic permissibility of withdrawing assent from p, or judging that one does not know that p. A failing of purely reliabilist accounts is their attempt to do just this.[23] The failing of a certain variety of evidentialism lies in its claim that one should *always* proportion one's beliefs to one's evidence.[24] Although one is epistemically permitted to proportion one's beliefs to one's evidence, one is not always epistemically obliged to do so, as the above quote from Adams suggests.

This theoretical difficulty, of being unable to specify in a non-circular, non-question-begging way the preservation conditions for the justification of belief, can elicit conflicting intuitions regarding the strength of evidence required for knowledge, and regarding the extent to which self-critical reflection is required if we are to avoid dogmatism and prejudice. On the latter point, on the one hand we may admire the fearless thinker who is unafraid to break with tradition and question that which everyone else takes for granted. On the other hand, we regard those who question certain truths, as cranks, or as those who are 'not in tune with reality'.[25]

These apparently conflicting intuitions are often remarked upon in the context of reflecting upon the now familiar contrast between the perspective of common sense and the perspective of philosophy.[26] As Gaita observes, 'Outside of philosophy common sense is generally thought to be a virtue. Within philosophy it is often treated with suspicion, because the philosophical tradition makes it seem so close to mere prejudice' (2000: 173). Compare, for example, the view of philosophy and self-critical reflection captured by Arendt in the following quote:

In the privacy of his posthumously published notes, Kant wrote, "I do not approve of the rule that if the use of pure reason has proved something, the results should no longer be subject to doubt, as though it were a solid axiom", and "I do not share the opinion . . . that one should not doubt once one has convinced oneself of something. In pure philosophy this is impossible. Our mind has a natural aversion to it". From which it follows that the business of thinking is like Penelope's web; it undoes every morning what it has finished the night before. For the need to think can never be stilled by allegedly definite insights of "wise men"; it can be satisfied only

---

[23] Note that the same kind of problem arises for proper function accounts.

[24] For a discussion and critique of deontological evidentialism, see Plantinga 1993a: chapter 1 and 2000: chapter 3.

[25] For a discussion of this point, see Gaita, 'Forms of the Unthinkable', in his 2000.

[26] See e.g. the discussion by Williams 1991: chapter 5.

through thinking, and the thoughts I had yesterday will satisfy this need today only to the extent that I will and am able to think them anew. (1978: 88)

That both perspectives can appear equally compelling is a natural consequence of the kind of epistemic liberty that we have as self-conscious agents capable of engaging in epistemic mental action—the kind of epistemic liberty that ensures a mutual interaction between the activity of conscious thinking and the standing attitude of belief. It is this mutual interaction between the mind's conscious agential epistemic activity and the bedrock of belief from which it constructs that endows the self-conscious subject with a form of responsibility for what she believes.

References

Adams, R. (1995). 'Moral Faith', *The Journal of Philosophy* 92: 75–95.

Addis, L. (1986). 'Pains and Other Secondary Mental Entities', *Philosophy and Phenomenological Research* 47(1): 59–74.

Adler, J. (2002). *Belief's Own Ethics*. Cambridge, MA: MIT Press.

Allen, K. (2011). 'Blur', *Philosophical Studies* 93(372): 17–25.

Anscombe, G.E.M. (1959). *An Introduction to Wittgenstein's Tractatus: Themes in the Philosophy of Wittgenstein*. Indiana: St. Augustine's Press.

Anscombe, G.E.M. (1963). *Intention*, 2nd. edn. Oxford: Blackwell.

Anscombe, G.E.M., and Geach, P.T. (1961). *Three Philosophers*. Oxford: Oxford University Press.

Arendt, H. (1978). *The Life of Mind*. New York: Harcourt Brace Jovanovich.

Aristotle (1984). *The Complete Works of Aristotle; Revised Oxford Translation*, ed. by J. Barnes. Bollingen Series. Princeton, NJ: Princeton University Press.

Armstrong, D.M. (1962). *Bodily Sensations*. London: Routledge and Kegan Paul.

Audi, R. (1999). 'Doxastic Voluntarism and the Ethics of Belief', *Facta Philosophica* 1: 87–109.

Austin, J.L. (1946). 'Other Minds', *Proceedings of the Aristotelian Society* 20: 148–87.

Aydede, M. (2007). 'Pain', *The Stanford Encyclopedia of Philosophy* (Winter 2007 Edition), ed. by E.N. Zalta. <http://plato.stanford.edu/archives/win2007/entries/pain/>.

Bayne, T. (2005). 'Divided Brains & Unified Phenomenology: An Essay on Michael Tye's "Consciousness and Persons"', *Philosophical Psychology* 18(4): 495–512.

Bayne, T. (2010). *The Unity of Consciousness*. Oxford: Oxford University Press.

Bayne, T., and Montague, M. (2011). *Cognitive Phenomenology*. Oxford: Oxford University Press.

Bell, D. (1979). *Frege's Theory of Judgement*. New York: Oxford University Press.

Bergson, H. (1911). *Creative Evolution*, trans. by A. Mitchell. New York: Dover.

Block, N. (1978). 'Troubles with functionalism', *Minnesota Studies in the Philosophy of Science* 9: 261–325.

Block, N. (1990). 'Inverted earth', *Philosophical Perspectives* 4: 53–79.

Block, N. (2003). 'Mental Paint', in M. Hahn and B. Ramberg (eds), *Reflections and Replies: Essays on the Philosophy of Tyler Burge*. Cambridge, MA: MIT Press.

Block, N., and Stalnaker, R. (1999). 'Conceptual Analysis, Dualism, and the Explanatory Gap', *The Philosophical Review* 108(1): 1–46.

Bonjour, L. (1980). 'Externalist Theories of Empirical Knowledge', in *Midwest Studies in Philosophy* 5: 53–73.

Brand, P.W., and Yancey, P. (1993). *Pain: The Gift Nobody Wants*. New York: HarperCollins Publishers.

Bratman, M. (1987). *Intention, Plans, and Practical Reasoning*. Cambridge, MA: Harvard University Press.

Bratman, M. (1992). 'Practical Reasoning and Acceptance in a Context', *Mind* 101(401): 1–16.

Bratman, M. (1999). *Faces of Intention: Selected Essays on Intention and Agency*. Cambridge: Cambridge University Press.

Bratman, M. (2000). 'Reflection, Planning, and Temporally Extended Agency', *The Philosophical Review* 109(1): 35–61.

Bratman, M. (2006). *Structures of Agency: Essays*. Oxford: Oxford University Press.

Brewer, B. (1995). 'Bodily Awareness and the Self', in J. Bermudez, A. Marcel, and N. Eilan (eds), *The Body and the Self*. Cambridge, MA: MIT Press.

Brewer, B. (2011). *Perception and its Objects*. Oxford: Oxford University Press.

Broad, C.D. (1923). *Scientific Thought*. London: Routledge.

Broad, C.D. (1925). *The Mind and its Place in Nature*. London: Routledge.

Brook, A. (2000). 'Judgments and drafts eight years later', in A. Brook, D. Ross, and D. Thompson (eds), *Dennett's Philosophy: A Comprehensive Assessment*. Cambridge, MA: MIT Press.

Buckareff, A. (2005). 'How (Not) to Think about Mental Action', *Philosophical Explorations: An International Journal for the Philosophy of Mind and Action* 8(1): 83–9.

Budd, M. (1989). *Wittgenstein's Philosophy of Psychology*. London: Routledge.

Burge, T. (1991). 'Vision and Intentional Content', in E. LePore and R. Van Gulick (eds), *John Searle and His Critics*. Oxford: Basil Blackwell.

Burge, T. (2010). *Origins of Objectivity*. Oxford: Oxford University Press.

Burnyeat, M. (1983). 'Can the Sceptic Live His Scepticism?', in M. Burnyeat (ed.), *The Skeptical Tradition*. Berkeley and Los Angeles: University of California Press.

Byrne, A. (2001). 'Intentionalism Defended', *Philosophical Review* 110(2): 199–240.

Byrne, A. (2004). 'What Phenomenal Consciousness is Like', in R. Gennaro (ed.), *Higher-Order Theories of Consciousness: An Anthology*. Amsterdam: John Benjamins.

Campbell, J. (2001). 'Memory Demonstratives', in C. Hoerl and T. McCormack (eds), *Time and Memory*. Oxford: Oxford University Press.

Campbell, J. (2002). *Reference and Consciousness*. Oxford: Oxford University Press.

Carruthers, P. (2000). *Phenomenal Consciousness: A Naturalistic Theory*. Cambridge: Cambridge University Press.

Carruthers, P. (2005). 'Conscious Experience versus Conscious Thought', in *Consciousness: Essays from a Higher-Order Perspective*. Oxford: Oxford University Press.

Cassam, Q. (2010). 'Judging, Believing and Thinking', *Philosophical Issues* 20(1): 80–95.

Cassam, Q. (2011a). 'How We Know What We Think', in *Revue de Métaphysique et de Morale* 68: 553–69.

Cassam, Q. (2011b). 'Knowing What you Believe', *Proceedings of the Aristotelian Society* 111(1): 1–23.

Chalmers, D.J. (1996). *The Conscious Mind: In Search of a Fundamental Theory*. New York: Oxford University Press.

Chalmers, D.J. (2004). 'The Representational Character of Experience', in B. Leiter (ed.), *The Future for Philosophy*. Oxford: Oxford University Press.

Chalmers, D.J., and Jackson, F. (2001). 'Conceptual Analysis and Reductive Explanation', *The Philosophical Review* 110: 315–61.

Conee, E., and Feldman, R. (2001). 'Internalism Defended', in H. Kornblith (ed.), *Epistemology: Internalism and Externalism*. Oxford: Blackwell Publishers Ltd.

Cook, J.T. (1987). 'Deciding to Believe Without Self-Deception', *The Journal of Philosophy* 84: 441–6.

Crane, T. (2003). 'The Intentional Structure of Consciousness', in Q. Smith and A. Jokic (eds), *Consciousness: New Philosophical Essays*. Oxford: Oxford University Press.

Crane, T. (2006). 'Is there a Perceptual Relation?', in T.S. Gendler and J. Hawthorne (eds), *Perceptual Experience*. Oxford: Oxford University Press.

Crowther, T. (2009a) 'Watching, Sight and the Temporal Shape of Perceptual Activity', *Philosophical Review* 118(1): 1–27.

Crowther, T. (2009b) 'Perceptual Activity and the Will', in L. O' Brien and M. Soteriou (eds), *Mental Actions*. Oxford: Oxford University Press.

Crowther, T. (2010). 'The Agential Profile of Perceptual Experience', *Proceedings of the Aristotelian Society* 110(2): 219–42.

Currie, G., and Ravenscroft, I. (2002). *Recreative Minds*. Oxford: Oxford University Press.

Dainton, B. (2000). *Stream of Consciousness: Unity and Continuity in Conscious Experience*. London: Routledge.

Dancy, J. (1995). 'Arguments from Illusion', *The Philosophical Quarterly* 45, 421–38.

Davidson, D. (2001a). *Essays on Actions and Events*, 2nd edn. Oxford: Clarendon Press.

Davidson, D. (2001b). *Inquiries into Truth and Interpretation*, 2nd edn. Oxford: Clarendon Press.

Dennett, D. (1991). *Consciousness Explained*. Boston: Little, Brown.

Dennett, D.C., and Kinsbourne, M. (1992). 'Time and the Observer: The Where and When of Consciousness in the Brain', *Behavioral and Brain Sciences* 15: 183–201.

DeRose, K. (1992). 'Contextualism and Knowledge Atrributions', *Philosophy and Phenomenological Research* 52: 913–29.

Descartes, R. (1984). *Philosophical Writings of Descartes*, volumes I–III, trans. by J. Cottingham, R. Stoothoff, and D. Murdoch; vol. III ed. by J. Cottingham, R. Stoothoff, D. Murdoch, and A. Kenny. Cambridge: Cambridge University Press.

Dorsch, F. (2009). 'Judging and the Scope of Mental Agency', in L. O' Brien and M. Soteriou (eds), *Mental Actions*. Oxford: Oxford University Press.

Dowty, D. (1979). *Word Meaning and Montague Grammar*. Dordrecht: Kluwer.

Dretske, F. (1995). *Naturalizing the Mind*. Cambridge, MA: MIT Press.

Dummett, M., (1973) *Frege: Philosophy of Language*: London: Duckworth.

Eilan, N. (2000). 'Primitive Consciousness and the "Hard Problem"', *Journal of Consciousness Studies* 7: 28–39.

Elster, J. (1979). *Ulysses and the Sirens*. Cambridge: Cambridge University Press.

Elster, J. (2000). *Ulysses Unbound*. Cambridge: Cambridge University Press.

Evans, G. (1982) *The Varieties of Reference*. Oxford: Oxford University Press.

Ewing, A.C. (1948). 'Mental Acts', *Mind* 57, 201–20.

Fine, K. (2005). 'Tense and Reality', in *Modality and Tense: Philosophical Papers*. Oxford: Oxford University Press.

Fitch, F.B. (1952). *Symbolic Logic*. New York: Ronald Press.

Flanagan, O. (2000). *Dreaming Souls: Sleep, Dreams and the Evolution of the Conscious Mind*. Oxford: Oxford University Press.

Fleming, N. (1976). 'The Objectivity of Pain', *Mind* 85(340): 522–41.

Foster, J. (1982). *The Case for Idealism*. London: Routledge.

Frankfurt, H. (1971). 'Freedom of the Will and the Concept of a Person', *The Journal of Philosophy* 68 (1): 5–20.

Frankfurt, H. (1978). 'The Problem of Action', *American Philosophical Quarterly* 15(2): 157–62.

Frankfurt, H. (1988). *The Importance of What We Care About*. Cambridge: Cambridge University Press.

Frege, G. (1906). 'On the Foundations of Geometry; Second Series', in *Collected Papers on Mathematics, Logic, and Philosophy*, ed. by B. McGuinness, trans. by M. Black. Oxford: Blackwell, 1984.

Frege, G. (1918). 'Negation', in *Collected Papers on Mathematics, Logic, and Philosophy*, ed. by B. McGuinness, trans. by M. Black. Oxford: Blackwell, 1984.

Frege, G. (1923). 'Compound Thoughts', in *Collected Papers on Mathematics, Logic, and Philosophy*, ed. by B. McGuinness, trans. by M. Black. Oxford: Blackwell, 1984.

Gaita, R. (1991). *Good and Evil: An Absolute Conception*. London: Macmillan Press Ltd.

Gaita, R. (2000). *A Common Humanity: Thinking about Love, Truth and Justice*. London: Routledge.

Geach, P. (1957) *Mental Acts*. London: Routledge and Kegan Paul.

Geach, P. (1969). *God and the Soul*. London: Routledge and Kegan Paul.

Gentzen, G. (1969). *The Collected Papers of Gerhard Gentzen*, ed. by M.E. Szabo. Amsterdam: North Holland.

Gibbons, J. (2009). 'Reason in Action', in L. O' Brien and M. Soteriou (eds), *Mental Actions*. Oxford: Oxford University Press.

Ginet, C. (1980). 'Knowing Less by Knowing More', *Midwest Studies in Philosophy* 5: 151–62.

Goldman, A. (1979). 'What is Justified Belief?', in G. Pappas (ed.), *Justification and Knowledge*. Dordrecht: Reidel. Reprinted in E. Sosa and J. Kim (eds), *Epistemology: An Anthology*. Blackwell Publishers, 2000.

Gombrich, E. (1964) 'Moment and Movement in Art', *Journal of the Warburg and Courtauld Institutes* XXVII, 293–306.

Graff, D. (2001). 'Phenomenal Continua and the Sorites', *Mind* 110(440): 905–35.

Grahek, N. (2001). *Feeling Pain and Being in Pain*. Oldenburg, Denmark: BIS-Verlag, University of Oldengurg.

Green, M. (2000). 'The Status of Supposition', *Nous* 34(3): 376–99.

Grice, H.P. (1961). 'The Causal Theory of Perception', *Proceedings of the Aristotelian Society Supplementary Volume* 35: 121–52.

Hampshire, S., and Hart, H.L.A. (1958). 'Decision, Intention and Certainty', *Mind* 67(265): 1–12.

Harman, G. (1973). *Thought*. Princeton, NJ: Princeton University Press.

Harman, G. (1984). 'Positive versus Negative Undermining in Belief Revision', *Nous* 18: 39–49.

Harman, G. (1986). *Change in View*. Cambridge, MA: MIT Press.

Harman, G. (1990). 'The intrinsic quality of experience', *Philosophical Perspectives 4: Action Theory and Philosophy of Mind*: 31–52.

Harman, G. (1999). 'Rationality', in *Rationality, Meaning and Mind*. Oxford: Oxford University Press.

Hatfield, G. (1990). *The Natural and the Normative: Theories of Spatial Perception from Kant to Helmholtz*. Cambridge, MA: MIT Press.

Hatfield, G. (1991) 'Representation in Perception and Cognition: Connectionist Affordances', in W. Ramsey, S.P. Stich, and D. Rumelhard (eds), *Philosophy and Connectionist Theory*. Hillsdale, NJ: Lawrence Erlbaum.

Hatfield, G. (2005). 'Introspective Evidence in Psychology', in P. Achinstein (ed.), *Scientific Evidence: Philosophical Theories and Applications*. Baltimore, MD: John Hopkins University Press.

Hatfield, G. (2009). *Perception and Cognition: Essays in the Philosophy of Psychology*. Oxford: Clarendon Press.

Hieronymi, P. (2009). 'Two Kinds of Agency', in L. O' Brien and M. Soteriou (eds), *Mental Actions*. Oxford: Oxford University Press.

Hill, C. (2006). 'Ow! The Paradox of Pain', in M. Aydede (ed.), *Pain: New Essays on Its Nature and the Methodology of Its Study*. Cambridge, MA: MIT Press.

Hoerl, C. (2001). 'The Phenomenology of Episodic Recall', in C. Hoerl and T. McCormack (eds), *Time and Memory*. Oxford: Oxford University Press.

Hofweber, T., and Velleman, J.D. (2011). 'How to Endure', *The Philosophical Quarterly* 61(242): 37–57.

Hookway, C. (2000). 'Epistemic Norms and Theoretical Deliberation', in J. Dancy (ed.), *Normativity*. Oxford: Blackwell Publishers Inc.

Horgan, T., and Tienson, J. (2002). 'The Intentionality of Phenomenology and the Phenomenology of Intentionality', in D.J. Chalmers (ed.), *Philosophy of Mind: Classical and Contemporary Readings*. New York: Oxford University Press.

Hornsby, J. (1997). *Simple Mindedness: In Defence of Naïve Naturalism in the Philosophy of Mind*. Cambridge, MA: Harvard University Press.

Husserl, E. (1905). *The Phenomenology of Internal Time-Consciousness*, ed. by M. Heidegger, trans. by J.S. Churchill. Bloomington: Indiana University Press, 1964.

Jackson, F. (1977). *Perception: A Representative Theory*. Cambridge: Cambridge University Press.

Jackson, F. (1982). 'Epiphenomenal Qualia', *Philosophical Quarterly* 32: 127–36

James, W. (1890). *The Principles of Psychology*. New York: Holt.

Johnston, M. (2004). 'The Obscure Object of Hallucination', *Philosophical Studies* 120: 113–83.

Kant, I. (1998). *Critique of Pure Reason*, ed. and trans. by P. Guyer and A.W. Wood. Cambridge: Cambridge University Press.

Kelly, S. (2005) 'The Puzzle of Temporal Experience', in A. Brook and K. Akins (eds), *Cognition and the Brain*. Cambridge: Cambridge University Press.

Kenny, A. (1963). *Action, Emotion and Will*. London: Routledge and Kegan Paul.

Korsgaard, C. (1996a). *The Sources of Normativity*. Cambridge: Cambridge University Press.

Korsgaard, C. (1996b). *Creating the Kingdom of Ends*. Cambridge: Cambridge University Press.

Korsgaard, C. (2009a). *Self-Constitution: Agency, Identity, and Integrity*. Oxford: Oxford University Press.

Korsgaard, C. (2009b). 'The Activity of Reason', Presidential Address of the Eastern Division of the American Philosophical Association, 2008, in *The Proceedings and Addresses of the American Philosophical Association* 83(2): 23–43.

Kosslyn, S. (1996). *Image and Brain: The Resolution of the Imagery Debate*. Cambridge, MA: MIT Press.

Kripke, S. (2011). *Philosophical Troubles: Collected Papers, Volume 1*. Oxford: Oxford University Press.

Kukso, B. (2006). 'The Reality of Absences', *Australasian Journal of Philosophy* 84(1): 21–37.

Kusch, M. (1999). *Psychological Knowledge: A Social History and Philosophy*. London: Routledge.

Langsam, H. (1995). 'Why Pains are Mental Objects', *The Journal of Philosophy* 92(6): 303–13.

Levi, I. (1980). *The Enterprise of Knowledge*. Cambridge, MA: MIT Press.

Levine, J. (1983). 'Materialism and Qualia: The Explanatory Gap', *Pacific Philosophical Quarterly* 64: 354–61.

Lewis, D. (1996). 'Elusive Knowledge', *Australasian Journal of Philosophy* 74: 549–67.

Lycan, W. (1996). *Consciousness and Experience*. Cambridge, MA: MIT Press.

Marcel, A. (2003). 'The Sense of Agency: Awareness and Ownership of Action', in J. Roessler and N. Eilan (eds), *Agency and Self-Awareness*. Oxford: Oxford University Press.

Martin, C.B. (1996) 'How It Is: Entities, Absences and Voids', *Australasian Journal of Philosophy* 74(1): 57–65.

Martin, M.G.F. (1992). 'Sight and Touch', in T. Crane (ed.), *The Contents of Experience* Cambridge: Cambridge University Press.

Martin, M.G.F. (1995). 'Bodily Awareness: A Sense of Ownership', in J. Bermudez, A. Marcel, and N. Eilan (eds), *The Body and the Self*. Cambridge, MA: MIT Press.

Martin, M.G.F. (1997) 'The Reality of Appearances', in M. Sainsbury (ed.), *Thought and Ontology*. Milan: FrancoAngeli.

Martin, M.G.F. (1999). 'Sense Modalities and Spatial Properties', in N. Eilan, R. McCarthy, B. Brewer (eds), *Spatial Representation: Problems in Philosophy and Psychology*. Oxford: Clarendon Press.

Martin, M.G.F. (2000). 'Beyond Dispute: Sense Data, Intentionality and the Mind-Body Problem', in T. Crane and S. Patterson (eds), *The History of the Mind-Body Problem*. London: Routledge.

Martin, M.G.F. (2001). 'Out of the Past: Episodic Recall as Retained Acquaintance', in C. Hoerl and T. McCormack (eds), *Time and Memory*. Oxford: Oxford University Press.

Martin. M.G.F. (2002). 'The Transparency of Experience', *Mind and Language* 17: 376–425.

Martin, M.G.F. (2004). 'The Limits of Self-Awareness', *Philosophical Studies* 103: 37–89.

Martin, M.G.F. (2006). 'On Being Alienated', in T.S. Gendler and J. Hawthorne (eds), *Perceptual Experience*. Oxford: Oxford University Press.

McDowell, J. (1978). 'On the Reality of the Past', in A. Hookway and A. Pettit (eds), *Action and Interpretation*: Cambridge and New York: Cambridge University Press.

McDowell, J. (1995). 'Knowledge and the Internal', *Philosophy and Phenomenological Research* 55: 87–93.

McGinn, C. (1988). 'Consciousness and content', *Proceedings of the British Academy* 74: 219–39.

McGinn, C. (1989). 'Can We Solve the Mind-Body Problem?', *Mind* 98(391): 349–66.

McGinn, C. (2004). *Mindsight: Image, Dream, Meaning*. Cambridge, MA: Harvard University Press.

McKenzie, J.C. (1968). 'The Externalization of Pains', *Analysis* 28: 189–93.

Mele, A. (2009). 'Mental Action: A Case Study', in L. O' Brien and M. Soteriou (eds), *Mental Actions*. Oxford: Oxford University Press.

Melnick, A. (1973). *Kant's Analogies of Experience*. Chicago: University of Chicago Press.

Miller, I. (1984) *Husserl, Perception, and Temporal Awareness*. Cambridge, MA: MIT Press.

Mole, C., Smithies, D., and Wu, W. (eds) (2011). *Attention: Philosophical and Psychological Essays*. Oxford: Oxford University Press.

Molnar, G. (2000). 'Truthmakers for Negative Truths', *Australasion Journal of Philosophy* 78(1): 72–86.

Moore, A. (1990). *The Infinite*. London: Routledge.

Moore, G.E. (1903). 'The Refutation of Idealism', *Mind* 12(48): 433–53. Reprinted in G.E. Moore, *Selected Writings*, ed. by T. Baldwin. London: Routledge, 1993.

Moore, G.E. (1925). 'A Defence of Common Sense', in J.H. Muirhead (ed.), *Contemporary British Philosophy, 2nd Series*. London: Allen and Unwin. Reprinted in G.E. Moore, *Selected Writings*, ed. by T. Baldwin. London: Routledge, 1993.

Moore, G.E. (1993). *Selected Writings*, ed. by T. Baldwin. London: Routledge.

Moran, R. (1999). 'The Authority of Self-Consciousness', *Philosophical Topics* 26(1–2): 179–99.

Moran, R. (2001). *Authority and Estrangement: An Essay on Self-Knowledge*. Princeton, NJ: Princeton University Press.

Mourelatos, A.P.D. (1978). 'Events, Processes and States', *Linguistics and Philosophy* 2: 415–34.

Mouton, D.M. (1969). 'Thinking and Time', *Mind* 78: 60–76.

Nabokov, V. (1947). *Bend Sinister*. New York: McGraw Hill.

Nagel, T. (1974). 'What is it Like to be a Bat?', *Philosophical Review* 4: 435–50.

Nagel, T. (1979). *The Possibility of Altruism*. Princeton, NJ: Princeton University Press.

Nagel, T. (1986). *The View From Nowhere*. New York: Oxford University Press.

Nasim, O. (2008). *Bertrand Russell and the Edwardian Philosophers: Constructing the World*. Basingstoke: Palgrave Macmillan.

Newton, N. (1989). 'On Viewing Pain as a Secondary Quality', *Nous* 23(5): 569–98.

Noordhof, P. (2002). 'Imagining Objects and Imagining Experiences', *Mind and Language* 17: 426–55.

O'Brien, L. (2007). *Self-Knowing Agents*. Oxford: Oxford University Press.

O'Shaughnessy, B. (1980). *The Will: A Dual Aspect Theory*. Cambridge: Cambridge University Press.

O'Shaughnessy, B. (2000). *Consciousness and the World*. Oxford: Oxford University Press.

O'Shaughnessy, B. (2008). *The Will: A Dual Aspect Theory*, 2nd edn. Cambridge: Cambridge University Press.

Owens, D. (2000). *Reason without Freedom*. London: Routledge

Parfit, D. (1984). *Reasons and Persons*. Oxford: Oxford University Press.

Pautz, A. (2010). 'Why Explain Visual Experience in Terms of Content?', in B. Nanay (ed.), *Perceiving the World*. Oxford: Oxford University Press.

Peacocke, C. (1985). 'Imagination, Conceivability and Possibility', in J. Foster and H. Robinson (eds), *Essays on Berkeley: A Tercentennial Celebration*. Oxford: Clarendon Press.

Peacocke, C. (1992) *A Study of Concepts*. Cambridge, MA: MIT Press.

Peacocke, C. (1999). *Being Known*. Oxford: Oxford University Press.

Peacocke, C. (2007). 'Mental Action and Self-Awareness (I)', in J. Cohen and B. McLaughlin (eds), *Contemporary Debates in the Philosophy of Mind*. Oxford: Blackwell.

Peacocke, C. (2009). 'Mental Action and Self-Awareness (II)', in L. O' Brien and M. Soteriou (eds), *Mental Actions*. Oxford: Oxford University Press.

Philips, I. (forthcoming). 'Hearing and Hallucinating Silence', in F. Macpherson and D. Platchias (eds), *Hallucination*. Cambridge, MA: MIT Press.

Pickard, H. (2004). 'Knowledge of Action Without Observation', *Proceedings of the Aristotelian Society* 104(1): 205–30.

Pink, T. (1996). *The Psychology of Freedom*. Cambridge: Cambridge University Press.

Pink, T. (2009). 'Reason, Voluntariness and Moral Responsibility', in L. O' Brien and M. Soteriou (eds), *Mental Actions*. Oxford: Oxford University Press.

Pitcher, G. (1970). 'Pain Perception', *The Philosophical Review* 79(3): 368–93.

Plantinga, A. (1993a). *Warrant: The Current Debate*. Oxford: Oxford University Press.

Plantinga, A. (1993b). *Warrant and Proper Function*. Oxford: Oxford University Press.

Plantinga, A. (2000). *Warranted Christian Belief*. Oxford: Oxford University Press.

Plato (2004). *The Republic*, trans. by C.D.C. Reeve. Indianapolis: Hackett.

Pollock, J. (1986). *Contemporary Theories of Knowledge*. Lanham, MD: Rowman and Littlefield.

Price, H.H. (1932). *Perception*. London: Methuen & Co. Ltd. Reprinted with a new Preface in 1954.

Radcliffe, D. (1997). 'Scott-Kakures on Believing at Will', *Philosophy and Phenomenological Research* 57: 145–51.

Rashbrook, O. (2011). 'The Continuity of Consciousness'. *European Journal of Philosophy*. doi: 10.1111/j.1468-0378.2011.00465.

Richardson, L. (2009). 'Seeing Empty Space', *European Journal of Philosophy* 18(2): 227–43.

Robinson, H. (1985). 'The General Form of the Argument for Berkeleian Idealism', in J. Foster and H. Robinson (eds), *Essays on Berkeley: A Tercentennial Celebration*. Oxford: Clarendon Press.

Robinson, H. (1994). *Perception*. London: Routledge.

Robinson, W.S. (1994). 'Orwell, Stalin, and Determinate Qualia', *Pacific Philosophical Quarterly* 75: 151–64.

Roessler, J. (2003). 'Intentional Action and Self-Awareness', in J. Roessler and N. Eilan (eds), *Agency and Self-Awareness*. Oxford: Oxford University Press.

Roorda, J. (1997). 'Fallibilism, Ambivalence and Belief', *The Journal of Philosophy* 94: 126–55.

Rosenthal, D.M. (1993). 'Multiple Drafts and Higher-Order Thoughts', *Philosophy and Phenomenological Research* 53: 911–18.

Rothstein, S. (2004). *Structuring Events*. Oxford: Blackwell.

Russell, B. (1903). *The Principles of Mathematics*. Cambridge: Cambridge University Press.

Russell, B. (1912). *Problems of Philosophy*: Oxford: Oxford University Press.

Russell, B. (1914). 'The Relation of Sense-data to Physics', *Scientia* 4: 1–27. Reprinted in B. Russell, *Mysticism and Logic*. London: Unwin Books, 1917.

Russell, B. (1992). *Theory of Knowledge: The 1913 Manuscript*. London: Routledge.

Ryle, G. (1949). *The Concept of Mind*. Chicago: University of Chicago Press.

Ryle, G. (1967–8). 'Thinking and Reflecting', *Royal Institute of Philosophy Lectures*, vol. 1. London: MacMillan and Co. Ltd. Reprinted in G. Ryle, *Collected Essays 1929–1968: Collected Papers, Volume 2*. London: Routledge, 2009.

Ryle, G. (1968). 'The Thinking of Thoughts: What is "Le Penseur" Doing?', University Lectures, The University of Saskatchewan. Reprinted in G. Ryle, *Collected Essays 1929–1968: Collected Papers, Volume 2*. London: Routledge, 2009.

Ryle, G. (2009). *Collected Essays 1929–1968: Collected Papers, Volume 2*. London: Routledge.

Salmon, W. (ed.) (2001). *Zeno's Paradoxes*. Indianapolis: Hackett Publishing Co.

Sartre, J.-P. (1948). *The Psychology of Imagination*. New York: Philosophical Library.

Scott-Kakures, D. (1994). 'On Belief and the Captivity of the Will', *Philosophy and Phenomenological Research* 54: 77–103

Searle, J. (1983) *Intentionality: An Essay in the Philosophy of Mind*. Cambridge: Cambridge University Press.

Sellars, W. (1962). 'Philosophy and the Scientific Image of Man', in R. Colodny (ed.), *Frontiers of Science and Philosophy*. Pittsburgh: University of Pittsburgh Press. Reprinted in K. Scharp and R.B. Brandom (eds) *In the Space of Reasons: Selected Essays of Wilfrid Sellars*. Cambridge, MA: Harvard University Press, 2007.

Sellars, W. (1963). 'Empiricism and the Philosophy of Mind', in *Science, Perception and Reality*. London: Routledge and Kegan Paul.

Sellars, W. (2007). *In the Space of Reasons: Selected Essays of Wilfrid Sellars*, ed. by K. Scharp and R. Brandom. Cambridge, MA: Harvard University Press.

Shear, J. (1997). *Explaining Consciousness: The Hard Problem*. Cambridge, MA: MIT Press.

Shoemaker, S. (1976). 'Embodiment and Behavior', in A. Rorty (ed.), *The Identities of Persons*. Berkeley: University of California Press. Reprinted in *Identity, Cause, and Mind*. Oxford: Oxford University Press, 2003.

Shoemaker, S. (1996). *The First-Person Perspective and Other Essays*. Cambridge: Cambridge University Press.

Siegel, S. (2003). 'Indiscriminability and the Phenomenal', *Philosophical Studies* 120: 90–112.

Siegel, S. (2011). *The Contents of Visual Experience*. New York: Oxford University Press.

Siewert, C. (1998). *The Significance of Consciousness*. Princeton, NJ: Princeton University Press.

Siewert, C. (2002). 'Consciousness and Intentionality', *The Stanford Encyclopedia of Philosophy* (Fall 2002 Edition), ed. by E.N. Zalta. <http://plato.stanford.edu/archives/fall2002/entries/consciousness-intentionality/>.

Siewert, C. (2004). 'Is Experience Transparent?', *Philosophical Studies* 117: 15–41.

Smith, A.D. (2002). *The Problem of Perception*. Cambridge, MA: Harvard University Press.

Smith, A.D. (2003). *Husserl and the Cartesian Meditations*. London: Routledge.

Smith, A.D. (2008). 'Translucent Experiences', *Philosophical Studies* 140: 197–212.

Snowdon, P. (1992). 'How to Interpret "Direct Perception"', in T. Crane (ed.), *The Contents of Experience*. Cambridge: Cambridge University Press.

Snowdon, P. (2003). 'Knowing How and Knowing That: A distinction Reconsidered', *Proceedings of the Aristotelian Society* 104: 1–29.

Snowdon, P. (2005). 'The Formulation of Disjunctivism: A response to Fish', *Proceedings of the Aristotelian Society* 105: 129–41.

Sorabji, R. (1983). *Time, Creation and the Continuum*. Chicago: University of Chicago Press.

Sorensen, R. (2008). *Seeing Dark Things*. Oxford: Oxford University Press.

Sosa, E. (2007). *A Virtue Epistemology: Apt Belief and Reflective Knowledge,* vol. 1. Oxford: Oxford University Press.

Soteriou, M. (2009). 'Mental Agency, Conscious Thinking and Phenomenal Character', in L. O' Brien and M. Soteriou (eds), *Mental Actions*. Oxford: Oxford University Press.

Stanley, J., and Williamson, T. (2001). 'Knowing How', *Journal of Philosophy* 98: 411–44.

Stephens, G.L., and Graham, G. (1987). 'Minding your P's and Q's: Pain and Sensible Qualities', *Nous* 21(3): 395–405.

Steward, H. (1997). *The Ontology of Mind: Events, Processes and States*. Oxford: Oxford University Press.

Stoljar, D. (2004). 'The Argument from Diaphanousness', in M. Ezcurdia, R.J. Stainton, and C. Viger (eds), *New Essays in the Philosophy of Language and Mind*. Calgary: University of Calgary.

Stoothoff, R. (1963). 'Note on a Doctrine of Frege', *Mind* 72(287): 406–8.

Strawson, G. (2003). 'Mental Ballistics *or* The Involuntariness of Spontaneity', *Proceedings of the Aristotelian Society* 103: 227–56.

Strawson, P. (1959). *Individuals*. London: Methuen.

Taylor, B. (1977). 'Tense and Continuity', *Linguistics and Philosophy* 1: 199–220.

Taylor, R. (1952). 'Negative Things', *Journal of Philosophy* 49(13): 433–49.

Travis, C. (2004). 'The Silence of the Senses', *Mind* 113(449): 57–94.

Travis, C. (2008). 'Thinking About Thinking'. Inaugural Lecture at King's College London. <https://sites.google.com/site/charlestraviswebsite/Home/current-and-recent-work>.

Tulving, E. (1982). *Elements of Episodic Memory*. Oxford: Oxford University Press.

Tye, M. (1992). 'Visual Qualia and Visual Content', in T. Crane (ed.), *The Contents of Experience*. Cambridge: Cambridge University Press.

Tye, M. (1995). *Ten Problems of Consciousness*. Cambridge, MA: MIT Press.

Tye, M. (1997). 'A Representational Theory of Pains and their Phenomenal Character', in N. Block, O. Flanagan, and G. Güzeldere (eds), *The Nature of Consciousness: Philosophical Debates*. Cambridge, MA: MIT Press.

Tye, M. (2000). *Consciousness, Colour and Content*. Cambridge, MA: MIT Press.

Tye, M. (2003). *Consciousness and Persons*. Cambridge, MA: MIT Press.

Tye, M. (2006). 'Another Look at Representationalism about Pain', in M. Aydede (ed.), *Pain: New Essays on Its Nature and the Methodology of Its Study*. Cambridge, MA: MIT Press.

Tye, M. (2010). 'The Puzzle of Transparency', in A. Byrne, J. Cohen, G. Rosen, and S. Shiffrin (eds), *The Norton Introduction to Philosophy*. New York: Norton.

Unger, P. (1974). 'An Argument for Skepticism', *Philosophical Exchange* 1: 131–55.

Van Gulick, R. (1993). 'Understanding the Phenomenal Mind: Are We All Just Armadillos?, in M. Davies and G. Humphreys (eds), *Consciousness: Psychological and Philosophical Essays*. Oxford: Blackwell.

Van Gulick, R. (1995). 'Dennett, Drafts, and Phenomenal Realism', *Philosophical Topics* 22: 443–55.

Velleman, J.D. (1989a). *Practical Reflection*. Princeton, NJ: Princeton University Press.

Velleman, J.D. (1989b). 'Epistemic Freedom', *Pacific Philosophical Quarterly* 70: 73–97. Reprinted in J.D. Velleman, *The Possibility of Practical Reason*. Oxford: Oxford University Press, 2000.

Velleman, J.D. (1996). 'The Possibility of Practical Reason', *Ethics* 106(4): 694–726. Reprinted in J.D. Velleman, *The Possibility of Practical Reason*. Oxford: Oxford University Press, 2000.

Velleman, J.D. (2000a) 'On the Aim of Belief', in *The Possibility of Practical Reason*. Oxford: Oxford University Press.

Velleman, J.D. (2000b). *The Possibility of Practical Reason*. Oxford: Oxford University Press.

Velleman, J.D. (2005a). 'A Brief Introduction to Kantian Ethics', in *Self to Self: Selected Essays*. Cambridge: Cambridge University Press.

Velleman, J.D. (2005b). *Self to Self: Selected Essays*. Cambridge: Cambridge University Press.

Velleman, J.D. (2007). 'What Good is a Will?', in A. Leist (ed.), *Action in Context*. Berlin: Walter de Gruyter.

Velleman J.D. (2009). *How We Get Along*. Cambridge: Cambridge University Press.

Vendler, Z. (1957). 'Verbs and Times', *Philosophical Review* 66: 143–60.

Vendler, Z. (1972). *Res Cogitans: An Essay In Rational Psychology*. London: Cornell University Press.

Vendler, Z. (1984). *Matter of Minds*. Oxford: Oxford University Press.

Williams, B. (1973a). 'Imagination and the Self', in B. Williams, *Problems of the Self*. Cambridge: Cambridge University Press.

Williams, B. (1973b). 'Deciding to Believe', in B. Williams, *Problems of the Self*. Cambridge: Cambridge University Press.

Williams, B. (1981). 'Persons, Character and Morality', in B. Williams, *Moral Luck*. Cambridge: Cambridge University Press.

Williams, M. (1991). *Unnatural Doubts*. Oxford: Blackwell.

Williamson, T. (2000). *Knowledge and Its Limits*. Oxford: Oxford University Press.

Winters, B. (1979). 'Willing to Believe', *The Journal of Philosophy* 76: 243–56.

Wittgenstein, L. (1953). *Philosophical Investigations*, trans. by G.E.M. Anscombe. Oxford: Basil Blackwell.

Index

.